Accounting: business reporting for decision making

SEVENTH EDITION

Jacqueline Birt

Keryn Chalmers

Suzanne Maloney

Albie Brooks

Judy Oliver

David Bond

Seventh edition published 2020 by
John Wiley & Sons Australia, Ltd
42 McDougall Street, Milton Qld 4064

Typeset in 10/12pt Times LT Std

A catalogue record for this book is available from the National Library of Australia.

Wiley
Terry Burkitt (Director, Publishing and Course Development), Mark Levings (Executive
Publisher), Kylie Challenor (Senior Manager, Knowledge & Learning Content Management),
Rebecca Campbell (Production Editor), Emily Echlin (Publishing Coordinator), Emily Brain
(Production Assistant), Laura Brinums (Copyright & Image Research), Delia Sala (Cover
Design)

Cover: © Pobytov / Getty Images Australia

Typeset in India by diacriTech

Printed in Singapore by
Markono Print Media Pte Ltd

10 9 8 7 6 5 4 3 2 1

BRIEF CONTENTS

CONTENTS

CHAPTER 9

Budgeting 336

CHAPTER 10

Cost–volume–profit analysis 370

CHAPTER 11

Costing and pricing in an entity 408

PREFACE

While this new edition of *Accounting: business reporting for decision making* covers both preparer and user issues of business reporting, it predominantly explores and reinforces the principles of financial and management accounting from a user perspective. Accounting is presented as a decision-making tool for business rather than as a record-keeping function.

In developing this new edition of the text, we have carefully considered the positioning of the chapters and the flow of the learning objectives, and we believe that the order of the topics presented will suit the sequence of topics covered in most accounting courses. In the majority of chapters, we have used JB Hi-Fi Ltd either as an illustrative case or as a basis for the chapter's exercises or problems, which provides students with interesting real-world examples to which they can relate and understand.

This text is most suitable for introductory accounting units that focus on financial decision making in business, rather than the preparation of financial reports. It is also highly suited to first-year units in accounting in business degrees, MBA introductory accounting units and accounting service units.

Key features

The text has several unique features.

- References to JB Hi-Fi Ltd's annual report enhance the understanding of the concepts covered in the chapters. Each of the chapters on financial reporting provides a step-by-step illustration of the components of the financial statements and how to prepare and use the financial statements.
- The interrelationship between accounting information, business decisions and sustainable business practices is considered.
- Running cases are integrated throughout the text focusing on two small businesses — a service provider and a manufacturer.

Learning toolkit

Each chapter contains the following pedagogical tools to support you with your studies.

- *Learning objectives* at the start of each chapter highlight the learning targets for the chapter.
- A *chapter preview* introduces the major topics to be covered in each chapter.
- *Value to business* vignettes positioned at the end of each main section in the text reiterate key issues and processes presented in the chapter.
- *Illustrative examples* located throughout the chapter aid in the conceptual understanding of the content. Examples provide a worked solution and explain the process.
- *Decision-making examples* located throughout the chapter emphasise the decision-making process (rather than computation) and provide students with experience in financial decision making.
- A *summary of learning objectives* is provided at the end of each chapter. After each learning objective, a short summary of the key points covered under that learning objective in the chapter is provided.
- A list of *key terms* is provided in alphabetical order at the end of each chapter.
- *Apply your knowledge* provides an exam-like question to test student knowledge of the chapter overall.
- *Self-evaluation activities* provide a worked solution as a model for the workings of the exercises that follow.
- *Comprehension questions* review the chapter content and help students understand the key concepts. Questions include multiple-choice questions, fill-in-the-blanks and review.
- *Exercises* test student knowledge of the concepts presented in the chapter and develop analytical, comparative, communication and reporting skills. They are graded according to difficulty: ★ basic, ★ ★ moderate and ★ ★ ★ challenging.
- *Problems* build knowledge and skill development and are graded according to difficulty: ★ basic, ★ ★ moderate and ★ ★ ★ challenging.
- *Decision-making activities* focus on developing awareness of accounting information and various generic professional skills. They cover a range of scenarios such as communication, preparing presentations, teamwork, financial interpretation, internet-based research and ethical issues.

Executive summary — key features of each chapter

Chapter	Key features
Chapter 1 Introduction to accounting and business decision making	• Introduces the process of accounting and illustrates the difference between bookkeeping and accounting • Outlines the role of accounting for various decision makers • Discusses the role of accounting information in the business planning process • Provides examples of the differences between financial and management accounting • Discusses business sustainability, its key drivers and principles • Describes sustainability reporting and disclosure (including integrated reporting) • Explains what is meant by digital disruption and how new technology is influencing the accounting profession
Chapter 2 Accounting in society	• Identifies the sources of company regulation in Australia • Explains the current standard-setting framework • Evaluates the role of the *Conceptual Framework* • Examines corporate governance guidelines and practices
Chapter 3 Business structures	• Defines the four different forms of business structure (sole trader, partnership, company and trust) • Outlines the advantages and disadvantages of each of the business structures
Chapter 4 Business transactions	• Explains the differences between business transactions, personal transactions and business events • Describes the concept of duality and illustrates the impact of the application of duality to the accounting equation and worksheet • Provides examples of common errors on the worksheet
Chapter 5 Statement of financial position	• Explains the nature and purpose of the statement of financial position • Outlines the criteria for identifying assets and liabilities • Illustrates the classification and format of the statement of financial position • Describes possible limitations of the statement of financial position
Chapter 6 Statement of profit or loss and statement of changes in equity	• Explains the reporting period concept and the differences between accrual accounting and cash accounting • Outlines the criteria for identifying income and expenses • Illustrates the classification of items in the statement of profit or loss • States the relationship between the statement of profit or loss, the statement of financial position, the statement of comprehensive income and the statement of changes in equity
Chapter 7 Statement of cash flows	• Explains the purpose of a statement of cash flows • Illustrates the direct method of preparing a statement of cash flows and explains the purpose of reconciling profit with cash flows from operating activities • Provides the steps to analyse the statement of cash flows
Chapter 8 Analysis and interpretation of financial statements	• Explains the nature and purpose of financial analysis • Describes ratios relative to profitability, asset efficiency, liquidity, capital structure and market performance • Explains the limitations of ratio analysis
Chapter 9 Budgeting	• Illustrates the key steps in the budgeting process • Links the budgeting process to strategic planning • Describes the different types of budgets and outlines the components of a production and cash budget
Chapter 10 Cost–volume–profit analysis	• Looks at cost behaviour and its impact on profit planning • Illustrates the concept of CVP analysis and outlines the key assumptions underlying CVP analysis • Explains how to analyse make or buy decisions and special orders

(continued)

(*continued*)

Chapter	Key features
Chapter 11 Costing and pricing in an entity	• Defines and classifies cost objects into direct and indirect costs • Provides illustrations of the allocation process for indirect costs • Explains pricing issues for products and services
Chapter 12 Capital investment	• Describes the different techniques to use when analysing capital investment decisions • Explains the advantages and disadvantages of each of the capital investment techniques
Chapter 13 Financing the business	• Explains and illustrates the different sources of finance for entities • Discusses issues of managing debtors and inventories • Describes new funding opportunities for business, such as crowdfunding, ICOs, angel investors and microcredit
Chapter 14 Performance measurement	• Presents performance measurement techniques for an organisation • Discusses characteristics of contemporary measurement systems

ABOUT THE AUTHORS

Jacqueline Birt

Professor Jac Birt, BEd Melb, BBus RMIT, MBus RMIT, PhD ANU, CPA, is a Professor of Accounting at the University of Western Australia and also the current Head of Department of Accounting and Finance at the University of Western Australia. Prior to the University of Western Australia, she held appointments at the University of Queensland, Monash University, the Australian National University, the University of Amsterdam and the University of Melbourne. Jac's teaching and research is in financial accounting and accounting education. Her PhD focused on segment reporting and examined issues such as value relevance and voluntary segment disclosures. She has published in journals such as *Abacus, Journal of Business Ethics, Australian Journal of Management, Accounting & Finance, Accounting in Europe, Australian Journal of Adult Learning, Australian Accounting Review* and *Accounting Education*. Jac has been the recipient of the Pearson Education Accounting/Finance Lecturer of the Year Award and also the ANU Faculty of Economics and Commerce Award for Teaching Excellence.

Keryn Chalmers

Professor Keryn Chalmers, BCom, Grad Dip, PhD, is Dean and Professor of Accounting at Swinburne Business School. Her prior roles include Deputy Dean (external and international) and Head of the Department of Accounting and Finance in the Faculty of Business and Economics at Monash University. During her academic career, she has been responsible for accounting-related curriculum development, quality assurance and delivery at the undergraduate and postgraduate level. Keryn's research in financial accounting and financial reporting is specifically in relation to accounting policy and disclosure choices of management. Keryn's academic accounting association appointments include President, International Association of Accounting Education and Research and Past President, Accounting and Finance Association of Australia and New Zealand.

Suzanne Maloney

Suzanne Maloney, BBus, MPhil, DipFinPlan, FCPA, GAICD, is an Associate Professor in the School of Commerce at the University of Southern Queensland. She has worked in the accounting and finance field, both in practice and academia, for the past 25 years. Suzanne works closely with professionals in practice and is the recipient of a number of teaching awards, including a National Citation for Outstanding Contributions to Student Learning. Her current research interests include accounting education, superannuation and retirement planning.

Albie Brooks

Dr Albie Brooks, BCom, DipEd, MBus, PhD, FCPA, is an Associate Professor in Accounting at the University of Melbourne. His teaching is predominantly in the areas of management accounting and managerial control. Albie's teaching experience includes both undergraduate and postgraduate levels in both domestic and international settings. He has a particular interest in creating and developing teaching materials that enhance student engagement in the study of accounting. His research activities relate to teaching and learning, and management accounting issues. Albie maintains strong connections with industry and the accounting profession through various engagement activities.

Judy Oliver

Dr Judy Oliver has held appointments at Swinburne University, University of Tasmania and Victoria University. Judy has had responsibility for first-year accounting and management accounting units at both the undergraduate and postgraduate levels. Her research interests are in management accounting control systems and corporate governance. She has published in journals such as *Australian Accounting Review, International Journal of Quality & Reliability Management* and the *Journal of Accounting & Organizational Change*.

David Bond

David joined the UTS Business School in 2003 and is currently a Senior Lecturer in the Accounting Discipline Group. He has published in journals including *Accounting & Finance*, *Journal of Accounting and Public Policy*, *Journal of Contemporary Accounting & Economics* and *Australian Accounting Review*. David is currently on the Board for the Accounting and Finance Association of Australia and New Zealand and the Sport Management Association of Australia and New Zealand. He has previously held the position of Academic Fellow at the International Financial Reporting Standards Foundation in London, as well as been a visiting academic at the London School of Economics. He has received a number of teaching awards, including an Australian Government Office for Learning & Teaching Citation.

CHAPTER 1

Introduction to accounting and business decision making

LEARNING OBJECTIVES

After studying this chapter, you should be able to:

1.1 explain the process of accounting

1.2 outline the importance of accounting and its role in decision making by various users

1.3 explain the differences between financial accounting and management accounting

1.4 explain the role of accounting information in the business planning process

1.5 discuss the globalisation of financial reporting

1.6 explain what is meant by digital disruption and how new technology is influencing the accounting profession

1.7 describe business sustainability, outline its key drivers and principles, and compare key theories in the area

1.8 describe sustainability reporting and disclosure (including integrated reporting)

1.9 provide examples of exciting opportunities for careers in accounting.

Chapter preview

What is accounting's role in business decision making? How can you use accounting to plan a business? What are the opportunities for careers in accounting? These questions and more are answered in this first chapter of this text. People in all walks of life rely on accounting information to make daily decisions concerning the allocation of scarce resources. For example, a retired rugby player may rely on accounting information to help guide investment decision making on the allocation of his earnings as a professional sportsman; a student might use budgeting tools to help plan an overseas trip to Japan at the end of her university year; and knowledge of expected costs could help a construction company quote for a job on a large-scale, multimillion-dollar building project. All of these scenarios would benefit from the input of accounting information to help reach the best decision based on the available resources.

In recent years, the responsibilities of the accounting profession have changed dramatically. The Enron Corporation and Arthur Andersen financial scandals at the start of the millennium resulted in major changes to public expectations of the accountant and underlined the importance of good accounting practices in companies. Changes in the structure of business entities, including the growth of the multinational and diversified entity, have also had consequences for the accounting profession. Digital disruption through the emergence of new technologies is also impacting on many aspects of the business world and of course the skill set required for tomorrow's accountant. The next decade will present many opportunities and challenges for the profession.

The role of the accountant is continually evolving and comprises a lot more than just the rudimentary preparation of financial statements and the traditional work areas of management and financial accounting. Accountants can work in exciting new growth areas such as artificial intelligence (AI), analytics, blockchain technology, fintech, forensic accounting, sustainability accounting, procurement and insolvency.

In addition to explaining the importance of accounting information in decision making such as planning a business, this chapter outlines the globalisation of financial reporting, the role of professional accounting associations, digital disruption, and the emergence of new technologies and new careers in accounting.

1.1 The accounting process

LEARNING OBJECTIVE 1.1 Explain the process of accounting.

Many students embarking on a first course in accounting not only have the wrong idea about what the course content is going to be, but also have a misconception of what an accountant actually does! Some anticipate that the course will be about recording transactions in journals and ledgers; others think that the course is all about balancing the books. Some people associate accountants with repetitive tasks such as data entry and see the role as rather dull. There is, however, a lot more to accounting and the role of an accountant than this. In accounting, we learn not only how to record and report transactions, but also the purpose of the information created and the many uses of accounting information in everyday living and business. Accounting provides users with financial information to guide them in making decisions such as planning a business. An understanding of accounting and its various roles in decision making will equip you with some important tools and techniques for understanding a broad range of accounting and business issues. The accounting and business issues we will explore throughout this text include the following.

- What is the blockchain and how could it change the role of the accountant?
- What are the differences between financial and management accounting?
- What is an SME?
- What type of financial reports do business entities prepare?
- What is meant by sustainability accounting?
- What is meant by integrated reporting?
- What is the meaning of IFRS?
- What does it mean to be ethical in business?
- What is governance and does it apply to all business entities?
- What does business analytics mean and how does it impact on accounting?
- How has accounting changed since corporate collapses such as Enron?

The word 'account' derives from the Latin words *ad* and *computend*, which mean 'to reckon together' or 'to count up or calculate'. **Accounting** can be defined as the process of identifying, measuring and communicating economic information about an entity to a variety of users for decision-making purposes. The first component of this definition is the process of identifying business transactions.

A **business transaction** is an event that affects the financial position of an entity and can be reliably measured and recorded. Business transactions include such events as withdrawals of cash by the owner(s), payment of wages and salaries, earning of fees revenue, purchase of an office photocopier, purchase of stationery, capital contributions by owners, incurring of interest on a bank loan and payment of quarterly GST (goods and services tax).

The second component of the definition is the measuring of information, which refers to the analysis, recording and classification of business transactions. This component identifies how transactions will affect the entity's position, and groups together similar items such as **expenses** and **income**. For example, the contribution of capital by the owners of an entity will have the effect of increasing the cash at bank (**asset**) of the entity and increasing the capital (**equity**) of the entity. The earning of fees revenue will have the effect of increasing the income of the entity and increasing the entity's assets. Depending on whether the fees earned were cash fees or on credit, the cash at bank or debtors of the entity, respectively, will increase. Throughout the accounting period, individual assets, expenses, income, equity and **liabilities** will be grouped (classified) together to summarise the information. For example, land, buildings, machinery, equipment and vehicles will be grouped together under the subheading 'property, plant and equipment' (PPE).

The final component is the communication of relevant information through accounting reports, such as the statement of profit or loss and the statement of financial position, for decision-making purposes for the various users. For example, the total of the PPE account will be reported on the statement of financial position. Different users require accounting information for making important decisions such as whether to invest in a business, what type of business structure would be appropriate, whether the entity should continue to manufacture a product or outsource this process to another entity, and whether the entity has the resources to pay its debts on time. All these decisions involve making the most of the scarce resource — money. The process of accounting assists users in the allocation of this scarce resource.

The practices of accounting and bookkeeping date back to ancient civilisations in China, Egypt, Greece and Rome, where families had to keep personal records of their receipts and payments. The title 'Father of accounting' belongs to the Italian mathematician Luca Pacioli, who in 1494 produced *Summa de Arithmetica, Geometrica, Proportioni et Proportionalita*, which included chapters based entirely on how to record business transactions using a double-entry system. Table 1.1 summarises the process of accounting.

TABLE 1.1	The process of accounting		
Identifying	**Measuring**	**Communicating**	**Decision making**
Transactions that affect the entity's financial position are taken into consideration. They must be able to be reliably measured and recorded.	This stage includes the analysis, recording and classification of business transactions.	Accounting information is communicated through various reports such as the statement of profit or loss, statement of financial positions and statement of cash flows.	Accounting information is used for a range of decisions by external and internal users.

VALUE TO BUSINESS

- Accounting is the process of identifying, measuring and communicating economic information about an entity for decision making by a variety of users.

1.2 Accounting information and its role in decision making

LEARNING OBJECTIVE 1.2 Outline the importance of accounting and its role in decision making by various users.

Accounting information is an important part of our everyday decision-making processes and, as summarised by this excerpt from the Jenkins Report (AICPA 1994, ch. 1), everyone is:

> affected by business reporting, the cornerstone on which our process of capital allocation is built. An effective allocation process is critical to a healthy economy that promotes productivity, encourages

innovation, and provides an efficient and liquid market for buying and selling securities and obtaining and granting credit.

Prospective and current investors, employees, consumers, regulatory bodies, government authorities and financial institutions are just some of the many individuals and groups that are interested in accounting information and require accounting to help them make decisions relating to the allocation of scarce resources.

Individuals and entities need accounting information to assist in making decisions, such as planning a business, and subsequent capital investment decisions. Planning a business is introduced later in this chapter and the appendix to this chapter provides more in-depth coverage of the main aspects of the business planning process. Accounting information is designed to meet the needs of both internal users and external users of such information. Accounting information is extremely valuable to an entity's owners or management (i.e. **internal users**). It is used to help owner(s)/managers achieve the following.

- Make decisions concerning the operations of a business entity. The information that owners or managers require is usually detailed enough to assist them in initial management planning processes, such as determining the appropriate sales mix and price of goods, forecasting profits and determining the capacity of assets such as plant.
- Evaluate the success of the entity in achieving its objectives. This is done by comparing the performance of the entity against budgets and assessing how well employees have achieved their set targets.
- Weigh up various alternatives when investing the resources of the business entity.

External users (stakeholders) include such parties as employees, shareholders, suppliers, banks, consumers, taxation authorities, regulatory bodies and lobby groups, all of whom have their own information needs. They have a 'stake' or interest in the performance of the entity. Accounting information is used to help external users achieve the following.

- Current shareholders of an entity will seek accounting information to help them evaluate whether the entity's managers have been appropriate stewards or custodians of the entity's assets. They will examine entity reports to glean how effectively management have invested the assets of the business entity and whether they have made appropriate business decisions on behalf of the investors. This is known as the stewardship function of management. The information in an entity's annual report can explain to the investors what areas of business the entity has expanded into and what the entity's strategic plan is for the next 12 months, 5 years, 10 years.
- Prospective investors will seek information from entity reports to determine whether or not a particular entity is a sound investment. Information such as the financial structure of the entity (level of debts versus level of equity), current financial performance and future growth prospects can help such external users to determine whether capital growth is expected for the entity.
- Suppliers and banks are interested in gauging the entity's ability to repay debt and the level of risk associated with lending funds to it. Statements such as the statement of cash flows and the statement of financial position enable them to evaluate whether the entity has sufficient funds to meet debt repayments and to cover interest expense.
- Employees are most concerned about the future prospects of the entity. Is there a likelihood that the entity will expand, consequently creating additional job opportunities? Is there a possibility of promotion? Or, if the entity is performing poorly, are jobs at risk? What is the remuneration of the highest paid executives and what are the financial details of the employee share ownership plan? Particular sections in the annual report such as the chief executive officer's (CEO's) report, directors' report, statement of comprehensive income and statement of cash flows will provide useful information to the employees of the entity.
- Government authorities such as the Australian Taxation Office (ATO) will be interested in the reported profit for the year and the associated GST paid, in order to calculate the amount of tax to be paid or refunded in a particular financial year. Regulatory bodies such as the **Australian Securities and Investments Commission (ASIC)** will seek to identify whether the business has complied with requirements of the *Corporations Act 2001* (**Cwlth**); for example, whether a **disclosing entity** has complied with the Australian Accounting Standards.

Table 1.2 summarises the accounting information required by different stakeholders for their decision making.

TABLE 1.2   Stakeholders and the accounting information they need for their decision making

Stakeholder	Accounting information and decision making
Shareholders	Information to assess the future profitability of an entity, the future cash flows for dividends and the possibility of capital growth of investment.
Banks	Information to determine whether the entity has the ability to repay a loan.
Suppliers	Information to determine the entity's ability to repay debts associated with purchases.
Employees	Information concerning job security, the potential to pay awards and bonuses, and promotion opportunities.
Consumers	Information regarding the continuity of the entity and its ability to provide appropriate goods and services.
Government authorities	Information to determine the amount of tax that should be paid and any future taxation liabilities or taxation assets.
Regulatory bodies	Information to determine whether the entity is abiding by regulations such as the Corporations Act and Australian taxation law.
Community	Information to determine whether the entity is contributing positively to the general welfare and economic growth of the local community.
Special interest groups	Information to determine whether the entity has considered environmental, social and/or industrial aspects during its operations.

VALUE TO BUSINESS

- Internal users are the owner(s) or management of an entity who use accounting information to assist with various decision-making activities.
- External users (also known as stakeholders) are groups outside an entity that use accounting information to make decisions about the entity.

1.3 Financial accounting and management accounting

LEARNING OBJECTIVE 1.3 Explain the differences between financial accounting and management accounting.

In a typical accounting degree, you will undertake studies in both financial accounting and management accounting. **Financial accounting** is the preparation and presentation of financial information for all types of users to enable them to make economic decisions regarding the entity. **General purpose financial statements (GPFS)** are prepared to meet the information needs common to users who are unable to command reports to suit their own needs, while **special purpose financial statements** are prepared to suit a specific purpose and do not cater for the generalised needs common to most users. This information is governed by the **generally accepted accounting principles (GAAP)**, which provide accounting standards for preparing financial statements. Financial accounting is also guided by rules set out in the Corporations Act and the **Listing Rules** of the **Australian Securities Exchange (ASX)**. Financial accounting is traditionally based on historical figures that stem from the original transaction; for example, the purchase of a building for $500 000 would be shown in the financial statement (the statement of financial position) as an asset of $500 000. Even though the $500 000 may not reflect the current market value of the building, the building is still shown at its **historical cost**, which is the original amount paid for the asset.

The **financial statements** consist of the entity's statement of cash flows, statement of financial position and statement of profit or loss (for companies, the statement of profit or loss and other comprehensive income and the statement of changes in equity). The **statement of cash flows** reports on an entity's cash inflows and cash outflows, which are classified into operating, investing and financing activities. The **statement of profit or loss** reflects the **profit** for the entity for a specified time period. (Profit is the excess of income over expenses for a period.) An entity's assets and its liabilities at a point in time are reported in the **statement of financial position**. Financial statements will suit a variety of different users, such as the management of the entity, investors, suppliers, consumers, banks, employees, government bodies and regulatory authorities.

Management accounting is a field of accounting that provides economic information for internal users, that is, owner(s) and management. The core activities of management accounting include formulating plans and budgets, and providing information to be used in the monitoring and control of different parts of an entity. Management accounting reports are bound by few rules and are therefore less formal. Because management accounting reports are prepared for and tailored to suit the needs of management, they can provide any level of detail. For example, if the human resources manager requires information on the number of employees who have opted to make additional superannuation contributions, then a report can be produced. Management accounting reports must be up to date and can be prepared at any time for any period. For example, a sales manager in the entity may demand information on the current day's sales by the end of that day.

Ultimately there will be an interaction between financial accounting and management accounting, because management accounting will provide economic information for internal users that is then reflected in the financial accounting statements for external users. One such example of the interaction between financial and management accounting is in the area of segment reporting by large and diversified companies. Large and diversified companies must disclose segment information as part of their accompanying notes to their financial statements. Reporting on segments assists users in helping to understand an entity's relative risks and returns of individual segments of the entity. The operating segments are reported according to how an entity is organised and managed, and hence this is known as the management approach. Therefore, management accounting determines the operating segments and financial accounting reports these operating segments to the various users of financial statements. Illustrative example 1.1 shows the reportable operating segments for the Qantas Group. As you can see, the revenue and results for the Qantas Group have been disaggregated into the operating segments of Qantas Domestic, Qantas International, Jetstar Group, Qantas Loyalty, etc. There are also additional breakdowns for depreciation and amortisation, operating leases and so on.

ILLUSTRATIVE EXAMPLE 1.1

Operating segments for the Qantas Group

(ii) Analysis by operating segment[1]

2018 $m	Qantas Domestic	Qantas International	Jetstar Group	Qantas Loyalty	Corporate	Unallocated Eliminations[4]	Consolidated
REVENUE AND OTHER INCOME							
External segment revenue and other income	5 535	6 515	3 646	1 386	18	(40)	17 060
Inter-segment revenue and other income	438	377	121	160	—	(1 096)	—
Total segment revenue and other income	5 973	6 892	3 767	1 546	18	(1 136)	17 060
Share of net profit/(loss) of investments accounted for under the equity method	4	4	7	—	—	—	15
Underlying EBITDAR[2]	1 473	1 005	890	402	(182)	(13)	3 575
Non-cancellable aircraft operating lease rentals	(76)	(64)	(132)	—	—	—	(272)
Depreciation and amortisation	(629)	(542)	(297)	(30)	(13)	(6)	(1 517)
Underlying EBIT	768	399	461	372	(195)	(19)	1 786
Underlying net finance costs					(182)		(182)
Underlying PBT					(377)		1 604
ROIC %[3]							22.0%

1. Qantas Domestic, Qantas International, Jetstar Group, Qantas Loyalty and Corporate are the operating segments of the Qantas Group.
2. Underlying EBITDAR represents underlying earnings before income tax expense, depreciation, amortisation, non-cancellable aircraft operating lease rentals and net finance costs.
3. ROIC % represents Return on Invested Capital (ROIC) EBIT divided by Average Invested Capital (refer to Note 1(C)).
4. Unallocated Eliminations represents unallocated and other businesses of Qantas Group which are not considered to be significant reportable segments including consolidation elimination entries.

Source: Qantas Airways Ltd 2018, p. 59.

Qantas is widely regarded as the world's leading long-distance airline and one of the strongest brands in Australia.

The main differences between financial accounting and management accounting are summarised in table 1.3.

TABLE 1.3	Differences between financial accounting and management accounting	
	Financial accounting	**Management accounting**
1. Regulations	Bound by GAAP. GAAP are represented by accounting standards (including those issued by both the Australian Accounting Standards Board (AASB) and the International Accounting Standards Board (IASB)), the Corporations Act and relevant rules of the accounting associations and other organisations such as the ASX.	Much less formal and without any prescribed rules. The reports are constructed to be of use to managers.
2. Timeliness	Information is often outdated by the time statements are distributed to users. The financial statements present a historical picture of the past operations of the entity.	Management reports can be both a historical record and a projection (e.g. a budget).
3. Level of detail	Most financial statements are of a quantitative nature. The statements represent the entity as a whole, consolidating income and expenses from different segments of the business.	Much more detailed and can be tailored to suit the needs of management. Of both a quantitative and a qualitative nature.
4. Main users	Prepared to suit a variety of users including management, suppliers, consumers, employees, banks, taxation authorities, interested groups, investors and prospective investors.	Main users are the owner(s)/managers in the entity, hence the term management accounting.

1.4 Role of accounting information in business planning

LEARNING OBJECTIVE 1.4 Explain the role of accounting information in the business planning process.

Accounting plays a crucial role in the business planning process. Starting and planning a business is a demanding task. Whether an individual or a group of investors buys an existing business or begins a brand-new business entity, there are many issues to deal with. One of the most important questions that faces prospective business owners is what type of business structure will suit the business. Will the business be a for-profit entity with the primary objective of making a profit from the resources the owners control in order to increase their wealth? Alternatively, is the entity's objective to maximise the services provided from the resources they control? This second type of entity is known as a not-for-profit entity. Examples include sporting clubs, hospitals and charities. Profit-oriented business structures include sole traders, partnerships and companies. Most business entities are classified as SMEs (small to medium-sized enterprises). Small businesses are entities with annual revenue between $2 million and $10 million. In Australia, more than 97 per cent of entities are SMEs and they employ approximately 44 per cent of the workforce. Larger business entities such as JB Hi-Fi Ltd, Qantas Group and BHP Group Ltd are listed on the ASX. In New Zealand, companies such as Air New Zealand Ltd, Fisher & Paykel Healthcare and The Warehouse Group are listed on the New Zealand Exchange (NZX) and have special reporting requirements. The business structures chapter will consider each form of business structure and the type of decision making that goes into the business planning process in order to choose the right form of business.

When contemplating commencing a business, an effective way to deal with the complex issues that arise is to draw up a business plan. Accounting has many inputs to this process, particularly in the area of financial projections. A business plan is a written document that explains and analyses an existing or proposed business. It explains the goals of the firm, how it will operate and the likely outcomes of the planned business. A business plan can be referred to as a 'blueprint', similar to the plans an architect would prepare for a new building, or a draft or specification that an engineer would prepare for a new machine.

Benefits of a business plan

There are a number of benefits to be gained from developing a business plan. The business plan provides a clear, formal statement of direction and purpose. It allows the management and employees of an entity to work towards a set of clearly defined goals in the daily operations of the business. It also assists the business entity in evaluating the business.

Operation of the business

As stated, accounting information provides managers and owners with the tools they require to make decisions regarding the daily running of the business entity and whether the goals set by the business entity in the planning process are being achieved. For example, the owner/managers will be able to see if they are selling the correct products and work out the right product mix to achieve their sales targets. The chapter on costing and pricing in an entity includes a systematic consideration of cost behaviour and the subsequent impact on profit planning. Cost–volume–profit analysis assists management in understanding how profits will change in response to changes in sales volumes, costs and prices. Accounting information also provides key information relating to large asset purchases by a business entity. Entities regularly make decisions to invest in new assets or new projects and need to determine which particular investments offer the highest returns and produce the requisite cash flows. The capital investment chapter provides a comprehensive discussion of the role of accounting information in capital investment decision making.

Evaluation of the business plan

Accounting information provides management with the tools necessary to evaluate the business plan and encourages the management and owners to review all aspects of the operations. The evaluation process, along with the decision-making process, allows a more effective use of scarce resources such as staff, equipment and supplies, and improvement in coordination and internal communication. Strategic planning and budgeting will be discussed in detail in the budgeting chapter. In the evaluation process, results are compared to budgeted results so that both favourable and unfavourable variances can be detected. Management can then take action if necessary to make changes to the entity's operating activities to ensure that it stays on track with the original business plan. Management may also modify the entity's original goals. Further information on the business planning process and an illustration of a business plan for the fictitious company Murphy Recruiting Pty Ltd are provided in the appendix to this chapter.

VALUE TO BUSINESS

- Accounting information plays a major role in business planning and in evaluating the business planning process.

1.5 Globalisation of accounting

LEARNING OBJECTIVE 1.5 Discuss the globalisation of financial reporting.

Even though the vast majority of our business entities are SMEs, our larger entities have become bigger, more diversified and multinational. Consider the National Australia Bank (NAB), which reports its operating segments as Australian Banking, NAB Wealth, NZ Banking, UK Banking, NAB UK Commercial Real Estate and Corporate Functions & Other. In 2018, NAB reported a profit of $5.6 billion and total assets of $806.5 billion. In 1996, its reported profit was $2.1 billion and total assets were $174 billion (approximately a fifth of the size of its assets 22 years later!). As entities become more diversified and multinational, they require more complex accountancy and auditing services. Accountants must ensure that they remain up to date with the local GAAP and global accounting standards. Currently, more than 166 countries worldwide prepare their financial statements following global accounting standards. These accounting standards are known as **International Financial Reporting Standards (IFRS)**.

1.6 Digital disruption and the impact on accounting

LEARNING OBJECTIVE 1.6 Explain what is meant by digital disruption and how new technology is influencing the accounting profession.

Digital disruption has been defined as 'New technologies and business models that impact, transform or re-invent existing goods and services, industries and business activities. It's a change that can be positive or negative, and can drive substantial changes across the economy' (Queensland Government Chief Information Office 2018). The business world has changed considerably over the past couple of decades, and in the next decade there will be more industry disruption and transformation (Birt et al. 2017). In recent years we have seen the emergence of the fintech industry, Big Data and data analytics, cloud computing, mobile phone technology, AI and social media, and all of these have consequences for the accounting profession.

Fintech companies include many aspects of finance, for example, borrowing money, foreign currency, e-commerce and government payments, and the growth of this sector is impacting on accounting systems and processes. With the streamlining of certain accounting processes due to the introduction of new technologies there will be less need for traditional accounting services, but at the same time there are additional opportunities for accountants in managing the regulatory, tax and financial implications of the fintech industry (ACCA 2016).

In today's world, the amount of data that is produced is phenomenal. It is very hard to quantify exactly how much data is produced every day, but the unit of measurement at the moment is quintillion bytes! Ninety per cent of the data in the world has been generated in the past two years alone, and this is only going to increase. It is important for accountants and other business professionals to have the skills to understand data analytics. Accountants need to be able to blend data from different sources (e.g. company reports, ASX data, government data, economic data), use analytical tools to draw insights from the data, make decisions based on the data and communicate their findings to other parties such as management, the board and investors. There are many business analytical tools that assist accountants, for example Excel and Tableau.

Blockchain technology supports cryptocurrencies such as Bitcoin. Bitcoin is a digital currency that allows for online payments to be made without going through a financial institution (Raymaekers 2014). A blockchain is a structure of data that represents a financial ledger entry (Hassell 2016). The blockchain's data is partitioned into blocks and these blocks are linked together using cryptographic signatures. The blockchain creates many opportunities and challenges for the accounting profession. Some of the current accounting and audit roles will diminish, as there will be less need for accountants and auditors to perform the transaction processing, reconciliation and control type tasks. However, there will be new opportunities for auditors in overseeing and auditing the blockchain.

AI is having an impact on many industries. Traditionally robots have been used in the manufacturing industry, but in recent years there has been adoption of robotic technology in the healthcare, agriculture and food-preparation industries. In auditing, drones are performing audits in remote areas that are difficult to access and would otherwise be too expensive or unsafe to send a human to.

1.7 Business sustainability, drivers, principles and theories

LEARNING OBJECTIVE 1.7 Describe business sustainability, outline its key drivers and principles, and compare key theories in the area.

Generally, a growing environmental and societal awareness has put pressure on entities to consider their non-financial impacts. More specifically, entities need to account for all resources used (labour, material, energy, forests, water, air etc.) and all outputs produced (products/services, carbon emissions, waste etc.). To cope with this expectation, new frameworks and techniques are being developed and adopted under an overarching theme of **business sustainability**. But what is business sustainability?

An often-cited definition of sustainability was put forward by Brundtland (1987):

> Sustainable development is development that meets the needs of the present without compromising the ability of future generations to meet their own needs. It contains within it two key concepts: the concept of needs, in particular the essential needs of the world's poor, to which overriding priority should be given; and the idea of limitations imposed by the state of technology and social organisation on the environment's ability to meet present and future needs.

Many reasons have been put forward in relation to the need for a focus on sustainability. Ceres (2010) suggests there are four key drivers of sustainability. These are outlined in figure 1.1.

| **FIGURE 1.1** | Key drivers of sustainability |

Competition for resources

The world's population is projected to increase to more than 9 billion people by 2050. Rising living standards will result in both expanded markets for goods and services, and unprecedented demands on the planet's natural resources. Many of the resources once considered renewable — like forests and fresh water — have become finite when we consider that human demands are growing more quickly than the ability of natural processes to replenish them. While the exhaustion of commodities can be monitored and measured, the impact of depletion on ecosystems is harder to gauge and often impossible to remedy. With resource depletion comes the risk of conflict as people struggle to meet their basic needs. Take water — population growth, economic development and climate change are straining access to fresh water globally. By 2025, two-thirds of the world's population will live in water-stressed countries, posing significant risks to the economic and social stability of entire regions and to the corporate operations in those regions.

Climate change

Our current fossil-fuel based economy has led to a growing concentration of greenhouse gases in the atmosphere that is driving more extreme weather events, more severe and frequent cycles of drought and flood, and rising sea levels. These phenomena are being met with new policies and regulations, including those designed to limit and put a cost on carbon emissions. Businesses need to plan for a policy environment increasingly hostile towards carbon emissions and for the costs of adaptation to climate change. A large number of businesses and investors have come together to call on governments at the national and global levels to implement comprehensive climate policy. These groups include the Business for Innovative Climate and Energy Policy (BICEP), US CAP, Prince of Wales Corporate Leaders Group on Climate Change, Investor Network on Climate Risk (INCR) and Institutional Investors Group on Climate Change (II GCC), among others. These businesses recognise the opportunity to profit from technologies that reduce emissions and create solutions to global warming.

Economic globalisation

The integration of national economies into the global economy brings opportunities for business, but often with significant risks. More and more companies operate in or source from multiple countries with wide disparities in enforced environmental and social standards. Whatever the local enforced standard, many stakeholder groups demand, at a minimum, that companies meet international expectations.

Connectivity and communication

Advances in digital communication over the last two decades have reduced not only the time it takes to build a reputation, but also the time it takes to destroy one. Communication is increasingly disaggregated across multiple social networks. Facebook has over 65 million users and is growing by more than 200% per year. Twitter, while having a 'mere' 7 million users, has shown year-to-year growth of over 1000%. Using these types of tools, it has never been easier for people to track a company's sustainability performance and to widely disseminate their perspectives on it. We have entered an era of 'radical transparency'.

Source: Ceres 2010, p. 8.

Widespread acceptance of the need for entities to become sustainable has led to a number of scholars, professional groups and corporations developing guidelines and principles to help shape the business sustainability movement. Table 1.4 presents the nine principles of business sustainability performance as outlined by Epstein and Roy (2003).

TABLE 1.4	Principles of business sustainability performance	
1	**Ethics**	The company establishes, promotes, monitors and maintains ethical standards and practices in dealings with all company stakeholders.
2	**Governance**	The company manages all of its resources conscientiously and effectively, recognising the fiduciary duty of corporate boards and managers to focus on the interests of all company stakeholders.
3	**Transparency**	The company provides timely disclosure of information about its products and services, and its activities, thus permitting stakeholders to make informed decisions.
4	**Business relationships**	The company engages in fair trading practices with suppliers, distributors and partners.
5	**Financial return**	The company compensates providers of capital with a competitive return on investment and the protection of company assets.
6	**Community involvement/ economic development**	The company fosters a mutually beneficial relationship between the corporation and the community in which it is sensitive to the culture, context and needs of the community.
7	**Value of products and services**	The company respects the needs, desires and rights of its customers, and strives to provide the highest levels of product and service values.
8	**Employment practices**	The company engages in human resource management practices that promote personal and professional employee development, diversity and empowerment.
9	**Protection of the environment**	The company strives to protect and restore the environment and sustainable development with products, processes, services and activities.

Source: Epstein and Roy 2003, p. 37.

Theories of business sustainability

The nine principles of business sustainability performance illustrate the heightened interest in business sustainability that has grown out of the expectation that corporations need to be socially responsible. This responsibility is assessed and examined through a number of theories including corporate social responsibility, **shareholder value**, stakeholder theory, stewardship theory and legitimacy theory. These theories are outlined briefly in the following sections.

Corporate social responsibility

Corporate social responsibility (CSR) refers to the responsibility an entity has to all stakeholders, including society in general and the physical environment in which it operates. Many reasons have been proposed as to why entities do act in socially responsible ways. Some commentators believe entities act in a socially responsible manner because there is ultimately some benefit to their profits. For example, by acting in the best interests of society generally, an entity may be able to seek higher prices or sell a greater volume of product, and therefore achieve the goal of maximising owner wealth. Others believe entities want to limit interference from governments or other groups and therefore do the minimum needed to retain control over their industry. Still others suggest managers are motivated simply by the desire to do the right thing and that there is no economic motive behind acting in a socially responsible manner. Motives aside, there is increasing acceptance that an entity has a responsibility to all stakeholders — not just the owners — and that the entity will be better off in the long term by acting in a socially responsible fashion.

The thought surrounding business sustainability was brought together by quite divergent groups working contemporaneously on issues that concerned them about the environmental and social impacts of business activity. These groups include John Elkington, an English environmentalist and the founder of Sustainability, who put forward the triple bottom line approach to corporate performance; Ceres, which was formed in the aftermath of the Exxon Valdez oil spill disaster in 1989; the International Union for Conservation of Nature (IUCN), which was concerned for the biosphere; and the Greenpeace movement. These are all examples of associations working to change the culture and shift the thinking about the role of business in contemporary society. Elkington tells the story in his famous book, *Cannibals with forks*, of a UK director attempting to explain the sustainability imperative to a US board in the early 1990s. He describes the event as one where metaphorical blood was spilled as the US board viewed the sustainability theme as a plot to transfer US knowledge to other countries and in support of communist ideals, thus undermining principles of capitalism. Suffice it to say that the view on sustainability has changed since that time, with many entities considering their obligations to a wider stakeholder audience.

A corporation usually has a large number of **stakeholders**, who are individuals or groups that have an interest in the entity's affairs. They include shareholders (the owners), employees, creditors, suppliers, governments and other interested parties (such as unions and environmental groups). Despite recognition that corporations should consider wider stakeholder interests, there is still a fundamental question regarding an entity's ultimate responsibility. Does the entity have a responsibility to consider all of them equally?

Shareholder value

In the Australian and New Zealand legal context, the responsibilities of a board of directors are set out, respectively, in the *Corporations Act 2001* and the *Companies Act 1993*. This legislation, together with the constitution of an entity, generally acknowledges the owners (shareholders) of the entity to be the primary focus. It is through the provisions of a company's constitution and the Corporations Act (Australia) and the Companies Act (NZ) that shareholders give power to the directors to make decisions and to act on their behalf. The legislation and a company's constitution set out various requirements, such as the need to publish financial reports and hold annual general meetings. It is the shareholders who vote at the annual general meeting and the shareholders who choose the directors. A well-known theory called **agency theory** is used to describe the relationship between the owners (shareholders) and managers of an entity. The shareholders appoint managers as their agents to run the business on their behalf. Given this separation of control between owners and managers, the owners need to set up mechanisms to ensure that managers make the decisions that they themselves would have made had they been in control. To this end, it is commonly accepted that a central part of business sustainability is to ensure the maximisation of shareholder value.

Stakeholder theory

Critics of shareholder value claim that many stakeholders other than shareholders invest in entities. **Stakeholder theory** holds that the purpose of an entity is to work for the good of all stakeholder groups, not just to maximise shareholder wealth. Employees, governments, customers and communities all have an interest in the affairs of the entity. Estes (1990, p. C1) argues that:

> These forgotten investors are owed an accounting because they, too, invest by committing valuable resources, including not only money but their work, their careers, sometimes their lives to the corporation.

Stewardship theory

Related to stakeholder theory is **stewardship theory**. This theory suggests that the motive for serving on a board goes beyond a perspective of pure self-interest. This motive may be guided by a code or company purpose, or directors may see themselves as stewards of a particular interest. It is generally under this banner that there has been an increase in the number of independent non-executive directors on boards, thus serving the interests of a large number of small shareholders, or the community and the environment. At times, key suppliers or debt providers may take a place on a board to help protect their relevant interests. No matter what the interest, they are stewards of some greater good, not just shareholder wealth. However, it may go beyond this, as summarised by Peter Weinberg (a former Goldman Sachs executive):

> Serving on a board is like taking on a position in public service … It is not (and should not be) a wealth creation opportunity but a chance to play a role in the proper workings of our marketplace (Nordberg 2008, p. 43).

Legitimacy theory

Another theory considered in the economic and sustainability realm is **legitimacy theory**. The basic tenet of this theory suggests that entities, to remain legitimate, must operate within the bounds and norms of society. In other words, society allows an entity to operate (to pursue its objectives and rewards) so long as the entity acts in a socially acceptable manner. Proponents of legitimacy theory call this the 'social contract'. The social contract represents the explicit and implicit expectations that society holds about how organisations should conduct their operations. An organisation must be responsive to these expectations, as they change over time. Sanctions, a reduced demand for products or a limitation on available resources could be some consequences of breaking the social contract. Proponents suggest that organisations will seek to legitimise their actions through the information they supply to the community, including that information contained in the financial statements. In other words, managers are motivated to ensure the community perceives them to be operating within societal norms.

1.8 Reporting and disclosure

LEARNING OBJECTIVE 1.8 Describe sustainability reporting and disclosure (including integrated reporting).

Integral to business sustainability is reporting. A company is required to issue an annual report that includes GPFS. The practice of issuing a voluntary business sustainability report (along with the annual report) is becoming widespread. In 2000, *A framework for public environmental reporting: An Australian approach*, released by the federal government agency Environment Australia, outlined the benefits of environmental reporting as:
- improving stakeholder relations
- creating market opportunities
- increasing control over environmental disclosure
- satisfying a mandatory or signatory reporting need
- gaining the confidence of investors, insurers and financial institutions
- triggering internal improvement in environmental performance
- gaining external recognition/awards.

Top senior finance professionals known as the Group of 100 cited the organisational benefits of sustainability reporting as:
- reputation and brand benefits
- securing a 'social licence to operate'
- attraction and retention of high-calibre employees
- improved access to the investor market
- establishing position as a preferred supplier
- reducing risk profile

- cost savings
- innovation aligning stakeholder needs with management focus
- creating a sound basis for stakeholder dialogue.

These lists illustrate the importance of reporting and disclosing environmental and social performance.

In New Zealand, the *Environmental Reporting Act 2015*, which outlines a reporting framework, was passed into law in September 2015 after a lengthy consultation process commencing in 2011. This highlights the importance of environmental reporting.

A number of frameworks have been proposed by governments and professional associations to help with the content of such reports, and a number of indices help to measure an organisation's performance in sustainability. For example, the Australian SAM Sustainability Index (AuSSI) has been used since 2005 to identify companies committed to good sustainability outcomes. Internationally, the Global Reporting Initiative (GRI) is a widely accepted and used reporting framework. The work and leadership of Ceres and the United Nations Environment Programme (UNEP) led to the formation of the GRI and the development of the *Sustainability Reporting Guidelines*. From 1 July 2018, the Guidelines were replaced with the GRI Standards. The **GRI Standards** (which can be accessed at www.globalreporting.org) contain four main parts:

1. Universal Standards, which are applicable to every entity preparing a sustainability report
2. Economic Standards, which are used to report on an entity's material impacts related to economic topics
3. Environmental Standards, which are used to report on an entity's material impacts related to environmental topics including:
   - Materials
   - Energy
   - Water and Effluents
   - Biodiversity
   - Emissions
4. Social Standards, which include Employment, Labour/Management Relations and Occupational Health and Safety.

The GRI Standards also include criteria to be applied by an entity in order to prepare its sustainability report 'in accordance' with the Standards, based on two options, the 'core' option and the 'comprehensive' option. Regardless of the option chosen by the entity, the focus of preparing the report is on the process of identifying any material economic, environmental and social aspects that would substantially influence the assessment of decisions of stakeholders.

Triple bottom line

The GRI Standards include performance indicators from the economic, environmental and social dimensions. These three dimensions are commonly accepted as the three 'pillars' of sustainability and are known as the **triple bottom line**. They are also frequently depicted in interlocking cycles, as shown in figure 1.2. Sometimes referred to as 'people, planet and profit', 3BL or TBL, the three concepts have been used widely to discuss and disseminate information regarding business sustainability.

Traditionally, business entities report their financial performance. Depending on the entity structure, this is required by law to help with capital funding applications, to lodge tax returns and to generally assess the financial performance of the entity. The business structures chapter will discuss the different business entities and their reporting requirements. However, the TBL approach advocates expanding the reporting of an entity's performance to include social and environmental performance. The underlying concept is in line with stakeholder theory as discussed earlier. That is, an entity exists to bring about interactions and transactions with various stakeholders on economic, environmental and social levels.

Economic performance is the traditional profit and return on capital performance. More recently, economic performance has been defined as the economic value created by the entity over a particular period of time. This is the profit minus the cost of the capital employed. All entities must turn a profit and deliver an adequate return on the capital employed in order to remain sustainable. It is this bottom line that captures the conventional concept of performance and the focus of the owners of the entity.

Environmental performance refers to an entity's activities relating to natural capital and whether its activities are environmentally sustainable. Natural capital falls into two main areas: 'critical natural capital and renewable, replaceable, or substitutable natural capital' (Elkington 1998, p. 79). So the environmental bottom line captures the effect an entity's operations have on natural capital and whether this is sustainable.

FIGURE 1.2 Triple bottom line reporting framework

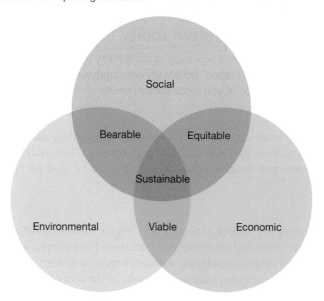

Source: Adams 2006.

Social performance refers to both human capital (the employees'/community's health, skills and education) and society's wealth creation potential (Elkington 1998). Fukuyama (1995) describes social capital as 'the ability of people to work together for common purposes in groups and organizations'. He argues that 'trust' in one another is a central element in social prosperity and that those organisations which trust one another and accept a common set of ethical norms will do business more efficiently and gather a greater variety of positive social relationships than those organisations which do not trust. As a result, doing business will be cheaper and the synergies from more positive social relations will help create sustained wealth. Examples of social capital are paying fair salaries to workers, not exploiting supplier relationships, providing safe working conditions and ensuring products/services are safe for consumers.

Inherent in the TBL framework is the trade-off between the three dimensions, and the need for environmental and social issues to be defined in accordance with financial viability. Critics of TBL contend that most social and environmental phenomena cannot be easily quantified. TBL and sustainability reporting in Australia and New Zealand is a growing trend despite lagging behind international levels (see www.kpmg.com.au/portals/0/ras_sustainability_reporting_aust200710.pdf). The GRI Standards are widely adopted to assist reporting across the TBL. The process of TBL reporting includes identifying stakeholders and the scope of the report, selecting appropriate indicators, data collection, measurement and verification, and finally the report presentation.

Beyond sustainability and towards abundance

Recently there has been a move to go beyond the concept of sustainability, which is seen by some as insufficient, and instead look at how we can improve the world around us. Critics argue that the focus on scarcity and lack is driving the creation of inappropriate business models and the inappropriate use of resources. The economy-of-scale thinking that developed during the Industrial Revolution may simply not be appropriate for today's ecological priority. Small-scale development, including encouraging SME development, would help serve regional communities and would be a more environmentally friendly way of strengthening economies.

The concept of abundance encourages businesses to embrace both literal abundance (what nature provides 'in abundance') and functional abundance (where scarce material is cycled endlessly via redesigned industrial models). Governments, businesses and people know that our current churn rate of limited natural resources is unsustainable, no matter how much measuring and reporting are done. However, switching to using resources that are naturally abundant makes good business sense. In natural systems, wastage due to abundance becomes feedstock for other parts of the system. Examples include green power, using hemp to make body panels on cars and using bacteria to extract precious metals from waste. Abundance thinking discourages the use of scarcity in determining 'price' as recommended by the basic economic supply and demand model. Price does not equate to value. Proponents argue that the use of the abundance concept to determine 'price' is a more useful approach. (For further research on the circular economy, see www.ellenmacarthurfoundation.org.)

Role of accountants in sustainability

The role of accountants in promoting and reporting sustainability is very broad. They can use their skills of aggregating data into useful information, help with cost analysis of environmental decisions and be involved with the audit and assurance of corporate social reports.

Reporting

Accountants are well versed in the application of standards for reporting, and their skills in this area can be applied to the reporting of an entity's sustainability performance. Their systems could also be modified to incorporate environmental and social information, which could be used for both external and internal reporting purposes.

Cost analysis

Comparison of two competing investment projects would require an analysis of economic profits in order to make decisions relating to social and environmental initiatives. For example, a development may require land to be brought back to its original condition; a decision may be needed as to what tyres to purchase given their costs and impacts on company-maintained roads; or the cost of implementing energy-efficient devices may need to be compared to the energy consumption costs. This could then be extended to the collection, analysis and reporting of non-qualitative information.

Audit and assurance services

The integrity of financial information and its collection can be safeguarded by putting in place clear processes and procedures known as internal control. This is familiar ground for accountants and makes them ideal candidates to help provide auditing and assurance on the CSR reports that are issued by entities. Apart from internal control, the systems in place and reports produced can be audited by external independent groups or individuals. The GRI Standards identify external assurance as important to the reporting process and list its key qualities. External assurance:

- is conducted by groups or individuals who are external, competent and independent of the reporting organisation
- is systematic, documented, evidence-based and characterised by defined procedures
- assesses whether the report provides a reasonable and balanced presentation of performance
- utilises groups or individuals that are not unduly limited by their relationship with the organisation or its stakeholders (i.e. they are impartial and independent)
- assesses the extent of the application of the GRI Standards
- results in an opinion or conclusion that is publicly available along with a statement outlining the relationship of the assurance provider to the report preparer (Global Reporting Initiative 2013).

VALUE TO BUSINESS

- Business sustainability has been increasing with the growing awareness that society and the environment cannot cope with the continued focus on economic growth.
- The GRI Standards encourage the reporting of sustainability practices. Sustainability reporting promotes the transparency and accountability of an entity's operations.
- The triple bottom line approach encourages a focus on the economic, social and environmental performance of an entity.
- Accountants can use their formal training to help organisations become more sustainable.

Integrated reporting

Integrated reporting (IR) refers to the integration of social, environmental, financial and governance information. In 2010 the International Integrated Reporting Council (IIRC) was formed, which has accelerated the implementation of IR. At present IR is mandated in South Africa and Japan, and each year more and more companies are producing integrated reports. IR brings together material information about an organisation's strategy, governance, performance and prospects in a way that reflects the commercial, social and environmental context within which the organisation operates. It provides a clear and concise representation of how an organisation demonstrates stewardship and how it creates and sustains value (International Integrated Reporting Council 2018). An integrated report is based on the six capitals — financial capital, manufactured capital, human capital, intellectual capital, natural capital and social and relationship capital.

1.9 Careers in accounting

LEARNING OBJECTIVE 1.9 Provide examples of exciting opportunities for careers in accounting.

The three traditional areas of employment for accountants have been in public accounting, the private sector and the government and not-for-profit sector. Public accountants can provide advice on the design of an accounting system such as MYOB and on investment, audit, forensic accounting and tax issues. Private sector accountants may work in a number of positions, such as management accounting, e-commerce or as chief financial officers (CFOs) in small, medium or large private companies. Accountants working in the government and not-for-profit sector could work for a government entity such as the Department of Defence, for which they would maintain government records and prepare government financial reports. Other public sector accountants could be employed by the ATO and would be responsible for checking company taxation returns and ensuring compliance with taxation laws. An accountant working in the not-for-profit sector could be employed at a public hospital and be responsible for setting up the hospital accounting system to record individual patient revenue and patient expenses.

New opportunities

There are exciting new opportunities for today's accounting graduates. These include positions in the area of forensic accounting, where accountants help to solve such crimes as computer hacking and the theft of large amounts of money through hoax schemes on the internet. In recent years, several Australian banks have been the targets of this type of crime, where customers have been sent an email, supposedly from the bank, requesting them to provide confidential personal banking details. Some of these customers have been misled and supplied personal details, resulting in unauthorised individuals accessing their personal funds. The burgeoning area of e-commerce also provides opportunities, as accountants are required to assist in designing web-based payment systems such as BPAY and helping to ensure the security of these systems. There are also opportunities in the administration of insolvency, where accountants may help failing companies by offering advice to improve the entity's future prospects or assist in selling the entity's assets if a decision is made to wind up the company.

Another important growth area is sustainability accounting and, more specifically, carbon accounting. A job as a carbon accountant could involve categorising and calculating greenhouse gas emissions, reviewing carbon reporting procedures, and evaluating the business risks and opportunities for reducing an entity's carbon footprint.

Figure 1.3 illustrates just some of the opportunities for accountants.

FIGURE 1.3 Accounting opportunities

Manager, Data Analytics (Data Management)
AE Business Bank
As Manager, Data Analytics, you will be responsible for the management of our data requirements, including appropriate reporting of data, management of data storage and of datasets.

Immediate start
Brisbane, CBD

Commercial Manager — Manufacturing
Bill Bloomburg Pty Ltd
Manage all commercial aspects of Bill Bloomburg's business ventures, with a focus on generating efficiencies, building profitability and ensuring accurate reporting.

Competitive salary
Sydney, western suburbs

Audit Manager
Joan Finance
In this key role, you will manage a team of auditors and be responsible for organising and overseeing all internal audits. You will also be responsible for developing and implementing internal auditing policies as well as undertaking risk management reviews.

Attractive remuneration package
Adelaide, CBD

▶

Senior Tax Accountant
The Best in Tax Ltd
Your responsibilities in this role include:
- lodging forms with the ATO and liaising with government departments
- reconciling accounts for the preparation of financial statements
- preparing financial statements
- providing taxation and business advice.

Flexible work environment
Melbourne, inner & western suburbs

Forensic Accountant — Senior Analyst
Linda Brown Recruitment Services
As our Forensic Accountant, you will investigate accounts and gather business information in order to analyse and report on areas of profit and loss. You will provide advice regarding strategic risk management and share information with company stakeholders.

Excellent career prospects
Perth, CBD

SAP Solution Specialist
Team Timmaco Group
Your responsibilities in this role include using SAP to manage all accounting and inventory processes. You will work with company managers to action SAP requests and to provide support as required.

Permanent position
Brisbane, outer suburbs

A background in accounting is beneficial for people working in various positions in an entity. There are many well-known accounting techniques to be discussed later in the text that are extremely important for management to understand and implement. Tools such as break-even analysis allow management to determine the selling point where total revenue will equal total costs. The process of capital investment decision making enables management to screen and analyse different capital projects in order to determine which projects should be undertaken by the entity to maximise the return on investment. The chapters on capital investment and performance management will examine these topics in detail.

SUMMARY OF LEARNING OBJECTIVES

1.1 Explain the process of accounting.

The process of accounting is one of identifying, measuring and communicating economic information about an entity for decision making by a variety of users.

1.2 Outline the importance of accounting and its role in decision making by various users.

Accounting information is an important part of the information used by individuals and entities in decision making regarding investment and other business opportunities. The internal users (i.e. management) use accounting information to make decisions concerning sales mix, which products to make or buy, and opportunities for expansion. Stakeholders (e.g. suppliers, consumers, banks, shareholders and regulatory bodies) require accounting information to help decide whether to lend money to the entity, whether to invest in the entity and whether to purchase goods from the entity.

1.3 Explain the differences between financial accounting and management accounting.

Management accounting concerns the creation of reports for use by management in internal planning and decision making. Management accounting reports are much less formal than financial accounting reports, as they are not bound by regulatory requirements. These reports can also be tailored to suit the needs of management. There is no time lag with management reports, so they are up to date. Financial accounting provides information for the use of external parties so that they can make economic decisions about the entity. Financial accounting is bound by the generally accepted accounting principles (GAAP). There is usually a time lag from the date of the report to when it is distributed to the various users. Financial accounting information is concise, as extra detail is disclosed in the notes to the financial statements. The users of financial statements include suppliers, consumers, banks, investors and regulatory bodies.

1.4 Explain the role of accounting information in the business planning process.

Accounting plays a major role in the business planning process. Accounting information assists owner(s)/managers in determining the type of business structure that would be appropriate for a business and in establishing goals for the business entity to achieve. Accounting information provides feedback for the owner(s)/managers on the daily operations of the business. It allows entities to determine the correct mix of goods to sell and the right prices at which to market the products. It also assists the business in making decisions relating to assets to purchase to help the business achieve its goals. Finally, accounting information assists the business in evaluating its business plan. Budgeted plans are compared to actual performance. Tools such as analysis and interpretation assist management in determining if the business entity is on track with its goals.

1.5 Discuss the globalisation of financial reporting.

In recent years, entities have become larger, more diversified and multinational. Currently, two-thirds of US investors own shares in foreign entities that report their financial information using IFRS. Over 166 countries worldwide have now adopted IFRS and, in years to come, the rest of the world will most likely adopt a single set of high-quality accounting standards that will meet the needs of all users.

1.6 Explain what is meant by digital disruption and how new technology is influencing the accounting profession.

Digital disruption is influencing many aspects of business and will provide opportunities and challenges for the accounting and auditing professions. New technologies and advances such as AI, drones, fintech, blockchain and Big Data are all influencing the role of the accountant and the skills required to perform accounting and auditing tasks.

1.7 Describe business sustainability, outline its key drivers and principles, and compare key theories in the area.

Business sustainability considers the use of the world's resources in a way that does not compromise the ability of future generations to meet their needs. Key drivers include the competition for resources, climate change, economic globalisation and connectivity and communication. Principles include ethics, governance, transparency, business relationships, financial return, community involvement/economic development, value of products and services, employment practices and protection of the environment. By necessity, decision making in business incorporates a certain level of ethical contemplation. This includes consideration of corporate social responsibilities, such as consideration of employees, the lifecycle of a product or service, the impact of the entity generally on society and the environment, and the need to report such effects, both positive and negative. Shareholder value is concerned with the increase in the wealth of the shareholders (owners of the corporation). Stakeholder theory suggests that many groups other than shareholders have a stake in the activities and performance of an entity, and that corporate governance needs to reflect the wider duty of care that society is placing on the decision makers of entities. Stewardship theory suggests that directors are stewards of some cause or group.

1.8 Describe sustainability reporting and disclosure (including integrated reporting).

The triple bottom line approach and the GRI Standards are two common methods used for reporting corporate social responsibility (CSR). The three dimensions of the triple bottom line approach espouse the need to report on economic, social and environmental dimensions. The GRI Standards support this view and outline principles and standard disclosures required, technical protocols and information relevant to different sectors. A standard sustainability report should contain the strategy and profile of an entity, the management approach and the entity's economic, social and environmental performance indicators. Accountants can help organisations to apply the GRI Standards by using their expertise in gathering, collating and reporting information, including sustainability-relevant information, in their analysis for business decisions and through the provision of auditing and assurance services. Integrated reporting combines social, environmental, financial and governance information. It is based on the six capitals of financial capital, manufactured capital, human capital, intellectual capital, natural capital and social and relationship capital.

1.9 Provide examples of exciting opportunities for careers in accounting.

Accountants are employed in public accounting roles, private and public sector accounting roles, and government and not-for-profit sector accounting roles. New opportunities for accountants exist in forensic accounting, environmental accounting, e-data analytics, blockchain, commerce, insolvency and international accounting.

KEY TERMS

accounting The process of identifying, measuring and communicating economic information about an entity to a variety of users for decision-making purposes.

agency theory A theory that describes the relationship between the owners (shareholders) and the managers of an entity.

asset A resource controlled by an entity as a result of past events and from which future economic benefits are expected to flow to the entity.

Australian Securities and Investments Commission (ASIC) Government body responsible for regulating companies, company borrowings and investment advisers and dealers.

Australian Securities Exchange (ASX) Australian marketplace for trading equities, government bonds and other fixed-interest securities.

business sustainability Use of the world's resources in a way that does not compromise the ability of future generations to meet their needs.

business transaction An occurrence that affects the assets, liabilities and equity items in an entity and must be recognised (recorded).

corporate social responsibility (CSR) The responsibility an entity has to all stakeholders, including society in general and the physical environment in which it operates.

Corporations Act 2001 **(Cwlth)** National scheme of legislation, administered by ASIC, dealing with the regulation of companies and the securities and futures industries in Australia.

disclosing entity An entity that issues securities which are quoted on a stock market or made available to the public via a prospectus.

equity Residual interest in the assets of an entity after all its liabilities have been deducted.

expenses Decreases in economic benefits during an accounting period in the form of outflows, decreases in assets or incurrences of liabilities that result in decreases in equity, other than those relating to distributions to equity participants.

external users (stakeholders) Parties outside an entity who use information to make decisions about the entity.

financial accounting Preparation and presentation of financial information for users to enable them to make economic decisions regarding an entity.

financial statements A set of statements directed towards the common information needs of a wide range of users.

general purpose financial statements (GPFS) Financial statements prepared to meet the information needs common to external users.

generally accepted accounting principles (GAAP) The specific rules and guidelines pertaining to a specific jurisdiction that entities use to help them prepare financial statements. These rules and guidelines vary from country to country.

GRI Standards The GRI Standards encourage the reporting of sustainability practices. Sustainability reporting promotes the transparency and accountability of an entity's operations.

historical cost Original amount paid or expected to be received for an item.

income Increase in economic benefits during an accounting period in the form of inflows, increases in assets or decreases in liabilities that result in increases in equity, other than those relating to contributions from equity participants.

internal users Owner(s) or managers of an entity who use financial information to assist in various aspects of business decision making.

International Financial Reporting Standards (IFRS) Accounting standards that are prepared and issued by the International Accounting Standards Board (IASB).

legitimacy theory A theory which suggests that entities, to remain legitimate, must operate within the bounds and norms of society.

liabilities Present obligations of an entity arising from past events, the settlement of which is expected to result in an outflow from the entity of resources embodying economic benefits.

Listing Rules Rules governing the procedures and behaviour of all ASX-listed companies.

management accounting A field of accounting that provides economic information for use by management in internal planning and decision making.

profit Income less expenses for a reporting period.

shareholder value The wealth of shareholders (owners of the corporation).

special purpose financial statements Financial statements prepared to suit a specific purpose.

stakeholder theory A theory which holds that the purpose of an entity is to work for the good of all stakeholder groups, not just to maximise shareholder wealth.

stakeholders Individuals or groups that have an interest in an entity's affairs. They include shareholders (the owners), employees, creditors, suppliers, governments and other interested parties (such as unions and environmental groups).

statement of cash flows A statement that reports on an entity's cash inflows and cash outflows for a specified period.

statement of financial position A statement that reports on the assets, liabilities and equity of an entity at a particular point in time.

statement of profit or loss A statement that reports on the income and expenses of an entity for a period and the resulting profit or loss.

stewardship theory A theory which suggests that the motive for serving on a board goes beyond a perspective of pure self-interest and that directors are stewards of some cause or group.

triple bottom line The TBL approach to reporting encourages a focus on the economic, social and environmental performance of an entity.

APPLY YOUR KNOWLEDGE
40 marks

(a) Provide an example of the different types of activities that would be performed by a management accountant and a financial accountant for a large public company listed on the ASX.   *5 marks*

(b) What are some of the advantages of business planning?   *5 marks*

(c) Sustainability accounting is a very important and huge growth area of accounting. Discuss the different stakeholders (and their information needs) that would be interested in sustainability reports. *10 marks*

(d) Integrated reporting is a type of reporting that has been adopted in countries such as South Africa. What do you think are the advantages and the disadvantages to a company of providing such disclosures?
10 marks

(e) What are the three elements of a business plan? Consider the situation of two sisters contemplating a new business hiring surfboards and providing surf lessons on the Sunshine Coast. Explain how the business plan would assist the sisters in planning their business venture.   *10 marks*

COMPREHENSION QUESTIONS

1.1 What is a business transaction and how does it relate to the accounting process? Illustrate the concept of a business transaction with five examples relating to an SME such as a provider of Chinese therapeutic massages. **LO1**

1.2 Differentiate between financial accounting and management accounting. Provide an example of how a management accounting report would be incorporated into financial accounting reports. **LO3**

1.3 Describe how accounting information helps shareholders and lenders to make decisions concerning the operations and performance of an entity. **LO2**

1.4 Provide an example each of a company that would produce a GPFS and a company that would produce a special purpose financial statement. Who are the likely stakeholders of both types of entities? **LO3**

1.5 One of the new opportunities for accounting graduates is forensic accounting. What does forensic accounting entail? Provide an example of a position as a forensic accountant. **LO9**

1.6 List five stakeholders of accounting information. Describe the information requirements for each one; for example, lenders would need information regarding a business's ability to repay debt and service a loan. **LO2**

1.7 Jackie Smith is considering purchasing a sushi bar in the inner Melbourne suburb of Albert Park. Outline the importance of a business plan for Jackie and the type of accounting information she will require to assist her in making the decision. **LO4**

1.8 What is stakeholder theory and how is it related to corporate governance? **LO7**

1.9 What are the challenges associated with digital disruption for accountants? **LO6**

1.10 Give an example each of the role accounting information plays in the investment planning for a retired footballer and a retired schoolteacher. **LO2**

1.11 Why has the globalisation of accounting become so important for accountants? **LO5**

1.12 How does data analytics help accountants make decisions? **LO6**

1.13 Explain the role of the blockchain in cryptocurrencies. **LO6**

1.14 What are the six capitals that an integrated report is focused on? **LO8**

1.15 What is the role of the International Integrated Reporting Council? What is its strategy? **LO8**

1.16 What is meant by business sustainability? **LO7**

1.17 Suggest ways in which suppliers and customers could work together to reduce their overall impact on the environment. **LO7**

1.18 What are the three pillars of sustainability? **LO7**

1.19 Growth areas for accountants in the future include sustainability reporting and, more specifically, carbon accounting. What are the costs and the benefits for entities in reporting their carbon greenhouse gas emissions? **LO9**

1.20 Outline the nine principles of business sustainability performance as put forward by Epstein and Roy (2003). **LO7, 8**

1.21 Outline some ways that accountants could contribute to the sustainability efforts of organisations. **LO7**

1.22 Suggest what the most important driver of sustainability would be and explain your rationale for its selection. **LO7**

1.23 List the qualities needed in providing external audit and assurance services to organisations in relation to CSR reports. **LO7**

1.24 Compare the principles underlying the GRI sustainability reporting Standards with the principles underlying the preparation of GPFS. **LO8**

PROBLEMS

★ BASIC | ★ ★ MODERATE | ★ ★ ★ CHALLENGING

1.25 Business sustainability ★ **LO7**

Read the article on environmental auditing at www.epa.vic.gov.au/our-work/environmental-auditing. What is environmental auditing? What is a 53V audit? What is the role of the auditor in the 53V process?

1.26 GRI framework ★   **LO8**

You are a CFO in an organisation that is considering reporting on CSR using the GRI Standards. The CEO has asked you to prepare a report for the board supporting such a proposal. In this report you should outline:

(a) the benefits of CSR reporting

(b) the likely costs of CSR reporting

(c) to whom the company will be reporting

(d) what will be covered in the report

(e) how this process will support the business strategy.

1.27 Business sustainability ★   **LO7**

Critique the role that regulation plays in encouraging business sustainability. In other words, assess whether you feel the government should regulate to protect the environment's and society's needs or whether companies would 'do the right thing' anyway. In your answer, define regulation and business sustainability. Give your opinion as to whether existing legislation such as work health and safety and industrial relations (such as award wages) are necessary or just an extra burden on business that destroys efficiency and productivity.

1.28 Business sustainability ★   **LO7**

'Human rights are rights inherent to all human beings, whatever our nationality, place of residence, sex, national or ethnic origin, colour, religion, language, or any other status. We are all equally entitled to our human rights without discrimination. These rights are all interrelated, interdependent and indivisible' (United Nations Human Rights Office of the High Commissioner 2018).

Required

Investigate the relationship of human rights to business sustainability. In your answer, examine the relationship from various angles, such as:

(a) human beings are a resource to be used as a means to an end

(b) individual human beings should be able to negotiate their own pay without the need for industrial laws

(c) if some people have more than others, then they must have worked harder and deserved it; the system is based on opportunities and everyone has to look out for themselves.

1.29 International convergence ★ ★   **LO5**

It is argued that the convergence of our accounting standards with international standards and their subsequent adoption have brought great benefits to the Australian economy. What are the benefits in relation to international trade?

1.30 IFRS adoption ★ ★   **LO5**

Go to the IFRS Foundation website, www.ifrs.org. Select 'Around the world' then 'Use of IFRS standards by jurisdiction'. Comment on the jurisdictions that have adopted IFRS. Which countries are yet to adopt IFRS? Can you think of reasons why certain countries have not adopted IFRS?

1.31 Sustainability reporting ★ ★ ★   **LO7**

BHP Group Ltd includes a sustainability report in its annual report. What key performance indicators (KPIs) are included in this report? Explain the different stakeholders that would be interested in this information.

DECISION-MAKING ACTIVITIES

1.32 Download the report *Triple bottom line reporting in Australia* at www.environment.gov.au/archive/settlements/industry/finance/publications/indicators/pubs/indicators.pdf. This guide puts forward a methodology to help entities report on their environmental impacts. The environment is one of the three pillars of TBL accounting. From the report:

(a) outline the five environmental management indicators stated

(b) for each of the environmental issues listed, give two examples of an environmental measure of environmental performance

(c) discuss how accountants could help an entity develop a TBL report.

1.33 After successfully running her SME recruitment agency for a number of years, Angelica feels it is now time to expand. Her friends in business have told her to 'get big or get out'. One of the options she is investigating is whether or not to list on the ASX. She has heard that the ASX has its own regulation in the form of Listing Rules.

(a) Go to www.asx.com.au and conduct a search under 'Regulation' for the 'ASX Listing Rules'.

(b) Give two examples of the Listing Rules that Angelica must abide by if she decides to list her recruitment agency on the ASX.

1.34 Go to the CSR Ltd website (www.csr.com.au) and locate the segment report in the company's latest financial statements.

(a) What do you think is the purpose of the segment report?

(b) What operating segments does CSR have?

(c) How do you think this information would benefit stakeholders of financial statements?

(d) Can you think of any disadvantages of disclosing this information for CSR Ltd?

1.35 Refer to the latest financial statements for JB Hi-Fi Ltd. (The notes to the 2018 consolidated financial statements of JB Hi-Fi Ltd appear in the appendix to this text and the statements are available online at http://investors.jbhifi.com.au.) For each of the following stakeholders, give an illustration of a report or a note that would be useful for decision-making purposes, state why the information is useful and give an example of how that information would be used.

(a) Prospective shareholders

(b) Customers

(c) Employees

(d) Suppliers to JB Hi-Fi Ltd

(e) Auditors

(f) Charity organisations

(g) Australian Taxation Office

1.36 In Amcor's *2017 GRI Report*, CEO Ron Delia stated that 'with our global scale, strong relationships and collaborative approach, Amcor is making improvements and breakthroughs that are raising the environmental profile of our entire industry'. Listed among Amcor's key achievements for the year, it was noted that the company earned gold awards and high ratings 'for packaging innovation and sustainability excellence, including from the DuPont Packaging Innovation Awards, the Flexible Packaging Association, EcoVadis, and the European Aluminium Foil Association' (Amcor 2017).

Required

Suggest why organisations would use resources to apply for sustainability awards and would be concerned about their rating on sustainability market indices.

1.37 Go to the Tableau website (www.tableau.com). Select 'Products' and 'Tableau Desktop'. Summarise the main features of 'Tableau Desktop' and how it can assist accountants in their daily tasks.

REFERENCES

ACCA 2016, *Professional accountants – the future: Drivers of change and future skills*, www.accaglobal.com/content/dam/members-beta/docs/ea-patf-drivers-of-change-and-future-skills.pdf.

Adams, WM 2006, *The future of sustainability: Re-thinking environment and development in the twenty-first century*, Report of the IUCN Renowned Thinkers Meeting, 29–31 January, The World Conservation Union, p. 2.

AICPA Special Committee on Financial Reporting 1994, *Improving business reporting: A customer focus* (The Jenkins Report), American Institute of Certified Public Accountants, New York, www.aicpa.org.

Amcor Ltd 2017, *2017 GRI Report*, www.amcor.com.

Birt, J, Wells, P, Kavanagh, M, Robb, A & Bir, P 2017, *ICT literature review*, www.iaesb.org/system/files/meetings/files/4-2-ICT-Literature-Review.pdf.

Brundtland, G 1987, *Our common future: Report of the World Commission on Environment and Development*, Oxford University Press, Oxford.

Ceres 2010, *The 21st century corporation: The Ceres roadmap for sustainability*, Creative Commons, San Francisco.

Elkington, J 1998, *Cannibals with forks: The triple bottom line of 21st century business*, New Society Publishers, Canada and Stony Creek, CT, USQ.

Environment Australia 2000, *A framework for public environmental reporting: An Australian approach*, www.environment. gov.au.

Epstein, MJ & Roy, M 2003, 'Improving sustainability performance: specifying, implementing and measuring key principles', in MJ Epstein 2008, *Making sustainability work: Best practices in managing and measuring corporate social, environmental and economic impacts*, Berrett Koehler Publishers, San Francisco.

Estes, R 1990, 'How to save corporate America, *Des Moines Register*', in TL Wheelen & JK Hunger (eds) 1992, *Strategic management and business policy*, Addison Wesley Publishing Company, New York, p. C1.

Fukuyama, F 1995, *Trust: The social virtues and the creation of prosperity*, Hamish Hamilton, London.

Global Reporting Initiative (GRI) 2013, *External assurance*, Global Reporting Initiative, Amsterdam, www.globalreporting.org.

Hassell, J 2016, 'What is blockchain and how does it work?', CIO from IDG homepage, www.cio.com/article/3055847/security/what-is-blockchain-and-how-does-it-work.html.

International Integrated Reporting Council 2018, *Integrated Reporting Framework*, http://integratedreporting.org/resource/international-ir-framework.

Nordberg, D 2008, 'The ethics of corporate governance', *Journal of General Management*, vol. 33, no. 4, pp. 35–52.

Qantas Airways Ltd 2018, *Annual report 2018*, www.qantas.com.au.

Queensland Government Chief Information Office 2018, *QGCIO Glossary*, www.qgcio.qld.gov.au/publications/qgcio-glossary/digital-disruption-definition.

Raymaekers, W 2014, 'Cryptocurrency Bitcoin: Disruption, challenges and opportunities', *Journal of Payments Strategy & Systems*, vol. 9, no. 1, pp. 1–40.

United Nations Human Rights Office of the High Commissioner 2018, 'What are human rights?', www.ohchr.org/en/issues/pages/whatarehumanrights.aspx.

ACKNOWLEDGEMENTS

Photo: © leungchopan / Shutterstock.com

Photo: © Ryan Fletcher / Shutterstock.com

Illustrative example 1.1: © Qantas Airways Ltd 2018

Figure 1.1: © Ceres 2010, *The 21st century corporation: The Ceres roadmap for sustainability*, Creative Commons, San Francisco, p. 8.

Figure 1.2: © Wiley. Adams, WM 2006, *The future of sustainability: Re-thinking environment and development in the twenty-first century*, Report of the IUCN Renowned Thinkers Meeting, 29–31 January, International Union for Conservation of Nature, www.iucn.org.

Table 1.4: © Braybrooke Press. Epstein, MJ & Roy, M 2003, 'Improving sustainability performance: specifying, implementing and measuring key principles', in MJ Epstein 2008, *Making sustainability work: Best practices in managing and measuring corporate social, environmental and economic impacts*, Berrett Koehler Publishers, San Francisco, p. 37.

APPENDIX 1

The business planning process

What is a business plan?

As discussed in this chapter, a business plan explains the goals of a firm, how it will operate and the likely outcomes of the planned business. A business plan can be referred to as a 'blueprint', similar to the plans an architect would prepare for a new building, or a draft or specification that an engineer would prepare for a new machine. Starting and organising a business is a demanding task. Whether you are buying an existing business or beginning a brand-new business entity, there are always many tasks to do and issues to deal with. One way is simply to deal with each question or problem as it arises. The other strategy, long favoured by business advisers and commentators, is to carefully draw up a business plan. A business plan is a written document that explains and analyses an existing or proposed business. As such, it is a forecast or forward projection of a potential business idea. It explains the goals of the business entity, how it will operate and the likely outcomes. At the conclusion of this appendix, you will find a business plan for the fictitious business Murphy Recruiting Pty Ltd.

A business plan can be referred to as a 'blueprint' and is a forward projection of a potential business idea.

Advantages of a business plan

There are several advantages stemming from the development of a business plan (Schaper 1996). A well-prepared business plan provides a clear statement of purpose and direction for a firm. It allows management and employees of the firm to work towards a set of clearly defined goals, thus enhancing the likelihood of the goals being reached. This allows the business to take the initiative in determining its fate, rather than just reacting to events that occur in the outside environment.

Planning also provides a suitable means of periodically evaluating the performance of the firm. Different quantifiable targets, such as sales revenue, the number of items sold, market share and profitability, can be compared with the actual results at the end of the plan period (Zimmerer, Scarborough & Wilson 2008). Business owners need to assess the reasons for substantial discrepancies between the forecast and the actual results, and initiate action to overcome the gaps.

Because it is a comprehensive document, a business plan encourages managers and owners to effectively review all aspects of their operations (Hormozi et al. 2002). The review and decision-making processes involved in business plan construction foster a more effective use of scarce resources, such as staff, time and money, and improve coordination and internal communication. An effective plan demarcates responsibilities, spelling out the roles of key personnel; it also helps clarify job expectations and improves the accountability of staff to the owners and managers.

In addition, the very processes of collecting information, analysing it and integrating it into a written document can help ensure that the small-business owner has adequately researched their business idea. If properly done, preparation of a business plan will foster skill development during the processes of balanced and objective data collection, systematic analysis of the positive and negative results revealed by the research, and development of a comprehensive business response strategy that integrates all activities of the proposed venture with its internal and external environments. This developmental effect has been shown to be particularly important for improving the growth prospects of less experienced entrepreneurs and for starting a new venture from scratch (Burke, Fraser & Greene 2010).

Disadvantages of a business plan

However, it is also important to bear in mind that business plans, in themselves, are not a guarantee of success. Although some research does indicate that failed firms are less likely to have had business plans than other businesses, the mere existence of a plan does not ensure survival (Perry 2001). Business plans do not eliminate uncertainty, because no business entity exists in a completely predictable environment. In addition, many entrepreneurs express the view that a high level of planning will reduce their flexibility and room to move, rather than enhancing it (Gibb & Davies 1990). In some cases, an inflexible over-reliance on a predetermined plan, even in the face of overwhelming evidence of significant changes taking place in the business environment, can do more damage to the business than might otherwise be the case. There is also evidence emerging that the process and focus of plans (on marketing, operations or finance) should change in response to the prevailing environmental circumstances (Gruber 2007).

There are several other pitfalls that may reduce the effectiveness of a plan. Common failings include a lack of sufficient detail in explaining the intentions of the small-business owner; reliance on outdated, limited or biased information; failure to undertake detailed market research to validate the sales forecasts, expense estimates and marketing plans of the business entity; and preparation of a document that appears self-evident to the writer, but cannot be understood by other readers (Merle Crawford 2003).

Just how effective are plans to the overall success of a business? A recent extensive study aggregating the findings of many incidences of business planning undertaken in the period 2007–10 provides perhaps strong evidence of the value of business planning (Burke, Fraser & Greene 2010). The aggregated analysis shows there is indeed a significant positive relationship between planning and performance. While planning was shown to be important for new firm performance, this need was identified as even stronger for existing firms, which can draw upon internal knowledge and data to aid in their future forecasting and planning.

Components of a business plan

There is no universal format for a business plan; however, most such plans contain a common mix of items, since there are universal issues that are dealt with by all business entities. The main issues covered in all business plans can be broadly grouped into those relating to marketing, operations and finance (see figure A1.1).

These three components — marketing, operations and finance — are universal. All business owners need to research their market, know their customers, understand the state of the industry they operate in and have a comprehensive knowledge of the products or services they sell. They must also be able to structure, manage and operate the business in a logical manner so that it can work effectively on a day-to-day basis. Finally, they must know how much money is required to start the business, its prospective sales turnover and what returns they are likely to receive from it. One possible format of a plan is discussed below. It covers these three core elements of marketing, operations and finance, and considers additional issues that help round out the business idea and explain it comprehensively. At the end of this section, there is an example business plan for the fictitious business Murphy Recruiting Pty Ltd which follows the same plan structure.

Title page

The title page normally shows the name of the business and that of the owner or owners, and provides contact details (addresses, phone and fax numbers, website URL and email addresses).

Executive summary

An executive summary is an introductory segment briefly summarising the key features that are explained in more detail later in the plan. It is a quick snapshot of the idea and is often critical in influencing a reader's judgement of the whole document. Typically, it discusses the following items.

- *Business ideas and goals.* This section provides an overview of the business project, what product or service is being sold and what the business owner's goals are. It also indicates where the business expects to be in a year's time and later.
- *Marketing.* How will the products or services of the business be sold? Who will be the main target markets (customer groups) and what are the main elements of the proposed advertising and promotional strategy for the firm?
- *Operations.* Where will the business be located? How many staff will there be and how will they be organised? What is the legal structure of the business? How will it be managed?
- *Finances.* What profit is the firm expected to make by the end of the business plan time period? What finance is required and what will it be used for? Where will such capital be obtained from and what will the repayments be?

If at all possible, it is advisable to keep the executive summary to one page and certainly no more than two pages in length. It is, after all, the quick teaser designed to make the potential buyer want to read on.

Background

In this section, the business owner sets down the issues driving the business project, including the following.

- *Mission statement.* What is the philosophy and overall vision that the owners have for the business? Why do they want to start and run such a venture?
- *Company history.* Many existing businesses already have well-established systems, products and operating processes, and a customer base. It is important to briefly outline these before discussing the changes planned for the future.
- *Business goals.* What are the goals of this business? It is useful to provide both short-term goals (those for the next 12 months) and long-term goals (those covering the next 2 or 3 years, perhaps even longer). It is always desirable to provide some specific, measurable targets (such as net profit sought, anticipated sales revenue, number of staff employed, product range offered and market share to be held).

An important but often overlooked aspect of goal setting is the development of an exit strategy — what the business owner needs to do to get out of the business. Many business owners hope to build their wealth by eventually selling their business. A proposed exit strategy is also important for venture capitalists and other investors, who usually want to know how their investment will be returned to them (McKaskill 2006).

Marketing

The marketing segment provides the rationale for the existence of the business. Among other things, it gives the business owner the opportunity to show what market research has been done, the likely level of demand for the firm's products, what exactly will be sold by the firm and the intended customer base.

- *Market research.* What research has been done to prepare the plan? It is a good idea to list the primary and secondary sources consulted, including any personal communication with experts and their credentials to speak as experts (Barringer 2009). If appropriate, attach the results of any surveys or other particularly relevant data as an appendix.
- *Market analysis.* What is the result of the research? It is especially important to cover the following issues:
  - *Industry.* What are the characteristics of the industry in which the firm will operate? This section is particularly concerned with providing an overview of the industry as a whole, rather than the individual business. What is the current state of that industry and what are the likely prospects for future growth?
  - *Seasonality.* Are sales in this industry likely to be affected by changes at different times of the year or is the business cyclical in some other way — perhaps peaking at different times of the day or week?
  - *Competitors.* How many competitors are there, both direct and indirect? Who are the main players and what is known about them, such as where they are located, what they sell, what prices they charge, how long they have been in the industry, their after-sales service, staffing and customers' views of them?
  - *Potential strategic allies.* Are there other firms that the business can work with on joint projects, such as cross-referral of work or other ways that provide mutual benefits?
  - *SWOT analysis.* Using the data acquired, as well as your own understanding of the business idea, it should be possible to construct a table or list that identifies the various *strengths* and *weaknesses* of the business, as well as the *opportunities* and *threats* that it faces.
- *Marketing plan.* In this section, the marketing mix is dealt with.
  - *Products/services and target market.* This describes or lists the main product(s) and/or service(s) to be sold by the business. If making a product, how will it be packaged? What is the target market (who are the main groups of customers for the product/service mix)?
  - *Placement (distribution channel).* How will goods be distributed to customers? What costs and legal issues may be involved?
  - *Promotions and advertising.* How will the entity's goods and services be advertised and promoted to consumers?
  - *ICT marketing strategy.* With the widespread adoption of internet-based technologies by small business, there is a need to focus upon information and communication technology (ICT) strategy, from both marketing and operations perspectives. This should include a discussion on the use of emerging communications platforms such as Facebook, LinkedIn, Twitter and others (which this text refers to collectively as social media).
  - *Pricing policy.* What prices will be set? What sort of pricing strategy will be used? Will there be any discounts for bulk purchases or special customer groups? Will credit terms be offered to any clients?
- *Evaluation of marketing.* How will the effectiveness of the marketing program be assessed? What performance indicators will be used to measure success and how often will this be done?

Operations and production

Organisational details, day-to-day operating processes and other issues that do not have a clear marketing or financial role are usually discussed here.

- *Legal and licensing requirements.* This includes the business name, the legal structure of the business and the laws and licences that the business operates under or must obtain.
- *Management details.* This provides background details about the business owner and/or manager, including full name, residential address, phone number, email address, date of birth, qualifications, special skills and job history. Is there any other information about the business owner/manager that could be important? Does the business owner have any outstanding loans, guarantees or other financial exposure? Have they ever been bankrupt or charged with an offence that could affect their ability to operate the business? What previous business experience does the owner have?
- *Organisational structure and staffing.* Who will do which jobs in the business? If there will be more staff than just the owner-operator, who else will be employed? What skills and qualifications do they

need? How will the firm recruit staff and at what rate of pay? What further training will staff need? If possible, include an organisational chart for the firm.

- *Professional advisers.* This provides the names and contact details of all the outside business and technical advisers the business expects to use. This may include an accountant, a bank manager, an insurance broker and management consultants.
- *Insurance and security needs.* What insurance will be required for the business and how much will it cost? Are there any special security precautions that need to be considered for the business's property and equipment?
- *Business premises.* This discusses and explains all the issues related to location. Where will the business be based? How accessible is this to customers? Is it convenient to local roads and transport services? If the proposed site is to be leased, what rent, lease period, payments and conditions apply? Are any special facilities required (that is, does the business need a certain building size, specialised customer access, special lighting, air-conditioning or toilets)?
- *Plant and equipment required.* What equipment does the business need? Provide a list of likely needs, along with the type and make, cost, life expectancy, running costs, and service and maintenance requirements.
- *Production processes.* This briefly explains how the product is made, including the supply of any raw materials or trading stock, production processes in the premises and any related issues.
- *Information and communication technologies.* This describes the extent to which ICT will support people and processes within the business from an operational standpoint. It typically focuses on technologies that will be used to enhance productivity and/or enable consistency and quality.
- *Critical risks and contingency plans.* All businesses face potential problems and threats that can derail the goals outlined in the business plan or possibly even destroy the organisation. Although not all of these can be identified in advance, major threats should be discussed here, along with strategies for dealing with such issues if they arise.

Financial projections

In this section, the financial documents are presented, along with background notes and information that help a reader make sense of the financial forecasts.
- *Basic assumptions and information*
  - This explains the assumptions made in estimating income and expenses, and in calculating the various figures. Justify any unusual items, significant omissions or unusual variations in the figures. What estimates have been made about inflation or increases in costs, wages and interest rates?
  - It may be useful to provide details about the bank accounts that the business operates. What financial institution are these with, what type of accounts are they (savings, cheque or cash management) and what fees are charged? Does the financial institution have the facilities that the business might need (e.g. credit card access, mobile credit card scanners, online banking)?
  - Does the business currently have any loans or overdrafts outstanding? Provide details about the lender, the amount borrowed, the current balance still outstanding and the terms of the loan.
  - If additional funds are needed by the business, how much and how are they to be raised? If this money is to be borrowed, provide information about the proposed lender, total amount sought, date required, monthly repayments due, interest rate, loan conditions and term (duration) of the loan.
- *Financial forecasts*
  - *Sales mix forecast.* This uses market research and/or past performance to determine likely sales revenue for the first 12 months. Estimate the number of items sold each month, sales income from these and cost of goods sold.
  - *Cash flow forecast.* A cash flow statement summarises the monthly amount of cash movements (cash inflows and cash outflows) and the resulting cash balance for a year.
  - *Projected profit and loss statement.* Also known as a statement of financial performance, this shows business revenues, expenses and net profit for the forthcoming year.
  - *Statement of financial position.* This reports a business's financial position at a specific time. It provides details about the assets (financial resources owned by the firm), liabilities (claims against these resources) and net worth of the business. A statement of financial position is usually not provided for a new business. (There is no statement of financial position in the sample plan in the appendix to this chapter because Murphy Recruiting Pty Ltd is a new business.)
  - *Personal expenses, assets and liabilities.* Since much of the capital funding for a new or small business venture is provided by the owner, it is often recommended that the business plan contain

details about the owner-manager's personal assets and liabilities. In addition, since the owner usually draws income from the business, it is a good idea to include an estimate of likely personal expenses that will need to be drawn from the business. It is important to build in some degree of variation in these estimates since, just like the business, the owner will have high-expense and low-expense months.

- *Analysis of financial forecasts*
  - From the data provided, it may be desirable to conduct ratio analysis or other pertinent calculations. These could include (but are not necessarily limited to) an estimation of break-even point, fixed and variable costs, contribution margins, mark-ups and margins, projected impact upon the value of the business and return on investment (ROI) consequences.

Implementation timetable

This section provides a schedule of the activities needed to set up and run the business. It is usually organised on a monthly basis, providing a set of milestones for the owner-manager to work by.

Appendices

This section includes any extra useful information such as the resumes of the business owner and key management personnel, credit information, quotes for major capital purchases, lease or buy/sell agreements, other legal documents, competitors' promotional material, maps of the business site, floor plans of the business premises, service blueprints, process flowcharts and reference sources, and key statistics collected during the market research process.

Time frame

A business plan can be geared for a short time period (anything up to a year) or it may have a longer perspective. Short-term plans can afford to be more detailed, whereas a long-term orientation means that the plan must be more generalised in its contents. Many researchers argue that business planning in small firms tends to be overwhelmingly short term in orientation and that it is unusual to find a small business with plans that extend beyond a two-year time horizon (Glen & Weerawardena 1996). Of course, there are always some exceptions to this rule — some firms have been able to successfully use a very long-term time frame to help turn their business around. In general, however, a shorter term focus is used by most small-business entities.

Preparing the document: the business planning process

Few business plans are written at one sitting. More typically, a plan is the result of a series of logical steps that most business owners work through, regardless of whether or not they are conscious of the business planning process involved (see figure A1.2). These steps are often iterative; people may go through some of them several times before finally developing a plan that all parties feel comfortable with.

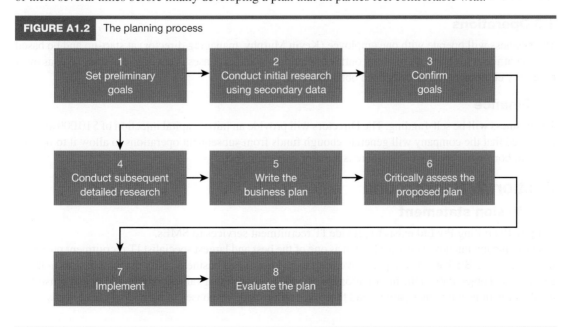

FIGURE A1.2 The planning process

1 Set preliminary goals → 2 Conduct initial research using secondary data → 3 Confirm goals

4 Conduct subsequent detailed research → 5 Write the business plan → 6 Critically assess the proposed plan

7 Implement → 8 Evaluate the plan

Summary

A business plan is a written outline of a business. It may be devised for an existing firm or for a new business entity that has not yet been launched. The main advantages of business planning include more complete information gathering, balanced decision making and assistance in raising finance. Disadvantages of a plan can include skewed information, incorrect assumptions, inflexibility and unrealistic expectations.

All business plans, whatever their structure, should cover the key issues of marketing, operations and finance. The major elements of a typical plan include an executive summary, background on the firm (if an existing enterprise), marketing details, operational arrangements, financial projections and a timetable for implementation.

Plans vary from one business to another. The format and sequence are often quite different, although all business plans should cover the basic issues. In addition, written business plans may have different levels of specificity, be written for different audiences and cover short-term or long-term time frames.

The business planning process is an ongoing process by which plans are constructed, implemented and evaluated. It includes the steps of preliminary goal setting, initial information gathering, formulation of set goals, detailed research, plan preparation, critical analysis of the proposed plan, implementation, and subsequent evaluation and revision.

Sample business plan: Murphy Recruiting Pty Ltd

Note: The business plan in this appendix is hypothetical and provided solely for the purpose of illustrating the nature and content of a completed plan. The business name, personal details, statistical data and references are all fictitious; no link with any actual person or organisation is intended.

Section 1. Executive summary

1.1 Business idea and goals

The main goal is to establish a small private (proprietary limited) company that specialises in IT recruitment services for the SME sector in Brisbane and other cities within the state of Queensland, Australia. The services to be provided are IT recruitment services for SME firms.

The owners plan to begin by employing one person full-time (Kevin Murphy, a major shareholder) and gradually grow to the point where the business employs three or four people within two to three years of inception. The business intends to generate sales revenue of about $200 000 and to make a $4000 profit by the end of its first year of trading.

1.2 Marketing

Murphy Recruiting Pty Ltd will provide specialist IT recruitment services to SMEs in the Brisbane metropolitan area. We will promote the business using a variety of methods, including direct mail, email canvassing, a Yellow Pages listing, networking, a website and testimonials.

1.3 Operations

The business will operate with one employee (Kevin Murphy, managing director) at start-up and be based from an office at his home. A minimal outlay of equipment and expenses is envisaged at this stage, as most necessary equipment has already been obtained.

1.4 Finance

The business will be self-funding. The Directors will provide an initial capital injection of $10 000 and it is envisaged that the company will generate enough funds from subsequent operations to allow it to operate on a 'no borrowing' policy unless there is a major change in focus.

Section 2. Background

2.1 Mission statement

Murphy Recruiting Pty Ltd exists to provide IT recruitment services to SMEs.

The company intends to become known as one of the best and largest specialist IT recruitment providers for SMEs in the Brisbane marketplace. We want to be known as a business entity that emphasises honesty, accuracy and objectivity in the information we provide to clients; that values confidentiality and sensitivity in all its relations with other parties; and that gives tailor-made responses to individual client needs.

In this way, Murphy Recruiting Pty Ltd seeks to promote the interests of the following.

- *Clients.* By providing these services, we can help our clients achieve the best-quality candidate who best suits the position offered.
- *The wider community.* Helping businesses with their recruitment processes ultimately stimulates local economic development, job creation and wealth distribution.
- *Our employees.* A well-paid, motivated and well-educated staff is essential to ongoing success. In return, employees should expect to receive secure employment, to continually expand and improve their business skills, to be encouraged to try new ideas and approaches, and to work in a comfortable, encouraging environment.
- *The owners of the company.* Successful achievement of the company mission should allow the company to operate profitably and to provide a fair return on effort and investment by the owners on a long-term basis.

2.2 Company history

This is a new business that springs from the existing experience of Kevin Murphy, who previously worked for several recruitment companies during the period 1995–2015. During this time, Kevin developed many skills including human resource management, recruitment and behavioural profiling of potential candidates to a range of clients.

2.3 Business goals

The business's goals for the short term (next 12 months) are to employ at least one person full-time on a salary of approximately \$65 320 per annum (gross), to meet all operating expenses and to generate a net profit of at least \$4000 for future investment. The long-term goals (next two or three years) are to establish a viable consultancy service employing up to five people and based in Brisbane, delivering services in IT recruitment from its own purchased building.

A future exit strategy has been agreed to by the three foundation shareholders/Directors, should any of them wish to liquidate their interest in the business at a later stage. The Directors have agreed that, after the end of the third year of trading, any shareholder will have the right to ask for the business to be independently valued; the remaining Directors will then have first option to buy out that person's interest. If they do not wish to exercise this right, the shareholder may sell to an outside party.

Section 3. Marketing

3.1 Market research

The following sources were used to prepare this business plan:
- Australian Bureau of Statistics
- Queensland Small Business Advisory Service
- personal interviews with several recruitment businesses in and around Brisbane
- Australian Institute of Human Resources
- a brief survey of SMEs that already use outside recruitment agencies
- other existing IT recruitment agencies
- a search of the relevant human resources literature
- conversations with several business brokers servicing greater Brisbane to establish valuation methods and benchmarks.

3.2 Market analysis

After a review of the industry, the following conclusions were drawn.
(a) *Industry analysis*
    There is a definite demand for specialist IT recruitment services in the SME market. Most services provided are aimed at larger corporations, which often already house their own recruitment division or capability. Accordingly, niche opportunities to provide these services best exist among small to medium-sized (mid-range) businesses (Ziericki 2007).
(b) *Seasonality*
    It is estimated that business declines in December and January, which represents the Christmas break and summer holiday period in Australia.
(c) *Competitors*
    They include other recruitment agencies (especially those that focus on IT recruitment).

(d) *Potential strategic alliances*

Potential exists to subcontract work from incubators.

(e) *SWOT analysis*

The above information was used to develop a list of potential strengths, weaknesses, opportunities and threats.

Potential strengths	Kevin's substantial recruitment experience Links to Queensland Small Business Advisory Service
Potential weaknesses	One-person operation at present Minimal track record in external consultancies Little skill in preparing tenders
Potential opportunities	Growth in external training programs Growth of ongoing mentoring services Good placement to qualify if sector becomes regulated
Potential threats	Competitors Sensitivity of SMEs to economic downturns

3.3 Marketing plan

3.3.1 Products/services and target market

Specialist IT recruitment services

Target markets:

- Small to medium-sized firms with an IT employee (10 to 100 employees)
- Brisbane metropolitan area
- Established companies (preferably two years or older)
- Approximately 600 such firms

Customer buying motives:

- SMEs often need specialist recruitment services to help find the right candidate for a position.
- It is often too difficult to do themselves, or a major recruitment agency may not have the specialist/ expertise to 'head hunt' the right candidate for the right position. SMEs want a high degree of service for the right price.

3.3.2 Placement

Since this is a home-based business dealing directly with clients at their premises, no particular distribution arrangements are envisaged as necessary.

3.3.3 Promotions and advertising

To start trading, the business already has a number of secure contracts in place. As such, it is not necessary to actively promote the enterprise to the general community. However, it would be useful to alert other potential clients to its existence, with a view to seeking work from them at a later stage. To this end, the following promotional tools will be used by the business:

- business cards and letterheads
- direct email followed up by telephone contacts
- listing in the next edition of the Brisbane Yellow Pages under 'IT Recruitment Consultants'
- promotional information — a series of web pages on the company website covering the staff of the organisation, services provided, benefits of using the company and a listing of previous clients
- networking — links to other practising professionals through membership of the Australian Institute of Human Resources and other local business bodies
- testimonials — a web page of positive testimonials from clients that can be used as references for future marketing
- public relations — as a start-up, we do not have the luxury of a significant focus on public relations initiatives. However, we will do what we can to ensure we are good corporate citizens and, as such, will have a triple bottom line perspective to external communications. This will need to be backed up with action on the ground (operations and finance).

3.3.4 ICT marketing strategy

There are few serious start-up businesses these days that achieve sustained success without an effective ICT strategy. We are talking here about something broader than just our e-commerce strategy or our website content; there is a need to include other forms of ICT that inform, service, retain, develop and generally communicate with a range of stakeholders. The range of tools to be used includes the following.

- *Internet.* A website will be created, displaying inbound links from other referring entities (such as government information agencies and online directories) as well as resources for other online information for customers. We will seek expertise to ensure the website is search engine optimised so that small businesses seeking advice in Brisbane can find us online easily. Once built, the website will be designed so that the content can be quickly updated by the owners or approved employees without need to rely on the developer to effect minor changes.
- *Social media.* The business will employ select social media tools to engage in a two-way conversation with key clients as a way of generating referral business and reinforcing existing relationships.
- *Software.* The business will use video-streaming software (and associated hardware) to develop and disseminate information in-house that educates the market about what we offer. We will also use customer relationship management (CRM) software which helps us maximise client value and repeat business (providers yet to be determined). Because our business places us on the road (mobile), a great deal of the time we will also utilise basic blogs and wikis for internal marketing-related communication.
- *Hardware.* We will utilise smartphones and tablets as sales and marketing tools for conveying concepts to clients in the field and for internal communications while out of the office.

3.3.5 Pricing policy

The standard price for providing recruitment services will be approximately $5000 per placement. This figure is very competitive and, if anything, slightly below the average fee. However, to help attract additional business in the first few months/year, Kevin thinks this is a good strategy. Terms of payment will be ten working days (two calendar weeks) and accounts will be tendered on the day that the final services are provided.

3.4 Evaluation of marketing

The effectiveness of our marketing strategy will be assessed on a six-monthly basis by analysing fees data to see what draws the company's work. For example, if most work is coming from the distribution of promotional emails, then this source of promotion will be considered effective.

Section 4. Operations

4.1 Legal and licensing requirements

(a) *Business name and legal structure*

Murphy Recruiting Pty Ltd (Australian Business Number 99 999 999 999) is a proprietary limited company. The company structure has already been registered and established with three shareholders:

Mart Box	(40% shareholding)
Kevin Murphy	(40% shareholding)
Tim Brunt	(20% shareholding)

who also serve as the Directors of the entity.

(b) *Operating laws and licences*

After checking with the Small Business Development Corporation's Business Licence Centre, it appears that no specific licences are needed to operate this business, except for a home-based business permit from the City of Brisbane.

4.2 Management details

The Managing Director of the company will be:

Kevin Murphy

Home address:	135 Central Boulevard, Yeronga QLD 4104
	Ph: (07) 9999 9999 Fax: (07) 9999 9998
Date of birth:	4 October 1966
Qualifications:	Bachelor of Business (distinction), Graduate Diploma in Human Resources Management
Experience:	Masterstaff Recruitment 1992–2001
	Interchange Recruitment 2001–2006
	IT HR & Recruit 2007–2014

4.3 Organisational structure and staffing

Initially, the following tasks of the business will be done by the Managing Director:

- executive IT recruitment
- general IT recruitment
- marketing and public enquiries
- bookkeeping and administration of the business.

  The following is an intended final staffing structure as part of the business's long-term goals (two to three years).

- *Managing Director — executive IT and general IT recruitment*

  Duties: Provide business planning, mentoring and occasional training to clients; undertake marketing of the business; provide administrative services and strategic development of the firm.

  Salary: Set at approximately $65 320 per annum in Year 1, rising to $75 400 by the end of Year 2.

  This role will be filled by Kevin Murphy.

- *Consultant — general IT recruitment*

  Duties: Conduct business planning and general management consultancy work for clients; undertake office management.

  Salary: $45 000 per annum commencing in Year 2.

  Qualifications required: Aptitude for dealing with the public; small-business background; experience in consulting; recruitment experience useful but not essential.

Professional associations

The managing director will continue membership with the Australian Institute of Human Resources (AIHR).

4.4 Professional advisers

Accountant
Sunshine Street Accountants
4 Sunshine Street, Yeronga QLD 4104
Ph: (07) 7999 9999 Fax: (02) 2222 9999 Email: info@sunshinestreet.com.au

Lawyer
Moot & Moot Partners
Suite 1, 1 Main Street, Yeronga QLD 4104
(Postal address: PO Box 1, Yeronga QLD 4104)
Ph: (07) 8999 9999 Fax: (02) 3999 9999 Email: reception@moot.net.au

Insurance broker
To be determined

Bank
MegaBank Australia
5 St Gregory Tce, Yeronga QLD 4104

Bank manager
Janine Sharma
Ph: (07) 2222 3333 Fax: (07) 2222 3334 Email: Janine.Sharma@megabank.com.au

Bookkeeper
To be determined. This will not be sought unless the Managing Director can no longer provide this service.

4.5 Insurance and security issues

The following insurance will be required for the business:

- professional indemnity
- public liability
- workers compensation
- director's liability (possibly).

  It is estimated that the combined cost for these insurances will be approximately $2500 in Year 1.

  Necessary security precautions for the business property and equipment include the provision of a locked filing cabinet for client records. Online security (anti-virus and other software) for the website will be needed and electronic data will be backed up regularly and stored off-site.

4.6 Business premises

(a) *Location*

The business will be based at Kevin's home at 135 Central Boulevard, Yeronga QLD 4104. A separate room with all necessary furniture and equipment, which can be used as a dedicated office, is available. The property concerned is owned by Kevin and his wife, so it has security of tenure indefinitely. No rent is payable and no special equipment or fixtures are required.

Training courses will be conducted at specialised venues that can be hired on a daily basis.

(b) *Council and government rules*

A home-based business licence will have to be obtained from the City of Brisbane. No other licences apply to the project. Trainers and business planners do not need to be licensed.

(c) *Ability to access target market*

Since most services will be provided at meetings at the customers' premises, the office will easily allow the business to access its target markets. The office is located close to most major roads and freeways. Clients will be scattered throughout the metropolitan area; therefore, the firm will need to travel to clients' preferred locations.

4.7 Equipment required

The equipment required for the business will be:
- answering machine
- telephone line
- smartphone
- computer, printer and scanner
- laptop or tablet
- high-speed internet access
- filing cabinet
- table
- ergonomic office chair.

Quotes from suppliers indicate that the total cost of these items will be approximately $8900. All materials required for the proposed training programs (such as TV, video and whiteboard) are provided by commercial training venues.

Likely future needs

Future computing needs will probably include an upgraded system.

4.8 Production processes

An operations manual, to be updated every six months, will explain procedures and processes within the office. This will also allow the company to apply for quality assurance certification at a later stage, if it wishes to do so.

4.9 Information and communication technologies

The business will use Microsoft Office® professional suite to manage most internal data and document handling needs and, in addition, will purchase MYOB® basics for our accounting software. We will use CRM tools from Salesforce.com for developing a knowledge base of our existing and future clients, and an online communications and e-commerce toolset developed by Woocom.com.au. Selected 'lead user' clients will also be given access to a private wiki that we hope will involve them in the development of process and product improvements over time.

4.10 Critical risks/contingency plans

The critical risks facing this business and contingencies to deal with them are:
- liability — to be covered by professional indemnity insurance
- injury to the Managing Director — to be covered by workers compensation
- excessive workload — other Directors may take on work, or it may be redirected to other consultancies with whom a strategic alliance has been developed.

Section 5. Financial projections

5.1 Basic assumptions and information

(a) *Calculation of income and expenses*

Expenses have been calculated based on market research and the manager's own knowledge of costs. It is assumed that all accounts revenue will be paid within the month issued (so there is no delayed income on a monthly basis). No provision has been made for the impact of inflation or increases in costs. Pricing and costs for the second year of operations will be reviewed in next year's business plan to take these factors into account.

Depreciation of equipment items purchased in July 2015 will be calculated using the straight-line method at 10% per annum of total initial outlay. Only one year's forecasts have been provided due to the difficulty of forecasting over a longer time period.

(b) *Financing of the business*

The Directors will provide an initial capital contribution to the business according to their shareholdings — Mart Box $4000, Kevin Murphy $4000, Tim Brunt $2000. Sales income for July 2015 is based on commitments or early orders from prospective clients, thus providing initial cash flow and removing the need for short-term debt financing. The overall financing strategy is to operate, wherever possible, with a cash surplus in the bank account at all times. Bank loans will not be required. If necessary, the Directors will reduce the wages paid to them during times of cash flow difficulty.

The bank account required for the business is one that:

- has mobile phone/internet banking access
- pays interest on sums below $5000
- provides monthly bank statements (for reconciliation with accounts)
- has credit card and EFTPOS facilities.

For security reasons, a minimum of two Directors will be required to verify all accounts.

(c) *Distribution of profits*

Profits in Year 1 will be retained in the business. In future years, annual net profit after tax will be divided in the following manner: three-quarters will be paid to the shareholders at the end of the financial year in accordance with their shareholdings and the remaining quarter will be kept as retained earnings. The retained capital will be used for reinvestment in the business, mainly to upgrade equipment and to meet unforeseen contingencies. If the business is highly profitable, some of the retained capital may eventually (in two to three years' time) be used to help fund the purchase of permanent business premises.

(d) *Goods and services tax*

No GST figures are shown in any of the financial documents; that is, all forecasts are net of tax.

(e) *Loans*

The firm has no current loans or debts.

5.2 Analysis of financial forecasts

(a) The owners have decided to use net profit margin and projected market and earnings-based valuations as the main indicators of the firm's performance. Based on the projections made in this document, it is estimated for Year 1 that this will be:

$$\text{Net profit margin \%} = \text{Net profit before tax/Fees revenue} = \$2320/\$95\,000 = 2.44\%$$

We expect margins to increase substantially in Year 2 and Year 3.

In future years, as more data are gathered, it will also be possible to use other ratios to help analyse the financial performance of the firm.

(b) *Break-even point*

Assuming there are no variable costs, the break-even point is the projected fixed costs.

$$\text{Projected fixed costs} = \$92\,680$$

(c) *Applying market-based and earnings-based valuations to a start-up*

While we are in the start-up phase, we do not expect our returns to be competitive. However, by benchmarking against industry norms, we are ensuring we are focused on what we need to do to be competitive. We understand through personal enquiry with Brisbane Consultancies that several businesses similar to ours have been offered for sale at an average industry multiplier of 0.8 times annual turnover this year in the greater Brisbane area. Using this benchmark, our business may theoretically be worth as much as $76 000 at the end of the first year.

$$\text{Market-based fees (revenue multiplier)} = \$95\,000 \text{ (fees)} \times 0.80 \text{ (multiplier)} = \$76\,000$$

In the medium term, revenue multipliers may be a quick, easy and useful measure. However, during the start-up phase a better measure of performance may be to calculate a price that reflects return on investment (ROI). The ROI expected in this industry is estimated (by comparison with three other similar businesses for sale) to be in the order of 75 per cent before allowing for the manager's salary (Kevin). Using this information to calculate the theoretical sale price suggests a much lower outcome.

$$\text{Earnings-based selling price (ROI)} = \$2320/0.75 = \$3093.33$$

This means that, in Year 1, the business is worth as little as $3093.33, effectively making it not at all saleable. Of course, both of these valuation methods have problems when applied to the first year of a start-up business, so how will we account for this apparent problem of newness?

Over the course of the first few years, we would expect the ROI-derived selling price to increase at least on par with the revenue multiplier method once the business's start-up costs had washed through the accounts. In today's dollar terms, if the turnover number was not increased, that would mean a target net profit of $57 000 was required.

$$\$76\,000 \text{ (required sale price)} \times 0.75 \text{ (expected ROI)} = \$57\,000 \text{ net profit}$$

When we exceed that net profit target (based on turnover of $95 000), then we will be doing better than the market would require in terms of net margins. Projecting our profits beyond the first year could be done to predict when this might occur, but we do not feel this is feasible given our lack of data as a start-up. In future years, we will certainly look to understand the trends and forward-plan to a more strategic time frame.

5.2.1 Fees forecast (all figures are in Australian dollars)

	Jul.	Aug.	Sep.	Oct.	Nov.	Dec.	Jan.	Feb.	Mar.	Apr.	May	Jun.	TOTAL
MURPHY RECRUITING PTY LTD **Fees forecast** for the period July 2018 to June 2019													
Item: Business planning Number of placements	0	1	1	1	2	0	0	2	2	3	3	4	19
Placement price	$0	$5 000	$5 000	$5 000	$ 5 000	$0	$0	$ 5 000	$ 5 000	$ 5 000	$ 5 000	$ 5 000	
Total fees income	0	5 000	5 000	5 000	10 000	0	0	10 000	10 000	15 000	15 000	20 000	$95 000
Total fees revenue	$0	$5 000	$5 000	$5 000	$10 000	$0	$0	$10 000	$10 000	$15 000	$15 000	$20 000	$95 000

5.2.2 Cash flow forecast (all figures are in Australian dollars)

MURPHY RECRUITING PTY LTD
Cash flow forecast
for the period July 2018 to June 2019

	Jul.	Aug.	Sep.	Oct.	Nov.	Dec.	Jan.	Feb.	Mar.	Apr.	May	Jun.	TOTAL
Income													
Fees revenue	$ 0	$5 000	$5 000	$5 000	$10 000	$ 0	$ 0	$10 000	$10 000	$15 000	$15 000	$20 000	$ 95 000
Capital	10 000												10 000
Sundry													
Total income	10 000	5 000	5 000	5 000	10 000	0	0	10 000	10 000	15 000	15 000	20 000	105 000
Expenses													
Accounting/legal services	1 500		800					200					2 500
Advertising	2 000	100	100	100	180	100	100	100	100	100	100	100	3 180
Bank fees	15	15	15	15	15	15	15	15	15	15	15	15	180
Equipment purchases	8 900												8 900
Equipment leases													0
Insurance	2 500												2 500
Light and power													0
Loan repayments													0
Motor vehicle — fuel	50	50	50	50	50	50	50	50	50	50	50	50	600
Motor vehicle — other													0
Petty cash	25	25	25	25	25	25	25	25	25	25	25	25	300
Postage, printing and stationery	400												400
Rent													0
Repairs and maintenance	100			100			100			100			400
Staff superannuation												6 000	6 000
Staff director's wages	5 400	5 340	6 700	5 220	5 340	5 400	5 220	5 340	5 400	5 220	5 340	5 400	65 320
Telephone and internet	50	50	50	50	50	50	50	50	50	50	50	50	600
Other	100	50	50	50	50	50	50	50	50	50	50	50	650
Total expenses	21 040	5 630	7 790	5 610	5 710	5 690	5 610	5 830	5 690	5 610	5 630	11 690	91 530
Cash surplus/(deficit)	$(11 040)	$ (630)	$(2 790)	$ (610)	$4 290	$(5 690)	$(5 610)	$4 170	$4 310	$9 390	$9 370	$8 310	$13 470
Bank balance ($)													
Start of month	0	(11 040)	(11 670)	(14 460)	(15 070)	(10 780)	(16 470)	(22 080)	(17 910)	(13 600)	(4 210)	(5 160)	
End of month	(11 040)	(11 670)	(14 460)	(15 070)	(10 780)	(16 470)	(22 080)	(17 910)	(13 600)	(4 210)	(5 160)	(13 470)	

5.2.3 Projected profit and loss statement (all figures are in Australian dollars)

MURPHY RECRUITING PTY LTD Projected profit or loss statement for the period July 2018 to June 2019	
Revenues	
Fees revenue	$95 000
Expenses	
Accounting/legal services	2 500
Advertising	3 180
Bank fees	180
Equipment purchases	8 900
Equipment leases	0
Insurance	2 500
Light and power	0
Loan repayments	0
Motor vehicle — fuel	600
Motor vehicle — other	0
Petty cash	300
Postage, printing and stationery	400
Rent	0
Repairs and maintenance	400
Staff superannuation	6 000
Staff director's wages	65 320
Telephone and internet	600
Other	650
Depreciation	1 150
Total expenses	92 680
Net profit	$ 2 320

5.2.4 Owner's personal expenses (all figures are in Australian dollars)

MURPHY RECRUITING PTY LTD
Owner's personal expenses: Kevin Murphy
for the period July 2018 to June 2019

Monthly commitments	Jul.	Aug.	Sep.	Oct.	Nov.	Dec.	Jan.	Feb.	Mar.	Apr.	May	Jun.	TOTAL
Food	$ 400	$ 400	$ 400	$ 400	$ 400	$ 400	$ 400	$ 400	$ 400	$ 400	$ 400	$ 400	$ 4 800
Health	100	100	100	100	100	100	100	100	100	100	100	100	1 200
Clothes	80		80			80			80			80	400
Entertainment	200	200	200	200	200	200	200	200	200	200	200	200	2 400
Transport	120	120	120	120	120	120	120	120	120	120	120	120	1 440
Education													0
Home loan payments	3 400	3 400	3 400	3 400	3 400	3 400	3 400	3 400	3 400	3 400	3 400	3 400	40 800
Car payments													0
Other loan repayments													0
Telephone and internet			100			100			100			100	400
Electricity and gas		120			120			120			120		480
Rates			1 300										1 300
Personal income tax	900	900	900	900	900	900	900	900	900	900	900	900	10 800
Credit cards	100												100
Other	100	100	100	100	100	100	100	100	100	100	100	100	1 200
Monthly drawings needed*	**$ 5 400**	**$ 5 340**	**$ 6 700**	**$ 5 220**	**$ 5 340**	**$ 5 400**	**$ 5 220**	**$ 5 340**	**$ 5 400**	**$ 5 220**	**$ 5 340**	**$ 5 400**	**$ 65 320**

*Shown as 'Staff — director's wages' in cash flow forecast

5.2.5 Owner's personal assets and liabilities (all figures are in Australian dollars)

MURPHY RECRUITING PTY LTD Owner's personal assets and liabilities: Kevin Murphy as at 1 July 2018	
Assets	
Own house (market value)	$700 000
Other real estate (market value)	0
Motor vehicle (insured value)	25 000
Cash (on hand or in bank)	6 000
Superannuation	84 000
Furniture and personal effects (insured value)	25 000
Other (list if appropriate)	0
Total assets	840 000
Liabilities	
Outstanding mortgage (on home)	201 500
Outstanding mortgage (on other real estate)	0
Personal loans	0
Credit cards	100
Current bills	0
Other debts	600
Total liabilities	202 200
Personal worth (total assets minus total liabilities)	**$637 800**

Section 6. Implementation timetable, 2018–19

2018	
July	Apply for home-based business licence
	Open business bank account
	Prepare letterheads, business cards
	Send copy of business plan to accountant and lawyer (for their information)
	Obtain all relevant insurance policies
August	Start direct email campaign
	Review contents of website
September	Start compiling operations manual
	Visit accountant re progress to date, recordkeeping
	Enquire re computing equipment required
October	Enquire with Institute of Management Consultants (Australia) re membership
November	Prepare promotional brochure
December	Print promotional brochure
2019	
January	Staff/Directors' retreat to review progress to date
	Review business plan
	Review effectiveness of marketing plan and analyse source of sales to date
	Review operations manual
February	Attend Small Business Development Corporation course on managing business growth
March	Implement benchmarking of advertising by outside adviser
April	Update website
May	Visit accountant re EOFY returns
June	Write business plan for 2019–20
	Review and write new marketing plan

Section 7. Appendix — references

Barringer, B 2009, *Preparing effective business plans*, Pearson Education, Upper Saddle River, NJ, p. 108.

Burke, A, Fraser, S & Greene, FJ 2010, 'The multiple effects of business planning on new venture performance', *Journal of Management Studies*, vol. 47, no. 3, pp. 391–415.

Gibb, A & Davies, L 1990, 'In support of frameworks for the development of growth models of the small business', *International Small Business Journal*, vol. 9, no. 1, pp. 15–31.

Glen, W & Weerawardena, J 1996, 'Strategic planning practices in small enterprises in Queensland', *Small Enterprise Research*, vol. 4, no. 3, pp. 5–16.

Gruber, M 2007, 'Uncovering the value of planning in new venture creation: A process and contingency perspective', *Journal of Business Venturing*, vol. 22, no. 6, pp. 782–807.

Hormozi, AM, Sutton, TS, McMinn, RD & Lucio, W 2002, 'Business plans for new or small businesses: paving the path to success', *Management Decision*, vol. 40, no. 7–8, pp. 755–64.

McKaskill, T 2006, *Finding the money: How to raise venture capital*, Wilkinson Publishing, Melbourne, p. 71.

Merle Crawford, C 2003, 'New study shows six critical business plan mistakes', *Business Horizons*, vol. 46, no. 4, p. 83.

Perry, SC 2001, 'The relationship between written business plans and the failure of small businesses in the US', *Journal of Small Business Management*, vol. 39, no. 3, pp. 301–9.

Schaper, M 1996, 'Writing the perfect business plan', *My Business*, October, pp. 26–7.

Small Business Development Corporation 2009, *Opportunities for new beginnings*, SBDC, Sydney.

Sydney Chamber of Commerce 2009, *Survey of small organisation professional development needs*, Sydney Chamber of Commerce, Sydney.

Ziericki, BB 2007, *Consulting: An overview of the personal services sector*, www.managementmyopia.com.

Zimmerer, TW, Scarborough, NM & Wilson, D 2008, *Essentials of entrepreneurship and small business management*, 5th edn, Pearson Education, Upper Saddle River, NJ, p. 1346.

ACKNOWLEDGEMENTS

Photo: © Jacob Lund / Shutterstock.com

CHAPTER 2

Accounting in society

LEARNING OBJECTIVES

After studying this chapter, you should be able to:

2.1 identify the sources of company regulation in Australia

2.2 explain the current standard-setting framework and the role of the professional accounting associations in the standard-setting process

2.3 evaluate the role of the *Conceptual Framework* and illustrate the qualitative characteristics of financial statements

2.4 explain the concept of corporate governance

2.5 outline corporate governance guidelines and practices

2.6 outline the role of ethics in business and compare ethical philosophies relevant to business decision making

2.7 explain the use of codes of ethical conduct and apply ethical decision-making methods to business situations

2.8 give examples of the limitations of accounting information.

Chapter preview

In the previous chapter you were introduced to the accounting process, the different types of accounting and the important role accounting plays in helping businesses plan and thrive in a global economy. The global economy has as its foundation many rules and regulations. This chapter introduces you to some of these rules and regulations in the Australian and New Zealand contexts. We look at sources of company regulation in Australia, the role of professional accounting associations and the *Conceptual Framework for Financial Reporting* (*Conceptual Framework*). This chapter also explores the important issue of corporate governance and the corporate governance guidelines and practices. Along with corporate governance, ethics plays an important role in business and, in particular, business decision making. The role of ethics is discussed along with ethical philosophies. The chapter concludes by considering the limitations of accounting information.

2.1 Sources of company regulation

LEARNING OBJECTIVE 2.1 Identify the sources of company regulation in Australia.

The Australian business sector in the late 1990s and the first decade of the new millennium witnessed many large-scale corporate collapses, activities of fraud by company employees, episodes of insider trading and the advent of hefty salary packages for company directors. Collapses in previously buoyant industries such as insurance resulted in several thousand small and large shareholders losing large amounts of cash and often their life savings. Corporate regulation in Australia is now under closer scrutiny than ever before. In the early part of the twenty-first century, there were a number of changes to the *Corporations Act 2001* (Cwlth). The main changes were in the areas of auditor responsibilities, disclosure requirements of directors, requirements for the preparation of concise annual reports, abolition of the concepts of authorised capital and par value, and the accounting standard-setting program. The **Australian Securities and Investments Commission (ASIC)** website provides detailed information on the changes to the Corporations Act (see www.asic.gov.au).

The role of company regulation is to protect different stakeholders (such as investors, consumers and lenders) and help promote a strong and vibrant economy. Regulation assists in monitoring the preparation, presentation and distribution of financial statements. Company regulation also helps liquidators to obtain records from bankrupt companies, carry out legal proceedings against directors and ensure that appropriate information is provided to the different stakeholders of listed companies.

The main source of company regulation in Australia is the Corporations Act, enforced through ASIC. The Act stipulates (among other things) that disclosing entities must prepare financial statements and, in doing so, comply with accounting standards and regulations. The other important sources of regulation are the Listing Rules of the ASX and the accounting principles, standards, ethics and disciplinary procedures of the accounting profession, represented by two main accounting associations: Chartered Accountants of Australia and New Zealand (CAANZ) and CPA Australia. The roles of ASIC, the ASX and other government organisations involved in company regulation and the role of the professional accounting associations are discussed in the following sections.

VALUE TO BUSINESS

- Corporate collapses and episodes of insider trading and company fraud have resulted in changes to corporate regulation.
- Corporate regulation protects the interests of different stakeholders and promotes confidence and investment in business and economic activities.
- The main source of company regulation is the Corporations Act, enforced through ASIC.

Australian Securities and Investments Commission (ASIC)

ASIC acts as the company watchdog and enforces company and financial services laws (such as the Corporations Act and the ASX Listing Rules) to protect consumers, investors and creditors.

ASIC's role, as stated in the *Australian Securities and Investments Commission Act 2001* (Cwlth), is to:
- uphold the law uniformly, effectively and quickly
- promote confident and informed participation in the financial system by investors and consumers

- make information about companies and other bodies available to the public
- improve the performance of the financial system and the entities within it.

ASIC administers and enforces several laws, including the Corporations Act, ASIC Act, *Business Names Registration Act 2011*, *Business Names Registration (Transitional and Consequential Provisions) Act 2011*, *Insurance Contracts Act 1984* (Cwlth), *Superannuation (Resolution of Complaints) Act 1993*, *Superannuation Industry (Supervision) Act 1993* (Cwlth), *Retirement Savings Accounts Act 1997* (Cwlth), *Life Insurance Act 1995* (Cwlth), *National Consumer Credit Protection Act 2009* and *Medical Indemnity (Prudential Supervision and Product Standards) Act 2003* (Cwlth).

Corporations Act 2001

By far the most important Act under the auspices of ASIC is the *Corporations Act 2001* (**Cwlth**). This Act is based on the legislative powers that the Australian government has under s. 51 of the Australian Constitution. The Act contains various sections that provide guidance for corporations in Australia. It includes such sections as the definition of a disclosing entity; the accounting requirements of a disclosing entity; exemptions by ASIC; a small-business guide; the basic features of a company; registering a company; company powers; annual financial reporting to members and the appointment of an auditor; and specific offences, including false or misleading statements and obstructing or hindering ASIC.

Australian Securities Exchange (ASX)

Stock exchanges around the world assist in regulating companies and ensuring that fair and orderly markets are maintained. Some stock exchanges worldwide include the New Zealand Exchange (www.nzx.com), the New York Stock Exchange (www.nyse.com), the London Stock Exchange (www.londonstockexchange.com), the Tokyo Stock Exchange (www.jpx.co.jp) and the Australian Securities Exchange (www.asx.com.au).

The **Australian Securities Exchange** (**ASX**) was formed in 1987 as the Australian Stock Exchange and provides in-depth market data and information to a variety of users. It operates as the primary Australian exchange for shares, derivatives and fixed-interest securities such as **debentures**. The New Zealand Exchange (NZX) was formed in 1974 through an amalgamation of a number of regional stock exchanges. The NZX is the only registered securities exchange in New Zealand and is also an authorised futures exchange. As of June 2018, the NZX had 301 listed securities with a combined market capitalisation of NZ\$164.6 billion (NZX Limited 2018).

Figure 2.1 shows the ASX home page on the internet. The ASX contributes to company regulation through its Operating and Listing Rules. The **Operating Rules** regulate how trading takes place on the ASX by overseeing the operations and behaviour of participating entities. The **Listing Rules** 'watch over' companies listed on the ASX and help to ensure these companies are providing adequate disclosures to various stakeholders and behaving appropriately. These rules are in addition to the regulations of the Corporations Act. The Listing Rules include rules on continuous disclosure, changes in capital and new issues, restricted securities and trading halts, suspension and removal.

Australian Competition and Consumer Commission (ACCC)

The Australian Competition and Consumer Commission (ACCC) administers the *Competition and Consumer Act 2010* (Cwlth). This Act covers anti-competitive behaviour and unfair market practices, mergers and acquisitions of companies, and product safety and liability. ACCC's primary role is protection of the consumer. With the reform of the tax system in 2001, it had a particular role to play in ensuring that there was no price exploitation in relation to the GST. The ACCC website is www.accc.gov.au.

Reserve Bank of Australia (RBA)

The Reserve Bank of Australia (RBA) is responsible for the stability of the Australian financial system and for setting monetary policy. The RBA website is www.rba.gov.au.

Australian Prudential Regulation Authority (APRA)

The Australian Prudential Regulation Authority (APRA) oversees financial institutions (banks, building societies, credit unions) and is responsible for ensuring that financial institutions can honour their commitments. It also has a role in promoting the safety of life and general insurance companies and larger superannuation funds. APRA's website is www.apra.gov.au.

FIGURE 2.1 The ASX home page

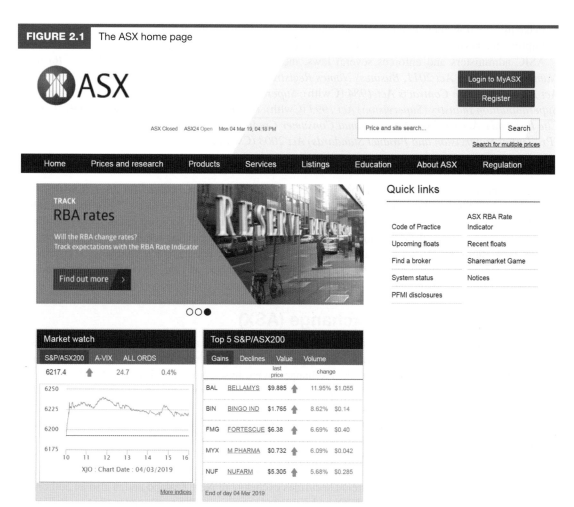

Source: Australian Securities Exchange 2019.

Australian Taxation Office (ATO)

At some stage in their lives, all Australians in one way or another will come into contact with the ATO. The ATO collects taxes (e.g. income tax and GST) and has a number of other responsibilities, such as overseeing all self-managed superannuation funds. The ATO website is www.ato.gov.au.

Other government agencies

There are other government agencies and initiatives that are targeted to particular areas of commercial operations. Although these agencies are not specifically aimed at commercial transactions, they do affect the operations of entities. For example, there are agencies dealing with the protection of information rights (www.oaic.gov.au), human rights (www.humanrights.gov.au) and consumer protection (www.accc.gov.au). There is also a central site (www.business.gov.au) for business access to all government information and services that can help with gaining information about business registration, trademarks, patents, licences, workers compensation and various other business responsibilities.

VALUE TO BUSINESS

- ASIC acts as the company watchdog and enforces company and financial services laws such as the *Corporations Act 2001*.
- The ASX regulates companies through its Operating and Listing Rules.
- The ASX Operating Rules govern the operations and behaviour of participating organisations of the ASX and affiliates.

- The ASX Listing Rules govern the procedures and behaviour of all ASX-listed companies.
- APRA is responsible for ensuring that financial institutions honour their commitments to their stakeholders.
- The ACCC administers the *Competition and Consumer Act 2010*, which covers anti-competitive behaviour and unfair market practices, mergers and acquisitions of companies, and product safety and liability.

2.2 Australian and international accounting standards

LEARNING OBJECTIVE 2.2 Explain the current standard-setting framework and the role of the professional accounting associations in the standard-setting process.

Prior to 2005, Australian Accounting Standards were largely developed by the **Australian Accounting Standards Board (AASB)**. However, since 1 January 2005, Australian entities have complied with **International Financial Reporting Standards (IFRS)**. The adoption of IFRS has ensured compliance with internationally agreed principles, standards and codes of best practice, resulting in the issue of various new standards and the amendment of many existing Australian standards. For some standards, the changes have been substantial; in other instances, the changes have been insignificant. The AASB is responsible for developing and maintaining high-quality financial reporting standards in Australia and contributing to the ongoing development of global accounting standards. The AASB provides input into current International Accounting Standards Board (IASB) projects by issuing exposure drafts of amended Australian Accounting Standards that incorporate the relevant clauses and requirements of IFRS. The functions and responsibilities of the AASB include:
- issuing Australian Accounting Standards
- significantly influencing the development of IFRS (such as providing significant input to the development of standards relating to the global financial crisis)
- promoting globally consistent application and interpretation of accounting standards.

The Corporations Act stipulates that disclosing entities, public companies and large proprietary companies must apply Australian Accounting Standards in preparing their financial reports. For other reporting entities (i.e. non-disclosing entities), preparers and auditors of **general purpose financial statements (GPFS)** have a professional obligation to apply the accounting standards. A **disclosing entity** is an entity that issues securities that are quoted on a stock market or made available to the public via a prospectus.

Financial Reporting Council (FRC)

The **Financial Reporting Council (FRC)** is a statutory body established under s. 225(1) of the *Australian Securities and Investments Commission Act 2001* (Cwlth), originally the *Australian Securities and Investments Commission Act 1989*. The FRC is responsible for overseeing the accounting and auditing standard-setting process for both the public and private sectors in Australia. The FRC is made up of key stakeholders from the business community, the professional accounting bodies, and governments and regulatory agencies (including the AASB). The FRC was also responsible for promoting the Australian adoption of IFRS, and monitors the operation of the Australian Accounting Standards to assess their relevance and effectiveness in achieving their objectives.

Development of accounting standards

The development of an accounting standard is a lengthy and rigorous process that can span several years. An accounting standard must go through a number of different steps before it can become an official standard to be applied under the Corporations Act. It is extremely important for any accounting issue to be carefully examined and debated prior to it being issued as an accounting standard. Although many of the Australian Accounting Standards stem from IFRS, the AASB provides input to the process. The examination and debate of an issue with consultative groups, advisory panels and interested parties are all part of a standard's **due process**. The due process of an accounting standard includes identifying a technical issue through submissions and other materials from interested parties; developing a project proposal to determine if the project is worthwhile; researching the issue comprehensively; issuing an exposure draft, discussion paper or invitation to comment; and issuing a draft interpretation. The outcome of the due process could be an accounting standard, an interpretation or a *Conceptual Framework* document.

The AASB's standard-setting process is illustrated in figure 2.2.

FIGURE 2.2 The AASB's current standard-setting process

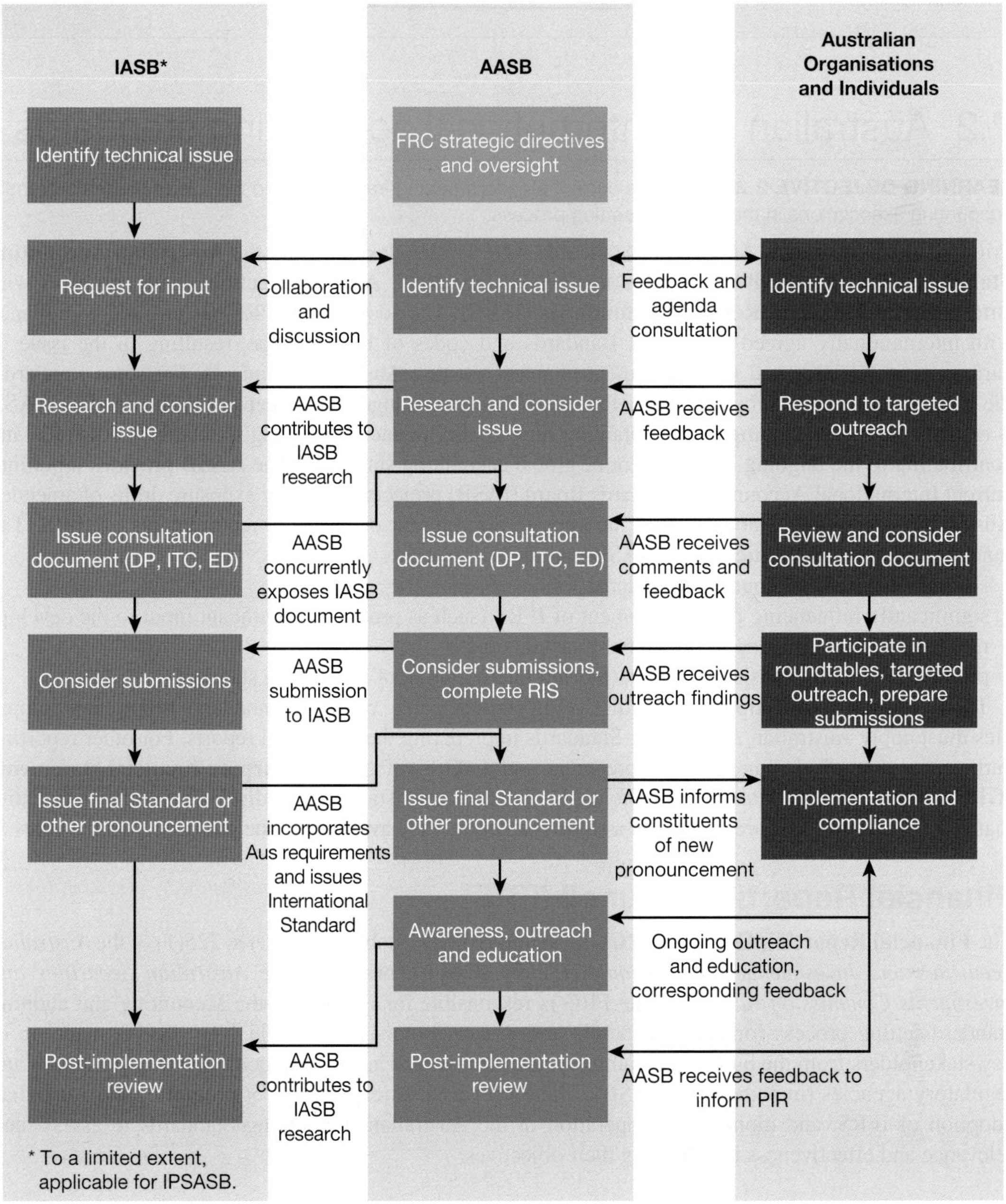

Source: Australian Accounting Standards Board 2018.

Regulation in New Zealand

Accounting and auditing standards in New Zealand are set by the External Reporting Board (XRB), which is an independent Crown Entity established under section 22 of the *Financial Reporting Act 1993* and subject to the *Crown Entities Act 2004*. For more information about the XRB refer to its website, www.xrb.govt.nz.

In 2011, the New Zealand government announced changes to the financial reporting requirements for New Zealand entities. These changes are enacted in the *Financial Reporting Act 2013*. The main change is that many small and medium-sized New Zealand companies will no longer need to prepare accounting reports using New Zealand **generally accepted accounting principles (GAAP)**. Complementary to this the XRB announced that, for financial reporting, New Zealand would change from a single set of sector-neutral accounting standards to a multi-standards approach. The full effect of these changes took place from 2016. Prior to these changes the reporting requirements between Australia and New Zealand were similar, particularly in having sector-neutral accounting standards. Now, New Zealand is similar to the international standards where for-profit publicly accountable entities use New Zealand equivalents to IFRS (NZ IFRS) and public benefit entities (not-for-profit and government sectors) report using PBE (public benefit entity) standards, which are based primarily on International Public Sector Accounting Standards (IPSAS), modified as necessary for the New Zealand environment by the XRB. Also, within the two-sector reporting regime there are four tiers. Tier one in both sectors uses the full standards, with fewer requirements as the tiers move from tier two to tiers three and four.

Public companies listed on the NZX must also comply with the NZX listing rules. The listing rules relating to financial reporting typically focus on disclosure of information. They also include industry-specific disclosure requirements. For example, the NZX requires listed companies operating in the mining industry to provide quarterly reports with full details of production, development and exploration activities. For more information about the NZX refer to its website, www.nzx.com.

Role of professional associations

Many countries have a professional accounting association and these are tending to become more global in their operations. In Australia, there are two main professional associations: CPA Australia and CAANZ. Other professional associations include the Association of Chartered Certified Accountants (ACCA) and Chartered Institute of Management Accountants (CIMA). CPA Australia and CAANZ play important roles in regulating Australian companies through stringent regulation of their members and through their input into the standard-setting process. Members of these bodies are required to ensure that the entities they are involved with comply with accounting standards when preparing their GPFS. The professional bodies have certain professional, ethical and legislative requirements that their members are required to uphold, such as maintaining independence during an audit, preparing financial statements according to Australian Accounting Standards and advising companies on disclosure according to the requirements of the Corporations Act. The professional bodies regulate the actions and conduct of their members according to their relevant code of conduct.

CPA Australia

CPA Australia provides education, guidance and support to students, accountants and businesses in Australia. A certified practising accountant (CPA) is a graduate who has completed an accounting qualification, the CPA program and three years of approved work experience, and who undertakes continuing professional development each year. To be admitted to the CPA program, you need to have completed prescribed accounting units in an undergraduate or postgraduate degree from a CPA-accredited provider or enrol in CPA foundation-level subjects. A CPA can work in various areas, including public accounting and public sector accounting.

Chartered Accountants Australia and New Zealand (CAANZ)

CAANZ provides education to its members and input to debates affecting the accounting profession and influencing regulators. A chartered accountant (CA) can be employed in a range of organisations to provide advice on areas such as running a business, future directions and complying with accounting standards. To become a CA, you need to have completed an approved university degree, passed the CA program and completed three years of approved work experience.

VALUE TO BUSINESS

- Australia adopted Australian equivalents of IFRS from 1 January 2005. The adoption of IFRS has helped ensure compliance with internationally agreed principles, standards and codes of best practice.
- The AASB remains the Australian accounting standard setter under the law and will continue to issue Australian Accounting Standards.
- The Financial Reporting Council (FRC) is responsible for overseeing the standard-setting process in Australia. The AASB is responsible for developing accounting standards for application to reporting entities under the Corporations Act.

▶

- The procedure for due process involves the following steps: identify a technical issue; develop a project proposal; research the issue; consult with stakeholders and prepare an exposure draft; send the exposure draft for comment to interested parties; issue an exposure draft for further comment; and finalise the accounting standard, interpretation or *Conceptual Framework* document.
- The professional bodies provide feedback on exposure drafts and forward any comments to the AASB. They also inform their members of any developments in accounting standards through newsletters and by conducting continuing professional education (CPE) sessions.

2.3 Role of the *Conceptual Framework*

LEARNING OBJECTIVE 2.3 Evaluate the role of the *Conceptual Framework* and illustrate the qualitative characteristics of financial statements.

The AASB's original conceptual framework contained Statements of Accounting Concepts (SACs) to assist in the preparation and presentation of financial statements. It also assisted standard setters in developing future accounting standards and helped users in interpreting information in financial statements. With the adoption of IFRS in 2005, it was necessary to adopt the IASB's *Framework for the Preparation and Presentation of Financial Statements* (*Framework*). The IASB and the US equivalent FASB (Financial Accounting Standards Board) undertook a joint project on the framework. The purpose of this joint project was to 'develop an improved common conceptual framework that provides a sound foundation for developing future accounting standards'. In 2010, the IASB issued a revised document titled *Conceptual Framework for Financial Reporting* (*Conceptual Framework*). This document has since been superseded, with the revised *Conceptual Framework* (issued in March 2018) becoming effective for annual reporting periods beginning on or after 1 January 2020. In 2018, the AASB was working on replacing the existing AASB *Framework for the Preparation and Presentation of Financial Statements* with the revised *Conceptual Framework*. This text will focus on the new revised *Conceptual Framework*, which was adopted in Australia in 2019.

The revised *Conceptual Framework* applies to entities that are required to prepare GPFS (note that these are called general purpose financial *reports* in the *Conceptual Framework*). As noted earlier in the chapter, GPFS are financial statements intended to meet the information needs common to users who are unable to command the preparation of statements tailored to suit their information needs. GPFS are in contrast to **special purpose financial statements**, which are prepared to suit a specific purpose and do not cater for the generalised needs common to most users. The components of the *Conceptual Framework* are as follows.

Objective of financial reporting

According to paragraph 1.2 of the *Conceptual Framework*, general purpose financial reporting provides a reporting entity's financial information in a way that is of use to 'existing and potential investors, lenders and other creditors in making decisions about providing resources to the entity'.

Qualitative characteristics of financial reports

The two *fundamental* qualitative characteristics of financial reports are relevance and faithful representation. The four *enhancing* qualitative characteristics are comparability, verifiability, timeliness and understandability.

Fundamental qualitative characteristics

Relevance

The characteristic of relevance implies that the information should have predictive and confirmatory value for users in making and evaluating economic decisions.

Faithful representation

The characteristic of faithful representation implies that financial information faithfully represents the phenomena it purports to represent. This depiction implies that the financial information is complete, neutral and free from error.

The relevance of information is affected by its nature and *materiality*. Information is material if omitting it or misstating it could influence decision making. A financial report should include all information which is material to a particular entity.

Enhancing qualitative characteristics

Comparability

The characteristic of comparability implies that users of financial statements must be able to compare aspects of an entity at one time and over time, and between entities at one time and over time. Therefore, the measurement and display of transactions and events should be carried out in a consistent manner throughout an entity, or fully explained if they are measured or displayed differently.

Verifiability

The characteristic of verifiability provides assurance that the information faithfully represents what it purports to be representing.

Timeliness

The characteristic of timeliness means that the accounting information is available to all stakeholders in time for decision-making purposes.

Understandability

The characteristic of understandability implies that preparers of information have classified, characterised and presented the information clearly and concisely. The financial reports are prepared with the assumption that its users have a 'reasonable knowledge' (para. 2.36) of the business and its economic activities.

The consolidated statement of profit or loss for the Qantas Group (shown in figure 2.3) illustrates these qualitative characteristics. It reports revenues less expenses in an easy-to-understand format in order to determine the **profit** for the year (understandability). The profit is relevant for determining the profitability of a company and can be used by a number of different stakeholders — investors, consumers, employees and lenders. The financial statement will show separately material items that are significant in nature. For example, the amounts in the Qantas Group report are in millions of dollars and the totals for expense groups (e.g. Manpower and staff related, Fuel) are shown, rather than the breakdowns of individual expenses (relevance).

FIGURE 2.3 Consolidated statement of profit or loss of the Qantas Group

QANTAS GROUP
Consolidated statement of profit or loss
for the year ended 30 June 2018

	Notes	2018 $m	2017 $m
REVENUE AND OTHER INCOME			
Net passenger revenue		14 715	13 857
Net freight revenue		862	808
Other	2(B)	1 483	1 392
Revenue and other income		17 060	16 057
EXPENDITURE			
Manpower and staff related		4 300	4 033
Fuel		3 232	3 039
Aircraft operating variable		3 596	3 436
Depreciation and amortisation		1 528	1 382
Non-cancellable aircraft operating lease rentals		272	356
Share of net (profit)/loss of investments accounted for under the equity method		(15)	7
Other	3	2 574	2 434
Expenditure		15 487	14 687
Statutory profit before income tax expense and net finance costs		1 573	1 370
Finance income	4	48	46
Finance costs	4	(230)	(235)
Net finance costs	4	(182)	(189)
Statutory profit before income tax expense		**1 391**	**1 181**
Income tax expense	5	(411)	(328)
Statutory profit for the year		**980**	**853**

Source: Qantas Airways Ltd 2018, p. 52.

An entity's statement of profit or loss reports profit for a prescribed period of time. Its format will be similar to that of other companies in the same industry, and this feature allows for comparison and analysis between companies. It also should not change significantly from period to period, thereby facilitating analysis within a company between the years (comparability).

An entity's statement of profit or loss, which will have been independently audited (verifiability), is a reliable representation of the company's income less expenses. In the audit report contained within the financial statements, the auditor will state whether the financial statements have been prepared in accordance with accounting principles and standards, and whether they are an accurate representation of performance for the period (faithful representation).

Finally, the financial statements of an entity will be made available to users within three months of the end of the financial period (timeliness).

Cost constraint on financial information

The benefits of providing financial information, such as improved effectiveness and efficiency of decision making by users, should outweigh the costs of providing it. Cost is the major constraint on the provision of financial information. The costs of providing financial information include those associated with the collecting, processing, verifying, disseminating and storing of the information.

Definition and recognition of the elements of financial statements

The revised *Conceptual Framework* establishes definitions of the elements of financial statements — assets, liabilities, equity, income and expenses — and specifies criteria for their inclusion in financial statements. These definitions will be explored in more detail in chapters 4 and 5 of this text.

Assets

Assets are present economic resources, resulting from past events, and are controlled by the entity (para. 4.3). Examples of assets for JB Hi-Fi Ltd are plant and equipment, cash, inventories, goodwill and intangible assets. For the Qantas Group, they include inventories, property, plant and equipment (PPE), intangible assets and investments.

Liabilities

Liabilities are present obligations 'to transfer an economic resource as a result of past events' (para. 4.26). Examples of liabilities for JB Hi-Fi Ltd are borrowings, trade payables and current tax payable. For the Qantas Group, they include payables, lease obligations, revenue received in advance and provisions.

Equity

Equity is the residual interest in the assets of the entity after deducting its liabilities. Equity is increased through the contributions of owners and through the excesses of the entity's income over its expenses. Equity is decreased by excesses of expenses over income and by distributions to owners. Examples of equity for JB Hi-Fi Ltd are capital contributions, dividends, reserves and retained earnings. Examples for the Qantas Group include issued capital, treasury shares, reserves and retained earnings. For sole traders and partnerships, the equity will be in the form of capital (owner(s) contributions). Withdrawals from the business will be in the form of drawings.

Income

Income is an increase in an asset, or a decrease in a liability, which results in an increase in equity, 'other than those relating to contributions from holders of equity claims' (para. 4.68). Examples of income for JB Hi-Fi Ltd are revenue, interest and dividend income from investments in other entities. Examples from the Qantas Group include passenger revenue and freight revenue.

Expenses

An **expense** is a decrease in an asset, or an increase in a liability, which results in a decrease in equity, 'other than those relating to distributions to holders of equity claims' (para. 4.69). Examples of expenses for JB Hi-Fi Ltd are sales and marketing expenses, rent expense, finance costs and salaries. Examples for the Qantas Group include fuel, depreciation and amortisation, impairment, aircraft operating variable, and manpower and staff related expenses.

- The revised *Conceptual Framework* establishes the objectives of financial statements and identifies the different users of GPFS.
- The revised *Conceptual Framework* deals with transactions and other events that are not currently included in the accounting standards.
- The revised *Conceptual Framework* identifies the qualitative characteristics that financial information should possess. The fundamental characteristics are relevance (including materiality) and faithful representation. The enhancing characteristics are comparability, verifiability, timeliness and understandability. It also discusses the cost constraint on the provision of relevant and faithfully represented information.
- The revised *Conceptual Framework* establishes definitions of the elements of financial statements and specifies what is required of each of these elements for inclusion in the financial statements.

2.4 Corporate governance

LEARNING OBJECTIVE 2.4 Explain the concept of corporate governance.

Central to discussion on business sustainability is the role that governance plays in determining the future of an entity. Although it can be fun and rewarding to be in charge, making decisions is a difficult task. The quality of those decisions determines the success or otherwise of an entity in meeting its objectives, and can influence the lives of many. People who make such decisions have power, but they also have responsibilities and are accountable for their actions. The business structures chapter outlines a number of different business structures and also discusses the differing reporting requirements for small and large entities. Regardless of whether an entity is small or large, there needs to be some type of governance structure (decision-making process) in place. Some of the guidelines and listing rules presented below are relevant only for large public entities. However, it is important that the owners, as directors, of small and medium-sized enterprises, most of which operate using a private company structure, also comply with legislation governing such structures.

What is corporate governance?

Generally, **corporate governance** refers to the direction, control and management of an entity. This includes the rules, procedures and structure upon which the organisation seeks to meet its objectives. The Organisation for Economic Co-operation and Development (OECD) (www.oecd.org) states that:

> Corporate governance deals with the rights and responsibilities of a company's management, its board, shareholders and various stakeholders. How well companies are run affects market confidence as well as company performance. Good corporate governance is therefore essential for companies that want access to capital and for countries that want to stimulate private sector investment. If companies are well run, they will prosper. This in turn will enable them to attract investors whose support can help to finance faster growth. Poor corporate governance on the other hand weakens a company's potential and at worst can pave the way for financial difficulties and even fraud.

The meaning of corporate governance has evolved over time but, in the strictest sense, is linked to the legislation that allows its existence. The law sets forth a corporation's rights and responsibilities. These can differ from country to country. In New Zealand, the Ministry of Business, Innovation and Employment oversees the Companies Office that administers a wide range of legislation including the *Companies Act 1993*, while in Australia ASIC oversees Commonwealth legislation including:

- *Corporations Act 2001*
- *Australian Securities and Investments Commission Act 2001*
- *Financial Services Reform Act 2001*
- *Insurance Contracts Act 1984*
- *Superannuation Industry (Supervision) Act 1993*
- *Superannuation (Resolution of Complaints) Act 1993*.

It is generally accepted, however, that corporate governance extends beyond the law to include a consideration of best practice and business ethics. The structure of corporate governance as put forward by Farrar (2005) and represented in figure 2.4 illustrates this relationship. When considering this relationship, it is worth remembering that a corporation is an artificial entity that has 'no physical existence, sentience, thought or will' (Shailer 2004, p. 1). The decisions and actions of a corporation are made by humans acting as representatives of the corporation. Thus, the perceived purpose of a corporation is as varied as the humans who interact with it. The issues surrounding the rights and responsibilities of corporations are complex and ever-changing as the financial markets become more global, corporations become larger and more powerful, and society's perceptions of the corporate role develop. The GRI reporting framework outlined in the introduction to accounting and business decision making chapter falls into the category of 'statements of best practice'. It is not a legal requirement for an entity to report on sustainability but many are doing so, as such reporting is increasingly being demanded by the community.

FIGURE 2.4	The structure of corporate governance

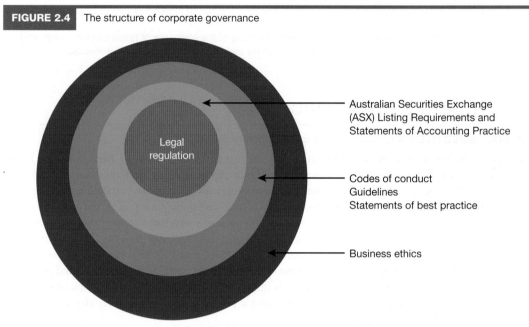

Source: Farrar 2005, p. 4.

Generally, corporate governance responsibilities rest with the board of directors. Both large public companies and small to medium private entities have directors. They are usually given broad powers to make decisions on behalf of the entity through the entity's constitution. The Corporations Act regulates companies generally, and specifically details the duties and responsibilities of company directors.

Specifically, directors owe the following legal duties to their company to:
- act in good faith, in the best interests of the company
- act with care and diligence
- avoid improper use of information or position
- avoid conflicts between their role as a director and any of their personal interests.

In addition, the Corporations Act specifically identifies numerous duties, responsibilities and potential liabilities. A common example of the latter is the personal liability that directors risk in allowing their company to continue to trade while it is insolvent.

Over the past decade, major corporate collapses, the global financial crisis, and environmental and social concerns have focused a spotlight on the governance of business entities. Investors, governments and other stakeholder groups are all looking for greater transparency and accountability in regards to the management of entities' assets by their boards of directors. This has led to a review of corporate governance laws, guidelines and practices, in an attempt to promote good governance and improve the quality of financial reporting and decision making.

2.5 Corporate governance principles, guidelines and practices

LEARNING OBJECTIVE 2.5 Outline corporate governance guidelines and practices.

There are a number of guidelines for directors that outline good corporate governance principles and practices. Generally, these guidelines cover such items as the functions and structure of the board of directors; the conduct of directors; the role of shareholders; the compensation of senior officers and directors; the roles of company accountants, auditors and audit committees; and customer and supplier relations. The *G20/OECD Principles of Corporate Governance* was reissued in September 2015. Likewise, the ASX Corporate Governance Council (CGC) reviewed and has just reissued the *Corporate Governance Principles and Recommendations*, 4th edition, in 2019. This document (available at www.asx.com.au) outlines the eight principles underlying the best practice guidelines. The principles are summarised in figure 2.5.

FIGURE 2.5 ASX CGC corporate governance principles

Eight central principles

1. *Lay solid foundations for management and oversight.* Establish and disclose the respective roles and responsibilities of board and management and how their performance is monitored and evaluated.
2. *Structure the board to add value.* Have a board of an effective composition, size and commitment to adequately discharge its responsibilities and duties.
3. *Act ethically and responsibly.*
4. *Safeguard integrity in corporate reporting.* Have formal and rigorous processes that independently verify and safeguard the integrity of its corporate reporting.
5. *Make timely and balanced disclosure.* Make timely and balanced disclosure of all matters concerning it that a reasonable person would expect to have a material effect on the price or value of its securities.
6. *Respect the rights of shareholders.* Respect the rights of its security holders by providing them with appropriate information and facilities to allow them to exercise those rights effectively.
7. *Recognise and manage risk.* Establish a sound risk management framework and periodically review the effectiveness of that framework.
8. *Remunerate fairly and responsibly.* Pay director remuneration sufficient to attract and retain high-quality directors and design its executive remuneration to attract, retain and align their interest with the creation of value for security holders.

Source: ASX Corporate Governance Council 2014.

The code of ethics for accountants presented later in this chapter has similar themes to those of the ASX guidelines for corporations presented above. Both require consideration of the public interest, both list the minimum standards expected (technical and professional standards for individuals, and best practice standards for corporations) and both stipulate the need for transparency and accountability. Important personal attributes for managers and directors referred to in the guidelines, and for accountants in the professional code of ethics, include competence, integrity and objectivity. Related to these attributes is independence. Independence is an important element in the provision of professional accounting services. It contributes enormously to the trust the public has in accountants and is included in the code of professional ethics. It is therefore not surprising that independent verification is an important element of principle 4 of the ASX guidelines, which relates specifically to safeguarding the integrity of corporate reporting.

Under principle 4 of the ASX guidelines for good corporate governance, it is recommended that the:
• board should establish an audit committee
• audit committee should consist of:
  – only non-executive directors
  – a majority of independent directors
  – an independent chairperson who is not chairperson of the board
  – at least three members
• entity should disclose the audit committee charter, details of those on the audit committee including their experience and qualifications, and the number of meetings and attendees of the audit committee, and explanations of any departures from the recommendations as stated above should be included in the corporate governance section of the annual report; it is also recommended that the procedures for selection and appointment of external auditors are made publicly available.

The use of audit committees and an independent external auditor to help promote the integrity of the financial system is key to providing the public with confidence. You are encouraged to obtain an annual report of a listed public company and investigate the information provided in the report to satisfy principle 4 of the ASX guidelines.

2.6 Ethics in business

LEARNING OBJECTIVE 2.6 Outline the role of ethics in business and compare ethical philosophies relevant to business decision making.

Related to the concept of governance and sustainability is ethics. In fact, the key to governance for sustainability may be determined by the extent of ethical consciousness. The business world has control of the world's resources, and makes decisions every day that affect those resources and the lives of millions of people, so it is imperative that those who operate within the business world have an understanding of various ethical philosophies to help guide their decision making.

Ethical philosophies have been central to the study of humankind for centuries. 'What ought one to do?' was asked by Socrates and argued by Plato as the fundamental question of ethics. Fundamental ethical principles such as virtue, duty, morals, prudence and justice have been proposed and debated throughout history.

Ethical philosophies

Two common approaches to the study of ethics are the teleological approach (sometimes called consequentialism) and the deontological approach (sometimes called idealism). **Teleological theories** are concerned with the consequences of a decision, whereas **deontological theories** are concerned with the action or decision itself. So in deciding 'what is the right thing to do' some would assess the benefits (short or long term) arising from an action, while others would consider the action based on some ethical principle or standing regardless of the outcome of the action.

Teleological theories

An accountant or manager making decisions that would optimise the greatest possible good for the greatest number of people is following a teleological approach to decision making. Two common forms of this approach are called utilitarianism and ethical egoism. **Utilitarianism** is derived from the work of the English philosopher Jeremy Bentham (1748–1832), who defined happiness as 'utility'. He espoused the need for individuals to maximise their utility and argued that, if all individuals did so, this would lead to society's utility being maximised also. The logic is that society's utility is the sum of each individual's utility. John Stuart Mill (1806–1873), however, advanced the theory that the maximisation of an individual's utility should not be at the expense of the group or community. He proposed that behaviour should be based on what provides the greatest good to the greatest number. So, the idea is to maximise the utility of society as a whole, rather than that of individuals. This thinking underlies the development of economics. Generally, in business, this basic principle fits nicely with the efficiency theme. That is, it is in the public's best interest if businesses focus on profitability, as this will ensure the maximum production from their limited resources.

Following on from utilitarianism is **ethical egoism**, where the individual decision maker decides what is best for himself or herself. This type of thinking underlies the assumptions in agency theory (Nordberg 2008) and is relevant to modern corporate governance. For example, it is widely assumed that CEOs will act in their own self-interest and, therefore, one job of the board of directors is to set up mechanisms that will allow the entity to prosper as a result of the CEO pursuing their own wealth-maximisation actions. Whether or not self-serving decisions are likely to be morally wrong compared to decisions made for the common good, the greed or profit-pursuing motive of individuals or entities has in the modern day taken precedence over the overall sense of corporate purpose for the good of society generally.

The self-interest theme underlies much debate throughout the centuries on the amount of government regulation. How much should a government step in and set rules to ensure that entities do the 'right thing'? Thomas Hobbes (1588–1679) felt that rationally people would want regulation for security and protection, while Adam Smith (1723–1790) believed that regulation impeded prosperity and that competitive self-interests were necessary in the commercial world to achieve overall public benefit. This debate is what spurred the American economist Milton Friedman (1912–2006) to write his famous words:

> There is one and only one social responsibility of business — to use its resources and engage in activities designed to increase its profit so long as it stays within the rules of the game, which is to say, engages in open and free competition without deception or fraud (Friedman 1970, p. 126).

Friedman's laissez faire economy, in which profit is the ultimate goal and there is very little regulation, is based on the idea that an entity taking on social costs becomes less efficient and will, in the long run, do more harm to society than good. However, the question remains as to what extent regulation is needed to protect the interest of the community while not stifling the risk-taking ventures of entrepreneurs that provide the impetus for wealthy nations. In other words, what are the rules of the game, and how and who decides on them?

Deontological theories

Accountants or managers taking actions based on their sense of duty subscribe to the deontological approach. That duty may be based on a set of rules or professional guidelines. Following rules of religion (for example, the Bible or the Koran) or various philosophical approaches (for example, Marxism or Rousseau's social contract) would require taking actions according to what they believe would be the principles of right and wrong relative to their beliefs despite the consequences of their decisions.

Another such philosophy is **Kantianism**. The German philosopher Immanuel Kant (1724–1804) proposed that an action is morally right if it is motivated by a good will that stems from a sense of duty. How do you determine whether an act is done in good will? Through what Kant proposed as the 'categorical imperative' (Kant 1964). This categorical imperative, according to Kant, provides a general rule that can be used in any given ethical situation. Two definitions of the categorical imperative that have been espoused are as follows.

1. I ought never to act except in such a way that I can also will that my maxim should become a universal law.
2. Act in such a way that you always treat humanity . . . never simply as a means, but always at the same time as an end.

The first of these maxims is similar to the 'do unto others as you would have them do unto you' philosophy. If you took out credit knowing that you couldn't pay it back, would you like a universal law that dictates that this is acceptable practice? If so, logic would suggest that eventually no-one would extend credit, thus grinding to a halt the cycle of the credit markets. In fact, the global financial crisis during 2008 was firstly a credit crisis that overflowed into the general business arena and significantly impacted on people's savings, investments and house prices.

The second maxim is that the end does not justify the means or, to put it another way, you should not take advantage of people in order to achieve a certain end. Kant's philosophy is grounded in the notion of respect for the individual, hence the requirement that people should be treated as ends and not as a means to others' ends. People themselves are not machinery, capital or commodities at the disposal of others for their self-interest. Some good examples that emphasise this human dignity aspect of Kant's philosophy are as follows.

- The auction on eBay of a human kidney was reported as attracting bids of up to $5.7 million before eBay terminated the auction. The selling of kidneys, no matter how utilitarian for the seller or society, was seen to be morally wrong.
- Many businesses have the relationships among their various stakeholders at the core of their mission statements or codes of conduct. Such companies include Nokia Corporation, Johnson & Johnson and Motorola.
- The Southwest Airlines action of not terminating the employment of staff after the September 11 terrorist attack led to a level of employee loyalty that resulted in staff working overtime for free until the public started flying again. Through this action, the organisation emphasised the importance of staff and the

substance of the company's values, according to which individual relationships with all stakeholders are treasured and stakeholders are not treated simply as a means to economic profitability. In fact, Southwest Airlines' financial success in contrast to most other airlines, which have been doing it tough in recent years, has been argued to be a consequence of its good relationship with its staff.

In summary, Kant's philosophy is embedded in duty or obligation and encompasses a dignity or respect for the individual. So, a business motivated by profits, despite doing respectful things, is acting in a prudential way and not a moral way. However, critics point out that Kant's universal obligations do not take into account particular situations. This is especially relevant in business situations where impartiality is assumed. Businesses undertake transactions at 'arm's length', give all employees equal opportunity and treat customers similarly. However, it is sometimes argued that there is a need to recognise special relationships and therefore to act with partiality. For example, in business the concept of supply chain management may warrant the building of special relationships between suppliers and customers. If supply is restricted, it is natural for suppliers to favour customers that order regular shipments and always pay on time. In fact, in some countries such as Japan, loyal, trusting relationships are treasured. The universal obligation to treat all customers equally would be seen to exploit that relationship. But when does partiality become immoral? Most people can accept a business doing favourable deals with its loyal customers, suppliers or employees. Discounts or favourable terms would be seen as a part of treating employees with respect and rewarding them for their hard work. However, large loans to employees, particularly top management, were the subject of bank scandals in the early 1990s. As a result, regulation and codes explicitly stating the need for 'arm's length transactions' or transactions on the same terms as those with outsiders were introduced for such situations.

In fact, impartiality and regulation are seen as essential components of a moral system. Would you trade on a securities exchange that you knew was rife with insider trading? If insider trading was the universal law and people could trade on inside knowledge, then if you weren't an insider and therefore didn't have access to this information, you would hardly risk placing your money in the system, and so the system would eventually collapse. Another example in business is the audit function. External auditors undertake their audit of financial statements on behalf of shareholders, creditors, employees and other stakeholders. The independence of external auditors to a company and its management is crucial to ensure the credibility of the audit. If an auditor has a partial relationship with their client, the objectivity of the audit could be, or could be perceived to be, impaired. There have been numerous cases where the impartial relationship between auditor and client has been tested in a court of law. A well-known example is that of the audit firm Arthur Andersen LLP and its client Enron. Suffice to say, in the Enron collapse the scrutiny paid to the audit firm showed partiality and favouritism in the audit engagement.

Ethics and regulation

According to Carroll (1979), the key responsibilities of business can be grouped into four categories: economic, legal, ethical and discretionary. Business entities have an economic responsibility to provide goods and services at a fair price, to repay their creditors and to seek a reasonable return for their shareholders. Legally, they are required to uphold the laws and regulations of government. Ethically, businesses are obliged to act in the way expected of them by society. Discretionary responsibilities are carried out voluntarily. These can become legal or regulatory responsibilities over time as expectations change. For example, dismissing women workers who got married was acceptable practice in the 1950s, but now discrimination against women is legally punishable. A contemporary example of a change in business responsibility from discretionary to legal can be found in the debate on the environment. The environment affects all of us and belongs to the world community; therefore, carbon or greenhouse gas emissions into the environment from business activity are gaining a lot of attention. Traditionally, it was not seen as the responsibility of business to consider carbon emissions. However, with the onset of climate change there is now an expectation that business considers the environmental costs of the technologies it employs. Some large companies such as BP, Toyota and British Airways joined forces in January 2005 at the World Economic Forum and took upon themselves the responsibility of monitoring their carbon emissions because they felt it was the right thing to do for the environment and their business (see World Economic Forum 2005). A number of countries, including Australia and New Zealand, have taken steps to regulate carbon emissions.

Other areas in which regulatory action has been required include price skimming, exploitation, the selling of harmful products, whistleblowing, bribery, insider trading and corporate governance. In some of these areas, there has been a move from discretionary responsibility to regulatory responsibility. Most countries would regulate the general areas of their securities exchange, financial system, company pricing and competition, industrial relations, privacy, e-commerce, consumer advocacy, human rights and tax system. An outline of the relevant regulatory bodies was presented at the start of this chapter.

Debate surrounding the impact of globalisation also has at its core the trade-off between the benefits of free enterprise, the promotion of private property rights and the encouragement of competition, thus leading to a greater level of overall national wealth, and the benefits of state ownership, planning and protection (Wolf 2004). However, it is becoming increasingly apparent that the free enterprise culture may be profiting at a high cost to social and environmental needs. This enlightenment is creating a wave of discontent throughout many communities, and has brought about a new interest in and questioning of appropriate political and ideological systems. Democratic capitalist systems that were accepted as the ideal for economic prosperity are now being questioned. Economic growth comes at a cost. Even the move towards sustainable development is being criticised, and the new call is now for sustainable communities and a more appropriate distribution of wealth. Advances in technology, free trade over global markets and changes in policy and regulation will always benefit some people more than others. Economic theory contends that winners gain more than losers lose (Peck 2011), but redistribution through government and policy can compensate for this. However, there is now widespread belief that this redistribution does not occur in practice. So, as class differences increase and the ecosystem struggles, the link between ethics, governance, sustainability and politics becomes stronger. Nordberg (2008) put forward a framework, presented in table 2.1, to help consider the relationship between these elements.

TABLE 2.1 Relationship between ethical theories and economic theories

	Personal	Corporate
Consequentialism (teleology)	Agency theory	Shareholder value
Ethical idealism (deontology)	Stewardship theory	Stakeholder theory

Source: Nordberg 2008, p. 44.

At a personal level, management and directors of corporations are acting in their own self-interest as suggested by agency theory or have some stewardship role on behalf of others or a cause, while at the corporate level the emphasis on shareholder value represents the self-interest teleological approach and the stakeholder view gives rise to consideration for others and what ought to be done.

2.7 Professional codes of ethics and ethical decision-making methods

LEARNING OBJECTIVE 2.7 Explain the use of codes of ethical conduct and apply ethical decision-making methods to business situations.

Many companies and professional bodies have developed their own codes of ethics. The two major accounting professional bodies have a joint code of ethics known as the *APES 110 Code of Ethics for Professional Accountants*. This code is issued by the Accounting Professional and Ethical Standards Board (APESB), established by CPA Australia and CAANZ as an independent body that issues the code of ethics and the standards that their members are required to abide by. Complying with the code is mandatory for all members of the two accounting professional bodies, and disciplinary action can take place if members do not comply. The code describes minimum acceptable standards of professional conduct and focuses on fundamental principles, but is not to be taken as a definitive statement on all matters. Members are encouraged to be guided by the spirit of the code. The code is divided into three main parts: A. the fundamental principles; B. issues relevant to members in an accounting public practice; and C. issues relevant to members in business. The overriding application of the code emphasises that 'a distinguishing mark of the accountancy profession is its acceptance of the responsibility to act in the public interest'. This means that accounting professionals need to safeguard the interests of their clients and employers, and accept their responsibility to the public at large. The five fundamental principles espoused in the code to guide a member's decision making are summarised as follows.

Integrity

- Be straightforward, honest and sincere in your approach to professional work.

Objectivity

- Do not compromise your professional or business judgement because of bias, conflict of interest or the undue influence of others.

Professional competence and due care

- Perform professional services with due care, competence and diligence. Carry out your professional work in accordance with the technical and professional standards relevant to that work.
- Maintain professional knowledge and skill at a level required.
- Refrain from performing any services that you are not competent to carry out unless assistance is obtained.

Confidentiality

- Respect the confidentiality of information acquired in the course of your work and do not disclose any such information to a third party without specific authority or unless there is a legal or professional duty to disclose it.
- Refrain from using confidential information acquired as a result of the professional engagement to your advantage or the advantage of third parties.

Professional behaviour

- Conduct yourself in a manner consistent with the good reputation of the profession and refrain from any conduct that might bring discredit to the profession.

Everyone is encouraged to think about their financial future.

DECISION-MAKING EXAMPLE

Applying the code of conduct

SITUATION You are currently the auditor for the Learning and Care Childcare Centre. It values your audit each year and your suggestions for improving its internal control and accounting systems. It has approached you to undertake some consultancy services for an information system upgrade. Do you take on the engagement?

DECISION Independence is a key attribute of auditing services. You have to be not only independent in fact, but independent in appearance. Taking on the consultancy might impair your independence. It would result in you auditing a system that you helped to install. The engagement might also impair your integrity and objectivity in the eyes of the investors and members of the childcare centre that you are auditing. An audit is an independent check on behalf of those investors and members. This could also lead to a breach of professional behaviour, as it might not be seen to enhance the reputation of the profession. A choice would need to be made between continuing as the auditor and taking on the consultancy engagement. Prior to accepting the consultancy engagement, you would need to ensure that you complied with the principles of competence and due care. You should not take on the engagement if you do not have expertise in the area.

One of the major criticisms of the financial planning industry is that financial planners are paid via commissions from the manufacturers (of investment products) rather than from direct fees for services rendered to clients. Comparisons to doctors receiving commissions from pharmaceutical companies have been made. This means there is a big question mark over financial planners' independence, and many people feel that financial planners are merely salespeople and not advisers or planners as they claim to be. For example, would a financial planner recommend an investment product because it fit the objective and risk profile of the client, or because the financial planner would receive a large commission?

Nowhere was this issue more apparent than in the Storm Financial collapse during the global financial crisis in 2008, where thousands of Australians lost their life savings and their homes due to the risky nature of their very highly leveraged (high debt) investments, which many of them could not possibly have understood. Essentially, a large number of everyday people were placed into high-risk plans and products that simply didn't fit their risk profiles. Despite claiming independence, Storm Financial had many links to institutional product suppliers.

Parts B and C of the *APES 110 Code of Ethics for Professional Accountants* illustrate how the fundamental principles can be applied in specific situations, namely by a member in public practice and a member in business. A member in public practice generally carries out a range of accounting services for a number of different clients, whereas a member in business may be an employee of a business or a government department who has been employed in a specific position to perform tasks relating to that position. Both parts stress the importance of accountants being aware of threats to their compliance with the fundamental principles. These threats include self-interest, self-review, advocacy, familiarity and intimidation. One major difference between a member in public practice and a member in business is independence. A member in public practice, especially one providing audit services, must maintain independence in fact and in appearance at all times. The value of a financial statement audit is linked closely to the credibility of that independence. A good example of where independence came under threat was the audit of the failed company Enron by the audit firm Arthur Andersen LLP. Arthur Andersen LLP provided non-audit services as well as audit services to the company, and a number of ex-Arthur Andersen LLP employees were employed by Enron. The impact of this situation on its independence was severe: the firm Arthur Andersen LLP no longer exists and many senior Enron employees were fined and jailed.

The concept of providing a code of ethics has not been without criticism. Some argue that providing a 'rule book' will do little to address potential problems and that such an approach — defining ethics as a set of rules — will encourage a minimum standard. They argue that an approach that goes beyond the rules is needed in order to encourage a culture that leads to highly ethical behaviour. Despite these criticisms, many entities and professional bodies have continued to issue codes of conduct to help communicate minimum standards. A good example of the usefulness of a code is that published by Nash (1993), which describes the ethical dilemma faced by James Burke, chairman of Johnson & Johnson. In 1982, several people in Chicago were poisoned after taking a tablet called Tylenol. Despite some commentators maintaining that the product tampering was localised to that area, Burke made the decision to pull the product from the market worldwide, at a cost to the company of millions of dollars. His response was in line with the entity's long-maintained 'credo' that its first responsibility is to the customers who use its products. The short-term loss of the action was outweighed by the long-term positive public response.

Ethical decision-making methods

A number of methods have been developed to help in decision making when there is an ethical issue at stake. Some methods provide a sequential approach, while other methods simply help to identify the issues that should be considered in the process of making a decision. An example of each of these methods is presented in figure 2.6.

The self-evaluation activity at the end of this chapter contains an example demonstrating the use of such models.

FIGURE 2.6 Ethical decision-making models

Langenderfer and Rockness (1990)
1. Determine the facts of the case.
2. Determine the ethical issues in the case.
3. Determine the norms, principles and values related to the case.
4. Determine the alternative courses of action.
5. Determine the best course of action consistent with 3 above.
6. Determine the consequences of each possible course of action identified in 4.
7. Decide the course of action.

The Ethics Centre (www.ethics.org.au)
1. What are the relevant facts?
2. Which of my values make these facts significant?
3. What assumptions am I making?
4. What are the weaknesses in my own position?
5. Would I be happy for my actions to be open to public scrutiny?
6. Would I be happy if my family knew what I'd done?
7. What will doing this do to my character or the character of my organisation?
8. What would happen if everybody took this course of action?
9. How would I feel if my actions were to impact upon a child or parent?
10. Have I really thought the issues through?
11. Have I considered the possibility that the ends may not justify the means?

Source: Langenderfer & Rockness 1990; The Ethics Centre.

VALUE TO BUSINESS

- Ethics is fundamental to the study of business and can aid those making decisions.
- Business decision making has at its roots ethical philosophies such as utilitarianism and Kantianism.
- Professional bodies issue codes of professional conduct that prescribe the minimum acceptable standards for their members.
- Ethical decision-making methods are available to help guide decision makers on the correct course to take.
- Regulation can increase as society expects more from business in meeting its responsibilities.

2.8 Limitations of accounting information

LEARNING OBJECTIVE 2.8 Give examples of the limitations of accounting information.

Accounting information provides a wide range of information for both internal and external users. However, for decision-making purposes other relevant business factors in addition to accounting information need to be considered. For example, if a prospective investor was considering purchasing shares in a company, they would spend some time analysing the financial statements of the company (i.e. looking at accounting information). To make an informed judgement, they would also need to consider other sources of information, such as the company's percentage of market share, how long the company has been in existence and the company's social and environmental policies (if any). When making investment decisions, investors are increasingly evaluating a company's social and environmental credentials as well as its financial situation.

Additionally, users of accounting information need to consider carefully a number of limitations of the information provided, especially in the financial statements. These limitations include the time lag in the distribution of the information to the various users, the historical nature of accounting information and the subjective nature of financial statements. These will now be discussed in more detail.

Time lag

There is a significant time delay from the end of the financial year until the information reaches users in the form of a financial report. Although the internet has assisted in decreasing the time lag, there is often a delay of up to three months from the end of the financial year until the information is published.

The problem with the time delay is that a lot can happen to business entities within a few months.

- An increase in market competition can dramatically change future demand for an entity's products.
- An unsettled legal dispute can be resolved in the months subsequent to the end of the financial year.
- Fire and flood can damage an entity's stockholdings.

While entities are required to disclose after reporting day events that are material, there will always be some information that is not accurately reported by the time the annual report is available to the users.

When making investment decisions, investors are increasingly evaluating a company's social and environmental credentials as well as its financial situation.

Historical information

Despite one of the major roles of accounting information being an assessment of the future performance of the entity, the information in financial statements is based on past transactions and therefore does not provide forecast information. For example, the expenses and income are reported in the statement of profit or loss for the financial period past. They are not an accurate indication of what the future income and expenses will be. Nevertheless, a review of the past is often a helpful guide to future performance.

Subjectivity of information

Accounting information is prepared based on GAAP, which provide accounting standards for preparing financial statements, but there is much subjectivity (choice) involved in the inclusion of items to be reported and the choice of accounting policies to adopt. For example, entities can choose the value that an asset will be reported at in the financial statements. They can report certain assets at either cost or current market value. JB Hi-Fi Ltd reports most assets at historical cost; however, certain financial assets and classes of PPE are revalued to fair value (current market value). There are also choices for inventory valuation methods, when to recognise revenue and the disclosure of additional financial information. JB Hi-Fi Ltd recognises revenue at the fair value of the consideration received or receivable.

Potential costs of providing accounting information

Providing accounting information to various users involves potential costs. The two types of costs discussed here are information costs and the cost of releasing information to competitors.

Information costs

Various costs are involved in gathering, summarising and producing the information contained in financial statements. The implementation of accounting software programs (such as MYOB, QuickBooks and other custom-made software) assists in decreasing these information costs, but there are still substantial collating and printing costs to be met in order to produce financial statements.

Consider the recording of the different assets that an entity such as the Qantas Group would have to keep updated. Figure 2.7 shows a snapshot of the PPE note (note 10) to the Qantas Group 2018 financial statements. As you can see, there are various categories of PPE reported along with their cost and accumulated depreciation during the periods 2017 and 2018.

FIGURE 2.7	The Qantas Group's property, plant and equipment

11. Property, plant and equipment

Qantas Group	2018 $m			2017 $m		
	At cost	Accumulated depreciation and impairment	Net book value	At cost	Accumulated depreciation and impairment	Net book value
Freehold land	49	—	49	50	—	50
Buildings	295	(216)	79	335	(226)	109
Leasehold improvements	1 392	(990)	402	1 413	(966)	447
Plant and equipment	1 511	(1 099)	412	1 563	(1 130)	433
Aircraft and engines	22 713	(11 964)	10 749	20 992	(10 960)	10 032
Aircraft spare parts	909	(414)	495	835	(405)	430
Aircraft deposits	665	—	665	752	—	752
Total property, plant and equipment	**27 534**	**(14 683)**	**12 851**	**25 940**	**(13 687)**	**12 253**

Source: Qantas Airways Ltd 2018, p. 65.

Release of competitive information

The information disclosed in an entity's financial report potentially contains proprietary information that could be used by competitors to strengthen their market positions. An example of this information is the disclosure of segment data that is found in the notes to financial statements. Consider the Qantas Group segment report in illustrative example 1.1 from the introduction to accounting and business decision making chapter. As you can see, it reports the entity's segment information, including different types of revenue and profit. This information does give the user (possibly a competitor) an insight into where the entity's main profits are derived from. It also informs potential competitors of the most cost-effective segments (highest profit margins). This is particularly interesting because in 2018 Qantas Group's most profitable segment was Qantas Domestic, which operates domestic flights in Australia. This would provide useful information to competitors such as Virgin Australia. Interestingly, apart from the Corporate segment, the least profitable was Qantas Loyalty.

SUMMARY OF LEARNING OBJECTIVES

2.1 Identify the sources of company regulation in Australia.

The main source of company regulation is the Corporations Act, administered by the Australian Securities and Investments Commission (ASIC). The other important sources of regulation are the Listing Rules of the Australian Securities Exchange (ASX) and the accounting principles, standards, ethics and disciplinary procedures of the professional accounting associations.

2.2 Explain the current standard-setting framework and the role of the professional accounting associations in the standard-setting process.

Prior to 2005, Australian Accounting Standards were largely developed by the Australian Accounting Standards Board (AASB). However, since 1 January 2005 Australian entities have complied with International Financial Reporting Standards (IFRS) developed by the International Accounting Standards Board (IASB). The AASB is responsible for developing and maintaining high-quality financial reporting standards in Australia and contributing to the ongoing development of international accounting standards by the IASB. In Australia, there are two main professional associations: CPA Australia and Chartered Accountants Australia and New Zealand (CAANZ). The professional associations provide feedback on exposure drafts and forward any comments to the AASB. They also inform their members of any developments in accounting standards through newsletters and by conducting continuing professional education (CPE) sessions.

2.3 Evaluate the role of the *Conceptual Framework* and illustrate the qualitative characteristics of financial statements.

The *Conceptual Framework* is designed to assist in the preparation and presentation of financial statements, guide the standard setters in developing future accounting standards and help users interpret information in financial statements. It specifies the objective of financial statements, their desirable qualitative characteristics, and the definition and recognition of elements in financial statements. The two fundamental qualitative characteristics of financial statements are relevance (including materiality) and faithful representation. The enhancing qualitative characteristics are comparability, verifiability, timeliness and understandability. Cost is a constraint on financial reporting.

2.4 Explain the concept of corporate governance.

Corporate governance refers to the direction, control and management of an entity. The board of directors is given the authority through a company's constitution and the *Corporations Act 2001* to act on behalf of the shareholders.

2.5 Outline corporate governance guidelines and practices.

Corporate governance guidelines foster improved corporate governance practices. An example is those put forward by the ASX Corporate Governance Council. These guidelines foster awareness of a director's responsibilities and help communicate society's expectations to the wider business community. Such guidelines generally include items such as board structure, financial reporting, ethics, stakeholders, remuneration and disclosure.

2.6 Outline the role of ethics in business and compare ethical philosophies relevant to business decision making.

Business decision makers influence the use of the world's resources and affect the lives of many people. Ethics is central to the study of humankind and so should be explored in a business context. Two key approaches are teleological and deontological theories. The teleological approach is concerned with the consequences of a decision, while the deontological approach is concerned with the action or decision itself.

2.7 Explain the use of codes of ethical conduct and apply ethical decision-making methods to business situations.

Codes of ethical conduct prescribe minimum ethical standards and are widely used in business to communicate a respect for the public good. The fundamental principles are integrity, objectivity, professional competence and due care, confidentiality and professional behaviour. The methods proposed by Langenderfer and Rockness and by The Ethics Centre have been presented. The application of ethical decision-making methods helps to identify the issues and clarify thought when making a business decision.

2.8 Give examples of the limitations of accounting information.

The limitations of accounting information include the time lag between production of the report and distribution to the users, the historical nature of financial statements and the subjective nature of financial statements. Costs associated with releasing accounting information include the costs of preparing and disseminating the information, and any losses from the potential release of proprietary information to competitors.

KEY TERMS

assets Present economic resources controlled by an entity as a result of past events and from which future economic benefits are expected to flow to the entity.

Australian Accounting Standards Board (AASB) Body responsible for developing accounting standards for application to Australian entities.

Australian Securities and Investments Commission (ASIC) Government body responsible for regulating companies, company borrowings, and investment advisers and dealers.

Australian Securities Exchange (ASX) Australian marketplace for trading equities, government bonds and other fixed-interest securities.

corporate governance Direction, control and management of an entity.

Corporations Act 2001 **(Cwlth)** National scheme of legislation, administered by ASIC, dealing with the regulation of companies and the securities and futures industries in Australia.

debentures Loan instruments that are normally secured by a fixed or floating charge over assets.

deontological theories Theories concerned with duty and an action or decision itself, as opposed to its consequences.

disclosing entity An entity that issues securities which are quoted on a stock market or made available to the public via a prospectus.

due process Course of formal proceedings that is carried out in accordance with established rules and principles for protecting and enforcing different individual views associated with standard setting.

equity Residual interest in the assets of an entity after all its liabilities have been deducted.

ethical egoism The moral position where a person ought to do what is in their own self-interest.

expenses Decreases in economic benefits during an accounting period in the form of outflows, decreases in assets or incurrences of liabilities that result in decreases in equity, other than those relating to distributions to equity participants.

Financial Reporting Council (FRC) Statutory body responsible for overseeing the accounting and auditing standard-setting processes for both public and private sectors in Australia.

general purpose financial statements (GPFS) Financial statements prepared to meet the information needs common to external users.

generally accepted accounting principles (GAAP) The specific rules and guidelines pertaining to a specific jurisdiction that entities use to help them prepare financial statements. These rules and guidelines vary from country to country.

income Increases in economic benefits during an accounting period in the form of inflows, increases in assets or decreases in liabilities that result in increases in equity, other than those relating to contributions from equity participants.

International Financial Reporting Standards (IFRS) Accounting standards that are prepared and issued by the International Accounting Standards Board (IASB).

Kantianism Theory proposed by Kant that an action is morally right if it is motivated by a good will that stems from a sense of duty.

liabilities Present obligations of an entity arising from past events, the settlement of which is expected to result in an outflow from the entity of resources embodying economic benefits.

Listing Rules Rules governing the procedures and behaviour of all ASX-listed companies.

Operating Rules Rules governing how trading takes place on the ASX by overseeing the operations and behaviour of participating entities.

profit Income less expenses for a reporting period.

special purpose financial statements Financial statements prepared to suit a specific purpose.

teleological theories Theories concerned with the consequences of decisions.

utilitarianism Theory that all individuals maximising their own utility will lead to society's utility being maximised also.

APPLY YOUR KNOWLEDGE

16 marks

Financial acumen may not be every director's strength but ignorance is no excuse when it comes to understanding company accounts. The former directors of property group Centro found this out the hard way when the Federal Court brought down its landmark decision against them regarding their lack of due diligence in the lead-up to the company's near collapse in 2007. The eight former directors and executives were found to have breached the Corporations Act by signing off on financial reports that failed to disclose billions of dollars of short-term debt. The case was watched closely by boards of directors across Australia, although the recently announced penalties were considered lenient. Declarations of contravention were made against all defendants.

Regardless of the lightness of the penalties, the case will continue to hold important lessons for Australian company directors. In his ruling, Federal Court judge John Middleton commented that the omission of more than A$2 billion of debt from the accounts could have been identified 'without difficulty'. What was required of the directors was 'critical and detailed attention', rather than relying on the information presented to them by management and Centro's auditors PricewaterhouseCoopers 'no matter how competent or trustworthy they may appear to be'. The Centro case will continue to be upheld as a prime example of what can go wrong when directors rely on others for information rather than make it their business to read the financial statements and check them.

'The judgement is more of a wake-up call to say "don't skim the accounts and don't rely on the assurances of others. You need to exercise judgement and use an inquiring mind". Which is consistent with the legal principals [sic] that directors have to be pro-active when it comes to understanding company affairs including its financial affairs,' [Anil Hargovan] says. Leigh Warnick, a partner with Lavan Legal in Perth, says there are two key messages company directors and their advisers should take home from the Centro judgement: directors are the last line of defence on financial reporting; and information overload is no excuse — directors must take control. Directors across Australia would be entitled to react to the Centro case with alarm if it obliged them to read financial statements with the eyes of an expert, but this is not the case, Warnick says. The requirements outlined by Justice Middleton were to have enough financial literacy to understand basic accounting conventions, and to exercise proper diligence in reading financial statements.

John Colvin, managing director and chief executive of the Australian Institute of Company Directors (AICD), says the judgement against the Centro directors highlights important issues and provides some timely reminders of the significant responsibilities that come with a board seat and just how difficult being a director can be. 'It is important for all company directors to have an understanding of the business they oversee, as well as a basic understanding of the financial position of the company,' says Colvin. However, in an environment where the complexity of financial reporting standards and their application continues to increase, the role of company directors continues to become even more onerous.

The Centro judgement reminds directors that they are entitled to rely on specialist knowledge and advice provided by management and external advisers, but cautions directors that there are limits to that reliance, according to Colvin. 'Board members should apply their individual, considered judgement to matters that are highly significant to the company before approving financial statements, and while we (at the AICD) agree that "directors are an essential component of corporate governance", we are of the view that it is not the role of non-executive directors to be involved in the day-to-day management of the company,' says Colvin.

'You may find that some directors are not confident about their ability to understand the basic accounting concepts in the financial statements,' says Warnick. 'The only safe option for directors in this position is to take an appropriate course to improve their skills.' (*BusinessThink* 2011)

Required

(a) Discuss the main issues for directors that are evident in the extract above.   **4 marks**

(b) Critique the judgement made in the case regarding the level of financial knowledge required of directors.

4 marks

(c) Suggest the consequence of the Centro decision for the diversity of Australian boardrooms.   **4 marks**

(d) A continuing controversial topic relating to management and the board is remuneration. Given the decision in the Centro case, predict the consequences for the remuneration of board members and the effect this would have on other stakeholders.   **4 marks**

SELF-EVALUATION ACTIVITIES

2.1 Westpoint Corporation is a property development company. Imagine that you are a financial adviser and have been approached by the directors of Westpoint Corporation to recommend their company as a good investment to your clients. You read their material and note that the return for investors is

12 per cent per annum. A number of your clients have expressed an interest in investing in property and would appreciate this high return. The information you receive seems reasonable given the buoyancy of the property market. You note that there is a cap on the amount the developers are collecting to fund developments. However, the investment would be mezzanine lending, and this means high risk. (The term 'mezzanine' in this scenario is used to describe a structure where a group of companies are formed in the middle, between the parent company and the property development projects. This makes the investment more complex, and makes it harder to trace and understand the flow of money and the property rights of each company.) The commission payable to you is double the normal rate of commission. This arouses your suspicions regarding the project, but the financial benefits to you would help fund the further growth of your own business.

Required

Would you recommend this investment to your clients? If yes, on what basis would you make the recommendation? Use the Langenderfer and Rockness method presented in the chapter to help answer these questions.

SOLUTION TO 2.1

Step 1. Determine the facts of the case.

The property investment is high risk due to mezzanine lending, which involves a complex company structure. The commissions payable are high, and the accuracy of the information received seems reasonable but also raises your suspicions.

Step 2. Determine the ethical issues in the case.

There is a duty to:

- ensure your clients are fully informed as to the risk inherent in the project
- disclose the amount of commission payable
- act in the best interests of your clients
- ensure that the investment is the best choice for your clients regardless of the commission payable.

Step 3. Determine the norms, principles and values related to the case.

You as the adviser should act with objectivity, integrity, honesty and trust.

Step 4. Determine the alternative courses of action.

These are the alternatives.

(a) Recommend the investment and fully disclose the risk involved and the commission payable.

(b) Recommend the investment and do not fully disclose the risk involved or the commission payable.

(c) Inform clients of the investment and, if a client wants to proceed with the project, refuse the commission.

(d) Do not recommend the investment.

Step 5. Determine the best course of action consistent with 3 above.

The best course of action is (c) or (d). The mezzanine funding structure, the high annual return of 12 per cent and the commissions payable at twice the normal rate should arouse your suspicions and warrant further investigation of the proposal. A key issue is that your clients trust you and are likely to invest in the project if you recommend it. Your objectivity could be clouded by the high commission rates. Your integrity and honesty will be shattered if you recommend the investment when you do not truly believe that the investment matches the risk profile and financial objectives of your clients.

Step 6. Determine the consequences of each possible course of action identified in 4.

These are the likely consequences.

(a) If the investment goes well, your clients will be grateful. However, if the investment fails, you will feel some responsibility due to the trust the clients placed on your recommendation — even if they were informed of the risk involved. Public perception of you and your business could be adversely affected if it were known that you recommended an investment that subsequently failed.

(b) If the investment goes well, your clients will be grateful. However, the non-disclosure of the commissions could weigh heavily on your conscience. Once again, public perception of you and your business could be adversely affected if the public found out about your recommendation and non-disclosure. If the project fails and your clients lose their money — possibly all their life savings — you would feel responsible. You would also risk professional negligence action if discovered.

(c) Because your clients were kept informed of all investment opportunities, there is no link between the clients' decisions (whether they invest or not) and the payment of your commission. Regardless of the success or otherwise of the investment, your conscience should be clear and your professional reputation would remain untarnished.

(d) If the investment fails, you will have a clear conscience about not recommending a highly speculative investment. Your clients would need to find other projects in which to invest their money, perhaps with a reduced rate of return. If, however, the investment pays off, the clients could blame you for a missed investment opportunity and withdraw their custom.

Step 7. Decide the course of action.

The best course of action is to investigate the proposal further. Be open and honest with your clients regarding the proposal, including the risk, the return and the commissions payable to you. If a client decides to go ahead with the investment, then you need to ensure that all details disclosed have been documented and satisfy yourself that the client is fully aware of the risk being taken.

2.2 A well-known fraud scandal in Australia involved the collapse of the Westpoint Corporation. Essentially, investors thought they were funding property development projects for a 12 per cent per annum return. However, Westpoint Corporation was a property development company that relied on mezzanine finance schemes. (As above, the term 'mezzanine' in this context is used to describe a group of companies in the middle, between the parent company and the property development projects.) The unsuspecting investors thought they were providing funding to a particular company for a particular property development. However, once the money was received it was farmed off by the parent company for distribution to other companies to pay for previous projects, the directors' large salaries, financial planner commissions and previous investor returns. In essence, more and more investors were needed to fund the previous investor returns and projects. The group of companies eventually collapsed. The following is typical of the media attention this collapse attracted.

> It's being called the biggest corporate collapse since HIH — and whether or not that's accurate, it's probably the most predictable property disaster since Henry Kaye collapsed. Depending on which report you read, as many as six thousand investors may lose as much as $1 billion after investing their savings with Perth-based Westpoint Corporation. Whatever the final numbers, it's going to be very big and very tragic. But, worst of all, it was all so predictable and avoidable.
>
> Westpoint . . . [was] . . . a property development company. It needs to find two types of investors — financiers to fund its apartment projects and then buyers to buy the apartments. To fund the building of its projects, financial predators (who call themselves financial planners) advised their trusting clients that Westpoint Corporation's projects were safe and secure. The investors effectively loaned their money to Westpoint in schemes known as Mezzanine Lending. Thanks to these financial planners, Westpoint raised hundreds of millions of dollars.
>
> So why did many financial planners recommend Westpoint to their clients? Because they're more predators than planners. When Westpoint offered extra big commissions, they knew it would attract the most predatory of the planners. Hundreds of millions of investors' money went into Westpoint's Mezzanine Finance schemes because of the financial planners. The second type of investors that Westpoint needed were buyers for its apartments. In order to pay big interest rates and big commissions, Westpoint needed a big price for its apartments, well above the true market price. Enter more predators.
>
> Australian Securities and Investments Commission chief Jeff Lucy said of the financial planners who steered their clients into Westpoint, 'They should have known better'. Yes, indeed, it was all so predictable. Now, it's all so tragic (Jenman 2006).

Required

(a) Outline the main issues of this case.

(b) Now that you have read the outcome of the Westpoint Corporation case, and particularly that investors lost millions of dollars, how do you feel about your recommendation in 2.1?

SOLUTION TO 2.2

The issues involved in the case include:

- financial planner independence and commission versus fee-based service
- code of ethics — honesty, integrity, trust and objectivity
- general philosophy viewpoint
  - obligation and sense of respect and dignity for your client, versus
  - a strict self-interest principle where everyone is expected to look after themselves.

The way you feel will depend on whether or not you recommended the investment in 2.1. Your sense of responsibility to your clients will also depend on whether you feel a sense of obligation towards your clients (under Kantianism) or you operate on a strict self-interest principle.

Note that Westpoint Corporation was classed as a 'ponzi' scheme (a high-return investment in which the dividends to earlier investors are paid from funds deposited by newer investors; ultimately the scheme falls apart when it fails to attract more new investors and there is no more money to continue paying dividends) and action was taken against it by ASIC. Claims of approximately $570 million were lodged in the courts against the directors of the nine Westpoint mezzanine companies, KPMG (the auditors of the Westpoint Group), seven financial planners and a trust that held an unsecured mezzanine note. To read more about the Westpoint collapse and subsequent recovery of monies, go to https://asic.gov.au/about-asic/news-centre/key-matters/westpoint.

COMPREHENSION QUESTIONS

2.3 Describe the structure of corporate governance as put forward by Farrar. **LO4**

2.4 Compare and contrast the view of Hobbes with those of Smith and Friedman. **LO6**

2.5 Outline the major maxims of Kantianism and describe what they mean. **LO6**

2.6 One of the limitations of accounting information is the historical nature of financial reports. Provide an example of an asset from the statement of financial position of Qantas Group where the asset's historical cost may not reflect its current value. **LO8**

2.7 What are the benefits of professional association membership for accounting graduates? **LO2**

2.8 Discuss whether an accountant should take on an appointment outside their area of expertise. **LO7**

2.9 Compare and contrast the roles of the Financial Reporting Council (FRC) and the Australian Securities Exchange (ASX). **LO2**

2.10 What is the difference between the revised *Conceptual Framework*'s fundamental qualitative characteristics of relevance and faithful representation? Can you think of any trade-offs between relevance and faithful representation? **LO3**

2.11 Imagine that you are a manager in a large entity and need to make a recommendation to the CEO on which tender to accept. The job being put out to tender by the entity is worth millions of dollars and you have a significant ownership share in one of the companies tendering. Outline the ethical issues to be considered. **LO7**

2.12 How can the professional accounting bodies assist in standard setting? **LO2**

2.13 Describe the major purpose of the ASX. What types of information does it provide for a novice investor? **LO1**

2.14 What are the four key responsibilities of business? Do you think that an entity should consider discretionary responsibilities? Why or why not? **LO6**

2.15 What is the impact of the qualitative characteristic of materiality on the preparation of financial statements? **LO3**

2.16 In your own words, explain the advantage of comparability and transparency of financial information due to the adoption of IFRS. **LO2**

2.17 'Complying with the law will always mean that you are acting ethically.' Discuss this statement. **LO2**

2.18 Are ethics and corporate governance important topics in the study of accounting and the business environment? Why or why not? **LO4**

2.19 Explain the relationship between the Australian Accounting Standards Board (AASB) and the International Accounting Standards Board (IASB). **LO2**

2.20 Briefly describe how the AASB develops accounting standards. **LO2**

2.21 Comment on the approach put forward by The Ethics Centre in deliberations of an ethical issue. **LO7**

2.22 How do accounting standards assist large companies? **LO2**

2.23 What is an IFRS and how does it impact on standard setting in Australia? **LO2**

2.24 Identify and discuss the five fundamental principles of the *APES 110 Code of Ethics for Professional Accountants*. **LO7**

2.25 What is risk management and why is it included in the ASX Corporate Governance Council (CGC) *Corporate Governance Principles and Recommendations*? **LO5**

2.26 Give some examples of each of Carroll's four key responsibilities of business. Have any of these changed from one responsibility grouping to another over the last decade? **LO6**

2.27 Explain: **LO4**
  (a) triple bottom line reporting
  (b) corporate governance
  (c) the relationship of stakeholders to corporate governance.

2.28 Outline the corporate governance principles and recommendations. **LO5**

2.29 Outline the legal duties that directors have to their company. **LO4**

2.30 Compare and contrast the professional code of ethics for individuals and the guidelines for corporations. **LO7**

2.31 What is the difference between business ethics and social and environmental responsibility? **LO6**

EXERCISES

★ BASIC | ★ ★ MODERATE | ★ ★ ★ CHALLENGING

2.32 Australian Accounting Standards ★ **LO2**

There are at least 60 Australian Accounting Standards. Go to the AASB website at www.aasb.gov.au and choose one. (*Hint*: Go to 'Quick Links' and select 'Table of Standards'.) One of the recent accounting standards is the standard on fair value measurement. Briefly describe the meaning of 'fair value' accounting. What is the purpose of this standard?

2.33 AASB and standard setting ★ **LO2**

The AASB, as part of its work program, offers comment on documents such as proposed agenda decisions, exposure drafts, draft exposure drafts, invitations to comment and discussion papers. Go to the 'Work in Progress' page of the AASB website at www.aasb.com.au and choose 'Pending'. One of the topics listed relates to the exposure draft — ED 259 *Classification of Liabilities*. Summarise the main changes to this proposed standard.

2.34 Fraud ★ **LO6**

A survey conducted by PricewaterhouseCoopers in 2018 shows that 45 per cent of organisations experienced customer fraud in the last two years. Likewise 43 per cent suffered a cyber attack. The most common types of cyber attacks were: phishing (48%), malware (39%) and network scanning (24%). External actors accounted for 64 per cent of economic crime in Australia.

Comment on whether fraud is just part of the cost of doing business. Outline five steps that organisations can take to fight against economic crime.

2.35 Professional institutions ★ **LO2**

CPA Australia and CAANZ have designated areas on their websites for technical resources and updates. Go to each of the respective bodies' websites (www.cpaaustralia.com.au and www.charteredaccountantsanz.com) and summarise the resources provided.

2.36 *Conceptual Framework* and accounting standards ★ **LO8**

Describe the relationship between the revised *Conceptual Framework* and the accounting standard AASB 116 *Property, Plant and Equipment*.

2.37 Corporate governance and sustainability ★ ★ **LO5**

> I put it to you that the directors are responsible to the shareholders for profit in perpetuity; and that this general expression of a principle permits, indeed requires, directors to pay full regard to their employees, to labour relations generally, to the community, to the country, in all their decisions for and on behalf of shareholders (Dunlop 1987).

Discuss the implications of Sir John Dunlop's statement as a company director.

2.38 Corporate governance ★ ★ **LO4**

Outline some of the legal constraints in legislating for the consideration of stakeholder interests.

2.39 Code of ethics ★ ★ **LO7**

Members of the two accounting professional bodies, CPA Australia and the Chartered Accountants of Australia and New Zealand (CAANZ), have to comply with the *APES 110 Code of Ethics for Professional Accountants*. This code lists several possible threats to the fundamental principles. Look up the APESB website (www.apesb.org.au) and outline some examples of each of the five threats.

2.40 Ethical decision-making models ★ ★ **LO7**

Your client MJM Ltd consults with you in relation to the new financial information system that it wishes to have installed. You are technically competent in this area, and so accept the engagement. You carry out an analysis of software available and make a recommendation that the client accepts. You continue to be involved while the software is being installed.

Discuss the effect of this engagement on you continuing as the client's auditor. Use the Langenderfer and Rockness model to help with your answer.

2.41 Corporate governance ★ ★ LO5

Comment on the following situations in relation to the ASX CGC *Corporate Governance Principles and Recommendations*.

(a) A member of a board of directors insists on being involved in the employment of personnel.

(b) The auditor of a company is the brother-in-law of one of the company's directors.

(c) The XYZ company ensures that as much information as possible about its operations and financial affairs is made available on the company website.

(d) The chairman of the board puts forward a proposal to remunerate the CEO. A member of the board questions the proposal, giving the opinion that 'in comparison to similar-sized entities, it seems excessive'.

(e) A board member is a major shareholder of a company that has tendered on a contract worth millions of dollars. When the board meets to consider the tenders received, the board member declares that she has a conflict of interest and leaves the meeting room while the tenders are being discussed.

2.42 Ethics ★ ★ LO7

As the director of a company, you need to make a decision regarding whether to shift the manufacturing operations offshore. Over recent years, the influx of cheap imports has made it harder to compete on a cost basis. However, shifting the operations offshore will create job losses for a large number of local people. Your company is a major employer in the region and the closure of the factory will have a significant economic effect in the area. Use The Ethics Centre method to identify the issues to consider.

2.43 Disciplinary action ★ ★ LO7

Every time there is a spate of corporate collapses, the accounting profession has been closely scrutinised and many members of the professional bodies have appeared before disciplinary hearings. The professional bodies publish a professional conduct annual report each year. Go to the CAANZ website at www.charteredaccountantsanz.com. Search for 'Member Complaints and Discipline'. Select 'Tribunal Decisions'. Summarise five of the tribunal hearings and the nature of the allegations against the members of the accounting profession.

2.44 Ethical decision-making models ★ ★ LO7

You are faced with the following situations. Use the Langenderfer and Rockness model to help determine the course of action you would take.

(a) You are a manager within a large entity and need to make a recommendation to the CEO on which tender to accept. The job being tendered for is worth millions of dollars and you have a significant share in one of the companies tendering.

(b) You are a small-business owner who wants to enter an overseas market. You arrange to meet with a government official of the country you wish to do business with in order to discuss your market entry. To be successful, you really need his support. During the discussion, you realise that he expects a monetary payment in exchange for his help.

2.45 Code of ethics for professional accountants ★ ★ ★ LO7

You are an accountant with XYZ Ltd and are confronted with the situations described below. State in each case whether there has been a breach of the *APES 110 Code of Ethics for Professional Accountants*.

(a) You are appointed the auditor of Jones Ltd, a supplier of electronic devices. While on the premises carrying out some audit work, you are offered a new tablet in appreciation of your work to date.

(b) You discover that your client, White Ltd, has overestimated its allowable deductions on its tax return. You ask the company to submit an amended return but it refuses.

(c) You approach one of your friends, who works for a lending institution, for an unsecured loan. You have been unable to obtain a loan elsewhere. Your friend approves the loan.

(d) You are on the local council works committee. It is considering a number of tenders for a library upgrade. Your best friend has submitted a tender and you argue strongly in favour of that tender.

(e) You have been approached to audit a large regional business. Your spouse is employed as a manager within the company.

2.46 Corporations and social responsibility ★ ★ ★ LO7

A corporation is an artificial entity. Discuss whether the rights of this artificial entity should ever take priority over the rights of individuals and communities.

2.47 Ethics ★ ★ ★   **LO6**

Compare and contrast teleological theories and deontological theories. Discuss whether you think these theories have a place in modern business society.

2.48 The Australian Accounting Standards Board (AASB) and international accounting standards ★ ★   **LO2**

What is the relationship between the AASB and international standard-setting bodies such as the IASB?

2.49 Ethics, corporate governance and sustainability ★ ★ ★   **LO6**

Underlying the professional code of ethics is an obligation to act in the public interest. Utilitarianism espouses the need to act and make decisions with consequences in mind. Practically, business decisions are often made based on a consideration of the decision's effect on the business. How can any business manager merge the principles of utilitarianism — acting in the public interest — while ensuring the growth and prosperity of the organisation they are managing? Discuss.

2.50 Corporate governance ★ ★ ★   **LO4**

Corporate governance relates only to large public enterprises and is therefore irrelevant for small business. Discuss this statement.

PROBLEMS

★ BASIC | ★ ★ MODERATE | ★ ★ ★ CHALLENGING

2.51 Corporate governance ★   **LO5**

The notes to the 2018 consolidated financial statements of JB Hi-Fi Ltd appear in the appendix to this text. Examine these notes together with other information from the website (http://investors.jbhifi.com.au) to investigate JB Hi-Fi Ltd's compliance with principle 4 (safeguard the integrity of financial reporting) of the ASX CGC *Corporate Governance Principles and Recommendations*.

Form teams to investigate the recommendations under principle 4 as presented in this chapter. The teams should examine one different recommendation each.

2.52 Ethics ★   **LO7**

Erle Smith is a financial controller with Accounting Success Ltd, an entity that sells software products to accounting firms and small businesses. At present, Erle is analysing a number of software packages that focus on job costing. He needs to pick one package that he can recommend to his clients. Each software vendor is keen to have their software selected, as it would result in a significant increase in sales for their company.

Anitah Loh is a salesperson for software company Catta Ltd. She has told Erle that he should go to Tokyo to analyse her company's software package properly, because the programming experts there could give him a thorough demonstration. Anitah has also suggested that he take his family, so that he feels relaxed in a foreign country and is in the right frame of mind to undertake his analysis. She says that Disneyland is worth visiting. Catta Ltd would pick up the expenses for the trip.

Required

(a) Do you think Erle should take the trip? Outline any ethical concerns involved.

(b) Do you think the management of Accounting Success Ltd should allow Erle to go on the trip?

(c) Do you think that Accounting Success Ltd should have a code of conduct? What would be the advantages and disadvantages to Accounting Success Ltd of having a code of conduct?

2.53 Business sustainability and ethics ★   **LO7**

Search the Johnson & Johnson website for its famous credo (www.jnj.com.au). (*Hint:* Access the credo from the drop-down menu called 'Our Company'.) Given that the credo was written nearly 60 years ago, comment on its appropriateness in today's business world. Further, reflect on the early philosophical writings (such as utilitarianism and Kantianism) and comment on the credo's relevance to these philosophies.

2.54 Ethics ★ ★ ★   **LO7**

The downturn in the economy during 2008 revealed one of the biggest cases of fraud in history. The fraud was masterminded by Bernie Madoff, a well-known American finance executive. The US$65 billion ponzi scheme, called Bernard L Madoff Investment Securities, resulted in a number of institutional and high-wealth individuals losing their money. Clients affected included Steven Spielberg, HSBC, Fortis, RBS, Baroness Thyssen-Bornemisza, Yeshiva University, top Merrill

Lynch executives and Eliot Spitzer, the New York governor. Many charities and organisations had to shut down due to losing their money. There were also various fund managers who channelled their clients' money into the Madoff investment. One French fund manager committed suicide when the extent of the disaster became known.

It seems that there were warning signals and general rumours over the years that Bernie's investment performance was too good to be true. The performance of the investment fund was never over the top, but was consistently good. One investor even tried to re-engineer the investment strategy by calculating each individual trade, but couldn't get the same investment return. He decided that it just didn't add up and something had to be wrong. The fact that there was never a down month, that Bernie had his own broker-dealer clearing trades, that a relative was his finance person, that the regulatory audit was performed by a too-small audit firm (it employed only three people, including an 80-year-old), that he didn't welcome questions and returned funds to investors who probed too much were all signs that something was too good to be true. The market's collapse in 2008 exposed the truth that the consistently good 6.8 per cent returns were being funded by fresh investments from new clients.

It seems that people invested because Bernie was 'a good bloke'. They trusted him. He wasn't a loudmouth, he belonged to the right clubs, he had the right connections and he seemed to perform consistently. Despite complaints and concerns about the business since 2000, and a number of discrepancies found by a Securities Exchange Commission (SEC) lawyer and inspector in 2004, the SEC did nothing. On 29 June 2009, Bernard Madoff was sentenced to 150 years in prison. His statement: 'I have left a legacy of shame, as some of my victims have pointed out, to my family and my grandchildren. This is something I will live in for the rest of my life. I'm sorry.' (Compiled from various Clusterstock.com, nydailynews.com and Cityfile New York articles.)

Some fund managers invested and lost clients' money in the Bernard L Madoff Investment Securities scheme. One example was that of the Fairfield Greenwich Group, which directed US$7.3 billion of client money into the fund over a five-year period.

Required

(a) If you were a client of Fairfield Greenwich Group, what minimum checks on recommended investments would you have expected your fund management to undertake?

(b) As a client, do you think you should be made aware if your fund manager or financial planner would gain a commission from your investment? Why or why not?

(c) If you, on the advice of your financial planner, had invested your money in the Bernard L Madoff Investment Securities scheme and then subsequently lost it, would you blame your financial adviser given that it was a well-orchestrated fraud? Why or why not?

(d) Would your answer in (c) be different if you knew that the Fairfield Greenwich Group earned US$500 million in commissions by directing the US$7.3 billion capital into the fund?

DECISION-MAKING ACTIVITIES

2.55 Corporate Governance and the Royal Commission

The Royal Commission into Misconduct in the Banking, Superannuation and Financial Services Industry was established in 2017.

There were 10 140 public submissions, mainly in the areas of personal financial, superannuation and small-business finance. A number of entities were asked to provide the Commission with information concerning instances of misconduct or conduct falling below community standards and expectations that the entity had identified in the past 10 years.

Required

Go to the Royal Commission website at https://financialservices.royalcommission.gov.au/Pages/default.aspx.

1. Select 'Submissions'.
2. Select 'Submissions in response to original request'.
3. Choose one of the companies that have been asked to provide further information.
4. Describe one instance of misconduct or conduct falling below community standards that has been identified for that company.
5. What has the company done recently to rectify the situation?
6. Do you think that the company has resolved the issue? Explain why or why not.

2.56 Ethics and the Royal Commission

Go to the Royal Commission website at https://financialservices.royalcommission.gov.au/Pages/default.aspx.

1. Select 'Submissions'.
2. Select 'Submissions in response to original request'.
3. Choose one of the companies that have been asked to provide further information.
4. Following Langenderfer and Rockness (1990), determine the facts of the case against this company.
5. Determine the ethical issues in the case.
6. Determine the norms, principles and values related to the case.

2.57 Revised *Conceptual Framework*

The IASB has published its revised *Conceptual Framework for Financial Reporting*.

Required

Go to the IFRS website and select the 'Project Summary' for the *Conceptual Framework* at www.ifrs.org/projects/2018/conceptual-framework/#supporting-material.

(a) Why was the *Conceptual Framework* revised?
(b) Summarise the main changes.
(c) Choose two chapters and comment on the specific changes to these chapters.

REFERENCES

Accounting Professional and Ethical Standards Board Limited (APESB) 2010, *APES 110 Code of Ethics for Professional Accountants*, APESB, Melbourne, www.apesb.org.au.

ASX Corporate Governance Council 2019, *Corporate governance principles and recommendations*, 4th edn, ASX Corporate Governance Council, Sydney, www.asx.com.au.

Australian Accounting Standards Board 2018, 'About the AASB', www.aasb.gov.au.

Australian Securities Exchange (ASX) 2019, ASX homepage, www.asx.com.au.

BusinessThink 2011, 'Directors' notes post Centro: How to avoid barking up the wrong tree', UNSW Australian School of Business, 13 September, www.businessthink.unsw.edu.au.

Carroll, AB 1979, 'A three-dimensional conceptual model of corporate performance', *Academy of Management Review*, October, pp. 497–505.

Dunlop, Sir J 1987, 'The responsibility of company directors: Formulation of the major policies of the company', *Dunlop on Directors*, The Institute of Directors in Australia, Sydney.

Farrar, J 2005, *Corporate governance: Theories, principles and practice*, 2nd edn, Oxford University Press, South Melbourne.

Friedman, M 1970, 'The social responsibility of business is to increase its profits', *New York Times Magazine*, 13 September, pp. 32–3, 122, 124, 126.

International Accounting Standards Board 2018, *The Conceptual Framework for Financial Reporting*, IFRS Foundation Publications Department, London.

JB Hi-Fi Ltd 2018, *Annual report 2018*, www.jbhifi.com.au.

Jenman, N 2006, 'The Westpoint disaster', *Jenman Real Estate Monitors*, 17 January, www.jenman.com.au.

Kant, I 1964, *Groundwork of the metaphysic of morals*, trans. Paton, HJ, Harper and Row, London, in GD Chryssides & JH Kaler 1995, *An introduction to business ethics*, Chapman & Hall, London, pp. 80–107.

Langenderfer, HQ & Rockness, J 1990, *Ethics in the accounting curriculum: Cases and readings*, American Accounting Association, Sarasota, in S Henderson & G Peirson, *Issues in financial accounting*, Prentice-Hall, Frenchs Forest, NSW, chapter 31.

Nash, L 1993, *Good intentions aside*, Harvard Business School Press, Boston, pp. 38–43.

Nordberg, D 2008, 'The ethics of corporate governance', *Journal of General Management*, vol. 33, no. 4, pp. 35–52.

NZX Limited 2018, *NZX Limited–Monthly Shareholder Metrics*, February 2018, www.nzx.com.

Organisation for Economic Co-operation and Development (OECD), 'Frequently asked questions about the OECD principles of corporate governance', www.oecd.org.

Peck, D 2011, 'Can the middle class be saved?', *The Atlantic*, September, www.theatlantic.com.

Qantas Airways Ltd 2018, *Annual report 2018*, www.qantas.com.au.

Shailer, GEP 2004, *An introduction to corporate governance in Australia*, Pearson Australia, Canberra.

The Ethics Centre, 'What is ethics? Ethical decision making', www.ethics.org.au.

Wolf, M 2004, *Why globalization works*, Yale University Press, New Haven, CT.

World Economic Forum 2005, *Statement of G8 Climate Change Roundtable*, World Economic Forum, Switzerland, 9 June, www.weforum.org.

ACKNOWLEDGEMENTS

Photo: © Westend61 / Getty Images

Photo: © marvent / Shutterstock.com

Photo: © mangostock / Shutterstock.com

Figure 2.1: © ASX Limited, ABN 98 008 624 691, ASX 2019. All rights reserved. This material is reproduced with the permission of ASX. This material should not be reproduced, stored in a retrieval system or transmitted in any form whether in whole or in part without the prior written permission of ASX.

Figure 2.2: © 2019 Australian Accounting Standards Board (AASB). The text, graphics and layout of this publication are protected by Australian copyright law and the comparable law of other countries. No part of the publication may be reproduced, stored or transmitted in any form or by any means without the prior written permission of the AASB except as permitted by law. For reproduction or publication, permission should be sought in writing from the AASB. Requests in the first instance should be addressed to the National Director, Australian Accounting Standards Board, PO Box 204, Collins Street West, Victoria 8007.

Figures 2.3, 2.7: © Qantas Airways Ltd 2018

Figure 2.4: Reproduced by permission of Oxford University Press Australia from John Farrar 2005, *Corporate governance, theories, principles and practice*, 2nd edn. © Oxford University Press, www.oup.com.au.

Figure 2.5: © ASX Corporate Governance Council 2014

Figure 2.6: © Langenderfer & Rockness 1990; © The Ethics Centre

Table 2.1: © Nordberg, D 2008, 'The ethics of corporate governance', *Journal of General Management*, vol. 33, no. 4, pp. 35–52.

Apply your knowledge question: © UNSW Australian School of Business 2011

Self-evaluation activity 2.2: © Neil Jenman 2006

CHAPTER 3

Business structures

LEARNING OBJECTIVES

After studying this chapter, you should be able to:

3.1 understand the different forms that business entities take

3.2 define the term 'sole trader' and discuss the main features of a sole trader

3.3 discuss the advantages and disadvantages of a sole trader

3.4 define the term 'partnership' and discuss the main features of a partnership

3.5 discuss the advantages and disadvantages of a partnership

3.6 define the term 'company'

3.7 identify the different types of companies and provide examples of each

3.8 discuss the advantages and disadvantages of a company

3.9 define the term 'trust'

3.10 discuss the advantages and disadvantages of a trust

3.11 compare financial statements for different business structures

3.12 explain the term 'differential reporting' and discuss the implications for disclosing entities.

Chapter preview

Individuals are regarded as separate business entities from the entities they invest in, trade with and are employed by. This means that, in establishing a business entity, business transactions will be recorded separately from the personal transactions involving the owner(s). This is known as the **accounting entity concept** and the application of this concept results in the preparation of separate financial statements for the business entity. When an individual establishes a business entity, the choice of the appropriate business structure is an important decision that will have a significant impact on the future direction of the entity. The type of business structure will have implications for such areas as tax, financing the entity, the role of the owners and the extent of liability of the owners.

This chapter introduces the different forms of business structure. It describes the differences between for-profit entities and not-for-profit entities (NFPs) and the concept of small and medium-sized enterprises (SMEs). It discusses the different focuses of business entities (i.e. manufacturing, trading and service). It outlines the main characteristics of each form of business structure, explains their relative advantages and disadvantages, and compares the financial statements for each type of structure. It also outlines the reporting requirements for disclosing entities and discusses the concept of differential reporting.

3.1 Forms of business entities

LEARNING OBJECTIVE 3.1 Understand the different forms that business entities take.

A business is an entity or organisation that engages in the trading of goods and/or services, but most frequently is established for making money. Business entities come in many shapes and forms, and the choice of an appropriate business structure is important for individuals contemplating commencing a business. Many factors must be taken into account when determining which form of business structure will best suit the needs of the entity. Some business entities do not have profit making as their main objective; these are known as NFPs. Businesses such as sporting clubs, hospitals, schools, local councils and charities are examples of NFPs. The government sector, which is also referred to as the public sector, consists of many departments which are largely NFPs.

For-profit entities are usually structured in one of the following ways: as a sole trader, partnership, company or trust. All of these structures have different features that make them attractive to individuals intending to go into business. The four for-profit business structures differ mainly in terms of owner liability, equity structure, funding opportunities, decision-making responsibilities and taxation.

The most common classification of a business entity is the SME — the small to medium-sized enterprise. SMEs are defined by the International Accounting Standards Board (IASB) as 'entities that do not have public accountability and publish general purpose financial statements for external users' (IASB 2015, para 1.2). The SME is the most common classification of a business entity in Australia and is the fastest growing sector. About 97 per cent of businesses trading in Australia are SMEs and they employ about 44 per cent of the Australian workforce (ABS 2018a, 2018b).

The focus of a business entity is one or more of manufacturing, trading or services. Business entities that trade in goods are either manufacturers of the goods or traders of the goods. Manufacturing entities are involved in the conversion of raw materials into finished goods. The finished goods are either used in more complex manufacturing operations or sold to wholesalers. Trading entities are involved in the buying of inventory (goods) at cost price and then selling the goods at sale price.

Service entities provide services to customers. The services provided may be either equipment-based or largely people-based. Examples of equipment-based services are classes at the gym and excavation of building sites. Examples of people-based services are plumbing and electrical services, motor mechanic services, professional services such as those provided by doctors, lawyers and accountants, and coaching or tuition services.

3.2 Definition and features of a sole trader

LEARNING OBJECTIVE 3.2 Define the term 'sole trader' and discuss the main features of a sole trader.

A **sole trader** is an individual who controls and manages a business. The business is not a separate legal entity and the owner is fully liable for all debts. For example, if the business incurs debts resulting from a warranty claim, then the individual will be held responsible for those debts and any claims will be made against the individual's personal assets. It is easy to commence operating as a sole trader, as the costs and paperwork associated with establishing the business are minimal. Basically a sole trader needs to complete the general registration requirements applying to all new businesses, which consist of applying for an **Australian Business Number (ABN)**. An ABN is an identifying number for dealings with the **Australian Taxation Office (ATO)** and other government departments and agencies. It is an eleven-digit number allocated by the ATO to businesses that assists them with transactions involving taxes such as the **goods and services tax (GST)** and fringe benefits tax (FBT). If a sole trader business has a GST turnover of $75 000 or more, then the business must also register for GST.

For tax purposes, the income of the sole trader is treated as the sole trader's individual income. Therefore, the individual owner is responsible for paying tax on the business income and must have a tax file number. Sole traders are not bound by any formal requirements such as accounting standards, so they can be quite flexible in their reporting of the entity's financial performance and position. However, some such entities use computerised accounting packages such as MYOB or Xero to assist in report preparation and determining business profit. Common examples of sole trader entities include most trades, for example, chefs, hairdressers and carpenters.

3.3 Advantages and disadvantages of a sole trader

LEARNING OBJECTIVE 3.3 Discuss the advantages and disadvantages of a sole trader.

As with all business structures, there are both advantages and disadvantages of this business form.

Advantages

Being a sole trader has several advantages. First, the sole trader entity is a quick, inexpensive and easy form of business to establish and can be inexpensive to wind down. The sole trader form is not subject to company regulation such as the *Corporations Act 2001*. The sole trader business does not pay separate income tax, as the individual owner reports business income or losses on their individual income tax return. The owner has total autonomy over business decisions and is therefore free to choose the direction of the business and its strategies and policies. A further advantage is that the owner claims all the profits of the business and all after-tax gains if the sole trader business is sold.

Disadvantages

As the sole trader's business is not a separate legal entity, if the business is involved in any form of legal dispute then the individual owner has **unlimited liability**, which means full responsibility for the business debts and any legal actions.

If a sole trader business is involved in any form of legal dispute, the individual owner has unlimited liability.

For example, the individual could be sued by one of the employees of the business for an act of negligence. If the owner is found guilty of negligence, then they will have to meet all the costs associated with the case and also the amount of damages paid to the employee. Taxation can be a disadvantage — the sole trader can pay more tax on business income because individual income tax rates are often higher than the rate applied to companies, which is currently 30 per cent (27.5 per cent for SMEs).

The sole trader is also limited by the skill, time and investment of the individual owner. This could be an issue if the sole trader wants to take time away from the business or wants to expand the business but is restricted by their own funds. The sole trader's business will cease to exist if the owner decides to leave the business.

The sole trader business structure can be restrictive for those businesses trying to secure opportunities with the government, as government departments may be reluctant to do business with sole traders because of their non-legal status. Further, if the business reports a loss, then the sole trader is ultimately responsible for the loss and cannot offset the loss with other business partners. Finally, if something happens to the individual, such as incapacitation or death, then the business will cease to exist. Illustrative example 3.1 demonstrates some of the issues facing sole traders.

ILLUSTRATIVE EXAMPLE 3.1

The sole trader

Nicholas Cash is the owner of Advantage Tennis Coaching (ATC), a Brisbane tennis-coaching clinic which provides services to customers in the form of tennis coaching. Recall that a service-based entity may provide equipment-based services or largely people-based services.

ATC leases a number of courts at the Brisbane Tennis Centre in Tennyson, Queensland. The business commenced operations on 1 September 2019 and is building a customer base consisting of beginners, competitive juniors, adult masters and retirees who would like to play social tennis.

One morning, one of the older players approaches the reception area of the Tennyson courts to book an extra lesson prior to an upcoming masters' tournament. Unfortunately, as she approaches the counter she loses her footing and slips on a recently washed area of the floor. She just misses hitting her head on a concrete structure beside the reception but falls heavily on her side and hip, which causes her to scream out in pain. Immediately Nicholas rushes over to assist her and the receptionist calls an ambulance. The retiree consequently spends three weeks in hospital with a dislocated hip and, while recuperating, contacts her lawyer to begin proceedings against ATC. Nicholas has insurance to cover such incidents, but the insurance will not cover all the costs involved.

Nicholas pays what he can out of the business's bank account, but he still needs over $100 000 to settle the lawsuit. In order to meet the remainder of the costs, Nicholas will need to mortgage his house to the bank and borrow against those funds.

VALUE TO BUSINESS

- A sole trader is the single owner of a business that is solely controlled and managed by that person.
- Sole trader entities have low start-up costs, with minimal paperwork required.
- Sole trader entities pay no tax. An individual owner includes business profits or losses in their individual tax return.
- There are no formal guidelines for sole trader entities to follow when producing financial statements.
- The main advantage of the sole trader structure is that the business is relatively simple and cheap to set up, and the owner has total autonomy in decision making.
- The main disadvantage of the sole trader structure is that the owner is totally responsible for all the debts and legal actions against the business, leaving the individual's personal assets at risk if the business runs into trouble.

3.4 Definition and features of a partnership

LEARNING OBJECTIVE 3.4 Define the term 'partnership' and discuss the main features of a partnership.

A **partnership** is an association of two or more persons or entities that carry on business as partners, and share profits or losses according to the ownership structures outlined in the partnership agreement. The association of two or more persons enables the sharing of ideas and also brings together individuals with different skills, knowledge and talent.

As with a sole trader, a partnership is easy and cheap to establish. Individuals do not have to complete any additional paperwork to form an ordinary partnership. However, they must fulfil the same registration requirements as any new business, for example, applying for an ABN and registering the business name. As with sole traders, there are no formal requirements for partnership financial statements, although many partnerships use MYOB or QuickBooks to assist in report preparation. The partnership does not pay separate taxation; however, the partnership will lodge an annual partnership income tax return to the ATO showing the partnership's income and deductions for the period. This return will also disclose each of the partners' income for the period and this amount will be taken into consideration for each partner's individual tax return. Partners are responsible for all the liabilities of the business.

Each Australian state has its own Partnership Act. For example, New South Wales is bound by the *Partnership Act 1892* (NSW), Victoria is bound by the *Partnership Act 1958* (Vic) and Western Australia is bound by the *Partnership Act 1895* (WA). The differences between states lie in the terms of the partnership and in areas such as dissolution of the partnership and rights of remaining partners if the partnership dissolves.

A partnership is suitable for many SMEs and is common in the areas of law and accounting.

The partnership agreement

While the owners of a partnership are not legally required to have a written partnership agreement, it is important that the partners draw up such an agreement to record the details of the partnership. The **partnership agreement** should include details such as the name of the partnership and the contributions of cash and other assets to the partnership made by each partner. It is especially important to set out the profit and loss sharing agreement, as there could be different contributions in terms of capital, skills or workload by each partner, and this should be reflected in the allocations of profit and the amounts that the partners can each withdraw. There are several different methods of sharing profits or losses. They include sharing according to each partner's capital contribution to the business, splitting profits or losses equally between the partners and sharing them based on salary requirements. If there is no partnership agreement, then the law assumes that all profits or losses will be shared equally between the partners.

The partnership agreement also provides details about responsibilities such as workloads, positions in the business and decision making. For example, one of the partners may be responsible for the bookkeeping activities of the business, another may be involved in marketing, and some partners may be more suited to serving customers. The partnership agreement should also set out the rights of each of the partners, detail the entry procedures for new partners into the partnership and stipulate what happens when a partner dies or leaves the partnership.

3.5 Advantages and disadvantages of a partnership

LEARNING OBJECTIVE 3.5 Discuss the advantages and disadvantages of a partnership.

Outlined below are the main advantages and disadvantages of partnerships for the potential businessperson.

Advantages

As is the case with sole traders, there are several advantages to partnerships. Like sole traders, partnerships are relatively easy to set up and are not required to prepare financial statements in accordance with accounting standards. The partnership itself does not pay tax on the income earned by the partnership. The main advantage of a partnership over a sole trader is that the partnership combines the skills, talents and knowledge of two or more people, allowing the decision making and workload to be shared among the partners.

Disadvantages

Similar to sole traders, the partnership is characterised by unlimited liability. Therefore, the partners are fully responsible for all business debts and obligations, irrespective of their involvement in the entity. Another major disadvantage of partnerships is that the partnership form has a limited life, as it will automatically dissolve if one of the partners dies or withdraws from the partnership or there is an irresolvable dispute. A great number of partnerships find themselves involved in disputes because of disagreements concerning profit sharing or decision making for the business. Further, in most forms of partnership, growth is limited due to a set number of partners allowed.

Another disadvantage is known as mutual agency. **Mutual agency** is when each partner is seen as an agent for the business, having the right to enter into contracts for the business and being bound by any partnership contract. Some of these contracts could be inappropriate or risky, involving the repayment of sums of money that the business cannot afford or involving relations with an unreliable third party.

Illustrative example 3.2 demonstrates one of the many ways in which a partnership can be constructed.

ILLUSTRATIVE EXAMPLE 3.2

The partnership

Martina, James and Brigitte met at the University of Western Australia when they were completing their Honours year of their Bachelor of Commerce degree in the early 2000s. The three maintained their friendship over the years and, after several years working in the public sector, they set up their own accounting practice in the Brisbane CBD in July 2018. They offer several accounting-related services such as taxation, budgeting and financial planning. Both Martina and James are CPAs and Brigitte is a CA. The three of them decided to form a partnership because they wanted to combine their different skills and expertise in three different accounting areas, thereby offering a range of services under the one business name. Each of the three partners contributed some form of asset to the business. Martina contributed cash of $100 000, James contributed a building valued at $400 000 that he inherited from a great aunt and Brigitte contributed office furniture worth $60 000. In their partnership agreement, they outlined that profits and losses would be split according to their respective capital contributions. The partners plan to expand their business and are already negotiating with a tax accountant from the firm Dunstan & Co.

VALUE TO BUSINESS

- A partnership is an association of two or more persons or entities who carry on business as partners and share the profits or losses according to their ownership structures, as outlined in the partnership agreement.
- Partnerships are relatively easy to set up, with minimal costs and resources required in order to commence operations.
- The individuals should complete a partnership agreement, which includes details such as the name of the partnership, the contributions of cash and other assets, and the profit and loss sharing arrangement.
- Partnerships have several advantages. They include minimal time and resources needed to set up a partnership and the ability to combine the skills, talent and knowledge of two or more people.
- There are several disadvantages to the partnership structure. They include the unlimited liability of the partners in relation to debts and legal actions against the partnership, and the automatic dissolution of the partnership if one of the partners dies or withdraws or there is an irresolvable dispute.

3.6 Definition and features of a company

LEARNING OBJECTIVE 3.6 Define the term 'company'.

A **company** is a form of business characterised by owners known as **shareholders**. A company is an independent **legal entity**, meaning that it is separate from the people who own, control and manage it. The separate legal status of the company has many implications for the entity. First, the company can enter into contracts, incur debts and pay taxes independently of its owners. Unlike sole traders and partners, a company's owners do not pay individual tax on all the company's profits. Instead, the owners pay individual taxes only on the company profits paid to them in the form of salaries, bonuses and dividends. A **dividend** is the distribution of part of a company's profit to shareholders. It is usually expressed as a number of cents per share.

The owners (that is, the shareholders) are not personally responsible for the debts of the company; they are liable only for the unpaid balance of shares they agree to purchase in the company. For example, if a company issued $2 shares, with $1.50 payable on application and the remaining 50 cents payable by future instalments, the shareholders' liability in the event of the company collapsing would be the remaining 50 cents on each share they own. This is known as **limited liability** of the shareholders. Unlike sole traders and partnerships, a company does not dissolve when its owners (shareholders) change or die. If the shareholders of a company decide to sell their shares in the company to another buyer, this transaction takes place in the 'market' and does not affect the company's statement of financial position; that is, a change in name of a shareholder does not affect the financial statements.

The main types of company are:

- proprietary companies
- companies limited by shares
- companies limited by guarantee
- no-liability companies
- unlimited companies.

Forming a company

Forming a company is more complicated than forming a sole trader business or partnership. Several steps are required to create a company. First, the individual must apply to the Australian Securities and Investments Commission (ASIC) for registration of the company and must register every person who agrees to be a shareholder, director or company secretary.

Once the company is registered, ASIC will allocate a unique **Australian Company Number (ACN)**. The ACN is a nine-digit number allocated to a company to ensure that it has adequate identification when transacting business. Companies will also register for an ABN.

Most companies follow the jurisdiction of the Corporations Act, which outlines the procedures, and accounting and reporting requirements for companies. Under this Act, companies must prepare financial statements in accordance with accounting standards, and these statements must be audited by an independent auditor and then lodged with ASIC.

Certain companies also require some form of licence or permit to operate legally in a Commonwealth, state, territory or local government jurisdiction. Because of the company's limited liability status, company owners must comply with certain formalities and submit additional paperwork to maintain this status. Companies must lodge an annual company tax return to report income and deductions for the period and the income tax that they are required to pay. The current tax rate for Australian companies is 30 per cent (27.5 per cent for SMEs).

3.7 Types of companies

LEARNING OBJECTIVE 3.7 Identify the different types of companies and provide examples of each.

Table 3.1 lists the various types of company structure in Australia and their characteristics.

TABLE 3.1	Company structures in Australia
Type	**Characteristics**
Proprietary company	Limited by shares
Public company	Limited by shares
	Limited by guarantee
	No-liability company
	Unlimited company

Proprietary companies

Proprietary companies, also known as private companies, are a common form of business structure adopted by SMEs in Australia. Private companies are largely family-owned and include entities such as plumbing supplies and kitchen renovation companies. Proprietary companies are denoted by the words 'Pty Limited' or 'Pty Ltd' in their names and, as these words imply, such entities cannot offer their shares to the public. The definition of 'proprietary' is ownership; hence Pty Ltd means 'ownership limited'. A proprietary company is relatively easy to set up — it can be done for as little as $1000. Proprietary companies have at least one shareholder but no more than 50, and may have one or more directors. Small proprietary companies do not have to prepare audited financial statements, but large proprietary companies must lodge audited financial statements with ASIC.

Illustrative example 3.3 shows some of the benefits and issues involved in forming a proprietary company.

Setting up Coconut Plantations Pty Ltd

Joanne (Jo) Geter commenced her own company, known as Coconut Plantations Pty Ltd, on Queensland's Sunshine Coast in August 2019. During the previous ten years, Jo had worked at a number of part-time jobs in food, fashion and homeware shops in Queensland. While at university studying for her Bachelor of Arts degree, she had developed a keen interest in sustainable materials and attended workshops on manufacturing such products.

After chatting with her parents, Jo decided that the best business strategy for her would be to establish a small business manufacturing her own sustainable products with the common ingredient coconut. Her idea was to manufacture coconut candles, soaps and dishwashing and laundry detergents. Coconut Plantations Pty Ltd would manufacture its own products using sustainable materials and sell its goods to wholesale traders throughout Australia and New Zealand. Down the track, Jo would love to export her coconut-based products overseas and would also consider online trading.

Jo decided to commence operations as a proprietary limited company because she knew this was the most efficient model for her business needs. She wanted to limit responsibility for her personal debts, and she also wanted to broaden her business activities through the additional avenues that come from incorporating a business. To set up the business, Jo had to pay the costs of registering the company (legal fees, government fees), advertising, website development, professional indemnity insurance and membership of fashion industry associations. She also purchased Quicken accounting software for bookkeeping and reporting.

Every three months, the company must lodge its **business activity statement (BAS)** with the ATO. (Entities use the BAS to report their business tax entitlements and obligations to the tax office.) If the company has paid more GST than it has received from its customers, then it will receive a refund from the ATO. The company must also complete a tax return at the end of each financial year.

Jo does not regret undertaking the proprietary limited form of business structure. While there were initial start-up costs and a fair bit of time involved in setting up the company, this company form has its advantages, especially limited liability. The company has subsequently secured a number of high-end accounts and is currently broadening its market into Australian regional areas.

Public companies

Table 3.1 listed four types of public company:
1. public companies whose capital is limited by shares
2. public companies whose capital is limited by guarantee
3. public companies which are no-liability companies
4. public companies whose capital is unlimited.

Each of these will now be explained in more detail.

Limited by shares

Public companies limited by shares are companies that offer shares to the public, and must have at least three directors and at least one shareholder. The shares can be classified broadly under two headings:
1. ordinary or common shares (see figure 3.1)
2. preference shares

FIGURE 3.1	Summary of ordinary shares for JB Hi-Fi Ltd

18 Contributed equity		
(a) Share capital	Parent entity	
	2018 Shares	2017 Shares
Ordinary shares — fully paid	114 883 372	114 421 403

Source: JB Hi-Fi Ltd 2018, p. 76.

Ordinary shares are the most common class of shares in Australia. **Preference shares** rank ahead of ordinary shares if an entity goes into liquidation, and the preference shares usually receive a fixed rate of dividend, which is paid out before the ordinary shareholders' dividend is paid.

A limited-by-shares company is commonly denoted by the word 'Ltd' in its name, signalling that the liability of the shareholders is limited to the subscription price of the shares. Public companies limited by shares can be either listed on the stock exchange or not listed. For a company to be listed on the stock exchange, it must meet certain financial criteria. Both listed and non-listed public companies must follow the requirements of the Corporations Act, but listed companies must also follow the Listing Rules requirements of the Australian Securities Exchange (ASX). The Listing Rules stipulate that listed companies must report announcements to the ASX to keep the different users up to date, and they must report profit results and other financial information within specific deadlines.

An example of a limited-by-shares Australian company is JB Hi-Fi Ltd (see illustrative example 3.4).

ILLUSTRATIVE EXAMPLE 3.4

JB Hi-Fi Ltd

JB Hi-Fi Ltd is an Australian limited-by-shares company specialising in home consumer products with a particular focus on consumer electronic and electrical goods and software. The company has headquarters in Victoria, Australia. The business commenced operations in 1974 in a small suburban shopping strip in Melbourne, selling a range of hi-fi equipment and records. In October 2003, the company was listed on the ASX and expanded its range to include LCD televisions, home theatre components, computers and laptops, mobile phones, MP3 players, cameras, DVDs and a large number of accessories. Profit after tax for the financial year ending 30 June 2018 was $233.2 million and total assets were approximately $2491.7 million. As at June 2018 there were 208 JB Hi-Fi stores and 103 The Good Guys stores across Australia and New Zealand. The company also operates JB Hi-Fi NOW — an online digital content platform — and JB Hi-Fi Solutions, which sells products and services to the commercial, government and education sectors (JB Hi-Fi Ltd 2018).

Limited by guarantee

Public companies can be limited by guarantee, which means that the owners guarantee to contribute an agreed amount of cash or other assets to the company in the event of the company winding up. This is normally a very small amount and would assist in the costs associated with winding up the company and paying the outstanding debts. This form of business structure is popular among sporting clubs and NFP organisations such as charities and social groups, which do not usually make a profit but need to be a separate legal entity. For example, Green Collect (www.greencollect.org) is an NFP social enterprise that works for sustainable social and environmental change. It became a company limited by guarantee to meet its goal of providing increased numbers of supported employment opportunities through ensuring its activities are viable and sustainable. Operating as a company limited by guarantee provides Green Collect with a framework to support the work involved in delivering environmental services. Green Collect builds inclusive workplaces that create sustainable change in the world. The company collects unwanted materials, such as printers, print cartridges, corks and mobile phones, and recycles or converts them into new products.

No-liability company

No-liability (NL) companies are companies that have shareholders who have no liability for the outstanding debts of the company, due to the risky nature of the company's operations. Shareholders are attracted to this type of company as there is the possibility of obtaining a good return on their investment. However, there is also obviously no guarantee. For that reason, if an NL company becomes insolvent, shareholders have no further responsibility (they don't even have to pay any outstanding amounts owed on their shares). In Australia, these companies are solely mining companies. Cougar Metals NL is an NL company incorporated in Australia in May 2002. It is listed on the ASX.

Unlimited company

Unlimited companies are characterised by members who have no limit placed on their liability. This form of company is usually restricted to investment-type organisations.

3.8 Advantages and disadvantages of a company

LEARNING OBJECTIVE 3.8 Discuss the advantages and disadvantages of a company.

As outlined earlier, companies in Australia are divided into two types, proprietary and public companies, the latter having several further divisions. Following is a broad overview of their advantages and disadvantages.

Advantages

The main advantage of forming a company is the limited liability that shareholders have for business debts. Other advantages include taxation, as company rates may be lower than some individual tax rates. As of 2018, the Australian company tax rate is 30 per cent (27.5 per cent for SMEs) and the top personal tax rate is much higher. (Current personal tax rates can be found on the ATO website, www.ato.gov.au.) The company form of ownership can also provide entities with additional opportunities to make income through expanded business networks, as some businesses and government departments are reluctant to trade with sole traders and partnerships because of their non-legal status. Companies also have the ability to raise large amounts of capital through public share offerings.

Disadvantages

There are several disadvantages of the company form of business structure. First, a company is more expensive and time-consuming to establish. Companies must comply with the Corporations Act and other legal requirements from which partnerships and sole traders are exempted. Most companies must hold annual shareholder meetings, prepare financial statements based on accounting standards and lodge their financial statements with ASIC. Companies are subject to the company rate of tax. The limited liability of companies can also be a negative characteristic. It can preclude certain suppliers and financiers from entering into business contracts with the company, because the individuals involved in the company are not personally responsible for the company's debts. This drawback, however, can be overcome by personal guarantees from the company directors.

Most companies must hold annual shareholder meetings.

Public companies can also be disadvantaged by the separation of ownership and control of the company. The owners of the company (the shareholders) have little say in the day-to-day operation of the company — this responsibility lies with the board of directors of the company. In certain situations, the company directors can be held personally responsible for the company's debts.

3.9 Definition and features of a trust

LEARNING OBJECTIVE 3.9 Define the term 'trust'.

A **trust** is a common form of business structure in Australia that involves a special entity (**trustee**) holding a sum of money or other assets for the benefit of others. The assets of the trust can be invested in a range of investments, such as shares and property. These investments will earn income that is then distributed to the beneficiaries of the trust in a tax-effective way, according to the tax status of each beneficiary. There are two common types of trust in Australia: family or discretionary trusts, and unit trusts.

A **family (or discretionary) trust** is usually established for the benefit of one family and its members. The trustee can distribute income and assets among the various family members, who will then be taxed individually. A **unit trust** holds a collection of assets on behalf of various parties, rather than family members. Income is distributed to these parties according to their respective unit holdings in the trust. Unit trusts usually concentrate on a particular investment such as equity, property or cash management.

3.10 Advantages and disadvantages of a trust

LEARNING OBJECTIVE 3.10 Discuss the advantages and disadvantages of a trust.

The main advantage of the trust form of business structure is that trusts minimise tax payments. The trust itself does not pay tax on income earned. Instead, the beneficiaries pay tax on the amount of income distributed to them. Trusts are also characterised by limited liability. They are relatively simple to form and are subject to little government regulation unless they are a trust (such as a property trust) listed on the ASX.

Additional laws apply to trusts, however, and these laws can be quite complex. A trust should be administered by a suitably qualified accountant with an up-to-date knowledge of the tax and legal implications of trusts.

3.11 Comparison of business reports

LEARNING OBJECTIVE 3.11 Compare financial statements for different business structures.

This section briefly outlines the main components of the financial statements for the sole trader, partnership and company business structures. A more in-depth discussion of these statements, including the content and definition of each of the elements, will be provided in the statement of financial position chapter and the statement of profit or loss and statement of changes in equity chapter.

Each form of business structure records and reports business transactions separately from the personal transactions of the owner(s). This is known as the accounting entity concept. If the owner uses the business entity's funds for personal use, this will be shown as a reduction in cash and a distribution of profits (reducing equity) — that is, not as an expense for the business entity.

Sole trader reports

The financial statements in illustrative example 3.5 have been prepared for the sole trader, Nicholas Cash, owner of Advantage Tennis Coaching (ATC). The statement of profit or loss shows income less expenses for Cash's ATC business and reports a profit of $16 370 in September 2019, the first month of operations. As you can see, the profit is reported on the statement of financial position as an addition to capital. The capital has been contributed by the owner of the business (N Cash) and the profit (loss) shown belongs to the owner.

ILLUSTRATIVE EXAMPLE 3.5

Financial statements for a sole trader

ADVANTAGE TENNIS COACHING Statement of profit or loss for one month ending 30 September 2019		
Income		
Coaching fees		$22 300
Expenses		
Website development	$2 000	
Wages	2 200	
Telephone	280	
Rent	1 000	
Electricity	450	5 930
Profit		**$16 370**

ADVANTAGE TENNIS COACHING Statement of financial position as at 30 September 2019		
ASSETS		
Current assets		
Cash	$71 270	
Accounts receivable	6 800	$78 070
Non-current assets		
Office furniture	3 200	
Office equipment	6 500	9 700
Total assets		87 770
LIABILITIES		
Current liabilities		
Accounts payable		1 400
Non-current liabilities		
Loan		50 000
Total liabilities		51 400
Net assets		**$36 370**
OWNER'S EQUITY		
Capital — N Cash		$20 000
Profit		16 370
Total equity		**$36 370**

Partnership reports

The financial statements in illustrative example 3.6 report on the financial performance and financial position of the partnership Martina, James and Brigitte — Accountants. Compared with a sole trader, the main difference in the distribution of profit (loss) here is that the profit (loss) is split according to each of the partner's original capital contributions, as stated in the partnership agreement. The main difference in the statement of financial position is that there are three capital accounts — one for each partner. There are also three current accounts that represent the combined sum of all the year's profits that have been left in the partnership less the drawings taken out of the business by each partner.

ILLUSTRATIVE EXAMPLE 3.6

Financial statements for a partnership

MARTINA, JAMES AND BRIGITTE — ACCOUNTANTS
Statement of profit or loss
for the period ended 31 December 2019

Income		
Fees		$40 000
Expenses		
Administrative expenses	$2 400	
Rates	4 000	
Finance expenses	400	
Depreciation of office furniture	2 000	
Depreciation of office equipment	1 000	9 800
Profit		**$30 200**
Distribution to partners		
Salary		
— Martina	$8 000	
— James	4 000	
— Brigitte	6 000	$18 000
Distribution of remaining profit to current accounts		
— Martina (100 000/560 000 · 12 200)	2 179	
— James (400 000/560 000 · 12 200)	8 714	
— Brigitte (60 000/560 000 · 12 200)	1 307	12 200
Total distributions to partners		**$30 200**

MARTINA, JAMES AND BRIGITTE — ACCOUNTANTS
Statement of financial position
as at 31 December 2019

Current assets		
Cash in bank	$ 95 200	$ 95 200
Non-current assets		
Office building		400 000
Office furniture	60 000	
Less: Accumulated depreciation — office furniture	2 000	58 000
Office equipment	30 000	
Less: Accumulated depreciation — office equipment	1 000	29 000
Total assets		582 200
Non-current liabilities		
Bank loan	10 000	
Total liabilities		10 000
Net assets		**$572 200**
Partners' equity		
Capital		
— Martina	$100 000	
— James	400 000	
— Brigitte	60 000	$560 000

MARTINA, JAMES AND BRIGITTE — ACCOUNTANTS		
Statement of financial position		
as at 31 December 2019		
Current		
— Martina	$ 2 179	
— James	8 714	
— Brigitte	1 307	$ 12 200
Total partners' equity		**$572 200**

Company reports — private company

The simplified financial statements in illustrative example 3.7 show the financial performance and position of Coconut Plantations Pty Ltd for four months to 31 December 2019. Here, the company's statement of profit or loss shows tax being deducted directly from company profit. As discussed earlier, sole traders and partnerships do not pay tax directly on business profits — it is up to the individuals to include the business income in their individual tax returns. Coconut Plantations Pty Ltd is a manufacturing company which is involved in the conversion of raw materials, such as coconut, other plant extracts and water, to produce coconut soaps, candles and detergents. These finished goods are then sold to wholesale retailers.

In the company statement of financial position, the shareholders' equity section shows share capital instead of owners' or partners' capital, and also reports **retained earnings**, which represent the sum of the profit retained in the business after the deduction of dividends or allocation to another equity account.

ILLUSTRATIVE EXAMPLE 3.7

Financial statements for a proprietary company

COCONUT PLANTATIONS PTY LTD		
Statement of profit or loss		
for 4 months ended 31 December 2019		
Income		
Sales		$500 000
Cost of sales		275 000
Gross profit		225 000
Other income		5 000
Operating expenses		
Warehouse	$32 000	
Distribution	10 000	
Sales and marketing	3 000	
Administration	30 000	
Finance	5 000	80 000
Profit before tax		**150 000**
Income tax expense		45 000
Profit after tax		**$105 000**

COCONUT PLANTATIONS PTY LTD		
Statement of financial position		
as at 31 December 2019		
Current assets		
Cash on hand	$51 557	
Accounts receivable	23 110	
Inventories (finished goods and raw materials)	60 000	
Prepayments	1 000	$135 667

Non-current assets		
Building	$200 000	$200 000
Equipment	40 000	
Less: Accumulated depreciation — office equipment	1 667	38 333
Total assets		374 000
Current liabilities		
Accounts payable		3 300
Accrued expenses		700
Income tax payable		45 000
Dividend payable		14 790
Non-current liabilities		
Bank loan — due 2022		20 000
Total liabilities		83 790
Net assets		**$290 210**
Shareholder's equity		
Share capital		$200 000
Retained earnings		90 210
Total equity		**$290 210**

Company reports — public company

JB Hi-Fi Ltd is an example of a public company limited by shares. JB Hi-Fi Ltd has to prepare its financial statements in accordance with the Corporations Act and accounting standards and interpretations. Accounting standards include Australian equivalents to the International Financial Reporting Standards (IFRS). The statement of profit or loss and statement of financial position in figures 3.2 and 3.3 respectively have been prepared for JB Hi-Fi Ltd for the period ended 30 June 2018. There are many similarities between the reports of JB Hi-Fi Ltd and Coconut Plantations Pty Ltd, as both entities are companies, but JB Hi-Fi Ltd has additional reporting requirements because it is a listed public company.

FIGURE 3.2 JB Hi-Fi Ltd's consolidated statement of profit or loss

JB HI-FI LTD
Consolidated statement of profit or loss
for the financial year ended 30 June 2018

		Consolidated	
	Notes	2018 $m	2017 $m
Revenue		6 854.3	5 628.0
Cost of sales		(5 384.1)	(4 397.5)
Gross profit		1 470.2	1 230.5
Other income		1.1	2.0
Sales and marketing expenses		(695.1)	(580.1)
Occupancy expenses		(305.7)	(248.6)
Administration expenses		(42.2)	(36.2)
Acquisition transaction and implementation expenses		—	(22.4)
Other expenses		(77.2)	(75.3)
Finance costs	5	(16.6)	(10.7)
Profit before tax		**334.5**	**259.2**
Income tax expense	6	(101.3)	(86.8)
Profit for the year attributable to Owners of the Company		233.2	172.4
		Cents	Cents
Earnings per share			
Basic (cents per share)	3	203.09	154.30
Diluted (cents per share)	3	201.11	152.94

Source: JB Hi-Fi Ltd 2018, p. 54.

JB Hi-Fi Ltd's consolidated statement of financial position

JB HI-FI LTD
Consolidated statement of financial position
for the financial year ended 30 June 2018

		Consolidated	
	Notes	2018 $m	2017 $m
ASSETS			
Current assets			
Cash and cash equivalents		72.0	72.8
Trade and other receivables	8	204.7	193.6
Inventories	7	891.1	859.7
Other current assets	9	42.7	41.4
Total current assets		1 210.5	1 167.5
Non-current assets			
Plant and equipment	10	198.0	208.2
Intangible assets	11	1 037.3	1 037.3
Other non-current assets	9	45.9	46.8
Total non-current assets		1 281.2	1 292.3
Total assets		2 491.7	2 459.8
LIABILITIES			
Current liabilities			
Trade and other payables	12	665.3	644.7
Deferred revenue	13	150.5	141.8
Provisions	14	83.5	76.3
Other current liabilities	15	8.3	9.0
Current tax liabilities		9.6	13.6
Total current liabilities		917.2	885.4
Non-current liabilities			
Borrowings	17	469.4	558.8
Deferred revenue	13	103.7	99.6
Deferred tax liabilities	6	5.7	16.1
Provisions	14	12.5	11.8
Other non-current liabilities	15	35.6	34.6
Total non-current liabilities		626.9	720.9
Total liabilities		1 544.1	1 606.3
Net assets		**947.6**	**853.5**
EQUITY			
Contributed equity	18	441.7	438.7
Reserves	19	42.7	33.2
Retained earnings		463.2	381.6
Total equity		**947.6**	**853.5**

Source: JB Hi-Fi Ltd 2018, p. 56.

3.12 Differential reporting

LEARNING OBJECTIVE 3.12 Explain the term 'differential reporting' and discuss the implications for disclosing entities.

In recent years, there has been much debate by preparers and users of financial statements in relation to the applicability of a full set of IFRS for all reporting entities. In response, the Australian Accounting Standards Board (AASB) reviewed the financial reporting framework in Australia. In June 2010, the AASB modified the reporting entity concept by classifying disclosing entities that prepare general purpose financial statements (GPFS) as either Tier 1 or Tier 2 entities. A Tier 1 entity is basically an entity that is publicly accountable, while a Tier 2 entity is an entity that is not publicly accountable (such as unlisted public companies, NFP private companies and some public sector entities). Tier 1 entities must still prepare GPFS and comply with the disclosure requirements of the AASB standards. Tier 2 entities apply a reduced-disclosure version of the AASB standards known as the reduced disclosure requirements. This difference in reporting requirements is known as **differential reporting**. The reduction in requirements for disclosing entities that are not publicly accountable includes disclosures relating to the usage of financial instruments, business combinations, income tax and financial statement presentation. The full implementation of these new requirements became applicable from 1 July 2013 and has since been updated with the new standard from 1 July 2015.

In 2018, the AASB released a number of research reports relating to public sector and for-profit private sector companies, and a staff paper on smaller entities. These reports are part of the Australian Financial Reporting Framework Project, which is investigating the future of financial reporting for the private and public sectors, and exploring a possible Tier 3 of financial reporting requirements.

SUMMARY OF LEARNING OBJECTIVES

3.1 Understand the different forms that business entities take.

Business entities take many shapes and forms. The most common classification of business entity is the SME (small to medium-sized entity). SMEs account for approximately 97 per cent of all Australian business entities. The four common types of business entities are sole trader, partnership, company and trust. Business entities may either be profit oriented (for-profit) or not-for-profit. NFP entities include clubs, hospitals, churches, private educational institutions and charities. These entities are largely classified as associations or companies limited by guarantee. An entity's focus will be manufacture of goods, trade in goods or provision of a service. Manufacturing entities' operations involve the conversion of raw materials into finished goods. Trading entities are involved in buying inventory and onselling it. Service entities provide services to customers; these services may be either equipment-based or largely people-based.

3.2 Define the term 'sole trader' and discuss the main features of a sole trader.

A sole trader is the single owner of a business that is controlled and managed solely by that person. The sole trader form of business has the following characteristics.
- Sole trader businesses have low start-up costs.
- Minimal paperwork is required to commence sole trader operations.
- Sole trader businesses pay no tax. The owner includes business profits or losses in their individual tax return.
- Owners have unlimited liability for the entity's debts and legal actions against the business.
- Sole traders have total responsibility for all business decisions and for all profits or losses.
- There are no formal guidelines to follow in terms of business reports.

3.3 Discuss the advantages and disadvantages of a sole trader.

The main advantages of a sole trader form of business are that the entity is relatively simple and cheap to set up, and the owner has total autonomy over any business decisions. The main disadvantage of a sole trader form of business is that the owner is totally responsible for all the debts and legal actions against the business. This means that the individual's personal assets are at risk if the business runs into trouble.

3.4 Define the term 'partnership' and discuss the main features of a partnership.

A partnership is an association of two or more persons or entities that carry on business as partners and share profits or losses according to the ownership structures outlined in the partnership agreement. Partnerships are relatively easy to set up, with minimal costs and resources required to commence operations. The individuals should complete a partnership agreement, which includes details such as the name of the partnership, the contributions of cash and other assets, and the profit and loss sharing arrangements.

3.5 Discuss the advantages and disadvantages of a partnership.

Partnerships have several advantages. Minimal time and resources are needed to set up a partnership, and the partnership has the benefit of the skills, talent and knowledge of two or more people. Partnerships have several disadvantages. They include the unlimited liability of the partners for debts and legal actions against the partnership; mutual agency; and the automatic dissolution of the partnership if one of the partners dies or withdraws from the partnership, or there is an irresolvable dispute.

3.6 Define the term 'company'.

A company is an independent legal entity normally characterised by the limited liability of its shareholders.

3.7 Identify the different types of companies and provide examples of each.

The main five different types of companies are private companies, companies limited by shares, companies limited by guarantee, no-liability companies and unlimited companies.

3.8 Discuss the advantages and disadvantages of a company.

The main advantages of companies are the limited liability of shareholders for business debts and the access to additional capital from the shareholders for business expansion. Their main disadvantages are the time and money needed to establish a company, and the complex regulatory requirements imposed on companies.

3.9 Define the term 'trust'.

A trust is a common form of business structure in Australia. It represents an obligation on a person to hold property for the benefit of others. Family trusts/discretionary trusts are established for the benefit of families and unit trusts are established for the benefit of various parties.

3.10 Discuss the advantages and disadvantages of a trust.

The main advantages of trusts are tax benefits and limited liability. The main disadvantage is the complexity of the law relating to trusts.

3.11 Compare financial statements for different business structures.

Each of the different types of financial statements reflects a business entity's financial performance and position separately from those of the owner(s). The main differences in the financial statements for each of the different business structures occur in the distribution of profit to the respective owners. For a sole trader, the individual owner has the sole right to any profits. For a partnership, the respective partners have rights to profits as outlined in the partnership agreement. For a company, the profit is distributed to its owners (shareholders) in the form of dividends. In the statement of financial position, the capital account in the equity section reflects the capital contributions of the owner(s). For a partnership, there are multiple owners and each of their contributions is shown in the statement of financial position. For a company, the share capital account reflects the contributions of the shareholders of the company. The undistributed profit for a partnership is included in each partner's current account on the statement of financial position. For a company, undistributed profits sit in retained earnings on the statement of financial position.

3.12 Explain the term 'differential reporting' and discuss the implications for disclosing entities.

In 2010, the AASB modified the reporting entity concept by allowing disclosing entities that are not publicly accountable (such as unlisted public companies) to apply a reduced disclosure version of the AASB standards, known as the reduced disclosure regime. All other reporting entities prepare GPFS. This difference in requirements of reporting is known as differential reporting.

KEY TERMS

accounting entity concept Business transactions are recorded separately from personal transactions involving the owner(s) because the business is regarded as a separate legal entity from the owner(s).

Australian Business Number (ABN) Eleven-digit identifier issued by the ATO for certain dealings with the ATO and other government departments and agencies.

Australian Company Number (ACN) Nine-digit number allocated to a company to ensure that it has adequate identification when transacting business.

Australian Taxation Office (ATO) The federal government's main revenue-collection agency.

business activity statement (BAS) Single form used by entities registered for GST to report their business tax entitlements and obligations to the ATO.

company Business structure that has a separate legal identity from its shareholders and is taxed on its taxable income.

differential reporting Framework under which entities have different financial reporting requirements.

dividend Distribution of company profit to shareholders.

family (or discretionary) trust Business structure usually established for the benefit of one family and its members.

goods and services tax (GST) Broad-based indirect tax levied on supplies of goods and services.

legal entity Entity that is separate from its owners and recognised at law.

limited liability Shareholder liability limited to the extent of the value of shareholders' shares or a guarantee.

mutual agency Each partner is an agent for an entity and has the right to enter into contracts for the entity.

ordinary shares Most commonly traded type of shares in Australia. Holders of ordinary shares are part-owners of a company and may receive payments in cash (called dividends). This class of shares has no preferential rights to dividends or capital on winding up.

partnership Group of people who come together in business with a common goal of making a profit.

partnership agreement Agreement between business partners that contains the details of that partnership.

preference shares Shares with characteristics of both debt and equity. They rank before ordinary shares in the event of liquidation of a company and usually receive a fixed rate of return.

retained earnings Cumulative profits made by an entity that have not been distributed as dividends or transferred to reserve accounts.

shareholders Part-owners of a company.

sole trader Individual who controls and manages a business and is solely liable for all the business debts.

trust Business structure in which a person holds property for others who are intended to benefit from the property or income of that property.

trustee Person or persons, or proprietary limited company, personally liable for all debts and other liabilities incurred on behalf of the trust.

unit trust Business structure established for the benefit of various parties, rather than family members.

unlimited companies Companies characterised by members who have no limit placed on their liability (usually restricted to investment-type entities).

unlimited liability When an individual or partnership is fully liable for all the debts of an entity.

APPLY YOUR KNOWLEDGE   *50 marks*

PART A

(a) Explain the advantages and disadvantages of the sole trader form of business structure compared to the partnership form of business structure.   *4 marks*

(b) Summarise the differences between a service and a manufacturing company.   *2 marks*

(c) Compare the liability requirements of members of a no-liability company and shareholders of a public company.   *4 marks*

(d) Describe the differences between a family trust and a unit trust. What are the tax advantages of the trust form of business structure?   *6 marks*

(e) Define limited liability. Provide an illustration of the term in relation to public companies.   *2 marks*

(f) What are the implications of the reduced disclosure regime for smaller companies: (1) to the entity; and (2) to other stakeholders?   *4 marks*

PART B

Ping and Juno decide to form a partnership on 30 June 2020. They secure the services of Timothy Legal to draw up their partnership agreement as follows.

1. Ping is to contribute:
   - his car, the fair value of which is $32 000
   - property with a book value of $120 000, but revalued to $150 000
   - a mortgage of $80 000; this was secured over the property and the partnership has agreed to assume this liability.

2. Juno is to contribute:
   - cash totalling $25 000
   - office equipment with a market value of $45 000.

It is also agreed that Ping will act as manager with an annual salary of $65 000, to be allocated at the end of each year. Profits or losses will be divided between Ping and Juno in the proportion 2/3 and 1/3 respectively.

Gross profit for the year ended 30 June 2021 is $165 000, with operating expenses of $105 000. Ping withdrew $19 500 and Juno withdrew $4000 during the year.

Required

(a) Prepare the statement of financial position of the partnership on its formation (30 June 2020). *8 marks*

(b) Calculate each partner's share of profit for the year ended 30 June 2021.   *6 marks*

PART C

The directors of Carlos Ltd provide you with the following financial information for the period ended 30 September 2019: selling expenses $96 000; occupancy expenses $12 000; finance expenses $26 400; loss due to legal action $5400; administrative expenses $20 400; cost of sales $180 000; ordinary share capital (100 000 shares issued) $300 000; sales revenue $720 000; other revenue $15 000; dividends declared (for current period) $14 400; retained earnings at beginning $258 000. Income tax is to be applied at a 30 per cent rate to profit before tax.

Required

(a) Prepare a statement of profit or loss for Carlos Ltd for the period ended 30 September 2019. *7 marks*

(b) Determine the closing balance of retained earnings at 30 September 2019.   *3 marks*

(c) Public companies have to comply with extensive reporting regulations, including the Corporations Act and the ASX Listing Rules. Explain the reasons why public companies have additional regulations compared to proprietary companies and how the additional reporting disclosures assist different users in making decisions about the allocation of scarce resources.   *4 marks*

SELF-EVALUATION ACTIVITIES

3.1 Charley Bucket has worked as a secondary school teacher for 15 years. Her dream had always been to work for herself selling a variety of confectionery types. In 2018, she inherited $80 000 cash from her grandmother and decided to use some of this money to purchase a lolly shop (called Freckles) in nearby Toowong.

For the financial year ended 30 June 2019, Charley provides you with the following details: lolly sales $144 000; cost of sales $64 000; administrative expenses $5120; rent of shop $22 400; casual wages $4800; interest on loan $9280; electricity and gas expenses $3200; cash at bank $19 680; shop fittings $20 000; cash on hand $6400; accounts payable $3680; display case (asset) $12 800.

Use the above information to prepare a statement of profit or loss and a statement of financial position for Charley operating Freckles as a sole trader. Calculate Charley's capital contribution.

SOLUTION TO 3.1

FRECKLES — CHARLEY BUCKET Statement of profit or loss for the financial year ended 30 June 2019		
Income		
Lolly sales		$144 000
Cost of sales		64 000
Gross profit		80 000
Expenses		
Administrative expense	$ 5 120	
Shop rental expense	22 400	
Casual wages expense	4 800	
Interest on loan	9 280	
Electricity and gas expense	3 680	
Total expenses		44 800
Profit		**$ 35 200**

FRECKLES — CHARLEY BUCKET Statement of financial position as at 30 June 2019		
Current assets		
Cash at bank		$19 680
Cash on hand		6 400
Non-current assets		
Shop fittings		20 000
Display case		12 800
Total assets		58 880
Current liabilities		
Accounts payable		3 680
Total liabilities		3 680
Net assets		**$55 200**
Equity		
Capital — C Bucket		$20 000
Profit		35 200
Total equity		**$55 200**

3.2 Xavier and Lauren agree to form a partnership to supply beer to restaurants. The business will be known as X&L Craft Beers. They agree on the following market values given to them by an independent valuer.

- Xavier's contribution: cash $15 400; inventory of beer $44 800; furniture $17 500; laptop computer $2000.
- Lauren's contribution: cash $41 000; inventory of beer $8000; accounts payable $1400.

Prepare the initial statement of financial position for X&L Craft Beers as at 1 April 2020, the date the partnership commenced.

SOLUTION TO 3.2

X&L CRAFT BEERS
Statement of financial position
as at 1 April 2020

Current assets	
Cash	$ 56 400
Inventory	52 800
Non-current assets	
Furniture	17 500
Laptop computer	2 000
Total assets	128 700
Current liabilities	
Accounts payable	1 400
Total liabilities	1 400
Net assets	**$127 300**
Partners' equity	
Capital	
— Xavier	$ 79 700
— Lauren	47 600
Total partners' equity	**$127 300**

3.3 Using the information from self-evaluation activity 3.2, assume the partnership had been in existence for three months, made a profit of $44 800 for the period ended 30 June 2020 and retained this as cash in the business. Prepare a new statement of financial position to incorporate this profit, assuming that no written partnership agreement exists.

SOLUTION TO 3.3

X&L CRAFT BEERS
Statement of financial position
as at 30 June 2020

Current assets	
Cash	$101 200
Inventory	52 800
Non-current assets	
Furniture	17 500
Laptop computer	2 000
Total assets	173 500
Current liabilities	
Accounts payable	1 400
Total liabilities	1 400
Net assets	**$172 100**
Partners' equity	
Capital	
— Xavier	$ 79 700
— Lauren	47 600
Current	
— Xavier	22 400
— Lauren	22 400
Total partners' equity	**$172 100**

3.4 Willow Deng operates Spinnaker Pty Ltd, a private company selling sailing accessories. The following information is available to you for Spinnaker Pty Ltd's first year of operations ended 30 June 2019: sales revenue $57 800; accounts receivable $13 600; inventory $6120; accounts payable $6800; rent expense $3600; bank loan $17 000; share capital $34 000; equipment $48 960; cost of sales $32 000; gas and electricity expenses $2840; insurance expense $1000; supplies expense $680; cash $3400; taxation expense $3400. No dividends were declared for the period.

Prepare a statement of profit or loss for the financial year ended 30 June 2019 and a statement of financial position as at 30 June 2019 for Spinnaker Pty Ltd.

SOLUTION TO 3.4

SPINNAKER PTY LTD
Statement of profit or loss
for the financial year ended 30 June 2019

Income		
Sales revenue		$57 800
Less: Cost of sales		32 000
Gross profit		25 800
Expenses		
Rent expense	$3 600	
Insurance expense	1 000	
Supplies expense	680	
Gas and electricity expense	2 840	8 120
Profit before tax		**17 680**
Taxation expense		3 400
Profit after tax		**$14 280**

SPINNAKER PTY LTD
Statement of financial position
as at 30 June 2019

Current assets	
Cash	$ 3 400
Accounts receivable	13 600
Inventory	6 120
	23 120
Non-current assets	
Equipment	48 960
Total assets	72 080
Current liabilities	
Accounts payable	6 800
Non-current liabilities	
Loan	17 000
Total liabilities	23 800
Net assets	**$48 280**
Shareholders' equity	
Share capital	$34 000
Retained earnings	14 280
Total shareholders' equity	**$48 280**

COMPREHENSION QUESTIONS

3.5 You are a friend of Penny Williams, who is thinking about starting a business to sell her personalised embroidered towels. Advise Penny on the four factors that should be considered before deciding what form of business structure to operate under. **LO1, 2, 3, 4, 5, 6**

3.6 Explain with examples the major differences between a company limited by shares (such as JB Hi-Fi Ltd) and a proprietary company (such as Coconut Plantations Pty Ltd). **LO6, 7**

3.7 What are two major advantages and disadvantages of a company structure? Provide an illustration with a company listed on the ASX (such as JB Hi-Fi Ltd, CSL Ltd, BHP Group Ltd). **LO8**

3.8 Illustrate with an example the difference in the format of the equity section of the statement of financial position between a sole trader, partnership and company. **LO2, 4, 6, 11**

3.9 Another relatively widespread business structure is a trust. What are the two main forms of trusts in Australia? What are the tax issues associated with family trusts? **LO9, 10**

3.10 Illustrate with an example how sole traders and partners are taxed in Australia. What are the advantages and disadvantages compared to paying company tax? **LO2, 3, 4, 5**

3.11 It is important that partners draw up a partnership agreement. What details should be specified in this agreement? **LO4**

3.12 Go to the ATO website (www.ato.gov.au) and provide a definition for each of the following. **LO6**
(a) Pay as you go (PAYG)
(b) Capital gains tax (CGT)
(c) Goods and services tax (GST)

(d) Tax file number (TFN)

(e) Wine equalisation tax (WET)

3.13 Differential reporting is applicable to which entities? Name four areas where the reduced disclosure requirements apply. **LO12**

3.14 What are the major differences in equity funding between a partnership and a public company? **LO4, 5, 6, 7**

3.15 What do the following terms mean? **LO3, 6, 7, 9**

(a) Unlimited liability

(b) Mutual agency

(c) Dividend

(d) Preference shares

(e) Unit trust

EXERCISES

★ BASIC I ★ ★ MODERATE I ★ ★ ★ CHALLENGING

Exercises 3.16 to 3.25 are multiple-choice questions. Select the correct answer for each.

3.16 ★ **LO2, 4, 6, 8**

A business organised as a separate legal entity that is owned by shareholders is a:

(a) family trust.

(b) company.

(c) sole trader.

(d) legal partnership.

3.17 ★ **LO6, 7**

The shareholders' equity section of the statement of financial position for a public company includes:

(a) share capital (contributed equity).

(b) retained earnings.

(c) reserves.

(d) all of the above.

3.18 ★ **LO6, 7**

Retained earnings represent a part of shareholders' equity resulting from profit that:

(a) was paid in by the original shareholders.

(b) has not been distributed as a dividend.

(c) must be paid to the government in the form of GST.

(d) must be used when a company makes a call on capital.

3.19 ★ **LO2**

Equity finance for a sole trader comes from:

(a) the issue of shares to the public such as an IPO (initial public offering).

(b) borrowings from the government.

(c) the owner and profit retained in the business.

(d) bank loans.

3.20 ★ **LO4**

Partnerships are most common among:

(a) doctors.

(b) accountants.

(c) lawyers.

(d) all of the above.

3.21 ★ **LO4**

For a partnership to be legal, the agreement should:

(a) be in writing.

(b) indicate a sharing of a bank account.

(c) indicate how profits or losses are to be shared.

(d) have any one or more of the above characteristics.

3.22 ★ **LO9**

In Australia, a trust:

(a) is an obligation on a person to hold property for the benefit of beneficiaries.

(b) pays income tax on profit.

(c) has unlimited liability.

(d) has all of the above characteristics.

3.23 ★ **LO10**

An advantage of a trust as a form of business structure is that it:

(a) is simple to set up, just like a sole trader or partnership.

(b) is generally tax effective.

(c) possesses limited liability.

(d) has all of the above characteristics.

3.24 ★ **LO9, 10**

Under a discretionary trust, a trustee can distribute income and assets:

(a) according to government acts.

(b) using wide discretionary powers.

(c) according to specific items in the Corporations Act.

(d) as advised by the principal beneficiary.

3.25 ★ **LO2, 3**

A sole trader in Australia is taxed at:

(a) the company tax rate of 30 per cent.

(b) the same as the rate of capital gains tax for the owner.

(c) the owner's marginal tax rate.

(d) both the rates in (b) and (c) above.

3.26 ★ **LO2**

Didi, a sole trader operating a small landscaping business, asks you to prepare her statement of financial position (showing her equity) for the year ended 30 June 2020: contributed capital $26 440; profit $5600; drawings $3600; cash $36 000; fixtures and fittings $10 800; accounts receivable $9000; accounts payable $13 500; bank loan $13 860.

3.27 ★ ★ **LO2, 4, 6, 9**

From the six scenarios described below, indicate (giving your reasons) the business form each one is likely to take — sole trader, partnership, company or trust.

(a) Conor and Ella wish to start an internet business marketing cosmetics. They are concerned about the legal issues (e.g. their personal liabilities) for this business once they start trading.

(b) Tommy has just commenced a home maintenance business by himself, with the help of $2000 inherited from a rich aunt. He wishes to employ his wife as the bookkeeper.

(c) As friends at university, Paul, Ingrid and Jasmine studied commerce. They are now setting up a small accounting business specialising in taxation returns and investment advice.

(d) Two brothers (Will and Chas), who are both married and are both trained and practising plumbers, wish to combine their businesses into one so that they can share resources and take more holidays.

(e) Three engineers (Azil, Danny and Jessica) wish to set up a prospecting business searching for gold and they want to list their business on the ASX.

(f) Four members of the Ng family wish to establish an investment business, with the proviso that additional family members can be admitted as they reach the age of 18 years.

3.28 ★ ★ **LO11**

Produce the shareholders' equity section of the statement of financial position for Geelong Davis Ltd, a public company. Use the following information: share capital (200 000 $1 ordinary shares and 30 000 $4 preference shares, all fully paid up); profit for this period $84 000 and retained earnings from last year $69 000; dividends paid during year $26 600.

3.29 ★ ★ **LO4, 11**

Jenny and Margaret agree to form a partnership on 16 September 2020 to supply first-aid kits to motor vehicle dealers. They agree on the following market values given to them by an independent valuer.

- Jenny's contribution:
  - cash $10 000
  - inventory $18 000
  - accounts receivable $7500 (less allowance for doubtful debts $1250)
  - computer table $1200

- Margaret's contribution:
  - cash $20 000
  - inventory $2000
  - accrued expenses $800

(a) Prepare the initial statement of financial position for Jenny and Margaret's partnership as at 16 September 2020.

(b) What would happen to the statement of financial position if, over the following four weeks, Jenny and Margaret made a cash profit of $14 000? (*Note:* Assume all other figures remain constant and Jenny and Margaret agree to split any profit or loss 50/50.)

3.30 ★ ★   **LO2, 11**

Presented below are financial statement items for Jupiter Planet (a sole trader) for the period ended 30 September 2020. Determine which items should appear in the statement of profit or loss and which items should appear in the statement of financial position.

(a) Cash	$ 99 000
(b) Accounts receivable	11 000
(c) Service revenue	26 400
(d) Advertising expense	8 800
(e) Accounts payable	6 600
(f) Expenses owing	3 960
(g) Rent expense	2 420
(h) Internet expense	660
(i) Petrol expense	6 160
(j) Insurance expense	880
(k) Equipment	132 000

3.31 ★ ★   **LO2, 11**

Using the information shown in exercise 3.30, produce a statement of profit or loss for the period ended 30 September 2020.

3.32 ★ ★   **LO2, 6**

Refer to the JB Hi-Fi Ltd statement of profit or loss in figure 3.2 to answer the following questions.

(a) What is the major difference between the format of this statement and that of a sole trader?

(b) What do you think is the purpose of the Notes column?

(c) What do you think is the purpose of providing the different profit figures (i.e. gross profit, profit before tax, profit for the year)?

(d) The statement of profit or loss and statement of financial positions are consolidated statements for JB Hi-Fi Ltd. What do you think is meant by the term 'consolidated'?

3.33 ★ ★   **LO4, 6**

Refer to the JB Hi-Fi Ltd consolidated statement of financial position in figure 3.3 to answer the following questions.

(a) What is the major difference between the format of this statement and that of a partnership?

(b) List two current assets and two current liabilities of JB Hi-Fi Ltd and explain what is meant by each one.

(c) Why do you think some items such as 'borrowings' and 'provisions' appear as both current and non-current liabilities?

(d) What information can external users (e.g. creditors and shareholders) obtain from this statement?

3.34 ★ ★   **LO2, 5, 11**

Lou and Stu are sole traders who run their own separate businesses providing accounting and bookkeeping services. On 31 December 2019, their individual statements of financial position show the following accounts.

	Lou	Stu
Cash	39 650	28 600
Accounts receivable	20 800	26 000
Inventory	36 400	39 000
Equipment	52 000	50 700
Capital	148 850	144 300

Starting in 2020, Lou and Stu have agreed to form a partnership trading as Lou and Stu Financial Services. The partnership agreement stipulates that all cash and other assets will be transferred to the partnership. In addition, Lou and Stu will invest an additional $8000 and $140 000 in cash respectively. Prepare a statement of financial position for Lou and Stu Financial Services as at 1 January 2020.

PROBLEMS

★ BASIC | ★ ★ MODERATE | ★ ★ ★ CHALLENGING

3.35 Researching the benefits of listing ★   **LO6, 7**

Go to the ASX website (www.asx.com.au). In the search window, type 'listing with ASX'. What are the key benefits of listing according to the ASX?

3.36 Researching business start-up strategies and advantages and disadvantages of business structures ★   **LO2, 4, 6, 9**

Go to the Business Queensland website (www.business.qld.gov.au) and select 'Starting a business', then 'Business types and legal structures'. Next select 'Setting up a legal business' under the heading 'Business legal structures'. List the various considerations that should be taken into account when deciding on a business structure. Compare the advantages and disadvantages of each of the four business structures.

3.37 Preparing a statement of financial position ★   **LO2, 11**

From the following information for sole trader J Pfahlert, software designer, draw up a statement of financial position as at the end of the financial year (30 June 2020). You are also required to determine the amount of owner's capital: accounts payable $9600; land $120 000; cash on hand $12 000; office building $276 000; bank mortgage $16 800; profit $800; accounts receivable $9180; computer equipment $1200.

3.38 Preparing a statement of profit or loss ★   **LO2, 11**

Teddy Thomas, a real estate agent, requires you to prepare a statement of profit or loss for the period ended 31 December 2020: donations $120; office wages $8400; sales salaries $30 000; sales commission expense $6000; advertising $4800; rent expense $2400; rates and land tax expenses $3600; stationery expense $960; fee revenue $324 000; interest paid on loan $5040; interest earned on term deposit $1440; mobile phone expense $1704.

3.39 Preparing a statement of profit or loss and a statement of financial position ★   **LO1, 11**

The following account balances, dated 30 September 2020, are of sole trader Victoria Stone (Stone Bike Hire): capital (V Stone) $108 125; hire revenue $45 000; bike maintenance $10 000; administrative expense $5000; rent expense $2750; wages $10 000; interest expense $22 500; cash at bank $3750; cash on hand $1250; office equipment $17 500; bicycles $125 000; gas and electricity expenses $3500; drawings $4375; accounts payable $8750; bank loan $43 750. Use this information to prepare a statement of profit or loss and a statement of financial position as at that date.

3.40 Preparing a statement of financial position ★ ★   **LO4, 11**

Julia and Evie, owners of competing businesses, agree to form a partnership on 1 July 2020. Their individual assets and liabilities are independently valued and on this basis the following values are assigned to the partnership.

	Julia	Evie
Cash at bank	80 000	40 000
Accounts receivable	—	40 000
Inventory	80 000	20 000
Equipment	70 000	40 000
Land	—	40 000
Building	—	70 000
Mortgage	—	60 000

Required

Prepare a statement of financial position for the new partnership as at 1 July 2020.

3.41 Preparing a statement of profit or loss ★ ★   **LO6, 11**

The directors of Pumpkin Ltd provide you with the following financial information for the period ended 31 December 2020: selling expense $76 050; interest expense $29 250; legal fees $4875; administrative expense $60 450; income tax expense $31 200; cost of sales $370 500; ordinary share capital (20 000 shares issued) $156 000; sales revenue $604 500; other revenue $146 250; dividends declared (for current period) $15 600; retained earnings at beginning $226 200.

Required

(a) Prepare a statement of profit or loss for Pumpkin Ltd for the period ended 31 December 2020.

(b) Determine the closing balance of retained earnings as at 31 December 2020.

3.42 Preparing a statement of financial position and calculating profit ★ ★   **LO4, 11**

Samuel and Vinnie decide to form a partnership on 1 January 2020. They secure the services of a solicitor to draw up their partnership agreement as follows.

(a) Samuel is to contribute:
  • his vehicle valued at $72 000
  • plant and equipment valued at $168 000
  • accounts receivable totalling $28 800.

(b) Vinnie is to contribute:
  • cash totalling $48 000
  • a building valued at $336 000
  • a mortgage of $192 000; this was secured over the building and the partnership agreed to assume this liability.

  It is also agreed that Samuel will act as manager with an annual salary of $120 000, to be allocated at the end of each year. Profits or losses will be divided between Samuel and Vinnie in the proportion 3/5 and 2/5 respectively.

  Gross profit for the year ended 31 December 2020 is $520 000, with operating expenses of $240 000. Samuel withdrew $24 000 and Vinnie withdrew $32 000 during the year.

Required

(a) Prepare the statement of financial position of the partnership on its formation (1 January 2020).

(b) Calculate each partner's share of profit for the year ended 31 December 2020.

3.43 Preparing a statement of profit or loss and statement of financial position ★ ★   **LO2, 11**

P Nightingale commenced business on 1 October 2020 as a beautician operating as Nightingale Beauty Salon. Transactions for the month of October were as follows.

2020		
October	1	Started business by contributing capital of $120 000.
	2	Paid rent for month of October $12 800.
	3	Purchased beauty supplies for the year $20 000 for cash.
	4	Bought fixtures and fittings for the beauty salon (chairs, coffee tables, cabinets, massage table, fountain) on credit from Wellness Supplies $48 000.
	8	Paid wages $2000 for first week's work.
	15	Banked takings from first full week of operations $3300. Paid wages $2000.
	18	Bought new light fitting for $2800 from local artist and paid cash.
	22	Banked takings from second week of operations $5000. Paid wages $3000.
	24	Withdrew $6000 cash from business for personal use.
	27	Banked takings $4700.
	31	Paid monthly electricity and gas $1680.

Required

(a) Prepare a statement of profit or loss for Nightingale Beauty Salon for the month ended 31 October 2020.

(b) Prepare a statement of financial position for Nightingale Beauty Salon as at 31 October 2020.

3.44 AASB differential reporting ★ ★ ★   **LO12**

Access the latest update on the Australian Financial Reporting Framework from the AASB website www.aasb.gov.au/admin/file/content102/c3/AASB_Financial_Reporting_Framework_Project_Summary.pdf) and summarise the current status of the project.

3.45 Comparing the differences between ownership ★ ★ ★

Refer to the statements of financial position for Advantage Tennis Coaching and Coconut Plantations Pty Ltd.

Required

(a) Summarise the differences in the ownership structure of the two business entities.

(b) What are the relative advantages and disadvantages of each form of ownership structure?

(c) What are the advantages of the JB Hi-Fi Ltd form of ownership compared to that of Coconut Plantations Pty Ltd? Discuss.

DECISION-MAKING ACTIVITIES

3.46 The introduction of differential reporting has resulted in many significant changes for Australian companies. Access a summary of the Differential Reporting Project update at the AASB website (www.aasb.gov.au).

Required

(a) Summarise the requirements for both for-profit entities and NFP entities.

(b) Compare this to the summary given in the Australian Financial Reporting Framework from the AASB website.

3.47 Kiki has just been offered a retirement package from her work as a sales representative with Makeup Magic. Her long-term goal has been to start up a day-spa resort on the Sunshine Coast in Queensland with her sister Cece, who is a marketing consultant. Kiki dreams of joining the 'sea change' set. A suitable building (an ex-holiday home) has become available at Sunrise Beach, Queensland. With their husbands (Mike, who is a builder, and Jim, who is a plumber), they decide to sell their homes in Brisbane and purchase this property. They think the potential for the business venture is enormous, but expect that additional capital will be required over the next five years for their dreams to be realised.

Required

(a) Do you think the two families have the necessary skills between them to run such a demanding venture? List the skills that you think are important.

(b) Go to the Queensland government business and industry portal (www.business.qld.gov.au). Select 'Starting a business' and then 'Legal obligations for business' under the heading 'Licensing, registrations and legal obligations'. Select 'Record keeping' under the heading 'Meeting your legal obligations'. What business records should the two partners keep for the next five years?

(c) Do you think their bank would be happier to lend the families finance to expand due to the fact that they are in partnership? Why?

3.48 From humble beginnings, Phil expanded his backyard business in Melbourne to produce and sell sports drink bottles for AFL, cricket, rugby league and rugby union football teams in 2019. Due to the success of his product and the fact that he was dealing with very wealthy football clubs, he was advised to form a proprietary company limited by shares so as to maintain his credibility. To comply with a previous requirement in the Corporations Act (whereby a company requires two directors), he insisted that his wife, Josephine (a school teacher), become a director. Phil was not renowned for his accounting skills and he overlooked the group tax liabilities for the company over the following two years. The case has ended up in court, with the ATO claiming that both Phil and Josephine are jointly liable.

Required

(a) Do you think Phil and/or Josephine should be liable for overlooking the tax liabilities for the company? Why or why not?

(b) What responsibilities do you think Phil and Josephine have as directors of the company?

REFERENCES

Australian Accounting Standards Board 2015, 'An update on the Differential Reporting Project', 12 January, www.aasb.gov.au/admin/file/content102/c3/Differential_Reporting_Project_Update_12_01_2015.pdf.

Australian Bureau of Statistics 2018a, 'ABS 8155.0: Australian industry', June 2016–2017, table 5.

Australian Bureau of Statistics 2018b, 'ABS 8165.0: Counts of Australian businesses including entries and exits',
    June 2013–2017, table 13.
International Accounting Standards Board (IASB) 2015, *International Financial Reporting Standard for Small and
    Medium-sized Entities (IFRS for SMEs)*, IFRS Foundation, UK.
JB Hi-Fi Ltd 2018, *Preliminary annual report 2018*, www.jbhifi.com.au.

ACKNOWLEDGEMENTS

Photo: © Hero Images / Getty Images
Photo: © Syda Productions / Shutterstock.com
Photo: © Robert Daly / Getty Images
Figures 3.1, 3.2, 3.3: © JB Hi-Fi Ltd 2018

CHAPTER 4

Business transactions

LEARNING OBJECTIVES

After studying this chapter, you should be able to:

4.1 describe the characteristics of business transactions

4.2 differentiate between a business transaction, a personal transaction and a business event

4.3 explain the accounting equation process of the double-entry system of recording

4.4 identify the impact of business transactions on the accounting equation

4.5 prepare an accounting worksheet and a simplified statement of profit or loss and statement of financial position

4.6 discuss how journals and ledger accounts can help in capturing accounting information efficiently and effectively

4.7 apply debit and credit rules, and record simple transactions in the journals and ledgers of a business

4.8 explain the purpose of a trial balance

4.9 detect errors in transaction analysis and investigate the origin of the errors.

Chapter preview

This chapter describes the typical characteristics of business transactions and illustrates the differences between business transactions, personal transactions and business events. It provides examples of business transactions and illustrates the concept of duality as applied to the accounting equation. The process and benefits of recording business transactions in the accounting worksheet are then explained. Common errors involved in recording transactions, such as transposition errors, are described with accompanying illustrative examples. A short introduction to recording in journals and ledgers is also provided towards the end of the chapter. The chapter concludes with an explanation and illustration of the trial balance.

4.1 Recognising business transactions

LEARNING OBJECTIVE 4.1 Describe the characteristics of business transactions.

Business transactions are occurrences — exchanges of resources between an entity and another entity or individual — that affect the assets, liabilities and owners' equity items of the entity. A business transaction is recorded in the accounting information system when there has been an exchange of resources between one business and another person or business, and where that exchange can be reliably measured in monetary terms and occurs at arm's length distance. An **arm's length distance** transaction can be described as when parties with equal bargaining positions make a deal and:

> neither party is subject to the other's control or dominant influence, and the transaction is treated with fairness, integrity and legality. If discovered by a taxing authority, the absence of an arm's length transaction may result in additional taxes incurred resulting from transfer at less than fair market value (Dictionary of Small Business 2018).

Every type of entity — sole proprietor, partnership, company and trust — must keep records of its business transactions separately from any personal transactions of the owner(s). This is known as the **entity concept** and it means that the owner of a business should not include any personal assets on the entity's **statement of financial position**, as this statement must reflect the financial position of the business alone. The entity concept also applies to the personal expenditures of the owner, which should not be included in the entity's expenses in the **statement of profit or loss**, as this statement must also reflect the financial performance of the business alone. Personal expenditures of the owner that involve the business entity's funds are known as **drawings**.

For every business transaction that occurs, there must be evidence provided of that transaction and the transaction must be measurable in monetary terms. The evidence can come from a number of source documents. **Source documents** are the original documents verifying a business transaction. They include:
- sales invoices
- purchase orders
- ATM receipts.

Examples of business transactions

The frequency and type of daily business transactions will vary greatly among entities. Some entities will have hundreds of transactions every day — small, large, cash and credit business transactions. Consider JB Hi-Fi Ltd: every day, thousands of transactions would be recorded. Some transactions would involve very small sums of money, while others would represent large purchases or sales. Some of JB Hi-Fi Ltd's transactions would involve the exchange of cash for goods or services — known as **cash transactions** — but others would be classified as **credit transactions**, where an amount will be paid or received at a later date.

Typical transactions for entities are:
- contribution of capital by owner(s)
- payment of wages
- receipt of bank interest
- payment of GST
- purchase of equipment
- payment of accounts payable
- sale of goods to customers
- provision of services to clients
- purchase of accounting software

- charging interest on overdue accounts receivable
- withdrawal of capital
- repayment of short-term loans to financial institutions
- cash purchases of office supplies
- payment for advertising.

4.2 Business and personal transactions and business events

LEARNING OBJECTIVE 4.2 Differentiate between a business transaction, a personal transaction and a business event.

It is important to distinguish between business transactions, personal transactions and business events. Business transactions involve an exchange of goods between an entity and another entity or individual. **Personal transactions** are transactions of the owners, partners or shareholders that are unrelated to the operation of the business. Such transactions are not classified as business transactions because they do not involve an exchange of goods between the business entity and another entity. For example, if the owner purchases a new iPad for home use, this is unrelated to the operations of the business entity and is therefore not classified as a business transaction. However, if the owner withdraws business funds to purchase the iPad for home use, it does become a business transaction. The withdrawal of cash for personal use will be recorded as drawings and so will not be included in the business expenses.

Business events are occurrences that have the potential to affect the entity in some way but will not be recorded as business transactions until an exchange of goods occurs between the entity and an outside entity or individual. Examples of such business events include negotiations between the entity and other entities or individuals. For example, if the entity negotiates a bank loan for the purchase of a new property, this will not be recorded as a loan by the entity until the loan is paid out to the business entity. Similarly, if the entity negotiates for a new employee to commence work from July and signs a contract for them to start at that time, no transaction is recorded for wages until the employee has completed the first week, fortnight or month of work.

Many business entities now use accounting software to keep a record of their daily transactions such as cash and credit purchases, cash and credit sales, withdrawals by the owner and capital contributions.

4.3 The accounting equation

LEARNING OBJECTIVE 4.3 Explain the accounting equation process of the double-entry system of recording.

The **accounting equation** expresses the relationship between the assets of an entity and how the assets are financed. **Assets** are resources controlled by the entity. They can be financed by outside fund providers, and so classified as **liabilities**, or through inside funds, known as **equity**. The liabilities and equity represent the claims against the entity's assets. For example, if CM Enterprises has assets totalling $5.6 million and liabilities of $4 million, then the amount of equity must be $1.6 million.

We can see this illustrated in the accounting equation as:

$$\text{Assets (A)} = \text{Liabilities (L)} + \text{Equity (E)}$$
$$\$5\,600\,000 = \$4\,000\,000 + \$1\,600\,000$$

The concept of duality

An important part of understanding the effect of business transactions on an entity's performance and position is the concept of **duality**. This simply means that every business transaction will have a dual effect. For example, the purchase of a new office building through a bank loan will increase an asset (the building) and increase a liability (the loan):

$$\text{Assets (A)} = \text{Liabilities (L)} + \text{Equity (E)}$$
$$\uparrow \text{Office Building} = \uparrow \text{Loan}$$

The financial statement known as the statement of financial position is based on the accounting equation. The statement of financial position reports the entity's assets, liabilities and equity. Its common format is to show assets net of liabilities (net assets), which are represented by the equity of the entity. We can also expand the equity section of the accounting equation to show the impact of the income earned and the expenses incurred by the entity, which will determine the entity's profit or loss for the reporting period. Recall from the introduction to accounting and business decision making chapter that **income** is inflows or other enhancements, or decreases in liabilities, which result in an increase in equity during the reporting period. **Expenses** are decreases in economic benefits that result in a decrease in equity during the reporting period. The profit (loss) will be added (subtracted) to opening equity in the equity section of the statement of financial position. Income increases equity and expenses reduce equity. Therefore, incorporating income and expenses into the accounting equation is illustrated as follows.

Statement of financial position

Assets (A) = Liabilities (L) + Equity (E)

Statement of profit or loss

Income (I) − Expenses (E)

Further:

Income (I) increases Equity (E)

Expenses (E) decrease Equity (E)

Therefore:

Assets (A) = Liabilities (L) + Opening Equity (E) + Income (I) − Expenses (E)

VALUE TO BUSINESS

- Business transactions are occurrences that affect the assets, liabilities and equity accounts of an entity. A business transaction should be recorded when there has been an exchange of resources between the entity and another entity or individual.
- For each business transaction recorded, there must be evidence of the transaction and the transaction must be measurable in monetary terms.
- It is important to distinguish between business transactions and personal transactions. Personal transactions are transactions of the owners of the business and do not relate to the business; consequently, they have no impact on the entity's financial records. Business events have the potential to affect the entity in some way but will not be recorded as a business transaction until an exchange of goods or services occurs between the business entity and another entity or individual.
- The accounting equation expresses the relationship between the assets of an entity and how the assets are financed. Assets are financed either by liabilities or by contributions by the owners.
- For each business transaction, there will be at least two effects on the accounting equation. This is known as the application of duality.
- The statement of financial position of an entity is an expression of the accounting equation, as it reports the entity's asset, liability and equity accounts. The equity section of the equation can be expanded to show the impact of income and expenses for the entity, which will determine the entity's profit or loss for the reporting period. A profit increases equity and a loss decreases equity.

4.4 Analysis of business transactions

LEARNING OBJECTIVE 4.4 Identify the impact of business transactions on the accounting equation.

The following illustrative examples (4.1 to 4.3) illustrate the analysis of business transactions using the accounting equation.

ILLUSTRATIVE EXAMPLE 4.1

Analysis of business transactions (capital contribution)

Nicholas Cash recently set up his own tennis coaching academy, Advantage Tennis Coaching (ATC). He contributes $20 000 of his personal savings into a business bank account under the name of Advantage Tennis Coaching. The impact of this initial transaction is that the business will have assets of $20 000 in cash and also $20 000 in equity, which represents $20 000 owed to the owner, Nicholas. This would be shown as both an increase in the cash account and an increase in the equity account. At this stage there are no liabilities against the assets.

The accounting equation would record the impact of the transaction as follows.

$$\text{Assets (A)} = \text{Liabilities (L)} + \text{Equity (E)}$$
$$\uparrow \text{Cash } \$20\,000 = \$0 + \uparrow \text{Capital } \$20\,000$$

Note that the total of the assets always equals the claims on the assets.

ILLUSTRATIVE EXAMPLE 4.2

Analysis of business transactions (asset purchase)

ATC purchases a new iPad for $500 from JB Teck Supplies for cash. The iPad is classified as an item of office equipment for the business. Therefore, this transaction will result in the cash account going down by $500 and the office equipment account going up by $500:

$$\text{Assets (A)} = \text{Liabilities (L)} + \text{Equity (E)}$$
$$\downarrow \text{Cash } \$500$$
$$\uparrow \text{Office equipment } \$500$$

Note that this transaction affects only the asset side; it has no impact on the liability and equity side (the claims against the assets). The effects on the asset side cancel each other out. Note also that transactions can result in changes to accounts on one or both sides of the equation.

The services provided by a tennis coaching entity will be recorded as income in the business's books.

ILLUSTRATIVE EXAMPLE 4.3

Analysis of business transactions (income earned)

ATC sends an invoice to Tennis Queensland for providing tennis coaching services totalling $3000. Tennis Queensland has 30 days' credit. Tennis Queensland will be recorded as an accounts receivable and the services rendered will be shown as income as follows.

$$\text{Assets (A)} = \text{Liabilities (L)} + \text{Equity (E)} + \text{Income (I)} - \text{Expenses (E)}$$

↑ Accounts receivable	↑ Coaching fees
$3000	$3000

Note that the $3000 of income recorded increases profit, thereby increasing equity. Hence, the accounting equation remains in balance.

VALUE TO BUSINESS

- A business transaction is recognised when there has been an exchange of resources between one entity and another person or entity, which must be at arm's length distance.
- Business transactions that involve the exchange of cash for goods or services are known as cash transactions; those where an amount will be paid or received at a later date are classified as credit transactions.
- The concept of duality means that every transaction will affect the accounting equation such that the equation remains in balance. The accounting equation expresses the relationship between the assets controlled and owned by the entity and the claims against those assets.

4.5 The accounting worksheet

LEARNING OBJECTIVE 4.5 Prepare an accounting worksheet and a simplified statement of profit or loss and statement of financial position.

The accounting worksheet summarises the duality associated with all business transactions. All the business transactions of an entity can be entered into the worksheet. This is especially useful when there are a large number of transactions to be analysed. If we kept analysing each transaction using just the accounting equation, it would be quite cumbersome to summarise the impact of all the transactions over a certain period. This could lead to errors that would ultimately affect the financial statements. Once the transactions have been entered into the worksheet, we can total the individual columns of the worksheet and use them as the basis for preparing the financial statements.

The following transactions occurred for ATC during September 2019. The first step in preparing the worksheet is to understand the effect of each business transaction on the accounting worksheet.

Date	Transaction	Effect on accounting equation
2019 September		
1	Nicholas contributed $20 000 cash into the business bank account.	*Increase* cash by $20 000 and *increase* equity by $20 000.
3	The business purchased an iPad for $500 cash from JB Teck Supplies.	*Increase* office equipment by $500 and *decrease* cash by $500. *Note:* We do not record individual asset items. Instead, we record them as a category of assets (in this case, office equipment).
4	The business sent an invoice to Tennis Queensland for services rendered of $3000.	*Increase* accounts receivable (i.e. debtors) by $3000 and *increase* income by $3000. We record the income in a new column called profit or loss, and the income is shown as an increase in profit. The profit or loss column summarises all income and expense transactions. The balance in the profit or loss column will be transferred to equity at the end of the reporting period.
5	The business banked cash received from coaching services of $10 000.	*Increase* cash by $10 000 and *increase* profit or loss to record income of $10 000 for coaching fees.
7	The business paid rent of $1000.	*Decrease* cash by $1000 and *decrease* profit or loss by $1000 to record rent expense.

8	The business negotiated with a contractor (Allan Faff) to perform 80 hours of work over the next two weeks for Indooroopilly Tennis Club.	This event is not a business transaction, as there is no exchange of resources between the business and another entity or individual.
9	The business banked cheques received from DT Tennis for coaching services provided of $5000.	*Increase* cash by $5000 and *increase* profit or loss by $5000 to record income for coaching fees.
10	The business paid salaries to part-time staff (A Rafter and L Pratt) of $2200.	*Decrease* cash by $2200 and *decrease* profit or loss by $2200 to record the salaries expense.
12	The business paid $1800 to Dickson Bros for office furniture.	*Decrease* cash by $1800 and recognise an asset (office furniture) of $1800.
14	The business paid $450 for electricity.	*Decrease* cash by $450 and *decrease* profit or loss by $450 to record the electricity expense.
15	The business invoiced TJB $3800 for coaching services.	*Increase* accounts receivable by $3800 and *increase* profit or loss by $3800 to record the income for coaching fees. The invoice is evidence of a credit transaction, so no cash has exchanged hands.
16	The business paid mobile phone charges of $280.	*Decrease* cash by $280 and *decrease* profit or loss by $280 to record the phone expense.
17	The business paid $2000 to Russell Solutions for website development.	*Decrease* cash by $2000 and *decrease* profit or loss by $2000. The website development is a business expense and could be categorised as a marketing expense.
19	Nicholas purchased a digital camera for home use for $300 from Dr Cameras using his personal credit card.	This event is a personal transaction, not a business transaction. According to the entity concept, only business transactions should be recorded in the books of the business.
20	The business bought an office desk on credit from Offices R Us for $1400.	*Increase* office furniture by $1400 and *increase* accounts payable by $1400.
21	The business banked $500 for coaching services provided to Ironside Primary School.	*Increase* cash by $500 and *increase* profit or loss by $500 to record coaching income.
25	The business bought a new computer server for $6000 from JB Teck Supplies for cash.	*Increase* office equipment by $6000 and *decrease* cash by $6000.
28	The business took out a bank loan to purchase equipment with Welcome Bank for $50 000, to be repaid in five years.	*Increase* cash by $50 000 and *increase* loan account by $50 000.

Once we understand the effect of each transaction on the accounting equation, we can enter the transactions into the accounting worksheet. Illustrative example 4.4 contains a worksheet with all the transactions of ATC for September 2019. It is designed around the columns that represent the types of account affected by each transaction. Typical columns included in a worksheet are cash, accounts receivable, equipment, motor vehicle, accounts payable, loan and capital. The column headings will change depending on the nature of the business entity. Two worksheet accounts will be affected for each transaction. Consider the transaction on 1 September 2019 as an example; the two accounts affected are the business cash account and the capital account. The $20 000 is recorded in the cash column, with a corresponding entry of $20 000 in the capital column. Both these amounts are recorded as positives because they increase the accounts. When the business makes a payment out of the cash account, as done in the transaction on 14 September, the balances of both the cash account and the profit or loss account are decreased. After each transaction, the worksheet should remain balanced.

These two examples affect both sides of the accounting equation. However, certain transactions will result in entries to only one side of the equation. Consider the transaction on 3 September, when the business purchases an iPad for cash. This transaction results in changes to two asset accounts, with the cash account decreasing and the office equipment account increasing. There is no overall change to the asset side of the worksheet resulting from this transaction, and no entries are made on the liability and equity side.

Worksheet for Advantage Tennis Coaching

2019 September	Cash	Accounts receivable	Office furniture	Office equipment	Accounts payable	Loan	Capital	Profit or loss
1	20 000						20 000	
3	(500)			500				
4		3 000						3 000
5	10 000							10 000
7	(1 000)							(1 000)
8	No transaction							
9	5 000							5 000
10	(2 200)							(2 200)
12	(1 800)		1 800					
14	(450)							(450)
15		3 800						3 800
16	(280)							(280)
17	(2 000)							(2 000)
19	No transaction							
20			1 400		1 400			
21	500							500
25	(6 000)			6 000				
28	50 000					50 000		
Total	71 270	6 800	3 200	6 500	1 400	50 000	20 000	16 370

Once all the transactions have been entered into the worksheet, each of the columns should be summed, and the total of the asset columns should be the same as the total of the liability and equity totals. In illustrative example 4.4, the assets total $87 770 and the liabilities and equity total $87 770. We can now prepare the statement of profit or loss and statement of financial position from this summarised information, based on the column totals at the bottom of the worksheet (see illustrative example 4.5).

Statement of profit or loss and statement of financial position for Advantage Tennis Coaching

ADVANTAGE TENNIS COACHING Statement of profit or loss for one month ending 30 September 2019		
Income		
Coaching fees		$22 300
Expenses		
Website development	$2 000	
Wages	2 200	
Telephone	280	
Rent	1 000	
Electricity	450	5 930
Profit		**$16 370**

ADVANTAGE TENNIS COACHING		
Statement of financial position		
as at 30 September 2019		
ASSETS		
Current assets		
Cash	$71270	
Accounts receivable	6800	$78070
Non-current assets		
Office furniture	3200	
Office equipment	6500	9700
Total assets		87770
LIABILITIES		
Current liabilities		
Accounts payable		1400
Non-current liabilities		
Loan		50000
Total liabilities		51400
Net assets		**$36370**
OWNER'S EQUITY		
Capital — N Cash		$20000
Profit		16370
Total equity		**$36370**

4.6 Capturing accounting information: journals and ledger accounts

LEARNING OBJECTIVE 4.6 Discuss how journals and ledger accounts can help in capturing accounting information efficiently and effectively.

Earlier in the chapter we discussed the concept of duality and how every transaction has a dual effect. Analysing each transaction by using the accounting equation is not appropriate for a large number of transactions. Instead, we can use the journal or ledger.

The journal

A **journal** is a book that records each business transaction shown on the source documents in chronological order. The journal entry will consist of the transaction date, the names of the two accounts affected by the transaction and whether each account is debited or credited. Transactions that occur frequently can be recorded in separate journals. For example, a business that deals mainly in cash will have a cash receipts journal and a cash payments journal. A business dealing with credit will also have a credit sales journal and a credit purchases journal.

Let us now use the journal to record the first transaction for ATC for the month of September 2019 (see illustrative example 4.6).

ILLUSTRATIVE EXAMPLE 4.6

Journal entry for Advantage Tennis Coaching

The transaction recorded in the journal below represents a contribution of $20000 cash by the owner (N Cash) on 1 September 2019. Cash is debited because the debit represents an increase in cash, and capital is credited because this represents an increase in equity.

Date	Name of account	Dr	Cr
1/9/19	Cash	$20000	
	Capital — N Cash		$20000

The ledger

A **ledger** is an account that accumulates all the information about changes in specific account balances. It can be used in place of a journal, or it can be used to record the summarised information from a journal. For example, if you use special journals to record similar transactions such as cash receipts or cash payments, then you will post the totals from these journals to the ledger account. There will be a separate ledger account for each item affected by the transaction, and each account will have a debit side and a credit side. The debit side is the left side and the credit side is the right side of the ledger account. The advantage of recording in a ledger rather than in a journal is that it allows us to summarise all the transactions affecting that ledger account (e.g. all the sales for a month).

Chart of accounts

A **chart of accounts** is a listing of the ledger account titles and their related numbers and/or alpha numbers, and is maintained in either or both a manual and ar computerised system like MYOB or QuickBooks. A chart of accounts assists in locating ledger accounts efficiently and identifies whether the entity is a sole trader, partnership or company. A chart of accounts should be flexible enough to cater for expansion of accounts as the business grows. As you can see in ATC's chart of accounts in figure 4.1, not every number has been assigned, which will allow for the insertion of new accounts in the future.

| FIGURE 4.1 | Example of chart of accounts for Advantage Tennis Coaching |

ADVANTAGE TENNIS COACHING Chart of accounts	
Assets (100–199)	
Cash at bank	100
Accounts receivable	110
Office furniture	120
Office equipment	130
Liabilities (200–299)	
Accounts payable	200
Loan	210
Equity (300–399)	
Capital — N Cash	300
Drawings — N Cash	310
Income (400–499)	
Coaching fees	400
Expenses (500–599)	
Wages	500
Website development	510
Telephone	520
Rent	530
Electricity	540

Let us now use the ledger to record the original capital contribution made by N Cash (see illustrative example 4.7). Note the number reference in the right-hand corner of the T account.

ILLUSTRATIVE EXAMPLE 4.7

Ledger entry for Advantage Tennis Coaching

Cash at bank				100
1/9	Capital — N Cash	20 000		
			Capital — N Cash	300
			1/9 Cash at bank	20 000

This transaction shows the capital contribution by the owner, N Cash, of $20 000 cash. It is recorded by a debit to the cash account (an asset account) and a credit to the capital account (an equity account).

4.7 Rules of debit and credit

LEARNING OBJECTIVE 4.7 Apply debit and credit rules, and record simple transactions in the journals and ledgers of a business.

The debit and credit rules that we have applied are summarised in table 4.1. Remember that debits and credits are opposites of each other so, whichever rule is applied to one, the opposite rule must be applied to the other.

TABLE 4.1	Debit and credit rules	
	Increase	**Decrease**
Debit	• Assets • Expenses	• Liabilities • Equity • Income
Credit	• Liabilities • Equity • Income	• Assets • Expenses

Let us now look at ATC's business transactions from 3 to 7 September as further examples of double-entry accounting using journal entries.

3/9 ATC purchased $500 office equipment and paid cash.

Date	Name of account	Dr	Cr
3/9	Office equipment	500	
	Cash		500

4/9 The business sent an invoice for services rendered for $3000.

Date	Name of account	Dr	Cr
4/9	Accounts receivable	3 000	
	Service fees		3 000

5/9 The business received $10 000 from coaching services.

Date	Name of account	Dr	Cr
5/9	Cash	10 000	
	Services fees		10 000

7/9 The business paid rent of $1000 for September.

Date	Name of account	Dr	Cr
7/9	Rent expense	1 000	
	Cash		1 000

When recording the transaction in the ledger, the description identifies the corresponding ledger entry. Instead of using journals, we could record these transactions in the ledger account.

		Cash			100
1/9	Capital — N Cash	20 000	3/9	Office equipment	500
5/9	Coaching fees	10 000	7/9	Rent	1 000
			30/9	Balance c/d	28 500
		30 000			30 000
1/10	Balance b/d	28 500			

Accounts receivable					110
4/9	Coaching fees	3 000			

Office equipment					130
3/9	Cash	500			

Capital — N Cash					300
			1/9	Cash	20 000

Coaching fees					400
			4/9	Accounts receivable	3 000
			5/9	Cash	10 000
					13 000

Rent expense					530
7/9	Cash	1000			

Examine the cash ledger account. It has been balanced at the end of the period by subtracting the side with the smallest balance from the side with the highest balance. The resulting amount is a cash balance of $28 500 on 30 September. This amount is c/d (carried down) to the start of the next period. On 1 October, the balance has been b/d (brought down) and this provides the opening balance for the new period.

Note that similar rules apply to the debits and credits as to the accounting equation: there will be dual effects for every transaction. For debits and credits, each transaction will have at least one debit and at least one credit. For example, for the transaction on 3 September it would be incorrect to record this by debiting office equipment and debiting cash. First, we have not recorded both a debit and a credit. Second, according to the debit and credit rules a debit to cash will increase the asset cash account, and that is not what we want to do — we want to decrease the cash account! This is achieved by crediting the account.

4.8 The trial balance

LEARNING OBJECTIVE 4.8 Explain the purpose of a trial balance.

The **trial balance** is a list of ledger account balances that is prepared at the end of the period. It is prepared to assist in the preparation of the financial statements and to check the accuracy of the ledger or journal entries. However, the trial balance will not detect all recording errors. Any errors that are made to both accounts affected by the transaction will not be detected by the trial balance. For example, if rent paid of $1000 is incorrectly recorded as $10 000 in both the rent and cash accounts, both sides of the trial balance will still be equal. Care must be taken to double-check that the correct accounts are being recorded for each transaction.

The trial balance has two columns: a debit column and a credit column. Illustrative example 4.8 shows the trial balance for ATC after recording all transactions to 7 September.

ILLUSTRATIVE EXAMPLE 4.8

Trial balance for Advantage Tennis Coaching

ADVANTAGE TENNIS COACHING Trial balance as at 7 September 2019		
Name of account	Dr	Cr
Cash	$28 500	
Accounts receivable	3 000	
Office equipment	500	
Capital — N Cash		$20 000
Coaching fees		13 000
Rent expense	1 000	
Total	**$33 000**	**$33 000**

The totals of the debit side and the credit side are shown at the bottom of the trial balance. Both sides are equal at $33 000. If the trial balance did not balance, we would then need to retrace the transactions to identify whether we have followed the double-entry rules and not made any errors as discussed later in the chapter (such as transposition errors or single-entry errors).

VALUE TO BUSINESS

- The accounting worksheet summarises the duality associated with all business transactions. The column totals can be used to prepare the statement of profit or loss and the statement of financial position.
- If the two sides of the worksheet do not balance, we should check carefully for errors in recording.
- The accounting equation can be used to solve for missing amounts.
- A journal is a book that records each business transaction shown on the source documents in chronological order.
- A ledger can be used in place of a journal, or it can be used to record the summarised information from a journal. There will be a separate ledger account for each item affected by the transaction, and each account will have a debit side and a credit side.
- The trial balance is a list of ledger account balances that is prepared at the end of the period. It is prepared to assist in the preparation of the financial statements and to check the accuracy of the ledger or journal entries.

4.9 Accounting errors

LEARNING OBJECTIVE 4.9 Detect errors in transaction analysis and investigate the origin of the errors.

Sometimes the asset side of the accounting equation might not balance with the claims side (the liabilities and equity) of the accounting equation. This could be evident through the preparation of a worksheet, trial balance or statement of financial position, and it could occur for a number of reasons. The main technique for rectifying the situation is to double-check every transaction entered and ensure the duality rules have been followed. The most common errors are single-entry errors, transposition errors and incorrect entry.

Single-entry error

The concept of duality must be applied to every transaction. If only one effect of the business transaction is entered, this will cause the two sides of the accounting equation to be out of balance. A **single-entry error** arises when only one part of a transaction is entered. For example, if a payment of wages of $2000 were recorded only as a decrease in bank, it would cause the asset side to be lower than the claims side. The correct dual entry would be to:
1. decrease cash $2000
2. decrease profit or loss $2000 (to record the expense of wages).

Transposition error

A **transposition error** occurs when two of the digits recorded in the transaction are transposed (switched). Imagine that office equipment of $8700 is purchased for cash and $8700 is shown as a decrease to the cash account but $7800 is mistakenly shown as an increase to the office equipment account. As we can see, the last two digits have been transposed. This can be identified as a transposition error because the difference of $900 is divisible by 9.

Here are some further examples.
- A business bought stationery for $541 and recorded it as a decrease of $514 to cash and a decrease of $541 to profit or loss. The difference is divisible by 9.
- The business banked takings of $3230 and recorded the takings as $3320 income. The difference is 90 and this amount is divisible by 9.

Incorrect entry

Another common error is to incorrectly record a business transaction as two increases (or decreases) to one side of the equation, or an increase on one side and a decrease on the other. All of these situations will also cause the equation (and therefore the worksheet) to be out of balance. Here are some examples.

- An entity records advertising expense of $3000 as a decrease to cash and an increase to profit or loss of $3000. This error will cause the claims side to be $6000 greater than the assets side.
- The entity purchases office equipment for $8000 cash and records the transaction as a decrease to cash of $8000 and a decrease to office equipment. This will result in the asset side being $16 000 less than the claims side.
- The owner withdraws cash of $3500 and records the transaction as an increase in cash of $3500 and a decrease in equity. The correct entry would be to decrease cash and decrease equity. The result of this error is that the asset side will be $7000 higher than the claims side.

Using the accounting equation to solve for missing figures

The accounting equation can also help us solve for missing figures. Remember that the assets side must equal the claims side in all situations. Here are some examples using the accounting equation to solve for missing figures.

1. A business has assets of $200 000 and liabilities of $40 000, but we do not know the amount of equity. Let us use the accounting equation to determine the missing item:

$$A = L + E$$
$$\$200\,000 = \$40\,000 + \,?$$
$$E = \$160\,000$$

2. A business has liabilities of $104 000 and equity of $182 000. What are the total assets?

$$A = L + E$$
$$= \$104\,000 + \$182\,000$$
$$= \$286\,000$$

3. The accounting equation can be used when we know the current assets but not the non-current assets. A business has current assets of $34 000, current liabilities of $8000, non-current liabilities of $80 000 and equity of $160 000. What is the amount of non-current assets?

$$A = L + E$$
$$\$34\,000 + \,? = \$8000 + \$80\,000 + \$160\,000$$
$$\$34\,000 + \,? = \$248\,000$$
$$? = \$214\,000$$

Therefore, the non-current assets are $214 000.

4. We can also use this equation to find missing figures for either income or expenses. The business has capital of $200 000, liabilities of $160 000, income of $180 000 and total assets of $500 000. What are the expenses for the period?

$$A = L + E$$
$$\$500\,000 = \$160\,000 + \$200\,000 + \$180\,000 + \,?$$
$$? = -\$40\,000$$

Therefore, the expenses for the period are $40 000. Recall that expenses reduce profit and therefore reduce equity.

SUMMARY OF LEARNING OBJECTIVES

4.1 Describe the characteristics of business transactions.

A business transaction involves the exchange of resources between an entity and another entity or individual, and must be at arm's length distance.

4.2 Differentiate between a business transaction, a personal transaction and a business event.

For a business transaction to be recognised, there must be an exchange of resources between an entity and another entity or individual (e.g. the purchase of office equipment for cash). Personal transactions do not involve an exchange of goods between the entity and another party. Similarly, no exchange of resources takes place when a business event occurs, such as when the contract of a new employee is being negotiated or when the entity is being advised that a loan interest rate will increase from 1 July in the current year. These two events will become business transactions at some later stage when the exchange of resources takes place.

4.3 Explain the accounting equation process of the double-entry system of recording.

The accounting equation expresses the relationship between the assets controlled and owned by the entity, and the claims on those assets — whether this is by outside funds (known as liabilities) or through inside funds (known as the equity of the business). The expanded accounting equation includes the profit or loss of the entity, which is represented by the entity's income less expenses.

4.4 Identify the impact of business transactions on the accounting equation.

Every business transaction will have a dual effect. As a result, the accounting equation remains in balance after each business transaction is recorded in the journals or ledgers of the entity. For the contribution of capital, the dual effect would be an increase in the cash account and an increase in the capital account. In the accounting equation, this would be illustrated by assets increasing and equity increasing, that is:

$$\uparrow \text{Cash (assets)} = \uparrow \text{Capital (equity)}$$

4.5 Prepare an accounting worksheet and a simplified statement of profit or loss and statement of financial position.

The accounting worksheet summarises the duality associated with each of the business transactions. The column totals provide the basis for the preparation of the financial statements. The information in the profit or loss column will be used to prepare the statement of profit or loss, and the profit or loss will be transferred to the equity section of the statement of financial position at the end of the reporting period. The information in the asset, liability and equity columns will form the basis of the statement of financial position.

4.6 Discuss how journals and ledger accounts can help in capturing accounting information efficiently and effectively.

Accounting information can be captured efficiently and effectively through the use of journals and ledger accounts. Frequent transactions such as cash receipts and cash payments are recorded in separate journals. Ledger accounts can be used in place of a journal, or to record the summarised information from the journal. Both journals and ledger accounts summarise and classify the information, thereby enabling the financial statements to be more easily prepared.

4.7 Apply debit and credit rules, and record simple transactions in the journals and ledgers of a business.

A debit entry is used to increase assets and expenses, and to decrease liabilities, equity and revenue. A credit entry is used to increase liabilities, equity and income, and to decrease assets and expenses. Each journal or ledger entry will consist of a debit entry and a credit entry to at least two separate accounts.

4.8 Explain the purpose of a trial balance.

A trial balance assists in the preparation of the financial statements and checks the accuracy of the ledger or journal entries. If the trial balance does not balance, then the preparer needs to retrace the transactions to ensure that the double-entry rules were correctly followed and the correct amounts were entered.

4.9 Detect errors in transaction analysis and investigate the origin of the errors.

The common recording errors are transposition errors, single-entry errors and incorrect entry. Transposition errors are easily identified if the difference between the total assets and total claims on those assets (liabilities plus equity) is divisible by 9.

KEY TERMS

accounting equation Expresses the relationship between assets controlled by an entity and the claims on those assets.

arm's length distance Parties deal from equal bargaining positions, neither party is subject to the other's control or dominant influence and the transaction is treated with fairness, integrity and legality.

assets Present economic resources controlled by an entity as a result of past events and from which future economic benefits are expected to flow to the entity.

business events Events that will probably affect an entity without any immediate exchange of goods and services between the entity and another entity.

business transactions Occurrences that affect the assets, liabilities and equity items of an entity and must be recognised (recorded).

cash transactions Business transactions involving the exchange of cash for goods or services.

chart of accounts Detailed listing/index that guides how transactions will be classified in the financial reporting system.

credit transactions Business transactions involving an exchange of goods and services on the proviso that cash will be received at a later date.

drawings Withdrawals of assets from an entity by the owner(s) that are recorded as decreases in equity.

duality Describes how every business transaction has at least two effects on the accounting equation.

entity concept Separation of business transactions from any personal transactions of the owner(s).

equity Residual interest in the assets of an entity after all its liabilities have been deducted.

expenses Decreases in economic benefits during the accounting period in the form of outflows or depletions of assets or incurrences of liabilities that result in decreases in equity, other than those relating to distributions to equity participants.

income Increases in economic benefits during an accounting period in the form of inflows, increases in assets or decreases in liabilities that result in increases in equity, other than those relating to contributions from equity participants.

journal Accounting record in which transactions are initially recorded in chronological order.

ledger Account that accumulates all of the information about changes in specific account balances.

liabilities Present obligations of an entity arising from past events, the settlement of which is expected to result in an outflow from the entity of resources embodying economic benefits.

personal transactions Transactions of the owner unrelated to the operations of a business.

single-entry error Error created by entering only one part of a transaction.

source documents Original documents verifying a business transaction.

statement of financial position A statement that reports on the assets, liabilities and equity of an entity at a particular point in time.

statement of profit or loss Statement that reports on the income and expenses of an entity for a period and the resulting profit or loss.

transposition error Error created by transposing (or switching) digits when recording transactions.

trial balance List of ledger account balances prepared at the end of the period.

APPLY YOUR KNOWLEDGE   *50 marks*

PART A

(a) Discuss the difference in the role of the journal and the ledger in capturing accounting information efficiently and effectively.   *4 marks*

(b) Outline the entity concept and how it impacts on the recording of personal and business transactions.
                                   3 marks

(c) Identify the type of errors that could be discovered by preparing a trial balance and provide examples of each.   *4 marks*

(d) Provide examples of two transactions and examine the application of the debit and credit rule. *4 marks*

PART B

The following business transactions relate to Colin Clark (financial planner) for his first month of business operations in August 2020.

2020		
August	1	Commenced business operations with a $300 000 cash injection of personal funds.
	2	Paid monthly rent $1500.
	4	Purchased office stationery $2000 on credit from Stationery Plus.
	7	Purchased office equipment on credit from Supplies Inc. $10 000.
	9	Sent invoice to client M Birt for services $3000.
	11	Purchased MYOB software for laptop computer $700 cash.
	13	M Birt paid amount outstanding.
	14	Met with prospective client and negotiated provision of financial advice for client and family, quoting $5000.
	17	Paid car parking permit $220.
	19	Withdrew cash from business of $2000 for personal use.
	22	Paid WWW Ltd for monthly internet use $182.
	29	Received interest from business bank account $15.

(a) State the impact on the accounting equation for each transaction above. For example:

1 Aug   ↑ Cash $300 000   ↑ Capital $300 000

(b) Prepare a worksheet for the month of August 2020 from the above information.   *15 marks*

PART C

(a) Using the business transactions in part B, record the transactions in the ledger of Colin Clark. *7 marks*
(b) Prepare a trial balance for Colin Clark as at 31 August 2020.   *5 marks*
(c) Prepare a statement of profit or loss for the month ending 31 August 2020.   *4 marks*
(d) Prepare a statement of financial position as at 31 August 2020.   *4 marks*

SELF-EVALUATION ACTIVITIES

4.1 Prepare an accounting worksheet to demonstrate the duality of each business transaction shown for Acacia Financials. Using the profit or loss column, identify the profit or loss for the month of October 2019.

2019		
October	1	Contributed $50 000 into the business bank account.
	2	Purchased desk and chair for office $6000 from Office Plus and paid cash.
	4	Paid for office stationery $560 from Suppliers Inc. Received $1960 for provision of investment services.
	8	Paid mobile phone bill $356.
	9	Received $1280 from a customer for investment services.
	10	Paid energy bill $404. Owner purchased for partner a new Tiffany ring with personal funds of $12 200.
	11	Purchased a computer and printer on credit from JB Technologies $5000.
	12	Paid advertising in local paper $600.
	13	Invoiced a client for investment advice $2800.
	14	Paid wages to a casual member of staff $1300.

SOLUTION TO 4.1

2019 October	Cash	Accounts receivable	Office furniture	Office equipment	Accounts payable	Equity	Profit or loss
1	50 000					50 000	
2	(6 000)		6 000				
4	(560)						(560)
4	1 960						1 960
8	(356)						(356)
9	1 280						1 280
10	(404)						(404)
10	No transaction						
11				5 000	5 000		
12	(600)						(600)
13		2 800					2 800
14	(1 300)						(1 300)
Balance	**44 020**	**2 800**	**6 000**	**5 000**	**5 000**	**50 000**	**2 820**

Note: From the above worksheet, the profit for the month of October 2019 is $2820. The profit is added to equity when preparing the statement of financial position.

4.2 From the following financial information on the business of Brampton Professional Services (owner — D Burton), prepare a worksheet and extract a statement of profit or loss for the period ending 31 December 2019 and a statement of financial position as at 31 December 2019.

2019	
December 5	Owner, D Burton, contributed $200 000 into the entity.
8	Purchased office furniture for cash $460.
9	Received from J Beaumont $1340 for services.
10	Paid electricity account $130.
11	Paid rent on building $2400.
12	New neon sign purchased for entity on credit for $1750.
14	Collected cash fees from clients $1600.
15	Paid wages to office executive assistant $790.
16	D Burton injected another $10 000 into the entity.
17	Sent invoice to a client for services provided $1800.
19	Received full payment on invoice of 17 December.
21	Received an invoice from CBD electronics for new office computer $1356.

SOLUTION TO 4.2

2019 December	Cash	Accounts receivable	Office furniture	Equipment	Accounts payable	Equity	Profit or loss
5	200 000					200 000	
8	(460)		460				
9	1 340						1 340
10	(130)						(130)
11	(2 400)						(2 400)
12				1 750	1 750		
14	1 600						1 600
15	(790)						(790)
16	10 000					10 000	
17		1 800					1 800
19	1 800	(1 800)					
21				1 356	1 356		
Balance	**210 960**	**0**	**460**	**3 106**	**3 106**	**210 000**	**1 420**

BRAMPTON PROFESSIONAL SERVICES		
Statement of profit or loss		
for period ending 31 December 2019		
Income		
Fees revenue		$4 740
Expenses		
Electricity	$ 130	
Wages	790	
Rent	2 400	3 320
Profit		**$1 420**

BRAMPTON PROFESSIONAL SERVICES		
Statement of financial position		
as at 31 December 2019		
ASSETS		
Current assets		
Cash		$210 960
Non-current assets		
Equipment	$3 106	
Office furniture	460	3 566
Total assets		214 226
LIABILITIES		
Current liabilities		
Accounts payable		3 106
Total liabilities		3 106
Net assets		**$211 420**
EQUITY		
Capital — D Burton		$210 000
Profit		1 420
Total equity		**$211 420**

4.3 Nicholas Cash, owner of Advantage Tennis Coaching (ATC), commenced business in September 2019. Refer to illustrative examples 4.1, 4.4, 4.5, 4.6 and 4.7 for background information relating to the operations of the business and transactions in the first month of trading, September 2019. The following transactions occurred in October 2019.

2019		
October	2	Received payment from Tennis Queensland for ATC invoice dated 4 September for $3000.
	7	Paid this month's rent $1000.
	10	The business banked $5600 cash from coaching fees.
	12	Nicholas withdrew $1500 for personal use.
	18	Paid invoice for $1400 received from Offices R Us for an office desk purchased last month.
	22	Paid A Faff $4500 for performing coaching services at Indooroopilly Tennis Club.
	25	Invoiced Indooroopilly Tennis Club $6900 for coaching services.
	26	Banked cash $12 000 from coaching fees.
	27	Received $3800 from TJB for services invoiced last month.
	28	Paid casual coaching wages $2500.
	30	Purchased coaching equipment for $48 800.

Required

(a) Prepare journal entries for the October transactions for ATC.

(b) Post journal entries to the general ledger accounts.

(c) Prepare a trial balance for ATC as at 31 October 2019. The trial balance will include transactions from September 2019.

SOLUTION TO 4.3

(a) Journal entries

Date	Name of account	Dr	Cr
2/10	Cash	3 000	
	Accounts receivable — Tennis Queensland		3 000
7/10	Rent expense	1 000	
	Cash		1 000
10/10	Cash	5 600	
	Coaching fees		5 600
12/10	Drawings — N Cash	1 500	
	Cash		1 500
16/10	Stationery expense	600	
	Cash		600
18/10	Accounts payable	1 400	
	Cash		1 400
22/10	Wages expense	4 500	
	Cash		4 500
25/10	Accounts receivable	6 900	
	Coaching fees		6 900
26/10	Cash	12 000	
	Coaching fees		12 000
27/10	Cash	3 800	
	Accounts receivable — TJB		3 800
30/10	Wages expense	2 500	
	Cash		2 500
30/10	Coaching equipment	48 800	
	Cash		48 800

(b) General ledger

Cash   **100**

1/10	Balance b/d	71 270	7/10	Rent	1 000
2/10	Accounts receivable	3 000	12/10	Drawings	1 500
10/10	Coaching fees	5 600	18/10	Accounts payable	1 400
26/10	Coaching fees	12 000	22/10	Wages expense	4 500
27/10	Accounts receivable	3 800	30/10	Wages expense	2 500
			30/10	Coaching equipment	48 800
			30/10	Balance c/d	35 970
		95 670			95 670
1/11	Balance b/d	35 970			

Accounts receivable   **110**

1/10	Balance b/d	6 800	2/10	Cash	3 000
25/10	Coaching fees	6 900	27/10	Cash	3 800
			31/10	Balance c/d	6 900
		13 700			13 700
1/11	Balance b/d	6 900			

Office furniture   **120**

1/10	Balance b/d	3 200			

Office equipment   **130**

1/10	Balance b/d	6 500			

Coaching equipment					140
30/10	Cash	48 800			

Accounts payable					200
18/10	Cash	1 400	1/10	Balance b/d	1 400

Loan					210
			1/10	Balance b/d	50 000

Capital — N Cash					300
			1/10	Balance b/d	20 000

Drawings — N Cash					310
12/10	Cash	1 500			

Coaching fees					400
			1/10	Balance b/d	22 300
			10/10	Cash	5 600
			25/10	Accounts receivable	6 900
			26/10	Cash	12 000
			1/11	Balance c/d	46 800

Wages expense					500
1/10	Balance b/d	2 200			
22/10	Cash	4 500			
30/10	Cash	2 500			
31/10	Balance c/d	9 200			

Website development					510
1/10	Balance b/d	2 000			

Telephone expense					520
1/10	Balance b/d	280			

Rent expense					530
1/10	Balance b/d	1 000			
7/10	Cash	1 000			
31/10	Balance c/d	2 000			

Electricity expense					540
1/10	Balance b/d	450			

(c) Trial balance

ADVANTAGE TENNIS COACHING Trial balance as at 31 October 2019		
Name of account	Dr	Cr
Cash	$ 35 970	
Accounts receivable	6 900	
Office furniture	3 200	
Office equipment	6 500	
Coaching equipment	48 800	
Loan payable		$ 50 000
Capital — N Cash		20 000
Drawings — N Cash	1 500	
Coaching fees		46 800
Website development	2 000	
Wages expense	9 200	
Telephone expense	280	
Rent expense	2 000	
Electricity expense	450	
Total	**$116 800**	**$116 800**

COMPREHENSION QUESTIONS

4.4 Explain what a transposition error is and identify how you can detect that one has occurred.　**LO9**

4.5 Distinguish between personal transactions and business transactions. Illustrate with five examples of each.　**LO1, 2**

4.6 Explain what is meant by an 'arm's length business transaction' when a business buys accounting software on credit.　**LO1, 2**

4.7 What is the purpose of a statement of profit or loss for an entity? List typical items that you would see in the statement of profit or loss for a computer service technician.　**LO5**

4.8 Describe how an accounting worksheet assists in the preparation of the statement of profit or loss and the statement of financial position.　**LO5**

4.9 What is meant by the concept of duality? Provide an illustration involving a business transaction where the business purchases furniture or a motor vehicle on credit.　**LO1, 2**

4.10 Both the journal and the ledger can be used to record a large number of transactions. Differentiate between financial recordkeeping in the journal and the ledger.　**LO6**

4.11 Discuss the purpose of a double-entry bookkeeping system.　**LO6**

4.12 Summarise the procedures you would undertake if an accounting worksheet does not balance.　**LO5, 9**

4.13 Illustrate three scenarios of incorrect recordings that may cause a trial balance to not balance.　**LO9**

4.14 Can errors still exist in the trial balance if the sum of the debit and credit columns equals the same amount? If so, provide an example.　**LO9**

EXERCISES

★ BASIC I ★ ★ 　MODERATE I ★ ★ ★ 　CHALLENGING

4.15 ★　　　　　　　　　　　　　　　　　　　　　　　　　　　　　**LO8, 9**

You are the bookkeeper for Chic Styles and, on review of the business's records and reports, you realise the trial balance does not balance. Your supervisor asks you to investigate why this occurred. Explain with examples what type of errors would have caused the trial balance not to balance.

4.16 ★　　　　　　　　　　　　　　　　　　　　　　　　　　　　　　**LO4**

Classify each of the following according to whether it is an asset, liability or equity account. Apply your learning from the definitions in the introduction to accounting and business decision making chapter to provide a justification for each classification.

(a) Trade receivables
(b) Intangible assets
(c) Borrowings
(d) Retained earnings
(e) Contributed equity
(f) Current tax liabilities
(g) Deferred revenue
(h) Inventory
(i) Plant and equipment
(j) Trade payables
(k) Cash and cash equivalents
(l) Prepayments

4.17 ★　　　　　　　　　　　　　　　　　　　　　　　　　　　　　　**LO4**

Using your knowledge of the accounting equation, solve the missing values in the following table.

Assets	=	Liabilities	+	Equity
$200 000	=	$58 000	+	a.
b.	=	66 000	+	$120 000
250 000	=	c.	+	38 000
22 400	=	11 600	+	d.

4.18 ★ ★   **LO4**

Determine the missing entries.

Current assets	Non-current assets	Current liabilities	Non-current liabilities	Capital	Income	Expense
$ 5 000	$ 9 000	$6 000	$ 1 400	$3 000	a.	$ 5 000
7 000	5 000	2 000	3 000	2 000	$26 000	b.
21 000	61 000	9 000	12 000	c.	60 100	41 000

4.19 ★ ★   **LO4**

From the following descriptions of business transactions, choose two appropriate column headings for the worksheet. Justify for each description your choice of heading.
(a) The owner contributes capital to the business.
(b) The business purchases cabinets and shelving for the business on credit from a furniture supplier.
(c) The business purchases computers, printers and a digital camera for business use.
(d) The owner withdraws cash for personal use.
(e) The business provides services on credit.

4.20 ★ ★   **LO4**

State the effect of each of the following business transactions for Trevor's Trampolines. For example, in (a) we increase cash and increase capital.
(a) P Trevor commenced business by injecting cash into her business.
(b) Paid wages.
(c) Purchased goods for sale on credit.
(d) Sold goods on credit.
(e) Received an invoice for annual insurance on building and paid the account.
(f) P Trevor withdrew an iPad from the business.
(g) Sold inventory for cash.
(h) M Kramer (accounts receivable) paid amount outstanding.
(i) Trevor's Trampolines paid accounts payable in full.

4.21 ★ ★   **LO4**

Complete the following table. (*Note:* Each row should be treated independently.)

Current assets	+	Non-current assets	=	Current liabilities	+	Non-current liabilities	+	Capital	Profit/ loss
$ 200	+	a.	=	$ 1 700	+	$ 1 100	+	$4 000	$ 700
6 400	+	$19 700	=	50	+	400	+	b.	750
15 100	+	8 400	=	3 900	+	2 200	+	11 100	c.
d.	+	5 700	=	10 700	+	17 900	+	3 500	5 300

4.22 ★ ★   **LO5, 9**

Cash sales of $2079 have caused the worksheet to be out of balance because a mistake was made when the figures were put into the worksheet. The bookkeeper accidentally increased the cash account by $2097 and increased the profit or loss account in the worksheet by $2079. This is often referred to as a transposition error. Discuss how this type of error can be quickly identified and corrected.

4.23 ★ ★   **LO3, 4**

Choose two appropriate account names for each of the following business transactions. State whether you would debit or credit each of the accounts.
(a) D Dango commenced business DD by contributing cash.
(b) Cash sales by DD to customer.
(c) Paid business registration fees.
(d) Paid wages to part-time employee.
(e) Made cash purchases of inventory.
(f) Sold goods on credit to customer.
(g) Borrowed money from Metro Bank.

(h) Purchased office chair for cash from Flare Office Furniture.

(i) Received interest from Metro Bank.

PROBLEMS

★ BASIC I ★ ★ MODERATE I ★ ★ ★ CHALLENGING

4.24 Understanding business transactions ★ LO3, 4

For each of the following transaction outcomes, describe an example of a transaction that would result in that outcome.

(a) Both asset and equity accounts decreased.

(b) Both asset and equity accounts increased.

(c) Liability account increased and equity account decreased.

(d) One asset account increased and another asset account decreased.

(e) One asset account increased, another asset account decreased and a liability account increased.

4.25 Understanding business transactions ★ LO3, 4

For each of the following independent scenarios, explain why each transaction is or is not a business transaction.

(a) Maggie, a sole trader, meets with her bank and negotiates a loan to provide additional finance to her business.

(b) Maggie, a sole trader, purchases inventory for her store using EFTPOS.

(c) Mulvey Ltd signs an employment contract for a new director two months before they actually start work.

(d) Smith & Co receives an invoice for internet expense.

(e) Smith & Co pays the internet expense outstanding.

(f) A partner from Dixon Associates withdraws a computer from the business for home use.

(g) Maggie, a sole trader, has lunch with a potential client and discusses a discount incentive scheme for future business between the two parties.

(h) The partner from Dixon Associates uses personal funds for a new home theatre system.

4.26 Preparing a worksheet and calculating profit or loss ★ LO4, 5

Enter the following transactions for the month of March 2020 in a worksheet and calculate the profit or loss for the period. Explain how the worksheet assists in the calculation of profit or loss.

2020		
March	3	Injected capital to commence business $250 000.
	4	Purchased office stationery $1600.
	7	Received cash fees $2400.
	8	Took out a loan from Taylor Bank $30 000.
	8	Paid rent for March $1800.
	10	Purchased office suite of furniture on credit $8000.
	12	Invoiced a customer for services $2200.
	17	Paid wages to executive assistant $1250.
	27	Invoiced a customer for services $2200.

4.27 Preparing a worksheet ★ ★ LO4, 5

The closing statement of financial position items are given below for Jason Woodstock in accounting equation form as at 30 June 2021. Transactions for the following month of July are also given.

	Assets		=	Liabilities	+	Equity
Cash at bank	+	Accounts receivable	=	Accounts payable	+	Capital
$39 400	+	$2 800	=	$1 200	+	$41 000

2021		
July	2	Received $2800 from accounts receivable.
	3	Paid $1000 of accounts payable.
	4	Paid rent for July $700.
	5	Sent invoice to customer $5600.
	7	Purchased office equipment for cash $2000.
	9	Recorded cash sales $800.
	10	Recorded credit sales $1500.
	14	Purchased office supplies for cash $330.
	23	Cash sales $2000.
	31	Drawings by Jason Woodstock $800.

Required

(a) Prepare worksheet entries for the business transactions for the month ended 31 July 2021.

(b) At the end of July, Jason realised that the customer invoice sent on 5 July 2021 was recorded incorrectly. The correct amount should be $6500. Explain what type of error Jason made and explain the impact of this error on the statement of financial position and the statement of profit or loss.

4.28 Preparing a statement of profit or loss and statement of financial position ★ **LO5**

Using the information in problem 4.27, prepare a:

(a) statement of profit or loss for the period ending 31 July 2021

(b) statement of financial position as at 31 July 2021.

4.29 Allocating transactions and demonstrating duality ★ ★ **LO4**

Choose appropriate account names and demonstrate the dual effect that occurs when the following business transactions for Brett Little take place. For example, in (a) we increase cash $14 000 and increase capital $14 000.

(a) Brett Little commenced business by contributing $22 000 cash.

(b) Received $8500 income for services performed.

(c) Paid telephone account $191.

(d) Brett Little withdrew cash from business $800.

(e) Purchased office stationery on credit $1900.

(f) Cash sales $700.

(g) Credit sales of $520.

(h) Brett Little withdrew office equipment from business $2000.

(i) Brett Little negotiated with a possible business partner to contribute $40 000 as a silent partner to the business.

(j) Brett Little purchased a meal for his partner's birthday on his personal credit card.

4.30 Preparing a worksheet and calculating profit ★ ★ **LO4, 5**

The following transactions were taken from the records of Anthony Reader, an interior designer, for the month ending 31 May 2020. You are required to design a suitable accounting worksheet for the period.

2020		
May	1	Commenced business with cash at bank of $80 000.
	2	Invoiced client for work completed $2100.
	3	Purchased second-hand vehicle for business $20 000 cash.
	5	Received cash payment for services rendered $1320.
	7	Paid casual wages $900.
	8	Paid rent for the past week $1000.
	9	Sent an invoice to a client $960.
	10	Paid electricity $180.

	11	Received an invoice from newsagent for stationery $253.
	15	Paid rent for the past week $1000.
	16	Paid casual wages $900.
	17	Paid gas and electricity $229.
	18	Received fees for services $880.
	19	Received fees for services $1200.
	21	Sent an invoice to client $350.
	22	Paid invoice received 11 May.
	23	Paid rent for the past week $1000.
	27	Received invoice from Cool Carpets $1500 for new office carpet.
	28	Paid phone bill $300.
	29	Sent invoice to client $1400.
	31	Won money at the Brisbane Cup and contributed a further $20 000 into business.

4.31 Recording in the ledger and trial balance and understanding the purpose of a trial balance ★ ★ ★   **LO6, 8**

Using the data in problem 4.30:
(a) Record the transactions in the ledger for Anthony Reader for the month of May 2020.
(b) Prepare a trial balance at 31 May 2020.
(c) What is the purpose of the trial balance? Illustrate, by example, situations that would cause the trial balance not to balance.

4.32 Preparing a statement of profit or loss and a statement of financial position ★ ★ ★   **LO5, 8**

Using the data from the trial balance in problem 4.31, prepare a statement of profit or loss for the period ending 31 May 2020 and a statement of financial position as at 31 May 2020.

4.33 Analysing business transactions and preparing a worksheet and a statement of financial position ★ ★ ★   **LO4, 5**

From the following business transactions of Kristy Jones, landscape consultant:
(a) State the impact on the accounting equation for each transaction. For example:

6 June   ↑ Cash $21 600   ↑ Capital $21 600

(b) Prepare a worksheet and a statement of financial position for the month of June 2020 from the following information.

2020		
June	6	Kristy Jones commenced business operations with a $21 600 cash injection.
	8	Paid internet advertising fees $713.
	11	Purchased drawing board on credit $2441.
	16	Paid electricity account $272.
	21	Purchased stationery for cash $380.
	22	Sent invoice to client for services performed $808.
	23	Purchased a new iPad for partner's birthday $1058 using personal funds.
	24	Paid business registration fee to local council $264.
	28	Withdrew cash from business $864.
	29	Paid advertising fees $637.
	30	Received interest from business bank account $32.

4.34 Recording in the ledger and trial balance and understanding the purpose of the ledger ★ ★ ★   **LO6, 8**

(a) Using the business transactions in problem 4.33, record the transactions in the ledger of Kristy Jones.
(b) What is the advantage of recording in the ledger compared to the journal?
(c) Prepare a trial balance for Kristy Jones at 30 June 2020.

4.35 Comprehensive problem of preparing a worksheet, statement of profit or loss and statement of financial position ★ ★ ★ LO5

Rotterdam Financial Services Pty Ltd, managed by Saphira Browne, provides accounting, taxation and financial planning services to clients residing in the inner Melbourne area. The statement of financial position for Rotterdam Financial Services Pty Ltd as at 1 October 2021 is as follows.

ROTTERDAM FINANCIAL SERVICES PTY LTD Statement of financial position as at 1 October 2021	
Assets	
Cash	$ 58 140
Accounts receivable	6 840
Supplies	13 680
Building	139 080
Total assets	**$ 217 740**
Liabilities	
Accounts payable	$28 500
Equity	
Capital	189 240
Total liabilities and equity	**$ 217 740**

During the three months from October to December, Rotterdam Financial Services Pty Ltd conducted the following transactions.

2021		
October	4	Invoiced customer for various accounting and tax services $10 032, to be paid by customer at end of month.
	4	Purchased new office furniture $17 400 cash.
	10	Invoiced customer for financial planning services completed $18 240.
	14	Received $9120 payment from customers who were previously billed.
	20	Paid supplier $4560 for office supplies purchased last month.
	28	Received a $5380 invoice from the *Melbourne Times* newspaper for advertising, due to be paid in two weeks.
	31	Received payment from customer invoiced on 10 October.
November	7	Paid employee salaries $17 680 cash.
	11	Paid invoice from the *Melbourne Times* received on 28 October.
	15	Received gas and electricity bill to be paid one month later $274.
	23	Provided tax services to customers $3876 cash.
	30	Paid employee salaries $1140 and shop rent $1368 cash.
December	8	Paid gas and electricity bill dated 15 November.
	15	Owners contributed a further $34 200 cash to the business.
	23	Provided accounting (Quicken) services to customers for $2280, with payment due in one month.
	29	Received water bill $536 to be paid in three weeks.
	30	Paid employee salaries $912.
		Paid bank fees incurred directly out of business's bank account $23.

Required

(a) Prepare a worksheet for Rotterdam Financial Services Pty Ltd for the business transactions from October to December 2021.

(b) Using the data given above, prepare a statement of profit or loss for the quarter ending 31 December 2021 and a statement of financial position as at 31 December 2021 for Rotterdam Financial Services Pty Ltd.

(c) Comment on the profit/loss for the business for the three months ending 31 December 2021.

4.36 Comprehensive problem of preparing a worksheet, statement of profit or loss and statement of financial position ★ ★ ★   **LO6**

The following business transactions and business events relate to Andrew's Business Services Pty Ltd.

2020		
June	1	Andrew commenced business with $15 000 given to him by his Aunt Kate.
	4	Purchased new computer for his business $1200 on credit.
	5	Received $500 for services rendered.
	6	Paid rent on office for June $400.
	7	Negotiated with Baxter and Michael possible casual employment contracts totalling $1500.
	8	Aunt Kate injected a further $2000 gift into Andrew's business.
	9	Billed a client $500 for services rendered.
	10	Received an invoice for new reception desk $3400.
	15	Paid for telephone connection fee $65.
	16	Sent a quote for a large prospective job $4800.
	16	Paid gas charges $231.
	23	Received $250 for consultation work completed.
	28	Paid in full for the reception desk bought on 10 June.
	30	Paid advertising $200.

Required

(a) Prepare a worksheet for the business transactions for June.
(b) Enter these transactions into ledger accounts for the business.
(c) Complete a statement of profit or loss and statement of financial position for Andrew's Business Services Pty Ltd for the period ending 30 June 2020.

DECISION-MAKING ACTIVITIES

4.37 Go to www.jbhifi.com.au and find the consolidated statement of profit or loss and the consolidated statement of financial position for JB Hi-Fi Ltd in the latest annual report.

Required

Use these statements to answer the following questions.
(a) What is meant by the JB Hi-Fi Ltd 'consolidated' statement of profit or loss?
(b) What is the total value of each of the following items at the end of the current reporting year in the JB Hi-Fi Ltd consolidated accounts? For each item, classify it as an asset, expense, revenue, equity or liability. Provide reasons for your classification.
  (i) Cash and cash equivalents
  (ii) Sales and marketing
  (iii) Occupancy expenses
  (iv) Cost of sales
  (v) Provisions
  (vi) Inventories
  (vii) Plant and equipment
  (viii) Intangible assets
(c) The key statistical data for JB Hi-Fi Ltd's Australia division is provided in the divisional performance section. For each item, summarise the change occurring between 2014 and 2018 and what this means for JB Hi-Fi Ltd.
(d) What is the purpose of providing two years of comparative figures for the financial statements (i.e. 2017 and 2018)? How would this information be useful to one of JB Hi-Fi Ltd's shareholders?

4.38 Go to the Westpac website (www.westpac.com.au) and download the latest annual report.

Required

Use these statements to answer the following questions.
(a) What is the total value of each of the following items at the end of the current reporting year in the Westpac consolidated accounts? For each item, classify it as an asset, expense, revenue, equity or liability. Provide reasons for your classification.

(i) Interest income
(ii) Cash and balances with central banks
(iii) Derivative financial instruments
(iv) Ordinary share capital
(v) Deposits and other borrowings
(vi) Debt issues
(vii) Property and equipment

(b) What is the main source of revenue for Westpac? Compare this to JB Hi-Fi Ltd. What is the main source of revenue for JB Hi-Fi Ltd? What implications does this have for receivables on the statement of financial position for both companies?

(c) Locate the 'Notes to the financial statements'. Note 1(a) provides the Basis of preparation for Westpac. What accounting standards and other regulation is Westpac complying with?

4.39 Go to the Australian Taxation Office website (www.ato.gov.au) and select the 'Business' tab, then select 'Businesses' under the 'Online Services' heading. Next, select 'Standard Business Reporting' and then 'What is Standard Business Reporting (SBR)?'

Required

(a) What is SBR?

(b) How does SBR work?

(c) What do you think are the benefits of SBR for companies?

REFERENCES

Dictionary of Small Business 2018, 'Arm's length transaction', http://small-business-dictionary.org/wiki/wiki-index/a/arms-length-transaction.

JB Hi-Fi Ltd 2018, *Annual report 2018*, www.jbhifi.com.au.

ACKNOWLEDGEMENTS

Photo: © Odua Images / Shutterstock.com
Photo: © Microgen / Shutterstock.com

CHAPTER 5

Statement of financial position

LEARNING OBJECTIVES

After studying this chapter, you should be able to:

5.1 identify the financial reporting obligations of an entity

5.2 explain the nature and purpose of the statement of financial position

5.3 outline the effects of accounting policy choices, estimates and judgements on financial statements

5.4 apply the asset definition criteria

5.5 apply the liability definition criteria

5.6 discuss the definition and nature of equity

5.7 apply the recognition criteria to assets, liabilities and equity

5.8 describe the format and presentation of the statement of financial position

5.9 describe the presentation and disclosure requirements for elements in the statement of financial position

5.10 discuss the measurement of various assets and liabilities in the statement of financial position

5.11 discuss the limitations of the statement of financial position.

Chapter preview

This chapter introduces financial statements and the choices, judgements and estimates underlying their preparation. The focus of this chapter is the financial statement that depicts the financial position of an entity at a point in time: the statement of financial position (also known as the balance sheet). The statement of financial position lists an entity's assets, liabilities and equity at a particular point in time. Simplistically, the assets can be thought of as the items that the entity owns (or, more precisely, controls), with the liabilities and equity representing the external and internal claims on those items, respectively. The purpose of this chapter is to examine in more detail the nature and purpose of the statement of financial position. We will explore the definition, recognition, measurement, classification and disclosure criteria applied to assets, liabilities and equity reported in the statement of financial position. Presentation aspects of the statement of financial position, including how this varies according to entity type, will be discussed. Potential limitations associated with using financial numbers in the statement of financial position will also be considered.

5.1 Financial reporting obligations

LEARNING OBJECTIVE 5.1 Identify the financial reporting obligations of an entity.

An entity's financial report can include four financial statements — a statement of financial position (also referred to as a balance sheet), a statement of profit or loss (also known as an income statement and included as part of a statement of comprehensive income), a statement of changes in equity and a statement of cash flows. This chapter focuses on the statement of financial position, while subsequent chapters focus on other statements.

Before examining the statement of financial position, a broader discussion of the reporting obligations of entities is warranted. The previous chapter introduced the business Advantage Tennis Coaching (ATC). What financial statements, if any, does ATC have to prepare? How does this differ to the financial statements that a listed company such as JB Hi-Fi Ltd has to prepare? What are the rules and regulations that govern the preparation of financial statements prepared by entities?

Some entities have a legal obligation to prepare financial statements. Entities that are structured as companies (incorporated entities) generally must lodge financial statements with a relevant regulatory body. For companies registered in Australia, this is the Australian Securities and Investments Commission (ASIC). For charities registered in Australia, this is the Australian Charities and Not-for-profits Commission (ACNC). For example, JB Hi-Fi Ltd has a legal obligation to prepare and lodge financial statements with ASIC. A charity such as Oxfam Australia has a legal obligation to lodge information with the ACNC. Similarly, legislative obligations exist for some public sector entities, such as hospitals and local councils, to prepare financial statements in order to discharge their accountability to the public.

For other entities, such as partnerships and sole traders, there is no legal requirement to prepare financial statements, as the businesses are not separate legal entities from their owners. A business such as ATC is not required to prepare financial statements. However, for taxation purposes records of the operations of the business are required so that the owner(s) can fulfil their taxation obligations. Further, if the owner(s) wanted to sell the business as a going concern, potential purchasers would wish to view financial statements. A lender to the business may also demand financial statements to assess the entity's ability to service debt obligations, when providing new, or renewing existing, financing facilities. Financial statements should also assist the owner(s) to assess the financial position and performance of the business.

General purpose and special purpose financial statements

In Australia, entities required to prepare financial statements prepare either **general purpose financial statements (GPFS)** or **special purpose financial statements (SPFS)**. Central to the determination of whether an entity prepares *general purpose* or *special purpose* financial statements is the **reporting entity** concept. This is not a legal concept, but an accounting concept linked to the information needs of users. Further, the concept is not used internationally to determine financial reporting requirements. An entity is assessed as a reporting entity when there are users who depend on GPFS for their decision making. The factors taken into consideration when deciding if an entity is a reporting entity include its size and indebtedness, the separation of the entity's management and ownership, and its economic or political significance. If an entity has indicators that suggest it is a reporting entity, then the entity should prepare GPFS. Further, the financial statements of a reporting entity should comply with specified accounting rules governing recognition, measurement, presentation and disclosure requirements. If an entity is assessed as a non-reporting entity, then it can prepare SPFS. For example, JB Hi-Fi Ltd is a reporting entity given its size and separation of ownership and management, as its decision making resides with management on behalf of the shareholders. Conversely, a private school limited by guarantee may not be assessed as a reporting entity and may produce SPFS.

What is the difference between GPFS and SPFS? Statements that are purported to be GPFS must be prepared in accordance with **generally accepted accounting principles (GAAP)**, whereas SPFS can be prepared without adhering to GAAP. GAAP are a set of rules and practices that guide the recording of transactions and financial reporting. The reporting entity concept and its role in determining financial reporting requirements are currently being reviewed by the Australian Accounting Standards Board (AASB). The project includes a reconsideration of the role that the reporting entity concept has in determining which entities must prepare GPFS. A two-tier reporting framework is still proposed, but an entity will no longer be able to opt out of standards by self-assessing as a non-reporting entity. The proposal is for Tier 1 of the reporting framework to continue to be fully IFRS compliant (see below) and mandatory for all entities with public accountability. For Tier 2, two options are proposed. Option 1 is the existing Tier 2 (reduced disclosure regime, RDR) disclosures. Option 2 is new Tier 2 disclosures which will encompass the disclosures in the accounting standards that were previously mandatory for SPFS plus some additional disclosures about related parties, revenue, impairment of assets and income tax.

A country's GAAP are usually specified in accounting standards. Accounting standards detail the specific recognition, measurement, presentation and disclosure requirements applicable to various types of transactions. For example, there are accounting standards governing accounting for inventory, property, plant and equipment (PPE) and revenue. Historically, accounting standards have varied by country. For example, Australia issued accounting standards that were different to the accounting standards issued in China, Japan, Germany and the United States. As markets have become increasingly borderless, considerable progress has occurred in developing a set of acceptable international accounting standards — International Financial Reporting Standards (IFRS). IFRS are particularly focused on for-profit entities and are issued by the International Accounting Standards Board (IASB). At the time of writing, 144 jurisidictions have adopted or converged their domestic standards with IFRS. Countries adopting IFRS include Australia, South Africa and all European Union countries. Countries substantially converging their domestic standards with IFRS include China and India. Notable countries that have not adopted or substantially converged their standards with IFRS are the United States and Japan, although IFRS may be permitted in such jurisdictions.

A set of public sector accounting standards — International Public Sector Accounting Standards (IPSAS) — issued by the International Public Sector Accounting Standards Board are also available for jurisdictions to adopt. In Australia's case, rather than adopting IPSAS, additional paragraphs have been included in the Australian-adopted IFRS to make them applicable to all entity types (e.g. for-profit, not-for-profit, private sector and public sector entities) required to prepare GPFS. References throughout this chapter and subsequent chapters are to IFRS.

Are there different versions of IFRS to use when preparing GPFS? The IASB has issued IFRS as well as *IFRS for Small and Medium-sized Entities* (IFRS for SMEs). IFRS for SMEs simplifies some of the recognition and measurement rules, omits topics not relevant to SMEs and reduces disclosure requirements. The use of IFRS or IFRS for SMEs when preparing GPFS depends on whether an entity has public accountability. Entities with public accountability must prepare GPFS using IFRS. **Public accountability** is applicable to entities with securities, debt or equity that are traded in a public market, and to entities that hold assets in a fiduciary capacity as their main business activity. For example, the shares of JB Hi-Fi Ltd are traded on the ASX; therefore, JB Hi-Fi Ltd is subject to public accountability. IFRS for SMEs are available for use by small and medium-sized entities (SMEs) that are not subject to public accountability but do publish GPFS.

Not all jurisdictions have accepted IFRS for SMEs. Some countries have followed a different path. Australia, for example, has introduced differential reporting. In Australia, entities preparing GPFS can be required to prepare the statements using full IFRS or IFRS with reduced disclosure requirements. The entities required to prepare GPFS that comply with full IFRS are for-profit private sector entities that have public accountability, and the Australian government and state, territory and local governments. JB Hi-Fi Ltd, being an entity with public accountability, is required to prepare GPFS using full IFRS. Universities are also deemed to have public accountability and must prepare GPFS using full IFRS. Entities that may prepare GPFS using the reduced disclosure requirements, rather than full IFRS, include all for-profit private sector entities that do not have public accountability, and all not-for-profit private sector entities.

New Zealand's approach is similar to Australia's approach. New Zealand has implemented a multi-standard framework, where the standards to be applied depend on the nature and classification of the entity. Entities with public accountability are required to comply with IFRS and some entities can use IFRS but with reduced disclosures. For public benefit entities, New Zealand is implementing 'public benefit standards' based on IPSAS. These are derived from IFRS but with differences to accommodate a public benefit objective rather than a for-profit objective.

5.2 Nature and purpose of the statement of financial position

LEARNING OBJECTIVE 5.2 Explain the nature and purpose of the statement of financial position.

A primary objective of a for-profit entity is the generation of profits and a strong financial performance. A not-for-profit entity's objective may be the provision of services to a community. To generate profits, or to provide services, entities need to invest in productive assets. Assets are items controlled by an entity that provide the entity with future economic benefits. Value creation can also occur if the assets in which an entity invests appreciate in value. Decisions concerning the acquisition and sale of assets are referred to as **investing decisions**. The acquisition of assets requires financing, which may be provided by external parties (e.g. lenders) and/or internal parties (e.g. the owners). The external claims on the entity's assets are termed liabilities. Interest-bearing debt is a category of liability. The internal claims on the entity's assets are referred to as equity. The mix of debt and equity financing that an entity chooses reflects its **financing decisions**.

The **statement of financial position** (also known as the balance sheet) is a financial statement that details the entity's assets, liabilities and equity as at a particular point in time — the last day of the reporting period. For example, entities with financial years ending on 30 June produce a statement of financial position as at 30 June each year. Note that a statement of financial position can be prepared more frequently than on an annual basis — indeed, it can be prepared as at any date. However, common practice is to prepare the statement of financial position semi-annually or annually as at the end of the reporting period.

The end of an entity's reporting period often coincides with the end of the financial year. This aligns the accounting period with the taxation period. For example, JB Hi-Fi Ltd's reporting period ends on 30 June. However, the end of the reporting period can be a date other than the end of the financial year. For example, Coca-Cola Amatil's year-end aligns with the end of the calendar year — 31 December — and Westpac Banking Corporation's year-end is 30 September.

The statement of financial position is a financial statement that documents:
- what the entity owns (or controls) as at a particular date — the assets
- the external claims on the entity's assets — the liabilities
- the internal claim on the entity's assets — the equity.

Recall from the previous chapter that the accounting equation specifies that an entity's assets equal the sum of the entity's liabilities and equity. The **duality** system of recording business transactions means that the business transactions have a dual effect on the accounting equation such that the equation remains in balance after the recording of each transaction. This is why a statement of financial position, prepared as at any point in time, will always balance.

An example of a statement of financial position for Advantage Tennis Coaching (ATC), a small business owned by Nicholas Cash, was shown in illustrative example 4.5 in the previous chapter. The statement of financial position for this tennis coaching business is reproduced as illustrative example 5.1. The assets of the business as at 30 September 2019 are $87 770. The external claims on the assets at this date — the liabilities — are $51 400 and the equity — the internal claim on the entity's assets — is $36 370. Thus, the assets ($87 770) equal the liabilities ($51 400) plus the equity ($36 370). 'Net assets' refers to the assets less the liabilities. As assets less liabilities equal equity, net assets equal equity. For ATC, the net assets are $36 370, representing the assets of $87 770 less the liabilities of $51 400.

Analysing a statement of financial position enables users to make a preliminary assessment as to the financial position of the entity. For example, ATC commenced the business with an investment of $20 000. As at 30 September 2019, Nicholas Cash has invested in some office furniture and equipment only. ATC has $71 270 cash in the bank and is unlikely to face **liquidity** issues (in relation to its ability to meet its financial commitments) in the short term. As the business grows, the investment and finance decisions will be reflected in the statement of financial position. For example, if ATC purchases ball machines and uses cash to finance the acquisitions, the cash balance will reduce and ball machines will appear as assets of ATC. If ATC purchases a minibus to transport junior players to tennis tournaments and finances the acquisition by a loan, its assets will increase and its liabilities will increase. By reviewing the statement of financial position, a user may make a preliminary assessment of the economic condition of an entity by identifying the types of assets in which the entity invests and its use of liabilities relative to equity to finance the assets, by appreciating the types and terms of liabilities used to finance the assets and the sources of equity used to fund assets, and by assessing the entity's financial solvency.

ILLUSTRATIVE EXAMPLE 5.1

A statement of financial position

ADVANTAGE TENNIS COACHING Statement of financial position as at 30 September 2019		
ASSETS		
Current assets		
Cash	$71 270	
Accounts receivable	6 800	$78 070
Non-current assets		
Office furniture	3 200	
Office equipment	6 500	9 700
Total assets		87 770
LIABILITIES		
Current liabilities		
Accounts payable		1 400
Non-current liabilities		
Loan		50 000
Total liabilities		51 400
Net assets		**$36 370**
OWNER'S EQUITY		
Capital — N Cash		$20 000
Profit		16 370
Total equity		**$36 370**

To further illustrate the information a user can obtain from a glance at a statement of financial position, consider the statement of financial position for Coconut Plantations Pty Ltd, shown in figure 5.1. This private company was incorporated in August 2019 and commenced operations in September 2019. As at 31 December 2019, the company has $374 000 in assets. These were financed by $83 790 of liabilities and $290 210 of equity, indicating that the company relies more on equity than debt to finance its assets. Coconut Plantations Pty Ltd has current assets amounting to $135 667 and investments in PPE of $238 333 (net of accumulated depreciation). The company keeps inventories of finished goods and raw materials ($60 000), which is not surprising given that it is a manufacturing entity rather than a service entity or a retail entity. Coconut Plantations has $63 790 in short-term (current) liabilities compared to $20 000 in longer term (non-current) liabilities. Its current assets are higher than its current liabilities, which indicates that the company's liquidity is satisfactory. Retained earnings of $90 210 indicate that the company has been profitable over its first four months of operation.

FIGURE 5.1	Statement of financial position of Coconut Plantations Pty Ltd

COCONUT PLANTATIONS PTY LTD Statement of financial position as at 31 December 2019	
	$
Current assets	
Cash on hand	51 557
Accounts receivable	23 110
Inventories of finished goods and raw materials	60 000
Prepayments	1 000
Total current assets	135 667

Non-current assets		
Property, plant and equipment		240 000
Less: Accumulated depreciation		(1 667)
Total non-current assets		238 333
Total assets		374 000
Current liabilities		
Accounts payable		3 300
Accrued expenses		700
Income tax payable		45 000
Dividend payable		14 790
Total current liabilities		63 790
Non-current liabilities		
Loan payable		20 000
Total non-current liabilities		20 000
Total liabilities		83 790
Net assets		**290 210**
Equity		
Share capital		200 000
Retained earnings		90 210
Total equity		**290 210**

Another illustration of the information a user can obtain from a statement of financial position is the statement of financial position for the Qantas Group reproduced in figure 5.2. Note that the Qantas Group uses the term 'balance sheet' rather than 'statement of financial position'. As at 30 June 2018, the group had $18 647 million in assets. These were financed by liabilities of $14 688 million and equity of $3959 million, indicating that the group relies more on debt than equity to finance its assets. The Qantas Group had considerable investments in cash ($1694 million) and PPE ($12 851 million). It keeps a relatively low level of inventories ($351 million), which is not surprising given that it is a service entity rather than a retail entity. The Qantas Group has $404 million in short-term (current) interest-bearing liabilities compared to $4344 million in longer term (non-current) interest-bearing liabilities. Its current assets are lower than its current liabilities and the movement from 2017 to 2018 indicates that the group's liquidity has not changed significantly. Retained earnings of $1084 million suggest that the Qantas Group has paid out less in dividends than the earnings it has generated over its period of operation.

FIGURE 5.2   Consolidated balance sheet of the Qantas Group

QANTAS GROUP
Consolidated balance sheet
as at 30 June 2018

	Notes	2018 $m	2017 $m
Current assets			
Cash and cash equivalents	15(A)	1 694	1 775
Receivables	8	908	784
Other financial assets	20(C)	474	100
Inventories		351	351
Assets classified as held for sale	9	118	12
Other	13	167	97
Total current assets		3 712	3 119
Non-current assets			
Receivables	8	100	123
Other financial assets	20(C)	112	43
Investments accounted for under the equity method		226	214
Property, plant and equipment	10	12 851	12 253
Intangible assets	11	1 113	1 025
Other	13	533	444
Total non-current assets		14 935	14 102
Total assets		18 647	17 221

QANTAS GROUP Consolidated balance sheet as at 30 June 2018			
Current liabilities			
Payables		2 295	2 067
Revenue received in advance	14	3 939	3 685
Interest-bearing liabilities	15(B)	404	433
Other financial liabilities	20(C)	34	69
Provisions	16	860	841
Liabilities classified as held for sale	9	64	0
Total current liabilities		7 596	7 095
Non-current liabilities			
Revenue received in advance	14	1 446	1 424
Interest-bearing liabilities	15(B)	4 344	4 405
Other financial liabilities	20(C)	25	56
Provisions	16	367	348
Deferred tax liabilities	12	910	353
Total non-current liabilities		7 092	6 586
Total liabilities		14 688	13 681
Net assets		**3 959**	**3 540**
Equity			
Issued capital	17(A)	2 508	3 259
Treasury shares		(115)	(206)
Reserves		479	12
Retained earnings		1 084	472
Equity attributable to the members of Qantas		3 956	3 537
Non-controlling interests		3	3
Total equity		**3 959**	**3 540**

This Consolidated balance sheet should be read in conjunction with the accompanying notes to the accounts as referenced in the 'Notes' column.

Source: Qantas Airways Ltd 2018, p. 54.

VALUE TO BUSINESS

- The statement of financial position is one of the financial statements prepared at the end of the reporting period. It details the assets, liabilities and equity of an entity as at the end of the reporting period. This information helps users to assess the entity's financial solvency and stability.
- The statement of financial position reflects the assets in which the entity has invested (investing decisions) and how the entity has financed the assets (financing decisions).

5.3 Accounting policy choices, estimates and judgements

LEARNING OBJECTIVE 5.3 Outline the effects of accounting policy choices, estimates and judgements on financial statements.

In introducing the statement of financial position, we have presented a statement of financial position for ATC, an entity that is not required to prepare financial statements, and for the Qantas Group, a group that is required to prepare GPFS in compliance with accounting standards. This and subsequent chapters explore some of the key recognition, presentation and disclosure requirements for financial statement elements contained in accounting standards. JB Hi-Fi Ltd's financial statements will be used to illustrate these requirements. The financial statements for many listed entities are available from the entities' websites. JB Hi-Fi Ltd's financial statements can be accessed at www.jbhifi.com.au or through databases that provide annual reports for listed companies such as those found at a university library. The relevant financial statements and notes for JB Hi-Fi Ltd are reproduced in the appendix to this text.

Even when preparing financial statements in compliance with accounting standards such as IFRS, the accounting standards offer options to preparers. Therefore, most items in the financial statements involve the exercise of judgement and estimation on the part of preparers. Users of financial statements need to appreciate that accounting flexibility and discretion exist, and to consider the potential impact these have on reported information in the statement of financial position and statement of profit or loss.

We will explore some of the permissible options in the recording of transactions and the estimations and judgements required by preparers. Accounting choices applied to the recognition and measurement of elements in the financial statements are referred to as **accounting policies**. This is why an analysis of an entity's accounting policies is important. There are numerous accounting rules that permit choices. Examples include the alternative methods of costing inventory, the measurement of PPE subsequent to its acquisition, the method for calculating depreciation and the treatment of development expenditure as an asset (known as capitalisation) or as an expense.

Examples of estimations that affect the values reported in the statement of financial position include the impairment of accounts receivable, the costs associated with a well-planned and documented business restructure, and the liabilities related to employee benefits (e.g. long service leave and sick leave entitlements). When reviewing financial statements, a user must be cognisant of the particular accounting policies used and of financial numbers that involve preparer estimations. Many accounting policy choices are transparent, as accounting standards require disclosure of such choices. However, entities are not obliged to detail all estimations used to derive various financial statement elements. For a listed entity such as JB Hi-Fi Ltd, the accounting policy disclosures are usually given in the first few notes accompanying the financial statements.

5.4 The definition of assets

LEARNING OBJECTIVE 5.4 Apply the asset definition criteria.

We have been referring to the elements of the statement of financial position (assets, liabilities and equity) and will now re-examine the definitions introduced in the introduction to accounting and business decision making chapter. Accounting professions and regulators in various countries, including Australia, New Zealand and the United States, have developed frameworks for the preparation and presentation of financial statements. Such frameworks address matters such as the objective of financial statements, the assumptions underlying financial statements and the qualitative characteristics of financial statements, and they define the elements of financial statements (assets, liabilities, equity, income and expenses) and identify the recognition criteria to be applied to these elements. They also guide the development of accounting standards. As is the case with the globalisation of accounting standards, conceptual frameworks are also converging. References throughout this chapter, and subsequent chapters, are to the IASB's *Conceptual Framework for Financial Reporting* (**Conceptual Framework**). The IASB recently revised the *Conceptual Framework* to improve financial reporting by providing a more complete, clear and updated set of concepts. The project focused on the reporting entity, elements of financial statements (including recognition and derecognition), measurement, presentation and disclosure. The revised framework was issued in March 2018 and is effective for financial reporting periods from January 2020. The focus in this chapter is on the revised definitions. The introduction of the reporting concept in the revised *Conceptual Framework*, different to the reporting concept used in financial reporting in Australia, was the catalyst for reviewing general and special purpose reporting in Australia.

Asset definition

The asset definition in the revised *Conceptual Framework* is 'an asset is a present economic resource controlled by the entity as a result of past events' where an economic resource is a right that has the potential to produce economic benefits. The essential characteristics of an **asset** are:
1. it is a present economic resource
2. the resource is controlled by the entity
3. the resource is a result of a past event.

Present economic resource

An economic resource is a right that has the potential to produce economic benefits. These rights can be established by contract or legislation, or arise from a constructive obligation of another party. In principle, each of an entity's rights is a separate asset. However, for accounting purposes related rights tend to be treated as a single asset. For example, the following rights may arise from legal ownership of a property: the right to use the property and the right to sell the property.

For the economic resource to have the potential to produce economic benefits, it is only necessary that the economic resource already exists and that there is at least one circumstance in which it will produce economic benefits. There is no requirement that it be certain, or even probable, that the resource will produce economic benefits. The provision of benefits can take the form of having goods and services desired by customers available for sale. It can also take the form of being able to satisfy human wants. For example, an item of plant and equipment that produces goods for sale is an asset because it provides service potential (that is, it produces goods that can be sold for cash). An art gallery's public collection of artworks is an asset, as the collection provides service potential to the gallery (that is, the collection attracts visitors to the gallery and enables the gallery to achieve its objective of attracting a certain number of visitors). The latter example highlights that the future benefits do not necessarily have to involve cash.

Control

An entity must control an item for that item to be considered an asset and recognised in the entity's statement of financial position. Legal ownership is synonymous with control; however, legal ownership is not a necessary prerequisite for control. The concept of control refers to the capacity of the entity to benefit from the asset in the pursuit of its objectives, and to deny or regulate the access of others to the benefit. To illustrate this concept, consider an entity that arranges to lease an asset required for its manufacturing process. The lessee (the entity) pays the lessor (the owner of the asset) a monthly rental. The lease contract specifies that the lease can be cancelled by the lessor with one month's notice. In this scenario, the entity is able to use the asset but it does not have control of the asset, given that the lessor can cancel the lease contract. It is the lessor who controls access to the asset. What if the contract was non-cancellable and the lessee had the right to purchase the asset at the end of the lease contract at a predetermined price? In this situation, it would be most likely that the lessee controlled the asset even in the absence of legal ownership. Other examples of assets where control is present in the absence of legal ownership are licences and management rights.

Past event

Another criterion necessary for an item to be defined as an asset is the existence of a past event that has resulted in the entity controlling the asset. Most assets are generated as a result of an exchange transaction, non-reciprocal transfer or discovery. Consider an office building that is to be used as a rental property. The first two asset definition criteria are satisfied, as the building creates future economic benefits in the form of rental income and the entity owns (and so controls) the building. If the building is purchased, an exchange transaction has occurred and the requirement that there be a past event is satisfied. If the building is bequeathed to the entity, a non-reciprocal transfer (a past event) is also deemed to have occurred. If the entity is in the process of finding a suitable property and has enlisted the services of a commercial real estate agent to assist in the task, the past event criterion is not satisfied as no exchange has occurred yet. The building is not considered an asset until this exchange has occurred.

VALUE TO BUSINESS

The essential characteristics of an asset are:
1. it is a present economic resource
2. the resource is controlled by the entity
3. the resource is a result of a past event.

5.5 The definition of liabilities

LEARNING OBJECTIVE 5.5 Apply the liability definition criteria.

We have just discussed the definition criteria applicable to assets. In this section, we consider the same issues as they apply to the liability definition, with reference to the revised *Conceptual Framework*.

Liability definition

The liability definition in the revised *Conceptual Framework* is 'a present obligation of the entity to transfer an economic resource as a result of past events'. The essential characteristics of a **liability** are:
1. it is a present obligation.
2. the obligation is to transfer an economic resource
3. the obligation is a result of past events.

Present obligation

An essential element of the liability definition is a present obligation to another entity, even if that entity cannot be identified. A legal contractual obligation clearly creates a present obligation; however, the 'obligation' for accounting definition purposes is more far-reaching than a legal obligation — it extends to the entity having no practical ability to avoid the transfer. For example, if any action necessary to avoid the transfer would cause significant business disruption or would have economic consequences significantly more adverse than the transfer itself, then there would be no practical ability to avoid the transfer. The obligation can arise as a result of a duty to do what is fair, just and right, or it can arise if a particular set of facts creates valid expectations in other parties that the entity will satisfy the obligation. If an entity has no realistic alternative to settling the obligation, the obligation is deemed a present obligation. For example, if an entity has entered into a binding non-cancellable contractual arrangement to purchase specialised equipment from a manufacturer and subsequently cancels the order, a liability will exist. The contract creates a legal obligation for the entity, and the entity will need to honour that obligation in the form of damages for breach of contract.

Consider an entity that is embroiled in a dispute that will be settled by a court of law. Does a liability exist? Until a judgement is handed down in court, there is no present obligation to make a future sacrifice of economic benefits. Consequently, the liability definition is not satisfied. Similarly, if you have accumulated annual leave in your job, does your employer have a liability? The employer does have a liability, as they will have to make a future sacrifice when you take your annual leave. The entitlement to annual leave is a legal obligation arising from the services you have rendered to your employer.

Transfer

An entity's obligation to transfer an economic resource must have the potential to require the entity to transfer the economic resource to another party. Transferring economic resources is associated with adverse financial consequences for the entity. For example, accounts payable involve future sacrifices of economic benefits, because the entity must remit cash to the supplier in the future. Similarly, a bank loan is a liability, as the entity must transfer an economic resource in the form of cash payments for interest and loan repayments to service the loan. The transfer does not necessarily have to be a cash sacrifice. For example, the requirement to transfer goods constitutes the transfer of an economic resource.

Past event

Another essential element for a liability is the existence of a past event. An event resulting in the future sacrifice of economic benefits must have occurred. Consider an entity that has contracted a company to undertake a major overhaul of its machinery. Until the overhaul is performed (the past event), there is no present obligation for the entity to pay the contractor and so the liability definition is not satisfied.

One of the contentious issues in financial reporting has been how lease financing should be addressed in financial reporting. If an entity leases assets, should the leased assets be recorded as assets and the future lease obligations as liabilities? The reporting of leased assets is covered by an accounting standard. Previously, the accounting treatment depended on the contractual terms of the lease and whether the substantial risks and benefits associated with the assets transferred from the lessor to the lessee. If they did, the leased assets were recorded as assets and needed to be amortised. Correspondingly, the lease obligations were recorded as liabilities. If the substantial risks and benefits associated with the assets remained with the lessor, then lease financing had no statement of financial position implications. The lease payment was recorded as an expense in the statement of profit or loss. This is why lease financing was referred to as 'off balance sheet financing'. However, a new *leases* standard (IFRS 16), effective 2019, requires the majority of leases to be recognised 'on balance sheet' as a right-of-use asset and lease liability. The new standard establishes the principles that entities must now apply to report useful information to investors and analysts about the amount, timing and uncertainty of cash flows arising from a lease.

5.6 The definition and nature of equity

LEARNING OBJECTIVE 5.6 Discuss the definition and nature of equity.

The remaining element of the statement of financial position to discuss is equity. **Equity** is defined in the revised *Conceptual Framework* para. 4.63 as 'the residual interest in the assets of the entity after deducting all its liabilities'. This definition means that equity cannot be determined without reference to assets and liabilities. The definition is such that the entity's assets less liabilities (that is, net assets) at a particular point in time equal its equity. The equity balance represents the owner's (or owners') claims on the assets of the entity. Equity is a difficult concept to define independently of assets and liabilities, as the equity section of a statement of financial position contains many different items. For example, one item within the equity section of the statement of financial position is contributions made by the owner(s). The terms given to the funds contributed by owner(s) are 'share capital' for a company or 'contributed capital' for a partnership or sole trader. Retained earnings, also referred to as 'unappropriated earnings' or 'undistributed profits', are another equity item. Retained earnings are the cumulative profits made by an entity since it commenced operation that have been retained in the entity for reinvestment rather than distributed to the owner(s). We will explore the classification of equity more formally later in this chapter.

5.7 Assets, liabilities and equity

LEARNING OBJECTIVE 5.7 Apply the recognition criteria to assets, liabilities and equity.

Only items that meet the definition of an asset, a liability or equity can be recognised in the statement of financial position and, as will be discussed in the statement of cash flows chapter, only items that meet the definition of income or expenses can be recognised in the statement of financial performance. The term **recognition** refers to the recording of items in the financial statements with a monetary value assigned to them. Therefore, 'asset recognition' or 'liability recognition' means that the asset or liability is recorded and appears on the face of the statement of financial position with its amount included in totals in the relevant statement. Central to the recognition principle is that items can be measured in monetary terms. This is referred to as the **monetary concept**. As money is the language used to quantify items recognised in the financial statements, if items cannot be assigned a monetary value then they cannot appear in the statement of financial position.

It is recognition that links the elements in financial statements — assets, liabilities, equity, income and expenses — and hence links the financial statements themselves. The linkage between the statements arises because the recognition of one element (or a change in one element) requires the recognition of an equal amount in one or more other elements (or changes in one or more other elements) as per the accounting equation. For example, income and expenses are recognised in the statement of financial performance only if an increase or decrease in the carrying amount of an asset or a liability is also recognised. Thus, the recognition of income occurs simultaneously with the initial recognition of an asset, or an increase in the carrying amount of an asset or the derecognition of a liability, or a decrease in the carrying amount of a liability. Consider the sale of goods for cash. Income is recognised (revenue from the sale of goods) and an asset is increased (cash at bank). Similarly, the recognition of expenses occurs simultaneously with the initial recognition of a liability, or an increase in the carrying amount of a liability or the derecognition of an asset, or a decrease in the carrying amount of an asset. Consider the payment of wages. An expense is recognised (wages) and there is a decrease in the carrying amount of an asset (cash).

The sale of goods is recognised as income and as an asset.

There are no definitive rules to assist the decision on whether an item should be recognised. The recognition decision requires judgement. The overarching consideration when deciding whether to recognise an asset or a liability (and any related income, expenses or changes in equity) is whether the recognition provides financial statement users with relevant information about the asset or the liability and about any income, expenses or changes in equity, a faithful representation of the asset or the liability and of any income, expenses or changes in equity, and information that results in benefits exceeding the cost of providing that information.

The factors to consider when making a recognition decision are as follows.

- *Uncertainty*. This is when it is uncertain whether an asset exists, or is separable from goodwill, or whether a liability exists. For example, customer relationships are not contractual and therefore uncertainty exists as to whether these are assets or whether they are separable from the business as a whole.
- *Probability*. This is when an asset or a liability exists, but there is only a low probability that an inflow or outflow of economic benefits will result. For example, an entity is being sued for a claimed act of wrongdoing but the probability of having to pay damages is assessed as low.
- *Measurement uncertainty*. This is when a measurement of an asset or a liability can be obtained, but the level of measurement uncertainty is high, impacting on the relevance of the information. For example, certain economic benefits are derived from modelling diverse scenarios with numerous assumptions and estimations such that the reasonableness of the estimation is questionable.

If due to uncertainty, low probability or unreliable measurement an asset or liability is not recognised, an entity always has the option to disclose information concerning the asset or liability in the notes to the accounts supporting the financial statements. The term '**contingent**' is often used to describe such assets or liabilities. For example, an entity may be embroiled in a court case, resulting in a contingency being disclosed in the entity's notes to the accounts.

Figure 5.3 provides a summary of the asset and liability definition and recognition criteria discussed in the preceding sections.

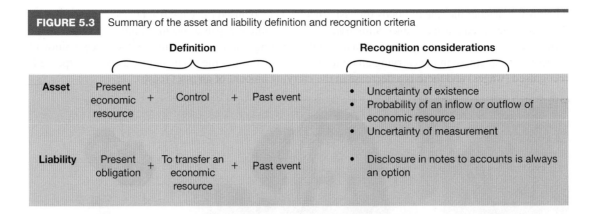

FIGURE 5.3 Summary of the asset and liability definition and recognition criteria

	Definition			Recognition considerations
Asset	Present economic resource	+ Control	+ Past event	• Uncertainty of existence • Probability of an inflow or outflow of economic resource • Uncertainty of measurement
Liability	Present obligation	+ To transfer an economic resource	+ Past event	• Disclosure in notes to accounts is always an option

5.8 Format and presentation of the statement of financial position

LEARNING OBJECTIVE 5.8 Describe the format and presentation of the statement of financial position.

The statement of financial position can be presented in a number of ways. A T-format is often used by smaller entities, whereas a narrative format tends to be used by larger entities. A T-format lists the assets on one side (left-hand side) and the liabilities and equity on the other (right-hand side). A narrative format presents the assets, liabilities and equity down the page. Examples of the narrative format were presented in illustrative example 5.1 and figure 5.1. While it is usual to list the assets first, with current assets listed before non-current assets, followed by the liabilities, with current liabilities listed before non-current liabilities, and then the equity section, there is no requirement to do so.

It is usual practice to present the statement of financial position for the previous reporting period in addition to the current reporting period. Known as **comparative information**, this allows users to see how an entity's financial position has changed from the previous period to the current period. When comparing the figures for the current and previous years, users should familiarise themselves with the entity's accounting policies to ensure that it is not a change in accounting policy that is the reason for the change in the reported figures. Whether the figures in the statement of financial position are expressed in whole dollars, or thousands or millions of dollars, is at the discretion of the entity. The entity should clearly identify in the statement the monetary value reported.

For companies which have investments in other companies that give them control of those entities' financial and operating policies, it is necessary to prepare financial statements for the group. Financial statements presented for the group are referred to as 'consolidated' or 'group' financial statements. Thus, a consolidated statement of financial position reports the combined assets, liabilities and equity for the parent entity and the controlled entities as a single economic entity, with inter-company transactions eliminated. A **parent entity** is an entity that controls another entity. A controlled entity is referred to as a 'subsidiary' entity. A principle-based approach is used to determine whether or not an entity controls another entity. Control is present when the investor has all of the following: power over the investee; exposure, or rights, to variable returns from its involvement with the investee; and the ability to use its power over the investee to affect the amount of the investor's returns. A fundamental consideration as to whether or not power exists is the extent of voting rights. Having more than half of the voting power in another entity is normally regarded as having power. However, even if less than 50 per cent of the voting power is held, an entity may still be regarded as controlling another entity if it has power to govern the financial and operating policies of the entity. For example, an entity may have a number of its directors on the board of another entity and therefore may have majority voting rights on the board of directors.

A **group (economic entity)** refers to a parent entity and all its subsidiaries. The concept of a group is illustrated in figure 5.4. Entity A (the parent entity) owns 80 per cent of Entity B and so controls Entity B via its majority share ownership. Hence, Entity B is regarded as a subsidiary of Entity A and part of the group. Parent entity financial statements portray the financial position of Entity A only, whereas consolidated financial statements portray the financial position of the group — both Entity A and Entity B. When preparing consolidated accounts, any transactions between entities in the group are eliminated. For example, assume Entity A sells goods to the value of $250 000 to Entity B. This is sales revenue for Entity A and the cost of sales for Entity B. However, when preparing the consolidated financial statements, such intercompany sales and purchases are eliminated. The sales for the consolidated entity will not include the $250 000 of sales from Entity A to Entity B, and the $250 000 of purchases by Entity B from Entity A will also be eliminated from the consolidated accounts.

FIGURE 5.4   Concept of parent entity and group

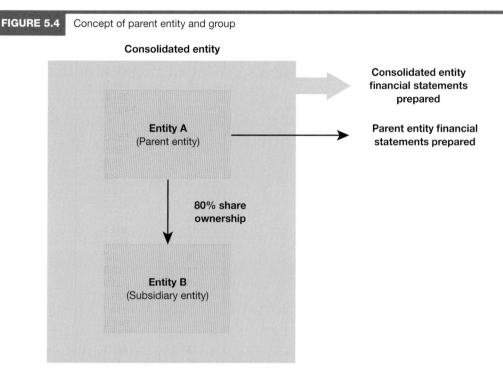

Entities are required to disclose the subsidiaries that they consolidate into their group accounts. If we use JB Hi-Fi Ltd as an illustration, JB Hi-Fi Ltd's notes to the financial statements identify that the parent entity (JB Hi-Fi Ltd) has control over 17 subsidiaries: JB Hi-Fi Group Pty Ltd, JB Hi-Fi (A) Pty Ltd, Clive Anthonys Pty Ltd, Rocket Replacements Pty Ltd, JB Hi-Fi Education Solutions Pty Ltd, JB Hi-Fi Group (NZ) Limited, JB Hi-Fi NZ Ltd, JB Hi-Fi (B) Pty Ltd, Muir Electrical Company Pty Ltd, Muir Electrical Service Co Pty Ltd, The Good Guys Discount Warehouses (Australia) Pty Ltd, Muir Group Employee Share Plan Pty Ltd, Muir Finance Company Pty Ltd, M. W. (Australia) Pty Ltd, Muir Electrical Company Pty Ltd as Trustee of the Muir Investment Unit Trust, The Good Guys Discount Warehouses (Australia) Pty Ltd as Trustee of the various store Trusts and Home Services Network Pty Ltd. As at the end of June 2018, JB Hi-Fi Ltd owned 100 per cent of the shares in each of these entities. The parent entity and the subsidiaries comprise the group. Financial statements are prepared for the group as a single economic entity. The parent entity financial statements reflect the performance and position of JB Hi-Fi Ltd only, whereas the consolidated financial statements reflect the performance and position for the parent and subsidiary entities.

The consolidated statement of financial position for JB Hi-Fi Ltd is illustrated in figure 5.5. Note that JB Hi-Fi Ltd uses the term 'balance sheet' rather than 'statement of financial position'. This is presented in a narrative format and reports the group's assets, liabilities and equity as at 30 June 2018. Note that the assets equal the liabilities plus equity.

FIGURE 5.5   JB Hi-Fi Ltd's consolidated balance sheet

JB HI-FI LTD **Consolidated balance sheet** as at 30 June 2018		Consolidated	
	Notes	2018 $m	2017 $m
Current assets			
Cash and cash equivalents		72.0	72.8
Trade and other receivables	8	204.7	193.6

	Notes	Consolidated 2018 $m	2017 $m
Inventories	7	891.1	859.7
Other current assets	9	42.7	41.4
Total current assets		1 210.5	1 167.5
Non-current assets			
Plant and equipment	10	198.0	208.2
Intangible assets	11	1 037.3	1 037.3
Other non-current assets	9	45.9	46.8
Total non-current assets		1 281.2	1 292.3
Total assets		2 491.7	2 459.8
Current liabilities			
Trade and other payables	12	665.3	644.7
Deferred revenue	13	150.5	141.8
Provisions	14	83.5	76.3
Other current liabilities	15	8.3	9.0
Current tax liabilities		9.6	13.6
Total current liabilities		917.2	885.4
Non-current liabilities			
Borrowings	17	469.4	558.8
Deferred revenue	13	103.7	99.6
Deferred tax liabilities	6	5.7	16.1
Provisions	14	12.5	11.8
Other non-current liabilities	15	35.6	34.6
Total non-current liabilities		626.9	720.9
Total liabilities		1 544.1	1 606.3
Net assets		**947.6**	**853.5**
Equity			
Contributed equity	18	441.7	438.7
Reserves	19	42.7	33.2
Retained earnings		463.2	381.6
Total equity		**947.6**	**853.5**

Source: JB Hi-Fi Ltd 2018, p. 56.

VALUE TO BUSINESS

- The statement of financial position is usually presented in a narrative format, although alternative presentation formats are acceptable.
- The statement of financial position should include relevant details for the current and comparative reporting periods.
- If a company controls other entities, the statement of financial position is presented for the group as a single economic entity.

5.9 Presentation and disclosure of elements in the statement of financial position

LEARNING OBJECTIVE 5.9 Describe the presentation and disclosure requirements for elements in the statement of financial position.

The presentation and disclosure of financial information are designed to communicate information to users in an effective and efficient manner which encompasses the qualitative characteristics of relevance, faithful representativeness, understandability and comparability. The statement of financial position details recognised assets, liabilities and equity as at a particular date. Relevant information is also conveyed through disclosures accompanying the financial statements. These disclosures include additional information pertaining to both recognised and unrecognised items, including their nature, measurement assumptions and estimations, and risks and uncertainties.

Accounting standards exist that prescribe the presentation and disclosure requirements for financial statements. In this section, we explore some of the key presentation and disclosure requirements applicable to the statement of financial position. Recall that all listed entities such as the Qantas Group and JB Hi-Fi Ltd are required to comply with the presentation and disclosure requirements of the accounting standards. Small entities with no public accountability, such as ATC, are not required to comply with the accounting standards. This means that they are unconstrained in the preparation of their financial statements. A small business operation such as ATC would not have raised equity or debt capital from the public, and would not have investors and shareholders who depend on financial statements to monitor and assess its investment decisions. Some entities with no public accountability voluntarily adopt presentation and disclosure practices required by accounting standards.

Current and non-current assets and liabilities

When preparing a statement of financial position, assets and liabilities should be presented in a current/non-current format unless an alternative presentation, such as listing the assets and liabilities in order of their liquidity, provides information that is more relevant and reliable. The distinction between **current assets** and **non-current assets** is based on the timing of the future economic benefits. Similarly, the distinction between **current liabilities** and **non-current liabilities** is based on the timing of the expected future sacrifices. If the economic benefits (outflow of resources) attached to the asset (liability) are expected to be realised within the next reporting period (assumed to be 12 months), then the asset (liability) is categorised as current. However, if the economic benefits (outflow of resources) attached to the asset (liability) are expected over a period extending beyond the next reporting period, a non-current categorisation is appropriate.

Grouping the assets and liabilities on a current/non-current basis is useful when assessing an entity's liquidity. Comparing the current assets and current liabilities is useful in assessing the likelihood that the entity will be able to pay its debts as they fall due. If an entity has a single, clearly identifiable time lapse between the purchase of assets for processing and the realisation of their economic benefits (referred to as the **operating cycle**) that extends beyond 12 months, then the length of the operating cycle can be used to categorise assets and liabilities as current or non-current.

To illustrate the current/non-current classification concept, consider an entity that has inventory available for sale. The inventory is categorised as a current asset, as the entity expects to sell the inventory and receive the cash within the next 12-month period. In contrast, the entity's machinery used to produce the inventory will generate economic benefits beyond the next reporting period and, accordingly, is categorised as a non-current asset. If an entity secures a loan in 2018 with the loan maturing in 2028, the portion of the loan that is to be repaid within the next 12 months is classified as a current liability, whereas the loan payments beyond the next 12 months are classified as a non-current liability.

In the statement of financial position, it is usual for an entity to show the total amounts for:
- current assets
- non-current assets
- current liabilities
- non-current liabilities.

Presentation and disclosure of assets, liabilities and equity

In the statement of financial position, assets are classified according to their nature or function. This means that the asset classifications can reflect an asset's:
- liquidity
- marketability
- physical characteristics
- expected timing of future economic benefits
- purpose.

Liabilities and equity are classified according to their nature. The factors that can be used to classify liabilities are:
- liquidity
- level of security or guarantee
- expected timing of the future sacrifice
- source
- conditions attached to the liabilities.

Classification of equity items in the statement of financial position can be based on their origin or source (that is, contributions from owners or retained earnings) and/or the rights attached to the item.

Now that we have an understanding of the elements of the statement of financial position, we will consider the different types of asset, liability and equity items (referred to as **classes**) that are likely to be found in the statement of financial position. Smaller entities often list all or some of their elements individually, without aggregating them into classes for the purpose of presenting the statement of financial position. However, larger entities aggregate their assets by class for the purpose of presentation in the statement of financial position and provide greater details on the various items within the asset, liability and equity classes in the notes to the accounts.

We will explore the classes of assets, liabilities and equity in the statement of financial position by referring to the 2018 consolidated statement of financial position for JB Hi-Fi Ltd. Recall that the relevant notes to the statement of financial position for JB Hi-Fi Ltd are reproduced in the appendix to this text.

Assets

An extract of the asset section of the 2018 statement of financial position for JB Hi-Fi Ltd is provided in figure 5.6. The first thing you should note is the segregation of assets into current and non-current assets, with subtotals for current and non-current assets.

| FIGURE 5.6 | Extract of JB Hi-Fi Ltd's 2018 balance sheet — asset section |

JB HI-FI LTD
Consolidated balance sheet (extract)
as at 30 June 2018

		Consolidated	
	Notes	2018 $m	2017 $m
Current assets			
Cash and cash equivalents		72.0	72.8
Trade and other receivables	8	204.7	193.6
Inventories	7	891.1	859.7
Other current assets	9	42.7	41.4
Total current assets		1 210.5	1 167.5
Non-current assets			
Plant and equipment	10	198.0	208.2
Intangible assets	11	1 037.3	1 037.3
Other non-current assets	9	45.9	46.8
Total non-current assets		1 281.2	1 292.3
Total assets		**2 491.7**	**2 459.8**

Source: JB Hi-Fi Ltd 2018, p. 56.

The various asset classes disclosed in the statement of financial position for a large entity such as JB Hi-Fi Ltd are as follows.

- **Cash and cash equivalents** — the cash resources that an entity has on hand at a particular point in time. Generally, we would not expect the cash amount to be substantial, as cash generates low returns relative to productive assets.
- Trade and other receivables — the cash the entity expects to receive from parties that owe it money. This class is often called **trade receivables (trade debtors** or **accounts receivable).**
- **Inventories** — the supplies of raw materials to be used in the production process (in the case of a manufacturing firm), work-in-progress and/or the finished goods that the entity has available for sale. The term 'stock' can be used interchangeably with 'inventories'. For JB Hi-Fi Ltd, the inventory would include items such as televisions, computers, DVDs, CDs, tablets, iPods and hi-fi equipment.
- Non-current assets classified as held for sale — a group of assets that the entity plans to dispose of as a group in a single transaction. Note that JB Hi-Fi Ltd has no non-current assets classified as held for sale.
- **Investments accounted for using the equity method** — this class of asset will appear only if the entity owns enough shares in another entity to enable it to exert significant influence (not control) over the other entity's decision making. This amount in the statement of financial position represents the cost of the shares acquired plus any share of the other entity's profits, less any dividends that the entity has received from the other entity. Note that JB Hi-Fi Ltd has no investments accounted for using the equity method.
- Other financial assets — a **financial asset** is any asset that is cash, a contractual right to receive cash or another financial asset, a contractual right to exchange financial instruments with another entity under conditions that are potentially favourable, or an equity instrument of another entity. Items included in this category are investments in shares. Often the other financial assets category includes derivative

financial assets. However, sometimes the derivative financial assets are separately listed. A **derivative financial asset** is a financial asset whose value depends on the value of an underlying asset, reference rate or index.

- **Property, plant and equipment (PPE)** — items of PPE controlled by the entity. This classification includes land, buildings, machinery and other items of plant and equipment. Note that JB Hi-Fi Ltd has plant and equipment only. Some of the items recorded in plant and equipment are leased assets.
- **Deferred tax assets** — accounting rules are used to determine accounting profit, and taxation rules are used to derive taxable income. Differences in the two sets of rules can give rise to expected taxation benefits that satisfy the asset definition and recognition criteria.
- **Agricultural assets (biological assets)** — living animals or plants such as grapevines, trees in a plantation, dairy cattle, fruit trees and sheep. Note that JB Hi-Fi Ltd has no agricultural assets.
- **Intangible assets** — assets do not have to be in physical form. An intangible asset is a non-monetary asset without physical substance. Intangible assets are identifiable in the sense that they can be individually identified, measured and recognised. Examples of **identifiable intangible assets** are trademarks, brand names, patents, rights, agreements, development expenditure, mastheads and licences. JB Hi-Fi Ltd's intangible assets include goodwill, brand names, location premiums and rights to profit share.
- **Goodwill** — this is classified as an unidentifiable intangible asset. Goodwill can be recognised in the statement of financial position only if it is acquired. The goodwill acquired is calculated as the excess of the consideration paid for a business over the fair value of the net assets acquired at the date of acquisition. Effectively, goodwill represents an amount the acquirer is paying for things such as an established client base, reputation, operational synergies and control. For example, in 2014 Facebook acquired WhatsApp for US$22 billion. As this price paid exceeded WhatsApp's net assets of approximately US$6.7 billion, Facebook recognised the goodwill associated with this acquisition at $15.3 billion. Goodwill on JB Hi-Fi Ltd's statement of financial position includes goodwill associated with the acquisition of The Good Guys, being $712.2 million.

An illustration of the calculation of goodwill is provided in illustrative example 5.2.

ILLUSTRATIVE EXAMPLE 5.2

Goodwill determination

On 17 March 2017, Cisco Systems Inc. acquired 100 per cent of the issued share capital of AppDynamics Inc., a private application intelligence software company. The acquisition sought to reinforce Cisco's strategic direction and its move to software-centric solutions (Cisco Systems Inc. 2017, p. 81).

Step 1. Determine the purchase consideration

1. What is the purchase consideration? This is the purchase price paid by Cisco Systems Inc. for AppDynamics Inc.:

$$\$3\,258\,000$$

Step 2. Determine the fair value of the net assets acquired

2. Determine the fair value of net assets acquired (fair value of assets acquired less fair value of any liabilities acquired):

$$\$610\,000$$

Step 3. Calculate goodwill

3. Calculate goodwill as the purchase consideration less the fair value of net assets acquired:

$$\$3\,258\,000 - \$610\,000 = \$2\,648\,000$$

To provide users with information that is useful for decision making, further information about the various asset classes in the statement of financial position should be provided in the notes to the accounts. Since the information in the financial statements consists of summarised and aggregated data, the financial statements contain cross-references to the notes, where greater detail is provided. Figure 5.7 provides the disaggregation of the asset classes in the extract of the 2018 statement of financial position for JB Hi-Fi Ltd to enable us to gain an appreciation of the assets comprising each asset class. This is not to say that every entity would necessarily have the same asset classes listed on its statement of financial position and/or the same assets within each asset class.

FIGURE 5.7 JB Hi-Fi Ltd's 2018 balance sheet — disaggregation of asset classes

JB Hi-Fi Ltd's assets on the balance sheet	Note	Disaggregation of asset class
Current assets		
Cash and cash equivalents		It is usual for the cash and cash equivalent asset class to include: • cash at bank, on hand and in transit • cash on deposit. If an entity is operating a bank overdraft, rather than having cash at bank, then the overdraft appears as a current liability.
Trade and other receivables	8	• Trade receivables (measured at their face value less any allowance for doubtful debts (impairment)) • Goods and services tax (GST) recoverable • Non-trade receivables Other types of receivables appearing in a statement of financial position include: • loans to other persons • employee share plan loans.
Inventories	7	• Finished goods (measured at the lower of the cost and net realisable value) If the entity is a manufacturer, other types of inventories on a statement of financial position include: • raw materials • work in progress.
Other	9	• Prepayments • Other deposits • Other assets
Non-current assets		
Plant and equipment	10	• Leasehold improvements • Plant and equipment • Equipment under finance lease JB Hi-Fi Ltd has plant and equipment and leasehold improvements only. It has no land or buildings. It is common for PPE to be grouped together in the statement of financial position.
Intangible assets	11	• Goodwill • Brand names • Location premiums • Rights to profit share Other types of intangible assets that may be found on a statement of financial position include patents, management rights and licences.
Other	9	Prepayments

Source: Information from JB Hi-Fi Ltd 2018, pp. 68–72.

Cash and cash equivalents in a statement of financial position comprise cash at bank, on hand, in transit and on short-term deposit. Receivables represent amounts owed to the entity by other entities/individuals (also referred to as 'debtors'). The **receivables** for JB Hi-Fi Ltd are divided into trade receivables (amounts due from customers for the sale of goods or services, also known as 'accounts receivable') and non-trade receivables. Non-trade receivables may include goods and services tax (GST) receivables arising due to an entity having paid more GST during the reporting period than it has collected. The entity is therefore entitled to receive the difference between GST paid and GST collected from the government. The trade and other receivables note for JB Hi-Fi Ltd details information concerning the receivables, such as the average credit period, the days that the receivables are overdue and receivables that have been assessed as being impaired (i. e. doubtful). As JB Hi-Fi Ltd is a retailer, its inventories consist of finished goods only. A manufacturing entity's inventories would include work-in-progress and raw materials. JB Hi-Fi Ltd also lists other assets in its statement of financial position. Its other assets include prepayments and deposits.

The PPE asset class is typically a large asset class, as it comprises the entity's physical non-current assets. Included in this asset class for JB Hi-Fi Ltd are plant and equipment, and leasehold improvements. The company has no land or property, as it leases all of its premises. Specific items within the PPE class are not disclosed. However, a smaller entity may list various types of plant and equipment in the statement of financial position. The plant and equipment note for JB Hi-Fi Ltd details information concerning acquisitions through business combination, additions, disposals, and depreciation and impairment charges for the reporting period.

JB Hi-Fi Ltd has both identifiable and unidentifiable intangible assets recognised in its statement of financial position. The identifiable intangibles listed are brand names, location premiums and rights to profit share. Goodwill is the unidentifiable intangible. Recalling our previous discussion, goodwill can be recognised only when an entity acquires another entity and the consideration exceeds the fair value of the net assets acquired. The recognition of goodwill in the statement of financial position indicates that JB Hi-Fi Ltd has been involved in business acquisitions in the current or previous reporting periods. The information disclosed in the notes to the accounts includes additions and write-downs during the reporting period.

Liabilities

To illustrate the classification of liabilities, an extract of the liability section of the 2018 statement of financial position for JB Hi-Fi Ltd is shown in figure 5.8. The various liability classes disclosed in the statement of financial position for a large entity such as JB Hi-Fi Ltd are as follows.

- Trade and other payables — the cash expected to be paid to entities or individuals to whom money is owed. This class is often called **trade payables (trade creditors or accounts payable)**.
- Borrowings — debt funding that requires interest payments. It is useful for users to be able to identify and separate the entity's liabilities requiring periodic servicing in the form of interest payments from the liabilities that do not involve regular interest payments.
- Tax liabilities — differences in the accounting and taxation rules used to determine accounting profit and taxable income respectively can result in the entity having future tax obligations.
- **Provisions** — these qualify as liabilities on the basis of satisfying the definition and recognition criteria. However, they are recorded as a liability subcategory on the basis that there is greater uncertainty in the amount or timing of the sacrifice of economic benefits relative to other liabilities.
- Other financial liabilities — a **financial liability** is any liability that is a contractual obligation to deliver cash or another financial asset to another entity, or a contractual obligation to exchange financial assets or financial liabilities with another entity under conditions that are potentially unfavourable to the entity. Often the other financial liabilities category includes derivative financial liabilities. However, sometimes the derivative financial liabilities are separately listed. A **derivative financial liability** is a financial liability whose value depends on the value of an underlying security, reference rate or index.

FIGURE 5.8	Extract of JB Hi-Fi Ltd's 2018 balance sheet — liability section

JB HI-FI LTD
Consolidated balance sheet (extract)
as at 30 June 2018

		Consolidated	
	Notes	2018 $m	2017 $m
Current liabilities			
Trade and other payables	12	665.3	644.7
Deferred revenue	13	150.5	141.8
Provisions	14	83.5	76.3
Other current liabilities	15	8.3	9.0
Current tax liabilities		9.6	13.6
Total current liabilities		917.2	885.4
Non-current liabilities			
Borrowings	17	469.4	558.8
Deferred revenue	13	103.7	99.6
Deferred tax liabilities	6	5.7	16.1
Provisions	14	12.5	11.8
Other non-current liabilities	15	35.6	34.6
Total non-current liabilities		626.9	720.9
Total liabilities		**1 544.1**	**1 606.3**

Source: JB Hi-Fi Ltd 2018, p. 56.

As with assets, more detailed information regarding the components of the various liability classes shown in the statement of financial position is available in the notes to the accounts. Smaller entities may provide disaggregated liabilities in the statement of financial position, rather than aggregating the information in the statement of financial position and providing greater detail in the notes to the accounts. To appreciate the types of liabilities within liability classes, an extract of the disaggregation of the liability classes in the 2018 statement of financial position for JB Hi-Fi Ltd is provided in figure 5.9.

FIGURE 5.9 JB Hi-Fi Ltd's 2018 balance sheet — disaggregation of liability classes

JB Hi-Fi Ltd liabilities on the balance sheet	Note	Disaggregation of liability class
Current liabilities		
Trade and other payables	12	• Trade payables • Goods and services tax payable • Other creditors and accruals
Deferred revenue	13	• Deferred revenue
Provisions	14	• Employee benefits • Lease provision
Other current liabilities	15	• Lease accrual • Lease incentive • Other financial liabilities
Current tax liabilities		• Income tax payable
Non-current liabilities		
Borrowings	17	• Bank loans
Deferred revenue	13	• Deferred revenue
Deferred tax liabilities	6	• Deferred tax liabilities
Provisions	14	• Employee benefits • Lease provision
Other non-current liabilities	15	• Lease accrual • Lease incentive

Source: Information from JB Hi-Fi Ltd 2018, pp. 72–76.

The notes to the accounts segregate the accounts payable amount in the statement of financial position into trade payables (e.g. trade creditors), GST payable, and other creditors and accruals. A creditor is an entity or individual to whom the entity owes money. The trade payables (or accounts payable or trade creditors) are those to whom money is owed for the goods and services provided. The term 'other creditors and accruals' refers to monies owed for non-trade related goods and services, including accrued expenses. Accrued expenses are expenses incurred but not yet paid; they will be explored in more detail in the next chapter. The GST payable relates to GST that has been collected by the company from customers and needs to be remitted to the government. The tax liability that JB Hi-Fi Ltd has in relation to income tax is disclosed in a separate class called current tax liabilities.

JB Hi-Fi Ltd's borrowings include bank loans. Figure 5.9 does not reflect the further segregation of borrowings into secured and unsecured, although this is provided in the relevant note. A provider of **secured debt** has a priority claim over the entity's assets in the event of the entity's demise. A provider of unsecured debt has no priority claim over the entity's assets; if the entity goes into receivership, the provider will recover its money, or part thereof, only if the proceeds from asset sales exceed the monies owed to secured debt holders. Shareholders are entitled to cash only if any funds remain after all the liabilities have been satisfied. Entities often disclose the assets offered as security for the borrowings and the interest rate range of the borrowings. While JB Hi-Fi Ltd has no other types of borrowings, debentures and notes are a type of borrowing often found in statements of financial position.

We stated earlier that provisions are liabilities for which uncertainty is associated with the amount or timing of the expected sacrifice of economic benefits. Consider the liabilities discussed thus far. There is a high degree of certainty associated with the timing and amount of payments to creditors and lenders, so these are not regarded as provisions. The provisions of JB Hi-Fi Ltd comprise lease provisions and employee benefits provisions.

- Provisions for employee benefits relate to payments expected to be made to employees in relation to benefits that the employees have accrued. The provision account represents an estimation of the amount owing in relation to entitlements such as annual leave, sick leave and long service leave.
- Lease provisions relate to the estimated amount required to return the group's leased premises to their original condition.
- Other types of provisions that we might find in the statement of financial position include provisions for warranties and restructuring costs, and provisions for dividends if the dividend has been declared, determined or publicly recommended by the entity but remains unpaid at the end of the reporting period. There are stringent accounting rules covering what can and cannot be recognised as provisions in the statement of financial position.

The disaggregation of JB Hi-Fi Ltd's assets and liabilities is not inclusive of all the assets and liabilities that could appear in a statement of financial position. Depending on an entity's operations and on changes in regulations, other assets and liabilities may arise. For example, earlier we discussed how lease financing may not result in statement of financial position applications. For example, JB Hi-Fi Ltd has leases, with terms of 5 to 15 years, relating to stores. As the company does not have an obligation to purchase the leased assets at the end of the lease period, there is no requirement to record the leased assets and liabilities in the statement of financial position. Nevertheless, entities with future lease commitments do need to disclose these commitments. JB Hi-Fi Ltd discloses its lease commitments in note 21. The note discloses that JB Hi-Fi Ltd has $684.4 million in future minimum lease payments. This is not recorded in its statement of financial position, yet it represents in excess of 44 per cent of JB Hi-Fi Ltd's total liabilities. However, after IFRS 16 *Leases* effective date of January 2019, it will have a significant impact on the group's consolidated financial statements commencing with the year ending 30 June 2020, as JB Hi-Fi Ltd will need to recognise a right-of-use asset and a related lease liability in its statement of financial position.

Another example of what we may see in statements of financial position in the future is carbon liabilities. There is currently no accounting standard governing reporting of carbon liabilities; however, some entities are voluntarily disclosing and measuring carbon-related information.

Equity

Depending on the entity structure, the terminology and equity classifications appearing in the statement of financial position will vary between entities. For example, in the case of ATC, a sole operator business, the equity comprises capital that the owner, Nicholas Cash, has contributed plus profits generated by the business since its commencement less any drawings. The equity section of the 2018 statement of financial position for JB Hi-Fi Ltd is typical of that for a large entity. Not dissimilar to a smaller entity, the equity of a company is categorised into three components in its statement of financial position:

1. share capital (contributed equity)
2. retained earnings (retained profits)
3. reserves.

Figure 5.10 provides an extract of the equity section from the JB Hi-Fi Ltd 2018 statement of financial position.

FIGURE 5.10   Extract of JB Hi-Fi Ltd's 2018 balance sheet — equity section

JB HI-FI LTD Consolidated balance sheet (extract) as at 30 June 2018			
		Consolidated	
	Notes	2018 $m	2017 $m
Equity			
Contributed equity	18	441.7	438.7
Reserves	19	42.7	33.2
Retained earnings		463.2	381.6
Total equity		**947.6**	**853.5**

Source: JB Hi-Fi Ltd 2018, p. 56.

Share capital

Share capital (also called issued capital or contributed equity) refers to the capital contributions to an entity made by the owner(s) of the entity. For large entities such as JB Hi-Fi Ltd, the capital is contributed as a result of shareholders paying money to the company in return for the company issuing them shares. Hence, it is usually given the term '**paid-up share capital**'. When shares are subsequently transacted in the market, the capital of the company does not change — the company receives no money from this transaction, because the transaction involves the exchange of shares that are already on issue between investors. An entity's share capital changes when it makes a new issue of shares through a public or private issue or via employee share plans. For entities that are not companies, such as ATC, capital usually takes the form of a cash injection and is referred to as **contributed capital**. However, a contribution of capital does not necessarily have to take the form of cash. Entities may receive a capital contribution in the form of plant and equipment. For example, when establishing a company, the vendor might contribute a property to the business in exchange for shares, or an individual starting their own business may contribute equipment. JB Hi-Fi Ltd's notes to the accounts detail the movement in the contributed equity during the reporting period. Note 18 details the number and dollar value of shares on issue at the start of the reporting period, any movements in ordinary share capital during the year by JB Hi-Fi Ltd, and the number and dollar value of shares on issue at the end of the reporting period.

Retained earnings

Retained earnings (also called retained profits or unappropriated profits) represent the sum of an entity's undistributed profits, being the profits the entity has generated since its inception that have not been distributed in the form of dividends or transferred to reserve accounts. Consider the following. Owners contribute $100 000 to commence a business. During the first year of operations, the entity reports a loss of $40 000. In year 2, a profit of $10 000 is recorded, increasing to $50 000 in year 3. Year 4's profit is $80 000 and a $20 000 dividend is distributed to the owners. A $110 000 profit is reported in year 5, and the entity increases the dividend to $30 000 and transfers $20 000 to a general reserve account. Table 5.1 shows the balance that would appear in the retained earnings as at the end of the reporting period. At the end of year 5, the retained earnings are $140 000, comprising the sum of the five years of profits, being $210 000 (–$40 000 + $10 000 + $50 000 + $80 000 + $110 000) less the $50 000 dividends distributed over this time, less the $20 000 transfer to the general reserve account.

TABLE 5.1   **Concept of retained earnings**

	Statement of profit or loss		Distribution of profits			Equity section of statement of financial position		
Year	Profit or loss	Dividends	Transfer to general reserve	Retained earnings at end of period	Contributed capital	Retained earnings	General reserve
1	$ (40 000)			$(40 000)	$100 000	$ (40 000)	
2	10 000			(30 000)	100 000	(30 000)	
3	50 000			20 000	100 000	20 000	
4	80 000	$20 000		80 000	100 000	80 000	
5	110 000	30 000	$20 000	140 000	100 000	140 000	$20 000

JB Hi-Fi Ltd had $463.2 million of retained earnings as at 30 June 2018. Figure 5.11 provides an extract from the 2018 statement of changes in equity for JB Hi-Fi Ltd. The company commenced the financial year with $381.6 million of retained earnings. The profit for the financial year ended 30 June 2018 was $233.2 million and the directors elected to distribute $151.6 million of dividends. Thus, as at 30 June 2018, the company had $463.2 million of retained earnings.

Reserves

Equity consists of various categories of items — capital contributions, retained earnings and reserves. **Reserves** are a component of equity that is difficult to define because they are accounts that can be created in a number of ways. Fundamentally, reserves represent the funds that are retained in the entity, in addition to retained profits. Examples of reserves that an entity may have include, but are not limited to, asset revaluation surplus, capital reserve and foreign currency translation reserve. A revaluation surplus will arise if an entity is using fair value rather than cost to measure its long-term assets such as property. The reserve reflects the increase in the fair value of the long-term assets. This increase is not a revenue item, so it is not part of retained earnings. Rather, the transaction involves increasing the asset and increasing the reserve account in recognition that additional funds are available to the owners as a result of this valuation adjustment. A capital reserve can be created by transferring funds from retained earnings to the capital reserve. This is signalling that the entity is isolating funds for the purpose of future capital investment.

| FIGURE 5.11 | Extract of JB Hi-Fi Ltd's 2018 statement of changes in equity — retained earnings |

	Consolidated	
	2018 $m	2017 $m
Retained earnings		
Balance 1 July	381.6	328.3
Net profit for the year	233.2	172.4
Dividends provided for or paid	(151.6)	(119.1)
Balance 30 June	**463.2**	**381.6**

Source: JB Hi-Fi Ltd 2018, p. 57.

A simple way of thinking about reserves is that they represent changes to an entity's assets and liabilities other than through what is captured in the capital contribution and retained earnings components of the statement of financial position. A small business such as ATC will typically not have reserve accounts; however, large companies do have reserve accounts. JB Hi-Fi Ltd has an equity-settled benefits reserve, a foreign currency translation reserve, a hedging reserve and other reserves. Descriptions of these reserve accounts, as well as other reserve accounts that could appear in a statement of financial position, are as follows.

- *Revaluation surplus.* As we will discuss later in this chapter, subsequent to acquisition entities can elect to revalue classes of PPE to fair value. Recalling the accounting equation, increasing the asset value requires a corresponding entry to keep the equation in balance. The corresponding entry is made to the revaluation surplus. This reserve will exist only if the entity revalues any of its PPE.
- *General reserve.* This reserve is created by management transferring funds from retained earnings to a general reserve. The transfer out of retained earnings reduces the equity balance, but the transfer to the general reserve increases equity. Therefore, the accounting equation remains in balance. The purpose of creating a general reserve is to indicate to owners that funds (not cash) have been set aside for a purpose to be determined in the future, and will not be available for distribution as dividends.
- *Foreign currency translation reserve.* This reserve will appear only if the entity has an overseas subsidiary. As previously discussed, consolidated accounts are prepared for the reporting entity, which comprises the parent entity and the entities that the parent controls. It is not possible to consolidate financial statements prepared in a domestic currency (e.g. A$) with non-domestic currency financial statements (e.g. yen). The accounts of the overseas entity must be converted into domestic currency before consolidation occurs. As different elements of the statement of financial position and statement of profit or loss are required by accounting standards to be converted at different exchange rates, the accounting equation no longer balances. The foreign currency translation reserve is effectively an equity account that is used to ensure that the accounting equation holds after the translation of the overseas currency financial statements into the domestic currency.
- *Share-based payment reserve (equity-settled benefits reserve).* This reserve account records the fair value at grant date of shares/options granted to employees and directors as a component of their remuneration. Amounts are transferred out of the reserve and into issued capital when the options are exercised.
- *Hedging reserve.* This reserve recognises gains or losses associated with derivative instruments that qualify as hedges. The cumulative deferred gain or loss on the hedging instruments is recognised in the profit or loss in the same period as when the hedged transaction affects the profit or loss.

It is important not to equate reserves with the availability of money. They do not reflect monies available to distribute to owners.

Non-controlling interests

In addition to paid-up capital, retained earnings and reserves, the other equity item that can appear in the statement of financial position is **non-controlling interests**. This item is presented in the consolidated accounts only if the parent entity does not own 100 per cent of the subsidiary entity. Non-controlling interests represent the claim on the net assets of the reporting entity that belongs to shareholders of an entity other than parent entity shareholders. JB Hi-Fi Ltd had no non-controlling interests as at 30 June 2018.

VALUE TO BUSINESS

- Assets and liabilities should be presented in a current or non-current format unless an alternative presentation — such as listing the assets and liabilities in order of their liquidity — provides information that is more relevant and reliable. The distinction between current and non-current assets (liabilities) is based on the timing of the expected future economic benefits (future sacrifices) — current if expected within the next 12 months and non-current if expected beyond the next 12 months.
- For the purpose of reporting in the statement of financial position, assets, liabilities and equity are usually aggregated and listed by class. Details of the assets, liabilities and equity within the various classes may be found in the notes to the accounts.
- The typical asset classes are cash; receivables; investments; financial assets; PPE; intangible assets; tax assets; and other assets.
- The liability classes typically found in the statement of financial position are payables, borrowings, tax liabilities and provisions.
- The four equity classes that may appear in the equity section of the statement of financial position are share capital (contributed equity), reserves, retained earnings (retained profits) and non-controlling interests.

5.10 Measurement of various assets and liabilities

LEARNING OBJECTIVE 5.10 Discuss the measurement of various assets and liabilities in the statement of financial position.

In this chapter thus far, we have discussed matters related to the definition, recognition, classification, presentation and disclosure of elements in the statement of financial position. We now consider how elements in the statement of financial position are measured.

The dollar value assigned to assets and liabilities in the statement of financial position is referred to as the **carrying amount (book value)**. What we need to assess is how carrying amounts are determined. Recall that equity is defined as the residual interest in the assets of an entity after all its liabilities have been deducted. As such, equity is not directly measured. The measurement of equity is the carrying value of all recognised assets less the carrying value of all recognised liabilities.

A number of measurement systems are used in financial reporting and these are discussed in the revised *Conceptual Framework*. Examples of alternative measurement systems for assets and liabilities, and the corresponding income and expense items, include historical cost and current value. The measurement principles discussed in this chapter relate to IFRS requirements.

Measurement principles

Historical cost is an entry value, as it reflects the value in the market in which the entity acquires the asset or incurs the liability. Historical cost is:
- for an asset — the cash or cash equivalents paid to acquire the asset
- for a liability — the amount of proceeds received in exchange for the obligation.

Current cost is also an entry value. It reflects the cash or cash equivalents that would have to be paid to replace the asset, or the undiscounted amount of cash or cash equivalents that would be required to settle the obligation at measurement date.

Current value measures provide monetary information about assets and liabilities (and income and expenses) using information that is updated to reflect conditions at measurement date. Compared to the previous measurement date, current values may have increased or decreased. There are a number of current value measurement bases. The two most common current value measurement bases are fair value and value-in-use for assets, and the fulfilment model for liabilities.

Fair value is defined as the price that would be received to sell an asset or paid to transfer a liability in an orderly transaction between market participants at the measurement date. A fair value is determined by considering various factors including estimates of future cash flows and their timing and uncertainty, the time value of money and liquidity. Fair value is an exit value, as it represents the perspective of market participants. If there is an active market, the fair value of an item will be observable and verifiable. For example, for an asset it would be the expected cash or cash equivalents from selling the asset in an orderly disposal. For a liability it would be the settlement value required for payment in the normal course of business. In the absence of an active market, valuation models are required to determine fair value. For example, a cash flow–based measurement model could be used, with an asset measured as the present discounted net cash flows associated with the asset and a liability measured as the present discounted value of the future net cash flows that are expected to be required to settle the liabilities in the normal course of business.

The value-in-use and fulfilment models are used for determining the value of the asset and liability to the entity. **Value-in-use** represents the present value of the cash flows that an entity expects to derive from the continuing use of an asset and its ultimate disposal. **Fulfilment value** applies to liabilities and is the present value of the cash flows that an entity expects to incur to satisfy a liability. As the valuation models are entity-specific, the assumptions factored into the models are entity-specific rather than market-based.

Given that the basis for measurement can be historical cost or current value (with options in each category), the question arises as to what is the preferred measurement basis. The *Conceptual Framework* discusses advantages and disadvantages associated with each of the measurement bases, noting that the measurement basis selection is context-specific and should be determined with reference to the desirable qualitative characteristics of financial information — relevance, faithful representation, comparability, verifiability and understandability.

Consider the following. At acquisition date, the historical cost and fair value of an item should be reasonably equivalent. However, the fair value and cost value of the item can diverge as time passes. Take the example of a property purchase. An entity pays $1 000 000 for a property. At acquisition date, the $1 000 000 represents both the property's historical cost and its fair value. Three years later, the property's cost price remains at $1 000 000. However, due to a property boom, its fair value based on the estimated selling price is $1 500 000. For financial reporting purposes, this presents a problem: subsequent to initial recognition, should the property be reflected in the statement of financial position at its original cost, its cost adjusted for changing prices associated with the inflation rate or its fair value?

In terms of accounting rules and regulations (the standards), some accounting standards do prescribe a particular measurement for items post-acquisition and other accounting standards provide account preparers with a choice of measurements that could be applied post-acquisition. From a conceptual viewpoint, the selected measurement basis should be the one that is most useful to financial statement users' decision making. In order to achieve this objective, financial information should be **relevant** (that is, assist users in their decision making) and a **faithful representation** of the economic phenomena it purports to represent (that is, be complete, neutral and free from error). Sometimes there is a trade-off between relevance and faithful representation. Take the case of the property purchased for $1 000 000. The cost price is objective and a faithful representation, but would users find the fair value — the estimated selling price of the property — more relevant for decision-making purposes?

Unless the accounting rules require otherwise, it is common to leave physical assets and liabilities at their historical cost, or historical cost adjusted for depreciation in the case of assets, in the statement of financial position. However, where a measurement choice exists, some entities elect to use fair value. This means that not all items in statements of financial position are recorded using the same measurement basis.

We will use the 2018 JB Hi-Fi Ltd statement of financial position to illustrate how items, particularly assets, can be measured for financial reporting purposes. Recall from earlier in the chapter that preparation of financial statements involves choices, estimates and assumptions. Measurement is an area where these are particularly evident.

Measuring receivables

The carrying amount of receivables in the statement of financial position is the expected cash to be received (the cash equivalent). This is the amount owing less an allowance (provision) for amounts expected to be uncollectable. The term '**allowance for doubtful debts**' (also referred to as provision for impairment or provision for doubtful debts) refers to the amount estimated to be irrecoverable. An entity makes an assessment as to the estimated irrecoverable amount based on objective evidence. A review of individual receivables and an examination of the age of the debtors may be useful in assessing the debts that will be uncollectable.

In the statement of financial position, receivables are usually shown at their net amount (that is, gross value less allowance for doubtful debts), with details of the gross value and the allowance for doubtful debts disclosed in the notes to the accounts.

Figure 5.12 provides an extract of the notes to the accounts from the current receivables section of the JB Hi-Fi Ltd 2018 financial statements. We can observe that the entity expected to receive $55.5 million from trade receivables. As the gross amount due was $56.6 million, the allowance for doubtful debts represented about 1.9 per cent of the balance owing.

| FIGURE 5.12 | Extract of JB Hi-Fi Ltd's 2018 notes to the accounts — trade and other receivables |

	Consolidated	
9. CURRENT ASSETS — TRADE AND OTHER RECEIVABLES	2018 $m	2017 $m
Trade receivables	56.6	54.2
Allowance for doubtful debts	(1.1)	(0.7)
	55.5	53.5
Non-trade receivables	149.2	140.1
	204.7	**193.6**

Source: JB Hi-Fi Ltd 2018, p. 68.

JB Hi-Fi Ltd discloses additional information related to its trade receivables. Note 8(a) details the terms and conditions of trade receivables. JB Hi-Fi Ltd has an average credit period of 30 days. It reviews individual debtors to estimate the amount irrecoverable. Note 8(b) discloses the ageing schedule of the trade receivables and note 8(c) details the movement in the allowance for doubtful debts account. The ageing of the impaired trade receivables is shown in note 8(d).

Measuring inventory

The accounting standards prescribe that the carrying amount of inventory must be the lower of its cost price and net realisable value. Measuring the cost or net realisable value of inventory is a particular issue for retail and manufacturing entities, but not for service entities as they do not manufacture or sell inventory. The process for determining the cost price of a retail or manufacturing firm's inventory depends on the inventory system that the entity is using. There are two types of accounting systems to record inventory — a perpetual inventory system and a periodic inventory system. The former involves keeping detailed records of inventory movements and tracking specific inventory items from purchase through to sale. With technological advances such as barcodes and optical scanners, using a perpetual inventory system is easier than it once was. Using a perpetual system, when inventory is purchased an asset account (inventory) is increased, with dual entry being a reduction in cash or an increase in accounts payable depending on whether the inventory was purchased for cash or on credit. When inventory is sold, the entity can identify the specific inventory that was sold (e.g. by the barcode). The accounting entry reduces the inventory account by the cost price of the inventory sold, with the dual entry being to increase an expense account — the cost of sales. Further, at the point of sale the entity records the sales proceeds as an increase in revenue, with the dual entry being to increase cash or accounts receivable depending on whether the transaction is for cash or on account. Given how the purchase and sale of inventory are recorded using a perpetual system, an entity will always have a record of the cost price of its inventory and the cost of the goods sold at any point in time.

In contrast, a periodic system of recording inventory does not keep a detailed record of the inventory on hand and the cost of the inventory sold. Using this system of recording inventory, when inventory is purchased an expense account (purchases) is increased, with the dual entry being a reduction in cash or increase in accounts payable depending on whether the purchase is for cash or on credit. When inventory is sold, sales revenue is increased and either cash increased (if the transaction is for cash) or accounts receivable increased (if the transaction is on account). Thus, while an entity will know its purchases and sales, it does not keep a continuous record of its inventory on hand and the cost of the inventory sold. To determine the inventory on hand, it is necessary for the entity to do a stocktake at the end of the reporting period. The stocktake will identify the inventory on hand (in quantities) but the entity will not necessarily know the particular cost price of that inventory, given that inventory items can be purchased multiple times during the year at different cost prices. Hence, if using a periodic system to record inventory, a cost flow assumption is needed to determine the cost price of the inventory on hand.

To illustrate these two different systems of recording inventory, consider the example of a retailer purchasing 200, 210, 175 and 200 units of the same inventory in month 1, month 3, month 7 and month 12, respectively, during a reporting period. The inventory's unit cost per batch is $44, $45, $48 and $46, respectively. Of the 785 units acquired during the year, 100 remain unsold at the end of the reporting period. There was no inventory on hand at the start of the reporting period. The inventory on hand at the end of the period needs to be measured for the statement of financial position, and the cost of inventory sold needs to be determined for the statement of profit or loss. What is the cost price of the inventory?

If the entity is using a perpetual inventory system, the inventory items will be tagged and specifically identified. This enables the entity to keep track of the cost of each item sold and the cost of the unsold items. Accordingly, the entity is keeping a running balance of the cost price of inventory and the cost of the inventory sold. As such, the entity will know the specific items that have been sold, and the specific items and their cost price of the 100 units that remain unsold at the end of the reporting period. This will be the balance in the inventory account, given that the inventory account is increased for every inventory item purchased and decreased for every inventory item sold.

While technological advances mean that it is becoming more feasible to track individual inventory items, many entities do not operate such systems. When inventory is not being tracked from purchase to point of sale, an entity is using a periodic inventory system. Under a periodic system, there is no running balance of the inventory on hand or the cost price of the inventory sold. Hence, an assumption about the inventory flow is necessary to determine the inventory on hand and the cost of inventory sold. There are only two cost flow assumptions permitted by IFRS: first-in, first-out (FIFO) and weighted-average. A method known as last-in, first-out (LIFO) is not permitted. The FIFO cost flow assumption is that the items sold are the ones that have been in inventory the longest (so the unsold items are the ones that have been purchased the most recently). The weighted-average cost flow assumption calculates a weighted-average cost of inventory purchased and on hand at the start of the period, and applies this to the number of units sold (unsold). The LIFO cost flow assumption would be that the items sold were the ones that had been in inventory the least amount of time (hence the unsold items were the ones inventory for the longest). The cost that is assigned to the inventory under the FIFO and weighted-average methods for an entity using a periodic inventory system is demonstrated in illustrative example 5.3.

ILLUSTRATIVE EXAMPLE 5.3

Inventory cost flow assumptions

FIFO method

Of the 785 inventory items acquired during the year, it is assumed that the items sold are from the earliest purchases and the items remaining are from the most recent purchases. The 100 units unsold at the end of the reporting period are assumed to be from the inventory purchased in month 12 at a unit cost price of $46. The value assigned to the inventory in the statement of financial position is 100 units @ $46 = $4600. The cost of the 685 units that have been sold is the 200 units purchased in month 1 for $44 ($8800) plus the 210 units purchased in month 3 for $45 ($9450) plus the 175 units purchased in month 7 for $48 ($8400) plus 100 of the 200 units purchased in month 12 for $46 ($4600). The total cost of sales is therefore $31 250. This is summarised below.

Inventory purchases	Inventory sales	Cost of sales	
200 units @ $44 (month 1) = $8800	685 units =	200 units @ $44 (from month 1 purchases)	= $8800
210 units @ $45 (month 3) = $9450		210 units @ $45 (from month 3 purchases)	= $9450
175 units @ $48 (month 7) = $8400		175 units @ $48 (from month 7 purchases)	= $8400
200 units @ $46 (month 12) = $9200		100 units @ $46 (from month 12 purchases)	= $4600
Total purchases = 785 units ($35 850)			
Closing inventory = 100 units @ $46 = $4600		**Total cost of sales = $31 250**	

The **net realisable value** is the expected selling price less the expected costs associated with getting the inventory to a saleable state plus the costs of marketing, selling and distribution. Consider an entity that has inventory on hand at the end of the reporting period that cost $4600. The entity has to ensure that recording the inventory at its cost price would not state the inventory at an amount higher than its net realisable value. If the inventory's net realisable value is assessed at $3500 due to some of the inventory being obsolete, the carrying amount of the inventory in the statement of financial position would have to be $3500, as this is lower than the cost price. The asset, inventory, would have to be reduced by $1100. The dual effect of reducing the inventory is to record an expense (inventory write-down) that increases expenses, reduces profit and therefore reduces equity. Thus, assets have decreased and equity has decreased. If the net realisable value is assessed at $6000, the inventory's carrying amount remains at its cost price given the rule that the carrying value is the lower of cost price or net realisable value.

Measuring non-current assets

All non-current assets with limited useful lives (**depreciable assets**) must be depreciated. Land is not required to be depreciated. **Depreciation** (the term 'amortisation' is used for non-physical non-current assets such as intangibles and also for leased assets) is the allocation of the depreciable amount of a depreciable asset over its estimated useful life. The concept of depreciation will be illustrated in the next chapter. **Accumulated depreciation** refers to the total depreciation charges for an asset from its acquisition to the end of the reporting period. The carrying amount of depreciable assets in the statement of financial position is their cost (or fair value) less the accumulated depreciation.

In general, each class of non-current assets can be carried at either cost, written-down cost or fair value. There are some notable exceptions.
- Goodwill cannot be revalued upwards and must be tested at least annually for impairment.
- Identifiable intangibles such as brand names can be revalued upwards only if an active and liquid market exists.
- Financial instruments are measured at their fair value.
- Agricultural assets are measured at their fair value less costs to sell.

Non-current assets carried at cost or written-down cost must not have a carrying amount that is greater than their recoverable amount. The **recoverable amount** of an asset is the higher of its expected fair value less costs of disposal, and its value-in-use. As noted above, value-in-use refers to the present value of the expected future cash flows associated with the use and subsequent disposal of the asset. This means that the carrying amount must be compared with the recoverable amount; if the latter is lower, the asset is deemed impaired. The asset's carrying amount must be reduced to its recoverable amount and an **impairment** loss (an expense) will be recognised immediately in the statement of profit or loss.

For entities electing to value one or more of their PPE classes at fair value, the fair value must be reviewed regularly. If the fair value of an asset increases from one reporting period to the next, the asset's carrying amount increases and the revaluation surplus increases. The exception is if the increase reverses a previous decrease recorded in the statement of profit or loss. In such a case, rather than increasing the revaluation surplus, the increase can be recorded in the statement of profit or loss to the extent of the decrement previously recorded. If an asset's fair value declines, the asset's carrying amount is reduced, with the corresponding entry recorded as an expense in the statement of profit or loss. The exception to this is if the decrease reverses a previous increase recorded in the revaluation surplus. In such a case, rather than recording an expense in the statement of profit or loss, the revaluation surplus is reduced to the extent of the revaluation previously recorded.

An extract of the notes to the accounts from the non-current assets section of JB Hi-Fi Ltd's 2018 financial statements is provided in figure 5.13. JB Hi-Fi Ltd records all classes of its plant and equipment at cost. It is not uncommon for entities to measure their PPE at cost and disclose the fair value, particularly of property, in the notes to the accounts. In 2018, JB Hi-Fi determined that some of its plant and equipment was impaired. Accordingly, the plant and equipment was written down via an impairment charge of $0.7 million. Goodwill is recorded at cost. It is not required to be amortised on an annual basis. Instead, entities must determine on at least an annual basis whether the goodwill value is impaired. If it is impaired, then the goodwill is written down, with the impairment amount charged as an expense in the statement of profit or loss. Goodwill cannot be revalued upwards. JB Hi-Fi Ltd did not write down any of its goodwill in 2018. In previous years, it has done so. In 2011, JB Hi-Fi Ltd determined that its goodwill associated with the acquisition of Clive Anthonys was impaired, resulting in the goodwill being written down by $4.6 million and an expense, impairment charge, recorded. Note 11(b) identifies the goodwill associated with JB Hi-Fi Ltd's business acquisitions and details the assumptions made in assessing the recoverable amount. JB Hi-Fi Ltd measures its identifiable intangible assets (brand names, location premiums and management rights to profit share) at cost. Identifiable intangible assets can only be upwardly revalued if their fair value can be determined by reference to an active and liquid market. JB Hi-Fi Ltd has determined that its intangible assets have an indefinite life and, hence, the assets are not amortised. As required by an accounting standard, these intangible assets with an indefinite useful life are tested for impairment annually and whenever indicators suggest they may be impaired. The cost of identifiable intangible assets with finite lives must be amortised over their useful lives.

| FIGURE 5.13 | Extract of JB Hi-Fi Ltd's 2018 notes to the accounts — non-current assets |

	Consolidated		
10. NON-CURRENT ASSETS — PLANT AND EQUIPMENT	Plant and equipment $m	Leasehold improvements $m	Total $m
Year ended 30 June 2018			
Opening net book amount	148.2	60.0	208.2
Exchange differences	(0.4)	(0.2)	(0.6)
Additions	35.9	18.5	54.4
Disposals	(2.2)	(0.7)	(2.9)
Depreciation charge	(40.8)	(19.6)	(60.4)
Impairment charge	(0.6)	(0.1)	(0.7)
Closing net book amount	**140.1**	**57.9**	**198.0**
At 30 June 2018			
Cost	336.4	188.1	524.5
Accumulated depreciation and impairment	(196.3)	(130.2)	(326.5)
Net book amount	**140.1**	**57.9**	**198.0**

11. NON-CURRENT ASSETS — INTANGIBLE ASSETS	Goodwill $m	Brand names $m	Location premiums $m	Rights to profit share $m	Total $m
Year ended 30 June 2018					
Opening net book amount	747.0	284.4	2.4	3.5	1 037.3
Impairment charge	—	—	—	—	—
Closing net book amount	**747.0**	**284.4**	**2.4**	**3.5**	**1 037.3**

Source: JB Hi-Fi Ltd 2018, pp. 70–71.

Because measurement choices exist, an entity should identify its measurement basis for various asset and liability classes in the accounting policy note. The measurement method will affect the carrying amount of assets. It is important for users of financial statements to be aware of the measurements employed, especially when making comparisons intra-entity and inter-entity. To facilitate the provision of useful information, an entity can also provide disclosures reconciling the carrying amount of the non-current asset classes at the start of the reporting period with the carrying amount of the classes at the end of the reporting period. This is also illustrated in figure 5.13.

The preceding discussion should make you appreciate that a statement of financial position does not portray the worth of an entity or the entity's value. Illustrative example 5.4 provides an extract from the non-current asset section of the statement of financial position of a fictitious company, Additive Pty Ltd. The total assets as per this statement of financial position are $143 350. This figure does not represent the amount of money that would be received if the assets were sold. Nor does it represent the aggregate historical cost of the assets acquired, as different measurement models are applied to different asset classes. The $143 350 is a combination of cash at bank, trade debtors at their estimated cash equivalent value, the price paid for the motor vehicle at the start of 2016 less two years of depreciation charges, the fair value of property, and the cost price less accumulated depreciation for machinery A and B acquired in 2013 and 2017 respectively.

To illustrate that this statement is not a statement of value, consider the motor vehicle. The statement of financial position is not proposing that the motor vehicle's resale value as at 31 December 2018 is $20 000. This figure simply reflects the vehicle's cost price less the future benefits deemed to have been used up (as represented by the accumulated depreciation). In reality, the vehicle's resale price two years after purchase will be considerably different to the carrying amount in the statement of financial position.

ILLUSTRATIVE EXAMPLE 5.4

Additive Pty Ltd — assets as at 31 December 2018123

ADDITIVE PTY LTD Statement of financial position (extract) as at 31 December 2018		
Current assets		
Cash at bank		$ 12 500
Trade receivables	$10 000	
Less: Allowance for doubtful debts	(150)	9 850
Total current assets		22 350
Non-current assets		
Motor vehicle[a] at cost	32 000	
Less: Accumulated depreciation	(12 000)	20 000
Property, at fair value		84 000
Machinery[b] at cost	19 000	
Less: Accumulated depreciation	(2 000)	17 000
Total non-current assets		121 000
Total assets		**$143 350**

[a] Acquired in 2016.
[b] Machinery A was acquired in 2013 and machinery B was acquired in 2017.

VALUE TO BUSINESS

- There are a number of alternative measurement systems that may be used for financial reporting purposes.
- Accounting standards prescribe different measurement bases for various statement of financial position assets and liabilities.
- The values assigned to items in the statement of financial position are referred to as the 'carrying amounts', 'carrying values' or 'book values'.
- Assets and liabilities are recorded initially at their cost price.
- Non-current assets with finite lives must be depreciated (or amortised).
- Receivables must be measured at their cash equivalent.
- Inventory must be measured at the lower of cost and net realisable value.

- Entities can choose to measure PPE at either cost or fair value. If using the cost basis, PPE cannot be measured at more than its recoverable amount. If using the fair value basis, the fair value must be regularly assessed and recorded.
- Goodwill cannot be revalued and must be tested for impairment at least annually. Identifiable intangibles can only be revalued if an active and liquid market exists.
- Some assets such as agricultural assets and derivative instruments must be measured at fair value.
- The statement of financial position does not portray the value of the entity.

5.11 Potential limitations of the statement of financial position

LEARNING OBJECTIVE 5.11 Discuss the limitations of the statement of financial position.

In later chapters, we will use information extracted from the statement of financial position to analyse an entity's financial performance and financial position. At this point, it is worth revisiting issues associated with the preparation of the statement of financial position because these issues have the potential to affect any analysis involving figures extracted from the statement of financial position.

The statement of financial position details an entity's assets, liabilities and equity as at a particular point in time, usually at the end of the reporting period. If the business is cyclical, the position reported by the statement of financial position may not necessarily be representative of the position at other times during the reporting period. For example, due to the peak retail Christmas period, the statement of financial position for a retail business with a December end of reporting period may be different if compared to a June end of reporting period statement of financial position for the same entity.

The statement of financial position does not reflect an entity's value. For example, the net assets of JB Hi-Fi Ltd as at 30 June 2018 totalled $947.6 million in its statement of financial position. The market value of the entity's equity as at 30 June 2018 — as calculated by the share price as at 30 June 2018 ($22.52) multiplied by the number of shares on issue (114.883 million) — was $2 587.2 million, significantly higher than the value depicted in the statement of financial position. The reasons why a statement of financial position is not a reflection of an entity's value include the following.

- Items creating value for the entity might not be recorded in the statement of financial position. Entities may have items that generate economic benefits or involve future obligations that fail the definition and/or recognition criteria. For instance, entities cannot recognise internally generated goodwill in the statement of financial position. For many entities, their employees are a valuable resource, but employees are not recognised as assets in the statement of financial position.
- Assets can be measured using different measurement systems and many are recorded at their written-down cost.
- Even if a single measurement system is applied (e.g. historical cost), no consideration is given to differences in cost prices due to changes in the purchasing power of money. For example, if historical cost is the measurement basis, land acquired in 2008 for $100 000 would be aggregated with land acquired in 2018 for $1 000 000, and the value assigned to land in the statement of financial position would be $1 100 000. If the entity elected to value the land at its fair value, independently assessed at $2 000 000, the same land could be recognised in the statement of financial position at $2 000 000.
- Preparation of the statement of financial position involves choices, assumptions and estimations on behalf of the manager or preparer of the statement. We have just seen how the choice of measurement for land would affect the value recognised in the statement of financial position. As another example, consider an entity with accounts receivable totalling $50 000. Identifying that 1 per cent of the accounts are impaired would reduce the carrying amount of the accounts receivable to $49 500. However, increasing the impairment to 5 per cent of the total amount owed would reduce the carrying amount of the accounts receivable in the statement of financial position to $47 500. This is just one example of how applying different choices, assumptions and estimations will alter the financial numbers in the statement of financial position.
- The exercise of judgement and discretion is illustrated by the following statement in JB Hi-Fi Ltd's notes to its accounts: 'estimates and judgements used in the preparation of these financial statements are continually evaluated and are based on historical experience and other factors' (JB Hi-Fi Ltd 2018,

p. 60). JB Hi-Fi Ltd's management makes critical judgements in relation to impairment of goodwill and other intangible assets and business combinations.

- The statement of financial position is essentially a historical representation, whereas expected future earnings and growth potential often influence value.

VALUE TO BUSINESS

- When using financial numbers extracted from the statement of financial position, we should be aware of the potential limitations associated with the preparation of the statement.
- The statement of financial position portrays an entity's assets, liabilities and equity at a point in time only, and this may not be representative of its position at other time points.
- The statement of financial position does not reflect an entity's value due to:
  - items that generate economic benefits or involve economic sacrifices not being recognised in the statement of financial position as they do not satisfy the definition criteria or there is considerable uncertainty regarding their measurement
  - assets and liabilities being recognised at historical cost or a combination of historical cost and fair value.
- The preparation of the statement of financial position involves management choices, judgements and estimations.

SUMMARY OF LEARNING OBJECTIVES

5.1 Identify the financial reporting obligations of an entity.

The reporting obligations of an entity vary depending on the nature of the entity. Entities with public accountability are required to prepare general purpose financial statements (GPFS) in accordance with approved accounting standards.

5.2 Explain the nature and purpose of the statement of financial position.

The statement of financial position lists an entity's assets, the external claims on the assets (the liabilities) and the internal claim on the assets (the equity). The statement of financial position reports the entity's financial position at a point in time. The financial position of an entity refers to the entity's:

- economic resources (assets)
- economic obligations (liabilities)
- financial structure
- financial solvency.

5.3 Outline the effects of accounting policy choices, estimates and judgements on financial statements.

Even when preparing financial statements in compliance with accounting standards, preparers are given accounting choices and are required to use estimations and judgements. Users of financial statements need to appreciate that accounting flexibility, discretion and incentives exist that may affect the preparer's choices, estimations and judgements, and therefore they need to be aware of the impact of these choices, estimations and judgements on the financial information reported.

5.4 Apply the asset definition criteria.

The essential characteristics of an asset are:

- it is a present economic resource
- the resource is controlled by the entity
- the resource is a result of a past event.

The item does not have to be tangible or exchangeable to be regarded as an asset. An entity can always disclose information about items that fail the definition criteria in the notes to the accounts.

5.5 Apply the liability definition criteria.

The essential characteristics of a liability are:

- it is a present obligation
- the obligation is to transfer an economic resource
- the obligation is a result of past events.

A legal obligation is a liability; however, a non-legal obligation may also be a liability. An entity can always disclose information about items that fail the definition criteria in the notes to the accounts.

5.6 Discuss the definition and nature of equity.

Equity is the residual interest in the assets of an entity after the liabilities have been deducted. The equity balance represents the owner's or owners' claims on the entity's net assets. The equity in the statement of financial position comprises capital that has been contributed by owners and gains (or losses) accruing to the entity that are undistributed.

5.7 Apply the recognition criteria to assets, liabilities and equity.

The term 'recognition' refers to recording items in the financial statements with a monetary value assigned to them. Therefore, 'asset recognition' or 'liability recognition' means that the asset or liability is recorded and appears on the face of the statement of financial position with its amount included in totals in the relevant statement. It is recognition that links the elements in financial statements — assets, liabilities, equity, income and expenses — and hence links the financial statements themselves. This linkage between the statements arises because the recognition of one element (or a change in one element) requires the recognition of an equal amount in one or more other elements (or changes in one or more other elements) as per the accounting equation. There are no definitive rules to assist with the decision on whether an item should be recognised. The recognition decision requires judgement. The overarching consideration when deciding whether to recognise an asset or a liability (and any related income, expenses or changes in equity) is whether the recognition provides financial statement users with relevant information about the asset or the liability and about any income, expenses or changes in equity, a faithful representation of the asset or the liability and of any income, expenses or changes in equity, and information that results in benefits exceeding the cost of providing that information. Factors of uncertainty and unreliable measurement may result in non-recognition. An entity always has the option to disclose information concerning items not recognised.

5.8 Describe the format and presentation of the statement of financial position.

The statement of financial position is usually presented in either a narrative format or a T-format. A statement of financial position in narrative format lists the assets, liabilities and equity in columns. The T-format lists the assets on one side, with the liabilities and equity on the other side. It is usual for the statement of financial position to report the financial figures for the current period and the corresponding previous reporting period. If an entity has subsidiary entities, then the statement of financial position reports the consolidated entity results.

5.9 Describe the presentation and disclosure requirements for elements in the statement of financial position.

Assets and liabilities are assigned either a current or non-current classification on the basis of when the economic benefits (sacrifices) are expected to occur. If the benefits (sacrifices) are expected to occur within 12 months of the end of the reporting period or within the entity's operating cycle, a current classification is appropriate. For assets (liabilities) where the benefit (sacrifice) is expected to occur beyond the next 12 months or operating cycle, a non-current classification results. Within the current and non-current sections, assets and liabilities are classified according to their nature or function. Typical asset classifications include cash; receivables; inventories; investments; property, plant and equipment (PPE); intangibles; tax assets; and other assets. Typical liability classifications include payables; interest-bearing liabilities; provisions; and tax liabilities. The equity classifications in the statement of financial position are capital (contributed equity), reserves, retained earnings and non-controlling interests.

A breakdown of the items within the various classifications is usually included in the notes to the accounts. The terms given to various elements in the statement of financial position, and the extent to which entities aggregate elements for the purposes of statement of financial position disclosure, vary according to the entity structure.

5.10 Discuss the measurement of various assets and liabilities in the statement of financial position.

Numerous measurement systems can be used to measure elements in the statement of financial position. These include historical cost and current value. The overarching consideration for selecting a measurement basis is the usefulness of information for users' decision making. At the time of acquisition, historical cost reflects an item's fair value. Subsequent to acquisition, receivables are recorded at their expected cash equivalent and inventory is measured at the lower of cost and net realisable value. Property, plant and equipment (PPE) can either remain at cost price or be revalued regularly to fair value. Regardless, the carrying amount of an asset must not exceed its recoverable amount. If it does, the asset is impaired and must be written down. There are some asset classes (such as agricultural assets and derivative financial instruments) where accounting rules specify that the assets must be recognised at their fair value. Non-current assets with limited lives must be depreciated. Goodwill cannot be revalued, and identifiable intangible assets can only be revalued if an active and liquid market exists. Goodwill and intangible assets must be tested for impairment at least annually. The value assigned to such assets in the statement of financial position is their cost or revalued amount, less the accumulated depreciation charges, less any impairment charges. It is important for a user to identify the basis for measuring assets and liabilities in the statement of financial position.

5.11 Discuss the limitations of the statement of financial position.

When analysing the financial numbers in the statement of financial position, it is necessary to consider issues associated with the preparation of the statement that potentially limit the inferences that can be made. The statement of financial position is a historical snapshot of an entity's economic resources and obligations at a point in time only, and this may not be representative of its resources and obligations throughout the reporting period. Further, the statement of financial position does not represent the value of the entity. This is due to the existence of assets and liabilities that are not reported in the statement of financial position, and the measurement systems used to recognise assets and liabilities. Finally, the definition and recognition of items in the statement of financial position involve management choices, estimations and judgements.

KEY TERMS

accounting policies Rules and practices, having substantial authoritative backing, that are recognised as a general guide for financial reporting.
accumulated depreciation Total depreciation charges for a particular asset.

agricultural assets (biological assets) Living animals or plants.

allowance for doubtful debts Estimate of the amount of accounts receivable expected to be uncollectable.

asset A resource controlled by an entity as a result of past events and from which future economic benefits are expected to flow to the entity.

carrying amount (book value) Dollar value assigned to an asset or liability in the statement of financial position.

cash and cash equivalents Cash held at bank, on hand and in short-term deposits.

classes Different types of asset, liability and equity accounts found in the statement of financial position.

comparative information Presentation of the financial statements of an entity for multiple years.

Conceptual Framework Document that sets out the objective of financial statements, assumptions underlying financial statements and qualitative characteristics of financial statements, and defines the elements of financial statements and the recognition criteria applied to the elements.

contingent Quality that the existence of an asset or liability arising from a past event may be confirmed only by uncertain future events not controllable by the entity.

contributed capital Funds contributed to a partnership or sole trader by the owner(s).

current assets Cash and other assets that are expected to be converted to cash or used in an entity within one year or one operating cycle, whichever is longer.

current cost Cost of replacing an asset or settling a liability today.

current liabilities Obligations that can reasonably be expected to be paid within one year or one operating cycle.

depreciable assets Non-current assets with limited useful lives.

depreciation Allocation of the depreciable amount of a depreciable asset over its estimated useful life.

derivative financial asset Financial asset whose value depends on the value of an underlying security, reference rate or index.

derivative financial liability Financial liability whose value depends on the value of an underlying security, reference rate or index.

duality Describes how every business transaction has at least two effects on the accounting equation.

equity Residual interest in the assets of an entity after all its liabilities have been deducted.

fair value The price that would be received to sell an asset or paid to transfer a liability in an orderly transaction between market participants at the measurement date.

faithful representation Information that is complete, neutral and free from error.

financial asset Cash, a contractual right to receive cash or another financial asset, a contractual right to exchange financial instruments with another entity under conditions that are potentially favourable, or an equity instrument of another entity calculated as the excess of the consideration paid for a business over the fair value of the net assets at acquisition date.

financial liability A contractual obligation to deliver cash or another financial asset to another entity or a contractual obligation to exchange financial assets or financial liabilities with another entity under conditions that are potentially unfavourable to the entity.

financing decisions Decisions involving the mix of debt and equity financing chosen by an entity.

fulfilment value Present value of the cash flows that an entity expects to incur to satisfy a liability.

general purpose financial statements (GPFS) Financial statements prepared to meet the information needs common to external users.

generally accepted accounting principles (GAAP) The specific rules and guidelines pertaining to a specific jurisdiction that entities use to help them prepare financial statements. These rules and guidelines vary from country to country.

goodwill An unidentifiable intangible asset (e.g. an established client base or reputation).

group (economic entity) Parent entity and all its subsidiaries.

historical cost Original amount paid or expected to be received for an item.

identifiable intangible assets Intangible assets that can be identified (e.g. trademarks, brand names, patents, rights, agreements, development expenditure, mastheads, licences).

impairment When an asset's carrying amount exceeds its recoverable amount.

intangible assets Non-current, non-monetary assets that do not have physical substance.

inventories Supplies of raw materials to be used in the production process, work-in-progress and/or the finished goods that an entity has available for sale.

investing decisions Decisions involving (a) the acquisition and sale of investments and productive non-current assets using cash; and (b) lending money and collecting on those loans.

investments accounted for using the equity method Carrying value of investments in another entity where the investing entity has the capacity to significantly influence (not control) the investee entity.

liability A present obligation of an entity arising from past events, the settlement of which is expected to result in an outflow from the entity of resources embodying economic benefits.

liquidity Ability of an entity to meet its short-term financial commitments.

monetary concept Use of money as the basis of quantifying items in financial statements.

net realisable value Expected selling price less the expected costs associated with getting the inventory to a saleable state, plus the costs of marketing, selling and distribution.

non-controlling interests Claim on the net assets of an entity that belongs to the shareholders of an entity other than parent entity shareholders.

non-current assets Assets not expected to be consumed or sold within one year or one operating cycle.

non-current liabilities Obligations expected to be paid after one year or outside one normal operating cycle.

operating cycle Length of time it takes for an entity to acquire and sell goods, and collect the cash from the sale.

paid-up share capital Total amount paid by shareholders for shares issued in a company.

parent entity An entity that controls another entity.

property, plant and equipment (PPE) Long-term assets that have physical substance, are used in the operations of an entity and are not intended for sale to customers.

provisions Liability class involving more uncertainty regarding the monetary value to be assigned to the future sacrifice of economic benefits.

public accountability Entities with securities, debt or equity traded in a public market or entities that hold assets in a fiduciary capacity as their main business activity.

receivables Cash an entity expects to receive from parties that owe it money.

recognition Recording of items in the financial statements with a monetary value assigned to them.

recoverable amount Higher of an asset's expected fair value (less costs of disposal) and its value in use (net selling price).

relevant Quality of information that is of value to users in making and evaluating decisions about the allocation of scarce resources.

reporting entity An entity with users who rely on the information in general purpose financial statements (GPFS) to meet their information needs.

reserves Equity accounts that originate in a variety of ways including asset revaluations (revaluation surplus), transfers of profits (general reserve) and movements in exchange rates (foreign currency translation reserve).

retained earnings Cumulative profits made by an entity that have not been distributed as dividends or transferred to reserve accounts.

secured debt Debt with a priority claim on an entity's assets in the event of the entity's demise.

share capital Funds contributed to a company by the owners.

special purpose financial statements (SPFS) Financial statements prepared to suit a specific purpose.

statement of financial position A statement that reports on the assets, liabilities and equity of an entity at a particular point in time.

trade payables (trade creditors or **accounts payable)** Amounts owed to suppliers for the purchase of goods or services.

trade receivables (trade debtors or **accounts receivable)** Amounts due from customers for the sale of goods or services.

value-in-use Present value of the cash flows that an entity expects to derive from the continuing use of an asset and its ultimate disposal.

APPLY YOUR KNOWLEDGE   *22 marks*

Following the collapse of the Toys"R"Us franchise in the United States, Toys"R"Us Australia went into administration on 21 May 2018, leaving 700 staff and 44 stores nationwide with an uncertain future.

Subsequent to the announcement of financial difficulties of Toys"R"Us, the administrator announced that gift vouchers would be honoured only if customers spent the equivalent amount of the voucher in store. Thus, customers attempting to use gift vouchers were being told they had to spend double the value of each voucher. As the administrator of Toys"R"Us Australia was unable to achieve a going-concern sale, the business was wound down and subsequently closed in August 2018. Gift card holders had until 5 July 2018 to have their cards honoured by Toys"R"Us.

Required

(a) Explain the initial recording that Toys"R"Us should prepare when a customer purchases a gift voucher for $100 cash. **3 marks**

(b) Using the definition and recognition of financial report elements contained in the revised *Conceptual Framework*, discuss why you have suggested the particular recording. **8 marks**

(c) Explain the recording that Toys"R"Us would prepare when a customer redeemed their $100 gift voucher by using it to purchase $100 worth of toys. The cost price of the toys that the customer purchased is $40. **6 marks**

(d) It was reported in the financial press that Toys"R"Us Australia had a total of $6.7 million in cash and inventory on hand of $47.5 million when it went into voluntary administration. Further, it had employee benefits (amounts owed to employees for annual leave) of $3.02 million and unsecured creditors of $94.9 million. Using the revised *Conceptual Framework*, explain the essential characteristics that categorise amounts owed to employees for annual leave as a liability. **5 marks**

SELF-EVALUATION ACTIVITIES

5.1 The following is a list of account balances for Fast Communications Pty Ltd for the financial years ended 31 March 2019 and 31 March 2020.

Account	31 March 2020 $	31 March 2019 $
Plant and equipment	25 124	22 136
Goodwill	5 245	4 020
Cash and cash equivalents	18 000	23 500
Accounts payable	23 241	20 557
Accounts receivable	20 120	19 852
Deferred tax assets	9 154	8 687
Deferred tax liabilities	15 356	14 524
Prepayments	6 859	5 274
Short-term borrowings	9 254	8 697
Long-term borrowings	14 652	14 328
Brand names	4 350	4 350
Licences	8 658	8 658
Issued capital	28 654	24 562
Inventories	6 854	5 277
Provisions for employee benefits (short term)	9 642	7 246
Patents	2 400	3 542
Provisions for employee benefits (long term)	8 198	5 469
Land and buildings	32 725	29 865
Accumulated depreciation — land and buildings	12 585	14 249
Accumulated depreciation — plant and equipment	5 684	3 245
Accumulated amortisation — brand names	2 864	1 468
Accumulated amortisation — patents	1 142	985
Accumulated amortisation — licences	3 568	2 500
Accumulated amortisation — software development cost	3 458	2 468
Other current assets	7 684	8 579
Retained earnings	9 184	25 262
Current tax liabilities	6 845	5 248
Software development cost	7 154	7 068

Required

(a) Prepare a narrative classified statement of financial position for Fast Communications Pty Ltd as at 31 March 2019 and 31 March 2020.

(b) Comment on Fast Communications Pty Ltd's liquidity and financing.

SOLUTION TO 5.1

(a) Narrative classified statement of financial position

FAST COMMUNICATIONS PTY LTD
Statement of financial position
as at 31 March

	2020 $	2019 $
ASSETS		
Current assets		
Cash and cash equivalents	18 000	23 500
Accounts receivable	20 120	19 852
Inventories	6 854	5 277
Prepayments	6 859	5 274
Other current assets	7 684	8 579
Total current assets	59 517	62 482
Non-current assets		
Property, plant and equipment	39 580	34 507
Intangible assets	16 775	20 217
Deferred tax assets	9 154	8 687
Total non-current assets	65 509	63 411
Total assets	125 026	125 893
LIABILITIES		
Current liabilities		
Accounts payable	23 241	20 557
Short-term borrowings	9 254	8 697
Current tax liabilities	6 845	5 248
Provisions for employee benefits (short term)	9 642	7 246
Total current liabilities	48 982	41 748
Non-current liabilities		
Long-term borrowings	14 652	14 328
Deferred tax liabilities	15 356	14 524
Provisions for employee benefits (long term)	8 198	5 469
Total non-current liabilities	38 206	34 321
Total liabilities	87 188	76 069
Net assets	**37 838**	**49 824**
EQUITY		
Issued capital	28 654	24 562
Retained earnings	9 184	25 262
Total equity	**37 838**	**49 824**

(b) Liquidity refers to an entity's ability to meet its short-term financial commitments. A preliminary assessment of the company's liquidity can be made by comparing the assets that the company can readily convert into cash (that is, cash, receivables and inventories) to the short-term cash demands on the company (that is, payables and short-term borrowings).

Looking at Fast Communications Pty Ltd's statement of financial position in 2019 and 2020, the company's liquid assets (that is, cash, receivables and inventories) have decreased by $3655 ($48 629 in 2019 compared to $44 974 in 2020). On the other hand, its short-term commitments (that is, payables and short-term borrowings) have increased by $3241 ($32 495 in 2020 compared to $29 254 in 2019). It should be recognised that inventories may take some time to sell and are not as liquid as cash.

For the time being, Fast Communications Pty Ltd appears to be able to repay its short-term commitments when they fall due, as the statement of financial position data show that its liquid assets exceed its short-term commitments in 2020. However, if the trend of decreased liquid assets and increased short-term commitments continues, Fast Communications Pty Ltd may have a liquidity problem in the future, which means the company may have difficulty paying its short-term liabilities.

Fast Communications Pty Ltd has financed more of its assets in 2020 with liabilities relative to 2019. Total liabilities in 2020 represent 70 per cent of total assets. In 2019, 60 per cent of assets were financed with liabilities.

5.2 In January 2021, business and information technology graduates Zac and Tran contribute $20 000 in total to commence their business, CloudIt Pty Ltd. During its first year of operations, the company reports a loss of $15 000. In year 2, a profit of $5000 is recorded, increasing to $20 000 in year 3. Year 4's profit is $45 000 and a total dividend of $12 000 is distributed to Zac and Tran. A $70 000 profit is reported in year 5 and, to take advantage of a market opportunity, Zac and Tran contribute another $50 000 in total.

Required

(a) Calculate the balance that would appear in the retained earnings as at the end of 2025.

(b) Prepare the equity section of CloudIt Pty Ltd's statement of financial position as at 31 December 2025.

SOLUTION TO 5.2

(a) CloudIt Pty Ltd — calculation of retained earnings as at 31 December 2025

Year	Profit or loss	Dividends	Retained earnings at end of period
1	$(15 000)		$(15 000)
2	5 000		(10 000)
3	20 000		10 000
4	45 000	$12 000	43 000
5	70 000		113 000

(b) CloudIt Pty Ltd — extract of equity section of statement of financial position as at 31 December 2025

CLOUDIT PTY LTD Statement of financial position (extract of equity section) as at 31 December 2025	
Equity	
Capital contributed[a]	$ 70 000
Retained earnings[b]	113 000
Total equity	**$183 000**

[a]$20 000 + $50 000
[b]See part (a) for calculation.

5.3 Due to poor health, the owners of Willow Pty Ltd, an importer, intend to sell their business. To facilitate the sale, the owners have prepared the following statement of financial position for prospective purchasers as at 30 April 2020. You are interested in purchasing the business and take this statement of financial position to your accountant for advice.

WILLOW PTY LTD Statement of financial position as at 30 April 2020	
Assets	
Cash	$ 6 000
Accounts receivable	14 000
Inventory	43 000
Prepayments	2 000
Plant and equipment	28 000
Goodwill	29 000
Total assets	122 000
Liabilities	
Accounts payable	9 000
Loan	20 000
Net assets	**$ 93 000**
Equity	
Capital	$ 60 000
Profit	33 000
Total equity	**$ 93 000**

Notes to the accounts

1. The entity also has a $10 000 bank overdraft.
2. The entity has borrowings of $100 000, on which it pays $20 000 (as shown in the statement of financial position) in interest and loan repayments per annum.
3. The capital of $60 000 represents the original capital contributed by the owners. It does not include subsequent capital injections.
4. The profit of $33 000 is the reported profit for the current reporting period.
5. The inventory is measured at cost price.
6. The goodwill represents the figure that was necessary to 'balance' the statement.
7. The plant and equipment is at cost.

Required

(a) Discuss at least five errors or divergences from acceptable accounting practices revealed by this statement of financial position.
(b) List three limitations of the statement of financial position.

SOLUTION TO 5.3

(a) The errors or divergences from acceptable accounting practices include the following.
- The statement of financial position does not provide information regarding the categorisation of the assets and liabilities as current and non-current. Furthermore, no subtotals for such items are detailed.
- Goodwill can be recognised only if it is purchased. Willow Pty Ltd should not be recognising any internally generated goodwill.
- The inventory is measured at cost price. Inventory should be measured at the lower of cost and net realisable value. Having the inventory at cost price is acceptable providing that the cost of the inventory is higher than the net realisable value.
- No allowance for doubtful debts is provided.
- Assets with limited useful lives must be depreciated, so the plant and equipment should be recorded at its cost less accumulated depreciation.
- The balance of retained earnings should be reflected in the statement of financial position, rather than just the current year's profit being included in the equity section.
- The $10 000 bank overdraft satisfies the liability definition and recognition criteria, and should be included in the statement of financial position as a current liability.
- The capital contribution should be the sum of all contributions to the business by the owners, rather than restricted to the contributions originally made.
- The borrowings of $100 000 should appear as a liability in the statement of financial position.

(b) First, the statement of financial position is a historical snapshot of an entity's economic resources and obligations at a point in time only, and the snapshot presented may not be representative of other times of the year. Second, it does not show the value of an entity, due to the existence of assets and liabilities that are not reported in the statement of financial position, and fair value not being the measurement system used to recognise all assets and liabilities. Third, the definition and recognition of items in the statement of financial position involve management choices, estimations and judgements.

COMPREHENSION QUESTIONS

5.4 Discuss whether the following statements are true or false.   **LO2, 9**
(a) The terms 'accounts payable and 'creditors' mean the same thing.
(b) The statement of financial position is a financial statement that shows the financial performance of an entity as at a point in time.
(c) Mr Startup invests his own cash to start a business. This transaction will increase the equity and assets of the business.
(d) All entities are legally obliged to prepare GPFS.
(e) The measurement system used in accounting is based on fair value.

5.5 The statement of financial position for Daffodil Pty Ltd reveals cash on hand of $8000, accounts receivable of $48 000, inventory measured at $50 000 and plant and equipment measured at $116 000. The liabilities of the entity are: accounts payable $28 000, bank overdraft $32 000 and long-term loan $180 000. Relate this information to the liquidity of the entity.   **LO2**

5.6 An entity has total assets measured at $220 000 in the statement of financial position. The entity's liabilities total $100 000, of which $60 000 is a bank loan. Calculate the entity's net assets. Discuss the entity's financing decision.   **LO2**

5.7 List three essential characteristics necessary to consider an item either as an asset or a liability.   **LO4, 5**

5.8 The High Cloud Software Company wants to increase its asset base by recognising its customer list as an asset. Discuss whether this is permissible under accounting standards.   **LO2**

5.9 JB Hi-Fi Ltd has a legal obligation to prepare and lodge financial statements. Access the notes to JB Hi-Fi Ltd's most recent financial statements and identify the rules and regulations that govern the basis for the preparation of the financial statements. Compare this with the basis for the preparation of the financial statements used by a not-for-profit organisation of your choice.   **LO1**

5.10 Knowing that you have some accounting experience, a friend has sought your advice regarding a business that she intends purchasing. The statement of financial position for the business shows total assets of $180 000 and liabilities of $90 000. The selling business has provided no notes to accompany the statement of financial position. On the basis of the information provided, your friend believes the business is worth $90 000. Advise your friend as to the accuracy of her assessment and what questions regarding the statement of financial position she should ask the seller of the business.   **LO2, 9, 10**

5.11 As an investor in the share market, you use the financial statements to assess the financial condition of entities. Discuss whether you would find it more useful to have items of PPE valued at historical cost or fair value.   **LO10**

5.12 Steam Kleen Ltd, a carpet steam-cleaning business, needs to acquire new machinery. The accountant has suggested that the entity should lease the machinery rather than taking out a loan to purchase it. When the owner enquires about why this would be preferable, the accountant says it is because structuring the lease in a certain way will keep the financing 'off-balance-sheet'. Explain the concept of off-balance-sheet financing and discuss whether this should be the entity's preferred option. Discuss whether you think that leased assets and lease liabilities should appear in the statement of financial position.   **LO4, 5**

5.13 Kookaburra Ltd is always running short of cash, despite growing sales volumes and its current assets exceeding its current liabilities. A review of its operations by a consultant finds that a considerable portion of the company's inventory is obsolete stock for which there is limited demand. Further, many of the accounts receivable are overdue by more than 60 days. The accounts receivable and inventory are carried at their gross amount and cost value, respectively, in the statement of financial position. Explain how the accounts receivable and inventory should be valued in the statement of financial position. If Kookaburra Ltd was to apply the correct measurement basis, determine the effects on: (1) profit; and (2) assets.   **LO10**

5.14 You are reviewing a statement of financial position and notice that goodwill appears in the statement. Relate this information to the entity's past investing decisions. Discuss how goodwill is measured: (1) at acquisition; and (2) post-acquisition.   **LO9, 10**

5.15 There are four financial statements: the statement of financial position, statement of profit or loss, statement of cash flows and statement of changes in equity. Describe the information conveyed by the statement of financial position relative to that conveyed by the statement of cash flows.   **LO2**

EXERCISES

★ BASIC | ★ ★ MODERATE | ★ ★ ★ CHALLENGING

5.16 ★   **LO6**

Advantage Tennis Coaching, a business owned by sole trader Nicholas Cash, had the following assets and liabilities as at the financial years ended 30 June 2019 and 30 June 2020.

	30 June 2020	30 June 2019
Assets		
Cash at bank	$15 000	$ 6 000
Accounts receivable	24 000	15 000
Prepaid insurance	5 000	2 500
Equipment (net)	7 000	6 000
Vehicle (net)	70 000	80 000
Liabilities		
Accounts payable	26 000	17 500
Accrued expenses	5 000	8 000
Bank loan	35 000	57 500

Required
(a) What is the equity as at the end of the two financial years?
(b) If Nicholas contributed an extra $15 000 capital during the financial year ending 30 June 2020 and made no drawings, determine his profit (or loss) for the year, assuming the above balances remain the same.
(c) If Nicholas had contributed an extra $20 000 and withdrew $15 000 during the year ending 30 June 2020, determine his profit (or loss) for the year, assuming the above balances remain the same.

5.17 ★ **LO8, 9**

From the following account balances of Platypus Pty Ltd as at 30 September 2019, prepare a statement of financial position in both the T-format and the narrative classified format.

Cash at bank	$ 55 000
Accounts receivable (net)	27 500
Inventory	50 000
Land	60 000
Fixtures and fittings	8 000
Loan payable	12 000
Tax payable	4 500
Share capital	50 000
Retained earnings	134 000

5.18 ★ **LO8, 9**

From the following account balances of Frosty Pty Ltd as at 30 June 2019, prepare a statement of financial position in both the T-format and the narrative classified format.

Cash at bank	$ 4 000
Accounts receivable (net)	49 000
Inventory	64 000
Plant and equipment	350 000
Goodwill	180 000
Accounts payable	35 000
Borrowings	184 000
Provisions	40 000
Share capital	240 000
Retained earnings	148 000

5.19 ★ **LO8, 9**

From the following account balances of Graceview as at 31 December 2019, prepare a statement of financial position in both the T-format and the narrative classified format. *Note:* You will need to determine the balance of the retained earnings.

Cash at bank	$ 12 000	
Accounts receivable (net)	56 000	
Inventory	88 000	
Other current assets	16 000	
Land and buildings	359 000	
Intangible assets	275 000	
Other financial assets (term deposits)	78 500	
Accounts payable	25 000	
Borrowings	200 000	
Provisions	56 000	
Share capital	500 000	
Retained earnings	?	

5.20 ★ **LO8**

Solve for the missing financial numbers as they would appear in the statement of financial position.

Current assets	Non-current assets	Total assets	Current liabilities	Non-current liabilities	Total liabilities	Share capital	Retained earnings	Total equity
$35 000	$46 000	a.	b.	$28 000	$37 000	$30 000	c.	$44 000
d.	84 000	e.	$29 000	f.	81 000	53 000	$7 000	60 000
159 000	g.	$295 000	55 000	102 000	157 000	h.	16 000	i.
j.	24 000	k.	6 900	16 000	22 900	l.	2 200	17 000
46 941	m.	129 127	n.	40 500	68 755	48 750	o.	60 372

5.21 ★ **LO8**

Identify whether the following assets would be classified as current or non-current as at the end of the reporting period, justifying your classification decision.
(a) Prepaid expenses
(b) Intangible assets
(c) Plant and equipment
(d) Accounts receivable
(e) Cash and cash equivalents
(f) Inventory

5.22 ★ **LO9**

Identify whether the following liabilities would be classified as current or non-current as at the end of the reporting period, justifying your classification decision.
(a) Provision for employee annual leave
(b) Long-term bank loan
(c) Payroll taxes payable
(d) Trade payables
(e) Bank overdraft
(f) GST payable

5.23 ★ **LO5**

Qantas Group has been ranked among the top six airlines of global carriers when it comes to the availability of frequent-flyer reward seats based on the ninth annual CarTrawler Reward Seat Availability Survey, which attempts to book award redemptions on carriers. The survey looks at 280 paired city flights, giving each airline a percentage for the time reward seats successfully booked, then assigning points up or down to show where the airlines have moved on the table since last year. Qantas' frequent flyer program, which has over 12 million members, was ranked six with a score of 90.7 per cent, reflecting the fact that 254 of 280 outbound and inbound date queries provided a minimum of one flight in each direction with at least two available reward seats (Sorensen 2018).

Required

Assume that the 12 million Qantas frequent flyer members had an average of 200 000 frequent flyer points. Referring to the revised *Conceptual Framework*, discuss whether the Qantas Group has a liability to record in relation to its frequent flyer program.

5.24 ★   **LO9**

Typical classifications of liabilities in the statement of financial position include: payables; borrowings; deferred revenue; deferred tax liabilities; provisions and other liabilities. The equity classifications for large entities are: share capital (contributed equity); reserves; non-controlling interests; and retained earnings. Categorise the following items.

(a) Employee benefits provision

(b) Equity-settled benefits reserve

(c) Lease provision

(d) Revenue received in advance

(e) Ordinary shares — fully paid

(f) Hedging reserve

(g) Unsecured bank loan

(h) Lease accrual

5.25 ★   **LO4**

Entities spend millions of dollars on marketing and advertising intended to promote and build brands, develop customers and sell services or products. Consider a new hotel being launched. Extensive marketing spend is required to create an awareness of the hotel and attract the first visitors. With reference to the revised *Conceptual Framework*, discuss whether the marketing costs incurred by the hotel can be capitalised and recognised in the statement of financial position.

5.26 ★   **LO4**

One of Google's largest acquisitions was Motorola Mobility for $12.5 billion in 2011. Google subsequently sold Motorola to Chinese giant PC producer Lenovo for $2.9 billion.

Required

Explain how the goodwill associated with Lenovo's acquisition would be determined.

5.27 ★   **LO10**

Chic Frames Ltd was acquired by Specsavers for $8 million. The fair value of the net assets acquired by Specsavers was assessed at $5 million. Prepare the double-entry transaction that would keep the accounting equation in balance.

5.28 ★   **LO4, 5, 6**

For each of the transactions identified, analyse how the asset, liability and/or equity accounts increase, decrease or remain unchanged. (*Hint:* Remember the accounting equation.)

	Assets (A)	Liabilities (L)	Equity (E)
a. Obtained a loan to purchase equipment for $55 000.			
b. The owners took $4000 in inventory for personal use.			
c. A trade receivable, who owes $6000, made a part payment of $2000.			
d. Purchased inventory for $10 000, paying $4000 cash and the balance on credit.			
e. Impaired a building from its acquisition cost less accumulated depreciation of $90 000 to its recoverable amount of $75 000.			
f. Inventory with a cost price of $42 000 had a net realisable value of $50 000.			

5.29 ★ ★   **LO8, 9**

A friend who owns a small entity trading as Fairies Galore knows that you are studying accounting and asks you to prepare the entity's classified statement of financial position in narrative format as at 30 June. The friend has provided you with the following list of assets and liabilities (the equity figure has not been provided).

Cash	$ 8 150
Motor vehicles	13 500
Equipment	8 000
Monies owed by customers	2 800
Monies owed to suppliers	4 900
Loan due to be paid in two years	14 300
Wages owed to employees	860
Rent paid in advance	400

5.30 ★ ★   **LO4**

Using the revised *Conceptual Framework* definition and recognition criteria, discuss whether each of the following items can be recorded as assets.
(a) Trade receivables
(b) Investments in shares
(c) Inventory
(d) Research expenditure

5.31 ★ ★   **LO1**

The accountant of a private secondary college, St Lucia, is preparing the school's financial statements. Discuss the justification for the school preparing SPFS rather than GPFS.

5.32 ★ ★   **LO3**

On 8 November 2011, the Australian Senate passed the 'carbon tax legislation' in relation to the government's clean energy proposal, including a mechanism for pricing carbon. The legislation was effective from 1 July 2012. Under the legislation approximately 500 of the largest emitters in Australia were liable to purchase and surrender carbon units for every tonne of carbon dioxide equivalent to what they produced. The carbon-pricing scheme had an initial price of $23 per tonne of emissions. On 17 July 2014, legislation to abolish the carbon tax was passed by the Senate and received the Royal Assent.

At the time the legislation was passed and subsequently repealed, there was no accounting standard governing the accounting treatment for emission schemes.

Access the websites of the IASB and AASB and report on the development of accounting standards governing the accounting treatment for emission schemes. Access the most recent financial report of one of the largest Australian companies and report on its accounting policy and disclosures in relation to carbon emissions.

5.33 ★ ★   **LO10**

Find the University of NSW (UNSW) asset revaluation policy on the internet. Summarise the measurement of UNSW's various asset classes. Discuss the advantages and disadvantages of the revaluation and cost measurement systems.

5.34 ★ ★   **LO10, 11**

You have a friend who is considering purchasing shares in Meridian Ltd. The shares are currently trading on the securities exchange at $3.58 each. The entity's financial statements suggest that its net assets are $250 000 and there are 150 000 shares on issue, giving a book value per share of $1.67. Your friend is confused as to why the financial statements do not reflect the measure of the entity's value. Explain this to your friend.

5.35 ★ ★   **LO5**

In calculating the provision for employee benefits, JB Hi-Fi Ltd includes the value attributable to employee long service leave entitlements. Explain how these entitlements differ from annual leave and sick leave entitlements. Given that most employment awards entitle the employee to long service leave after 10 or 15 years of service, apply the definition and recognition criteria for liabilities to suggest when an entity should start providing for long service leave.

5.36 ★ ★   **LO3**

Seek Ltd discloses areas involving critical accounting estimates and assumptions in the relevant notes to its financial statements. Locate the most recent annual report for Seek Ltd and identify the accounting areas that management believe have the greatest potential impact on its consolidated financial statements due to its associated assumptions and estimations. Select one area and explain the critical accounting estimates and assumptions involved in measuring the item for the purposes of the statement of financial position.

PROBLEMS

★ BASIC | ★ ★ MODERATE | ★ ★ ★ CHALLENGING

5.37 Analysing retained earnings ★   LO6

Golden Pineapples Pty Ltd had the following assets and liabilities at financial year end in 2019 and 2020.

	31 December 2020	31 December 2019
Assets		
Cash on hand	$131 658	$ 46 321
Accounts receivable	90 800	21 500
Inventory	175 000	60 000
Prepayments	4 500	1 000
Buildings and equipment (net)	350 000	230 000
Liabilities and equity		
Accounts payable	39 400	5 800
Accrued expenses	7 500	4 600
Income tax payable	63 215	33 187
Dividend payable	90 000	32 000
Bank loan	150 000	20 000
Share capital	200 000	200 000
Retained earnings	?	?

Required

(a) What is the balance of retained earnings as at the end of the two financial years?

(b) If the company reported profit after tax of $264 200 for the year ended 31 December 2020, what amount (if any) of dividends were declared during the year?

5.38 Analysing a statement of financial position ★   LO8, 9

Select an Australian Securities Exchange (ASX) listed company and visit its website to access the latest annual report. From the company's statement of financial position, identify the:

(a) company's total assets

(b) percentage of total assets that are:
   (i) current assets
   (ii) non-current assets

(c) company's total liabilities

(d) percentage of total liabilities that are:
   (i) current liabilities
   (ii) non-current liabilities

(e) company's liquidity, by comparing the current assets and current liabilities amounts

(f) company's financing of its assets, by comparing the total liabilities to total equity.

5.39 Analysing trade receivables ★   LO3, 4

The following table shows the balance of an entity's trade receivables for each of the past four years.

	Year 1	Year 2	Year 3	Year 4
Trade receivables	$60 000	$70 000	$105 000	$120 000

As the table indicates, the trade receivables have increased in absolute value each year. Discuss why entities are required to disclose the amounts receivable for trade receivables separately from the amounts receivable from other debtors. To assess the reasonableness of the increase in the trade receivables, list other financial item(s) trends that would be useful to investigate.

5.40 Measurement of assets ★   LO4, 10

Flight Centre Ltd's 2017 financial report notes that PPE is carried at cost less accumulated depreciation and any impairment charges. The notes to the accounts (pp. 48 and 81) note a gain on the sale of the NZ Head Office in 2016 of $6 264 000. The head office had a carrying amount of $10 186 000 in the statement of financial position prior to disposal.

Required

Discuss the usefulness of measuring assets such as property and buildings at cost less accumulated depreciation and any impairment charges. Explain why an entity may elect to measure property at cost in the statement of financial position and disclose its fair value.

5.41 Auditor's responsibilities and declaration ★ ★   **LO3, 11**

Using the company that you selected in question 5.38, read the independent auditor's report. Given the estimations and assumptions involved in preparing financial statements, discuss what the auditor's report is stating about the 'accuracy' of the financial statements.

5.42 Measurement of assets ★ ★   **LO3, 4, 10**

Australian Agricultural Company Ltd was formed with a grant of one million acres and the stated aim of cultivating and improving the wastelands of the colony of New South Wales. Today the company is a cattle producer with a significant position in the Australian food industry and is the largest beef cattle producer in Australia. The company's most significant asset is its cattle. In the statement of financial position as at 31 March 2018, the cattle were recorded as biological assets. The trading cattle, classified as current assets, were valued at $259 104 000. The commercial and breeding stud cattle, classified as non-current assets, were valued at $369 182 000.

Required

(a) Identify the basis for measuring biological assets.

(b) List the market indicators that inform the values of Australian Agricultural Company Ltd's cattle.

(c) Describe how Australian Agricultural Company Ltd determines the net market value of its biological assets. Discuss the information required to determine the measurement. Suggest how revaluation increases and decreases, related to the cattle, are accounted for.

5.43 Measurement of assets ★ ★   **LO3, 10**

The Commonwealth Bank of Australia measures its property assets (land and buildings) on a fair value measurement basis using independent market valuations. As at 30 June 2018, the land and buildings were valued in the statement of financial position at $440 million. If the land and buildings had been measured using the cost model rather than fair value, the carrying value would have been $229 million.

Required

Discuss which figure is more useful for decision making. Analyse how revaluation increases and decreases, related to the land, are accounted for. Explain if this is consistent with accounting for movements in the net market value of biological assets (refer to question 5.42).

5.44 Measuring goodwill ★ ★   **LO3, 4, 10**

Simply Better Pty Ltd has just acquired the Cutie Pie business. The fair value of Cutie Pie's net assets as at the date of acquisition is $1 855 000. Simply Better Pty Ltd has agreed to pay the owners of Cutie Pie $1 000 000 in cash and give them 100 000 shares in Simply Better Pty Ltd, valued at $10 per share. Calculate the goodwill that would be recognised in Simply Better Pty Ltd's statement of financial position immediately after the acquisition. How would this goodwill be treated subsequent to its recognition?

5.45 Business acquisition ★ ★   **LO3, 4, 5, 10**

When Microsoft acquired Skype, it agreed to pay US$8.5 billion. This was the most expensive acquisition Microsoft had made at that point, but was viewed as an important acquisition to compete with key business rivals. It was recorded at the time of acquisition that '[a]bout 170 million people use Skype's services every month but the vast majority are making free video calls from one computer to another ... Skype has yet to record a profit in its seven-year history, reporting a loss of US$7 million on revenue of US$860 million in 2010' (Corrigan 2011, p. 29).

Required

Generate a list of the factors that Microsoft would have considered in determining the price to pay for Skype. Compose a memorandum detailing how Microsoft would account for the acquisition of Skype:

(a) at acquisition date

(b) one year post-acquisition.

5.46 Impaired assets ★ ★   **LO4, 10**

EY's analysis of the accounts of 16 European utilities reveals that almost €17.7 billion (US$23.4 billion) was written off statements of financial position between 2010 and 2011. A large proportion (58 per cent) of this lost value was concentrated among just three utilities, while only four companies posted impairments of €150 million (US$198 million) or less.

Mergers and acquisitions activity may have left some companies lamenting costly acquisitions, notably those in southern Europe. Deals concluded at high prices had failed to deliver promised value in the current economic climate, leading to impairments to goodwill. Assets, meanwhile, accounted for the largest share of lost value, with almost €13.6 billion (US$18 billion) written off between 2010 and 2011 (EY Global 2012).

Required

(a) Discuss when entities can recognise goodwill in the statement of financial position.

(b) Once recognised, explain the annual reporting requirements for goodwill.

(c) Explain the factors that would have contributed to European utilities' impairment of goodwill.

5.47 Research and development expenditure ★ ★   **LO3, 4, 10**

Samsung considers innovation to be crucial to its business. It values speed and exploration of new markets in order to remain competitive in a market with a constant influx of new technologies. Samsung has outlined that '[t]hrough the interplay of creative, imaginative people; a global R&D network; an organisation that encourages collaboration and cooperation among business partners all along the supply chain; and a strong commitment to ongoing investment, Samsung has put R&D at the heart of everything we do' (Samsung 2013).

Investment in research and development (R&D) has been highlighted by Samsung as a key way in which it responds to 'highly uncertain' and 'increasingly competitive' markets, and assists it in securing intellectual property rights and standardising technology. In 2013, Samsung outlined that 9 per cent of its sales revenue was invested in R&D each year (Samsung 2013). Samsung furthered this investment in 2017 when it invested more than US$15.53 billion in R&D. Only US$413.78 million of the development costs were capitalised (as an intangible asset) and Samsung 'considers technical feasibility and future economic benefits when capitalising development costs' (Jin-young 2018).

Required

(a) Construct an argument justifying research costs being expensed, rather than capitalised and recorded as assets in the statement of financial position.

(b) List the factors to be considered in determining the probability of a development project generating future economic benefits.

(c) Imagine that development costs were capitalised, but it subsequently became apparent that the project would not generate future economic benefits. Report on how to account for this.

(d) Samsung notes that its team of talented researchers and engineers is its strongest asset. More than a quarter of all Samsung employees work every day in R&D, collaborating on strategic technologies for the future and original technologies designed to forge new market trends and set new standards for excellence at the company's research facilities around the world. From a financial accounting perspective, discuss whether employees are assets to be recognised in the statement of financial position.

5.48 Classifying items ★ ★   **LO5, 6**

When corporations found their traditional funding revenues drying up during the global financial crisis, one solution adopted by banks was to issue convertible bonds. Convertible bonds are often referred to as 'hybrid financing' as they have the characteristics of both debt and equity. Differentiate the features of a convertible bond from those of an ordinary bond. Given that convertible bonds have debt and equity characteristics, explain how they should be classified in the statement of financial position.

5.49 Understanding a statement of financial position ★ ★   **LO8, 9, 10**

Access the latest financial report for Maybank Banking Corporation on its corporate website and answer the following questions.

(a) The financial institution is not following the current/non-current asset and liability classification. On what basis do you think the assets and liabilities are listed in the statement of financial position, and why would this format be appropriate and acceptable?

(b) What is the rationale for reporting financial numbers for two reporting periods?

(c) Explain the meaning of 'consolidated' figures. What is the rationale for providing consolidated figures?

5.50 Valuing inventory ★ ★   **LO10**

Koala Furniture Ltd, an office furniture retailer and wholesaler, carries a particular brand of office chair. During the year ended 30 June, the following purchases occurred.

August	50 chairs at $45
October	60 chairs at $54
December	55 chairs at $60
March	60 chairs at $58

As at 1 July, Koala Furniture Ltd had 18 chairs in inventory, costed at $42 per unit. As at 30 June, an inventory count revealed 21 chairs in inventory.

Required

(a) Explain why the inventory costing method affects the financial reporting numbers.

(b) Compare the value of the office chairs on hand as at 30 June to be included in the inventory balance in the statement of financial position, under the following cost flow assumptions:
   (i) FIFO
   (ii) weighted-average.

5.51 Assigning a cost to inventory ★ ★ ★   **LO10**

As a trainee accountant, you have been asked to determine the monetary value that should be assigned to the inventory of sporting equipment on hand as at the end of the financial year for Outdoor Adventures Ltd. You are currently looking at the inventory levels of a training shoe that is very popular. The number of pairs of shoes on hand at the start of the accounting period was 200 and these had a monetary value of $10 000 assigned to them. During the year, a further 1500 pairs of the training shoe were purchased and, at the end of the year, a stocktake revealed that there were 60 pairs unsold. The purchases were made throughout the year. Five hundred pairs of shoes were purchased at a unit price of $60, a further 500 pairs of shoes at a unit price of $65 and a further 500 pairs at a price of $63.

Required

(a) Differentiate the cost assigned to the inventory of training shoes using: (1) FIFO; and (2) weighted-average cost methods.

(b) LIFO is a permitted cost assignment method in the United States but is not permitted under IFRSs. Compare the effect on assets and profits if LIFO was used rather than FIFO in times of rising cost prices.

5.52 Fair value ★ ★ ★   **LO4, 5**

There is an IFRS on fair value measurement. The objective of this standard is to define fair value and specify the framework for measuring fair value. Identify the characteristics of assets and liabilities that should be considered when determining fair value.

DECISION-MAKING ACTIVITIES

5.53 Liability criteria

During the global financial crisis in July 2008, National Australia Bank (NAB) was exposed to collateralised debt obligations (CDO). Consequently, NAB wrote down $1 billion associated with these risky instruments, with its share price plummeting and shareholders losing $450 million. A shareholder class action was initiated against NAB. The class action was settled in 2010, with NAB agreeing to pay $115 million — a fraction of the loss to shareholders. The lawsuit claimed NAB failed to disclose the extent of its subprime investments. Yet, despite the settlement, NAB denied liability and advised that the settlement was reached on a 'commercial basis' only (Wilkins 2012).

Required

(a) Referencing the *Conceptual Framework*, discuss whether NAB should record a liability when a lawsuit is launched.

(b) Access the 2010 and 2011 NAB annual reports and identify how NAB disclosed and/or recognised the lawsuit.

(c) The *Conceptual Framework* refers to a present obligation being a legal or constructive obligation. With reference to an example, describe your understanding of a constructive obligation.

(d) Identify the changes, if any, to the liability definition and recognition criteria as a result of the revised *Conceptual Framework*.

5.54 In a significant accounting-related court case, the Australian Securities and Investments Commission (ASIC) took the directors of Centro to court over the misclassification of liabilities. On 27 June 2011, the Federal Court found the directors had breached their duty of care. The judge found that each director knew of the interest-bearing securities and should have been aware of the relevant accounting principles that would have alerted them to the error in signing off accounts that classified billions of dollars as long-term, rather than short-term, debt. Each month the directors had received a 450-page board package containing 65 documents with 93 sets of complex financial statements. The directors' defence was that the board papers were voluminous and they could not be expected to absorb that amount of information.

Required

(a) Discuss when a liability should be classified as a current liability.

(b) Explain why Centro's debt should have been classified as short term.

(c) Outline the duties of directors in relation to the financial statements.

5.55 The following article extract refers to the 'goodwill glob' and implies that it produces data that lack serviceability. Clarke and Dean (2011, p. 63) outline that there will come a time when challenges are made to the data used in company financial statements:

> that ASIC has 'let through' ... yields the financial indicators for which it is habitually used to determine. And the ... answer will have to be 'no'. That means it is neither true nor fair in any meaningful sense, for the products of many of the current standards fail miserably. They contain fictions.

(a) Provide a counterargument to that of the financial statements containing 'fictions'.

(b) Each year ASIC conducts a surveillance program of companies' financial reporting. Identify the areas that ASIC focused on in its most recent surveillance program.

5.56 The most recent financial statements for the Brisbane City Council are available at www.brisbane. qld.gov.au. Referring to these statements, address the following questions.

(a) Discuss why the Council is preparing GPFS.

(b) Summarise the measurement basis for the Council's various classes of PPE and relate the choice of measurement to the concepts of relevance and faithful representation.

(c) Contrary to some jurisdictions, Australia has adopted a transaction-neutral approach to financial reporting. Explain the meaning of 'transaction-neutral'.

(d) List two arguments each for and against having a different set of accounting rules for private sector and public sector entities.

5.57 Despite Australia adopting IFRS issued by the IASB, the AASB has not adopted the *International Financial Reporting Standard for Small and Medium-sized Entities* (IFRS for SMEs). Instead, the AASB has introduced a differential reporting framework, referred to as the Reduced Disclosure Requirements (RDR).

The following publications are technical updates provided by Deloitte, an accounting firm, discussing IFRS for SMEs and the RDR.

- Deloitte Touche Tohmatsu 2009, *IAS plus update — Simplified financial reporting — IASB provides relief for SMEs*, update, July, www.iasplus.com
- Deloitte Touche Tohmatsu 2010, *Accounting alert 2010/02 — AASB's 'Reduced Disclosure Regime' (RDR) — no laughing matter*, accounting alert, February, www.deloitte.com

Required

Read the technical updates to:

(a) discuss the aims of IFRS for SMEs

(b) identify if and how the measurement of various asset and liability classes under IFRS for SMEs varies from the full IFRS principles outlined in this chapter

(c) compare the IASB's IFRS for SMEs approach with that of the AASB's RDR

(d) analyse whether a community bank operating in Australia should be permitted to prepare its GPFS using the RDR

(e) explain any recent developments in Australia in relation to the reporting entity concept being the basis for determining entities required to prepare GPFS.

REFERENCES

Brisbane City Council 2017, *Annual report 2016–17*, www.brisbane.qld.gov.au.

Cisco Systems Inc. 2017, *Annual report 2017*, p. 81.

Clarke, F & Dean, G 2011, 'Fresh focus on "true and fair"', *Australian Financial Review*, 29 June, p. 63, www.afr.com.

Corrigan, B 2011, '$8.5 bn . . . Will Microsoft's heart Skype a beat?', *Australian Financial Review*, 14–15 May, p. 29.

EY Global 2012, 'Europe's utilities take multi-billion Euro asset impairment hit', *Utilities Unbundled*, iss. 12, www.ey.com.

JB Hi-Fi Ltd 2018, *Preliminary final report 2018*, www.jbhifi.com.au.

Jin-young, C 2018, 'Samsung Electronics spends over $15 billion in R&DF in 2017', *BusinessKorea*, www.businesskorea.co.kr/news.

Qantas Airways Ltd 2018, *Annual report 2018*, www.qantas.com.au.

Samsung 2013, *Research and development*, www.samsung.com/au.

SEEK Ltd 2015, *Preliminary annual report 2015*, www.seek.com.au/about/investors/reports-presentations.

Sorensen, J 2018, 'American and Turkish Airlines show dramatic increase in reward seat availability with Southwest staying on top', IdeaWorksCompany and CarTrawler, 16 May.

Wilkins, G 2012, 'NAB pays $115m to settle class action', *Sydney Morning Herald*, 10 November.

ACKNOWLEDGEMENTS

Photo: © Zadorozhnyi Viktor / Shutterstock.com

Photo: © Monkey Business Images / Shutterstock.com

Figure 5.2: © Qantas Airways Ltd 2018

Figures 5.6, 5.7, 5.9, 5.11, 5.12, 5.13, 5.14: © JB Hi-Fi Ltd 2018

CHAPTER 6

Statement of profit or loss and statement of changes in equity

LEARNING OBJECTIVES

After studying this chapter, you should be able to:

6.1 explain the purpose and importance of measuring financial performance
6.2 explain the reporting period concept and the difference between accrual accounting and cash accounting
6.3 outline the effects that accounting policy choices, estimates and judgements can have on financial statements
6.4 describe the measurement of financial performance
6.5 discuss the definition and classification of income
6.6 discuss the definition and classification of expenses
6.7 apply the recognition criteria to income and expenses
6.8 identify presentation formats for the statement of profit or loss
6.9 differentiate between alternative financial performance measures
6.10 explain the nature of the statement of comprehensive income and the statement of changes in equity
6.11 explain the relationship between the statement of profit or loss, the statement of financial position, the statement of comprehensive income and the statement of changes in equity.

Chapter preview

In this chapter, we examine the financial statement that reflects the success of a business in generating profits from its available resources during a specified time period. This statement is referred to as the 'statement of profit or loss'. Other terms used to describe this statement are the 'profit or loss statement', 'income statement' and 'statement of financial performance'. The importance of this statement in an overall assessment of the financial wellbeing of an entity is discussed. We also examine the statement of comprehensive income and the statement of changes in equity. The statement of comprehensive income commences with the profit or loss for the reporting period, as reported in the statement of profit or loss, and includes other income and expense items that are required by accounting standards to be taken directly to equity. The statement of changes in equity explains movements in equity, hence assets and liabilities, from the beginning to the end of the reporting period.

6.1 Purpose and importance of measuring financial performance

LEARNING OBJECTIVE 6.1 Explain the purpose and importance of measuring financial performance.

Profit or loss, a measure of financial performance, is an important item in financial statements. Profit reflects the outcome of an entity's investment and financing decisions. An entity should periodically report its performance to enable internal and external users to make informed decisions. The profit or loss will inform internal decisions such as the entity's pricing of goods and services and the need to review cost structures. The profit or loss will inform external decisions such as whether or not to invest in, or lend to, the business. An entity that generates losses rather than profits is not sustainable.

For example, Nicholas Cash commenced a sole trader business, Advantage Tennis Coaching (ATC) (see illustrative example 3.1 in the chapter on business structures). ATC's financial statements after one month of operations are provided as an example of financial statements for a small business. The statement of profit or loss of ATC was further analysed in illustrative example 4.5 (see the chapter on business transactions), which is reproduced here as illustrative example 6.1. The statement of profit or loss identifies that the business has generated a profit of $16 370 for the one-month period ended 30 September 2019. Assuming the financial information for September 2019 is representative, the profit suggests that the owner, Nicholas Cash, is operating a financially viable business with the income from fees for tennis coaching exceeding the expenses associated with delivering the coaching. A lender would be reasonably confident in the ability of the business to support a small loan to purchase ball machines. It would be useful to compare the profit this month to that of future months in order to better evaluate the performance of the business. Comparing the profit with the equity and the assets in the business used to generate the profit will allow Nicholas Cash to better assess the success of his business.

ILLUSTRATIVE EXAMPLE 6.1

A statement of profit or loss

ADVANTAGE TENNIS COACHING Statement of profit or loss for the month ending 30 September 2019		
Income		
Coaching fees		$22 300
Expenses		
Marketing	$2 000	
Wages	2 200	
Telephone	280	
Rent	1 000	
Electricity	450	5 930
Profit		**$16 370**

One of the main financial objectives of an entity is to create value for its owners. For a company listed on a securities exchange, such as the Australian Securities Exchange (ASX) or the Shanghai Stock Exchange, the value creation (or lack thereof) is generally evidenced by movements in the company's share price. For business entities with no observable share price, value creation is realised when the business is sold. The two aspects that determine value creation are return and risk, higher risk being synonymous with higher return. The **statement of profit or loss** reflects the accounting return for an entity for a specified time period. The accounting return is formally referred to as the profit or loss of the entity.

While the focus of this chapter is on the statement of profit or loss and the reporting of profits, the importance of sustainable business practices must be understood. Sustainability considerations often factor into the risk and return analysis. While many entities aim for profit maximisation, the importance of sustainable business practices means that decisions may be made that are not necessarily profit maximising, but are beneficial for the environment or the community. Entities often articulate their governance, environmental and social policies, and report on their environmental and social performance in addition to their financial performance; this is referred to as **triple bottom line reporting** or **environmental, social and governance (ESG) reporting**. More recently, the concept of integrated reporting has emerged. **Integrated reporting** conveys information on how an entity's strategy, governance, performance and prospects are leading to the creation of value. Refer to the introduction to accounting and business decision making chapter for a discussion of sustainability reporting.

For example, JB Hi-Fi Ltd's 2018 annual report includes governance, environmental and social statements, and notes that the company recognises the importance of all these matters to its shareholders, suppliers and customers. Putting this into practice, JB Hi-Fi Ltd discusses its governance policies and procedures, details its initiatives to reduce the impact of its business on the environment, and lists its programs designed to 'give back' to the community.

It must also be remembered that a profit objective is not relevant for all entities. Many entities are not-for-profit entities. For example, the mission of the Bill and Melinda Gates Foundation is to help all people lead healthy, productive lives. As we see in this chapter, the profit or loss figure is not a measure of the change in an entity's value from the start of the reporting period to the end of the reporting period. This is because **profit or loss** is determined as income less expenses and, for accounting purposes, not all value changes result in income or expenses that are recognised in the statement of profit or loss. The reported profit figure is also not a measure of the cash that the entity has accumulated during the period, because income and expense recognition is not contingent on cash being received or paid. The definition of 'income' encompasses both:

- revenue arising in the ordinary course of activities (e.g. sales, fees and dividends)
- gains (e.g. gains on disposal of non-current assets and unrealised gains on revaluing assets).

While some gains are recognised in the statement of profit or loss, other gains are taken directly to equity, depending on the prescribed accounting treatment stated in various accounting standards. For example, property, plant and equipment (PPE) assets can be measured at their fair value. In electing to measure such assets at fair value, any value increase is an unrealised gain and increases the revaluation surplus in the equity section of the statement of financial position, rather than being included as income in the measurement of profit or loss for the reporting period. Other gains, such as the gain on disposal of PPE, are required to be recognised as income and included in the determination of profit or loss.

Given that revenue is a subset of income, the terms 'revenue' and 'income' both appear throughout the discussions. Do not let this confuse you. Remember **revenue** is the term that applies to income arising in the ordinary course of an entity's activities.

Periodic determination of an entity's profit or loss is necessary because users need to assess the profitability of an entity throughout its life. Users rely on periodic profit or loss figures to evaluate past decisions, revise predictions and make future decisions. An entity cannot remain viable in the long term if it continually generates losses. Without producing a periodic statement of profit or loss, management will be unaware of the entity's profitability. This would impede their decision making. For example, if a declining profit is not identified by management, they are unable to take corrective action to improve profitability. Further, owners would not be able to gauge the capacity of the entity to make distributions in the form of drawings or dividends, or to assess the return on their investment, if profit or loss was not measured periodically.

It is common practice for an entity to prepare a statement of profit or loss for a 12-month period to the end of its reporting period, often 30 June of each year. Large companies are subject to statutory reporting requirements and are required to prepare a statement of profit or loss for a 12-month period in addition to producing and lodging a semi-annual statement. However, a statement of profit or loss can be produced for management for any period of time (e.g. monthly or quarterly). More frequent profit determination and reporting provide timely information for managers, enabling them to assess performance against budgets and react to undesirable profit trends.

> **VALUE TO BUSINESS**
>
> - The statement of profit or loss is one of the financial statements prepared at the end of each reporting period. It reflects the profit or loss of the entity for a specified time period. Periodic determination of an entity's profit or loss is necessary because users need to assess the profitability of an entity throughout its life. Users rely on periodic profit or loss figures to evaluate past decisions and revise future predictions.
> - Profit or loss is determined as income less expenses. The statement of profit or loss is therefore a summary of the income and expense transactions occurring during the reporting period.
> - Income comprises both revenue and gains, with revenue being income arising in the ordinary course of activities.

6.2 Accounting concepts for financial reporting

LEARNING OBJECTIVE 6.2 Explain the reporting period concept and the difference between accrual accounting and cash accounting.

When discussing the statement of profit or loss, it is important to appreciate what is meant by the term 'reporting period' and to understand the distinction between cash accounting and accrual accounting.

The reporting period

As discussed previously, parties with an inherent interest in the financial performance of an entity need to be informed on a regular basis as to the profit or loss generated by the entity. For example, an investor who contributes capital to an entity will not want to wait until the entity is sold or wound up before ascertaining whether their investment has been financially rewarding. Management need timely information, as they must make informed decisions such as the price to charge for an entity's products. The financial statements assume that an entity is a going concern, but the life of the entity is divided into arbitrary **reporting periods**, also known as accounting periods. For external reports, the convention is that the arbitrary reporting period is yearly, and so the entity prepares financial statements at the end of each 12 months (not necessarily a calendar year). For internal reports, managers may divide the life of the business into time periods of less than one year. The reporting period to which the statement of profit or loss relates should be prominently displayed.

Many countries require interim reporting. In Australia and the United Kingdom, most listed entities are required to report financial results to the relevant securities exchange on a semi-annual basis. In contrast, the United States and Canada have quarterly reporting, whereas the state government of Victoria requires monthly reporting by all public hospitals.

Accrual accounting versus cash accounting

Accounting standards require that financial statements are prepared on the basis of accrual accounting, as distinct from cash accounting. **Accrual accounting** is a system in which transactions are recorded in the period to which they relate, rather than in the period in which the entity receives or pays the cash related to the transaction. This means that the reported profit or loss based on the accrual system is the difference between income and expenses for the period. This is not synonymous with cash. A **cash accounting** system, in contrast, determines cash profit or loss as the difference between the cash received in relation to income items and the cash paid for expenses for the period. Under an accrual basis of accounting, the entity does not have to receive cash associated with a transaction for that transaction to be regarded as income, so cash received in the reporting period may not result in income being recognised. Similarly, the entity does not have to pay cash for that transaction to be regarded as an expense, so cash paid in the reporting period may not result in the recognition of an expense. Accrual accounting involves recognising the income and expense transactions when they occur, not when cash is paid or received.

The purpose of accrual accounting is to better reflect the performance of the entity for a reporting period. The timing of cash payments and cash receipts has the potential to distort performance in a period if a cash basis of accounting is used to measure financial performance. Therefore, an entity required to comply with accounting standards must prepare its financial statements on an accrual basis. Entities not required to comply with accounting standards, such as many small businesses, may prepare their financial statements on a cash basis.

We formally define and examine the income and expense elements later in the chapter. In the meantime, to illustrate the concept of accrual accounting versus cash accounting, consider illustrative examples 6.2 to 6.5 relating to Advantage Tennis Coaching (ATC). ATC's business transactions for September 2019 were recorded in the accounting worksheet in illustrative examples 4.1 to 4.3 in the chapter on business transactions. The transactions described below relate to the reporting period ended December 2019.

ILLUSTRATIVE EXAMPLE 6.2

Recognising income without receiving cash (accrued income)

ATC conducts a holiday clinic for a tennis club on 20 December 2019. The club is invoiced $8000 for the coaching clinic by ATC, but as at 31 December 2019 (the end of the reporting period) the invoice has not been paid. In recording the transaction in ATC's accounting worksheet, the asset account, accounts receivable (i.e. debtors) will be increased by $8000 and income (coaching fees) in the profit or loss column will be increased by $8000, thereby increasing profit and hence equity. It is appropriate to recognise the $8000 in the accounts as income in December, because ATC conducts the clinic and renders the services in December. The income has been earned even though it has not yet been received in cash — it is accrued income. **Accrued income** is income that has been earned but not received in cash. The club will not pay the invoice until January 2020. If ATC was operating a cash accounting system, there would be no transaction recorded in December 2019. No income would be recognised in ATC's accounts in relation to this invoice for the month ended 31 December 2019, because no cash has been received for the services rendered. Under a cash system, the income would be recognised in January 2020 when ATC received the $8000 from the club. In January 2020, the entry in the accounting worksheet under a cash system will be to increase an asset (cash) by $8000 and to increase income (coaching fees) in the profit or loss column by $8000.

ILLUSTRATIVE EXAMPLE 6.3

Receiving cash but not recognising income (income received in advance)

ATC is commissioned in December 2019 by Tennis Australia to conduct a four-week intensive training squad for elite players to take place in January 2020. Tennis Australia pays ATC an up-front payment of $12 000, which is banked by ATC. The transaction recorded by ATC is to increase an asset account (cash) and increase an income account (coaching fees). However, as at 31 December 2019 (the end of the reporting period) ATC has not commenced the training squad. The sessions will not be conducted until January 2020. Under a cash accounting system, income of $12 000 would be recognised in ATC's accounts for December 2019 because the money has been received by ATC. Under an accrual accounting system, no income in the current reporting period should be recognised in ATC's accounts because ATC has not rendered any services to Tennis Australia in December 2019. To reflect this in the accounts, it is necessary to do an adjusting entry. The initial recording of the transaction has resulted in income being overstated by $12 000 for December 2019. The adjusting entry necessary will be to reduce income by $12 000, thereby reducing profit and hence equity. The dual nature of the transaction will be reflected with a corresponding entry recognising that the business has a liability at the end of the reporting period, as it owes services to Tennis Australia. This liability is **income received in advance** (cash received for goods or services not yet provided) related to the coaching program. In January 2020, when ATC conducts the training squad, the liability will decrease and the income will be recognised.

ILLUSTRATIVE EXAMPLE 6.4

Recognising an expense without paying cash (accrued expense)

ATC uses a mobile telephone for business purposes. At the end of the reporting period, being 31 December 2019, ATC has not paid the December telephone charges, estimated to be $500. This account will be paid in January 2020. Under a cash accounting system, no expense would be recognised in ATC's accounts in relation to the December mobile phone charges, as no payment has been made to the mobile phone service provider. Under a cash system, this would be recorded as an expense in the month that it was paid (i.e. January 2020). Under an accrual accounting system, the expense associated with December mobile phone usage will be recognised in ATC's accounts because the coach has been using the mobile phone during December. An adjusting entry at the end of December 2019 is required to record the expense. The transaction will be recorded by increasing expenses by $500, thereby reducing profit and hence equity. The corresponding entry to keep the accounting equation in balance is to record a liability at the end of December 2019. This liability is an **accrued expense**, being the December mobile phone charges owed by ATC to the provider of the mobile phone service. When ATC pays the mobile phone bill in January 2020, the liability will decrease and an asset account (cash) will decrease.

ILLUSTRATIVE EXAMPLE 6.5

Paying cash but not recognising an expense (prepaid expense)

ATC pays a $2400 12-month premium for public liability insurance at the start of December 2019. The transaction recorded is a decrease in an asset account (cash) and an increase in an expense account (insurance), which reduces profit and hence equity. Under a cash accounting system, an expense of $2400 would be recognised in the statement of profit or loss at the end of the reporting period of 31 December 2019, because the premium has been paid. Under an accrual accounting system, it is necessary to consider what expense has been incurred in December 2019. ATC has received the benefit for only one month of the insurance premium as at the end of December. Therefore, the expense recognised in December will be 1/12 of the annual premium (1/12 of $2400 = $200). Given how the transaction was initially recorded, as an increase in expenses of $2400, the expense for December is overstated. An adjusting entry is needed. The transaction to be recorded to adjust the accounts is to reduce the expense from $2400 to $200, a decrease of $2200. Further, the dual nature of this transaction will be reflected in ATC's accounts, with a corresponding entry recognising that ATC has an asset at the end of December representing the unused insurance premium. This asset is a **prepaid expense** or **prepayment**, the amount paid in cash and recorded as an asset until the economic benefits are used or consumed. The prepayment is the $2200 of insurance premium for the next 11 months that has already been paid for by ATC.

The preceding illustrative examples have used timing differences to distinguish between the accrual and cash concepts of profit or loss that arise under the accrual and cash systems of accounting respectively. If an entity reported its profit or loss at the end of its life rather than periodically throughout its life, there would be no difference between the accrual and cash concepts of profit. For example, assume that ATC's business as described in the illustrative examples had a life of two years. As illustrated in table 6.1, the income and expenses recognised over the two-year life would be identical despite the accrual and cash profit figures being different in the reporting periods ended 31 December 2019 and 31 December 2020. This is because timing transactions reverse over the life of the entity.

TABLE 6.1 Accrual and cash profits compared between reporting periods ended December 2019 and December 2020

	Reporting period ended December 2019	Reporting period ended December 2020	Over the two years
Accrual-based profit			
Income recognised	$8000 for coaching fees	$12 000 for coaching fees	$20 000
Expenses recognised	$500 mobile phone $200 insurance	$2200 insurance	$ 2900
Accrual profit (loss) for period (income less expenses)	$7300	$9800	$17 100
Cash-based profit			
Income recognised	$12 000 coaching fees received in advance	$8000 received for coaching fees provided in 2019	$20 000
Expenses recognised	$2400 insurance premium paid	$500 mobile phone account paid	$ 2900
Cash profit (loss) for period	$9600	$7500	$17 100

Depreciation

There are other expenses recognised under accrual accounting that do not involve cash flows. For example, depreciation and amortisation are expenses recognised in the statement of profit or loss that do not involve any outflow of cash. All PPE assets must be depreciated and certain intangible assets must be amortised. **Depreciation (amortisation)** is the systematic allocation of the cost of a tangible (intangible) asset over its useful life. Depreciation (amortisation) expense recognises that the asset's future economic benefits have been used up in the reporting period. Depreciation and amortisation do not represent the reduction in the asset's market value from the start to the end of the reporting period. This is another reason why profit or loss does not represent the change in an entity's value from the start to the end of the reporting period.

Consider the following example of how depreciation can be calculated. An entity purchases a car for $40 000, with an estimated useful life of four years and expected residual value of $8000. If we assume that the benefits of using the car will be derived evenly over its useful life, then the straight-line depreciation method is used. Other depreciation methods are discussed later in this chapter. Straight-line depreciation results in the same depreciation expense being recorded each year for the asset's useful life. Straight-line depreciation is calculated using the equation below.

$$\text{Annual depreciation expense} = \frac{\text{Cost of asset} - \text{Expected residual value}}{\text{Asset's expected useful life (years)}}$$
$$= \frac{\$40\,000 - \$8000}{4\,\text{years}}$$
$$= \$8000$$

The annual depreciation expense to be recognised in the statement of profit or loss is $8000. The transaction will be recorded by increasing an expense (depreciation) and increasing accumulated depreciation. **Accumulated depreciation** is the account used to capture the total depreciation that has been charged to statements of profit or loss for a particular asset. The accumulated depreciation account is referred to as a **contra account**. In the statement of financial position, the accumulated depreciation account is deducted from the relevant asset account. Thus, when recording depreciation expense, the dual nature of the transaction is represented by an expense account increasing, thereby reducing profit and hence equity, and the contra account, the accumulated depreciation, increasing, thereby reducing assets. The asset account, cash, is unaffected by the recording of depreciation expense. Referring back to the example, after one year the carrying amount of the car reported in the statement of financial position is $32 000. The $32 000 represents the car's cost price ($40 000) less the accumulated depreciation expense ($8000). The $32 000 is not necessarily equivalent to the market value of the car at the end of the reporting period, so the financial statements do not reflect the change in the car's market value. In the second year, another $8000 depreciation expense is recognised in the statement of profit or loss. Hence, after two years the carrying amount of the car reported in the statement of financial position is $24 000, being the car's cost price ($40 000) less the accumulated depreciation, which is now $16 000. The $16 000 accumulated depreciation amount is the sum of the depreciation expense for the car in year 1 and year 2. After four years the accumulated depreciation is $32 000, being four years of the annual depreciation charge of $8000. At the end of year 4 the carrying amount of the car is $8000, being its cost price ($40 000) less the accumulated depreciation ($32 000). Thus, at the end of the asset's useful life, in this example four years, the asset's carrying value is its residual value. This accumulated depreciation represents the asset's future economic benefits that have been used up in the four years since its purchase.

6.3 Effects of accounting policy choices, estimates and judgements on financial statements

LEARNING OBJECTIVE 6.3 Outline the effects that accounting policy choices, estimates and judgements can have on financial statements.

As discussed in the statement of financial position chapter, even when preparing financial statements in compliance with the accounting standards, these accounting standards provide preparers with choices. Further, estimations and assumptions are necessary. Users of financial statements need to appreciate that accounting flexibility and discretion exist, and they need to consider the potential impact of this on the quality of the reported financial information.

Preparers of financial statements need to make choices, estimations and judgements when recording transactions.

Just as some of the permissible choices in the recording of transactions and estimations and judgements required by preparers of statement of financial positions were explored in the chapter on the statement of financial position, in this section we focus on the pertinent elements of the statement of profit or loss where similar considerations may be required. Earlier in this chapter we discussed the straight-line method of depreciation; however, this is not the only depreciation method permitted under approved accounting standards. An entity can choose the straight-line, diminishing balance or units of production depreciation methods. The method selected should be representative of the pattern by which the asset's benefits are expected to be consumed. Further, when selecting the depreciation method, estimates and judgements need to be made in relation to the asset's useful life and residual value. Consider an asset that is purchased for $30 000 at the start of the reporting period and has an estimated useful life of three years, with $3000 residual (salvage) value. Employing **straight-line depreciation** (where the annual depreciation on the asset is the same each year), an expense of $9000 would be recognised in the statement of profit or loss for each of the next three reporting periods. Using the calculation formula provided above, the annual depreciation expense is the asset's cost price less the residual value divided by the useful life (($30 000 – $3000)/3 years). If the asset is acquired partway through a reporting period, the annual depreciation is pro rata. For example, if the asset was purchased at the start of the seventh month of the reporting year, the depreciation expense for that reporting period would be $4500 ($9000 annual depreciation charge × 6 months/12 months).

The **diminishing balance depreciation** method assumes that the economic benefits of using the asset will decrease over its useful life. Consequently, depreciation expense is higher in the asset's earlier years relative to later years. Diminishing balance is calculated by applying a constant percentage to the asset's carrying amount at the start of each reporting period. Assume the asset is depreciated using a 50 per cent diminishing balance depreciation method. The depreciation expense for each of the next three years will be $15 000 in year 1 (50 per cent of $30 000), $7500 in year 2 (50 per cent of ($30 000 – $15 000)) and $3750 in year 3 (50 per cent of ($30 000 – ($15 000 + $7500)). Employing diminishing balance depreciation, the annual depreciation is higher in earlier years relative to later years. The asset's carrying value at the end of the third year is $3750, being its cost price of $30 000 less the accumulated depreciation of $26 250.

The **units of production depreciation** method charges depreciation expense based on the activity or output in the reporting period relative to the asset's total expected activity or output. Units of production depreciation is calculated using the following equation.

$$\text{Depreciation expense (for the period)} = \frac{\text{(Cost of asset − Expected residual value)}}{\text{Total estimated units}} \times \text{Units in the period}$$

Suppose that the asset used in this illustration is a machine with a useful life of 100 000 units of production. The depreciation charge each year will be a function of the yearly units produced. Assume the machine produces 50 000, 30 000 and 20 000 units in years 1 to 3, respectively. Using the units of production method, the depreciation expense in the statements of profit or loss for the next three reporting periods will be: $13 500 in year 1 calculated as (($30 000 − $3000)/100 000) × 50 000 units; $8100 in year 2 calculated as (($30 000 − $3000)/100 000) × 30 000 units; and $5400 in year 3 calculated as (($30 000 − $3000)/100 000) × 20 000 units. The asset's carrying value at the end of the third year is $3000, being its cost price of $30 000 less the accumulated depreciation of $27 000 in years 1, 2 and 3.

Table 6.2 presents a comparison of annual and total depreciation expenses for the three methods. Given that the depreciation expense differs according to the depreciation method employed, the estimated useful life and the estimated residual value, the reported profit or loss in a particular reporting period will vary according to these selections and estimations, as will the carrying value of the assets subject to depreciation.

TABLE 6.2	Comparison of depreciation methods			
		Year		
		1	2	3
Straight-line				
Asset carrying value at start of year		$30 000	$21 000	$12 000
Annual depreciation expense		9 000	9 000	9 000	$27 000
Asset carrying value at end of year		$21 000	$12 000	$ 3 000
Diminishing balance				
Asset carrying value at start of year		$30 000	$15 000	$ 7 500
Annual depreciation expense		15 000	7 500	3 750	$26 250
Asset carrying value at end of year		$15 000	$ 7 500	$ 3 750
Units of production				
Asset carrying value at start of year		$30 000	$16 500	$ 8 400
Annual depreciation expense		13 500	8 100	5 400	$27 000
Asset carrying value at end of year		$16 500	$ 8 400	$ 3 000

Figure 6.1 compares the depreciation patterns over the three years by showing the carrying value of the asset at the end of each of the three years for the different depreciation methods. Under the straight-line method, with an equal depreciation expense each year, the asset's carrying value reduces evenly over each of the three years. Under the diminishing balance method, with higher depreciation expense in earlier than in later years, the carrying value reduces at a faster rate in earlier years relative to the outcome of straight-line depreciation. Under the units of production method, with the depreciation expense varying with the usage each year, the reduction in carrying value each year is dependent on the asset's usage in that year.

FIGURE 6.1	Patterns of depreciation

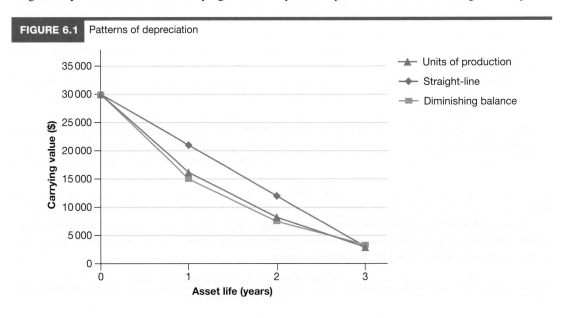

As just demonstrated through the depreciation example, an entity's accounting choices, estimates and judgements will affect the profit or loss figure. This also has implications for statement of financial position items. For example, depreciation expense affects accumulated depreciation, which in turn affects the carrying amount of the asset.

Other examples of estimations that affect the magnitude of expenses recognised in the statement of profit or loss in a particular reporting period, and statement of financial position items, include estimating any impaired accounts receivable, estimating costs associated with a well-planned and well-documented business restructure, and estimating the expense in a particular period associated with employee benefits (e.g. long service leave and sick leave).

When reviewing the financial statements, a user must be cognisant of the particular accounting policies used and of financial numbers that involve preparer estimations. Many accounting policy choices are transparent, as reporting entities are required to disclose such choices. However, entities are not obliged to detail all estimations used to derive various items recognised in the financial statements. For a listed entity such as JB Hi-Fi Ltd, the accounting policy disclosures are usually in the first few notes accompanying the financial statements.

Quality of earnings

Given that preparers of financial statements have discretion with respect to accounting policies and estimations, it is necessary to consider the quality of the profit or loss figure, often referred to as the 'quality of earnings'. Are the earnings persistent? Earnings derived from an entity's repetitive operations are regarded as persistent or sustainable, or core earnings. Are the earnings being managed? **Earnings management** refers to managers' use of accounting discretion via accounting policy choices and/or estimations to portray a desired level of profit in a particular reporting period. Reported profits are used in entities' contractual arrangements and to value entities, and are therefore an important financial number. Managers' choices may be determined by their desire to portray the economic reality of the entity in the statement of profit or loss; however, their choices may also be driven by self-interest. A particular profit range may be desirable for a number of reasons, including to avoid breaching loan covenants, to maintain the share price or to maximise salary bonuses. An independent audit of financial statements provides assurance that, based on the audit evidence, the financial statements give a true and fair view of the entity's financial position and performance, and comply with required accounting standards. In a demonstration of good corporate governance, the chief executive officer (CEO) and chief financial officer (CFO) may be required to sign a declaration certifying the accuracy of the financial statements.

Earnings management often occurs via the accruals process. In a later chapter, you will examine the statement of cash flows. This financial statement details the net cash inflows and outflows for an entity during the reporting period. It is useful to compare an entity's profit or loss with its cash flows from operations. This is synonymous with comparing profit or loss calculated under accrual accounting with profit or loss calculated under cash accounting. Remembering that timing differences associated with accrual accounting even out over the life of the entity, such a comparison enables the user to determine any unusual trends in accruals that may suggest the profit figure reported is being managed.

VALUE TO BUSINESS

- Many entities are required to prepare their statements of profit or loss using accrual accounting. This means that income and expenses are included in the statement of profit or loss when they occur. This differs from cash accounting, where income is recognised when the cash is received and expenses are recognised when the cash is paid.
- Generally accepted accounting principles permit and require preparer choices as to when transactions are recorded and measured.
- The profit or loss figure is a function of the entity's portfolio of accounting choices, estimations and judgements.

6.4 Measuring financial performance

LEARNING OBJECTIVE 6.4 Describe the measurement of financial performance.

Recall that the revised *Conceptual Framework for Financial Reporting* discussed in the statement of financial position chapter identifies the objectives of financial reporting, the assumptions underlying financial statements and the qualitative characteristics of financial statements, and defines the elements of financial statements (assets, liabilities, equity, income and expenses) and the recognition criteria applied to these elements. In the next sections, we discuss the definition and recognition criteria applicable to income and expenses.

'Profit or loss' is not formally defined in the revised *Conceptual Framework*, but is instead identified as being measured as the difference between income and expenses in a reporting period. To measure the profit or loss of an entity, it is therefore necessary to identify and measure all income and expense items attributable to the reporting period. This necessitates an understanding of what attributes are required by a transaction in order for it to be classified as an item of income or expense.

The revised *Conceptual Framework* specifies definition criteria for income and expenses. It also discusses the recognition process that applies to these elements. A transaction must satisfy the definition and recognition criteria in order to be included in the statement of profit or loss. We will see that the definitions of income and expenses are integrally linked with assets and liabilities.

6.5 Income

LEARNING OBJECTIVE 6.5 Discuss the definition and classification of income.

For a transaction to be recorded as income in a particular reporting period, the income definition criteria must be satisfied. These criteria are examined in the following sections.

Income definition

Income is defined in the revised *Conceptual Framework* (para. 4.68) as an increase in an asset, or a decrease in a liability, which results in an increase in equity (other than those relating to equity-holder claim contributions).

Recall that income comprises both revenue and gains, with revenue arising in the ordinary course of an entity's activities. Gains also represent increases in economic benefits, but they may or may not arise in the ordinary course of an entity's activities.

Income must be associated with an increase in assets or a decrease in liabilities. When deciding if the income definition criteria are satisfied, it is necessary to ascertain whether a new asset exists or an existing asset has increased, or whether an existing liability has been reduced. Recalling the duality principle, an increase in an asset or a reduction in a liability must be accompanied by an increase in equity. Thus, income increases equity.

Consider a retail operation that is making credit and cash sales. A cash sale satisfies the definition of income, as it results in an inflow or increase in economic benefits — the entity has increased its cash at bank. Similarly, a credit sale also satisfies the income definition criteria, as it results in the creation of an account receivable — representing a present economic resource. The later transaction in which the customer settles this account by paying cash to the business does not satisfy the income definition. While the retail operation has more cash, due to the customer paying, assets have not increased in total because another asset — accounts receivable — has been extinguished and therefore offsets the increase in cash. Thus, there is no increase in assets as a result of this latter transaction.

If a transaction involves a contribution by owners or contributed capital (such as a cash injection to the business from the owner's personal account), the income definition criteria are not satisfied. For example, the owners of a retail business contribute $100 000 to their business to fund a store refurbishment. The receipt of the $100 000 will not be recorded as income by the business (to be reported in the statement of profit or loss) because it results from a transaction with the owners of the business. Instead, cash (an asset) will increase and capital contributions (an equity item) will increase.

Income classification

Income arising in the ordinary course of an entity's activities (i.e. revenue) is generated from various activities; typically these include providing goods and services, investing or lending, and receiving contributions from parties other than owners. As well as diversity in income-generating activities, there are diverse income types, such as sales, fees, commissions, interest, dividends, royalties, rent and non-reciprocal transfers.

6.6 Expenses

LEARNING OBJECTIVE 6.6 Discuss the definition and classification of expenses.

As with income, definition criteria must be satisfied before an expense is recorded in the statement of profit or loss. The following sections discuss these criteria.

Expense definition

Expenses are defined in the revised *Conceptual Framework* (para. 4.69) as a decrease in an asset, or an increase in a liability, which results in a decrease in equity (other than those relating to equity-holder claim distributions).

The word 'expenses' refers to expenses arising in the ordinary course of the entity's activities, as well as losses (both realised and unrealised). When deciding if the expense definition criteria are satisfied, it is necessary to ascertain that assets have been reduced or liabilities have increased. A reduction in an asset or an increase in a liability must be accompanied by a reduction in equity for the definition to be satisfied. Thus, expenses decrease equity. The qualification to this definition is that the transaction does not involve a **distribution to owners** (i.e. a dividend distribution or return of capital to equity participants). This qualification eliminates dividend distributions and capital returns to owners from being recognised as expenses.

Consider a retail operation. The main expense incurred by the business is the **cost of sales**. In order to sell goods and generate revenue, the entity must purchase goods for resale. Remembering that financial statements are prepared using accrual accounting, the cost of sales expense comprises the entity's purchases during the reporting period and the change in the inventory balance from the beginning to the end of the reporting period (calculated using the equation below).

$$\text{Cost of sales} = \text{Inventory at beginning of period} + \text{Purchases} - \text{Inventory at end of period}$$

Imagine that the entity purchases goods on credit from a supplier on 15 June. For the reporting period ended 30 June, the purchases will be included in the cost of sales determination even though no cash has been paid to the supplier by 30 June. The critical feature of an expense is that an asset has been reduced or a liability increased, with a consequent reduction in equity. In the transaction described, the entity has an obligation to pay the supplier, so a liability is increased (accounts payable). The dual side of the transaction is that an expense, purchases, has increased and thereby reduced equity. When the supplier is paid, the liability account (accounts payable) is reduced and an asset account (cash) is also reduced, with no corresponding reduction in equity. Hence, the payment does not involve the recognition of an expense.

Other expenses associated with selling goods include advertising, sales staff salaries, store displays and wrapping materials. Generally, an expense will arise as a result of the payment of cash (asset reduction) or the recognition of an accrued expense or accounts payable (liability increase). Expenses are also associated with administrative functions, and investing and financing activities. Administrative expenses include items such as rent, office wages and salaries, utility charges and supplies. Finance-related expenses include interest on borrowings, lease payments and bank charges.

The acquisition of certain assets (such as items of PPE) is not an expense of the reporting period, as there is no reduction in equity associated with the transaction. If the asset is acquired for cash, cash at bank is reduced but the reduction is offset by an increase in another asset class — PPE. Such items are expected to provide the entity with future economic resources over a period extending beyond the current reporting period, so it would be inappropriate to recognise the acquisition as an expense in the period when it occurs. What is periodically recognised as an expense is the depreciation of such assets. The **carrying amount (book value)** (the dollar value assigned to the asset in the statement of financial position) of the asset must be allocated over the asset's useful life, representing future economic benefits of the asset that have been consumed during the reporting period. Further, when the value of the asset is lower than its carrying amount, the asset is impaired; in such circumstances, the asset must be written down to its recoverable amount and the write-down will be recognised as an **impairment** expense in the reporting period in which it occurs.

Expense classification

Entities have a choice as to how they display and classify expenses in the statement of profit or loss. Smaller entities will often list all their expenses in the statement of profit or loss, whereas larger entities will aggregate their expenses into certain classes for reporting purposes. Entities required to comply with accounting standards must classify their expenses by nature or function. For example, if an entity classified expenses by nature, expense categories in its statement of profit or loss might include employee benefits expense, and depreciation and amortisation expense. If the entity classified expenses by function, expense categories in its statement of profit or loss might include distribution, marketing, occupancy and administrative expenses, and borrowing costs expense.

Look at the statement of profit or loss for JB Hi-Fi Ltd in figure 6.2. The entity has classified its expenses by function; namely, cost of sales, sales and marketing expenses, occupancy expenses, administrative expenses, acquisition transaction and implementation expenses, finance costs and other expenses. Further disclosures regarding the disaggregation of expenses are minimal. Only certain expenses must be disclosed (e.g. amortisation and depreciation charges, lease rentals, auditor's fees and finance costs). Sometimes entities voluntarily provide details of other expenses.

FIGURE 6.2	JB Hi-Fi Ltd's statement of profit or loss

JB HI-FI LTD
Consolidated statement of profit or loss
for the financial year ended 30 June 2018

	Notes	Consolidated 2018 $m	Consolidated 2017 $m
Revenue		6 854.3	5 628.0
Cost of sales		(5 384.1)	(4 397.5)
Gross profit		1 470.2	1 230.5
Other income		1.1	2.0
Sales and marketing expenses		(695.1)	(580.1)
Occupancy expenses		(305.7)	(248.6)
Administrative expenses		(42.2)	(36.2)
Acquisition transaction and implementation expenses		—	(22.4)
Other expenses		(77.2)	(75.3)
Finance costs	5	(16.6)	(10.7)
Profit before tax		**334.5**	**259.2**
Income tax expense	6	(101.3)	(86.8)
Profit for the year attributable to Owners of the Company		**233.2**	**172.4**
		Cents	Cents
Earnings per share			
Basic (cents per share)	3	203.09	154.30
Diluted (cents per share)	3	201.11	152.94

Source: JB Hi-Fi Ltd 2018, p. 54.

6.7 Applying recognition criteria to income and expenses

LEARNING OBJECTIVE 6.7 Apply the recognition criteria to income and expenses.

The recognition process was discussed in the previous chapter. Recapping, the term **recognition** refers to recording items in the financial statements with a monetary value assigned to them. Therefore, 'income recognition' and 'expense recognition' mean that the income or expense is recorded and appears in the statement of profit or loss. Central to the recognition principle is that items can be measured in monetary terms. This is referred to as the monetary concept. As money is the language used to quantify items recognised in financial statements, if items cannot be assigned a monetary value then they cannot appear in financial statements.

It is recognition that links the elements in the statement of financial position (assets, liabilities and equity) and the statement of profit or loss (income and expenses). Given the definitions of income and expenses, the recognition of one of these elements requires the recognition of an equal amount of another element. For example, recognising income simultaneously requires recognising an increase in assets or a decrease in liabilities. Similarly, recognising an expense simultaneously requires recognising a decrease in assets or an increase in liabilities. For example, recognising tennis fee income for ATC requires recognising an increase in an asset (e.g. cash at bank if the fees are paid in cash or accounts receivable if the fees are outstanding). Recognising an expense for ATC, such as paying court hire, requires simultaneously recognising a decrease in an asset (e.g. cash). Recognising a mobile phone expense that is due but has not been paid requires simultaneously recognising an increase in a liability (accrued expense or payables).

As discussed in the previous chapter, there are no definitive rules to assist the decision about whether an item should be recognised. The recognition decision requires judgement. The overarching considerations when deciding to recognise an income or an expense (and any related asset or liability) are whether the recognition provides financial statement users with relevant information about the asset or the liability and about any income, expenses or changes in equity, whether it is a faithful representation of the asset or the liability and of any income, expenses or changes in equity, and whether the information results in benefits exceeding the cost of providing that information.

The factors to consider when making a recognition decision, framed in terms of whether an asset or liability is recognised, are as follows.

- *Uncertainty* — if it is uncertain whether an asset exists or is separable from goodwill, or whether a liability exists. For example, customer relationships are not contractual and therefore uncertainty exists as to whether these are assets or whether they are separable from the business as a whole.
- *Probability* — if an asset or a liability exists, but there is only a low probability that an inflow or outflow of economic benefits will result. For example, an entity is being sued for a claimed act of wrongdoing but the probability of having to pay damages is assessed as low.
- *Measurement uncertainty* — if measurement of an asset or a liability can be obtained, but the level of measurement uncertainty is high, affecting the relevance of the information. For example, the estimated economic benefits are derived from modelling diverse scenarios with numerous assumptions and estimations, so the reasonableness of the estimation is questionable.

If the uncertainty surrounding existence is high, the probability of inflows or outflows of economic benefits is low or measurement uncertainty is high, then it is less likely that the asset or liability, and hence income or expense, will be recognised.

Income (revenue) recognition

The determination of when an increase in assets or a reduction in liabilities has arisen, and hence when income can be recognised, can be difficult and it demands consideration of relevance assessed with reference to uncertainty, probability and measurement. Consider the following transactions: (1) a customer made a 50 per cent non-cancellable deposit for goods worth $5000; and (2) a customer made a $10 cancellable deposit for goods worth $5000. The inflow of economic benefits associated with collecting the remaining cash for the $5000 of goods sold is less likely to arise in the second scenario of the customer paying a $10 deposit. For income recognition purposes, the first transaction would result in income of $5000 being recognised in the statement of profit or loss for the reporting period, but the probability factor would be unlikely to be satisfied in the second transaction.

It is difficult to be prescriptive as to the appropriate point in time when income should be recognised. In fact, accounting standard setters have been grappling with producing a standard on revenue recognition. Instances of earnings management where income has been recognised in earlier, rather than later, reporting periods (in order to increase earnings) have focused regulators' attention on the income-recognition policies used by entities. To determine whether income should be recognised, consideration should be given to the following.

- Does an agreement for the provision of goods and services exist between the entity and a party external to the entity?
- Has cash been received, or does the entity have a claim against an external party that is for a specified consideration and is unavoidable without penalty?
- Have all acts of performance necessary to establish a valid claim against the external party been completed?
- Is it possible to reliably estimate the collectability of debts?

A positive response to all of these questions would result in income being recognised in the statement of profit or loss. However, it is not necessary for all these suggested tests to be satisfied in order for income to be recognised — it depends on the circumstances of the situation.

Reporting entities generally disclose their income recognition policies in the notes to the accounts that summarise their accounting policies. JB Hi-Fi Ltd discloses its revenue recognition policies in note 31(a). These notes are reproduced in the appendix to this text. Examining JB Hi-Fi Ltd's accounting policy, note 31(a) reveals that the company measures revenue at the fair value of the consideration received or receivable, with amounts disclosed as revenue being net of returns, trade allowances, rebates and amounts collected on behalf of third parties. Figure 6.3 identifies the specific recognition criteria that must be met before revenue associated with the sale of goods, interest and dividends is recognised.

FIGURE 6.3	JB Hi-Fi Ltd's revenue recognition

(a) Revenue recognition

Revenue is measured at the fair value of the consideration received or receivable. Amounts disclosed as revenue are net of returns, trade allowances, rebates and amounts collected on behalf of third parties.

The Group recognises revenue when the amount of revenue can be reliably measured, it is probable that future economic benefits will flow to the entity and specific criteria have been met for each of the Group's activities as described below. The Group bases its estimates on historical results, taking into consideration the type of customer, the type of transaction and the specifics of each arrangement.

Revenue is recognised for the major business activities as follows:

(i) *Sale of goods*

Revenue from the sale of goods is recognised when the Group has transferred to the buyer the significant risks and rewards of ownership of the goods. Risks and rewards are considered passed to the buyer at the point of sale if the goods are taken by the customer at that time, or on delivery of the goods to the customer.

(ii) *Commissions*

When the Group acts in the capacity of an agent rather than as the principal in a transaction, the revenue recognised is the net amount of commission made by the Group.

(iii) *Rendering of services*

Revenue from a contract to provide services is recognised by reference to the portion of services provided in accordance with the contract. Revenue from time and material contracts is recognised at the contractual rates as labour hours are delivered and direct expenses are incurred.

Source: JB Hi-Fi Ltd 2018, pp. 90–91.

Expense recognition

Recognising an expense involves determining if a decrease in assets or an increase in liabilities is required, paying due attention to relevance as assessed in considering the factors of uncertainty, probability and measurement uncertainty. In many instances, this is straightforward (e.g. goods to a known value have been sold or an invoice for advertising expenses has been received). Other transactions involve greater uncertainty about the occurrence and measurement of the outflow of economic benefits (e.g. employee benefits expense and asset impairments).

As a result of the economic climate, many entities have suffered impairment losses. The accounting rules require entities to write down the carrying amount of their assets if the carrying amount is higher than the asset's recoverable amount. The **recoverable amount** is the higher of the asset's value in use and its net selling price.

Prior to the *Conceptual Framework* and the definitions of income and expense contained in it, considerable emphasis was placed on the matching principle when recognising income and expenses in a reporting period. The matching principle required matching the income earned with the expenses incurred in a reporting period. Applying the income and expense definitions and the recognition criteria — summarised in figure 6.4 — will generally involve a matching of income and expenses. This occurs when:

- items of income and expense result directly and jointly from the same transaction (e.g. the concurrent recognition of sales and cost of sales)
- income is matched with progressive performance (e.g. a borrower recognises the interest expense associated with a loan throughout the loan's life even if all the interest is to be paid at the loan's maturity)
- expenses are matched with the entity's productivity (e.g. the recognition of depreciation on a systematic basis according to the asset's useful life is allocating the depreciation expense according to asset productivity).

FIGURE 6.4 Summary of the definition criteria and recognition process for income and expenses

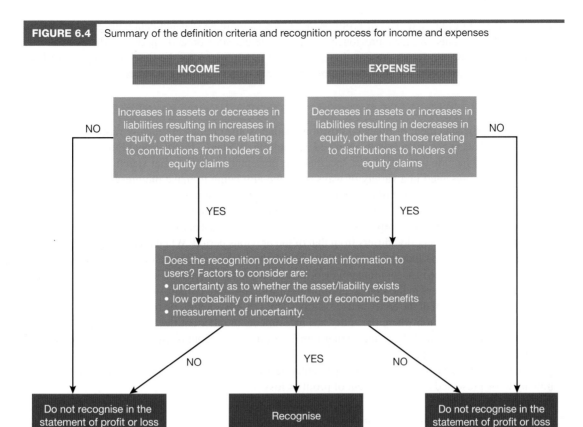

VALUE TO BUSINESS

- Measuring the profit or loss of an entity necessitates identifying, measuring and recognising all income and expense items attributable to the reporting period.
- Income is defined as increases in assets or decreases in liabilities that result in increases in equity for the entity, other than those relating to contributions from holders of equity claims.
- Expenses are defined as decreases in assets or increases in liabilities that result in decreases in equity for the entity, other than those relating to distributions to holders of equity claims.
- To recognise income and expenses in the statement of profit or loss, consideration is given to the following factors that influence the relevance of the information: (1) uncertainty regarding the asset's or liability's existence; (2) the probability of the inflow (outflow) of economic benefits associated with the asset (liability); and (3) the extent of measurement uncertainty.
- Income and expenses are generated from various activities. Income comprises revenue and gains. Sources of income include the provision of goods and services (sales), investing or lending, selling assets and receiving contributions such as government grants. Items of expense include the costs of providing goods and services (cost of sales), wages and salaries, depreciation and amortisation, and selling, administrative, investing and financing expenses.

6.8 Presenting the statement of profit or loss

LEARNING OBJECTIVE 6.8 Identify presentation formats for the statement of profit or loss.

In the statement of financial position chapter, the difference in appearance of the statement of financial position depending on the type of entity and the choice of entity was explored. Nonetheless, the statement of financial position contains common elements, such as assets, liabilities and equity. Similarly, the appearance of the statement of profit or loss differs depending on whether the statement is being prepared for internal or external reporting purposes, and whether the preparing entity is required to comply with accounting standards. For example, the statement of profit or loss presented for ATC, a non-reporting small business in illustrative example 6.1, looks quite different from that presented for JB Hi-Fi Ltd, a listed company. While the two statements of profit or loss have common elements, such as income, expenses and profit, JB Hi-Fi Ltd's statement of profit or loss contains more aggregated data with greater detail in the notes to the accounts. We have previously discussed the classifications of income and expenses. The following sections examine other presentation and content requirements for the statement of profit or loss, with a focus on requirements for entities required to comply with accounting standards.

Prescribed format for general purpose financial statements

As discussed in the statement of financial position chapter, some entities are legally required to prepare financial statements in accordance with approved accounting standards. International Financial Reporting Standards (IFRS) include a standard that specifies the presentation of financial statements. Income and expenses may be presented in a variety of ways, with the aim being to make the presentation consistent and relevant to external users. We now explore some of the presentation issues.

The statement of profit or loss for the previous reporting period in addition to the current reporting period is presented. Known as **comparative information**, it allows users to see how the entity's financial performance in the current period differs from that of the previous period. When comparing the figures for the current and previous periods, users should familiarise themselves with the entity's accounting policies to ensure that some change in accounting policy is not the reason for the change in the reported figures. The presentation of the numbers in the statement of profit or loss in whole dollars, or thousands or millions of dollars, is at the discretion of the entity, but the entity should clearly identify on the statement the monetary value reported. In a situation where the entity has investments in other entities, the statement of profit or loss for the group is presented. The concept of group (consolidated) accounts was explored in the statement of financial position chapter.

The accounting standard governing the presentation of the statement of profit or loss requires the following to be presented on the statement of profit or loss:
• revenue
• cost of sales (if revenue from sales is disclosed)
• finance costs
• share of profit or loss of associates and joint ventures accounted for using the equity method
• tax expense
• profit or loss.

If an entity has discontinued part of its operations during the reporting period, the entity must segregate profit or loss from continuing operations and from discontinued operations. This allows users of the financial statements to better analyse the financial performance — past, current and future. For example, Telstra's 2016 statement of profit or loss showed a loss from discontinued operations (net of tax) of $2017 million. The notes disclose that during the financial year 2015–16 Telstra made significant divestments including the completed sale of Autohome Group. In accordance with accounting standards, the Autohome Group business was disclosed as a discontinued operation.

Entities are permitted to disclose additional line items, headings and subtotals in the statement of profit or loss if these are relevant to users in assessing the financial performance of the entity. For example, figure 6.2 illustrates that JB Hi-Fi Ltd included the additional subtotal 'gross profit' in its statement of profit or loss.

Material income and expenses

To enhance the usefulness of information for decision making, entities are required to separately disclose any item of income or expense that is material or significant. The determination of whether an item is material is based on the size and/or nature of the item and whether its non-disclosure could influence users' decision making. This disclosure can occur via the notes to the accounts or in the statement of profit or loss. It is important to identify and separately disclose **material items**, as this helps users to identify permanent versus transitory earnings charges and thereby better predict future earnings. Situations that may result in material items of income and expenses are disposals of PPE, asset impairments and restructuring activities. JB Hi-Fi Ltd did not report any significant items in its 2018 statement of profit or loss. However, in its statement of profit or loss for the financial year ended 30 June 2011, it reported a significant expense of $33 352 000. This item related to the company's strategic review of its Clive Anthonys business. The result of the review was to restate the carrying amount of Clive Anthonys assets to their recoverable amount based on the revised strategy and to record any related liabilities. The components of the charge against profit included goodwill written off, inventory write-downs, and plant and equipment write-offs.

A typical statement of profit or loss format for entities preparing general purpose financial statements (GPFS) was presented in figure 6.2, which shows the 2018 statement of profit or loss for JB Hi-Fi Ltd. The information in figure 6.2 is used to discuss disclosures around income and expense items in figure 6.5.

FIGURE 6.5 JB Hi-Fi Ltd's statement of profit or loss for 2018 and disclosure requirements

JB HI-FI LTD
Statement of profit or loss
for the financial year ended 30 June 2018

	Note	Consolidated 2018 ($m)	Description and disclosure requirements
Revenue		6 854.3	The components of income may be shown in the statement of profit or loss or in the accompanying notes to the accounts. The sub-classifications of income may include sale of goods, rendering of services, rents, royalties and dividends. JB Hi-Fi Ltd reports only one source of revenue — the sale of goods.
Cost of sales		(5 384.1)	Entities disclosing revenue from the sale of goods are required to also disclose the cost of sales.
Gross profit		1 470.2	Gross profit is the revenue from the sale of goods less the cost of the sales.
Other income		1.1	Other income may include gains arising from the disposal of assets. JB Hi-Fi Ltd reports interest income and 'other' income in this category.
Sales and marketing expenses		(695.1)	Total expenses excluding financing costs must be reported in the statement of profit or loss.
Occupancy expenses		(305.7)	Disaggregated expense components may be shown either in the statement of profit or loss or in the notes to the accounts. Expenses must be classified into their components according to their nature (e.g. employee benefits, depreciation and amortisation, lease expenses) or function (e.g. distribution, marketing, occupancy and administrative). JB Hi-Fi Ltd has elected the latter classification. Specific expenses must be disclosed (e.g. depreciation) and JB Hi-Fi Ltd has disclosed these in note 5.
Administration expenses		(42.2)	
Other expenses		(77.2)	
Finance costs	5	(16.6)	Finance costs must be disclosed separately in the statement of profit or loss. Finance costs include interest costs, lease finance charges, amortisation of discounts or premiums relating to borrowings, and amortisation or ancillary costs incurred in arranging financing. Finance income includes interest received.
Profit before tax		**334.5**	This is income less expenses (excluding income tax expense).
Income tax expense	6	(101.3)	This is the income tax expense relating to the entity's continuing operations.
Profit for the year attributable to Owners of the Company		**233.2**	This is income less expenses (including income tax expense). This line item is often referred to as the 'bottom line' profit. It represents the reporting period's profit that is available to distribute to the entity's shareholders. If the entity has controlled entities that are not 100% owned, then it is necessary to recognise that not all of the consolidated profit (loss) belongs to the entity's owners. A line item referred to as 'non-controlling interests' reflects the interest in the financial performance of the entity by outside equity interests. JB Hi-Fi Ltd has no non-controlling interests, as it fully owns its subsidiaries.

	Note	Consolidated 2018 ($m)	Description and disclosure requirements
Earnings per share			
Basic (cents per share)	3	203.09	These items express the profit or loss relative to the number of shares that have been on issue during the reporting period. It is the growth in earnings per share from one reporting period to another that users are most interested in.
Diluted (cents per share)	3	201.11	

Source: Adapted from JB Hi-Fi Ltd 2018, p. 54.

Format for entities not required to comply with accounting standards

Entities not required to prepare GPFS complying with accounting standards have freedom in their presentation of the statement of profit or loss. While the presentation and classification of items can exhibit great diversity, the purpose of the statement of profit or loss does not change: to report the profit or loss for the entity for the reporting period. As shown previously in illustrative example 6.1, the statement of profit or loss for an entity not required to comply with accounting standards is usually more detailed and less aggregated than one prepared in accordance with accounting standards, as the statement is typically prepared for internal rather than external users. For example, consider illustrative example 6.6.

ILLUSTRATIVE EXAMPLE 6.6

Statement of profit or loss format for an entity not required to comply with accounting standards

COCONUT PLANTATIONS PTY LTD Statement of profit or loss for the 4 months ended 31 December 2019		
Income		
Sales		$500 000
Cost of sales		275 000
Gross profit		225 000
Other income		5 000
Operating expenses		
Warehouse	$32 000	
Distribution	10 000	
Sales and marketing	3 000	
Administrative	30 000	
Finance	5 000	80 000
Profit before tax		**150 000**
Income tax expense		45 000
Profit after tax		**$105 000**

In the statement presented, the entity has grouped income into sales-related and other income. The entity's other income could consist of items such as dividends received, interest revenue and royalties. Entities may choose to list other income items individually. Expenses have been grouped into six categories: cost of sales; warehousing; distribution; selling and marketing; administration; and finance. Entities can elect to aggregate or disaggregate expenses, as there are no fixed formatting requirements.

The cost of sales for a retailer represents the opening inventory value, plus purchases, less closing inventory value. For a manufacturing operation such as Coconut Plantations Pty Ltd, the cost of sales represents the opening value of the finished goods, plus the **cost of goods manufactured** (the cost of materials, labour and overheads used in manufacturing the goods), less the closing value of the finished goods.

Typical items included in warehouse expenses could be warehouse rent, wages and salaries of warehouse staff, insurance for stored inventory, depreciation of warehouse plant and equipment, and utilities (e.g. electricity, telephone, gas) consumed by the warehouse. Distribution expenses could include courier fees, fleet management costs, and postage and handling. Selling and marketing expenses could include advertising, sales staff salaries and promotional events. Items that comprise administrative expenses could include general staff costs and head office expenses such as stationery, utilities, rates, depreciation of office furniture and equipment, and general insurance. Finance costs could include interest on borrowings, bank fees and lease charges.

6.9 Financial performance measures

LEARNING OBJECTIVE 6.9 Differentiate between alternative financial performance measures.

We saw earlier that the statement of profit or loss complying with accounting standards must disclose a number of required profit figures such as profit before and after tax. There are additional profit figures that may be referenced in the financial statements or referred to in the financial press. The following sections introduce these profit figures.

Gross profit

Gross profit refers to revenue less the cost of sales, and is applicable to manufacturing and retail operations. The gross profit measures the revenue remaining after deducting the cost of sales. An entity cannot be sustainable unless it has a positive gross profit, meaning that it is selling its goods at a price exceeding their cost. Gross profit reflects the percentage by which an entity marks up the cost of its products to sell them to its customers. It also reflects an entity's relationship with suppliers and its purchasing power. Both of these are intrinsically linked to the competitiveness of the industry in which it operates. For example, the 2018 statement of profit or loss of JB Hi-Fi Ltd shows a gross profit of $1470.2 million, calculated as revenue ($6854.3 m) less the cost of sales ($5384.1 m). This represents a gross profit margin (gross profit divided by revenue) of 21 per cent. This is a relatively low mark-up, reflecting the high-volume nature and competitiveness of the industry in which JB Hi-Fi Ltd operates.

Profit

'Profit' is the term commonly given to the gross profit less all other expenses incurred in operating the business. Effectively, it is the entity's income less expenses for the reporting period.

Profit pre- and post-tax

Profit performance measures can be referred to on a pre- and/or post-tax basis. Taxation is an expense of a company, because companies have an obligation to pay tax on their business activities. The tax that a company pays is based on taxable income as calculated by applying taxation rules. In contrast, the profit reported in the statement of profit or loss is measured by applying accounting rules. To the extent that the taxation and accounting rules differ, the tax expense of a company will not be simply the pre-tax accounting profit multiplied by the applicable tax rate. Taxation and accounting rules can diverge due to:

- income not being assessable for taxation purposes
- expenses not being deductible for taxation purposes.

Consider a company that sold a building in the current reporting period for a $100 000 gain. The building was purchased prior to the introduction of the capital gains tax so, although the $100 000 will be included in the determination of accounting profit for the period, it is not assessable income for taxation purposes. As we will see in the analysis and interpretation of financial statements chapter, profit before and after tax is used to assess the profitability of an entity. An owner is more interested in the profit after tax, because tax obligations must be satisfied before profits can be distributed as dividends. Conversely, a financial analyst will be interested in the profit before tax, because this reflects the outcomes of the entity's investing and financing activities without the effect of a variable (taxation) that is determined by forces outside the control of the entity, namely the government.

Profit pre- and post-interest

As previously noted, profit reflects the effects of an entity's investing and financing decisions and the taxation consequences thereof. To isolate the returns associated with the investment decision only, profit before interest and tax is the relevant figure; this is more commonly referred to as **earnings before interest and taxation (EBIT)**. The interest figure refers to the net effect of finance-related income and expenses. **Net finance costs** are defined as interest income less interest expense (including finance lease charges). If the entity is a net lender (e.g. a bank) with interest income exceeding interest expense, it will be necessary to subtract the net interest from the profit before tax figure to derive EBIT. If the entity is a net borrower, with interest expense exceeding interest income, it will be necessary to add the net interest to the profit before tax figure to derive EBIT. The 2018 EBIT figure for JB Hi-Fi Ltd is not disclosed in its 2018 statement of profit or loss. Some entities do disclose their EBIT. The steps involved in calculating EBIT are shown in figure 6.6. Applying these steps, the EBIT for JB Hi-Fi Ltd is $351.1 million. This is JB Hi-Fi Ltd's profit before tax of $334.5 million with finance costs of $16.6 million added back.

FIGURE 6.6	Calculation of EBIT

Step 1. Identify the entity's profit from continuing operations before income tax but after interest.
Step 2. Calculate the entity's net finance income (cost):

$$\text{Finance income} - \text{Finance costs} = \text{Net finance income (costs)}$$

Step 3. If the entity has net finance income, deduct the net finance income from profit from continuing operations before tax to give EBIT. If the entity has net finance costs, add the net finance costs to profit before tax to give EBIT.

Profit pre- and post-depreciation and amortisation

Depreciation and amortisation are non-cash expenses included in the statement of profit or loss. **Earnings before interest, tax, depreciation and amortisation (EBITDA)** refers to the profit before net interest, taxation and depreciation/amortisation expense. It is a measure of the raw operating earnings of an entity, as it excludes asset diminution in addition to tax and financing charges. EBITDA is used for a number of purposes, including financial statement analysis and credit analysis. It was used traditionally as a substitute for a cash-based profit measure; because cash flows associated with operating activities are available in the statement of cash flows, the need to approximate cash flows from operations via EBITDA is no longer necessary.

Profit pre- and post-material items

Items of income and expense can be labelled as material (or significant) on the basis of their size or nature. Many users of financial statements are interested in an entity's maintainable earnings. Often this is taken to be the income less expenses from 'ordinary' activities, excluding the material items. It can be argued that the exclusion of material items from profit provides a better reflection of the trend and sustainability of profit. This does not mean that users should ignore material items. Due consideration should still be given to these items, as interesting trends in relation to them may emerge.

Profit from continuing and discontinued operations

If an entity has sold or plans to sell a part of its business during the reporting period, information must be disclosed that enables users of the financial statements to evaluate the financial effects of the discontinued operations. The entity must disclose separately the profit or loss after tax associated with the discontinued operations from that of the continuing operations. This assists users to better predict future profits.

Pro forma earnings

It has become popular for entities to refer to pro forma earnings in addition to earnings determined by generally accepted accounting principles (GAAP). **Pro forma earnings** refer to earnings that are not in accordance with GAAP earnings. The inclusion of pro forma earnings is often regarded as selective reporting by entities, because it allows them to include items of their choosing in the determination of profit. Consequently, it is usual for pro forma earnings to be higher than GAAP-reported earnings. Entities reporting pro forma earnings justify the pro forma figure by claiming that it is useful to decision makers because it 'normalises' earnings. Unusual items (particularly expense items) tend to be excluded in the calculation of pro forma earnings.

VALUE TO BUSINESS

- Profit (earnings) can be measured at various levels.
- Profit measures include:
  - gross profit
  - profit before and after tax
  - earnings before interest
  - earnings before interest, tax, depreciation and amortisation (EBITDA)
  - profit before and after material items
  - profit from continuing and discontinued operations
  - pro forma earnings.

6.10 The statement of comprehensive income

LEARNING OBJECTIVE 6.10 Explain the nature of the statement of comprehensive income and the statement of changes in equity.

So far in this chapter we have concentrated on the statement of profit or loss. The statement of profit or loss reports the profit or loss for the reporting period. Entities that are required to comply with accounting standards must also prepare a **statement of comprehensive income**. In addition to the income and expenses recognised in the determination of profit or loss, there are other income and expense items that are required or permitted by some accounting standards to be taken directly to equity, rather than being recognised in profit or loss; for example:

- non-current asset revaluations directly taken to a revaluation surplus
- net exchange differences associated with translating foreign currency–denominated accounts of a subsidiary into the reporting currency of the group
- adjustments to equity allowed pursuant to the operation of a new accounting standard.

Such items are included in the determination of an entity's 'other comprehensive income' for an accounting period, but they are not taken into account when determining the entity's profit or loss for the period. This is a product of having accounting standards that permit some transactions to bypass the statement of profit or loss. There is no rule or rationale explaining why this is permitted in some circumstances. **Other comprehensive income** refers to all changes in equity during the reporting period other than profit or loss in the statement of profit or loss and those resulting from transactions with owners as owners (such as dividends and capital contributions). Entities can elect to present all items of income and expense in a reporting period in a single statement of comprehensive income or in two statements: (1) a statement of profit or loss showing the income and expenses associated with the determination of profit (or loss) for the reporting period; and (2) a statement beginning with profit or loss and displaying components of other comprehensive income (statement of comprehensive income). In its 2018 financial report, JB Hi-Fi Ltd elected to present a statement of profit or loss showing the profit or loss for the reporting period and a statement of comprehensive income beginning with profit or loss and displaying components of other comprehensive income. Figure 6.7 shows the statement of comprehensive income from the 2018 financial report of JB Hi-Fi Ltd.

JB HI-FI LTD
Statement of comprehensive income
for the financial year ended 30 June 2018

	Consolidated	
	2018 $m	2017 $m
Profit for the year	**233.2**	**172.4**
Other comprehensive income		
Changes in the fair value of cash flow hedges (net of tax)	1.9	(1.1)
Exchange differences on translation of foreign operations	(1.3)	(0.1)
Other comprehensive income/(loss) for the year (net of tax)	0.6	(1.2)
Total comprehensive income attributable to Owners of the Company	**233.8**	**171.2**

Source: JB Hi-Fi Ltd 2018, p. 55.

The statement of changes in equity

When assessing the change in an entity's financial position, in addition to users being informed of the profit or loss for the reporting period, users should also be able to identify the change in equity from the start to the end of the reporting period and the reasons for the change. For example, if ATC earned a profit of $45 000 for the 3-month period 1 October 2019 to 31 December 2019 and Nicholas Cash, the owner, withdrew $30 000 during that period, the change in equity would be an increase of $15 000. Equity at the end of 2019 would be $51 370 comprising equity at 30 September 2019 ($36 370) plus the increase in equity ($15 000). Figure 6.8 shows the statement of changes in equity for ATC, a sole trader, for the year ended 31 December 2019.

FIGURE 6.8   ATC statement of changes in equity for 3 months ended 31 December 2019

ADVANTAGE TENNIS COACHING
Statement of changes in equity
for the 3 months ended 31 December 2019

Capital, N Cash, as at 1 October 2019	$36 370
Plus: Profit for three months	45 000
Less: Drawings	30 000
Capital, N Cash, as at 31 December 2019	**$51 370**

Entities required to comply with accounting standards must present a **statement of changes in equity**; this statement shows the change in an entity's equity between two reporting periods. Effectively, the statement of changes in equity is showing the impact of all of the changes in assets and liabilities during the reporting period. The statement shows all changes in equity arising from transactions with owners in their capacity as owners (such as equity contributions, dividends paid and shares purchased) separately from non-owner changes in equity (e.g. profit). The purpose is to provide users with better information by requiring aggregation of items with similar characteristics and separation of items with different characteristics. Figure 6.9 shows JB Hi-Fi Ltd's 2018 statement of changes in equity. The shareholders' equity balance at 1 July 2017 was $853.5 million and the closing balance at 30 June 2018 was $947.6 million. JB Hi-Fi Ltd's statement of changes in equity shows a reconciliation between the opening and closing balance disaggregated by contributed equity, reserves and retained earnings. The illustration shows the following.

- The reconciliation between the opening retained earnings balance at 1 July 2017 of $381.6 million and the closing balance at 30 June 2018 of $463.2 million; the $233.2 million profit for the reporting period (as shown in the statement of profit or loss) has increased the retained earnings. JB Hi-Fi Ltd paid dividends of $151.6 million that reduced the retained earnings balance.
- The reconciliation between the opening equity-settled benefits reserve balance at 1 July 2017 of $34.6 million and the closing balance as at 30 June 2018 of $43.5 million; the change in equity-settled benefits reserve relates to the issue of shares under share-option plans.

- The reconciliation between the opening foreign currency translation reserve balance at 1 July 2017 of $4.9 million and the closing balance as at 30 June 2018 of $3.6 million; the change relates to the foreign currency translation differences.
- The reconciliation between the opening hedging reserve balance at 1 July 2017 of $0.2 million and the closing balance as at 30 June 2018 of $1.7 million; the change in the value of cash flow hedges has, as allowed or required by accounting standards, bypassed the statement of profit or loss and gone directly to reserve accounts in equity.
- The reconciliation between the opening common control reserve balance at 1 July 2017 of $6.1 million and the closing balance as at 30 June 2018 of $6.1 million; there was no change in this reserve for the 2018 financial year.
- The reconciliation between the opening contributed equity at 1 July 2017 of $438.7 million and the closing contributed equity at 30 June 2018 of $441.7 million; the change in contributed equity during the reporting period is due to issuing shares under the entity's share-option plan.

FIGURE 6.9　JB Hi-Fi Ltd's extract of statement of changes in equity for the financial year ended 30 June 2018

JB HI-FI LTD
Statement of changes in equity
for the financial year ended 30 June 2018

Consolidated	Notes	Contributed equity $m	Equity-settled benefits reserve $m	Foreign currency translation reserve $m	Hedging reserves $m	Common control reserve $m	Retained earnings $m	Total $m
Balance at 1 July 2017		**438.7**	**34.6**	**4.9**	**(0.2)**	**(6.1)**	**381.6**	**853.5**
Profit for the year		–	–	–	–	–	233.2	233.2
Cash flow hedges (net of tax)		–	–	–	1.9	–	–	1.9
Exchange differences on translation of foreign operations		–	–	(1.3)	–	–	–	(1.3)
Total comprehensive income for the year		**–**	**–**	**(1.3)**	**1.9**	**–**	**233.2**	**233.8**
Issue of shares under share-option plan	18	3.0	–	–	–	–	–	3.0
Dividends provided for or paid	4	–	–	–	–	–	(151.6)	(151.6)
Share-based payments— expense		–	7.8	–	–	–	–	7.8
Share-based payments— income tax		–	1.1	–	–	–	–	1.1
Balance at 30 June 2018		**441.7**	**43.5**	**3.6**	**1.7**	**(6.1)**	**463.2**	**947.6**

Source: JB Hi-Fi Ltd 2018, p. 57.

6.11 The link between the financial statements

LEARNING OBJECTIVE 6.11 Explain the relationship between the statement of profit or loss, the statement of financial position, the statement of comprehensive income and the statement of changes in equity.

It is important to understand the relationships between the different financial statements, rather than viewing each statement in isolation. We have already seen how the income and expense definitions are linked to the asset and liability definitions. The recognition of income occurs simultaneously with the increase in assets or decrease in liabilities. Similarly, the recognition of expenses occurs simultaneously with the decrease in assets or increase in liabilities. The fundamental purpose of the statement of profit or loss is to present the entity's financial performance for a period of time. The entity's profit or loss for the reporting period belongs to the entity's owners. The profit or loss for the reporting period is added to the undistributed profits from previous periods (**retained earnings, retained profits** and **accumulated profits** are interchangeable terms used to describe undistributed profits in the entity). The retained earnings at the end of the reporting period are the retained earnings at the start of the period plus the current period's profits less any distributions (e.g. dividends or drawings) made to owners during the reporting period. The retained earnings balance at the end of the reporting period is an equity item in the statement of financial position. Items of income and expense directly recognised in equity, and transactions with owners as owners (as per the statement of changes in equity), also result in changes in the equity balance from the beginning to the end of the reporting period. This relationship between the statement of profit or loss, the statement of comprehensive income, the statement of financial position and the statement of changes in equity is illustrated in figure 6.10.

FIGURE 6.10 Relationship between the statement of profit or loss, statement of comprehensive income, statement of financial position and statement of changes in equity

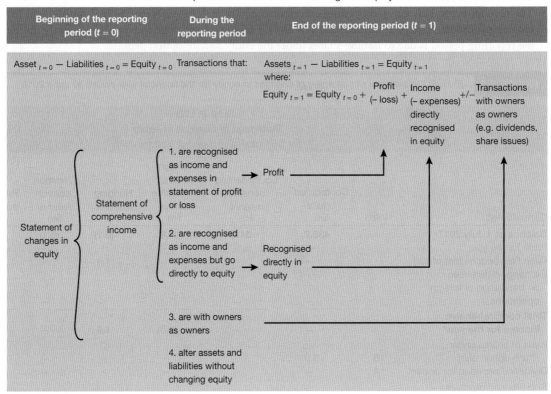

- The statement of profit or loss presents the profit or loss made by the entity during the reporting period. The statement of comprehensive income reports the profit or loss and other comprehensive income. The statement of financial position shows the financial position of the entity as at the end of the reporting period. The statement of changes in equity explains the changes in equity from the start to the end of the reporting period.
- The profit or loss for the reporting period is added to the retained earnings as at the start of the period.
- The entity can make distributions from retained earnings (e.g. dividends or drawings) and transfers to or from retained earnings.
- The balance of the retained earnings as at the end of the reporting period is included as an equity item in the statement of financial position.

SUMMARY OF LEARNING OBJECTIVES

6.1 Explain the purpose and importance of measuring financial performance.

It is important to measure financial performance periodically so that users, both internal and external, can assess the profitability of the entity. The primary objective of preparing financial statements is to provide information that is useful for decision making. Knowledge of the profit or loss is crucial in assessing past performance and forming an opinion as to expected future performance for a for-profit entity.

6.2 Explain the reporting period concept and the difference between accrual accounting and cash accounting.

The fundamental concepts underlying the preparation of the statement of profit or loss are the accounting or reporting period, accrual accounting and generally accepted accounting principles (GAAP). The GAAP are the accounting rules that determine the recognition, measurement and presentation of financial information. The financial performance of an entity is measured over a period of time — the life of the entity is arbitrarily divided into reporting periods. The profit measurement for a reporting period should include all transactions affecting profit in that reporting period. Accrual accounting, as distinct from cash accounting, means that the profit determination is independent of whether cash is received or paid in relation to profit items during the reporting period.

6.3 Outline the effects that accounting policy choices, estimates and judgements can have on financial statements.

Even when preparing financial statements in compliance with approved accounting standards, preparers are provided with choices and are required to use estimation and judgement. Therefore, users of financial statements need to appreciate that accounting flexibility and discretion exist, consider the incentives that may affect the choices, estimations and judgements being made, and be aware of the impact of these choices, estimations and judgements on the financial information reported.

6.4 Describe the measurement of financial performance.

Profit or loss for a reporting period is measured as the income during the reporting period less the expenses in the reporting period. If income exceeds expenses in a particular reporting period, a profit results. If expenses exceed income, the entity reports a loss for that reporting period.

6.5 Discuss the definition and classification of income.

Income is defined as increases in economic benefits — in the form of inflows, increases in assets or decreases in liabilities of the entity — that result in increases in equity during the reporting period. Contributions by owners are not regarded as income. Income comprises revenue and gains.

6.6 Discuss the definition and classification of expenses.

Expenses are defined as decreases in economic benefits — in the form of outflows, decreases in assets or increases in liabilities — that result in decreases in equity during the reporting period. Distributions to owners are not regarded as expenses. Expenses can be classified according to their nature or function.

6.7 Apply the recognition criteria to income and expenses.

The term 'recognition' refers to recording items in the financial statements with a monetary value assigned to them. Therefore, 'income recognition' or 'expense recognition' means that the income or expense is recorded and appears in the statement of profit or loss. It is recognition that links the elements in financial statements — assets, liabilities, equity, income and expenses — and hence the financial statements. This linkage between the financial statements arises because the recognition of one element (or a change in one element) requires the recognition of an equal amount (or change) in one or more other elements as per the accounting equation. There are no definitive rules to assist the decision about whether an item should be recognised. The recognition decision requires judgement. The overarching considerations when deciding to recognise an asset or a liability (and any related income, expenses or changes in equity) are whether the recognition provides financial statement users with relevant information about the asset or the liability and about any income, expenses or changes in equity, whether it is a faithful representation of the asset or the liability and of any income, expenses or changes in equity, and whether the information results in benefits exceeding the cost of providing that information. The factors of uncertainty and unreliable measurement may result in non-recognition. An entity always has the option to disclose information concerning items not recognised.

6.8 Identify presentation formats for the statement of profit or loss.

There is an accounting standard governing the presentation of the statement of profit or loss for entities that are required to comply with accounting standards. This standard prescribes the line items that must be disclosed in the statement of profit or loss or in the notes to the accounts, but permits discretion as to the presentation format.

6.9 Differentiate between alternative financial performance measures.

Various profit measures may be used. Gross profit is restricted to revenue less the cost of sales. Other derivations of profit include:
- profit before and after tax
- earnings before interest
- earnings before interest, tax, depreciation and amortisation (EBITDA)
- profit before and after material items
- pro forma earnings
- profit from continuing and discontinued operations.

6.10 Explain the nature of the statement of comprehensive income and the statement of changes in equity.

Entities required to comply with accounting standards must present a statement of comprehensive income and a statement of changes in equity. The statement of comprehensive income reports profit or loss and other comprehensive income. The statement of changes in equity explains the change in an entity's equity for the reporting period. The statement discloses: income and expenses recognised in the statement of profit or loss; income and expenses recognised directly in equity; and transactions with owners as owners.

6.11 Explain the relationship between the statement of profit or loss, the statement of financial position, the statement of comprehensive income and the statement of changes in equity.

The statement of profit or loss reports the profit or loss generated in the reporting period that belongs to the owners of the business. It is added to the retained earnings from previous periods to determine the pool of retained earnings available for distribution to owners. Retained earnings are included in the equity section of the statement of financial position as at the end of the period. The statement of comprehensive income details the profit or loss for the period (i.e. the statement of profit or loss) as well as items of income and expense that are not recognised as profit or loss as required or permitted by accounting standards. These items of income and expense bypass the statement of profit or loss and are recorded directly in the equity section of the statement of financial position. The statement of changes in equity explains the change in equity from the start to the end of the reporting period. These changes relate to profit or loss for the period, other comprehensive income and transactions with owners as owners. These statements are also related, given that recognising income and expenses involves simultaneously recognising (or reducing) assets or liabilities.

KEY TERMS

accrual accounting Transactions and events being recorded in the periods when they occur, rather than in the periods when the cash is received or paid.

accrued expense Amounts not yet paid for economic benefits that have been used or consumed.

accrued income Amounts not yet received for goods or services that have been provided.

accumulated depreciation Total depreciation charges for a particular asset.

amortisation Allocation of the cost of an intangible asset over its estimated useful life.

carrying amount (book value) Dollar value assigned to an asset or liability in the statement of financial position.

cash accounting Transactions being recorded in the period when the cash is received or paid.

comparative information Presentation of the financial statements of an entity for multiple years.

contra account An account that is offset against another account.

cost of goods manufactured The total cost of materials, labour and overheads used in manufacturing goods.

cost of sales Cost of inventory sold during a period. Recall the discussion of the periodic and perpetual inventory systems in the statement of financial position chapter; in a perpetual inventory system, continuous records of inventory on hand and cost of sales are maintained, while in a periodic inventory system, where continuous records of inventory on hand and cost of sales are not maintained, the cost of sales is determined by the opening inventory balance plus purchases less closing inventory balance. To determine the closing inventory balance in a periodic system, a stocktake must be performed.

depreciation Allocation of the depreciable amount of a depreciable asset over its estimated useful life.

diminishing balance depreciation Depreciation method that results in decreasing depreciation expense each reporting period over the asset's useful life; also referred to as reducing balance depreciation.

distribution to owners The resources (e.g. dividends) distributed to owners.

earnings before interest and taxation (EBIT) The profit before net interest and taxation expense.

earnings before interest, tax, depreciation and amortisation (EBITDA) The profit before interest, taxation and depreciation/amortisation expense.

earnings management Managers' use of accounting discretion via accounting policy choices and/or estimates to report a desired level of profit.

expenses Decreases in economic benefits during an accounting period in the form of outflows, decreases in assets or incurrences of liabilities that result in decreases in equity, other than those relating to distributions to equity participants.

gross profit Excess of net sales revenue over the cost of sales.

impairment When an asset's carrying amount exceeds its recoverable amount.

income Increases in economic benefits during an accounting period in the form of inflows, increases in assets or decreases in liabilities that result in increases in equity, other than those relating to contributions from equity participants.

income received in advance Amounts received from customers and recognised as liabilities before services are performed or goods are provided.

integrated reporting Reporting on the value created by an entity's strategy, governance, performance and prospects.

material items Items that are likely to influence a financial statement user's decision making.

net finance costs Interest income less interest expense (including finance lease charges).

other comprehensive income All changes in equity during the reporting period other than profit or loss and those resulting from transactions with owners as owners.

prepaid expense (prepayment) Amounts paid in cash and recorded as assets until the economic benefits are used or consumed.

pro forma earnings Earnings that are not in accordance with GAAP earnings.

profit or loss Income less expenses for a reporting period.

recoverable amount Higher of an asset's expected fair value (less costs of disposal) and its value in use (net selling price).

recognition Recording of items in the financial statements with a monetary value assigned to them.

reporting period Period of time to which financial statements relate; also called accounting period.

retained earnings (retained profits, accumulated profits) Cumulative profits made by an entity that have not been distributed as dividends or transferred to reserve accounts.

revenue Income arising in the ordinary course of an entity's activities.

statement of changes in equity Statement showing the change in an entity's equity between two reporting periods.

statement of comprehensive income Statement showing all items of income and expense during a reporting period, including those recognised in determining profit or loss as well as items of other comprehensive income taken directly to equity.

statement of profit or loss A statement that reports on the income and expenses of an entity for a period and the resulting profit or loss.

straight-line depreciation Depreciation method that results in a constant depreciation expense each reporting period over an asset's useful life.

triple bottom line reporting (environmental, social and governance (ESG) reporting) Reporting on environmental, social and financial performance.

units of production depreciation Depreciation method that results in a varying depreciation expense each reporting period over an asset's useful life.

APPLY YOUR KNOWLEDGE
20 marks

PART A

Nicholas Cash, the sole proprietor of Advantage Tennis Coaching (ATC), has met with his accountant to discuss preparation of ATC's financial statements for the year ended 31 December 2020. The following issues were discussed.

---

1. St Lucia Tennis Club owes $12 000 for a junior coaching clinic held in December 2020. St Lucia Tennis Club has not yet been invoiced for this service. ATC has not recorded the service revenue in its accounting information system.
2. ATC has $2000 unpaid wages as at 31 December 2020 that are not recorded in the accounting information system.
3. ATC has unpaid utility expenses (telephone, gas and electricity) amounting to $1500 for the three months ended 31 December 2020 that are not recorded in the accounting information system.
4. An annual membership fee of $800 was paid to the National Tennis Coaching Association on 1 March 2020. This payment was initially recorded as a prepaid membership.
5. ATC has office furniture and office equipment that cost $9700. The equipment has a zero residual value and is being depreciated over five years using the straight-line method.

Required

(a) Prepare the relevant general journal adjusting entries (narrations required) for each of the issues identified.   **5 marks**
(b) State whether the profit, assets or liabilities would be understated, overstated or unaffected in the absence of the adjusting entry for each of the five issues above. Consider each issue individually.

3 marks

(c) Explain the difference between cash accounting and accrual accounting for determining profit for a reporting period. Provide an example of a transaction that would appear as revenue for a reporting period under accrual accounting but would not appear under cash accounting.   **4 marks**

PART B

JB Hi-Fi Ltd's 2018 annual report includes governance, environmental and social statements, and notes that the company recognises the importance of all these matters to its shareholders, suppliers and customers. Putting this into practice, JB Hi-Fi Ltd discusses its governance policies and procedures, and details the initiatives that it is taking to reduce the impact of its business on the environment.

Required

(a) Explain your understanding of triple bottom line reporting. Include in your discussion three examples of JB Hi-Fi Ltd's initiatives to reduce the impact of its business on the environment.   **5 marks**
(b) Your friend believes that an entity's value is exclusively determined by its earnings and that, in analysing an entity, the emphasis should be on profit measures. Explain to your friend why entities would volunteer to provide their policies and practices in relation to environmental and social matters in addition to their financial performance.   **3 marks**

SELF-EVALUATION ACTIVITIES

6.1 B Thomas operates a retail clothing store. In preparing the financial reports, her accountant has made the following adjustments.
1. Reduced prepaid advertising by $2000.
2. Increased accumulated depreciation by $3600.
3. Reduced income received in advance by $1175.
4. Increased wages payable by $480.

Required

Given double-entry accounting for each of these adjustments, explain the corresponding entry and the rationale for the decision to make the adjustment.

SOLUTION TO 6.1

1. Reduced prepaid advertising by $2000 — the corresponding entry for this adjustment is an increase in advertising expense by $2000. The adjustment recognises that some of the future economic benefits of advertising paid in advance, and therefore recorded as an asset, have been used up during the period. The adjustment reduces the asset account (Prepaid advertising) and increases the expense account (Advertising expense).

2. Increased accumulated depreciation by $3600 — the corresponding entry for this adjustment is an increase in depreciation expense. Depreciation is the systematic allocation of the cost of an asset over its useful life. The depreciation expense recognises that some of the asset's future economic benefits have been used up in the reporting period.

3. Reduced income received in advance by $1175 — the corresponding entry for this adjustment is an increase in income. Income received in advance is a liability, as it represents cash that has been received for services yet to be provided. If this liability account has been reduced, it is due to some of the income having been earned.

4. Increased wages payable by $480 — the corresponding entry for this adjustment is an increase in wages expense. At the end of the reporting period, some wages have been incurred but have not been paid. The adjustment recognises the wages expense incurred in the period (increasing wages expense) but not yet paid (increasing a liability account — wages payable).

6.2 Coconut Plantations Pty Ltd is a manufacturer of coconut-based products that commenced operations in September 2019. Refer to the chapter on business structures for information relating to this private company and its financial statements for the four months to 31 December 2019. Assume now that Coconut Plantations Pty Ltd has been trading for a further year to 31 December 2020 and has the following balances in various accounts. There have been no additional shares issued. Prepare a statement of profit or loss for Coconut Plantations Pty Ltd for the year ended 31 December 2020, classifying operating expenses by function. Also prepare a statement of changes in equity for the year ended 31 December 2020.

Cash on hand	$ 145 367	Telephone expense	$ 5 000
Accounts receivable	93 010	Advertising expense	59 000
Inventory (finished goods, raw materials)	175 000	Warehouse insurance expense	15 000
Property, plant and equipment (net)	381 333	Warehouse rates expense	21 000
Accounts payable	42 500	Utilities expense	9 500
Loan	131 000	Depreciation of warehouse	12 000
Income tax payable	98 400	Sales salaries	72 000
Sales revenue	1 550 000	Interest expense	14 000
Cost of sales	902 500	Delivery costs and postage	18 000
Interest income	1 000	Dividend	130 000
Administration salaries	90 000	Income tax	98 400
		Depreciation of office equipment	5 000

SOLUTION TO 6.2

COCONUT PLANTATIONS PTY LTD
Statement of profit or loss
for the year ended 31 December 2020

Income	
Sales	$1 550 000
Cost of sales	902 500
Gross profit	647 500
Other income	1 000
Expenses	
Warehouse	48 000
Distribution	18 000
Sales and marketing	131 000
Administrative	109 500
Finance	14 000
Total expenses	320 500
Profit before income tax	**328 000**
Income tax	98 400
Profit	**$ 229 600**

			COCONUT PLANTATIONS PTY LTD		
			Statement of changes in equity		
			for the year ended 31 December 2020		
Share capital as at 1 January 2020					$200 000
Additional contributed equity during year					–
Contributed equity as at 31 December 2020					200 000
Retained earnings as at 1 January 2020					90 210
Plus: Profit					229 600
Less: Dividends					130 000
Retained earnings as at 31 December 2020					189 810
Shareholders' equity as at 31 December 2020					**$389 810**

6.3 (a) The rows in the following table represent independent cases. Fill in the missing items.

Income	Cost of sales	Other expenses	Profit	Total assets	Total liabilities	Share capital	Retained earnings
650 000	–	85 000	40 000	–	30 000	140 000	30 000
550 000	380 000	–	55 000	1 000 000	–	600 000	160 000
–	115 000	81 000	11 500	510 000	33 500	230 000	–
498 000	400 000	–	38 000	848 500	68 500	–	400 000
244 000	162 000	32 000	–	340 000	–	125 000	125 000

(b) For each of the independent cases presented, calculate the gross profit. Discuss the decisions that can influence an entity's gross profit margin.

SOLUTION TO 6.3

(a)

Income	Cost of sales	Other expenses	Profit	Total assets	Total liabilities	Share capital	Retained earnings
650 000	525 000	85 000	40 000	195 000	30 000	140 000	30 000
550 000	380 000	115 000	55 000	1 000 000	240 000	600 000	160 000
207 500	115 000	81 000	11 500	510 000	33 500	230 000	246 500
498 000	400 000	60 000	38 000	848 500	68 500	380 000	400 000
244 000	162 000	32 000	50 000	340 000	90 000	125 000	125 000

(b) The gross profit for each of the independent cases is: $125 000; $170 000; $92 500; $98 000; and $82 000. The gross profit margin is gross profit divided by sales and represents the percentage of a sales dollar that ends up as gross profit. As such, an entity's gross profit is influenced by its pricing decisions, discounting decisions and purchasing expertise.

COMPREHENSION QUESTIONS

6.4 Describe the users who would be interested in the financial position and performance of an entity and explain their interest. **LO1**

6.5 Explain whether the following statements are true or false for an entity using the accrual method of accounting. **LO1, 2**

(a) Statements of profit or loss are used only by users external to the entity.

(b) Revenue from sales is included in the statement of profit or loss when it is received, not when it is earned.

(c) At the end of a reporting period, accrued expenses need to be included in the profit or loss determination.

(d) At the end of a reporting period, revenue received for services not yet provided needs to be excluded from the profit or loss determination.

6.6 Discuss the difference between profit or loss and comprehensive income. **LO10**

6.7 Explain the three methods of depreciation. **LO3**

6.8 What is the main expense incurred by a retail business? Comment on how this differs to: (1) a service business; and (2) a manufacturing business. **LO6**

6.9 Explain how you would determine if an income or expense item is material. **LO4**

6.10 Discuss the importance of showing profit or loss from continued operations separately from profit or loss from discontinued operations. **LO8**

6.11 Describe the items that are likely to be present in a statement of changes in equity. **LO10**

6.12 Items of income and expense may be included in a statement of profit or loss only if they can be measured with certainty. Discuss. **LO3, 7**

6.13 If an entity uses an asset evenly over its useful life, predict the method of depreciation the entity would use. **LO3, 4, 7**

6.14 Explain the difference between income and revenue. **LO5**

6.15 Explain the difference between profit or loss, gross profit and EBIT. **LO9**

EXERCISES

★ BASIC | ★ ★ MODERATE | ★ ★ ★ CHALLENGING

6.16 ★ **LO5**

Consider each of the following transactions and examine whether they satisfy the income definition criteria using the accrual method of accounting.

(a) Received cash for services to be provided in the next reporting period.

(b) Borrowed money from a bank.

(c) Credit sale of goods.

(d) Received cash for goods sold.

(e) Owner contributed $15 000 to fund a new product line.

(f) Received a grant from a government body to assist with an export program.

6.17 ★ **LO6**

Consider each of the following transactions and examine whether they satisfy the expense definition criteria under the accrual method of accounting.

(a) Paid salaries owing from the previous reporting period.

(b) Owner withdrew money to purchase a motor vehicle for private use.

(c) Money owed to Optus for internet charges this reporting period.

(d) Office equipment is depreciated.

(e) Paid a supplier for goods that had been purchased on credit.

(f) Purchased a perpetual inventory system to computerise the inventory records.

6.18 ★ **LO3**

(a) Classify the following as either accounting policy choices or accounting estimations.

 (i) Impairment of assets.

 (ii) Employee benefits (long service leave).

 (iii) First in, first out (FIFO) method of costing inventory.

 (iv) Depreciation method of motor vehicles used for business.

 (v) Useful life of motor vehicles used for business.

(b) Explain the factors that would influence an entity's decision as to the choice of depreciation method.

6.19 ★ **LO4**

Solve the missing items for each independent case. The cost of sales is 60 per cent of sales revenue for each case.

Sales revenue	Cost of sales	Other expenses	Profit	Total assets	Total liabilities	Share capital	Retained earnings
180 000	a.	b.	40 000	c.	589 000	250 000	25 000
d.	102 000	e.	38 000	621 000	f.	225 000	201 000
204 500	g.	115 000	h.	180 000	75 000	80 000	i.
875 000	j.	k.	95 000	645 000	450 000	l.	50 000
m.	66 000	32 000	n.	o.	186 000	400 000	29 000

6.20 ★   **LO3, 4**

Coconut Plantations Pty Ltd purchased machinery for its manufacturing process on 1 March 2019. The machinery cost $900 000. Coconut Plantations Pty Ltd estimates that the machinery has a useful life of five years and will have a $75 000 residual value. Using straight-line depreciation, estimate the depreciation expense to be recorded in the statement of profit or loss for the year in which the machine was purchased and the subsequent year, assuming Coconut Plantations Pty Ltd's reporting period ends on 31 December.

6.21 ★   **LO3, 4**

Using the information relating to Coconut Plantations Pty Ltd in 6.20, recalculate the depreciation expense to be recorded in the statement of profit or loss for the year in which the machine was purchased and the subsequent year using the diminishing balance method and the units of production method. In recalculating the depreciation expense, use the following assumptions:

Diminishing balance — the machinery is depreciated using a $33\frac{1}{3}$ per cent depreciation rate.

Units of production — the machinery is expected to produce 300 000 units over its useful life. In the period March to December in year 1, 30 000 units are produced. In year 2, 70 000 units are produced.

6.22 ★   **LO2**

You have just completed the statement of profit or loss for the reporting period. The CEO (who has no accounting background) is reviewing the statement and asks you to explain why the profit is relatively low compared to the increase in the cash at bank during the reporting period. Prepare a report for the CEO offering some suggestions that would explain this.

6.23 ★   **LO6**

Categorise each of the following expenses into one of the expense types listed at the heads of the columns.

	Cost of sales	Selling and distribution	Administration and general	Finance
Purchases				
Depreciation of office equipment				
Sales commission				
Interest expense				
Lease charges				
Sales staff salaries				
General staff salaries				
Advertising				
Freight charges on purchases				
Bank charges				
Utility expenses				

6.24 ★   **LO2, 4**

In its first year of operation, Harrington Pty Ltd earned $150 000 in services revenue, $30 000 of which was on account and still outstanding at the end of the reporting period. The remaining $120 000 was received in cash from customers. The company paid expenses of $40 000 in cash. Included in the $40 000 paid is $12 000 for insurance coverage that will not be used until the second year. Additionally, there is $22 000 still owing on account at the end of the reporting period.

Required

(a) Apply cash accounting to calculate the first year profit of Harrington Pty Ltd.

(b) Apply accrual accounting to calculate the first year profit of Harrington Pty Ltd.

(c) Explain which basis of accounting you think is more useful for decision making.

6.25 ★ ★   **LO2, 4**

(a) Compare the adjustments necessary on the accounts (income or expense only) of Peter Burrows to reflect: (1) a cash-based; and (2) an accrual-based accounting system (assume the accounting period is for 12 months ending on 31 December 2018).

   (i) Accrued wages and salaries of $1200 are due to be paid on 1 January 2019.

   (ii) Peter depreciates his business computer purchased on 1 January 2017 over three years at $800 per annum.

   (iii) Insurance premium of $12 000 for one year was paid on 1 December 2018.

   (iv) A client paid Peter $4000 on 1 September 2018 for work not yet done.

   (v) A client owes $2000 for work started and completed in October 2018.

   (vi) Peter tendered for work totalling $3600 on 4 December 2018. He has not heard whether or not he has been successful by 31 December 2018.

   (vii) Peter paid his quarterly electricity bill of $350 on 30 September 2018.

(b) Discuss why the profit for the period is different depending on whether a cash- or accrual-based accounting system is used. Justify the preference to use accrual-based accounting.

6.26 ★ ★   **LO2, 4**

The accountant at AppsGalore, a technology business, has determined that the following adjustments should be made in the entity's accounts for the year ended 30 June using an accrual-based system.

1. Income earned but not invoiced totalling $21 000.
2. Unpaid wages and salaries of $1150.
3. Equipment depreciation expense of $5200.
4. Cash received for applications not yet developed of $4000.
5. An annual insurance premium of $1500 paid to the Insure Company on 1 January.

Required

For each item, analyse:

(a) the nature of the adjustment that needs to be made (e.g. prepaid expense, accrued income, income received in advance or accrued expense)

(b) whether the profit for the reporting period would have been under- or overstated without the adjustment occurring.

6.27 ★ ★   **LO4, 9**

Myer shares slumped when the department store posted a 23.1 per cent slide in profit for the first half of the 2014–15 year.

> Myer's profit was mostly hit by a 24-basis-point fall in gross profit margin and a 6.2 per cent increase in the cash cost of doing business. Myer's capital expenditure increased almost 36 per cent ... due to investment in new stores and refurbishment, ongoing investment in its website and other initiatives (Janda & Morgan 2015).

Required

(a) Explain how capital expenditure may have contributed to the drop in after-tax profit.

(b) Discuss the reasons for the gross profit margin decreasing and the cash cost of doing business increasing.

(c) Discuss if Myer's profit performance improved in the second half of the year.

6.28 ★ ★   **LO4, 8**

The following information was obtained from the financial records of Broadbeach Ltd for the year ended 30 June 2018. Prepare the statement of profit or loss for the year ended 30 June 2018.

	$'000
Retained earnings 1 July 2017	180
Sales revenue from continuing operations for the year	1 200
Finance costs	49
Estimated income tax expense for the year ended 30 June 2018	101
Interim dividends paid (ordinary shares)	40
Provision for final dividend on ordinary shares	62
Transfer retained earnings to general reserve	12
Amortise goodwill	12
Write off research and development costs	8
Share capital (1 million $1 shares)	1 000
General reserve (1 July 2017)	80
Expenses from ordinary activities (excluding finance costs)	500

6.29 ★ ★　　　　　　　　　　　　　　　　　　　　　　**LO4, 8**

A list of account balances for Mr Tanner's business Robotics at the end of the 30 June 2020 reporting period is shown below. Prepare the statement of profit or loss for the reporting period, and the equity balance at the end of the year.

	$'000
Cash	52 000
Receivables	28 000
Office supplies	2 400
Prepaid insurance	1 300
Plant and equipment	250 000
Accumulated depreciation — plant and equipment	58 600
Accounts payable	41 200
Salaries payable	12 000
Rent received in advance	24 000
Share capital	150 000
Retained earnings	32 000
Service revenue	356 000
Rent revenue	28 000
Supplies expense	35 000
Rent expense	59 000
Insurance expense	4 200
Depreciation expense	41 300
Salaries expense	228 600

6.30 ★ ★　　　　　　　　　　　　　　　　　　　　　**LO4, 11**

'The profit represents the increase in the value of an entity during the reporting period.' Critically evaluate this statement.

6.31 ★ ★　　　　　　　　　　　　　　　　　　　　　　**LO9**

You are the assistant accountant at Sunshine Plantations Pty Ltd and have prepared the following statement of profit or loss for the year ended 31 December 2021.

SUNSHINE PLANTATIONS PTY LTD Statement of profit or loss for the year ended 31 December 2021	
Sales	$1 675 000
Cost of sales	1 025 000
Other income	1 500
Warehouse expenses	57 000
Distribution expenses	20 000
Sales and marketing	105 000
Administrative expenses	115 000
Finance expenses	18 000
Profit before tax	**$ 336 500**

Additional information
- The 'Other income' comprises $800 of interest income.
- Administrative expenses include $6000 for the depreciation of office equipment.
- Finance expenses of $18 000 represent interest expense on a bank loan.
- Administration expenses include the write-off of the amount owed by a major customer ($22 000) who has gone bankrupt.
- Warehouse expenses include $27 000 for the depreciation of manufacturing equipment.

Required

The accountant has asked you to produce the following financial information.

(a) Gross profit

(b) Profit before interest

(c) Profit before material items

(d) Earnings before interest, tax and depreciation

PROBLEMS

★ BASIC ⏐ ★ ★ MODERATE ⏐ ★ ★ ★ CHALLENGING

6.32 Assessing comparative statement of profit or loss ★   LO4, 9

The statement of profit or loss for JB Hi-Fi Ltd for the financial year ended 30 June 2018 was provided in figure 6.2. It reports that JB Hi-Fi Ltd increased its gross profit from $1230.5 million in 2017 to $1470.2 million in 2018. Its profit for 2018 was $233.2 million compared to $172.4 million in 2017. Financial performance allows a manager to assess previous decisions and inform future decisions. Hypothesise as to the reasons or business decisions contributing to the increase in the gross profit in 2018. Assess why the profit in 2018 was higher than in 2017.

6.33 Preparing an accrual-based statement ★ ★   LO2, 4

Beatrice has prepared a statement of profit or loss for the 12-month reporting period ended 30 June on a cash basis, showing a $64 800 profit. The cash-based statement shows the following.

Sales	$416 100
Inventory purchased	246 000
Gross profit	170 100
Expenses	
Salary and wages	42 600
Rent	13 800
Insurance	5 160
Advertising	8 400
Administration	28 200
Interest	7 140

Additional information
- The accounts receivable and accounts payable balances at the start of the reporting period were $24 600 and $14 700 respectively. At the end of the reporting period, Beatrice had accounts receivable of $31 800 and accounts payable of $29 640.
- The opening inventory was $48 000 and the closing inventory was $57 000.
- An advertising invoice of $4440 had not been paid.
- The business has equipment that cost $60 600. This has a useful life of five years and an expected salvage value of $6600.
- The insurance expense represents the 12-month premium on a policy that was taken out on 30 April.

Required

(a) Prepare an accrual-based statement of profit or loss for Beatrice for the period ended 30 June.

(b) As a user of financial statements, critique why accrual accounting is preferred to cash accounting to measure financial performance.

6.34 Recognition and classification of income ★ ★   LO3, 5, 7

The following are the revenue recognition policies of Flight Centre Travel (FLT) Group as detailed in the company's 2017 annual report (pp. 47, 103–104).

Accounting policy

The group recognises revenue when:
- The amount of revenue can be reliably measured
- It is probable that future economic benefits will flow to the entity; and
- Specific requirements have been met for each of the group's activities.

Revenue is measured at the fair value of the consideration received or receivable. Revenue from the sale of travel services is recognised as set out below.

Revenue from the sale of travel services

Revenue from the sale of travel services is recorded when travel documents are issued, consistent with an agency relationship. Revenue relating to volume incentives, including override revenue, is recognised at the amount receivable when it is probable the annual targets will be achieved.

Revenue from our tour operations is derived from the Top Deck Tours Limited and Back Roads Touring Co. Limited companies. It is recognised upon tour departure, net of associated cost of sales.

Additional information on other revenue accounting policies is included in note 1(e).

Critical accounting estimates, assumptions and judgements — override revenue

In addition to commission payments, FLT is eligible for override payments from its suppliers, as included in revenue from the provision of travel. These overrides are negotiated with individual suppliers and will typically include a combination of guaranteed payments and volume incentives (super overrides).

The volume incentives are recognised at the amount receivable when it is probable the annual targets will be achieved.

The override revenue accrual process is inherently judgmental and is impacted by factors which are not completely under FLT's control. These factors include:
- Year-end differences — as supplier contract periods do not always correspond to FLT's financial year, judgements and estimation techniques are required to determine revenues from customers anticipated to travel over the remaining contract year and the associated override rates applicable to these forecast levels
- Timing — where contracts have not been finalised before the start of the contract period, override and commission earnings may have to be estimated until agreement has been reached. Information on override receivables is included in note F3.

Other revenue recognition policies

Lease income: Lease income from operating leases is recognised as income on a straight-line basis over the lease term.

Interest income: Interest income is recognised on a time proportion basis using the effective interest method. When a receivable is impaired, the group reduces the carrying amount to its recoverable amount, being the estimated future cash flow discounted at the instrument's original effective interest rate, and continues unwinding the discount as interest income. Interest income on impaired loans is recognised using the original effective interest rate.

Dividends: Dividends are recognised as revenue when the right to receive payment is established. This applies even if they are paid out of pre-acquisition profits. However, the investment may need to be tested for impairment as a consequence.

Royalties: Royalty revenue is recognised on an accrual basis in accordance with the substance of the relevant agreement.

Required

(a) Identify Flight Centre Travel Group's sources of revenue.
(b) In your own words, reconcile the revenue recognition criteria applied by Flight Centre Travel Group for travel services with the definition and recognition criteria in the *Conceptual Framework*.

6.35 Recognising and classifying revenue ★ ★   **LO5, 7**

On 31 December 2018, Narvey Horman sold whitegood appliances to a customer for $8000. The customer paid cash for the whitegoods. Narvey Horman includes a three-year warranty service with the sale of all its whitegoods.

Required

(a) Explain Narvey Horman's obligations arising from the sale.
(b) Narvey Horman recorded this transaction by increasing revenue by $8000 and increasing cash at bank by $8000. With due consideration of the *Conceptual Framework*, examine the appropriateness of recording the transaction and recognising the revenue in this manner. Justify an alternative way of recording the transaction.

6.36 Adjusting income, expense, asset and/or liability accounts ★ ★   **LO2, 4**

Generate the adjustments needed to the income, expense, asset and/or liability accounts for Board Games Pty Ltd to reflect the following transactions in the entity's financial statements for the 12-month reporting period ended 31 December 2019 using the accrual system.

(a) The fortnightly salaries and wages bill of $8400 for December 2019 is due to be paid on 1 January 2020.

(b) The entity has $60 000 of office furniture and equipment with a $10 000 residual value that it depreciates over five years on a straight-line basis.

(c) A client owes $3500 for services rendered in December 2019.

(d) Board Games Pty Ltd's utility services bill (water, telephone, electricity) for the quarter ended December 2019 has not yet been received. Based on previous bills, the quarterly expense is expected to be $1800.

(e) Board Games Pty Ltd has a two-year subscription to a trade magazine at a cost of $1600. The subscription was paid on 1 March 2019.

(f) A customer has commissioned work and paid $2500. As at 31 December 2019, the work has not been performed.

(g) Board Games Pty Ltd expects to lose a court case over a breach of contract. If it loses, the damages awarded could be in the range of $25 000 to $50 000.

(h) Board Games Pty Ltd tendered for work totalling $12 000 in November 2019. It has been advised that its tender is one of three being considered.

(i) One of Board Games Pty Ltd's clients was placed into liquidation in December 2019. This client owes Board Games Pty Ltd $1300.

(j) Board Games Pty Ltd has a property with a carrying value of $155 000. An assessment has determined that its recoverable amount is $125 000.

6.37 Preparing a statement of profit or loss ★ ★   **LO4**

Jacinta Williams had prepared the financial statements for her business, a sole proprietorship, to take to her accountant. Unfortunately, she has misplaced the statement of profit or loss. Her accountant assures her that the profit or loss for the period can be determined so long as she has her statement of financial position for the previous and current reporting periods. This is presented below.

JACINTA WILLIAMS BUSINESS Statement of financial position		
	As at 30 June 2020	As at 30 June 2019
Cash	$ 6 700	$ 3 800
Receivables	14 600	10 000
Inventory	30 200	39 500
Prepayments	3 510	2 100
Total current assets	55 010	55 400
Land	34 600	33 500
Plant and equipment	21 600	29 200
Total non-current assets	56 200	62 700
Total assets	**$111 210**	**$118 100**
Bank overdraft	$ —	$ 9 700
Accounts payable	15 000	16 700
Accrued expenses	6 000	3 300
Total current liabilities	21 000	29 700
Loan	23 800	28 100
Total liabilities	**$ 44 800**	**$ 57 800**
Equity	**$ 66 410**	**$ 60 300**

In addition, Jacinta Williams tells her accountant that she has made drawings totalling $27 000 during the reporting period.

Required

Analysing the information provided, determine the profit or loss for Jacinta Williams for the year ended 30 June 2020.

6.38 Accounting judgements and estimation uncertainty ★ ★   **LO3**

Note 1(d) of JB Hi-Fi Ltd's 2018 (p. 60) notes to the financial statements states:

> Estimates and judgements used in the preparation of these financial statements are continually evaluated and are based on historical experience and other factors, including expectations of future events that may have a financial impact on the Group and that are believed to be reasonable under the circumstances.
>
> The estimates and assumptions that have a significant risk of causing a material adjustment to the carrying amounts of assets and liabilities within the next financial year are included in the following notes:

Judgement area	Note
Impairment of goodwill and other intangible assets	11
Business combination	25

Required

(a) Identify the critical accounting estimates and assumptions noted by JB Hi-Fi Ltd.

(b) Note 1(d) of JB Hi-Fi Ltd's 2018 notes to the financial statements refer to critical judgements in applying the entity's accounting policies. Identify the accounting areas noted by JB Hi-Fi Ltd as requiring critical judgements and the critical judgements to be made in relation to these areas.

(c) Explain the impact on the profit and equity of the net realisable value of inventories being lower than their carrying amount. What accounts would be affected?

6.39 Understanding a statement of profit or loss, statement of comprehensive income and statement of changes in equity ★ ★ ★   **LO7, 8, 9**

Locate the most recent annual financial statements for Samsung Group from its website. Examine the information in the report and answer the following questions about Samsung Group's statement of changes in equity.

Required

(a) Identify and state Samsung Group's total comprehensive income for the period.

(b) Identify and state Samsung Group's profit for the period.

(c) Explain why Samsung Group's total comprehensive income and expense differ from its profit.

(d) Identify and state the amount of Samsung Group's transactions with equity holders as equity holders during the period.

(e) Identify if the profit in the statement of changes in equity agrees with that in the statement of profit or loss.

(f) Identify if the balance of retained earnings at the end of the period agrees with that in the statement of financial position.

6.40 Global citizenship ★ ★ ★   **LO1, 9**

Samsung Group upholds a belief in shared responsibility — to its people, the planet and society. Samsung Electronics produces a sustainability report that includes the company's profiles as well as its economic, environmental and social performance indicators to ensure the full sharing of information across all sectors.

Required

(a) Describe the Samsung Group's business principles.

(b) Discuss five ways that Samsung Group acts as a responsible citizen.

(c) List some of the quantitative indicators used to report on Samsung Group's sustainability performance.

(d) Discuss whether sustainability performance enhances or hinders financial performance.

(e) The sustainability report is produced using the Standards of the Global Reporting Initiative (GRI). Summarise the GRI. Your summary should include the organisation, its priorities, the Standards and the global reach of GRI.

6.41 Changes in accounting policies and estimations ★ ★ ★   **LO3, 4**

True Blue Ltd is reviewing its accounting policies and estimations. Detailed below are its current policies and estimations. Using these current policies, the company's calculated profit figure is $840 000. What would True Blue Ltd's profit be if the alternative accounting policies and estimations are applied?

	Current	Alternative
Depreciation rate for plant and equipment with a cost price of $600 000 and residual value of $100 000	20% straight-line	50% diminishing balance
Accounts receivable impairment	2% of gross accounts receivable	5% of gross accounts receivable
Accounts receivable (gross)	$200 000	
Development expenditure	$40 000 expensed	$40 000 capitalised

6.42 Revenue recognition ★ ★ ★   **LO5, 7**

The International Accounting Standards Board (IASB) and the US accounting standard–setting board worked on a joint project to develop a new standard on revenue recognition. Podcasts summarising the project are available on various websites including that of the IASB.

Required

Access the information available on the IASB website and answer the following questions.

(a) Summarise the timeline associated with the development of the revenue recognition standard, indicating the major milestones.

(b) Provide the rationale as to why a new revenue recognition standard was required.

(c) An area of debate in revenue recognition is the presentation of the adjustments to revenue for the uncollectibility of revenue associated with customer credit risk. Explain what difference it makes to the statement of profit or loss, and to key items within the statement, if uncollectible charges are deducted from revenue or included in operating expenses.

6.43 Calculating revenue ★ ★ ★   **LO4, 5, 9**

Jim St Cloud operates a wholesale clothing operation called St Cloud's Designs. All the sales and purchases of the business are made on credit. The opening and closing balances for accounts receivable, inventory and accounts payable are shown below.

	At start of period	At end of period
Accounts receivable	$ 4 000	$ 6 800
Inventory	13 000	16 200
Accounts payable	5 000	7 100

During the reporting period, Jim St Cloud received $60 000 from accounts receivable and paid $38 000 to suppliers.

Required

Calculate the revenue from sales, cost of sales and gross profit for the reporting period for St Cloud's Designs.

DECISION-MAKING ACTIVITIES

6.44 Groupon is a US company with a deal-of-the-day website that features discounted gift certificates usable at local or national companies. Since its formation, it has faced a number of questions relating to its accounting practices. Here are two examples of Groupon's questionable accounting practices.

- In 2011, Groupon restated its financial results for the three years prior in order to correct what it called an error in the way that it reported its revenue.

  Before, the company reported as revenue all the money it collected from customers, including cash that was later paid out to Groupon's merchant partners. Now, Groupon is reporting what it calls 'net revenues', which exclude the retailer payouts (De La Merced & Rusli 2011).

- In 2012, Groupon outlined that it had underestimated customer refunds for its more expensive offers and that this had led to problems with the way the company calculated its results. While Groupon collects more revenue on its more expensive offers (for example, laser eye surgery), it also experiences a higher rate of refunds.

The company honors customer refunds for the life of its coupons, so those payments can affect its financials at various times. Groupon deducts refunds within 60 days from revenue; after that, the company has to take an additional accounting charge related to the payments (De La Merced 2012).

Required

(a) Use the following to illustrate the difference between reporting gross and net revenue. Groupon collected US$1.52 billion in revenue from customers during a six-month period. Of this, US$0.832 billion was paid to merchant partners.

(b) Explain if the reporting of gross billings or net revenue affects the company's bottom line.

(c) Discuss what factors Groupon should consider when estimating customer refunds.

(d) Hypothesise how the share price of Groupon may have reacted to announcements of accounting irregularity. Identify the trend in Groupon's share price since its listing in 2008.

(e) In 2011, Groupon was criticised by the corporate regulator for its use of a pro forma profit measure. Discuss the pro forma profit measure that Groupon was using and why the regulator objected to its use.

6.45 Depreciation expense is an allocation of the cost of an asset over the asset's useful life. Entities assess the useful lives of their various assets. The notes to the accounts for two airlines reveal the following variation in useful-life estimates.

Air New Zealand Ltd (2018, p. 15) depreciates its aircraft on a straight-line basis to an estimated residual value over their economic lives as follows.

Aircraft	18 years	Residual values are reviewed annually
Engine overhauls		Period to next overhaul

Qantas Airways (2018, p. 90) depreciates its aircraft as follows.

Aircraft and engines	2.5–20 years	0–20% residual value
Aircraft spare parts	15–20 years	0–20% residual value

Required

(a) Comment on the effect of these differing depreciation rates on the profits of Air New Zealand Ltd and Qantas Airways.

(b) Can you suggest any reasons why the choice of useful lives would differ across these entities?

(c) Debate whether you believe entities should have discretion to choose the depreciation method and useful lives applicable to various asset classes.

(d) What do you think would affect the useful lives of assets such as aircraft?

6.46 In its 2018 annual report, Qantas Airways referred to 'underlying profit' and 'statutory profit'. Identify the differences in these profit figures. Debate the merits of reporting non-statutory profit figures.

6.47 The 2017 statement of profit or loss (referred to as consolidated income statement) for Wesfarmers is provided below.

WESFARMERS
Consolidated income statement
for the year ended 30 June 2017

	Note	2017 $m	2016 $m
Revenue	1	68 444	65 981
Expenses			
Raw materials and inventory		(46 359)	(45 525)
Employee benefits expense	2	(9 132)	(8 847)
Freight and other related expenses		(1 096)	(1 078)
Occupancy-related expenses	2	(3 229)	(2 959)

Depreciation and amortization	2	(1 266)	(1 296)
Impairment expenses	2	(49)	(2 172)
Other expenses	2	(3 346)	(3 107)
Total expenses		(64 477)	(64 984)
Other income	1	288	235
Share of net profits of associates and joint venture	18	147	114
Earnings before interest and income tax expense (EBIT)		4 402	1 346
Finance costs	2	(264)	(308)
Profit before income tax		**4 138**	**1 038**
Income tax expense	3	(1 265)	(631)
Profit attributable to members of the parent		**2 873**	**407**
Earnings per share attributable to ordinary equity holders of the parent	13		
Basic earnings per share		254.7	36.2
Diluted earnings per share		254.2	36.2

Source: Wesfarmers 2017, p. 94.

Required

Using the above information, answer the following questions.

(a) Give an example of an expense that would be included in each of the Wesfarmers expense categories.

(b) Calculate EBITDA for Wesfarmers.

(c) Explain the purpose of EBIT and EBITDA.

(d) What are the items of other comprehensive income?

6.48 Review the following quote from Colquhoun (2013).

> Investors assessing the recent reporting season of publicly listed companies will base their opinions of corporate performance largely on a handful of key numbers, all expressed in dollar terms and all dealing with the most recent financial year. This fixation with the bottom line and the profit and loss statement has existed for 100 years or so and, at its most extreme, has produced a short-term focus for investors that's been blamed for many failings, from poor corporate governance to the massaging of accounts to please the market and drive the share price — and, with that, executive remuneration.
>
> In recent times, more progressive elements within the accountancy profession have championed the concept of widening reporting criteria. In the past decade the Global Reporting Initiative (GRI) promoted sustainability reporting and introduced the idea of the triple bottom line, now adopted by about 4000 organisations around the world.
>
> ... GRI as principles of sustainability combine with traditional financial reporting to deliver a holistic vision of corporate performance, which goes behind publishing the sustainability report and the financial accounts in the same document. A significant milestone in this evolution was reached in April with the release of the Consultation Draft of the International Integrated Reporting Framework.

Required

Prepare a memorandum for a board of directors that: (a) defines integrated reporting; (b) discusses the various types of capital; and (c) describes the pilot program on integrated reporting.

6.49 The ASX convened the ASX Corporate Governance Council (ASXCGC) in August 2002, prompted by suggestions from ASIC and government that ASX take a leadership role in formulating a non-legislative response to the corporate governance issues arising following a number of corporate collapses in 2000. Many of these collapses were associated with poor financial reporting. The ASXCGC released the first edition of *Principles of good corporate governance and best practice recommendations* in March 2003; a second edition was released in 2007, a third edition in 2014 and a fourth edition in 2019. Eight principles are identified as underlying good corporate governance. One of these principles, principle 4, relates to safeguarding the integrity of financial reporting.

Required

(a) Discuss the recommendations in principle 4 of the ASXCGC guidelines for safeguarding the integrity of financial reporting.

(b) Access the JB Hi-Fi Ltd 2018 corporate governance statement in its annual report. Discuss the company's compliance with principle 4.

(c) The 2018 annual report of JB Hi-Fi Ltd contains a directors' declaration. Identify the functions and activities that are covered by the directors' declaration.

(d) The ASXCGC adopts an 'if not, why not?' approach to compliance with its recommended corporate governance practices. Explain what this approach means. How does this approach vary with the approach adopted in the United States?

REFERENCES

Air New Zealand Ltd 2018, *2018 Annual financial report*, www.airnewzealand.com.au.

Colquhoun, L 2013, 'Capital ideas afloat in integrated reporting: bringing all the strands of corporate reporting together will help reduce the risk of short-termism', *INTHEBLACK*, 14 June.

De La Merced, M 2012, 'Groupon's shares fall on revision', *New York Times*, 30 March.

De La Merced, M & Rusli, E 2011, 'Accounting change cuts Groupon's revenue', *New York Times*, 23 September.

Flight Centre Travel Group 2017, *2017 Annual report*, www.flightcentrelimited.com.

Janda, M & Morgan, E 2015, 'Myer management defends lack of warning on surprise 23pc profit slump', *ABC News*, 19 March.

JB Hi-Fi Ltd 2018, *Preliminary final report 2018*, www.jbhifi.com.au.

Qantas Airways Ltd 2018, *Annual report 2018*, www.qantas.com.au.

Telstra 2016, *Annual report 2016*, www.telstra.com.au.

Wesfarmers 2017, *Annual report 2017*, www.wesfarmers.com.au.

ACKNOWLEDGEMENTS

Photo: © Sergey Nivens / Shutterstock.com

Photo: © Blend Images / Getty Images

Figures 6.2, 6.3, 6.5, 6.7, 6.9: © JB Hi-Fi Ltd 2018

Problem 6.34: © Flight Centre Travel Group 2017

Problem 6.38: © JB Hi-Fi Ltd 2018

Decision-making activity 6.47: © Wesfarmers Ltd 2017

Decision-making activity 6.48: © Lachlan Colquhoun / *INTHEBLACK*

CHAPTER 7

Statement of cash flows

After studying this chapter, you should be able to:

7.1 assess the purpose and usefulness of a statement of cash flows

7.2 outline the format and the classification of cash flows in the statement of cash flows

7.3 produce a statement of cash flows using the direct method and a reconciliation using the indirect method

7.4 evaluate an entity's performance using a statement of cash flows.

Chapter preview

Previous chapters presented the statement of profit or loss, statement of comprehensive income, statement of changes in equity and statement of financial position; this chapter introduces the statement of cash flows. The statement of cash flows is useful for users of financial statements as it provides information to help assess an entity's ability to generate cash flows and meet its obligations, and appreciate why its assets and liabilities have changed. This chapter outlines the purpose of the statement of cash flows, its relationship to the statement of profit or loss and the statement of financial position, and its general format. Also discussed are the preparation and interpretation of the statement of cash flows.

7.1 The purpose and usefulness of a statement of cash flows

LEARNING OBJECTIVE 7.1 Assess the purpose and usefulness of a statement of cash flows.

Cash flows are the lifeblood of a business. Without cash flows the business will wither and die. We have seen many companies and countries during the global financial crisis (GFC) and its aftermath stall or come to a halt due to a cash shortage. Therefore, it makes sense to prepare a report that shows the cash flows of a business. This is the purpose of a **statement of cash flows**.

The flows of cash are important for the **working capital** management of an entity. Working capital is needed to fund inventory and accounts receivable while awaiting receipts from sales. The flow of cash through purchases and payments of inventory and labour to the receipt of cash can be simply depicted, as shown in figure 7.1.

FIGURE 7.1	Flow of cash in business cycle

The greater the number of times an entity can cycle through this process, generally the more profit it can make (as long as prices are set appropriately). However, cash is very important through the cycle as there is normally an outflow of funds for inventory and wages prior to the inflow from sales. The statement of cash flows helps ascertain the cash generation from this cycle and whether or not the entity is collecting its receipts in a timely manner.

The statement of profit or loss shows the income earned and expenses incurred through this cycle, while the statement of cash flows shows the actual cash receipts and payments through this cycle. It is important that we differentiate between a sale (revenue generated) and cash received, or between a purchase and a payment.

DECISION-MAKING EXAMPLE

Impact of cash flows on investment

SITUATION You are an investor who has been given an investment recommendation by your finance broker. The main reason for the recommendation is the extra tax benefits due to the primary production nature of the business. Being an accounting scholar, you decide to download the financial statements of the recommended business from the last couple of years and you discover the following.

	2019 $'000	2018 $'000
Profit attributable to equity holders of the parent	44 607	65 713
Net cash (used in)/provided by operating activities	(29 775)	(44 725)

Should you act on the recommendation and invest?

DECISION The negative cash flow should signal a warning to you that the business is not bringing in cash from its operations. So it will need to get cash either from borrowing money or by asking investors to put up more money. Sustaining a cash outflow can't be done in the long term.

Difference between cash and accrual accounting

Recall from the chapter about the statement of profit or loss and the statement of changes in equity that reporting entities must calculate their profit or loss using an accrual system of accounting. However, the accrual system focuses on when a transaction takes place (i.e. the sale) and not when the payment for that transaction occurs. In contrast, the statement of cash flows is concerned with cash receipts and payments, and not the timing of the underlying transaction.

This difference is highlighted in illustrative example 7.1. The statement of profit or loss of Mum's Choc Heaven Pty Ltd reports a profit of $7900, while the statement of cash flows reports that the net cash provided by operating activities for the reporting period is ($6000). Why the difference?

For entities using accrual accounting, such as an entity providing chocolate products, the timing of cash receipts and payments will differ from when the transaction takes place.

ILLUSTRATIVE EXAMPLE 7.1

Difference in profit and cash position

According to the statement of profit or loss for Mum's Choc Heaven Pty Ltd, the entity made a profit of $7900 for the month of March 2019. The statement of profit or loss reflects the transactions for the month, which include sales of products worth $20 000 ($5000 of which has been collected), rent paid of $1000 and wages paid of $4000. The depreciation relates to shop fixtures and fittings that the entity has been depreciating over a period of time. The entity also purchased and paid for $6000 worth of products from its supplier, but the cost of the products sold during the month amounted to $5600. (The other $400 will form part of inventory and be recorded as an asset on the statement of financial position.) The statement of cash flows shows that the entity's cash position is negative $4000 (i.e. the bank account is in overdraft) at the end of March 2019, despite having a $2000 credit balance at the beginning of the month.

A comparison of the two statements shows that, although Mum's Choc Heaven Pty Ltd was quite profitable for the month of March, the business will have trouble meeting its financial obligations. This illustrates the importance of the statement of cash flows: it allows users of the statement to quickly see what money is coming in and how the money is being used. The following statements demonstrate that, although income of $20 000 was generated, only $5000 of the sales were collected in cash during the period. It also demonstrates that, while depreciation is an expense incurred by the entity, it does not involve an outflow of cash and, as such, is a non-cash item. Mum's Choc Heaven Pty Ltd needs to address the collection of debts if the entity is going to survive and meet its financial obligations when they fall due. As you can observe, a quick glance at the statement of cash flows can show a user if an entity has a good cash position or not. In general, for an entity to survive, the net cash flows from operating activities should be positive.

MUM'S CHOC HEAVEN PTY LTD Statement of profit or loss for the month of March 2019		
Income		$20 000
Cost of sales		5 600
Gross profit		14 400
Expenses		
Rent	$1 000	
Wages	4 000	
Depreciation	1 500	6 500
Profit		**$ 7 900**

MUM'S CHOC HEAVEN PTY LTD Statement of cash flows for the month of March 2019			
Beginning cash balance			$ 2 000
Cash flows			
Receipts from sales		$ 5 000	
Payments for inventory	$(6 000)		
Payments for rent	(1 000)		
Payments for wages	(4 000)	(11 000)	
Net cash flows			(6 000)
Closing cash balance			**$(4 000)**

The above example reinforces the importance of working capital. The following timeline highlights the necessity of having enough cash to manage through the operating cash cycle of the entity.

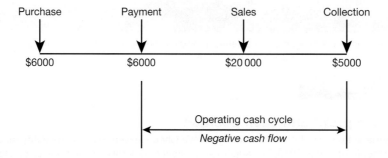

The time between the payment of inventory, wages and so on and the collection of debts is called the operating cash cycle. By minimising this time, an entity can save on funding costs (i.e. interest). Prudent companies tightly manage their working capital requirements and their operating cash cycle. Companies such as Woolworths Ltd have a positive operating cash cycle. This means they collect funds from sales/accounts receivable prior to paying their accounts payable. So rather than paying funding costs through this period, they are earning interest on funds collected prior to paying their accounts payable. This can be a great competitive advantage over rival companies.

The statement of cash flows is needed as it summarises the cash and types of cash flows coming into and flowing out of the entity. The statement of financial position does show the beginning and ending cash balances, but the statement of cash flows shows the various categories of cash flows. For instance, if the entity received cash from bank loans but no cash was coming into the entity through normal operations, this would indicate to a user that it would not be a good business to invest in. Likewise, if ample cash was coming in through the entity's normal operations and it therefore had no need for cash from borrowing, this would indicate to a user that it would be a good entity to invest in.

The importance of cash to the ongoing survival of a business cannot be overstated. An entity needs to have enough ready cash to ensure that it can meet its financial obligations in a timely manner, yet not too much — there are costs associated with keeping a supply of ready cash (e.g. interest payments on debt, lost investment opportunities). The ability of an entity to manage the flow of cash in and out of the business is critical for success. Paying for supplies, converting sales into cash and paying for assets are central to managing a business. Entities can be quite profitable and yet still falter due to poor cash management.

Relationship of the statement of cash flows to other financial statements

Illustrative example 7.1 emphasised the importance of the statement of cash flows by highlighting the additional information it contains. The financial statements comprise the:
1. statement of profit or loss and statement of comprehensive income — which show the results of an entity's performance for the reporting period
2. statement of financial position — which shows the entity's financial position at a particular point in time
3. statement of changes in equity — which shows the change in an entity's equity between two reporting periods
4. statement of cash flows — which shows the entity's cash inflows, outflows and net cash flow for the reporting period.

The statement of cash flows was introduced because the statement of profit or loss and statement of financial position did not provide a complete picture of an entity's economic activities. That is, a statement of profit or loss summarises an entity's income and expense transactions, but does not identify the flow of funds relating to those transactions; and a comparison of successive statements of financial positions would show the change in cash position from one point in time to another, but would not expose the cash flows associated with that change. **Cash flows** refer to the movement of cash resulting from transactions with external parties. As discussed in the statement of financial position chapter, the statement of financial position lists the assets (investing decisions) and the liabilities and equity (financing decisions) of an entity. The statement of cash flows also helps to identify changes in items in the statement of financial position. For example, the sale or purchase of an asset for cash would have an effect on both the statement of financial position and the statement of cash flows. Similarly, borrowing money and paying a dividend to the owners of the entity are examples of transactions that affect both statements.

So, the purpose of a statement of cash flows is to give information additional to the information provided by the other statements. Generally, the information provided should assist decision makers in assessing an entity's ability to:
1. generate cash flows
2. meet its financial commitments as they fall due, including the servicing of borrowings and the payment of dividends
3. fund changes in the scope and/or nature of its activities
4. obtain external finance.

Together, the statement of profit or loss and the statement of financial position (based on accrual accounting) and the statement of cash flows provide a rich source of information regarding the profitability, liquidity and stability of an entity.

Let's look at a simple case study to:
• understand more clearly the relationship of the statement of cash flows to the statement of profit or loss and statement of financial position
• gain an appreciation of the types of information the statement of cash flows contains and therefore the format of the statement of cash flows.

The simple case study is that of a sole trader, Teresa Tang, starting a business, Teresa's Carpets and Rugs. Teresa is unhappy in her present job as an office administrator for an import and export company. She wants to do something more fulfilling and challenging. Teresa loves textiles and feels that there is a business opportunity in selling imported rugs and carpets. She knows that you have completed studies in accounting and asks for your help.

Teresa is willing to invest her savings of $20 000 into the business known as Teresa's Carpets and Rugs, but she also knows that she will need to borrow money to get the business started. Her aunt is willing to lend her $50 000 at commercial rates. According to the terms of the loan, the interest is based on a 6 per cent variable rate tied to commercial bank rates. The loan is to be paid back by 2029. So, on 1 April 2019, Teresa creates a business account with her bank, transfers her $20 000 and banks her aunt's cheque for $50 000.

In summary, Teresa has:
1. injected $20 000 of her own money into the business
2. borrowed $50 000 from her aunt, due for repayment in 2029.

Teresa's opening statement of financial position as at 1 April 2019 is shown in illustrative example 7.2. When reading the statement of financial position, remember the accounting equation:

$$\text{Assets} = \text{Liabilities} + \text{Equity}$$

ILLUSTRATIVE EXAMPLE 7.2

Statement of financial position

TERESA'S CARPETS AND RUGS			
Statement of financial position			
as at 1 April 2019			
ASSETS		LIABILITIES	
Cash	$70 000	Loan	$50 000
		EQUITY	
		Capital contributed — T Tang	20 000
	$70 000		$70 000

Teresa's opening statement of cash flows for the period 1 April 2016 is shown in illustrative example 7.3.

ILLUSTRATIVE EXAMPLE 7.3

Statement of cash flows

TERESA'S CARPETS AND RUGS	
Statement of cash flows	
for 1 April 2019	
Cash flows	
Proceeds from loan	$50 000
Proceeds from capital (equity) contributed	20 000
Net cash flows	70 000
Beginning cash balance	—
Ending cash balance	**$70 000**

Teresa needs a shop in which to sell her rugs. She finds the right shop in a boutique shopping precinct featuring arts galleries, antique shops, coffee shops and smaller retail shops. She leases the shop for a period of five years. The cost of the lease has two components. The first is a lease premium of $10 000.

This is payable immediately and gives Teresa the right to occupy the shop for the next five years. The second is a yearly rental of $12 000 payable in monthly instalments. On 2 April 2019, she signs the lease and writes a cheque for $10 000 in favour of the lessor.

Teresa's statement of financial position as at 2 April is shown in illustrative example 7.4.

ILLUSTRATIVE EXAMPLE 7.4

Statement of financial position

TERESA'S CARPETS AND RUGS
Statement of financial position
as at 2 April 2019

ASSETS		LIABILITIES	
Current		Non-current	
Cash	$60 000	Loan	$50 000
Non-current		EQUITY	
Lease prepayment	10 000	Capital contributed — T Tang	20 000
	$70 000		$70 000

Teresa's statement of cash flows for the period 1–2 April 2019 is shown in illustrative example 7.5.

ILLUSTRATIVE EXAMPLE 7.5

Statement of cash flows

TERESA'S CARPETS AND RUGS
Statement of cash flows
for the period 1–2 April 2019

Cash inflows	
Proceeds from loan	$50 000
Proceeds from capital (equity) contributed	20 000
Total cash inflows	70 000
Cash outflows	
Lease payment	10 000
Total cash outflows	10 000
Net cash flow	60 000
Beginning cash balance	—
Ending cash balance	**$60 000**

Teresa needs to fit out the shop in order to display the wares she has for sale. On 3 April 2019, she contracts a builder to complete the fitout for $20 000. The next day the builder finishes the fitout and Teresa writes a cheque for $20 000 in favour of the builder. Teresa expects the life of the shop fittings to be five years.

Teresa's statement of financial position as at 4 April 2019 is shown in illustrative example 7.6.

ILLUSTRATIVE EXAMPLE 7.6

Statement of financial position

TERESA'S CARPETS AND RUGS
Statement of financial position
as at 4 April 2019

ASSETS		LIABILITIES	
Current		Non-current	
Cash	$40 000	Loan	$50 000

▷

TERESA'S CARPETS AND RUGS			
Statement of financial position			
as at 4 April 2019			
Non-current			
Shop fittings	$20 000	EQUITY	
Lease prepayment	10 000	Capital contributed — T Tang	$20 000
	$70 000		$70 000

Teresa's statement of cash flows for the period 1–4 April 2019 is shown in illustrative example 7.7.

ILLUSTRATIVE EXAMPLE 7.7

Statement of cash flows

TERESA'S CARPETS AND RUGS	
Statement of cash flows	
for the period 1–4 April 2019	
Cash inflows	
Proceeds from loan	$50 000
Proceeds from capital (equity) contributed	20 000
Total cash inflows	70 000
Cash outflows	
Purchase of shop fittings	20 000
Lease payment	10 000
Total cash outflows	30 000
Net cash flow	40 000
Beginning cash balance	—
Ending cash balance	**$40 000**

Teresa now needs to purchase her inventory of rugs and carpets. She approaches several companies and decides to buy her inventory from Carpetable Pty Ltd. On 5 April, she selects a range of small, medium and large rugs and carpets of varying textures, colours and fabrics from Carpetable Pty Ltd at a cost of $35 000, delivered immediately and payable in 28 days.

Teresa's statement of financial position as at 5 April 2019 and statement of cash flows for the period 1–5 April 2019 are shown in illustrative examples 7.8 and 7.9.

ILLUSTRATIVE EXAMPLE 7.8

Statement of financial position

TERESA'S CARPETS AND RUGS			
Statement of financial position			
as at 5 April 2019			
ASSETS		LIABILITIES	
Current		Current	
Cash	$ 40 000	Accounts payable	$ 35 000
Inventory	35 000	Non-current	
Non-current		Loan	50 000
Shop fittings	20 000	EQUITY	
Lease prepayment	10 000	Capital contributed — T Tang	20 000
	$ 105 000		$ 105 000

Statement of cash flows

TERESA'S CARPETS AND RUGS
Statement of cash flows
for the period 1–5 April 2019

Cash inflows	
Proceeds from loan	$50 000
Proceeds from capital (equity) contributed	20 000
Total cash inflows	70 000
Cash outflows	
Purchase of shop fittings	20 000
Lease prepayment	10 000
Total cash outflows	30 000
Net cash flow	40 000
Beginning cash balance	–
Ending cash balance	**$40 000**

Note that the statement of cash flows for the period 1–5 April is the same as for 1–4 April. No cash changed hands in the inventory transaction. The statement of financial position has changed to reflect the purchase of carpets (inventory) but cash did not decrease as we recorded an accounts payable amount equal to the inventory amount. During April, Teresa sold $20 000 worth of inventory for $40 000. Interest expense was $250 for the month and depreciation on fittings was $334 ($20 000/5 years/12 months). The monthly rent was $1000. In relation to the prepaid lease payment of $10 000 for five years, this is an asset as it gives Teresa the right to use the shop over the next five years. According to the *Conceptual Framework* recognition criteria (see the chapters on the statement of financial position, the statement of profit or loss and the statement of changes in equity), we should account for the proportion of the lease cost that is used each period. Therefore, the cost of the lease each month is $167 ($10 000/5 years/12 months). The profit for the period is calculated as:

$$\$40\,000 \text{ (sales)} - \$20\,000 \text{ (cost of sales)} - \$250 \text{ (interest)} - \$334 \text{ (depreciation)} -$$

$$\$1000 \text{ (lease payment)} - \$167 \text{ (lease amortisation)} = \$18\,249$$

Teresa's statement of financial position as at 30 April 2019 and statement of cash flows for the month ended 30 April 2019 are shown in illustrative examples 7.10 and 7.11.

Statement of financial position

TERESA'S CARPETS AND RUGS
Statement of financial position
as at 30 April 2019

ASSETS			LIABILITIES	
Current			Current	
Cash		$ 78 750	Accounts payable	$ 35 000
Inventory		15 000	Non-current	
Non-current			Loan	50 000
Shop fittings	$20 000			
Less: Accumulated depreciation	334	19 666		
			EQUITY	
Lease prepayment	$10 000		Capital contributed — T Tang	20 000
Less: Accumulated amortisation	167	9 833	Retained earnings	18 249
		$123 249		$123 249

Statement of cash flows

TERESA'S CARPETS AND RUGS
Statement of cash flows
for the month ended 30 April 2019

Cash inflows	
Proceeds from loan	$ 50 000
Proceeds from sales	40 000
Proceeds from capital (equity) contributed	20 000
Total cash inflows	110 000
Cash outflows	
Purchase of shop fittings	20 000
Lease payment	10 000
Payment for monthly lease expense	1 000
Payment for interest	250
Total cash outflows	31 250
Net cash flow	78 750
Beginning cash balance	—
Ending cash balance	**$ 78 750**

Note that we determined the profit in two lines above. With only one month of trading, this was simple enough to do as it is easy to remember the amounts and the revenue and expenses they represent. However, as time moves on and the business incurs more and varied income and expenses, it is best to determine the profit or loss as per the statement of profit or loss in illustrative example 7.12.

Statement of profit or loss

TERESA'S CARPETS AND RUGS
Statement of profit or loss
for the month ended 30 April 2019

Sales		$40 000
Less: Cost of sales		
Beginning inventory	$ —	
Add: Purchases	35 000	
Less: Ending inventory	(15 000)	20 000
Gross profit		20 000
Less: Other expenses		
Lease payment	1 000	
Depreciation	334	
Interest expense	250	
Lease amortisation	167	1 751
Profit		**$18 249**

Note the difference between the statement of cash flows and the statement of profit or loss. First, the statement of cash flows includes the total cash outlay for the lease and the shop fittings, while the statement of profit or loss only includes that portion of the outlay that relates to the month of April. Second, the statement of cash flows does not include any cash outlay for goods purchased as there has not yet been any payment for the goods, while the statement of profit or loss includes an expense for inventory as the cost of sales.

Let's now look at another month of trading. On 2 May, Teresa bought another $50 000 worth of inventory on credit and paid the account owing from her previous inventory purchases. She decided to spend some money on advertising to try to boost her business's name in the area. This marketing cost $5000. Teresa paid for this in cash. Throughout May, Teresa sold $55 000 worth of rugs for $100 000 ($80 000 for cash and $20 000 on credit).

Teresa's statement of profit or loss and statement of cash flows for May 2019 and statement of financial position as at 31 May 2019 are shown in illustrative examples 7.13, 7.14 and 7.15 respectively.

Again note the differences in flows between the statement of profit or loss and the statement of cash flows: the statement of profit or loss reports the flows of income and expenses, while the statement of cash flows reports the flows of cash.

ILLUSTRATIVE EXAMPLE 7.13

Statement of profit or loss

TERESA'S CARPETS AND RUGS Statement of profit or loss for the month ended 31 May 2019		
Sales		$100 000
Less: Cost of sales		
Beginning inventory	$15 000	
Add: Purchases	50 000	
Less: Ending inventory	(10 000)	55 000
Gross profit		45 000
Less: Other expenses		
Marketing	5 000	
Lease payment	1 000	
Depreciation	334	
Interest expense	250	
Lease amortisation	167	6 751
Profit		**$ 38 249**

ILLUSTRATIVE EXAMPLE 7.14

Statement of cash flows

TERESA'S CARPETS AND RUGS Statement of cash flows for the month ended 31 May 2019	
Cash inflows	
Proceeds from sales	$ 80 000
Total cash inflows	80 000
Cash outflows	
Payment to suppliers for rugs and carpets	35 000
Payment for marketing	5 000
Payment for monthly lease expense	1 000
Payment for interest	250
Total cash outflows	41 250
Net cash flow	38 750
Beginning cash balance	78 750
Ending cash balance	**$117 500**

Statement of financial position

TERESA'S CARPETS AND RUGS
Statement of financial position
as at 31 May 2019

ASSETS			LIABILITIES	
Current			Current	
Cash		$117 500	Accounts payable	$ 50 000
Accounts receivable		20 000	Non-current	
Inventory		10 000	Loan	50 000
Non-current				
Shop fittings	$20 000			
Less: Accumulated depreciation	668	19 332		
			EQUITY	
Lease prepayment	10 000		Capital contributed	20 000
Less: Accumulated amortisation	334	9 666	Retained earnings	56 498*
		$176 498		$176 498

*Retained earnings comprise the profit for April 2019 ($18 249) plus the profit for May 2019 ($38 249).

Note that, to be accurate, we should split the loan into its current and non-current components. The first $5000 is payable by the end of the year so should be listed as current, with the remaining $45 000 listed as non-current. This gives the user more information about when the loan is payable.

In the above example, we presented the cash flows in the statement of cash flows under two headings: **cash inflows** and **cash outflows**. In practice, it would be cumbersome to present every individual cash inflow and outflow as we have done above. To ensure that the statement of cash flows does not become too lengthy, generally the cash inflows and outflows are grouped into activities: operating activities, investing activities and financing activities. Grouping the cash flows in this way means that we can easily differentiate the cash flows from normal operations from the cash flows associated with investment and the cash flows associated with financing the business. Teresa's statement of cash flows for the months of April and May is presented in this grouped format in illustrative example 7.16 to show the various categories of cash flows and the activities they relate to.

Statement of cash flows

TERESA'S CARPETS AND RUGS
Statement of cash flows
for the period April–May 2019

Cash from operating activities	
Receipts from customers ($40 000 + $80 000)	$120 000
Payments to suppliers and employees ($35 000 + $2000 + $5000)	(42 000)
Dividends received	–
Interest received	–
Interest paid	(500)
Income taxes paid	–
Net cash from operating activities	77 500
Cash from investing activities	
Payments for lease rights and property, plant and equipment ($10 000 + $20 000)	(30 000)
Proceeds from sale of property, plant and equipment	–
Net cash from investing activities	(30 000)

Cash from financing activities	
Proceeds from capital contribution	20 000
Proceeds from borrowings	50 000
Repayment of borrowings	–
Distributions paid	–
Net cash from financing activities	70 000
Net increase/decrease in cash for the year	117 500
Cash at the beginning of the period	–
Cash at the end of the period	**$ 117 500**

Compare the presentation format of the statement of cash flows in illustrative example 7.16 with the format we used earlier. The cash flows are now separated into cash flows relating to operating, investing and financing activities. Operating activities relate to the normal activities of the entity. For Teresa's Carpets and Rugs this relates to the sales of merchandise, the payment for supplies and normal running expenses such as interest payments, lease costs and marketing expenses. Investing activities relate to the investments in non-current assets that will help generate positive cash flows in the future. For Teresa, this is the shop fittings and the right to lease the shop for five years. Financing activities relate to how the entity is structuring itself in relation to debt and equity. Teresa financed the business by injecting $20 000 of her own money into the business and borrowing $50 000. The statement of cash flows shows that the business is generating good cash from operations and so will probably need little debt finance in the future. However, if Teresa were to expand the business, the good cash flow from operations could be used to expand or to pay for higher interest costs if she did decide to borrow more funds.

Throughout the case study, you should note the relationship between items in the statement of cash flows and in the statement of profit or loss and in the statement of financial position. The items in the cash flows from the operating activities section can be compared to the income and expense items in the statement of profit or loss and in turn to the current assets and liabilities in the statement of financial position. For example, the cash at the end of the period should correspond to the cash appearing in the statement of financial position. The items in the cash flows from investing activities can be compared to the non-current assets in the statement of financial position, and the items in the cash flows from financing activities can be compared to the non-current liabilities and equity in the statement of financial position. This is summarised in table 7.1.

TABLE 7.1	Relationships between items in the statement of cash flows, statement of profit or loss and statement of financial position
Cash from operating activities	Revenue and expenses in the statement of profit or loss Current assets and liabilities in the statement of financial position
Cash from investing activities	Non-current assets in the statement of financial position
Cash from financing activities	Non-current liabilities and equity in the statement of financial position

VALUE TO BUSINESS

- The management of cash flow is critical for business success.
- The statement of cash flows presents all the cash inflows and outflows of an entity over a period of time.
- The statement of cash flows is prepared on a cash basis, whereas the statement of profit or loss and the statement of financial position are prepared on an accrual basis.
- The purpose of the statement of cash flows is to provide users with information about the movements of cash flows, and the increase or decrease in cash over a period, to help ascertain an entity's ability to generate funds and meet financial commitments.
- The statement of cash flows is one of the financial statements included in the general purpose financial statements (GPFS) of an entity.

7.2 Format of the statement of cash flows

LEARNING OBJECTIVE 7.2 Outline the format and the classification of cash flows in the statement of cash flows.

For the purposes of the preparation and interpretation of the statement of cash flows, **cash** refers to cash and cash equivalents. The definition of cash includes **cash on hand** and demand deposits (such as bank deposits). **Cash equivalents** are highly liquid investments and short-term borrowings that are subject to an insignificant risk of change in value. Examples of these are investments with three months or less to maturity and bank overdraft facilities repayable on demand. The movement of cash and cash equivalents resulting from transactions with external parties that fall into the definition of 'cash' is included in the statement of cash flows.

Like the statement of profit or loss and the statement of financial position, the classification, presentation and format of the statement of cash flows are governed by accounting standards. As outlined above, the statement of cash flows reports: the cash on hand at the start of the reporting period; the cash inflows, outflows and net cash flow for the reporting period; and the cash balance at the end of the reporting period. The statement of cash flows is classified into three main sections: operating activities, investing activities and financing activities.

The statement of cash flows for JB Hi-Fi Ltd in figure 7.2 shows the types of activities classified as operating, investing and financing. Figure 7.2 also presents note 16 from the JB Hi-Fi Ltd 2018 financial statements, which shows the reconciliation of the cash flow from operating activities with the profit. Let's discuss each of these sections in turn.

FIGURE 7.2 | JB Hi-Fi Ltd's statement of cash flows and reconciliation net cash inflow (outflow) from operating activities to profit (loss)

JB HI-FI LTD
Statement of cash flows
for the financial year ended 30 June 2018

	Notes	Consolidated 2018 $m	Consolidated 2017 $m
Cash flows from operating activities			
Receipts from customers		7 551.9	6 205.5
Payments to suppliers and employees		(7 130.5)	(5 908.8)
Interest received		0.5	1.7
Interest and other finance costs paid		(15.0)	(9.3)
Income taxes paid		(114.8)	(98.5)
Net cash inflow from operating activities	16	292.1	190.6
Cash flows from investing activities			
Payment for business combination, net of cash acquired	25	—	(836.6)
Payments for plant and equipment	10	(54.4)	(49.1)
Proceeds from sale of plant and equipment		(0.4)	0.2
Net cash (outflow) from investing activities		(54.0)	(885.5)
Cash flows from financing activities			
Proceeds from issues of shares	18	3.0	395.9
(Repayment)/proceeds of borrowings		(89.7)	450.0
Payments for debt issue costs		(0.8)	(1.7)
Share issue costs		—	(9.2)
Dividends paid to Owners of the Company	4	(151.6)	(119.1)
Net cash (outflow) inflow from financing activities		(239.1)	715.9
Net (decrease) increase in cash and cash equivalents		(1.0)	21.0
Cash and cash equivalents at the beginning of the financial year		72.8	51.9
Effects of exchange rate changes on cash and cash equivalents		0.2	(0.1)
Cash and cash equivalents at end of year		**72.0**	**72.8**
16 Notes to the cash flow statement			
Reconciliation of net cash inflow from operating activities to profit			
Profit for the year		233.2	172.4
Depreciation and amortisation		60.4	53.9

Impairment of plant and equipment			0.7	1.1
Impairment of goodwill			—	14.7
Non-cash employee benefits expense — share-based payments			7.8	5.3
Net loss on disposal of non-current assets			2.5	4.5
Fair value adjustment to derivatives			1.9	(1.1)
Change in operating assets and liabilities net of effects from acquisition of businesses:				
(Increase) decrease in inventories			(33.0)	(56.3)
(Increase) decrease in current receivables			(10.7)	3.0
(Increase) decrease in other current assets			(0.4)	(3.0)
(Decrease) increase in deferred tax liabilities			(10.4)	(8.5)
(Decrease) increase in current payables			22.4	(14.7)
(Decrease) increase in current provisions			7.3	4.2
(Decrease) increase in other current liabilities			(0.7)	1.4
(Decrease) increase in deferred revenue			12.8	15.0
(Decrease) increase in non-current provisions			0.7	(0.2)
(Decrease) increase in other non-current liabilities			0.7	2.2
(Decrease) increase in current tax liabilities			(3.1)	(3.3)
Net cash inflow from operating activities			**292.1**	**190.6**

Source: JB Hi-Fi Ltd 2018, pp. 58, 75.

Operating activities

Operating activities are those activities that relate to the provision of goods and services, and other activities that are neither investing nor financing activities. These activities relate to the normal activities of the entity. Examples of cash inflows from operating activities are the cash sale of goods or services, cash received from customers and the receipt of interest or dividends. Examples of cash outflows from operating activities are payments to suppliers, the payment of salaries and wages, and the payment of tax and interest.

Before a closer examination of each component is undertaken, it is important to remember that entities will normally collect and record information regarding their business transactions based on the accrual method of accounting. As explained in the statement of profit or loss and statement of changes in equity chapter, the reasons for this generally relate to the appropriate recognition of all transactions affecting income, expenses, assets, liabilities and equity for a given period. Recording transactions in this way is necessary for the preparation of the statement of profit or loss and the statement of financial position. Given that the statement of cash flows is concerned with when receipts and payments are made, and not with the appropriate recognition of income and expense transactions, some adjustments need to be made to the information collected. For example, the recording of a sale does not necessarily correspond to when a receipt is received. This is because a sale may be made on credit, with the payment received a month or more later. Illustrative example 7.1 shows how each transaction affects the profit and cash position differently. Therefore, a sale may increase profit (in the statement of profit or loss) but, if the amount owing is not collected, it will have no effect on the cash position (in the statement of cash flows).

Examine the cash flows from operating activities for JB Hi-Fi Ltd as presented in figure 7.2. The statement shows that JB Hi-Fi Ltd had a positive net cash flow from operating activities of $292.1 million. Compare this figure to the profit figure in JB Hi-Fi Ltd's statement of profit or loss (presented in the statement of profit or loss and statement of changes in equity chapter): the profit is $233.2 million. So, the profit is lower than the cash flow from operating activities. Is this normal? Yes, normally profit would be lower than cash from operating activities as the profit includes non-cash deductions such as depreciation and amortisation.

The net cash flow from operating activities is an important measure to gauge an entity's ability to generate cash, to meet its obligations, to continue as a going concern and to expand. It represents the cash flow from normal business operations. If an entity has negative cash flows from operations, it may be struggling to meet its financing and investing obligations or to attract new investment and finance. In the long term, an entity cannot rely solely on finance and investing activities to maintain cash levels. Few people would want to invest in or finance an entity that cannot generate enough funds through its normal activities to meet interest or dividend payments.

Investing activities

Investing activities are those activities that relate to the acquisition and/or disposal of non-current assets (including property, plant and equipment (PPE) and other productive assets), as well as investments (such as securities) not falling within the definition of cash. This section of the statement of cash flows usually identifies the investment decisions of an entity that are reflected in the non-current asset section of the statement of financial position. These activities are generally associated with the change in non-current assets; that is, the cash paid for non-current assets and that received from the sale of non-current assets. Ideally, investments in the non-current assets will positively increase the cash flow in forthcoming years. Examples of cash inflows are the sale of PPE, the sale of shares and the collection of loans from other entities. Examples of cash outflows are the purchase of PPE, the purchase of shares and the lending of money to other entities.

The items under this classification allow a user to analyse an entity's future direction by studying the major asset acquisitions and disposals. Remember, the entity must invest in order to generate future income and cash flows. As an investor in an entity, you would probably prefer that the entity invest in assets that will at least maintain current operations. If the entity has a desire to grow, you would expect that the net cash flow from investing activity would be negative.

The investing activities shown in the 2018 JB Hi-Fi Ltd statement of cash flows are presented in figure 7.2. In 2018, the total cash outflow for investment was $54 million. The 2017 comparative figure shows that the total cash outflow for investment was $885.5 million. The huge difference in investment activity across the two periods is due to the company's acquisition of The Good Guys in 2017. The negative cash outflow for investment activities is a good indicator that JB Hi-Fi Ltd is at least maintaining current operations. It is difficult to gauge the split in investment spend between maintaining existing operations and new investment. Generally, reading through the annual report will help to ascertain any growth plans. JB Hi-Fi Ltd reports an increase to 311 stores, following the increase of eight stores in 2018, so modest growth is being pursued.

As a user of the financial statements, you must make a personal decision as to whether this is good or bad. On the one hand, growth in the number of stores should lead to growth in sales and consequently more profit and more cash from operations. If you were an investor, this would increase the value of your investment and/or lead to greater dividends. On the other hand, growing more stores means a greater future maintenance bill. This could be a drain on the company cash and siphon off money that could go towards paying down debt and increasing dividends. It is a personal opinion that each investor would reach based on their view of the world economic environment, the retail trends of online versus bricks-and-mortar shopping and a comparison of profit and cash flow in relation to the number of store openings over the last few years.

Financing activities

Financing activities are those activities that change the size and/or composition of the financial structure of an entity (including equity) and borrowings not falling within the definition of cash. These activities are generally associated with changes in non-current liabilities and equity (i.e. the cash received from the issue of shares or debt, less the cash paid to shareholders or to repay debt). Again, these cash flows can be traced back to the statement of financial position. Examples of cash inflows from financing activities are cash received from the issue of the entity's own shares and cash from borrowings. Examples of cash outflows from financing activities are dividends paid to shareholders, the repurchase of shares from shareholders and the repayment of borrowings.

The financing activities shown in the 2018 JB Hi-Fi Ltd statement of cash flows are presented in figure 7.2. The statement shows a negative net cash flow from financing activities in 2018. The major outflows are the payment of dividends of $151.6 million and the repayment of borrowings of $89.7 million. The largest inflow is the proceeds from the issue of equity securities of $3 million. However, this amount is minor when compared to the payment of debt and dividends. In 2017, the company increased borrowings by $450 million. This large borrowing reflects the acquisition of The Good Guys. Now the focus appears to be on debt reduction. The reduction of debt has been a common theme across many businesses during the 2017–2018 period. This is in response to the world economic environment, in particular the slowing of major economies, the austerity measures of governments and the uncertainty of the wholesale debt market. It seems wise and prudent management that JB Hi-Fi Ltd lowered its debt levels during this time. The dividend payout in 2018 was higher than it was in 2017. This is in line with the increase in profit and cash from operations.

JB Hi-Fi Ltd's outflow of funds for financing activities is not typical. It is typical for an entity to have a positive inflow of cash from financing activities, as generally entities borrow cash to fund expansion. This can be viewed as a healthy step towards growth. However, if over a long period of time borrowings are significant and the cash from operating activities is struggling to pay the interest costs, then this would indicate a solvency problem. As mentioned previously, the current economic environment is not the best condition under which to borrow heavily for quick expansion. It is forcing many companies to delay investment and refocus on their debt to equity structures. JB Hi-Fi Ltd borrowed heavily in 2017 for the purpose of acquiring The Good Guys and is now using its surplus cash from operations to reduce this debt. So, with the information presented in the JB Hi-Fi Ltd statement of cash flows and the equity and liability section of the statement of financial position, we can ascertain that the financial structure of the entity changed from 65 per cent debt and 35 per cent equity in 2017 to 62 per cent debt and 38 per cent equity in 2018, thus slightly decreasing the statement of financial position risk.

Reconciliation of cash from operating activities with operating profit

In the section above, we outlined that the cash from operating activities contained all the cash flows relating to the operations for the entity. This can be compared to the statement of profit or loss, as the transactions affecting the statement of profit or loss reflect the cash flows relating to the operations of the entity. Why aren't these two figures the same? Recall from the previous chapter that the statement of profit or loss is prepared based on accrual accounting, while the statement of cash flows is prepared on a cash basis. Comparing the cash flow from operating activities to the profit or loss in the statement of profit or loss produces a reconciliation of these two figures showing the differences in accrual transactions and cash flow. For example, depreciation is an expense but not a cash flow, and a sale could be for cash or credit. The reconciliation of cash from operating activities with the profit from the statement of profit or loss is presented in order to reinforce the link between the cash received from operating activities and the profit or loss reported in the statement of profit or loss. As discussed in previous two chapters, operating accounts in the statement of financial position are related to the revenues and expenses in the statement of profit or loss. Sales, cost of sales and expenses in the statement of profit or loss are directly linked to accounts such as accounts payable, accounts receivable, inventory, expense prepayments and accruals in the statement of financial position. These accounts in the statement of financial position are necessary because of accrual accounting. For example, if a sale is made on credit (i.e. no cash flow), then a record in the accounts receivable account is made. The reconciliation picks up changes in these operating accounts from one year to the next. By doing so, it can help users to quickly ascertain the changes in operating accounts brought about by the use of the accrual basis versus the cash basis of accounting. Sometimes these accounts are referred to as *working capital* as they represent the normal capital required to run the business. Examining the working capital accounts shows whether the profit and flows of cash are being utilised wisely within the entity's normal operations.

The reconciliation usually starts with the profit or loss after tax, as per the statement of profit or loss, and ends with the cash from operating activities. To reconcile the two amounts, it is necessary to think about the differences between the statement of profit or loss and the cash from operating activities.

The reconciliation must be disclosed in the financial statements as a note to the accounts. The reconciliation of profit to net cash flows provided by operating activities for JB Hi-Fi Ltd in 2018 was disclosed as note 16(a) in its 2018 financial statements. An inspection of the JB Hi-Fi Ltd reconciliation in figure 7.2 firstly presents the profit for 2018 of $233.2 million. This figure is taken from the statement of profit or loss. Adjustments are then made to allow for non-cash items that were contained in the profit (e.g. depreciation expense). Further adjustments need to be made relating to current assets and liabilities (e.g. accounts receivable (debtors) and accounts payable (creditors)). This is due to the accrual recording system explained previously. For example, inspection of the 2018 JB Hi-Fi Ltd statement of financial position (see the statement of financial position chapter) and the reconciliation in figure 7.2 shows that the company had an increase in inventory for the year. Assuming that there were no price increases, this means that it bought more inventory than it sold. Its accounts receivable balance increased, which means that there were more sales made on credit in the period relative to the cash received from accounts receivable, thus decreasing cash received from sales. The increase in 'other assets' means that JB Hi-Fi Ltd has increased these assets (i.e. prepayments), thus saving cash.

The 2018 reconciliation also shows that JB Hi-Fi Ltd had an increase in accounts payable. Therefore, cash paid to suppliers for the period was lower than the purchases appearing in the statement of profit or loss. The provisions also increased. This means that JB Hi-Fi Ltd has paid out less in provision-related expenses than expenses incurred for the period.

Changes in current assets and liabilities are expected, as balances fluctuate throughout the year. These changes should be considered in light of other information in the report. For example, examining the reconciliation of JB Hi-Fi Ltd shows an increase in inventories. This would be expected given the increase in the number of stores and in online sales.

A summary of the reconciliation of profit to net cash flows from operating activities is shown in figure 7.3.

FIGURE 7.3 | Summary of reconciliation adjustments

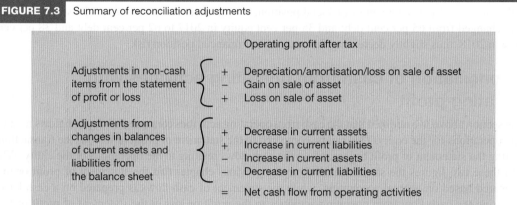

Presentation of the statement of cash flows

The statement of cash flows can be completed by bringing together all the sections and calculating the net increase or decrease in cash for the reporting period and ending cash balance for the year. Refer back to the 2018 JB Hi-Fi Ltd statement of cash flows in figure 7.2. Observe how the entity has classified its cash flows and how it has presented the total net cash flows for the period, as well as the opening and closing cash balances.

Overall, the JB Hi-Fi Ltd statement of cash flows shows that the net cash flows from operating activities of $292.1 million almost covered the investing activities of $54 million and the financing activities of $239.1 million. The shortfall of $1 million decreased cash. Note that cash flows from financing activities would be positive at times, to help pay for investment activity. In summary, the statement of cash flows contains:

- net cash flows from operating activities
- net cash flows from investing activities
- net cash flows from financing activities
- total net cash flow (increase or decrease in cash held for the period)
- the beginning cash balance
- the ending cash balance
- comparative figures from the previous year.

The ending cash balance should equate with the cash amount appearing in the statement of financial position. The JB Hi-Fi Ltd statement of financial position reports an asset of cash and cash equivalents of $72 million, which reconciles with the ending cash balance in the statement of cash flows.

To help your understanding of the purpose, use and interpretation of the statement of cash flows, it is worthwhile appreciating how a statement of cash flows is prepared. A comprehensive example illustrating this process is presented next.

7.3 Preparing the statement of cash flows

LEARNING OBJECTIVE 7.3 Produce a statement of cash flows using the direct method and a reconciliation using the indirect method.

The statement of cash flows can be prepared by analysing the cash receipts and payments records (as was done in the Teresa's Carpets and Rugs example presented earlier) or by evaluating the statement of profit or loss and statement of financial position. For the purposes of this chapter, the latter method will be utilised.

Normally, an entity will collect information regarding its business transactions based on the accrual method of accounting. The reasons for this have been explained in previous chapters and generally relate to the appropriate recognition of all transactions affecting income, expenses, assets, liabilities and equity for a given period. Recording transactions in this way helps in the preparation of the statement of profit or loss and the statement of financial position. Given that the statement of cash flows is concerned with when receipts and payments are made, and not with the recognition of income and expense transactions, there will need to be some adjustments made to the information collected. For example, the recording of a sale does not necessarily correspond to when cash is received. This is because the sale may be made on credit, with the payment due a month later. The example in figure 7.2 illustrated that transactions had different effects on the profit and cash position.

Therefore, in preparing the statement of cash flows there needs to be a conversion from the accrual basis to the cash basis. This conversion can be approached in one of two ways. These are: (1) the direct method; and (2) the indirect method. The **direct method** discloses major classes of gross cash receipts and gross cash payments. The **indirect method** adjusts profit or loss for the effects of transactions of a non-cash nature and deferrals or accruals of operating revenue and expenses. The International Financial Reporting Standards (IFRS), Australian Accounting Standards and New Zealand Accounting Standards give an entity a choice between presenting cash flows from operating activities using either the direct or indirect methods. In Australia and New Zealand, entities are encouraged to use the direct method.

To illustrate the preparation of the statement of cash flows (using the direct method) and the reconciliation (using the indirect method) we will use the example of Coconut Plantations Pty Ltd, a manufacturer of coconut-based products that commenced business in September 2019. Illustrative example 7.17 presents the 2020 statement of profit or loss and the 2019 and 2020 statements of financial position for Coconut Plantations Pty Ltd. Details relating to the nature of the operating expenses in the statement of profit or loss below are given in self-evaluation activity 6.2 in the previous chapter and reproduced in illustrative example 7.17.

ILLUSTRATIVE EXAMPLE 7.17

Coconut Plantations Pty Ltd statement of profit or loss and statement of financial position

COCONUT PLANTATIONS PTY LTD
Statement of profit or loss
for the year ended 31 December 2020

Income			
Sales			$1 550 000
Less: Cost of sales			
Inventory — direct materials 1 January 2020	$ 5 000		
Plus: Purchases of direct materials	650 000		
Inventory — direct materials 31 December 2020	15 000		
Direct materials used		$ 640 000	
Direct labour		245 000	
Manufacturing overhead		122 500	
		1 007 500	
Inventory — finished goods 1 January 2020		55 000	
Inventory — finished goods 31 December 2020		160 000	902 500
Gross profit			647 500
Other income (interest received)			1 000
Operating expenses			
Warehouse		48 000	
Distribution		18 000	
Sales and marketing		131 000	
Administrative		109 500	
Finance		14 000	320 500
Profit before income tax			**328 000**
Income tax expense			98 400
Profit			**$ 229 600**

COCONUT PLANTATIONS PTY LTD
Statement of profit or loss
for the year ended 31 December 2020

Details of nature of operating expenses included earlier			
Administrative salaries			$ 90 000
Depreciation office equipment			5 000
Telephone expense			5 000
Advertising expense			59 000
Warehouse insurance expense			15 000
Warehouse rates expense			21 000
Utilities expense			9 500
Depreciation of warehouse			12 000
Sales salaries			72 000
Interest expense			14 000
Delivery costs and postage			18 000
Total			**$320 500**

COCONUT PLANTATIONS PTY LTD
Statement of changes in retained profits
for year ended 31 December 2020

Contributed equity	
Initial issue of shares	$200 000
Retained earnings	
Balance 1 January 2020	$ 90 210
Profit for the year ended 31 December 2020	229 600
Less: Dividend for the year	130 000
Retained earnings at 31 December 2020	**$189 810**

COCONUT PLANTATIONS PTY LTD
Statement of financial position
as at 31 December 2019

Current assets		
Cash on hand	$ 51 557	
Accounts receivable	23 110	
Inventories (finished goods and raw materials)	60 000	
Prepayments	1 000	$135 667
Non-current assets		
Building	200 000	
Less: Accumulated depreciation	0	200 000
Equipment	40 000	
Less: Accumulated depreciation	1 667	38 333
Total assets		374 000
Current liabilities		
Accounts payable	3 300	
Accrued expenses	700	
Dividend payable	14 790	
Income tax payable	45 000	63 790
Non-current liabilities		
Bank loan — due 2022		20 000
Total liabilities		83 790
Net assets		**$290 210**
Shareholders' equity		
Share capital		$200 000
Retained earnings		90 210
Total equity		**$290 210**

COCONUT PLANTATIONS PTY LTD
Statement of financial position
as at 31 December 2020

Current assets		
Cash on hand	$145 367	
Accounts receivable	93 010	
Inventories (finished goods and raw materials)	175 000	
Prepayments	4 500	$417 877
Non-current assets		
Building and manufacturing equipment	360 000	
Less: Accumulated depreciation	12 000	348 000
Office equipment	40 000	
Less: Accumulated depreciation	6 667	33 333
Total assets		799 210
Current liabilities		
Accounts payable	42 500	
Accrued expenses	7 500	
Dividend payable	130 000	
Income tax payable	98 400	278 400
Non-current liabilities		
Bank loan		131 000
Total liabilities		409 400
Net assets		**$ 389 810**
Shareholders' equity		
Share capital		$200 000
Retained earnings		189 810
Total equity		**$ 389 810**

Note that, in addition to the above, the notes from the financial statements reveal that extensions were made to the manufacturing facility that cost $100 000 and new manufacturing equipment was acquired at a cost of $60 000. There were no disposals of PPE. There were no new issues of shares. A new loan of $140 000 was taken out and the existing loan of $20 000 was repaid. Retained earnings increased from $90 210 to $189 810 as a result of profit of $229 600 less dividends of $130 000.

To complete the statement of cash flows using the direct method and the reconciliation using the indirect method it is necessary to work through each classification activity (operating, financing and investing).

Step 1. Determine the cash flows from operating activities

Recall that the cash flows from operating activities, as illustrated in figure 7.2, include:
- receipts from customers
- payments to suppliers and employees
- dividends received
- interest and bill discounts received
- interest and other costs of finance paid
- income taxes paid.

Using the listed cash flows as a guide, work through each in turn using the information from the other financial statements. Receipts from customers and payments to suppliers and employees must be calculated. The other components can be read directly from the financial statements.

Step 1a. Calculate the receipts from customers

The receipts from customers are related to the sales in the statement of profit or loss and the accounts receivable in the statement of financial position. The opening balance of the accounts receivable represents what was owed by customers at the beginning of the year and the closing balance represents what was owed by customers at the end of the year. The sales state the customer activity for the current year. In our example:

Opening balance accounts receivable	$ 23 110
+ Sales for the current year	1 550 000
= Total amount that could be received from customers	1 573 110
− Closing balance accounts receivable	(93 010)
= **Cash received from customers**	**$1 480 100**

Cash from customers = Opening accounts receivable + Sales − Closing accounts receivable

▶

Step 1b. Calculate payments to suppliers and employees

Payments to suppliers can take two forms: payments to inventory suppliers and payments to other suppliers (e.g. for electricity, telephone, rent). Payments to employees are for wages. Accounts that relate to suppliers and employees include:

- inventory purchases from the statement of profit or loss and accounts payable from the statement of financial position
- operating expenses from the statement of profit or loss and prepaid expenses and accrued expenses from the statement of financial position.

Let's deal with each of these in turn.

The same logic used for step 1a can be applied to payments to suppliers. Firstly, payments to suppliers for inventory are related to the beginning and closing balances of accounts payable in the statement of financial position and the inventory purchases in the statement of profit or loss. In our example:

Opening balance accounts payable	$ 3 300
+ Inventory purchases	650 000
= Total amount that could be paid	653 300
– Closing balance accounts payable	(42 500)
= Cash paid to inventory suppliers	**$610 800**

Cash paid to suppliers = Opening accounts payable + Purchases – Closing accounts payable

Other payments to suppliers are related to other expenses in the statement of profit or loss and accrued and prepaid expenses in the statement of financial position. Accrued expenses are those expenses that are due to be paid but have not been paid yet (such as rates owing). Prepaid expenses are those expenses that have been paid for in advance (such as prepaid insurance). This is a little more complicated than calculating payments for inventory, as we are dealing with two accounts from the statement of financial position. Using logic you can deduce that:

1. if the balance of prepayments increases, then we have paid more for expenses, thus decreasing cash flow
2. if the balance of accruals increases, then we have a greater amount owing and have therefore paid less, thus increasing cash flow.

For our example:

Other expenses (from the statement of profit or loss, excluding interest, payments to employees, depreciation)		
Manufacturing overhead		$122 500
Warehouse		36 000
Distribution		18 000
Sales and marketing		59 000
Administrative		14 500
		250 000
Other expenses (excluding depreciation)		
Prepayments (from the statement of financial position):		
Opening balance prepaid expenses	$1 000	
Closing balance prepaid expenses	4 500	
+ Increase (– decrease) in prepayments		3 500
Accruals (from the statement of financial position):		
Opening balance accruals	700	
Closing balance accruals	7 500	
+ Decrease (– increase) in accruals		(6 800)
= Cash paid to other suppliers		**$246 700**

Cash paid to other suppliers = Other expenses + / – Increase (decrease)
in prepayments + / – Decrease (increase) in accruals

Remember that depreciation is not a cash item. So if other expenses contains an amount for depreciation (as in our example), this will need to be subtracted prior to the adjustment for prepayments and accruals.

Payments to inventory suppliers	$ 610 800
Payments for other expenses	246 700
Payments to employees ($245 000 + $72 000 + $90 000)	407 000
Total	**$1 264 500**

Step 1c. Calculate other payments for expenses and receipts for income

There are other cash flow items — in addition to receipts from customers and payments to suppliers and employees — that need to be included in operating activities. Other outflows include interest paid and income tax, and inflows include dividends and interest received. Although interest paid, and interest and dividends received, are normally classified as operating cash flows, there may be instances where they are classified as financing or investing cash flows.

In our example:

- there were borrowing costs in the form of interest paid of $14 000
- there was income tax payable in 2019 of $45 000, which would be paid in 2020 (generally income tax paid lags one year behind when it is payable)
- there were no dividends received
- there was no interest received and there were no bill discounts.

Putting steps 1a to 1c together, the net cash flows from operating activities are as follows.

Cash flows from operating activities	
Receipts from customers	$1 480 100
Payments to suppliers and employers	(1 264 500)
Dividends and interest received	1 000
Interest paid	(14 000)
Income taxes paid	(45 000)
Net cash from operating activities	**$ 157 600**

Step 2. Determine the cash flows from investing activities

Recall that the cash flows from investing activities mainly deal with changes in non-current assets in the statement of financial position. As illustrated in figure 7.2, cash flows from investing activities include:

- proceeds from repayment of related party loans
- payments for PPE
- proceeds from sale of PPE
- payments for businesses.

Examining the non-current assets in the statement of financial position and the note in our example reveals that there was an extension to the manufacturing facility that cost $100 000 and an acquisition of manufacturing equipment that cost $60 000. No businesses were acquired, nor were any proceeds from related party loans obtained. The cash flows from investing activities are therefore as follows.

Cash flows from investing activities	
Payments for property, plant and equipment	$(160 000)
Proceeds from sale of property, plant and equipment	—
Net cash from investing activities	**$(160 000)**

Step 3. Determine the cash flow from financing activities

Recall that the cash flows from financing activities mainly deal with changes in non-current liabilities and equity in the statement of financial position. As illustrated in figure 7.2, cash flows from financing activities include:

- proceeds from issue of equity securities (shares)
- proceeds from borrowings
- repayment of borrowings
- dividends paid.

Examining the non-current liabilities and equity in the statement of financial position in our example should help to decipher changes in the financial structure of Coconut Plantations Pty Ltd. For our example the following applies.

1. Comparing the loan payable under non-current liabilities shows there was an increase of $111 000. The accounting standard requires net amounts, not gross amounts, to be presented. The note reveals that a new loan of $140 000 was taken out and the existing loan of $20 000 was repaid. The difference in the balance means that $9000 of the new loan was also repaid.
2. The dividend payable at 31 December 2019 for $14 790 would have been paid during 2020.

The cash flows from financing activities are therefore as follows.

Cash flows from financing activities	
Proceeds from borrowings	$140 000
Repayment of borrowings	(29 000)
Dividend paid	(14 790)
Net cash from financing activities	**$ 96 210**

Step 4. Calculate the net cash flow and the ending cash balance for the year (the direct method)

The statement of cash flows can be completed by bringing together the sections compiled above and calculating the net cash flow and ending cash balance for the year. The beginning cash balance can be extracted from the statement of financial position. The ending cash balance calculated should equate with the ending cash balance in the statement of financial position.

COCONUT PLANTATIONS PTY LTD Statement of cash flows for the year ended 31 December 2020	
Cash flows from operating activities	
Receipts from customers	$1 480 100
Payments to suppliers and employees	(1 264 500)
Dividends received	—
Interest received	1 000
Interest paid	(14 000)
Income taxes paid	(45 000)
Net cash from operating activities	157 600
Cash flows from investing activities	
Payments for property, plant and equipment	(160 000)
Proceeds from sale of property, plant and equipment	—
Net cash from investing activities	(160 000)
Cash flows from financing activities	
Proceeds from borrowings	140 000
Repayment of borrowings	29 000
Distributions paid	(14 790)
Net cash from financing activities	96 210
Net increase (decrease) in cash held	93 810
Cash at beginning of the reporting period	51 557
Cash at the end of the reporting period	**$ 145 367**

Step 5. Reconcile cash from operating activities with operating profit (the indirect method)

The statement of cash flows presented in step 4 was prepared and presented using the direct method. The IFRS also requires the indirect method to be used to present a reconciliation of the cash flows from operating activities with the profit in the statement of profit or loss. This is normally presented as a note to the statement of cash flows. Generally, the reconciliation starts with the profit or loss after tax as per the statement of profit or loss and ends with the cash from operating activities. To reconcile the two amounts, it is necessary to think about the differences between them. In determining the cash flows from operating activities in step 1 above, we used the operating expenses in the statement of profit or loss and the current assets and liabilities in the statement of financial position (accounts receivable, accounts payable, inventory, prepaid expenses and accruals). So it would be these items that need to be considered in reconciling the cash from operating activities with the profit. The profit or loss would contain non-cash expenses such as depreciation and loss on sale of an asset, so these would need to be added back to the profit or loss. There would also be differences in non-cash current assets and liabilities such as inventory, accounts receivable and payable, and prepayments and accruals, as these are the items that were considered above when preparing the statement of cash flows. The form of the reconciliation will be:

$$\text{Profit or loss after tax} + \text{Non-cash expenses} + / - \text{Changes in non-current assets and liabilities}$$

For our example, the reconciliation would be as follows.

Profit after tax	$229 600
+ Depreciation	17 000
(**Increase**)/decrease in inventory	(115 000)
(Increase)/**decrease** in accounts receivable	(69 900)
(Increase)/**decrease** in prepaid expenses	(3 500)
Increase/(**decrease**) in accounts payable	39 200
Increase/(decrease) in tax payable	53 400
Increase/(decrease) in accruals	6 800
Net cash flow from operating activities	**$157 600**

Let's consider these items in turn.

The profit or loss would contain an adjustment for depreciation. Depreciation is a non-cash item and therefore does not form part of the statement of cash flows. It therefore needs to be added back into the profit.

An increase in a current asset such as inventory, accounts receivable or prepayments means a reduction in cash; that is, we would have had to spend more on them than we received over the year for there to be an increase. Coconut Plantations Pty Ltd had an increase in inventory for the year. This means that it bought more inventory than it sold. The increase in prepayments means it used up cash. The accounts receivable balance also increased, which means that fewer debts were collected from customers, reducing cash.

> Increase in current assets means a reduction in cash
>
> Decrease in current assets means an increase in cash

An increase in current liabilities such as accounts payable and accruals means that we have not paid as much over the period as we have expensed, thus increasing cash. Conversely, a decrease in current liabilities means that we have paid out more over the year than we have expensed and therefore a decrease in cash results. Coconut Plantations Pty Ltd had an increase in accounts payable, which means it conserved cash and increased its debt. The accruals increased, thus saving cash. The direction of changes in current assets and liabilities is consistent with a growing business.

> Increase in current liabilities means an increase in cash
>
> Decrease in current liabilities means a decrease in cash

Step 6. Complete notes to the statement of cash flows

The IFRS requires other explanatory notes to the statement of cash flows. These notes would generally cover items such as non-cash financing and investing activities, the disaggregated cash flows concerning acquisitions and disposals of entities, and a reconciliation of cash amounts shown in the statement of financial position and those shown in the statement of cash flows. These items are included as notes to the statement to ensure users have adequate information concerning the cash flows of the entity. They have not been prepared for our example but, as a potential user of financial statements, you should be aware that some notes are required to help in the evaluation of an entity.

Let's summarise the discussion above relating to the preparation of the statement of cash flows as follows.

- The preparation of the statement of cash flows requires the conversion of accrual accounts (statement of profit or loss and statement of financial position) to a cash basis.
- The statement of cash flows can be prepared using the direct method or the indirect method (reconciliation).
- A review of processes needed to convert the accrual basis to the cash basis under the direct method is:

> Cash from customers = Opening accounts receivable + Sales − Closing accounts receivable
>
> Cash paid suppliers = Opening accounts payable + Purchases − Closing accounts payable
>
> Cash paid to other suppliers = Other expenses + / − Increase (decrease)
> in prepayments + / − Decrease (increase) in accruals

- A review of processes needed to convert the accrual basis to the cash basis under the indirect method (reconciliation) is:

> Increase in current assets means a reduction in cash
> Decrease in current assets means an increase in cash
> Increase in current liabilities means an increase in cash
> Decrease in current liabilities means a decrease in cash

- The operating, investing and financing activities are linked to components in the statement of profit or loss and the statement of financial position. A summary of the common links is shown in table 7.2.

TABLE 7.2 Activity classification in the statement of cash flows

	Cash inflows	Cash outflows	Link to other statements
Operating activities	• Receipts from customers • Interest received • Dividends received	• Payments to suppliers and employees • Interest paid • Taxes paid	• Revenue and expense items in the statement of profit or loss and current assets and current liabilities in the statement of financial position

(continued)

TABLE 7.2 *(continued)*

	Cash inflows	Cash outflows	Link to other statements
Investing activities	• Sale of property, plant and equipment • Receipt of loan payments • Sale of other businesses	• Purchase of property, plant and equipment • Making loan payments • Purchase of other businesses	• Non-current assets in the statement of financial position
Financing activities	• Borrowing cash • Proceeds from issuing shares	• Repaying borrowed cash • Payments to acquire or redeem the entity's shares • Payment of dividends	• Non-current liabilities and equity in the statement of financial position

Using cash flows to evaluate loan applications

SITUATION You are a bank lending officer and are evaluating a loan application. The applicant has been in business for three years and is seeking to expand. Examine the figures below and make a recommendation to your manager.

	Year 1 $'000	Year 2 $'000	Year 3 $'000
Profit attributable to equity holders of the parent	56	75	120
Net cash (used in)/provided by operating activities	70	100	130
Net cash (used in)/provided by investing activities	(27)	(54)	(40)
Net cash (used in)/provided by financing activities	(40)	(40)	(40)

DECISION There is a profit and a positive cash flow each year over the three years. The cash flow from operations is greater than the profit and this is normal as there would be some non-cash items such as depreciation included in the profit figure. Over the three-year period funds have been invested into the business, presumably to help grow the business. The funds withdrawn from the business under financing activities point to a payment to the owners each year. The distributions back to the owners seem reasonable given the cash flow the business is generating. Certainly the withdrawal of funds plus the money invested into the business are less than the total cash flow provided by the operations each year. This would mean the business has a healthy cash balance. Based on the cash information provided, the loan could be recommended. It seems that the business is looking at growing at a greater rate than what can be achieved using its own generation of cash. Obviously, suitable loan limits and covenants would need to be considered.

- 'Cash' is defined as cash on hand and cash equivalents.
- The statement of cash flows classifies an entity's cash flows into operating, financing and investing activities.
- To prepare the statement of cash flows, adjustments need to be made to convert the accrual statements (statement of profit or loss and statement of financial position) to a cash basis.
- The direct method and the indirect method are two approaches that can be used to prepare and present the statement of cash flows.

In the past, the statement of profit or loss and the statement of financial position have taken centre stage when assessing future earnings. However, it is now becoming widely recognised in the investment community that the management of earnings can result in accounting manipulations in the statement of profit or loss. This heightened recognition has led to an increase in reliance on the statement of cash flows for extra information about the earnings potential of an entity. The comparison of profit or loss with the cash flow from operating activities can highlight how an entity is managing its working capital requirements.

The lending world is also showing interest in the statement of cash flows. It is argued that lenders can use the statement of cash flows to answer questions about the performance of an organisation's management or whether an organisation has generated or can generate sufficient cash. On the other hand, entities can manipulate items on the statement of cash flows just as easily as they can on the statement of profit or loss or statement of financial position to make performance appear more favourable.

7.4 Analysing the statement of cash flows

LEARNING OBJECTIVE 7.4 Evaluate an entity's performance using a statement of cash flows.

The purpose of preparing financial statements is to allow users to evaluate an entity's operations and financial performance. Understanding how the statements are prepared helps in the evaluation. The previous sections highlighted that the statement of cash flows helps to evaluate the cash generated by the operating activities in order to service the needs of the investing and financing activities.

For JB Hi-Fi Ltd, the following general observations for 2018 can be made from the statement of cash flows (see figure 7.2).
- Net cash flow from operating activities was $292.1 million, which was slightly higher than the profit of $233.2 million. Profit includes an amount for depreciation and amortisation so, as a general rule, the cash from operating activities should be higher.
- The reconciliation (which is produced in note 16(a) of the financial statements and reproduced in figure 7.2) reveals increases and decreases in current assets and current liabilities. This illustrates the heart of working capital management (the cycle of cash, inventory, accounts receivable and accounts payable). A build-up of inventory and delayed collection of debts mean that a company has to finance the increase in its working capital requirements. The level and management of cash in working capital are vital business factors. Many entities have failed from poor cash management rather than poor profitability. The reconciliation of profit to net cash from the operating activities of JB Hi-Fi Ltd shows a slight increase in receivables. This could indicate that the accounts receivable collection process has slackened; however, given that sales increased marginally, a slight increase would be expected. It is imperative that businesses keep a close eye on their accounts receivable balances. The reconciliation also shows an increase in the inventory balance between 2018 and 2017, although the increase is less than the increase of the previous year. Too much inventory can tie up cash unnecessarily. Given that JB Hi-Fi Ltd opened new stores and improved its online sales, it seems reasonable that inventory levels would increase. There is also a significant increase in accounts payable. A delay in settling accounts payable would have the effect of increasing cash from operating activities. In some instances, this could signal a company in distress that cannot pay its accounts payable. An inspection of the statement of financial position shows that the inventory is greater than the accounts payable. Comparing these two figures gives some insight into the entity's inventory management. If the balances are approximately equal, this may point to a self-funding inventory model. This means that the entity is trying to turn over inventory prior to having to pay suppliers. That is, it is selling inventory and collecting the cash from accounts receivable prior to paying suppliers for the cost of the inventory. This is great working capital management and, if inventory turnover is reasonable and it continues to work towards a self-funding inventory model, healthy future cash flows should result. Therefore, the inventory management, together with the reduction in borrowings (and consequently in interest payments), suggest that JB Hi-Fi Ltd is actively trying to manage its cash resources in this tough retail environment.
- Net cash flows from investing activities were $(54) million. This amount is significantly lower than in 2017 due to the acquisition of The Good Guys in 2017. Note that the investment in PPE was $(54.4) million, while the proceeds from The sale of PPE were $0.4 million. A judgement needs to be made about whether the investment in PPE is adequate to maintain existing operations or whether the investment will increase or decrease cash flows in the future.

- The major financing activities included repayment of borrowings of $(89.7) million and a dividend of $(151.6) million. The repayment of borrowings would decrease statement of financial position risk and relieve future cash flows of paying interest in future years. The payment of dividends is payment back to shareholders and thus increases the risk for accounts payable. However, most investors expect some return on their investment. In fact, a reduction in the dividend paid could signal to the investment market that there may be some financial trouble. Note that in 2017 there was a share buy-back. The share buy-back, according to the preliminary final report, is to stop the dilution of company shares through employee share options. Each year the company intends to buy back shares on the open market to appropriately cost and account for the employee salary arrangements.
- Overall, JB Hi-Fi Ltd seems to be in a healthy position. The GFC started in early 2008 and from all reports the retail sector was one of the hardest hit. However, the company shows good profit and good cash from operating activities despite the downturn in the economy. The cash from operating activities is helping the company to invest in PPE. The entity appears to be in a healthy cash position. However, its growth strategy needs to be carefully conducted as too much debt would weigh the company down. This would be risky in a weak retail economic environment.

How do you know how much cash is enough? The statement of cash flows for JB Hi-Fi Ltd shows cash on hand slightly decreasing from $72.8 million in 2017 to $72 million in 2018. From the statement of financial position, we can calculate that this cash amount represents about 7.6 per cent of net assets and 2.9 per cent of total assets in 2018 (2017: 8.5 per cent and 3.0 per cent for net assets and total assets respectively). The appropriate amount of cash to keep on hand depends on the type of business and the risk profile of management. Keeping too much cash means capital is tied up in low-return investments; however, sufficient cash must be available to provide flexibility during business downturns. Entities that operate in high-risk industries or are of a cyclic nature may prefer to have high cash reserves. Some business managers prefer to have limited reserves of cash and to manage the cash-flow cycle using short-term debt. Financing arrangements will be covered in more detail in the chapter about financing the business.

Keeping too much cash means capital is tied up in low-return investments; however, sufficient cash must be available to provide flexibility during business downturns.

Generally, an analysis of the statement of cash flows would include identification of cash-flow warning signals. These would include the following.

- *Cash received is less than cash paid.* Overall, the cash inflows should be greater than the cash outflows; otherwise there would be a depletion of cash on hand over time.
- *Operating outflows.* The cash flows from operating activities represent the cash flows from normal business operations. This is an important measure to gauge an entity's ability to generate cash, meet its obligations, carry on as a going concern and to expand. If the entity has negative cash flows from operations, it might have difficulty in meeting its finance and investing obligations.
- *Cash receipts from customers are less than cash payments to suppliers and employees.* This could indicate that insufficient cash is being generated from the entity's operations. Possible reasons for this situation include the entity underpricing its goods, having too few sales or not being paid by its customers. In any case, immediate action is warranted for the entity's long-term survival.
- *Net cash from operating activities is lower than profit after tax.* Profit includes non-cash items such as depreciation, so generally cash from operating activities should be higher.
- *Proceeds of share capital are used to finance operating activities.* Once again, this indicates that the entity might be having difficulty meeting its financial obligations.
- *Inflows from investing activities are inconsistent.* Generally, spending cash on investments (outflow) indicates healthy growth of the entity. It is these investments that will generate future cash flow. Inconsistent inflows from investing activities would mean that the entity is selling off major assets, indicating that it is downsizing or needing to sell assets to pay debts.
- *Proceeds from borrowing are continually much greater than the repayment of borrowings.* If proceeds from borrowings are significantly greater than the repayment of borrowings over a long period, this might indicate that borrowings are continually being used to finance investment and operations. Again, it is important for the cash flows from operations to be positive to ensure the entity's long-term survival.

Trend and ratio analysis

The preceding section provided a general analysis of the statement of cash flows. Such analysis gives a broad feel for the activities of a business, but trend and ratio analysis can provide a more detailed evaluation of an entity. This will be discussed in more detail in the chapter on analysis and interpretation of financial statements.

Trend analysis is conducted by comparing information about an entity (including key financial data and ratios) over a long period of time. Recall that figures from the previous year are often presented for comparison purposes in financial statements. Figure 7.4 shows key figures from the statement of cash flows of JB Hi-Fi Ltd over the period 2008–18. Examining each component over the ten years can help identify trends and give the user a picture of past and current performance.

In figure 7.4, comparing the statement of cash flows for 2017 and 2018 indicates that the cash position of JB Hi-Fi Ltd has decreased. The overall cash position at the beginning of 2018 was $72.8 million compared to $72.0 million at the end of 2018. Cash flows from operating activities, which provide the lifeblood of the entity, increased from $190.6 million to $292.1 million. Given the general economic downturn, this is a great result. Comparing the operating cash-flow individual balances across 2017 and 2018 shows that receipts have increased more significantly than payments to suppliers. This was discussed earlier in regards to the management of that inventory cycle and points to firm management of the working capital cycle that was introduced at the beginning of the chapter.

In 2017, significant investments were made both in payments for PPE and in buying other businesses as compared to previous years. The group bought a 100 per cent stake in The Good Guys. In the other years, the group carried out its strategy of opening new stores across Australia and New Zealand. The overall inflows of cash from financing activities had been relatively low from 2008, and then in 2011 and 2017 large borrowings were drawn. Except in the years 2008 and 2009, there does seem to be significant payment of dividends each year relative to the cash from operating activities.

Generally, a comparison of the years from 2008 to 2018 shows that cash from operating activities fluctuated, major businesses were acquired and significant dividends were paid.

FIGURE 7.4 JB Hi-Fi Ltd's selected financial statement items and ratios 2008–18

	2018 $m	2017 $m	2016 $m	2015 $m	2014 $m	2013 $m	2012 $m	2011 $m	2010 $m	2009 $m	2008 $m
Selected financial statement items											
Cash from operating activities	292.1	190.6	185.1	179.9	41.3	156.4	215.0	109.9	152.1	145.6	42.4
Cash from investing activities											
Outflow (purchase of assets)	(54.4)	(885.7)	(52.3)	(44.9)	(38.9)	(39.5)	(46.1)	(45.1)	(56.8)	(44.4)	(59.8)
Inflow (sale of assets)	0.4	0.2	0.3	0.5	0.7	1.2	1.3	1.1	1.1	0.6	0.2
	(54.0)	(885.5)	(52.0)	(44.4)	(38.2)	(38.3)	(44.8)	(44.0)	(55.7)	(43.8)	(59.6)
Cash from financing activities											
Outflow (dividends, repayment of debt)	(242.1)	(130.0)	(136.5)	(132.7)	(103.2)	(92.1)	(161.2)	(263.5)	(87.0)	(68.5)	(16.9)
Inflow (borrowings, share issue)	3.0	845.9	6.0	3.1	75.6	1.1	3.5	172.6	6.8	4.2	8.8
	(239.1)	715.9	(130.5)	(129.6)	(27.6)	(91.0)	(157.7)	(90.9)	(80.2)	(64.3)	(8.1)
Beginning cash balance	72.8	51.9	49.1	43.4	67.4	39.7	27.2	51.7	35.8	(1.5)	23.7
End cash balance	72.0	72.8	51.9	49.1	43.4	67.4	39.7	27.2	51.7	35.8	(1.5)
Dividends paid	(151.6)	(119.1)	(93.2)	(87.2)	(77.2)	(65.3)	(77.0)	(88.4)	(67.1)	(33.2)	(16.9)
Payment for property, plant and equipment	(54.4)	(49.1)	(52.3)	(42.4)	(35.9)	(35.3)	(46.1)	(45.1)	(54.5)	44.4	(51.6)
Information from other reports											
Net sales	6854.3	5628.0	3954.5	3652.1	3483.8	3308.4	3127.8	2959.3	2731.1	2327.3	1828.6
Current liabilities	917.2	885.4	446.8	380.3	352.2	442.4	439.5	345.9	363.1	323.7	239.4
Non-current liabilities	626.9	720.9	140.8	171.2	213.0	157.1	187.2	268.9	57.9	108.7	132.5
Ratios											
Cash adequacy ratio	1.42 times	1.13 times	1.27 times	1.39 times	0.37 times	1.55 times	1.75 times	0.82 times	1.25 times	1.87 times	0.55 times
Cash flow ratio (liquidity)	0.32 times	0.22 times	0.41 times	0.47 times	0.12 times	0.35 times	0.49 times	0.32 times	0.42 times	0.45 times	0.18 times
Debt coverage ratio (solvency)	2.15 times	3.78 times	0.76 times	0.95 times	5.15 times	1 time	0.87 times	2.45 times	0.38 times	0.75 times	3.13 times
Cash flow to sales ratio (profitability)	0.04 times	0.03 times	0.05 times	0.05 times	0.01 times	0.05 times	0.07 times	0.04 times	0.06 times	0.06 times	0.02 times
Free cash flow ($m)	$237.7	$141.5	$132.8	$137.4	$5.4	$121.1	$168.9	$64.9	$95.3	$101.1	$(17.3)

Source: Adapted from JB Hi-Fi Ltd 2008–17 and 2018.

Ratio analysis is a method to help the user interpret key items in the financial statements in order to assess the health of an entity. Normally, one key amount is divided by another key amount for the purpose of expressing their relationship as a ratio or percentage. The concept of ratio analysis, as it applies to information in the statement of cash flows, will be discussed further in the chapter on analysis and interpretation of financial statements. However, to complete our evaluation of the statement of cash flows, some relevant ratios are presented in figure 7.5 and discussed in the following sections.

FIGURE 7.5 Cash-based ratio analysis

Ratio	Calculation	JB Hi-Fi Ltd for 2018 ($m)
Cash adequacy ratio	$\dfrac{\text{Cash from operating activities}}{\text{Capital expenditure + Dividends paid}}$	$\dfrac{\$292.1}{\$54.4 + \$151.6} = 1.42$ times or 142%
Cash flow ratio (liquidity)	$\dfrac{\text{Cash from operating activities}}{\text{Current liabilities}}$	$\dfrac{\$292.1}{\$917.2} = 0.32$ times or 32%
Debt coverage ratio (solvency)	$\dfrac{\text{Non-current liabilities}}{\text{Cash from operating activities}}$	$\dfrac{\$626.9}{\$292.1} = 2.15$ times or 215%
Cash flow to sales ratio (profitability)	$\dfrac{\text{Cash from operating activities}}{\text{Net sales}}$	$\dfrac{\$292.1}{\$6854.3} = 0.04$ times or 4%
Free cash flow	Cash from operating activities – Capital investments for property, plant and equipment to maintain existing operations	$\$292.1 - \$54.4 = \$237.7$

Source: Adapted from JB Hi-Fi Ltd 2018.

Cash adequacy ratio

The **cash adequacy ratio** expresses the cash flows from operating activities as a percentage of the capital expenditure plus dividends paid for the period. In other words, the ratio shows an entity's ability to reinvest in its operations and to make distributions to owners from its operating cash flow. The cash adequacy ratio for JB Hi-Fi Ltd over the period 2008 to 2018 is calculated in figure 7.4. It shows that cash from operating activities could cover the current capital investment and dividends 1.42 times in 2018. A ratio greater than 1 over several years suggests good performance. The trend for JB Hi-Fi Ltd shows that the cash adequacy ratio has fluctuated over the period since 2008. Investors inspecting the cash adequacy ratio after 2008 would have been happy to see positive ratios, as they show that the purchases improved future cash flow. However, in 2011 and 2014 the ratio slipped below 1. As discussed in the previous section, there was a large dividend paid. The dividends paid were 80 per cent and 190 per cent, respectively, of the cash flows generated from operating activities. Dividends deplete the resources the entity can use to invest in operating assets that can fund future cash flows.

Cash flow ratio

The **cash flow ratio** compares the cash flows from operating activities with the current liabilities and is used to assess liquidity. **Liquidity** measures the ability of an entity to meet its financial obligations. As shown in figure 7.5, JB Hi-Fi Ltd had a cash flow ratio in 2018 of 0.32 times or 32 per cent. This means that the cash flows from operating activities could cover 32 per cent of JB Hi-Fi Ltd's current obligations. The higher the ratio, the better the entity's ability to meet its obligations. The equivalent accrual-based ratio is the current ratio, measured as current assets over current liabilities. (For JB Hi-Fi Ltd, the current ratio in 2018 was 1.32 times. In 2017, it was also 1.32 times.) The big difference between the cash flow ratio and the current ratio is due to the accounts receivable and inventory balances.

It is often argued that the cash flow ratio is a better measure of liquidity than the current ratio because it utilises cash flows generated over a whole reporting period, rather than the current assets at a particular point in time. Examining the trend in the cash flow ratio over the ten years, as shown in figure 7.4, again reveals an improvement after the 2008 year when a significant payment was made for businesses, but the slump probably also points to the risky nature of the electronics business environment and the start of the GFC. A point worth noting in relation to liquidity is that it is trying to measure an entity's ability to meet its short-term obligations.

Debt coverage ratio

The **debt coverage ratio** links the cash flows from operating activities to long-term debt (in contrast to the cash flow ratio, in which the link is to short-term liabilities). This ratio is a measure of an entity's ability to survive in the longer term and remain solvent. As seen in figure 7.5, the debt coverage ratio of JB Hi-Fi Ltd in 2018 was 2.15 times or 215 per cent. This informs us that, at the current operating level (i.e. if cash from operations remains constant), it would take 2.15 years to repay the existing long-term debts. This can be compared to previous years and also to the current loan term. Again, the comparison between the ratios over the years, as shown in figure 7.4, indicates a fluctuating performance. This can be linked to the weak collection of receipts and the large capital investment in 2017 and the large debt acquired during 2011 and 2017.

Cash flow to sales ratio

The **cash flow to sales ratio** measures the relative amount of cash flow generated by each sales dollar. It is used to help interpret the profitability of an entity. As shown in figure 7.5, the cash flow to sales ratio of JB Hi-Fi Ltd in 2018 was 0.04 times or 4 per cent. This means that, for every sales dollar received, the entity generated an operating cash flow of 4 cents. Again, this ratio needs to be compared with the previous years' ratios to determine whether it is reasonable. It also should be compared to the equivalent accrual-based ratio of return on sales, which is calculated by profit divided by net sales. (The entity's return on sales was 0.034 times in 2018 and 0.031 times in 2017.) Any significant differences should be investigated. JB Hi-Fi Ltd's cash flow to sales ratio has been steady over the last ten years, as shown in figure 7.4.

Although ratios help with the evaluation of financial statements, they do not stand alone. They need to be interpreted in light of other ratios, compared with past ratios and industry ratios (e.g. manufacturing industries tend to have higher capital expenditures than service industries) and considered along with other information presented in the financial statements.

Free cash flow

Another indicator of performance sometimes used is **free cash flow**, which represents the free cash a company has available to repay debt, pay dividends and expand operations. The measure is calculated by taking the amount spent on capital investments for PPE to maintain existing operations and subtracting it from the cash from operating activities. For JB Hi-Fi Ltd, free cash flow for 2018 was $237.7 million (compared to $141.5 million in 2017). (Note that, in calculating this figure, the payment for PPE was assumed to be for maintaining existing operations.)

There are a number of different definitions and calculations for free cash flow; so, if this performance indicator is reported by an entity, it is important to understand how it was calculated. One drawback of the calculation is that it is difficult to assess how much of the capital investment in PPE is to maintain existing operations and how much is for expansion. For JB Hi-Fi Ltd, the $54.4 million payment in 2018 probably includes some capital expenditure for expansion, and thus this portion should be excluded from the calculation. Unfortunately, the information in the statement of cash flows does not distinguish between the two. The comparison of the free cash flow over the years, as presented in figure 7.5, should bear this in mind, as the free cash flow fluctuates when significant expansion (e.g. in 2008 and 2017) occurs.

Complexity of transactions

It is difficult to compute cash inflows and cash outflows directly from an entity's published statement of profit or loss and statement of financial position. The number and types of adjustments are beyond the scope of this chapter, but they include transactions relating to bad debts, discounts, timing of tax and dividend payments, and acquisition of controlled entities. Although the array of transactions can become complex, it is not necessary for report users to prepare a statement of cash flows with complex scenarios. When interpreting the statement of cash flows, what you need to remember is that it basically shows cash received and cash paid, and that accrual adjustments have been made from the statement of profit or loss and the statement of financial position.

- The difficulty in manipulating the statement of cash flows increases its usefulness.
- The evaluation of the statement of cash flows includes a general analysis, as well as the use of trend and ratio analysis.
- Cash-based ratios include the cash adequacy ratio, the cash flow ratio, the debt coverage ratio, the cash flow to sales ratio and free cash flow.
- It is important to consider appropriate cash warning signals when analysing financial statements.
- Despite the complexity of transactions undertaken in business, when interpreting the statement of cash flows it is important to remember that its basic purpose is reporting what cash came in and what cash went out.

SUMMARY OF LEARNING OBJECTIVES

7.1 Assess the purpose and usefulness of a statement of cash flows.

The purpose of a statement of cash flows is to show the cash flows of an entity over a set period, in order to assess the entity's ability to generate cash and to meet future obligations. Heightened awareness of the management of earnings in the statement of profit or loss has elevated the importance of reviewing the statement of cash flows in conjunction with the statement of profit or loss.

7.2 Outline the format and the classification of cash flows in the statement of cash flows.

The statement of cash flows presents the beginning and ending cash balances and the cash inflows and outflows of a reporting period. The cash inflows and outflows are classified into operating, investing and financing activities. A reconciliation of the cash from operating activities with the profit in the statement of profit or loss is presented in a note to the accounts.

7.3 Produce a statement of cash flows using the direct method and a reconciliation using the indirect method.

Cash flows from operating activities are determined by examining the income and expenses in the statement of profit or loss and the non-current assets and non-current liabilities in the statement of financial position. Cash flows from investing activities are determined from changes in statement of financial position items dealing with non-current assets. Cash flows from financing activities are determined from changes in statement of financial position items associated with non-current liabilities and equity.

7.4 Evaluate an entity's performance using a statement of cash flows.

The interpretation of the statement of cash flows requires a general evaluation, as well as the use of trend and ratio analysis. Cash-flow warning signals can also indicate a cash-flow problem. Cash-based ratios include the cash adequacy ratio, the cash flow ratio, the debt coverage ratio, the cash flow to sales ratio and free cash flow. Despite the complexity of transactions, the basic purpose of a statement of cash flows is to report what cash came in and how it was spent.

KEY TERMS

cash Cash and cash equivalents.

cash adequacy ratio Cash from operating activities divided by capital expenditure plus dividends paid.

cash equivalents Highly liquid investments and short-term borrowings.

cash flow ratio Measure of liquidity calculated as cash from operating activities divided by current liabilities.

cash flow to sales ratio Measure of profitability calculated as cash from operating activities divided by net sales revenue.

cash flows Cash movements resulting from transactions with parties external to the entity.

cash inflows Cash movements into the entity resulting from transactions with an external party.

cash on hand Notes and coins, and deposits at call with a financial institution.

cash outflows Cash movements out of the entity resulting from transactions with an external party.

debt coverage ratio Capital structure ratio calculated as non-current liabilities divided by net cash flows from operating activities.

direct method Method of preparing a statement of cash flows that discloses major classes of gross cash receipts and gross cash payments.

financing activities Those activities that change the size and/or composition of the financial structure of the entity (including equity) and borrowings not falling within the definition of cash.

free cash flow The cash from operating activities less the amount spent on capital expenditure to maintain the existing level of operations.

indirect method Method of preparing a statement of cash flows that adjusts profit or loss for the effects of transactions of a non-cash nature and deferrals or accruals of operating revenue and expenses. (The indirect method is the reconciliation of the profit/loss with the cash flows from operating activities discussed earlier.)

investing activities Those activities that relate to the acquisition and/or disposal of non-current assets (e.g. property, plant and equipment, and other productive assets and investments) not falling within the definition of cash.

liquidity Ability of an entity to meet its short-term financial commitments.

operating activities Relate to the provision of goods and services and other activities that are neither investing nor financing activities.

ratio analysis Examination of the relationship between two quantitative amounts with the objective of expressing the relationship in ratio or percentage form.

statement of cash flows A statement that reports on an entity's cash inflows and cash outflows for a specified period.

trend analysis Method of examining changes, movements and patterns in data over a number of time periods.

working capital Difference between current assets and current liabilities.

APPLY YOUR KNOWLEDGE

20 marks

The consolidated statement of cash flows for CSR Ltd for the year ended 31 March 2018 is presented below.

CSR LTD Statement of cash flows for the year ended 31 March 2018		Consolidated	
	Notes	2018 $m	2017 $m
Cash flows from operating activities			
Receipts from customers		2 930.4	2 726.0
Payments to suppliers and employees		(2 652.7)	(2 424.6)
Dividends and distributions received	23	9.5	14.2
Interest received		2.6	1.9
Income tax (paid) received		(40.6)	(52.7)
Net cash from operating activities		249.2	264.8
Cash flows from investing activities			
Purchase of property, plant and equipment and other assets		(120.6)	(93.2)
Proceeds from sale of property, plant and equipment and other assets		62.6	44.7
Purchase of controlled entities and businesses, net of cash acquired	8	(0.3)	(3.5)
Costs associated with acquisition of businesses	8	(18.5)	(3.4)
Loans and receivables advanced		(2.0)	(5.3)
Net cash (used in) from investing activities		(78.8)	(60.7)
Cash flows from financing activities			
On-market share buy-back	15	(0.6)	(4.3)
Net (repayment) drawdown of borrowings		(2.5)	28.3
Dividends paid[1]		(163.2)	(146.7)
Acquisition of shares by CSR employee share trust	17	(5.8)	(5.4)
Interest and other finance costs paid		(4.1)	(3.4)
Transactions with non-controlling interests	8	—	(126.4)
Net cash used in financing activities		(176.2)	(257.9)
Net decrease in cash held		(5.8)	(53.8)
Net cash at the beginning of the financial year		19.1	73.1
Effects of exchange rate changes		0.4	(0.2)
Net cash at the end of the financial year		**13.7**	**19.1**
Reconciliation of net profit attributable to shareholders of CSR Ltd to net cash from operating activities			
Net profit attributable to shareholders of CSR Ltd	2	188.8	177.9
Net profit attributable to non-controlling interests	21	17.8	27.2
Depreciation and amortisation	5	84.4	88.5
Impairment of assets		1.5	11.1
Costs associated with acquisition of business		—	(1.5)
Share of profits of associates not received as dividends or distributions		(3.2)	(0.5)
Net gain on purchase of associate	8	—	(4.1)
Share-based payments	17	3.7	3.2
Finance cost net of discount unwind		4.1	3.3
Profit on disposal of assets	5	(51.0)	(16.9)
Net change in current receivables		14.3	5.7
Net change in current inventories		(57.2)	(15.7)

	Notes	Consolidated	
		2018 $m	2017 $m
Net change in current payables		33.8	19.7
Movement in product liability provision		(23.4)	(22.1)
Net change in other provisions		(0.1)	(2.9)
Movement in current and deferred tax balances		34.4	1.7
Net change in other assets and liabilities		1.3	(9.8)
Net cash from operating activities		**249.2**	**264.8**

[1] During the year ended 31 March 2018, within the $163.2 million of dividends paid, dividends to CSR Ltd shareholders were $133.7 million. Of the $133.7 million in dividends, $8.6 million was used to purchase CSR shares on market to satisfy obligations under the Dividend Reinvestment Plan (DRP) and the remaining $125.1 million was paid in cash.

Note: Sales in 2018 were $2606.2 million and in 2017 were $2468.3 million.

Source: CSR Ltd 2018, p. 58.

Required

(a) What information does the statement of cash flows provide? *2 marks*

(b) Outline the two different methods of preparing the statement of cash flows. Examine the CSR Ltd statement of cash flows and report on its method used. *2 marks*

(c) Describe the three sections of the statement of cash flows. *2 marks*

(d) Discuss the difference between the statement of cash flows and the statement of profit or loss. *2 marks*

(e) Assess how each section in the statement of cash flows relates to the statement of financial position. *2 marks*

(f) Examine the CSR Ltd statement of cash flows and compare the cash from operating activities with the operating profit after tax. Are they similar? If not, suggest why. *2 marks*

(g) Compare the cash from operating activities for 2017 and 2018. Are they similar? If not, ascertain why. *2 marks*

(h) What money did CSR Ltd spend on investing activities? How does this compare to the previous year? *2 marks*

(i) What financing activities were undertaken by CSR Ltd? Compare the borrowings from the previous year and suggest reasons for any major changes. Were there any payments made to shareholders? *2 marks*

(j) Generate an opinion about the company's cash position. *2 marks*

SELF-EVALUATION ACTIVITIES

7.1 Listed below are transactions that occurred in the current financial year for Fraser Pty Ltd. Classify each transaction into an operating, investing or financing activity, or a non-cash transaction. If a cash transaction, indicate whether it is a cash inflow or a cash outflow.

(a) Paid dividend of $1 million to shareholders.
(b) Collected $285 000 from a major account receivable.
(c) Recorded depreciation of $28 000 for some equipment.
(d) Paid $84 000 to a supplier.
(e) Acquired a parcel of land in exchange for some shares.
(f) Received a dividend from an investment in another company.
(g) Paid yearly insurance by cash.
(h) Purchased a new truck for $40 000 cash.
(i) Sold a major piece of equipment for cash.
(j) Paid salaries and wages.

SOLUTION TO 7.1

Transaction	Classification	Inflow/outflow
(a) Paid dividend of $1 million to shareholders.	Financing	Outflow
(b) Collected $285 000 from a major account receivable.	Operating	Inflow

(c)	Recorded depreciation of $28 000 for some equipment.	Non-cash	Not recorded in statement of cash flows
(d)	Paid $84 000 to a supplier.	Operating	Outflow
(e)	Acquired a parcel of land in exchange for some shares.	Non-cash	Recorded in notes to statement of cash flows
(f)	Received a dividend from an investment in another company.	Investing/ operating	Inflow
(g)	Paid yearly insurance by cash.	Operating	Outflow
(h)	Purchased a new truck for $40 000 cash.	Investing	Outflow
(i)	Sold a major piece of equipment for cash.	Investing	Inflow
(j)	Paid salaries and wages.	Operating	Outflow

7.2 The statement of profit or loss for Summer Ltd for the year ended 31 December 2020, and the statement of financial positions as at 31 December for 2019 and 2020, are shown below. You are required to complete a statement of cash flows and reconcile the cash from operating activities to the profit after tax.

SUMMER LTD
Statement of profit or loss
for the year ended 31 December 2020

	$'000	$'000
Sales		368
Cost of sales		
Opening inventory	25	
+ Inventory purchases	264	
	289	
+ Closing inventory	32	257
Gross profit		111
Operational expenses (including depreciation $7000)	43	
Interest expense	6	49
		62
Interest received		4
Profit before tax		**66**
Tax		20
Profit after tax		**46**
Retained earnings, 31 December 2019		23
		69
Dividend proposed		20
Retained earnings, 31 December 2020		**49**

SUMMER LTD
Statement of financial positions
as at 31 December 2019 and 2020

	2020 $'000	2019 $'000
Current assets		
Cash at bank	8	12
Accounts receivable	46	43
Inventory	32	25
Prepaid expenses	12	6
Total current assets	98	86
Non-current assets		
Land and buildings	240	110
Plant and machinery (net)	370	250
Total non-current assets	610	360
Total assets	**708**	**446**

	2020	2019
	$'000	$'000
Current liabilities		
Accounts payable	68	67
Income tax payable	20	28
Accrued expenses	21	28
Total current liabilities	109	123
Non-current liabilities		
Loan	350	150
Total liabilities	459	273
Equity		
Paid-up ordinary capital	200	150
Retained earnings	49	23
Total equity	249	173
Total liabilities and equity	**708**	**446**

Additional information
- There were no disposals of PPE throughout the year.
- An existing long-term loan of $50 000 was paid out.
- A share issue of $50 000 was made to help finance planned expansions.
- A long-term loan of $250 000 was taken up.
- A dividend of $20 000 was paid.

SOLUTION TO 7.2

Step 1. Determine the cash flows from operating activities

Step 1a. Calculate the receipts from customers

$$\text{Cash from customers} = \text{Opening accounts receivable} + \text{Sales} - \text{Closing accounts receivable}$$
$$= \$43 + \$368 - \$46$$
$$= \$365$$

Step 1b. Calculate payments to suppliers and employees

$$\text{Cash paid to suppliers} = \text{Opening accounts payable} + \text{Purchases} - \text{Closing accounts payable}$$
$$= \$67 + \$264 - \$68$$
$$= \$263$$

$$\text{Cash paid to employees} = \text{Other expenses} +/- \text{Increase (decrease) in prepayments} +/- \text{Decrease (increase) in accruals}$$
$$= \$36 + \$6 + \$7$$
$$= \$49$$

Total paid to suppliers and employees = $263 + $49 = $312

Step 1c. Calculate other payments for expenses and receipts for income

Interest received	$ 4 000
Interest paid	6 000
Tax paid	28 000

Step 2. Determine the cash flows from investing activities

Investing activities generally relate to the assets in the statement of financial position. Inspection of the assets in the Summer Ltd statement of financial position reveals the following changes in the asset values.

	2020 $'000	2019 $'000	Change $'000
Land and buildings	$240	$110	$130
Plant and machinery	377[a]	250	127
Total change			**$257**

[a] The book value of the plant and machinery in the statement of financial position was $370 000. The depreciation in the statement of profit or loss for the year was $7000. Depreciation is not a cash flow, so it should be added back before calculating the increase or decrease in the investment in assets. Note also that the question indicates that there were no disposals of PPE throughout the year. So, the change is all due to an increase in investment in PPE.

Step 3. Determine the cash flow from financing activities[a]

	$'000
Proceeds from shares issue	$ 50
Proceeds from borrowings	250
Repayment of borrowings	(50)
Distributions paid	(20)

[a] Financing activities generally relate to the liabilities and equity in the statement of financial position.

Examining the differences between the 2020 and 2019 balances shows that there was a share issue of $50 000. The loan account difference is $350 000 – $150 000 = $200 000. The notes to the accounts indicate that a new loan of $250 000 was acquired and an old loan of $50 000 was paid out. The dividends payable show a 2019 balance of $35 000 and a 2020 balance of $20 000. However, the statement of profit or loss indicates that a dividend of $20 000 was proposed in 2017, so the dividend paid in 2020 must have been $35 000 ($35 000 + $20 000 – $20 000).

Step 4. Calculate the net cash flow and the ending cash balance for the year

SUMMER LTD Statement of cash flows for the year ended 31 December 2020	
	$'000
Cash flows from operating activities	
Receipts from customers	365
Payments to suppliers and employees	(312)
Interest received	4
Interest paid	(6)
Income taxes paid	(28)
Net cash flows from operating activities	23
Cash flows from investing activities	
Payments for property, plant and equipment	(257)
Net cash flows from investing activities	(257)
Cash flows from financing activities	
Proceeds from shares issue	50
Proceeds from borrowings	250
Repayment of borrowings	(50)
Distributions paid	(20)
Net cash flows from financing activities	230
Net increase/decrease in cash for the year	(4)
Cash at beginning of the financial year	12
Cash at the end of the financial year	**8**

Step 5. Reconcile cash from operating activities with profit

	$'000
Profit after tax	46
+ Depreciation	7
(Increase)/decrease in inventory	(7)
(Increase)/decrease in accounts receivable	(3)
(Increase)/decrease in prepaid expenses	(6)
Increase/(decrease) in accounts payable	1

	$'000
Increase/(decrease) in tax payable	(8)
Increase/(decrease) in accruals	(7)
Net cash flows from operating activities	**23**

7.3 Examine the statement of cash flows prepared for Summer Ltd in self-evaluation activity 7.2. Evaluate the cash performance of Summer Ltd by conducting a general evaluation and ratio analysis.

SOLUTION TO 7.3

- The cash flow from operating activities of $23 000 is lower than the operating profit of $46 000. The reconciliation shows that, generally, current asset accounts have increased while liability accounts have decreased. This means that the entity now has more cash tied up in working capital than it had in the previous year.
- There was a large investment in PPE. This was funded by an increase in borrowings of $200 000 and a share issue of $50 000.
- The increase in borrowings means that there will be an increase in interest payable in the future. This, together with an increase in equity, will put pressure on the cash from operating activities to fund larger future interest and dividend payments. A watchful eye over working capital will be needed. Hopefully, the planned expansions will result in increased sales and profit, and thereby an increase in cash from operating activities.
- Ratio analysis shows the following.

Ratio	Calculation	Summer Ltd
Cash adequacy ratio	$\dfrac{\text{Cash from operating activities}}{\text{Capital expenditure} + \text{Dividends paid}}$	$\dfrac{\$23}{\$257 + \$20} = 0.08$ times or 8%
Cash flow ratio (liquidity)	$\dfrac{\text{Cash from operating activities}}{\text{Current liabilities}}$	$\dfrac{\$23}{\$109} = 0.211$ times or 21.1%
Debt coverage ratio (solvency)	$\dfrac{\text{Non-current liabilities}}{\text{Cash from operating activities}}$	$\dfrac{\$350}{\$23} = 15.22$ times or 152.1%
Cash flow to sales ratio (profitability)	$\dfrac{\text{Cash from operating activities}}{\text{Net sales}}$	$\dfrac{\$23}{\$368} = 0.062$ times or 6.25%

- The cash adequacy ratio shows that the cash from operating activities funded 8 per cent of the expansion and dividend payout.
- The cash flow ratio shows that the cash from operating activities covers 21.1 per cent of the current liabilities.
- The debt coverage ratio shows that it will take 15.22 years at the current operating level to pay off the long-term debt.
- The cash flow to sales ratio reveals that, at the current operating level, every sales dollar achieved resulted in 6.25 cents in cash flows from operating activities.
- Generally, the cash flow data reveal a low performance and a watchful eye is needed. Although the ratios reveal some information about Summer Ltd's operation, it is best to trace these ratios over time and to compare them to industry norms.

COMPREHENSION QUESTIONS

7.4 What is meant by the term 'cash'? **LO3**

7.5 What is the purpose of a statement of cash flows? **LO1**

7.6 Which of the following are not disclosed in a statement of cash flows? **LO2**
  (a) Net cash flows from financing activities.
  (b) The cash on hand at the end of the reporting period.
  (c) The amount of depreciation for a reporting period.
  (d) The proceeds from borrowings.

7.7 Outline the format of a statement of cash flows, identifying each of the activity classifications. **LO2**

7.8 Valley Company had a positive net cash flow for the year, but its statement of profit or loss reported a loss for the period. Explain. **LO1**

7.9 Outline some cash-flow warning signals. **LO4**

7.10 Fill in the blanks in the following statement by choosing the words from those in brackets that best complete the statement. **LO3**

Changes in non-current liabilities and equity would usually be classified as cash flows from (operating, financing or investing) activities and changes in non-current assets would usually be classified as cash flows from (operating, financing or investing) activities.

7.11 Choose the correct response. **LO1**

The primary purpose of a statement of cash flows is to provide relevant information about:

(a) an entity's ability to meet future obligations.

(b) the differences between profit and associated cash receipts and payments.

(c) the ability of an entity to generate future cash flows.

(d) the cash receipts and cash payments of an entity during a reporting period.

7.12 Outline the difference between the direct method and the indirect method of reporting cash flows. Why is it necessary to present the cash flows using both methods? **LO2**

7.13 List four ratios that could help evaluate an entity's cash adequacy, liquidity, solvency and profitability. **LO4**

7.14 Outline the difference between the cash and the accrual bases of accounting. **LO1**

EXERCISES

★ BASIC | ★ ★ MODERATE | ★ ★ ★ CHALLENGING

7.15 ★ **LO3**

The following ledger account shows the transactions in an entity's cash account during the month.

Cash

Opening balance	15 000	Drawings paid	10 000
Receipts from customers	156 000	Payments for wages	54 000
Dividends received	3 000	Payments for inventory	70 000
Sale of motor vehicle	16 000	Expenses payments	6 000
Proceeds from loan	30 000	GST paid	5 000
		Interest paid	3 000
		Closing balance	72 000
	220 000		220 000

Required

Prepare a statement of cash flows based on the cash account.

7.16 ★ **LO3**

Three sisters formed a partnership, FreshGlow, to sell skincare products made from organic ingredients. They have been operating for one year. The bank balance at the end of the year is $34 500. A summary of business transactions is as follows.

Sales to customers	$128 000
Receipts from customers	108 500
Payments for inventory	49 000
Payments for electricity, telephone, rent and insurance	2 500
Purchase of a motor vehicle	13 000
Drawings	25 000
Payment of interest	4 000
Loan proceeds	10 500
Interest received	500
Equity injection	10 500

Required

Prepare a statement of cash flows.

7.17 ★   **LO2**

In what section of the statement of cash flows (operating, investing or financing) would each of the following items appear?
(a) Cash paid to employees.
(b) Cash received from debentures.
(c) Payment of income tax.
(d) Gain/loss from sale of motor vehicle.
(e) Cash outlay for purchase of office equipment.
(f) Dividends paid to shareholders.
(g) Proceeds from issue of shares.
(h) Repayment of debt.
(i) Change in accounts payable.
(j) Profit.

7.18 ★   **LO1**

Consider the following transactions.
- Credit purchases, $12 000.
- Cash paid to suppliers, $16 000.
- Credit sales, $21 000.
- Cost of sales, $15 000.
- Cash payments received on accounts receivable, $14 000.
- Salaries accrued, $2500.
- Machine purchased, $8000 cash.
- Depreciation expense, $2250.
- Dividends declared, $3000.
- Rent received, $2000.
- Declared dividends paid, $3000.
- Lease paid, $1200.

Required

(a) Indicate the effect on the statement of financial position categories only, in the following format.

Transaction number	Cash	Other current assets	Non-current assets	Current liabilities	Non-current liabilities	Equity

(b) State, for the transactions affecting cash, whether they relate to an operating, investing or financing activity.

7.19 ★   **LO3**

Compute the cash from operations in each of the following cases (A and B). All sales and purchases have been made on credit.

	A	B
Sales revenue	$60 000	$80 000
Depreciation expense	5 000	12 000
Cost of sales	30 000	76 000
Other expenses	3 000	1 400
Dividends paid	10 000	
Increase/(decrease) in:		
Inventories	8 000	(20 000)
Accounts receivable	7 000	4 000
Prepayments	(1 000)	(2 000)
Accounts payable	(30 000)	9 000
Other current liabilities	16 000	(20 000)

7.20 ★   **LO3**

The cash flows below were extracted from the accounts of Martin Jones, a music shop owner.

Repayment of loan	$420 000
Sale of property	390 000
Interest received	1 560
Payments to employees	63 000
Receipts from customers	295 000
Expenses paid	16 500
Computer equipment purchase	24 000
GST paid	970
Payments to suppliers	156 000
Income taxes paid	3 120
Beginning cash balance	8 800

Required

Prepare a statement of cash flows using the direct method.

7.21 ★   **LO2**

Molly Winter Pty Ltd has the following items in its accounts.
- Bank interest received.
- Depreciation of delivery van.
- Cash purchase of office equipment.
- Sale of goods for cash.
- GST payable.
- Receipts from share capital issue.
- Cash from debenture.
- Dividends payable.
- Purchase of goods on credit.

Required

State whether each of the items listed would appear in the statement of cash flows and, if so, under which classification it would appear (investing, operating or financing).

7.22 ★   **LO3**

Smith and Jones Partnership provides specialist financial planning services to its clients. The following information relates to the year just ended.

	2020	2019
Cash	$63 000	$36 000
Accounts receivable	66 000	53 000
Prepaid expenses	22 000	20 000
Accounts payable	44 000	47 000
Sales revenue		$156 000
Operating expenses[a]		105 000
Profit		51 000

[a] Operating expenses include depreciation of $7000.

Required

Using the direct method, prepare the operating activities section of the statement of cash flows for the period ending 30 June 2020.

7.23 ★   **LO1**

'We made a profit of $124 000, so why is there only $15 000 in the bank?' exclaimed Mr Charlton, the owner of the local fish and chip shop. Explain to Mr Charlton the relationship between profit and cash flow, to help him understand the reason why there is such a big difference between profit and cash in the bank.

7.24 ★   **LO3**

On inspection of the financial statements, you note that sales are $67 500, and the beginning and closing accounts receivable balances are $49 500 and $63 000 respectively. What were the cash receipts from customers?

7.25 ★   **LO4**

The sole trader of Rhode Store has approached you for a loan. You note that the closing cash balances for the last two years were $15 920 and $18 650 respectively. Rhode Store also took out a loan of

$27 750 for the current year and sold plant worth $59 600 over the past two years. The cash from operating activities last year was negative $35 940 and in the preceding year was $9550. Indicate whether you would advance the loan. Give reasons.

7.26 ★   **LO4**

Wattle Ltd has cash from operating activities of $57 246. It has incurred capital expenditure of $47 350, of which $33 900 was for additional equipment. Calculate the entity's free cash flow. Comment on what the figure indicates.

7.27 ★ ★   **LO4**

Fresh Food Catering Ltd's capital expenditure for the current year on new equipment was $196 900. Current liabilities and non-current liabilities were $98 590 and $732 800 respectively. Sales for the current year were $331 650 and cash flows from operating activities totalled $108 760. Compute the cash adequacy ratio, cash flow ratio, debt coverage ratio and cash flow to sales ratio.

7.28 ★ ★   **LO1**

An entity is converting its accrual-based accounting records to a cash basis. The amount of $53 000 (including $7000 depreciation) was shown as 'Other expenses' in the statement of profit or loss. On inspection of the statement of financial position, you find that the beginning and closing balances for 'Prepaid expenses' were $13 000 and $15 000 respectively. Also, the beginning and closing balances of 'Accrued expenses' were $5000 and $11 000 respectively.

Required

(a) What is the actual amount of cash paid for other expenses during the period?
(b) Compare the cash basis of accounting with the accrual basis of accounting.
(c) Assess the information benefits of both accounting approaches.

7.29 ★ ★   **LO3**

The following list contains activities that may be added or subtracted from operating profit when reconciling to cash flows from operating activities. Indicate whether each activity is added, subtracted or irrelevant.

(a) Decrease in accrued expenses.
(b) Increase in interest payable.
(c) Decrease in PPE.
(d) Depreciation expense.
(e) Increase in inventory.
(f) GST paid.
(g) Increase in prepaid expenses.
(h) Proceeds from sale of shares.
(i) Receipt from a customer.
(j) Increase in long-term debt.

7.30 ★ ★   **LO3**

Tom and Clancy Partners reported a profit of $76 000 for the year. The statement of profit or loss also showed depreciation expense of $8000 and a loss on the sale of a motor vehicle of $2000. The statement of financial position showed an increase in accounts receivable of $5000 for the year, a decrease in inventory of $3000 and an increase in accounts payable of $4000.

Required

Prepare a reconciliation of profit to cash flows from operating activities using the indirect method as illustrated in the chapter.

7.31 ★ ★   **LO3**

Design Homes Ltd had a $58 000 net loss for 2020. A dividend of $22 000 was paid during the year and depreciation expense was $15 000. Inspection of the statement of financial position shows the following working capital accounts.

	1 Jan 2020	31 Dec 2020
Cash	$10 000	$ 8 000
Accounts receivable	12 000	14 000
Inventory	16 000	10 000
Prepayments	4 500	3 000
Accounts payable	14 000	18 000
Accrued expenses	6 000	8 000

Required

Calculate whether Design Homes Ltd generated any cash from its operations during 2020.

7.32 ★ ★   **LO4**

The financial information below has been extracted from the accounts of Misty Wines Pty Ltd. Peta Stevens, the sole shareholder, wants to evaluate the cash position of her company and understands she will need to calculate some cash-based ratios to do this. She has asked for your assistance, as you are studying a course in accounting. Help your friend by calculating some cash-based ratios.

Cash from operating activities	$ 157 600
Capital expenditure	160 000
Current liabilities	278 400
Non-current liabilities	131 000
Sales	1 550 000
Dividend paid	14 790

7.33 ★ ★   **LO1**

Outline how a creditor, an investor and an employee would each interpret this statement of cash flows of Fruit Plantations Pty Ltd.

FRUIT PLANTATIONS PTY LTD		
Statement of cash flows		
	4 months 2019 $	12 months 2020 $
Cash flows from operating activities		
Receipts from customers	476 890	1 480 100
Receipts from other income	5 000	1 000
Payments to suppliers and employees	(405 333)	(1 264 500)
Payment of interest	(5 000)	(14 000)
Payment of income tax	0	(45 000)
Net cash inflows from operating activities	71 557	157 600
Cash flows from investing activities		
Payment for buildings and equipment	(200 000)	(160 000)
Payment for office equipment	(40 000)	
Net cash outflows from investing activities	(240 000)	(160 000)
Cash inflows from financing activities		
Proceeds from capital contribution	20 000	
Proceeds from borrowings	20 000	140 000
Repayment of borrowings	0	(29 000)
Dividend paid to shareholder	0	(14 790)
Net cash inflows from financing activities	20 000	96 210
Net cash inflows during the period	51 557	93 810
Cash at the beginning of the period	0	51 557
Cash at the end of the period	**51 557**	**145 367**

7.34 ★ ★   **LO2**

Refer to the data on Fruit Plantations Pty Ltd in exercise 7.33 and answer the following questions.

(a) Fruit Plantations Pty Ltd's profit after income tax for the 4 months to 31 December 2019 was $105 000 and for the 12 months to 31 December 2020 was $229 600. These are higher than the respective net cash flows from operations. Is this normal? Why?

(b) The net cash flows from investing activities are negative in both periods. Is this normal? Why?

(c) What do you see as the most important cash activity for an entity? Why?

PROBLEMS

★   BASIC I ★ ★   MODERATE I ★ ★ ★   CHALLENGING

7.35 Preparing a statement of cash flows ★   **LO3**

Presented below is information for Sarah Waters, a sole trader, for the year ended 31 December 2020. Use the information to prepare a statement of cash flows.

Cash balance, 31 December 2020	$17 085
Cash paid to employees and suppliers	72 825
Cash received from sale of land	12 605
Cash paid as GST	5 600
Cash received from money market borrowings	8 400
Depreciation expense for the period	3 360
Cash paid to purchase equipment	14 000
Cash balance, 1 January 2020	12 885
Cash paid as drawings	17 645
Cash received from customers	92 425
Cash received as interest	2 240
Cash paid for interest	1 400

7.36 Preparing a statement of cash flows ★ **LO3**

Presented below is information for the Hudson Partnership for the year ended 31 December 2019. Use the information to prepare a statement of cash flows.

Cash balance, 31 December 2019	$ 51 618
Cash paid to employees and suppliers	220 013
Cash received from sale of land	38 079
Cash paid as GST	16 924
Cash received from debentures	25 386
Cash paid to purchase truck	30 000
Cash balance, 1 January 2019	38 925
Cash paid as drawings	53 311
Cash received from customers	279 247
Cash received as interest	6 770
Cash paid for interest	4 231
Cash paid to purchase equipment	12 310

7.37 Cash flow as a performance indicator ★ **LO4**

The importance of cash flow to people both inside and outside an entity is apparent by a quick look through financial papers and internet sites. For instance, Foster's Group Ltd eagerly announced in the press that it has curtailed its negative cash flow for its operations in China. BHP Group also announced that its cash flow was benefiting from a strong oil price and Austar United Communications Ltd announced a major debt restructure to help it meet its goal of having free cash flow.

Required

(a) Outline why companies are eager to share positive news about their cash-flow performance.

(b) What is free cash flow? Is it a good measure of cash-flow performance?

7.38 Calculating net cash flows and cash flow ratios ★ **LO4**

Information for Fred and Ginger's Dance Pty Ltd has been extracted from its financial statements and is presented below.

	30 June 2020	30 June 2019
Total current liabilities	$200 000	$180 600
Total non-current liabilities	41 400	48 800
Trade debtors	134 200	122 000
Trade creditors	102 400	87 800
Accrued expenses	24 400	31 800
Income tax payable	73 200	61 000
Prepaid expenses	18 400	22 000
Inventory	23 400	29 200

Information relating to the year ended 30 June 2020 is as follows.

Total asset expenditure	$102 000
Sales	890 000
Cost of sales	503 000
Depreciation expense	61 000
Income tax expense	73 200
Operating expenses (excluding depreciation)	134 200
Dividends paid	24 400

Required

(a) Calculate the net cash flows from operating activities.

(b) Compute the cash adequacy ratio, the cash flow ratio, the debt coverage ratio and the cash flow to sales ratio.

7.39 Reading and interpreting financial information ★ ★ LO4

Dick Smith Holdings Ltd was a company operating in the consumer electronics goods area. Dick Smith commenced this business in 1968. It was acquired by Woolworths during the early 1980s and was sold to Anchorage Capital Partners Pty Ltd in November 2012. In December 2013, Dick Smith held a successful initial public offering (IPO) and became the ultimate holding company of the Dick Smith business operations. Its cash flows from operations and investment from 2013 to 2015 are outlined below.

	2013 $'000	2014 $'000	2015 $'000	Total 2013–15 $'000
Net cash flow from operating activities	117 621	52 177	(3 940)	165 858
Net cash flow from investing activities	(81 083)	(54 005)	(31 615)	(166 703)
Cash flow after investing	36 538	(1 828)	(35 555)	(845)
Dividends paid	—	—	(35 476)	(35 476)
Other cash flows from financing activities	10 000	(15 000)	70 500	65 500
Funding surplus/(gap)	**46 538**	**(16 828)**	**(531)**	**29 179**

Source: Adapted from Dick Smith Holdings Ltd 2015, p. 55 and Dick Smith Holdings 2014, p. 52.

Required

(a) Examine each line item. Outline what the cash flow data is communicating to you about the operations of Dick Smith Holdings Ltd.

(b) The business collapsed in 2016 when its cash resources were insufficient to meet its current and future obligations, despite outstanding sales performance. Explain why cash is important to the ongoing survival of a business.

(c) Calculate the cash adequacy ratio for each of the three years and comment on your findings.

7.40 Preparing a statement of cash flows ★ ★ LO3

A comparative statement of financial positions as at 31 December 2019 and 2020 for Flowers Ltd is shown below.

FLOWERS LTD Statement of financial positions as at 31 December 2019 and 2020		
	2020	2019
Assets		
Cash	$ 4835	$ 3554
Accounts receivable	11 372	8 529
Inventory	22 034	15 637
Prepaid expenses	1 421	2 132
Property, plant and equipment	63 972	49 755
Less: Accumulated depreciation	(18 480)	(14 215)
Total assets	**$85 154**	**$65 392**
Liabilities and equity		
Accounts payable	$ 7108	$10 490
Debentures	12 794	
Paid-up capital (ordinary shares, par value $1)	35 000	35 000
Retained earnings	30 252	19 902
Total liabilities and equity	**$85 154**	**$65 392**

Sales for 2020 were $180 000 and profit after tax was $16 350. Cost of sales was $136 456. Dividends of $6000 were declared and paid during the year. Interest earned and received was $2340, and interest incurred and paid was $1654. Tax expense for the period was $3000 and this was paid in the period. Other expenses (including depreciation) were $24 880. PPE were purchased for cash.

Required

Prepare a statement of cash flows for Flowers Ltd for 2020.

7.41 Preparing a reconciliation of cash flow ★ ★ ★   LO3

Prepare a reconciliation of cash flows from operating activities and profit after tax for Flowers Ltd from problem 7.40.

7.42 Evaluating a statement of cash flows ★ ★ ★   LO4

Refer to problems 7.40 and 7.41 and complete an evaluation of the statement of cash flows of Flowers Ltd.

7.43 Preparing a statement of cash flows ★ ★ ★   LO3

Financial statements of Food and Wine Ltd are presented below.

FOOD AND WINE LTD		
Statement of profit or loss		
for the year ended 31 December 2020		
	$'000	$'000
Sales		272
Cost of sales		
Opening inventory	20	
+ Inventory purchases	147	
	167	
– Closing inventory	20	147
Gross profit		125
Expenses		
Wages and salaries	16	
Interest expense	7	
Depreciation expense	8	
Other expenses	9	40
		85
Interest received		1
Profit before tax		**86**
Tax		26
Profit after tax		**60**
Retained earnings 31 December 2019		11
		71
Dividends paid		21
Retained earnings 31 December 2020		**50**

FOOD AND WINE LTD				
Statement of financial positions				
as at 31 December 2019 and 2020				
	2020 $'000		2019 $'000	
Current assets				
Cash at bank		11		2
Accounts receivable		50		56
Inventory		16		16
Prepaid expenses		9		11
		86		85
Non-current assets				
Land and buildings		129		97
Plant and machinery at cost	216		203	
Less: Accumulated depreciation	51	165	43	160
		294		257
Total assets		**380**		**342**
Current liabilities				
Accounts payable		36		62
Income tax payable		26		18
Accrued expenses		10		8
		72		88
Non-current liabilities				
Loan		125		120
Equity				
Paid-up ordinary capital		133		123
Retained earnings		50		11
		183		134
Total liabilities and equity		**380**		**342**

The notes from the financial statements reveal that there were no disposals of land, plant or machinery. There was a new share offer of $10 000. A new loan of $15 000 was taken out and an existing loan of $10 000 was paid. A dividend of $21 000 was paid.

Required

Prepare a statement of cash flows for Food and Wine Ltd for 2020.

7.44 Preparing a reconciliation of cash flows ★ ★ ★　　　　　　　　　　　　　　**LO3**

Prepare a reconciliation of cash flows from operating activities and profit after tax for Food and Wine Ltd from problem 7.43.

7.45 Evaluating a statement of cash flows ★ ★ ★　　　　　　　　　　　　　　　　**LO4**

Refer to problems 7.43 and 7.44 and evaluate Food and Wine Ltd's statement of cash flows.

7.46 Preparing and analysing a statement of cash flows ★ ★ ★　　　　　　　　　**LO4**

Jenny Jones and Wendy Wilson are discussing the results of their Crystal Partnership. Presented below is the Crystal Partnership statement of cash flows for the year ended 31 December 2020.

CRYSTAL PARTNERSHIP Statement of cash flows for the year ended 31 December 2020		
Beginning cash balance, 1 January 2020		$ 120 000
Cash inflows		
Inventory sales	$500 000	
Plant and equipment sales	130 000	
Interest on investments	8 000	
Depreciation	12 000	
Sale of land	200 000	
Injection of equity capital	100 000	
Loan	80 000	
Total cash inflows		1 030 000
Cash outflows		
Inventory purchases	240 000	
Salaries and wages	100 000	
Car purchase	50 000	
Drawings	200 000	
Interest expenses	20 000	
Land purchase	250 000	
Loan	30 000	
Other expenses paid	70 000	
Total cash outflows		960 000
Cash increase (decrease)		70 000
Ending cash balance		**$ 190 000**

Jenny is impressed and pleased that the partnership has done so well. However, Wendy is disappointed in the results and criticises the presentation of the statement of cash flows.

Required

(a) Assess why Jenny is impressed.

(b) Using the information presented, prepare the statement of cash flows in accordance with approved accounting standards and give your view of the results of the Crystal Partnership.

DECISION-MAKING ACTIVITIES

7.47 Acquire a statement of cash flows for a company you are interested in evaluating. Normally, the financial statements are available on the company website. If you have trouble locating the financial statements of a company, ask at your library.

Required

Write a report for potential investors, evaluating the company by outlining its strengths and weaknesses. Your analysis should include an evaluation of the cash flows from operating, financing and investing activities.

7.48 The global financial crisis (GFC) was brought about by a bank-induced liquidity squeeze in August 2007. Globally, banks realised that their statements of financial position contained highly toxic subprime mortgages, and their derivatives and hedge-fund managers started liquidating their positions to try to reduce debt, thus producing a bear market in stocks. Short selling on the American bank Lehmann Brothers led to its bankruptcy. Earlier, the US Federal Reserve had stepped in to rescue other American banks such as Bear Stearns, Fannie Mae, Freddie Mac and Washington Mutual.

The whole debacle led to a shutdown in credit markets that affected share markets and trade globally. Letters of credit for shipping, manufacturing goods export and building programs all collapsed. Trust had gone out of the market and banks held onto what capital they had, thus drying up funding for business investment and expansion. Governments the world over started spending to try to stimulate their economies. The process of transferring private debt (mainly large bank debt) to the public sphere (government) had started. Now, years on from the start of the GFC, the world is worried about government debt and how on earth the people are going to pay for it.

Most governments have brought in a combination of tax increases and reduced social spending to help pay the interest costs and reduce the debt. In some parts of the world, citizens have not taken kindly to such measures. Most feel that the greed of the bankers, through their bonuses and commissions on selling subprime mortgages and derivatives, led to the mess and yet they have not been punished or brought to account. In fact, some commentators argue that the banks have just taken their government bailouts and started the process all over again.

Examine the following articles on the internet that give various views of the crisis.

- *People get naked to 'expose Wall Street'* 2011, video recording, CNN, New York, 4 August, http://edition.cnn.com.
- O'Neill, B 2011, 'Class antagonisms or mollycoddled youth?', *The Australian*, 10 August, www.theaustralian.com.au.
- Klein, N 2011, 'Looting with the lights on', *The Guardian*, 17 August, www.guardian.co.uk.

Required

(a) Hypothesise why cash and future cash flow are so important for an individual, business or country, and why it is necessary to report such information.

(b) Many critical commentators throughout the press have called for an end to a 'debt is money' style of thinking. Differentiate between solvency and liquidity and their relationship to debt.

(c) Make a judgement about governments' economic stimulus efforts. Should governments have bailed out the banks? In answering this question, assess a government's duty to provide an economic framework that encourages investment, employment, opportunities and social infrastructure along with its desire to keep the banking system intact and credit forthcoming.

(d) In Europe, the European banks have been forgiven for not valuing some of their asset holdings (creditors that owe them money) in Greek, Portuguese, Irish and Spanish securities in line with the required market-to-market accounting rules. This means that they have not revalued these assets downward to what they are really worth. (One could argue that they are worthless.) If they did, their equity would be wiped out. Assess this situation by commenting on the transparency of this approach, whether this is sound accounting practice and the effect of this position in the long term.

(e) Appraise the reactions of both the nudists and the looters to their government's response to the changing global economy.

REFERENCES

CSR Ltd 2018, *Annual report* 2018, www.csr.com.au.
Dick Smith Holdings Ltd 2015, *Annual report 2015*, www.asx.com.au/asxpdf/20150818/pdf/430kvhrl8cpg0l.pdf.
Dick Smith Holdings Ltd 2014, *Annual report 2014*, www.asx.com.au/asxpdf/20140819/pdf/42rkd9b1rh2wkd.pdf.
JB Hi-Fi Ltd 2018, *Preliminary annual report 2018*, www.jbhifi.com.au.
JB Hi-Fi Ltd 2008–17, annual reports from the years 2008 to 2017, www.jbhifi.com.au.

ACKNOWLEDGEMENTS

Photo: © Naluenart Pimu / Shutterstock.com
Photo: © avs / Shutterstock.com
Photo: © Jamie Farrant / Shutterstock.com
Figures 7.2, 7.4: © JB Hi-Fi Ltd 2018
Apply your knowledge: © CSR Ltd 2018

CHAPTER 8

Analysis and interpretation of financial statements

After studying this chapter, you should be able to:

8.1 explain why different user groups require financial statements to be analysed and interpreted

8.2 describe the nature and purpose of financial analysis

8.3 apply the analytical methods of horizontal, trend, vertical and ratio analysis

8.4 define, calculate and interpret the ratios that measure profitability

8.5 define, calculate and interpret the ratios that measure asset efficiency

8.6 define, calculate and interpret the ratios that measure liquidity

8.7 define, calculate and interpret the ratios that measure capital structure

8.8 define, calculate and interpret the ratios that measure market performance

8.9 explain the interrelationships between ratios and use ratio analysis to discuss the financial performance and position of an entity

8.10 discuss the limitations of ratio analysis.

Chapter preview

In earlier chapters, the various financial statements were introduced: the statement of financial position, the statement of profit or loss, the statement of comprehensive income, the statement of changes in equity and the statement of cash flows. A fundamental purpose of preparing these statements is to provide useful information to assist users in their decision making. The financial data in these statements are expressed in monetary terms, with corresponding figures for the comparative year provided. To better understand the consequences of an entity's operating, investing and financing decisions, it is necessary to analyse the relationships between the numbers in the financial statements, rather than relying on the absolute values in one particular period or one particular statement.

Fundamental analysis refers to analysing many aspects of an entity to assess the entity. Fundamental analysis involves reviewing the state of the industry in which the entity operates, as well as the entity's financial statements, its management and governance, and its competitive positioning. While fundamental analysis is conducted on historical data and current information, the purpose of the analysis is to make predictions about the entity's future.

One aspect of fundamental analysis is financial analysis. **Financial analysis** uses the reported financial numbers to form opinions about the entity's financial performance and position. It is typically associated with, but not restricted to, the calculation and interpretation of ratios. The calculation phase is a mechanical process, with the real benefit of financial analysis being the interpretative stage. When interpreting a ratio, it is important to understand what the ratio is measuring and to compare it to an appropriate benchmark. It must be remembered that the inputs to financial analysis are the numbers reported in financial statements. Given that an entity's accounting policy choices and management estimations affect the reported numbers, consideration must be given to this when comparing ratios over time or across entities.

This chapter describes the importance of financial analysis for financial statement users. Financial analysis adds further meaning to the reported numbers, allowing users to make a better assessment of an entity's profitability, efficiency, liquidity, capital structure and market performance. Consider Advantage Tennis Coaching (ATC), the tennis coaching business described in earlier chapters, and JB Hi-Fi Ltd. What are you able to infer from knowing that ATC generated a $16 370 profit for a particular month and that JB Hi-Fi Ltd generated a $233.2 million profit in 2018? Your assessments would be enhanced if you could compare these profit figures with prior years, those of other similar entities and the resources invested to generate the profits. This chapter discusses how the reported numbers can be compared with other reported numbers to assist users' decision making. Just as an absolute dollar figure is limited in its usefulness, a ratio is also of limited use unless it can be benchmarked. We also discuss the benchmarks that can be used, in addition to noting the limitations associated with financial analysis.

8.1 Users and decision making

LEARNING OBJECTIVE 8.1 Explain why different user groups require financial statements to be analysed and interpreted.

As discussed in the introduction to accounting and business decision making chapter, the users of financial statements can be categorised as resource providers (e.g. creditors, lenders, shareholders and employees); recipients of goods and services (e.g. customers and debtors); and parties performing an overview or regulatory function (e.g. the Australian Taxation Office (ATO), corporate regulators or a statistical bureau). User groups are interested in different aspects of the entity and various information sources are available to interested parties to facilitate their decision making. Such information sources include the financial press, trade-related magazines, research reports from broking houses, industry publications, online databases (e.g. Dun & Bradstreet) and government statistics. Another important source of information is financial statements. With a knowledge and understanding of the information contained in financial statements, financial analysis can provide information specific to the users' needs. Financial analysis is an analytical method in which reported financial numbers are used to form opinions as to the entity's past and future performance and position.

The decisions that users make vary. For example, before deciding whether to supply goods and services on credit to an entity, creditors would be interested in the entity's ability to pay the debts within the credit period provided. Professionals who assess the credit status of entities are referred to as *credit analysts*. A financial institution contemplating a loan to an entity would be interested in the ability of the entity to generate cash flows to service the loan over the loan period and the security that the entity could provide to the lender. They are interested in assessing the entity's credit risk. A shareholder or potential investor is interested in the ability of an entity to generate profits that allow it to distribute dividends and/or retain the profits to invest with the expectation of capital appreciation in its share price. Professionals known as *equity analysts* provide investment recommendations on entities' shares and use financial analysis as part of their fundamental analysis toolkit to assess what they believe to be the value of the entity. Employees are concerned about being paid for services rendered and long-term job security, so they would be interested in the entity's liquidity and profitability. Although the rules for determining taxable income and accounting profit differ, the ATO relies on financial numbers generated from the accounting information system in its assessments of tax payable. Management also uses financial statements in its decision-making capacity, but managers have the advantage of being able to command information from the accounting information system and so do not need to rely solely on external financial statements when conducting financial analysis.

Statement users generally share a common objective: to evaluate past decisions and make informed decisions about future events. In this sense, reported financial numbers have a role to play. The financial statements depict historical information. When making predictions about future events, an evaluation of past events is often the most useful starting point. For example, assessing an entity's past **profitability** (defined as the entity's ability to generate profits from the available resources) will shape an investor's expectations as to the entity's future profitability. Financial analysis involves expressing the reported numbers in relative terms rather than relying on the absolute numbers, and can highlight the strengths and weaknesses of entities. It is an important decision-making tool for evaluating the historical health of an entity and predicting the entity's future financial wellbeing.

VALUE TO BUSINESS

- Financial statements are employed by a range of users making a variety of decisions. The purpose of financial statements is to provide the information useful for decision making concerning the allocation of scarce resources.
- Financial analysis is an analytical tool that involves expressing the reported financial numbers in relative terms.
- Financial analysis helps statement users to evaluate an entity's past decisions and form an opinion as to the entity's future financial health.

8.2 Nature and purpose of financial analysis

LEARNING OBJECTIVE 8.2 Describe the nature and purpose of financial analysis.

We have identified that financial analysis involves expressing reported numbers in financial statements in relative terms. Relying on the absolute values contained in the financial statements is not meaningful when trying to evaluate an entity's past decisions and predict future rewards and risks. For example, if you are examining an entity's statement of profit or loss and note that the profit figure has increased from $200 000 in the previous year to $300 000 in the current year, does this mean that the entity has become more profitable? Similarly, if the entity's interest-bearing liabilities have increased from $1 million to $2 million, does this mean that the entity has become more reliant on external funding? The answer to both of these questions is 'not necessarily'. The entity's absolute dollar values of profit and external debt have increased, but this does not necessarily mean that the entity is more profitable or more reliant on debt. For example, if the entity's asset base increased twofold over the comparative period — from $2 million to $4 million — then the profit generated when expressed per dollar of investment in assets would have fallen. Likewise, if an increase in assets of $2 million was funded by only $500 000 of interest-bearing liabilities, the entity's reliance on external debt relative to equity would have fallen.

Similar analogies can be drawn when comparing two entities. For example, just because Entity A reports a profit of $50 000 and Entity B reports a profit of $10 000, this does not necessarily make Entity A more profitable relative to Entity B. Entity A's absolute dollar value of profit is indeed larger, but it is not possible to make an informed judgement on the relative profitability without comparing the profit generated to the resources available to generate it (e.g. the investment in assets).

These examples emphasise the need to express the reported numbers in relation to other numbers, enabling relationships to be revealed and the financial statements to tell a story about the entity's financial health. This process typically involves comparing figures to:
- the equivalent figures from previous years
- other figures in the financial statements.

The processes of comparison can be categorised as horizontal analysis, trend analysis, vertical analysis and ratio analysis. These are described in the next section.

8.3 Analytical methods

LEARNING OBJECTIVE 8.3 Apply the analytical methods of horizontal, trend, vertical and ratio analysis.

In this section we introduce the analytical techniques of horizontal, trend, vertical and ratio analysis. This chapter focuses on ratio analysis, but horizontal, trend and vertical analysis are important complementary tools to ratio analysis. All analytical methods involve comparing one item in the financial statements with another.

Horizontal analysis

Horizontal analysis compares the reported numbers in the current period with the equivalent numbers for a previous period, usually the immediate preceding period. Financial statements are usually presented in a two-column format containing the figures for the current reporting period and the figures for the comparative reporting period. This permits the user to readily calculate the absolute dollar change and the percentage change in the reported numbers between periods. The dollar change is calculated as shown in the equation below:

$$\text{Current period's number}$$
$$\textit{less} \text{ Previous period's number}$$

The percentage change is calculated as shown in the following equation:

$$\frac{\text{Current period's number } \textit{less} \text{ Previous period's number}}{\text{Previous period's number}} \times 100$$

The percentage change cannot be calculated if the equivalent reported figure for the previous year was zero. Care must also be exercised when ascertaining and interpreting the direction of the change. For example, if expenses or cash outflows are greater in the current year than in the previous year, the direction of the change is upwards but this has a negative, rather than a positive, impact on reported profit or cash flows.

The 2018 and 2017 statement of financial position, statement of profit or loss and statement of cash flows for JB Hi-Fi Ltd are provided in figures 8.1 to 8.3 respectively. (The statement of comprehensive income and statement of changes in equity have not been provided in this chapter.) Note that JB Hi-Fi Ltd's annual reports are available from the company's website at www.jbhifi.com.au. Information from these statements and supporting notes will be used throughout the chapter to illustrate concepts as they are introduced. The columns headed A and B are the absolute dollar figures in the financial statements. The column headed C shows the change in the absolute dollar amount from 2017 to 2018 and the column labelled D represents the percentage change in the reported amounts from 2017 to 2018. From an inspection of the financial statements, it is easy to identify which reported numbers have increased or decreased. By performing horizontal analysis, the magnitude and significance of the dollar changes becomes apparent.

As can be seen in figure 8.1, JB Hi-Fi Ltd's total assets increased by $31.9 million (1 per cent), total liabilities decreased by $62.2 million (4 per cent) and equity increased by $94.1 million (11 per cent). There are some items that in absolute dollar terms appear to have changed significantly, but the percentage change is relatively small. Similarly, there are some items that in percentage terms appear to have changed significantly, but the absolute dollar change is relatively small. Columns C and D provide insights not easily revealed by columns A and B. The horizontal analysis reveals that JB Hi-Fi Ltd was holding slightly less cash and cash equivalents as at 30 June 2018 than at the same time in 2017 (down $0.8 million, 1 per cent) and more trade and other receivables (up $11.1 million, 6 per cent), while the changes in most other asset classes were less than 5 per cent. Trade and other payables increased by $20.6 million (3 per cent). JB Hi-Fi Ltd reduced its reliance on borrowings in 2018 relative to 2017, with borrowings down $89.4 million (16 per cent). As shown, horizontal analysis identifies significant changes between reporting periods, alerting the user to matters that warrant further investigation.

FIGURE 8.1 JB Hi-Fi Ltd's statement of financial position

	Notes	Consolidated		Change	
		A 2018 $m	B 2017 $m	C $m	D %
Current assets					
Cash and cash equivalents		72.0	72.8	(0.8)	(1)
Trade and other receivables	8	204.7	193.6	11.1	6
Inventories	7	891.1	859.7	31.4	4
Other current assets	9	42.7	41.4	1.3	3
Total current assets		1 210.5	1 167.5	43.0	4
Non-current assets					
Plant and equipment	10	198.0	208.2	(10.2)	(5)
Intangible assets	11	1 037.3	1 037.3	0.0	0
Other non-current assets	9	45.9	46.8	(0.9)	(2)
Total non-current assets		1 281.2	1 292.3	(11.1)	(1)
Total assets		2 491.7	2 459.8	31.9	1
Current liabilities					
Trade and other payables	12	665.3	644.7	20.6	3
Deferred revenue	13	150.5	141.8	8.7	1
Provisions	14	83.5	76.3	7.2	9
Other current liabilities	15	8.3	9.0	(0.7)	8
Current tax liabilities		9.6	13.6	(4.0)	(29)
Total current liabilities		917.2	885.4	31.8	4
Non-current liabilities					
Borrowings	17	469.4	558.8	(89.4)	(16)
Deferred revenue	13	103.7	99.6	4.1	(4)
Deferred tax liabilities	6	5.7	16.1	(10.4)	(65)
Provisions	14	12.5	11.8	0.7	6
Other non-current liabilities	15	35.6	34.6	1.0	3
Total non-current liabilities		626.9	720.9	(94.0)	(13)
Total liabilities		1 544.1	1 606.3	(62.2)	(4)
Net assets		**947.6**	**853.5**	**94.1**	**11**
Equity					
Contributed equity	18	441.7	438.7	3.0	(1)
Reserves	19	42.7	33.2	9.5	29
Retained earnings		463.2	381.6	81.6	21
Total equity		**947.6**	**853.5**	**94.1**	**11**

Source: Data (excluding analysis) from JB Hi-Fi Ltd 2018, p. 56.

Columns C and D of figure 8.2 respectively show the dollar change and percentage change for items affecting JB Hi-Fi Ltd's profit. The entity's profit attributable to equity holders of the company is up by $60.8 million (35 per cent). Its gross profit is up $239.7 million (19 per cent) reflecting the increase in sales revenue (up $1 226.3 million, 22 per cent) in 2018, outstripping the increase in the cost of sales. The higher sales are associated with the roll-out of JB Hi-Fi Home branded stores, new stores, maturation of previously opened stores and growth in online operations. Consistent with the higher sales volumes, the cost of sales increased by $986.6 million (22 per cent) and sales and marketing expenses associated with generating higher sales were up $115 million, 20 per cent). Occupancy expenses also increased (up $57.1 million, 23 per cent) and this may be attributable to factors such as higher store rents and higher utility charges. The finance costs (up $5.9 million, 55 per cent) were higher in 2018 due to increased borrowings.

Analysing the change in the numbers reported in the cash flow statement (figure 8.3) reveals that JB Hi-Fi Ltd's cash at the end of the 2018 year was $0.8 million less (down 1 per cent) than it was at the start of the year. Net cash flows from operating activities increased by $101.5 million (53 per cent). Investing activities used net cash in 2018 of $54 million compared to $885.5 million in 2017, a decrease of $831.5 million (94 per cent). JB Hi-Fi Ltd's payments for property, plant and equipment (PPE) were higher in 2018 relative to 2017. The company's financing activities in 2018 resulted in a net outflow of $239.1 million compared to a net outflow in 2017 of $715.9 million (down $476.8 million). This decrease in outflow relates to the repayment of borrowings in 2018 compared to an increase in borrowings in 2017.

FIGURE 8.2 | JB Hi-Fi Ltd's statement of profit or loss

	Notes	Consolidated		Change	
		A **2018** **$m**	**B** **2017** **$m**	**C** **$m**	**D** **%**
Revenue		6 854.3	5 628.0	1 226.3	22
Cost of sales		(5 384.1)	(4 397.5)	986.6	22
Gross profit		1 470.2	1 230.5	239.7	19
Other income		1.1	2.0	(0.9)	(45)
Sales and marketing expenses		(695.1)	(580.1)	115.0	20
Occupancy expenses		(305.7)	(248.6)	57.1	23
Administrative expenses		(42.2)	(36.2)	6.0	17
Acquisition transaction and implementation expenses		—	(22.4)	(22.4)	(100)
Other expenses		(77.2)	(75.3)	1.9	3
Finance costs	5	(16.6)	(10.7)	5.9	55
Profit before tax		**334.5**	**259.2**	**75.3**	**29**
Income tax expense	6	(101.3)	(86.8)	14.5	17
Profit for the year attributable to Owners of the Company		**233.2**	**172.4**	**60.8**	**35**
		Cents	Cents	Cents	%
Earnings per share					
Basic (cents per share)	3	203.09	154.30	48.79	32
Diluted (cents per share)	3	201.11	152.94	48.17	31

Source: Data (excluding analysis) from JB Hi-Fi Ltd 2018, p. 54.

FIGURE 8.3 | JB Hi-Fi Ltd's statement of cash flows

	Notes	Consolidated		Change	
		A **2018** **$m**	**B** **2017** **$m**	**C** **$m**	**D** **%**
Cash flows from operating activities					
Receipts from customers		7 551.9	6 205.5	1 346.4	22
Payments to suppliers and employees		(7 130.5)	(5 908.8)	1 221.7	21
Interest received		0.5	1.7	(1.2)	(10.5)
Interest and other finance costs paid		(15.0)	(9.3)	5.7	61
Income taxes paid		(114.8)	(98.5)	16.3	17
Net cash inflow from operating activities	16	292.1	190.6	101.5	53
Cash flows from investing activities					
Payment for business combination, net of cash acquired	25	—	(836.6)	(836.6)	(100)
Payments for plant and equipment	10	(54.4)	(49.1)	5.3	11
Proceeds from sale of plant and equipment		0.4	0.2	0.2	100
Net cash (outflow) from investing activities		(54.0)	(885.5)	(831.5)	(94)
Cash flows from financing activities					
Proceeds from issue of shares	18	3.0	395.9	(392.9)	(99)
(Repayment)/proceeds of borrowings		(89.7)	450.0	(539.7)	(120)
Payments for debt issue costs		(0.8)	(1.7)	(0.9)	(53)
Share issue costs		—	(9.2)	(9.2)	(100)
Dividends paid to owners of the company	4	(151.6)	(119.1)	32.5	27
Net cash (outflow) inflow from financing activities		(239.1)	(715.9)	(476.8)	(67)
Net (decrease) increase in cash and cash equivalents		(1.0)	(21.0)	(20)	(95)

Cash and cash equivalents at the beginning of the financial year	72.8	51.9	20.9	40
Effect of exchange rate changes on cash and cash equivalents	0.2	(0.1)	0.3	300
Cash and cash equivalents at the end of year	**72.0**	**72.8**	**(0.8)**	**(1)**

Source: Data (excluding analysis) from JB Hi-Fi Ltd 2018, p. 58.

VALUE TO BUSINESS

- Horizontal analysis compares the reported numbers in the current period with the equivalent numbers for a preceding period.
- This permits the user to readily calculate the absolute dollar change and the percentage change in the reported numbers between periods.
- The dollar change is calculated as the reported number in the current reporting period less the reported number in the previous reporting period.
- The percentage change is calculated as the dollar change in the reported number between the current and the previous reporting periods, divided by the value of the reported item in the previous year.
- Horizontal analysis highlights the magnitude and significance of the dollar changes.

Trend analysis

Trend analysis tries to predict the future direction of various items on the basis of the direction of the items in the past. To calculate a trend, at least three years of data are required. A public company often provides a historical summary of various financial items in its annual report. The sales revenue, earnings before interest and taxation (EBIT) and profit after tax data for JB Hi-Fi Ltd for 2010 to 2018 are provided in figure 8.4. To identify the trends in these data over the six-year period, it is useful to convert the numbers into an index. Using 2010 as the base year and setting the base year at an index of 100, every subsequent figure is expressed relative to the base year (i.e. relative to 2010). For example, to calculate the trend in sales revenue, the following calculations are made:

Step 1. Set 2010 as the base year, assigning it a commencing index value of 100.

Step 2. Divide the 2011 revenue by the 2010 revenue and express this as an index by multiplying the answer by 100:

$$\frac{\$2\,959.3\,\text{million}}{\$2\,731.3\,\text{million}} \times 100 = 108$$

Step 3. Divide the 2012 revenue by the 2010 revenue and express this as an index by multiplying the answer by 100:

$$\frac{\$3\,127.8\,\text{million}}{\$2\,731.3\,\text{million}} \times 100 = 115$$

Step 4. Each subsequent year's sales revenue is divided by the 2010 sales revenue and expressed as an index by multiplying the answer by 100.

Analysing the trend figures in figure 8.4 identifies that sales revenue has increased each year over 2010–2018. In 2011 and 2012 EBIT and profit after tax declined, but have since trended upwards.

FIGURE 8.4 Trends in sales revenue, EBIT and profit after tax figures for JB Hi-Fi Ltd for the period 2010 to 2018

	2018	2017	2016	2015	2014	2013	2012	2011	2010
Absolute figures ($m)									
Sales revenue	6 854.3	5 628.0	3 954.5	3652.1	3 483.8	3 308.4	3 127.8	2 959.3	2 731.3
EBIT	351.1	269.9	221.7	189.6	191.5	178.2	161.4	162.6	175.1
Profit after tax	233.2	172.4	152.2	136.5	128.4	116.6	104.6	109.7	118.7

	2018	2017	2016	2015	2014	2013	2012	2011	2010
Trend analysis									
Sales revenue	251	206	145	134	128	121	115	108	100
EBIT	201	154	127	108	109	102	92	93	100
Profit after tax	196	145	128	115	108	98	88	92	100

Trend figures can be graphed to visually depict the direction and magnitude of financial items of interest. For example, a graph of the trends in JB Hi-Fi Ltd's sales revenue, EBIT and profit after tax for the period 2010 to 2018 is shown in figure 8.5. As we will see later in the chapter, examining trends in financial ratios — instead of focusing on trends calculated on absolute dollar values — is an important analytical tool, as such trends are useful in formulating predictions. For example, the graph in figure 8.5 depicts that the growth in sales revenue outstripped the growth in EBIT and profit after tax. This suggests that JB Hi-Fi Ltd's sales volume and revenue have not increased at a greater rate than the increase in the operating and financing costs of the business, and hence the trend in profits is not as positive as the trend in sales.

FIGURE 8.5 Graph of trends in JB Hi-Fi Ltd's sales revenue, EBIT and profit after tax for 2010 to 2018

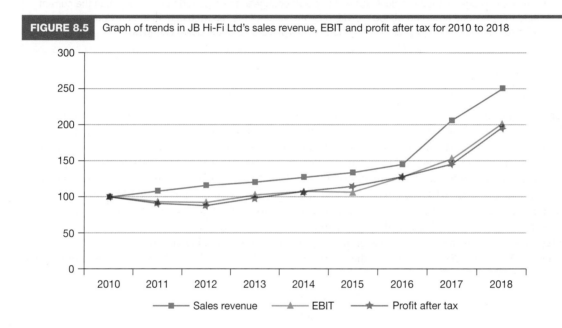

VALUE TO BUSINESS

- To calculate a trend, it is necessary to have at least three years of data.
- Trend analysis of a particular item involves expressing the item in subsequent years relative to a selected base year. The base year is typically given a value of 100.
- Trend analysis is useful in identifying the significance of an item relative to a base amount.
- Identifying trends is useful in formulating predictions as to the future prospects of an entity.

Vertical analysis

Vertical analysis is another method of converting the absolute dollar values in financial statements into more meaningful figures. Whereas horizontal analysis compares reported figures over time, **vertical analysis** compares the items in a financial statement to other items in the same financial statement. When expressed in this way, the financial statements are often referred to as 'common size' statements. This involves using a reported item as an anchor point against which other items are compared. When performing vertical analysis on the statement of profit or loss, the anchor point is the revenue figure and every item in the statement of profit or loss is expressed as a percentage of the income item. When performing vertical analysis on the statement of financial position, the anchor point is the total asset figure and every item in the statement of financial position is expressed as a percentage of the total asset figure.

The concept of vertical analysis is illustrated in figures 8.6 and 8.7 for JB Hi-Fi Ltd. The total asset figure in the statement of financial position (figure 8.6) is $2491.7 million. So, every item in the statement is divided by this total asset figure and multiplied by 100. For example, the plant and equipment constitute 8 per cent of the total asset figure (($198.0 million/$2491.7 million) × 100) with the current assets accounting for 49 per cent of the total asset figure. As a percentage of total assets, total liabilities are 62 per cent (($1544.1 million/$2491.7 million) × 100) with equity being 38 per cent. This informs us that the entity is more reliant on debt to finance its assets than on equity.

FIGURE 8.6 Vertical analysis of a statement of financial position: JB Hi-Fi Ltd

		Consolidated	
	Notes	**2018 $m**	**% relative to total assets**
Current assets			
Cash and cash equivalents		72.0	3
Trade and other receivables	9	204.7	8
Inventories	10	891.1	36
Other current assets	14	42.7	2
Total current assets		1 210.5	49
Non-current assets			
Plant and equipment	12	198.0	8
Intangible assets	13	1 037.3	42
Other non-current assets	14	45.9	2
Total non-current assets		1 281.2	51
Total assets		2 491.7	100
Current liabilities			
Trade and other payables	12	665.3	27
Deferred revenue	13	150.5	6
Provisions	14	83.5	3
Other current liabilities	15	8.3	0
Other current tax liabilities		9.6	0
Total current liabilities		917.2	37
Non-current liabilities			
Borrowings	17	469.4	19
Deferred revenue	13	103.7	4
Deferred tax liabilities	6	5.7	0
Provisions	14	12.5	1
Other non-current liabilities	15	35.6	1
Total non-current liabilities		626.9	25
Total liabilities		1 544.1	62
Net assets		**947.6**	**38**
Equity			
Contributed equity	18	441.7	18
Reserves	19	42.7	2
Retained earnings		463.2	19
Total equity		**947.6**	**38**

Source: Data (excluding analysis) from JB Hi-Fi Ltd 2018, p. 56.

FIGURE 8.7 Vertical analysis of a statement of profit or loss: JB Hi-Fi Ltd

		Consolidated	
	Notes	**2018 $m**	**% relative to revenue**
Revenue		6 854.3	100
Cost of sales		(5 384.1)	79
Gross profit		1 470.2	21
Other income		1.1	0
Sales and marketing expenses		(695.1)	10
Occupancy expenses		(305.7)	4

	Notes	Consolidated 2018 $m	% relative to revenue
Administrative expenses		(42.2)	1
Other expenses		(77.2)	1
Finance costs	4	(16.6)	0
Profit before tax		**334.5**	**5**
Income tax expense	5	(101.3)	1
Profit for the year attributable to Owners of the Company		**233.2**	**3**

Source: Data (excluding analysis) from JB Hi-Fi Ltd 2018, p. 54.

The vertical analysis of the statement of profit or loss highlights the importance of an item relative to the revenue figure. Each item in the statement is divided by the revenue figure and expressed as a percentage of that figure. In figure 8.7, the anchor point for the vertical analysis of the statement of profit or loss is revenue ($6 854.3 million). The gross profit and profit before tax are 21 per cent and 5 per cent respectively, suggesting that every dollar of sales generates on average 21 cents of gross profit and 5 cents of profit before tax. Aside from the cost of sales, the main expenses of the entity are sales and marketing expenses, constituting 10 per cent of revenue. This suggests that JB Hi-Fi Ltd spends around 10 cents of every sales dollar on sales and marketing. delivery

VALUE TO BUSINESS

- Vertical analysis compares items in a financial statement to an anchor item in the same statement. The anchor item in the statement of financial position is total assets; in the statement of profit or loss it is revenue.
- All asset, liability and equity items are expressed as a percentage of total assets, and all income and expense items are expressed as a percentage of revenue.
- A vertical analysis identifies the importance of an item relative to the anchor item.

Ratio analysis

The financial analysis tool that we will concentrate on for the remainder of the chapter is ratio analysis. A ratio is simply a comparison of one item in a financial statement relative to another item in a financial statement — one item is divided by another to create the ratio. **Ratio analysis** examines the relationship between two quantitative amounts with the objective of expressing the relationship in ratio or percentage form. In the statement of cash flows chapter, you were introduced to some ratios calculated using information from the statement of cash flows. The amounts compared do not necessarily have to be in the same statement, because it is often meaningful to compare items in the statement of profit or loss or statement of cash flows to those in the statement of financial position. However, comparisons between these statements are not always straightforward, because the statement of profit or loss and statement of cash flows involve **flow items** that are generated over a period of time, whereas the statement of financial position reports **stock items** at a point in time. For example, consider an entity that generated a profit of $50 000. The entity's investment in assets was $500 000 for the majority of the reporting period, but rose to $1 000 000 following the purchase of an asset close to reporting year end. For the majority of the year, the entity had investments of $500 000 from which to generate profit. If the $50 000 profit generated over the year is compared to the assets at the end of the year (i.e. $1 000 000), the profit per dollar of investment will be understated and not reflect the fact that the $1 000 000 investment existed for only a small portion of the year. As a result, when calculating ratios involving a comparison of a stock and a flow item, the average of the stock item during the year is often used instead of the year-end figure. To calculate the average, the beginning year value and the ending year value are added, with the sum being divided by two. The ratio calculations in this chapter use average balances when comparing stock and flow items. For simplicity, often the year-end balance of stock items is used in ratio analysis.

Ratio analysis is a three-step process.

Step 1. Calculate a meaningful ratio by expressing the dollar amount of an item in a financial statement by the dollar amount of another item in a financial statement.

Step 2. Compare the ratio with a benchmark.

Step 3. Interpret the ratio and seek to explain why it differs from previous years, from comparative entities or from industry averages.

The purpose of ratio analysis is to express a relationship between two relevant items that is easy to interpret and compare. In this chapter, we will categorise ratios into five groups:

1. profitability ratios
2. efficiency ratios
3. liquidity ratios
4. capital structure ratios
5. market performance ratios (relevant to companies listed on an organised securities exchange).

The ratios in each of these categories help users in their decision making concerning the allocation of scarce resources. The **profitability ratios** inform users as to the profit associated with their equity investment. The **efficiency ratios** shed light on management's effectiveness in managing the assets entrusted to it. An entity's ability to meet its short-term commitments is indicated by **liquidity ratios**, while its long-term stability and financing decisions are reflected in capital structure ratios. The **market performance ratios (market test ratios)** generally require share price data; for this reason they are usually confined to listed companies, relating the company's financial numbers to its share price, and indicate the market's sentiment towards the company. It is important to recognise that there is not necessarily a consensus regarding the ratios that should be calculated in each category or the method of calculating a particular ratio.

Benchmarks

Just as a financial number expressed as an absolute dollar amount is limited for decision-making purposes, a ratio is of limited usefulness unless it is compared to a relevant benchmark. Ratios are useful when the returns and risks for entities over time are compared with those of entities in different industries or entities in the same industry. Comparing the ratio with a benchmark enables the favourableness or otherwise of the ratio to be assessed. The various comparisons that can be made include the following.

- *A comparison of the entity's ratios over time to identify trends.* This permits users to assess the stability and/or directional changes in the ratios over time. Unfavourable trends should be investigated by financial statement users.
- *A comparison of the entity's ratios with those of other entities operating in the same industry, referred to as intra-industry analysis.* For example, a potential investor who wishes to invest in banking shares has identified four entities operating in that economic industry sector. The investor can use ratios to compare their respective returns and risks.
- *A comparison of the entity's ratios with the industry averages.* An industry norm is a relevant benchmark that enables a user to assess a particular entity's return and risk relative to its competitors, to determine if it is outperforming or lagging behind its peers. Industry averages for various economic industry sectors are available through commercial databases.
- *A comparison of the entity's ratios with those of entities operating in different industries or with the norms of other industries, referred to as inter-industry analysis.* Caution is needed when such an analysis is being undertaken, as differences in industry structures will affect the ratios.
- *A comparison of the entity's ratios with arbitrary standards.* It is not possible to specify what a ratio should be, but users operate on rules of thumb that serve as crude points of initial assessment. For example, a rule of thumb may be that a debt to equity ratio should not exceed 100 per cent. However, given that the 100 per cent is arbitrary, if an entity has a higher ratio than this it cannot be concluded that the ratio is unsatisfactory and the entity is in financial distress.

When comparing an entity's ratios over time or across industries, it is assumed that industry and entity risk remain constant. If risk changes, then returns should also change. Caution needs to be exercised when comparing entities within the same industry, as no two entities have identical products and product markets. Similarly, caution is needed when judging the favourableness of an entity's ratio with that of entities in other industries, as industry characteristics affect ratios. For example, a supermarket's gross profit generated per dollar of sales revenue would be substantially lower than that of a car manufacturer.

Financial ratios are also affected by an entity's accounting policy choices and assumptions. Before comparing the ratios for different entities, the degree of consistency in the accounting policies and assumptions of the entities should be reviewed. Similarly, before comparing an entity's ratios over time, the consistency of that entity's accounting policy choices and assumptions should be checked. For example, an entity that revalues its PPE may generate lower returns from its assets relative to an entity that measures its PPE at cost, assuming that the value of PPE assets is increasing.

In the remainder of this chapter, we will introduce ratios in each of these categories, calculate the ratios, compare them with relevant benchmarks and interpret the ratios. The 2018 JB Hi-Fi Ltd financial statements will be used for this purpose and the comparative benchmark will be the ratio for the previous year. Other comparisons could include competitors' ratios, such as those of other listed companies operating in the consumer retail industry, or industry averages. When performing ratio analysis for a company with subsidiaries, consolidated figures should always be used. Although the calculation process may appear to be fairly mechanical, the benefit of ratio analysis comes from interpreting and interrelating the ratios to answer the 'why' questions — for example, why did profitability decline? Why has liquidity improved? Why is the entity's efficiency declining? A summary of the ratios presented in this chapter is provided in the summary section of this chapter.

VALUE TO BUSINESS

- A ratio compares one item in the financial statements with another item in the financial statements with the aim of expressing a relationship between two relevant items that is easy to interpret.
- Ratios can be grouped into the following categories:
  - profitability ratios
  - efficiency ratios
  - liquidity ratios
  - capital structure ratios
  - market performance ratios (relevant only to entities listed on an organised securities exchange).
- To interpret the favourableness or otherwise of ratios, it is necessary to compare the ratios with relevant benchmarks.

8.4 Profitability analysis

LEARNING OBJECTIVE 8.4 Define, calculate and interpret the ratios that measure profitability.

An entity's ability to generate profits and return on investment is one of the prime indicators of its financial health. In this section, we introduce the ratios that are useful in assessing an entity's profitability.

Return on equity

Owners are interested in the return that the entity is generating for them. This test of an entity's performance is the return on equity. The **return on equity (ROE)**, expressed as a percentage, is computed by relating the profit that the entity has generated for its owners during the period to the owners' investments in the entity. For a non-company entity, the ROE is the profit available to the owners divided by the owners' equity in the business. When calculating the ROE for a company, we are interested in the profit available to the ordinary equity holders of the parent entity relative to the ordinary shareholders' equity in the company. The equity comprises any capital invested, retained earnings and reserves:

$$\frac{\text{Profit available to owners}}{\text{Average equity}} \times 100 = x\%$$

Profit is the current year's profit available for distribution to the owners. The numerator, profit, is obtained from the statement of profit or loss. The denominator, equity, is obtained from the equity section of the statement of financial position. When analysing a company, some analysts exclude the impact of significant items, which can distort the ratio by their size or nature and so distort the trends in the ratio over time. It is also necessary to exclude any dividends due to preference shareholders (should they exist), as the preference shareholders are entitled to receive their dividends before any distributions of profit can be made to ordinary shareholders. The equity figure before minority interests and preference capital is obtained from the statement of financial position. As the numerator of this ratio is a flow item and the denominator is a stock item, the stock item is averaged by summing the balance at the start and end of the reporting period and dividing this by 2. This assumes that any change between opening and closing balances occurred evenly throughout the reporting period.

The ROE indicates the annual return (in cents) that the entity is generating for owners for each dollar of owners' funds invested in the entity. It is advantageous for this ratio to show an upward trend over time. However, a sustained high ROE will attract new competitors to the industry and eventually erode excess ROE. The adequacy of the ROE is assessed by comparing it with the returns on alternative investment opportunities (of equivalent risk) available to owners. Inability to generate an adequate ROE will restrict an entity's capacity to attract new capital investment and adversely affect its ability to be sustainable in the long term.

The ROE is a ratio that reflects an entity's profitability, efficiency and capital structure. Changes in the ratio over time, and differences in the ratio across entities, will reflect the direction of an entity's profitability, asset efficiency and capital structure. We will now consider the ratios that have an impact on an entity's ROE.

Return on assets

The **return on assets (ROA)** is a profitability ratio that compares an entity's profit to the assets available to generate the profits. Effectively, the ratio reflects the results of the entity's ability to convert sales revenue into profit and its ability to generate income from its asset investments. In the numerator, profit or the EBIT figure can be used. For the purpose of our analysis, the profit figure is used. The ratio can be calculated including (or excluding) the effect of significant items from the profit figure. The ratio is calculated as:

$$\frac{\text{Profit (loss)}}{\text{Average total assets}} \times 100 = x\%$$

Given that the ROA reflects an entity's profitability (ability to convert income dollars into profit) and asset efficiency (ability to generate income from investments in assets), change in the ROA can be explained by changes in the entity's profitability and asset efficiency. The profitability ratios that reflect the ability of the entity to generate profits from income include the gross profit margin and the profit margin, as discussed next.

Profit margin ratios

Ratios that relate profit to sales revenue generated by the entity include the gross profit margin and the profit margin. The **gross profit margin** compares an entity's gross profit to its sales revenue, reflecting the proportion of sales revenue that results in gross profit. Given that gross profit is sales revenue less cost of sales, 100 per cent less the gross profit margin is the cost of sales as a percentage of sales revenue. The gross profit margin calculation is:

$$\frac{\text{Gross profit}}{\text{Sales revenue}} \times 100 = x\%$$

Both the numerator and denominator are sourced from the statement of profit or loss. The gross profit margin reflects the gross profit (in cents) generated per dollar of sales revenue and reflects an entity's pricing strategy. It is not possible to specify the gross profit range that would be desirable. This is because the gross profit is interrelated with sales volume. Entities with high (low) turnover tend to have smaller (larger) gross margins. For example, the gross margin for a supermarket is between 2 and 5 per cent. This is sustainable given the high-volume turnover of a supermarket. However, a gross profit margin of between 2 and 5 per cent would not be satisfactory for a luxury car sales business, as the volume of trade would not justify such a low margin.

An entity must meet all other expenses from its gross profit. The comparison of sales revenue and profit is referred to as the **profit margin**; this ratio reveals what percentage of sales revenue dollars results in profit (loss). As with the ROA, it is not uncommon to see the profit margin computed with EBIT rather than profit (loss) as the numerator. Any change in the profit margin over time must be attributable to changes in the gross profit margin and/or changes in the expenses as a percentage of sales (**expense ratios**). The ratio is calculated as:

$$\frac{\text{Profit (loss)}}{\text{Sales revenue}} \times 100 = x\%$$

As discussed in the statement of cash flows chapter, a cash-based measure of profitability is the ratio of cash flow (from operating activities) to sales. The **cash flow to sales ratio** measures the relative amount of cash flow generated by each sales revenue dollar. It is useful to compare this ratio with the equivalent accrual-based ratio, namely, the profit margin. The ratio is calculated as:

$$\frac{\text{Cash flow from operating activities}}{\text{Sales revenue}} \times 100 = x\%$$

Analysis of profitability: JB Hi-Fi Ltd

In this section we will calculate the profitability ratios for JB Hi-Fi Ltd for the 2018 and 2017 reporting periods, interpret the information that they convey and comment on their adequacy. The profitability ratios for JB Hi-Fi Ltd for 2017 and 2018 are presented in figure 8.8.

FIGURE 8.8	Analysis of JB Hi-Fi Ltd's profitability

2018	2017
Return on equity (ROE)	
$\left(\dfrac{\$233.2}{(\$947.6 + \$853.5)/2}\right) \times 100 = 25.90\%$	$\left(\dfrac{\$172.4}{(\$853.5 + \$404.7)/2}\right) \times 100 = 27.40\%$
Return on assets (ROA)	
$\left(\dfrac{\$233.2}{(\$2491.7 + \$2459.8)/2}\right) \times 100 = 9.42\%$	$\left(\dfrac{\$172.4}{(\$2459.8 + \$992.4)/2}\right) \times 100 = 9.99\%$
Gross profit margin	
$\left(\dfrac{\$1470.2}{\$6854.3}\right) \times 100 = 21.45\%$	$\left(\dfrac{\$1230.5}{\$5628.0}\right) \times 100 = 21.86\%$
Profit margin	
$\left(\dfrac{\$233.2}{\$6854.3}\right) \times 100 = 3.40\%$	$\left(\dfrac{\$172.4}{\$5628.0}\right) \times 100 = 3.06\%$
Cash flow to sales	
$\left(\dfrac{\$292.1}{\$6854.3}\right) \times 100 = 4.26\%$	$\left(\dfrac{\$190.6}{\$5628.0}\right) \times 100 = 3.39\%$
Expense ratios	
Sales and marketing	
$\left(\dfrac{\$695.1}{\$6854.3}\right) \times 100 = 10.14\%$	$\left(\dfrac{\$580.1}{\$5628.0}\right) \times 100 = 10.31\%$
Occupancy	
$\left(\dfrac{\$305.7}{\$6854.3}\right) \times 100 = 4.46\%$	$\left(\dfrac{\$248.6}{\$5628.0}\right) \times 100 = 4.42\%$
Administrative	
$\left(\dfrac{\$42.2}{\$6854.3}\right) \times 100 = 0.62\%$	$\left(\dfrac{\$36.2}{\$5628.0}\right) \times 100 = 0.64\%$
Finance	
$\left(\dfrac{\$16.6}{\$6854.3}\right) \times 100 = 0.24\%$	$\left(\dfrac{\$10.7}{\$5628.0}\right) \times 100 = 0.19\%$
Other	
$\left(\dfrac{\$77.2}{\$6854.3}\right) \times 100 = 1.13\%$	$\left(\dfrac{\$97.7}{\$5628.0}\right) \times 100 = 1.74\%$
Total expenses	
$\left(\dfrac{\$1136.8}{\$6854.3}\right) \times 100 = 16.59\%$	$\left(\dfrac{\$973.3}{\$5628.0}\right) \times 100 = 17.29\%$

Note: All numbers are in $m.

As shown in figure 8.8, in 2018 relative to 2017 the ROE declined to 25.9 per cent from 27.4 per cent. While the numerator, profit, was higher in 2018 relative to 2017, the denominator, equity, was larger in 2018 than 2017. An investment of $1 of shareholders' equity in 2018 returned 25.9 cents of earnings available for distribution to shareholders. In 2017, an equivalent investment generated 27.4 cents of earnings available for distribution to shareholders. The decline in the ROE is due to a decline in the ROA. JB Hi-Fi Ltd generated 9.42 cents of profit per dollar of investment in assets in 2018; its profit-generating ability was higher in 2017 when $1 of investment in assets generated 9.99 cents of profit. Increased profitability and asset efficiency can contribute to an ROA improvement.

In terms of profitability, JB Hi-Fi Ltd's gross profit margin was higher than 20 per cent in both years. This reflects the company's low pricing strategy. The gross profit margin for JB Hi-Fi Ltd decreased slightly, with $1 of sales revenue in 2018 resulting in 21.45 cents of gross profit (21.86 cents in 2017). If $1 of sales revenue resulted in 21.45 cents (21.86 cents) of gross profit in 2018 (2017), the cost of sales must therefore have accounted for 78.55 cents of each sales dollar in 2018 (78.14 cents in 2017). This suggests that either (1) input prices increased, and/or (2) JB Hi-Fi Ltd decreased selling prices more in 2018 than in 2017. The change in the gross margin could also reflect a change in the mix of products sold by JB Hi-Fi Ltd. Some product categories would have higher margins relative to those of other product categories. Selling a higher proportion of higher margin products would be beneficial to JB Hi-Fi Ltd's gross profit margin. For example, the establishment of its online store could have changed the product mix.

JB Hi-Fi Ltd converted $1 of sales revenue into 3.06 cents of profit in 2017 and this increased to 3.40 cents in 2018. Users would have been pleased with this improved profit margin. The profit margin for an entity is a function of the industry it operates in. Low-volume businesses have higher profit margins, while high-volume businesses tend to operate with lower profit margins. The increase in profit margin reflects the company's higher gross profit margin in 2018 relative to 2017. The profit margin is also affected by expense ratios, so attention now turns to these.

An entity's expenses (excluding the cost of sales) can be expressed (in aggregate or individually) as a percentage of sales revenue to determine which expenses have increased or decreased relative to sales revenue. From JB Hi-Fi Ltd's statement of profit or loss (figure 8.2), the sum of the entity's sales and marketing, occupancy, administration, significant items and other expenses (including acquisition, transaction and implementation costs) totalled $1136.8 million in 2018 ($973.3 million in 2017). Expressed relative to sales revenue, these expenses represented 16.59 cents of every sales dollar in 2018 (17.29 cents in 2017). This analysis identifies that JB Hi-Fi Ltd's costs were slightly lower as a proportion of revenue in 2018 relative to 2017. All expense ratios increased in 2018 relative to 2017 except for sales and marketing, administration and other expenses. The increase in the occupancy expense ratio reflects the growth in the number of stores. The increase in the finance expense ratio, with finance costs representing 0.24 cents (0.19 cents) of $1 of revenue in 2018 (2017), was due to lower borrowings as well as higher interest rates.

The cash flow to sales ratio for JB Hi-Fi Ltd suggests that every dollar of sales revenue generated 4.26 cents of net operating cash flows in 2018, compared to 3.39 cents in 2017. Any improvement in this ratio is favourable, although cash-flow timing affects this ratio.

VALUE TO BUSINESS

- The return on equity (ROE) ration calculates the profit that the entity has generated for its owners during the period to the owners' investments in the entity. It is a measure that reflects the return on an equity investment.
- The return on assets (ROA) is a profitability ratio that compares an entity's profits to the assets that are available to generate the profits. It reflects an entity's profitability from revenue and profitability from investments in assets.
- The gross profit margin relates an entity's gross profit to its revenue, reflecting the proportion of sales revenue that ends up as gross profit.
- The profit margin compares profit to sales revenue and reveals what percentage of sales revenue ends up as profit. The profit margin is a function of the entity's gross profit margin and expense ratio margins.

8.5 Asset efficiency analysis

LEARNING OBJECTIVE 8.5 Define, calculate and interpret the ratios that measure asset efficiency.

In this section, we introduce the ratios that assist in judging an entity's efficiency in using its assets.

Asset turnover ratio

Entities invest in assets in anticipation that the investment will generate returns. **Asset efficiency ratios** measure the effectiveness of an entity in generating sales revenue due to investments in current and non-current assets. An entity's overall efficiency in generating income per dollar of investment in assets is referred to as the **asset turnover ratio**. The asset turnover ratio is calculated as:

$$\frac{\text{Sales revenue}}{\text{Average total assets}} = x \text{ times}$$

An entity's asset efficiency, as depicted by the asset turnover, will depend on the efficiency with which it manages its current and non-current investments. A large component of an entity's investments in assets, one that requires significant management, is inventory and accounts receivable. It is therefore useful to assess management's efficiency in managing these assets, and this is done by calculating the entity's inventory and accounts receivable turnover. The accounts receivable turnover is also referred to as the 'debtors turnover'. A largely cash-based service business, such as Advantage Tennis Coaching introduced earlier in the text, does not have inventory and debtors to manage, so these ratios are not as applicable to such an entity.

Days inventory and days debtors ratios

The **days inventory** indicates the average period of time it takes for an entity to sell its inventory. The **days debtors** indicates the average period of time it takes for an entity to collect the money from its trade-related accounts receivable. Funds invested in inventory and accounts receivable are earning a zero rate of return, so it is advantageous for an entity to turn over its inventory and accounts receivable as quickly as possible (i.e. convert them into sales revenue and receive the cash). Accordingly, lower days inventory and days debtors generally reflect better management efficiency. However, a lower days inventory could also suggest that the entity is carrying insufficient levels of inventory. The calculation of these ratios is as follows.

Days inventory:

$$\frac{\text{Average inventory}}{\text{Cost of sales}} \times 365 = x \text{ days}$$

Days debtors:

$$\frac{\text{Average trade debtors}}{\text{Sales revenue}} \times 365 \text{ days} = x \text{ days}$$

It is common to calculate the number of times per annum that the inventory (times inventory turnover) and trade debtors (times debtors turnover) are turned over, rather than the number of days this occurs. These calculations are as follows.

Times inventory turnover:

$$\frac{\text{Cost of sales}}{\text{Average inventory}} = x \text{ times}$$

Times debtors turnover:

$$\frac{\text{Sales revenue}}{\text{Average trade debtors}} = x \text{ times}$$

The higher the times turnover ratios, the more efficient an entity would appear to be in converting inventory and accounts receivable to cash. It should be noted that dividing the times inventory turnover and times debtors turnover into the number of days per annum (365) will yield the days inventory ratio and days debtors ratio respectively. For the purpose of our analysis, we will refer to the turnover in days rather than times.

It is not possible to prescribe what an appropriate days inventory ratio is, as it will vary according to the type of inventory being sold. For example, a supermarket would have a significantly faster inventory turnover than an exclusive jewellery store. Remember, however, that the supermarket's gross margin would be significantly lower than that of the jewellery store. Similarly, the appropriateness of the days debtor turnover depends on the credit terms offered by the entity. Accounts receivable arise as a result of credit sales. Note that sales revenue from both cash and credit sales is used in the ratio calculation, as entities do not disclose the cash and credit components of sales. It would be expected that an entity offering its customers 30-day settlement terms would have a longer days debtors compared with an entity offering credit terms of only 10 days. A 30-day settlement term means that the customer is expected to pay within 30 days of the end of the purchase month. If purchasing goods on the first day of the month, the customer effectively receives 60 days' credit. As an arbitrary rule of thumb, the days debtors figure is expected to be around 1.3 times the settlement terms offered by the entity. When analysing an entity's efficiency in managing its debtors and inventory, concerns would be raised if the ratios showed an upward trend.

We can consider the days inventory and days debtors turnovers in conjunction to reflect the entity's **activity cycle (operating cycle)**; if an entity sells only on credit terms, then summing the days inventory and days debtors will reflect the average period of time it takes to convert inventory into cash (the activity cycle). As inventory can be purchased on credit terms, there is often a delay between receiving the inventory and paying for the inventory (this is referred to as 'days creditors'). This is why the activity cycle is longer than the cash cycle.

A period of time elapses between an entity paying for the inventory, selling the inventory, and receiving cash for the inventory; this period is the **cash cycle**. During this time, the entity is effectively financing the investment in inventory and incurring negative cash flows. Suppose that an entity's days inventory is 45 days, with days debtors of 55 days and days creditors of 25 days. Its activity cycle (illustrative example 8.1) and cash cycle are 100 days and 75 days respectively. The length of the activity and cash cycles will have a significant impact on the entity's liquidity position. Given that the entity has to finance the investment in inventory and debtors, the shorter the activity cycle, the better the entity's efficiency and liquidity.

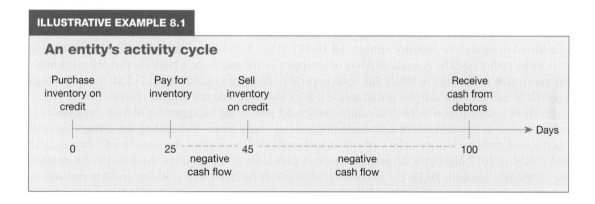

ILLUSTRATIVE EXAMPLE 8.1

An entity's activity cycle

Analysis of asset efficiency: JB Hi-Fi Ltd

We will now calculate and interpret the asset efficiency ratios for JB Hi-Fi Ltd for 2018 and 2017. Asset efficiency ratios measure the efficiency with which an entity manages its current and non-current investments, and converts its investing decisions into sales dollars. The ratios are presented in figure 8.9.

JB Hi-Fi Ltd's ability to convert a dollar investment in assets into sales revenue dollars has decreased over the two years. In 2018 an investment of $1 in assets generated $2.77 of sales revenue, compared to $3.26 in 2017.

FIGURE 8.9 Analysis of JB Hi-Fi Ltd's asset efficiency

2018	2017

Asset turnover ratio

$$\left(\frac{\$6854.3}{(\$2491.7 + \$2459.8)/2}\right) = 2.77 \text{ times} \qquad \left(\frac{\$5628.0}{(\$2459.8 + \$992.4)/2}\right) = 3.26 \text{ times}$$

Days inventory

$$\left(\frac{(\$891.1 + \$859.7)/2}{\$5384.1}\right) \times 365 = 59 \text{ days} \qquad \left(\frac{(\$859.7 + \$546.4)/2}{\$4397.5}\right) \times 365 = 58 \text{ days}$$

Note: The inventory includes the current portion of finished goods, raw materials and work in progress.

Days debtors

$$\left(\frac{(\$204.7 + \$193.6)/2}{\$6854.3}\right) \times 365 = 11 \text{ days} \qquad \left(\frac{(\$193.6 + \$98.1)/2}{\$5628.0}\right) \times 365 = 9 \text{ days}$$

The trade and other receivables comprise trade receivables and non-trade receivables (refer to note 8 to the company's accounts). The latter includes rebates receivable from suppliers for purchases of inventories. Recalculating days inventory using trade receivables only yields the following:

$$\left(\frac{(\$56.6 + \$54.2)/2}{\$6854.3}\right) \times 365 = 3 \text{ days} \qquad \left(\frac{(\$54.2 + \$31.5)/2}{\$5628.0}\right) \times 365 = 3 \text{ days}$$

Note: All numbers are in $m, and days inventory and days debtors are rounded to the nearest whole day.

When calculating the days debtors, only the gross value of current trade-related debtors should be included in the numerator. Recall that the gross value of debtors is the value prior to the deduction of the allowance for impairment losses. In 2018, JB Hi-Fi Ltd took on average 59 days to sell its inventory items — one day more than the average days taken in 2017. The suitability of this ratio needs to be considered in light of the industry average. JB Hi-Fi Ltd is a high-volume business and relies on turning over its inventory quickly. A quick turnover of inventory is imperative for a business that sells perishable inventory such as food items. While this same imperative does not exist for JB Hi-Fi Ltd, it requires high turnover to maintain low margins and to ensure that its inventories do not become obsolete.

JB Hi-Fi Ltd's business is predominantly cash-based and so the management of trade receivables is not as critical as it would be for a business that sells on credit terms. Calculating the debtors turnover (days) using gross trade receivables, rather than trade and other receivables, the turnover of 3 days in 2018 and 3 days in 2017 highlights the predominance of cash sales in the business. As stated in the notes to the company's accounts, JB Hi-Fi Ltd does sell some goods on credit with a 30-day credit period and no interest charged on trade receivables. With inventory turning over on average every 60 days and most sales being cash sales, JB Hi-Fi Ltd's asset efficiency is strong and its activity cycle is relatively short. This short activity cycle provides liquidity to the business.

VALUE TO BUSINESS

- The asset turnover ratio measures an entity's efficiency in generating sales revenue per dollar of investments in assets, and impacts on the entity's ROA.
- The days inventory and days debtors ratios reflect management's efficiency in managing these current assets. It is desirable for these ratios to be as short as possible. While the days inventory ratio is critical for a retail, wholesale or manufacturing business, it is not a significant ratio for a service-oriented business that carries little inventory. Similarly, a days debtors ratio is important for a business selling goods or services on credit, but it is not as meaningful for a business that sells most of its products or services for cash.
- The sum of the days inventory and days debtors represents the entity's activity cycle. Given that the entity needs to finance investments in inventory and debtors, a shortening activity cycle suggests that asset efficiency is improving.

8.6 Liquidity analysis

LEARNING OBJECTIVE 8.6 Define, calculate and interpret the ratios that measure liquidity.

An entity's inability to pay its debts when they fall due can result in creditors taking legal action against the entity to recover their monies. The survival of the entity therefore depends on its ability to pay its debts when they fall due. This ability to discharge short-term cash-flow obligations is referred to as an entity's **liquidity**. A number of ratios can be calculated to determine an entity's liquidity. Because liquidity is a measure of events over the short term, the ratios concentrate on an entity's current assets and current liabilities. The excess from current assets and current liabilities is referred to as an entity's **working capital**. An entity must have sufficient working capital to satisfy its short-term requirements and obligations. However, excess working capital is undesirable because the funds could be invested in other assets that would generate higher returns.

Current ratio and quick ratio

The current ratio and quick ratio are commonly used to assess an entity's liquidity position. These ratios are calculated as follows.

Current ratio:

$$\frac{\text{Current assets}}{\text{Current liabilities}} = x \text{ times}$$

Quick ratio:

$$\frac{\text{Current assets} - \text{Inventory}}{\text{Current liabilities}} = x \text{ times}$$

The **current ratio** (**working capital ratio**) indicates the dollars of current assets the entity has per dollar of current liabilities. It is undesirable to have a ratio that is too low, as this suggests that the entity will have difficulty in meeting its short-term obligations. However, a high current ratio is not necessarily good, as it could be due to excess investments in unprofitable assets — cash, receivables or inventory.

The **quick ratio** (**acid-test ratio**) measures the dollars of current assets available (excluding inventory) to service a dollar of current liabilities. It is a more stringent test of liquidity, as it excludes current inventory from the numerator. Inventory is excluded because it is the current asset that takes the longest period of time to convert into cash.

The difference between the current and quick ratios will be significant for manufacturing and retail entities with large inventory holdings, but insignificant for entities that are in service-related industries.

When assessing the current ratio, an arbitrary rule of thumb is that it should be around $1.50 of current assets for every $1 of current liabilities. The arbitrary benchmark ratio for the quick ratio is around $0.80 of current assets (excluding inventory) for every $1 of current liabilities. In calculating the quick ratio, bank overdrafts can be deducted from the denominator. This is done in recognition that bank overdrafts are permanent sources of funding to an entity but are classified as current because they are repayable on demand. Similarly, prepayments can be deducted from the numerator because they will not produce a cash inflow. A ratio that is higher (lower) than the arbitrary ratios should not be interpreted as a positive (negative) signal. The adequacy of the liquidity ratios needs to be assessed in conjunction with the entity's activity cycle. A short activity cycle will support a lower level of liquidity, whereas a longer activity cycle will require more liquidity.

Cash flow ratio

Another ratio that helps to assess liquidity is the cash flow ratio. Based on net cash flows from operating activities, the **cash flow ratio** indicates an entity's ability to cover its current obligations from operating activity cash flows. The higher the ratio, the better the position of the entity to meet its obligations. It is argued that the cash flow ratio is a better measure of liquidity than the current ratio, because it uses cash flows generated over a whole reporting period rather than the current assets at a particular point in time. The ratio is calculated as follows.

$$\frac{\text{Net cash flows from operating activities}}{\text{Current liabilities}} = x \text{ times}$$

Analysis of liquidity: JB Hi-Fi Ltd

JB Hi-Fi Ltd's current ratio, quick ratio and cash flow ratio (liquidity) for 2018 and 2017 are presented in figure 8.10.

FIGURE 8.10	Analysis of JB Hi-Fi Ltd's liquidity

2018	2017
Current ratio	
$\left(\dfrac{\$1210.5}{\$917.2}\right) = 1.32$ times	$\left(\dfrac{\$1167.5}{\$885.4}\right) = 1.32$ times
Quick ratio	
$\left(\dfrac{\$1210.5 - \$891.1}{\$917.2}\right) = 0.35$ times	$\left(\dfrac{\$1167.5 - \$859.7}{\$885.4}\right) = 0.35$ times
Cash flow ratio (liquidity)	
$\left(\dfrac{\$292.1}{\$917.2}\right) = 0.32$ times	$\left(\dfrac{\$190.6}{\$885.4}\right) = 0.22$ times

Note: All numbers are in $m.

JB Hi-Fi Ltd had $1.32 of current assets for every $1 of current liabilities in 2017 and 2018. As JB Hi-Fi Ltd has a relatively short activity cycle, the company can operate with lower levels of liquidity. Given that JB Hi-Fi Ltd has a large investment in inventories, the quick ratio should be significantly lower than the current ratio. The quick ratio was 0.35 times in 2017 and 2018. This suggests that JB Hi-Fi Ltd had approximately $0.35 of current assets, excluding inventory, for every dollar of current liabilities. For a retail operation, this is not unusual. In 2018, JB Hi-Fi Ltd had $0.32 of net operating cash flows for every $1 of current liabilities. This significantly increased from $0.22 of net operating cash flows for every $1 of current liabilities in 2017, suggesting that the company has capacity to meet its current obligations from its net operating activities cash flows.

VALUE TO BUSINESS

- An entity's liquidity is the ability of the entity to meet its short-term obligations. Liquidity ratios focus on relating current assets and cash availability to current liabilities.
- The current ratio and quick ratio are two measures of an entity's liquidity. The ratios indicate the dollar value of the entity's current asset relative to the entity's dollar value of current liabilities.
- Low liquidity ratios can reflect liquidity problems. High liquidity ratios are not desirable either, as they indicate excess investment in unproductive current assets.

8.7 Capital structure analysis

LEARNING OBJECTIVE 8.7 Define, calculate and interpret the ratios that measure capital structure.

An entity's **capital structure** is the proportion of debt financing relative to equity financing and reflects an entity's financing decisions. As per the accounting equation, an entity's assets equal its liabilities plus equity. Investments in assets are funded externally by liabilities, or internally by owner's equity. Expressing any of these three items — assets, liabilities and equity — relative to each other will reveal how an entity has used debt relative to equity to finance assets. **Capital structure ratios** (also referred to as 'gearing ratios' or 'solvency ratios') depict the proportion of debt to equity funding and are useful when assessing an entity's long-term viability. Achieving a balance between debt and equity funding affects the entity's

ROE. The use of debt can be advantageous, as debt funding is cheaper than equity funding. The lower cost of debt reflects the:
- lower returns required by debt holders, given the lower risk borne by debt holders relative to equity holders
- tax deductibility of interest expense.

However, excessive debt levels can be burdensome for an entity if the cost of servicing the debt exceeds the return generated by investments in assets (i.e. the cost of debt exceeds the return on assets), and this will depress the return on equity. If the debt is being used profitably and the return on assets financed with debt exceeds the cost of borrowing, then the benefit accrues to the owners in the form of higher returns on equity.

Capital structure ratios

The ratios that reflect an entity's use of debt relative to equity to finance assets are as follows.

Debt to equity ratio:
$$\frac{\text{Total liabilities}}{\text{Total equity}} \times 100 = x\%$$

Debt ratio:
$$\frac{\text{Total liabilities}}{\text{Total assets}} \times 100 = x\%$$

Equity ratio:
$$\frac{\text{Total equity}}{\text{Total assets}} \times 100 = x\%$$

It is necessary to calculate only one of the above three capital structure ratios, as they all indicate the entity's use of debt relative to equity to finance its investments in assets. We will focus on the **debt ratio**, which indicates how many dollars of liabilities exist per dollar of assets. If this exceeds 50 per cent, then the entity finances its investments in assets by relying more on debt relative to equity. If the debt ratio is less than 50 per cent, then the entity finances more of its assets with equity than with debt. The **debt to equity ratio** indicates how many dollars of debt exist per dollar of equity financing. If this ratio exceeds 100 per cent, then the entity is more reliant on debt funding than equity funding. The **equity ratio** suggests the dollars of equity per dollar of assets. If this ratio is less than 50 per cent, then the entity is more reliant on debt funding than equity funding.

Illustrative example 8.2 shows these ratios for an entity with $100 million of assets, $70 million of debt and $30 million of equity on its statement of financial position. The entity is more reliant on debt relative to equity, as indicated by the ratios. The debt ratio indicates that the entity uses $2.33 of debt per dollar of equity. Other ways of expressing this are: the debt ratio tells us that the entity funds every $1 of assets with $0.70 of debt; and the equity ratio indicates that every $1 of assets is financed by $0.30 of equity. The debt ratio divided by the equity ratio gives the debt/equity ratio, and the sum of the debt ratio and equity ratio equals 100 per cent.

ILLUSTRATIVE EXAMPLE 8.2

Capital structure ratios measuring the use of debt relative to equity funding

Assets = Liabilities + Equity
$100m = $70m + $30m

Capital structure ratios
Debt/equity ratio = 70/30 = 233%
Debt ratio = 70/100 = 70%
Equity ratio = 30/100 = 30%
Debt ratio + equity ratio = 100%

What is the appropriate level of debt funding relative to equity funding? Debt funding increases an entity's financial risk and the variability of cash flows to equity holders. The ability of an entity to absorb financial risk depends on the variability of its cash flows, which in turn is influenced by the entity's business risk. An entity that operates in a seasonal or risky industry will experience greater variability in its cash flows from operations and therefore have less ability to assume large financial risk. It is common to find variations in capital structure ratios across industries, but entities within an industry tend to operate at similar gearing levels.

An arbitrary benchmark that is used for a debt ratio is 50 per cent — an entity should use equal portions of debt and equity to finance its assets. This is not to say that a ratio exceeding 50 per cent proves that the entity's long-term financial viability is jeopardised. Many mature entities have debt ratios larger than 50 per cent.

When looking at how an entity has financed assets, the extent of current borrowings should also be examined. An entity that relies on current borrowings needs to refinance on a regular basis and may face the situation, when the current debt is due, of the financing not being available or only being available at a higher cost. For example, the global financial crisis made it more difficult for entities to access debt, and entities with short-term debt maturing had difficulty refinancing.

Capital structure ratios (as well as interest coverage ratios) are often used in lending contracts as a means of protecting the lender's wealth. For example, a loan contract could include a covenant specifying that the entity's debt ratio must not exceed 70 per cent. If the entity breaches this covenant by allowing its debt to assets ratio to exceed 70 per cent, the lender has the right to withdraw the loan facility and demand that the entity repay the loan. This illustrates how accounting numbers are used in entities' contractual arrangements. Users should focus on the trend in the ratio, as an increasing reliance on debt over a number of years would be of concern. When analysing an entity's capital structure, it is also relevant to examine the type of interest-bearing debt the entity is using, the breakdown of the debt into short and long term, and the maturity structure of the long-term debt.

Interest servicing ratios

The financial risk of an entity can also be assessed using the **interest coverage ratio (times interest earned)**, which measures the number of times an entity's EBIT covers the entity's net finance costs. It indicates the level of comfort that an entity has in meeting interest commitments from earnings. The calculation is:

$$\frac{\text{EBIT}}{\text{Net finance costs}} = x \text{ times}$$

The interest coverage ratio is inversely related to an entity's financial risk. A ratio less than 1 suggests that an entity's net finance costs exceed its EBIT — a situation that is unsustainable in the long run. The interest coverage ratio will exceed 1 so long as the EBIT is greater than net finance costs. As an arbitrary guide, the interest coverage ratio should not be below three times.

Debt coverage ratio

Debt needs to be serviced from cash flow, so it is useful to relate the entity's cash-generating capacity to its long-term debt. The **debt coverage ratio** links the cash flows from operating activities with long-term debt and is found by dividing non-current liabilities by cash from operating activities. It is also a measure of an entity's ability to survive in the longer term and remain solvent, as it indicates how long it will take to repay the existing long-term debt commitments at the current operating level. The ratio is calculated as:

$$\frac{\text{Non-current liabilities}}{\text{Net cash flows from operating activities}} = x \text{ times}$$

Analysis of capital structure: JB Hi-Fi Ltd

Figure 8.11 reports the capital structure ratios for JB Hi-Fi Ltd for 2018 and 2017. It shows that JB Hi-Fi Ltd funded every $1 of assets with 62 cents of debt in 2018, compared to 65 cents of debt in 2017. Funding approximately 62 per cent of assets with debt reflects a medium reliance on debt and suggests that the entity's exposure to financial risk is not high. During recent past years, JB Hi-Fi Ltd has pursued a debt-reduction strategy with declining long-term borrowings. As revealed by the statement of cash flows, the company was a net borrower in 2017 (cash proceeds from borrowings are shown as $450 million), whereas in 2018 JB Hi-Fi Ltd repaid more debt than it borrowed (cash repayments associated with borrowings are shown as $89.7 million).

FIGURE 8.11   Analysis of JB Hi-Fi Ltd's capital structure

2018	2017
Debt ratio	
$\left(\dfrac{\$1544.1}{\$2491.7}\right) \times 100 = 61.97\%$	$\left(\dfrac{\$1606.3}{\$2459.8}\right) \times 100 = 65.30\%$
Interest coverage ratio	
$\left(\dfrac{\$351.1}{\$16.6}\right) = 21.15\,\text{times}$	$\left(\dfrac{\$269.9}{\$10.7}\right) = 25.22\,\text{times}$
Debt coverage ratio	
$\left(\dfrac{\$626.9}{\$292.1}\right) = 2.15\,\text{times}$	$\left(\dfrac{\$720.9}{\$190.6}\right) = 3.78\,\text{times}$

Note: All numbers are in $m.

The EBIT of JB Hi-Fi Ltd adequately covers its net finance costs, suggesting the company does not have interest-bearing debt that is a financial strain. The interest coverage is a function of interest-bearing liability levels, interest rates and profitability levels. The higher finance costs, combined with higher EBIT, have decreased the interest coverage ratio from 25.22 times in 2017 to 21.15 times in 2018. This means that JB Hi-Fi Ltd's EBIT covers its net finance costs about 21 times over, representing more than an adequate safety margin.

The debt coverage ratio for 2018 indicates that, if JB Hi-Fi Ltd maintains its net operating cash flow, it would take the company on average 2.15 years of operating cash flows to repay its non-current liabilities. This is significantly less than the 3.78 years indicated by the 2017 ratio.

Entities complying with accounting standards disclose further details about their borrowings, such as the weighted average interest rate, overdraft facilities and other secured debt. This provides users with further information about entities' debt funding and the facilities available to the entities. JB Hi-Fi Ltd makes this disclosure in note 20.

VALUE TO BUSINESS

- An entity's assets must be financed by debt, contributions by owners or retained earnings. The ratios that depict an entity's reliance on debt funding relative to equity funding are capital structure (gearing) ratios.
- Capital structure ratios can express debt relative to assets (debt ratio), debt relative to equity (debt/equity ratio) or equity relative to assets (equity ratio). An entity's capital structure ratios indicate the entity's exposure to financial risk.
- The interest coverage ratio and cash debt coverage ratio indicate the ability of an entity to meet its interest commitments. The ratios reflect the entity's safety margin of profits or cash flows to meet debt-servicing charges.

8.8 Market performance analysis

LEARNING OBJECTIVE 8.8 Define, calculate and interpret the ratios that measure market performance.

We will briefly examine market performance ratios (also referred to as 'market test ratios') in this section. These ratios are most applicable to companies listed on organised securities exchanges, as the ratios relate reported numbers to the number of shares on issue or the market price of the share. The ratios we will introduce are ratios that are commonly referred to in the financial press.

Net tangible assets per share

The **net tangible asset backing (NTAB) per share** provides an indication of the book value of the company's tangible assets (as reported in the statement of financial position) per ordinary share on issue. The intangible assets, such as goodwill, are excluded from the calculation due to their lack of identifiability. The NTAB per share is not an indication of the cash that would be available per share if the company's assets were liquidated and the proceeds used to discharge the company's debts, due to the peculiarities of asset values in the statement of financial position. Remember from previous chapters that the book values of assets do not necessarily reflect their realisation value. It is useful to compare a company's NTAB per share with its share price, which will normally exceed the NTAB per share. The magnitude of the excess reflects the market's assessment of the entity's future growth prospects. A company trading at a much lower price than its NTAB per share is a prime candidate for a takeover, as this indicates that the value obtained from buying the company and then selling off its assets is higher than the price that would have to be paid to acquire the company in the marketplace. The NTAB per share is calculated as:

$$\frac{\text{Ordinary shareholders' equity} - \text{Intangible assets}}{\text{Number of ordinary shares on issue at year end}} = x \text{ cents/share}$$

Earnings, cash flow and dividend per share

A measure of the profit generated for each ordinary share on issue is the earnings per share. **Earnings per share (EPS)** are the entity's profit expressed relative to the number of ordinary shares on issue. Companies seek to achieve growth in earnings per share, as this signals to the market a company's earning ability. Companies are required to disclose their earnings per share at the bottom of their statement of profit or loss, as well as the numerator and denominator used in the calculation. In recognition of the importance of cash flows, the **operating cash flow per share (CFPS)** can be calculated. This ratio reflects the net cash flows from operating activities that are available to pay dividends to shareholders and to fund future investments. The difference in the EPS and CFPS highlights the differences that arise from preparing accounts on an accrual, rather than a cash, basis.

An investment in shares can generate returns in the form of dividends and/or share price appreciation. The **dividend per share (DPS)** is the former of these measures of return and indicates the distribution of the company's profits in the reporting period via dividends expressed relative to the number of ordinary shares on issue. Like the EPS, the DPS is reported in a company's financial statements.

The formulas below detail the basic calculations for these ratios.

Earnings per share:

$$\frac{\text{Profit available to ordinary shareholders}}{\text{Weighted number of ordinary shares on issue}} = x \text{ cents/share}$$

Operating cash flow per share:

$$\frac{\text{Net cash flows from operating activities} - \text{Preference dividends}}{\text{Weighted number of ordinary shares on issue}} = x \text{ cents/share}$$

Dividend per share:

$$\frac{\text{Dividends paid or provided to ordinary shareholders in current reporting period}}{\text{Weighted number of ordinary shares on issue}} = x \text{ cents/share}$$

Dividends can be distributed from current profits or from previous years' profits. Most companies pay a similar dividend each year or distribute a constant percentage of EPS as dividends. Expressing the DPS as a percentage of EPS results in the **dividend payout ratio**, which indicates the proportion of current year's profits that are distributed as dividends to shareholders. The profit not distributed remains in the entity for reinvestment.

Price earnings ratio

The **price earnings ratio (PER)** is a market value indicator that reflects the number of years of earnings that investors are prepared to pay to acquire a share at its current market price. The formula for the PER is:

$$\frac{\text{Current market price}}{\text{Earnings per share}} = x \text{ times}$$

If a company's current market price is $15.00 and its latest reported EPS is $2.50, the reported PER would be six times. This suggests that market participants are prepared to pay six years of current earnings to acquire the company's shares. The PER fluctuates as share prices change. The ratios vary across industries and are normally higher for high-growth companies. It is useful to compare the PER of a company with that of its competitors, as this highlights the market's assessment of the company's future performance relative to its peers. As a general rule, PERs for industrial companies are commonly between 10 and 15 times, although this varies according to the strength of the equity market.

Analysis of market performance: JB Hi-Fi Ltd

Because the market performance ratios are often available in the annual report of listed companies, as well as in the financial press, we will not calculate the ratios for JB Hi-Fi Ltd. Instead, the market performance ratios for the company over the past five years are summarised in table 8.1.

TABLE 8.1   Market performance ratios for JB Hi-Fi Ltd

	2018	2017	2016	2015	2014	2013
NTAB per share	$ (0.78)	$ (1.61)	$ 3.23	$ 2.62	$ 2.12	$ 1.61
EPS	$ 2.01	$ 1.53	$ 1.52	$ 1.36	$ 1.27	$ 1.17
Operating cash flow per share (CFPS)	$ 2.52	$ 1.69	$ 1.85	$ 1.81	$ 1.67	$ 1.59
DPS	$ 1.32	$ 1.18	$ 1.00	$ 0.90	$ 0.84	$ 0.72
Dividend payout ratio	65.67%	77.123%	65.79%	65.42%	66.20%	61.53%
PER	11.20	15.27	15.86	14.28	14.42	14.37
Year-end share price	$22.52	$23.37	$24.10	$19.48	$18.30	$16.81

Source: Adapted from JB Hi-Fi Ltd 2018, pp. 31, 54, 63, 64; JB Hi-Fi Ltd 2016, pp. 55, 64, 65.

The trends in the market performance ratios for JB Hi-Fi Ltd are generally positive. The EPS has gone from $1.17 in 2013 to $2.01 in 2018. It is worth noting that JB Hi-Fi Ltd repurchased shares in 2014, 2015 and 2016, and issued new shares in each of these years. A reduction in the number of shares on issue will improve any ratio that involves the number of shares in the denominator, all else being equal. The EPS disclosed by JB Hi-Fi Ltd at the bottom of its statement of profit or loss is based on the weighted average number of shares on issue during the year, as opposed to the number of shares on issue at the end of the year (as in table 8.1 for the years 2013 to 2015). The CFPS is higher than the EPS, but the operating cash flow ratio reported may not be restricted to operating cash flows only. Cash flow ratios are also generally higher than profit-based ratios because cash flows do not include depreciation and amortisation, as these are non–cash flow expenses.

The company's dividend payout ratio hovers around 60 per cent. JB Hi-Fi Ltd is distributing more than half of its current reporting period's profit as dividends to its shareholders. The consistency in the payout ratio reflects the company's preference to not significantly vary dividends each year even if profits vary. The PER suggests that investors in 2018 were prepared to pay 11.2 years of earnings to acquire a share in JB Hi-Fi Ltd. This is lower than the PER in any other year and reflects factors such as lower market sentiment. JB Hi-Fi Ltd's share price increased from $16.81 in 2013 to $22.52 in 2018. The total return to shareholders from any share investment is the capital growth plus dividends.

VALUE TO BUSINESS

- Market performance ratios are applicable to companies listed on organised securities exchanges, as the ratios relate reported financial numbers to the number of shares on issue or the market price of the shares.
- Some common market performance ratios are the net tangible asset backing per share, earnings per share, dividends per share and price earnings ratio.

8.9 Ratio interrelationships

LEARNING OBJECTIVE 8.9 Explain the interrelationships between ratios and use ratio analysis to discuss the financial performance and position of an entity.

Financial analysis is used to assess an entity's financial health, both past and future. The value of conducting ratio analysis, a key tool of financial analysis, lies in interpreting ratios and explaining why the ratios may be different from those of:
- previous years
- competitors
- industry averages
- entities in unrelated industries.

Ratio analysis is a convenient starting point for isolating and explaining reasons for differences. Understanding what each ratio is measuring, and how the ratios interrelate, helps users to answer the 'why' questions. For example, as demonstrated in the previous sections, any change in an entity's ROE will be attributable to changes in the entity's ROA and its financial risk. To analyse the underlying reason for the change in ROE, it is necessary to examine what has happened to an entity's ROA and its financial risk. Similarly, an entity's ROA reflects its asset efficiency and profitability; explaining why the ROA has changed therefore necessitates an examination of profitability ratios and asset efficiency ratios.

Figure 8.12 illustrates the disaggregation of the ROA. It can be seen that the ROA is the product of the profit margin and the asset turnover ratio. An entity's profit margin is affected by its gross profit margin and expense ratios. An entity's asset efficiency significantly depends on the efficient management of inventory and debtors.

| **FIGURE 8.12** | The interrelationships between ratios using JB Hi-Fi Ltd as the example |

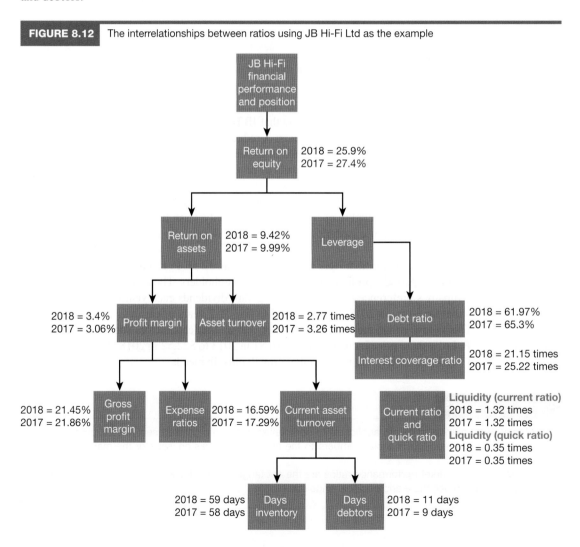

In presenting the 2018 and 2017 profitability, asset efficiency, liquidity, capital structure and market performance ratios for JB Hi-Fi Ltd, an attempt has been made to link these ratios to describe the financial health of the entity. For example, ratio analysis reveals that the decline in the ROE was due to a decline in the ROA. The ROA decreased from 2017 to 2018, reflecting a higher profit margin and lower asset efficiency. The profit margin improved from 3.06 per cent in 2017 to 3.4 per cent in 2018. This improvement is attributable to a slightly lower gross profit margin (21.45 per cent in 2018 and 21.86 per cent in 2017) that was partly offset by a lower expense ratio. The asset efficiency worsened slightly, with the asset turnover at 2.77 times in 2018 compared to 3.26 times in 2017. The inventory and the days debtors remained consistent from 2017 to 2018, with both higher by one or two days.

The interrelationships between ratios are depicted in figure 8.12. This provides a useful template to use when conducting ratio analysis or structuring a report on an entity's financial position and performance. For the purpose of illustration, the ratios for JB Hi-Fi Ltd for the years 2017 and 2018 have been included in this diagram.

It is important to remember, however, that ratios can be affected by the individual accounting policies applied to a company's financial data or by significant changes to accounting standards. For example, the implementation of International Financial Reporting Standards (IFRS) distorted PER figures due to significant changes in rules for determining certain revenue and expense items.

Ratio analysis, in conjunction with other considerations, is an important input to the process of valuing an entity or business. Analysts' reports, prepared to inform investors' investment decisions and other user decisions, always refer to the financial analysis that has been conducted on the entity, as well as other factors that influence the likely success of the entity in the future.

8.10 Limitations of ratio analysis

LEARNING OBJECTIVE 8.10 Discuss the limitations of ratio analysis.

There are a number of limitations of ratio analysis. Some limitations relate to the nature of the financial statements and the data disclosed (or not disclosed), while others are inherent in the nature of the financial ratios themselves. The limitations of the analytical process need to be considered when interpreting and relying on the ratios to form an opinion about an entity's financial health, past, present and future.

Ratio analysis relies on financial numbers in financial statements. Accordingly, the quality of the ratios calculated is dependent on the quality of an entity's financial reporting. This quality may be affected by inadequate disclosures and details in the entity's financial statements and/or in its accounting policy choices and estimations. Financial statements often aggregate numbers, with some separate figures reported in the notes to the accounts. The information needed to calculate a particular ratio may not be available, so an alternative financial number will have to be used instead. There exist a variety of ways to account for some transactions (e.g. the measurement of PPE). If ratios are being calculated for different entities, it is important to establish whether the entities account for transactions in the same manner. If the entities adopt different methods of accounting, their ratios may not be comparable. We have also seen that many of the reported accounting numbers involve estimations (e.g. doubtful debts), so it is important to consider how such estimations affect the ratios.

Many of the ratios that we have calculated rely on asset, liability or equity numbers reported in the statement of financial position. Remember that this statement reflects the financial position of an ongoing entity at a particular date and may not be representative of its financial position at other times of the year. For example, an entity may sell (buy) substantial assets close to the end of the reporting period. Using the figures from year end will therefore overstate (understate) the return on assets, all else being equal. We have tried to compensate for this by using average balances when comparing stock and flow items. However, such an averaging process is an approximation and, for assets sold (purchased) close to year end, the averaging process used will understate (overstate) the 'real' average asset balance.

Financial statements are historical statements reflecting past transactions. Often the past is a good guide to the future, but the use of information outside the financial statements needs to be considered when forming predictions as to an entity's financial health. For example, what are the technological advances, swings in consumer tastes and changes in economic conditions that may affect an entity's future operations? Financial data alone cannot adequately reflect the intricacies of an entity's operations. Effective analysis and interpretation of financial statements generally require a comprehensive analysis of an entity, its management, its competitors, its location and the industry in which it operates, and the surrounding economic conditions.

The information provided by financial statements alone is not enough to form predictions about an entity's financial health.

Users are also becoming more concerned about non-financial aspects of a business, particularly sustainability aspects. As discussed earlier in the introduction to accounting and business decision making chapter, an entity's environmental and social performance is often factored into users' assessments of the entity (triple bottom line reporting). Many entities prepare a sustainability report either in addition to, or contained within, their annual report. Often the sustainability report contains non-financial ratios designed to provide users with information on how effectively the entity manages the environmental and social impacts of its business activities. Some entities have developed environmental targets and publicly report against those targets.

For example, Fuji Xerox Australia produces a sustainability report. The report lists all of the company's carbon output as an eco-efficiency factor, reflecting how many millions of dollars of revenue are earned per tonne of carbon produced. Other measures reported by Fuji Xerox Australia include the percentage of waste that goes to landfill relative to the total waste generated, the water usage per capita at various business sites and the proportion of recycled paper used. As Fuji Xerox Australia's sustainability report demonstrates, economic, social and environmental performance is important to users when making decisions about an entity.

There is a movement to reshape reporting by entities to make reports more useful to users. In July 2011, the International Integrated Reporting Committee (IIRC) released a discussion paper titled 'Towards integrated reporting — communicating value in the 21st century'. The concept of integrated reporting is that reports should be strategically focused, connect information, be future oriented and be responsive to and inclusive of all stakeholders, and the information should be concise, reliable and material.

VALUE TO BUSINESS

- Examining the ratio interrelationships helps to explain changes or differences in performance and financial position.
- Limitations of the analytical process need to be considered when interpreting and relying on the ratios to form an opinion of an entity's financial health, past, present and future.
- Limitations of ratio analysis are often related to limitations of financial statements. For example, the required information may not be disclosed, the information may be outdated or comparability may be impeded by accounting policy and estimation choices.
- Ratio analysis is only one financial analysis tool. Comprehensive and effective financial analysis considers information beyond the financial statements.
- Non-financial considerations, such as environmental performance, are also taken into consideration by users when assessing an entity's performance.

SUMMARY OF LEARNING OBJECTIVES

8.1 Explain why different user groups require financial statements to be analysed and interpreted.

The financial statements assist users in their decision making. The decisions being made by users vary. For example, a decision may involve whether to advance credit to an entity, purchase or sell an ownership stake in an entity or lend money to an entity to acquire assets. Irrespective of the decision being made, analysis of an entity's financial statements can inform the decision-making process. Analysing the past financial performance and position of an entity is useful in predicting the entity's future performance and profitability. Such analysis allows users to detect changes in an entity's performance, to gain an insight as to why the changes have occurred and to assess the entity's performance and position relative to its peers, industry averages or unrelated entities.

8.2 Describe the nature and purpose of financial analysis.

Financial analysis refers to the assessment of an entity's financial position and profitability. Conducting financial analysis gives the user an enhanced understanding and appreciation of an entity's financial health. The reported numbers are of limited usefulness, given that they are in absolute dollar amounts. By expressing the numbers in relative terms, the financial statements become more meaningful and useful in evaluating an entity's past decisions and predicting future rewards and risks.

8.3 Apply the analytical methods of horizontal, trend, vertical and ratio analysis.

A reported number or ratio on its own is of limited usefulness. The analytical methods of horizontal analysis, trend analysis, vertical analysis and ratio analysis are designed to add a comparative dimension to the number or ratio. Using horizontal analysis, the current reporting period's number or ratio is compared with that in previous years, permitting the absolute dollar change and percentage change to be computed. If the comparative period extends further, trends can be depicted. Such a comparison is referred to as trend analysis. Alternatively, the reported numbers in the statement of profit or loss (or the statement of financial position) can be expressed as a percentage of a base number in the statement of profit or loss (or the statement of financial position). Items in the statement of financial position are expressed as a percentage of total assets and items in the statement of profit or loss are expressed as a percentage of sales revenue. Ratio analysis involves expressing one item in the financial statements relative to another item in the financial statements to add meaning to the reported numbers. Through ratio analysis, users can explore relevant relationships between reported financial numbers and gain a better understanding of an entity's financial health.

8.4 Define, calculate and interpret the ratios that measure profitability.

Profitability refers to an entity's performance during the reporting period or over a number of reporting periods. Profitability is not identical to profit. Profitability relates an entity's profit to the resources (assets or equity) available to generate profits and to an entity's effectiveness in converting income into profits. In comparison, profit is an amount measured in absolute dollars. The distinction is important because one entity can generate less profit than another entity but be more profitable than that other entity. Assessing an entity's historical profitability helps users to form an opinion about its expected future profitability. The ratios that measure an entity's profitability include the return on equity, return on assets, gross profit margin, profit margin and expense ratios.

8.5 Define, calculate and interpret the ratios that measure asset efficiency.

Asset efficiency refers to the effectiveness of an entity's investment in assets to generate income. The ratios in this category typically relate a particular class of assets to income. The asset turnover is calculated as income divided by total assets and reveals the average sales dollars generated for every dollar invested in assets. The asset efficiency ratios that are commonly referred to are the days debtors and days inventory. The former measures the average period of time it takes to collect cash from debtors, while the latter reflects the average length of time inventory is in stock before it is sold. A lower days ratio is desirable, as it reflects a quicker turnover of debtors and inventory.

8.6 Define, calculate and interpret the ratios that measure liquidity.

Liquidity refers to the ability of an entity to meet its short-term commitments. Creditors and employees expect to be paid for services and goods provided, and liquidity ratios indicate the likelihood that an entity will be able to make such payments. The two common liquidity measures are the current ratio and quick ratio. Expressing current assets relative to current liabilities indicates the dollar value of current assets available per dollar of current liabilities. Recognising that inventory is the least liquid current asset, the quick ratio removes inventory from current assets when comparing current assets to current liabilities.

8.7 Define, calculate and interpret the ratios that measure capital structure.

To be viable in the long term, an entity must be able to satisfy its long-term commitments. The ability to do so depends on an entity's financial risk and profitability. An entity must finance its investments in assets using new equity, retained earnings or debt. An entity's capital structure refers to the entity's relative use of debt and equity funding to finance assets. Capital structure ratios relate the proportion of debt funding relative to equity funding in financing an entity's assets. Financial risk increases as the proportion of debt funding relative to equity funding increases. The debt ratio expresses the total liability figure relative to total assets, thereby reflecting an entity's reliance on debt to finance investments in assets. Variations of this ratio include expressing equity as a proportion of assets and debt as a proportion of equity. The ability of an entity to absorb interest costs associated with borrowings is measured using the interest coverage ratio. This ratio indicates an entity's ability to meet interest commitments from its current year's profits.

8.8 Define, calculate and interpret the ratios that measure market performance.

Market performance ratios are relevant only for entities listed on organised securities exchanges, as they relate reported numbers to the number of shares on issue or the market price of the share. The common market performance ratios that are introduced in this chapter include net tangible asset backing per share, earnings per share, dividend per share, the dividend payout ratio and the price earnings ratio. It is common practice to compare these ratios with those of the entity's competitors, and to assess the trends in the ratios.

8.9 Explain the interrelationships between ratios and use ratio analysis to discuss the financial performance and position of an entity.

Calculating a ratio and ascertaining how it varies (compared with previous years or other entities) raises the question of why the variation occurs. Recognising that various ratios are interrelated enables a user to explore why a variation occurs. For example, in explaining why the return on equity (ROE) has improved or declined, the user can see what has happened to an entity's return on assets (ROA) and financial risk. Explanations as to why the ROA has changed can be explored by calculating the profit margin and asset efficiency ratios. Appreciating the interrelationships enriches explanations and understanding of an entity's financial circumstances. Rather than focusing solely on what the ratio is and how it has changed, analysing the interrelationships between ratios helps to better explain why variations occurred.

8.10 Discuss the limitations of ratio analysis.

Ratio analysis provides valuable insights into the financial position and performance of an entity, but the process has its limitations. Due consideration must be given to such limitations when interpreting and relying on the ratios to form an opinion about an entity's financial health, both past and present. These limitations can relate to the quality of the financial statements and the data disclosed (or not disclosed). Comprehensive and effective fundamental analysis considers information beyond, and in addition to, reported financial numbers. In particular, social and environmental performance is becoming increasingly important.

SUMMARY OF RATIOS

Ratio	Calculation	Interpretation
Profitability ratios		
Return on equity (ROE)	$\dfrac{\text{Profit available to owners}}{\text{Average equity}} \times 100$	Measures the rate of return earned on equity provided by owners
Return on assets (ROA)	$\dfrac{\text{Profit (loss)}}{\text{Average total assets}} \times 100$	Measures the rate of return earned as a result of investment in assets
Gross profit margin	$\dfrac{\text{Gross profit}}{\text{Sales revenue}} \times 100$	Measures gross profitability per dollar of sales revenue

Profit margin	$\dfrac{\text{Profit (loss)}}{\text{Sales revenue}} \times 100$	Measures net profitability per dollar of sales revenue
Cash flow to sales ratio	$\dfrac{\text{Cash flows from operating activities}}{\text{Sales revenue}} \times 100$	Measures the cash flow generated from operating activities for each dollar of sales revenue

Asset efficiency ratios

Asset turnover ratio	$\dfrac{\text{Sales revenue}}{\text{Average total assets}}$	Measures the sales revenue dollar generated per dollar investment in assets
Days inventory	$\dfrac{\text{Average inventory}}{\text{Cost of sales}} \times 365$	Measures the average length of time taken to sell inventory
Days debtors	$\dfrac{\text{Average trade debtors}}{\text{Sales revenue}} \times 365$	Measures the average length of time taken to collect the monies due from trade debtors
Times inventory turnover	$\dfrac{\text{Cost of sales}}{\text{Average inventory}}$	Measures the number of times per annum that inventory is turned over
Times debtors turnover	$\dfrac{\text{Sales revenue}}{\text{Average trade debtors}}$	Measures the number of times per annum that trade debtors is turned over

Liquidity ratios

Current ratio	$\dfrac{\text{Current assets}}{\text{Current liabilities}}$	Measures the dollars of current assets per dollar of current liabilities
Quick ratio	$\dfrac{\text{Current assets} - (\text{Inventory} + \text{Prepayments})}{\text{Current liabilities}}$	Measures the dollars of current assets (excluding inventory) per dollar of current liabilities
Cash flow ratio	$\dfrac{\text{Net cash flows from operating activities}}{\text{Current liabilities}}$	Measures the ability of the entity to meet its current obligations from operating activities' cash flows

Capital structure ratios

Debt to equity ratio	$\dfrac{\text{Total liabilities}}{\text{Total equity}} \times 100$	Measures the dollar of liabilities per dollar of equity
Debt ratio	$\dfrac{\text{Total liabilities}}{\text{Total assets}} \times 100$	Measures the dollar of liabilities per dollar of assets
Equity ratio	$\dfrac{\text{Total equity}}{\text{Total assets}} \times 100$	Measures the dollar of equities per dollar of assets
Interest coverage ratio	$\dfrac{\text{EBIT}}{\text{Net finance costs}}$	Measures the entity's ability to meet its net finance costs out of current year profits before interest and tax
Debt coverage ratio	$\dfrac{\text{Non-current liabilities}}{\text{Net cash flows from operating activities}}$	Measures the payback period for the coverage of long-term debt

(continued)

(*continued*)

Ratio	Calculation	Interpretation
Market performance ratios		
Net tangible asset backing per share	$$\frac{\text{Ordinary shareholder's equity} - \text{Intangible assets}}{\text{Number of ordinary shares on issue at year end}}$$	Measures the value of tangible assets (as reported in the statement of financial position) per ordinary share on issue
Earnings per share	$$\frac{\text{Profit available to ordinary shareholders}}{\text{Weighted number of ordinary shares on issue}}$$	Measures the profit generated for ordinary shareholders per ordinary share on issue
Dividend per share	$$\frac{\text{Dividends paid or provided to ordinary shareholders in the current reporting period}}{\text{Weighted number of ordinary shares on issue}}$$	Measures the dividend declared or paid to ordinary shareholders per ordinary share on issue
Dividend payout ratio	$$\frac{\text{Dividends per share}}{\text{Earnings per share}}$$	Measures the percentage of current period profits declared or paid as dividends
Operating cash flow per share	$$\frac{\text{Net cash flows from operating activities} - \text{Preference dividends}}{\text{Weighted number of ordinary shares on issue}}$$	Measures the operating cash flows generated per ordinary share on issue
Price earnings ratio	$$\frac{\text{Current market price}}{\text{Earnings per share}}$$	Measures the number of years of earnings that the market is capitalising into share price

KEY TERMS

activity cycle (operating cycle) The length of time it takes for an entity to acquire goods, sell them to customers and collect the cash from the sale.

asset efficiency ratios Measures of the efficiency with which an entity manages its current and non-current assets, and converts its asset decisions into sales dollars.

asset turnover ratio Asset efficiency ratio calculated as sales revenue divided by average total assets.

capital structure An entity's financing decisions (i.e. how it finances its investments in assets).

capital structure ratios Gearing or solvency ratios that measure how an entity finances its investments in assets.

cash cycle Period of time that elapses between paying for inventory, selling the inventory and receiving cash for the inventory.

cash flow ratio Measure of liquidity calculated as cash from operating activities divided by current liabilities.

cash flow to sales ratio Measure of profitability calculated as cash from operating activities divided by net sales revenue.

current ratio (working capital ratio) Liquidity ratio calculated by dividing current assets by current liabilities.

days debtors Debtor efficiency ratio calculated by dividing average trade debtors balance by sales revenue and multiplying by 365 days.

days inventory Inventory efficiency ratio calculated as average inventory balance divided by cost of sales and multiplied by 365 days.

debt coverage ratio Capital structure ratio calculated as non-current liabilities divided by net cash flows from operating activities.

debt ratio Capital structure ratio calculated by dividing total debt by total assets.

debt to equity ratio Capital structure ratio calculated as total liabilities divided by total equity.

dividend payout ratio Market performance ratio calculated as dividend per share divided by earnings per share.

dividend per share (DPS) Market performance ratio calculated as ordinary dividends paid or provided out of current year's profits divided by the number of ordinary shares on issue.

earnings per share (EPS) Market performance ratio calculated as profit divided by the weighted average ordinary shares.

efficiency ratios Measure of sales generated per dollar invested in assets.

equity ratio Capital structure ratio calculated by dividing total equity by total assets.

expense ratios Profitability ratios calculated as expenses divided by sales revenue.

financial analysis Analysing reported financial numbers to form opinions as to an entity's past and future performance and position.

flow items Items in the financial statements that are generated over a period of time.

fundamental analysis Analysing many aspects of an entity to assess the entity.

gross profit margin Profitability ratio calculated as gross profit divided by sales revenue.

horizontal analysis Analysing a series of financial statement data over a period of time.

interest coverage ratio (times interest earned) Capital structure ratio calculated as EBIT divided by net finance costs.

liquidity Ability of an entity to meet its short-term financial commitments.

liquidity ratios Measure of the short-term ability of the entity to pay its maturing obligations and to meet unexpected needs for cash.

market performance ratios (market test ratios) Ratios that generally relate an entity's financial numbers to the entity's share price.

net tangible asset backing (NTAB) per share Market performance ratio calculated as tangible assets divided by the number of issued shares.

operating cash flow per share (CFPS) Market performance ratio calculated as cash flows from operating activities divided by weighted average ordinary shares on issue.

price earnings ratio (PER) Market performance ratio calculated as the market price of the share divided by earnings per share.

profit margin Profitability ratio calculated as profit divided by sales revenue.

profitability An entity's performance (profit) during the reporting period measured in relative terms.

profitability ratios Measure of the profit relative to the resources available to generate the profit.

quick ratio (acid-test ratio) Stringent liquidity ratio calculated as the sum of cash, marketable securities and net receivables divided by current liabilities.

ratio analysis Examination of the relationship between two quantitative amounts with the objective of expressing the relationship in ratio or percentage form.

return on assets (ROA) Profitability ratio calculated as profit divided by average total assets.

return on equity (ROE) Profitability ratio measuring profit earned for each dollar invested by the owners, calculated as profit available to owners divided by average equity.

stock items Items in the financial statements as at a point in time.

trend analysis Method of examining changes, movements and patterns in data over a number of time periods.

vertical analysis Analysing financial statement data by expressing each item in a financial statement as a percentage of a base amount.

working capital Difference between current assets and current liabilities.

APPLY YOUR KNOWLEDGE

15 marks

Commentary in *Decore Ltd's yearly summary FY18* notes:

Our net profit remained the same as in FY17, the main reason being the contribution we made to our co-worker loyalty program, Give ($100 million), as well as the growing number of co-workers taking part in our bonus program ($49 million). However, adjusting for these expenses, our cost percentage decreased. The gross margin decreased by 0.4% to 42.9%. This was expected and is due to larger price reductions compared to FY17. But the negative effect on margins was partly balanced by lower purchase prices and lower transport costs.

(a) Decore's 2018 financial year end shows Decore's revenue at $14 646 million in 2018 and $14 253 million in 2017. Further, its cost of sales increased from $7898 million in 2017 to $8186 million in 2018. Calculate and evaluate Decore's 2017 and 2018 gross profit margin. **4 marks**

(b) In 2018, Decore's profit was $1665 million compared to $1659 in 2017. Calculate and evaluate the net profit margin. **5 marks**

(c) Decore's most recent statement of financial position is presented below. Calculating the appropriate ratios, evaluate Decore's liquidity and solvency. **6 marks**

DECORE Statement of financial position as at 31 December		
	2018 $ million	2017 $ million
Cash and securities	8 443	8 000
Receivables	1 274	1 097
Inventory	2 464	2 129
Total current assets	**12 181**	**11 226**
Property, plant and equipment	8 661	8 518
Other fixed assets	1 492	1 267
Total non-current assets	**10 153**	**9 785**
Short-term liabilities	2 198	2 382
Other payables	2 627	2 260
Total current liabilities	**4 826**	**4 642**
Long-term liabilities	775	999
Other non-current liabilities	929	946
Total non-current liabilities	**1 704**	**1 845**
Equity	**15 804**	**14 524**

SELF-EVALUATION ACTIVITIES

8.1 The statement of financial position of Helidon Ltd is presented as follows. **LO3**

HELIDON LTD Statement of financial position as at 30 June		
	2020	2019
Current assets		
Cash and cash equivalents	$ 23 092	$ 18 952
Accounts receivable	29 588	25 750
Inventories	18 966	25 094
Prepayments	11 740	14 600
Other current assets	21 000	17 530
Total current assets	104 386	101 926
Non-current assets		
Property, plant and equipment	87 174	71 722
Agricultural assets	53 748	49 368
Intangible assets	32 970	40 904
Total non-current assets	173 892	161 994
Total assets	278 278	263 920

Current liabilities				
Accounts payable			34 738	27 156
Short-term borrowings			44 000	56 000
Current tax liabilities			29 250	25 086
Total current liabilities			107 988	108 242
Non-current liabilities				
Long-term borrowings			92 500	78 000
Deferred tax liabilities			43 316	49 748
Total non-current liabilities			135 816	127 748
Total liabilities			243 804	235 990
Net assets			**$ 34 474**	**$ 27 930**
Equity				
Issued capital			$ 21 000	$ 17 000
Retained earnings			13 474	10 930
Total equity			**$ 34 474**	**$ 27 930**

Required

Prepare (a) a horizontal analysis and (b) a vertical analysis of the statement of financial position.

SOLUTION TO 8.1

(a) Horizontal analysis

HELIDON LTD Statement of financial position as at 30 June				
			Change	
	2020	2019	$	%
Current assets				
Cash and cash equivalents	$ 23 092	$ 18 952	4 140	21.84
Accounts receivable	29 588	25 750	3 838	14.90
Inventories	18 966	25 094	(6 128)	(24.42)
Prepayments	11 740	14 600	(2 860)	(19.59)
Other current assets	21 000	17 530	3 470	19.79
Total current assets	104 386	101 926	2 460	2.41
Non-current assets				
Property, plant and equipment	87 174	71 722	15 452	21.54
Agricultural assets	53 748	49 368	4 380	8.87
Intangible assets	32 970	40 904	(7 934)	(19.40)
Total non-current assets	173 892	161 994	11 898	7.34
Total assets	278 278	263 920	14 358	5.44
Current liabilities				
Accounts payable	34 738	27 156	7 582	27.92
Short-term borrowings	44 000	56 000	(12 000)	(21.43)
Current tax liabilities	29 250	25 086	4 164	16.60
Total current liabilities	107 988	108 242	(254)	(0.23)
Non-current liabilities				
Long-term borrowings	92 500	78 000	14 500	18.59
Deferred tax liabilities	43 316	49 748	(6 432)	(12.93)
Total non-current liabilities	135 816	127 748	8 068	6.32
Total liabilities	243 804	235 990	7 814	3.31
Net assets	**$ 34 474**	**$ 27 930**	**6 544**	**23.43**
Equity				
Issued capital	$ 21 000	$ 17 000	4 000	23.53
Retained earnings	13 474	10 930	2 544	23.28
Total equity	**$ 34 474**	**$ 27 930**	**6 544**	**23.43**

(b) Vertical analysis

HELIDON LTD Statement of financial position as at 30 June				
	2020	% to assets	2019	% to assets
Current assets				
Cash and cash equivalents	$ 23 092	8	$ 18 952	7
Accounts receivable	29 588	11	25 750	10
Inventories	18 966	7	25 094	10
Prepayments	11 740	4	14 600	6
Other current assets	21 000	8	17 530	7
Total current assets	104 386	38	101 926	39
Non-current assets				
Property, plant and equipment	87 174	31	71 722	27
Agricultural assets	53 748	19	49 368	19
Intangible assets	32 970	12	40 904	15
Total non-current assets	173 892	62	161 994	61
Total assets	278 278	100	263 920	100
Current liabilities				
Accounts payable	34 738	12	27 156	10
Short-term borrowings	44 000	16	56 000	21
Current tax liabilities	29 250	11	25 086	10
Total current liabilities	107 988	39	108 242	41
Non-current liabilities				
Long-term borrowings	92 500	33	78 000	30
Deferred tax liabilities	43 316	16	49 748	19
Total non-current liabilities	135 816	49	127 748	48
Total liabilities	243 804	88	235 990	89
Net assets	$ 34 474	12	$ 27 930	11
Equity				
Issued capital	$ 21 000	8	$ 17 000	6
Retained earnings	13 474	5	10 930	4
Total equity	$ 34 474	12	$ 27 930	11

8.2 Selected information for two companies competing in the retail clothing industry is presented below.

LO4, 7

	Forever30	Bardod
Sales revenue	$ 2 000 000	$1 000 000
Cost of sales	(1 410 000)	(420 000)
Gross profit	590 000	580 000
Less: Expenses	(315 000)	(327 000)
Profit	$ 275 000	$ 253 000
Total assets	$ 490 000	$ 475 000

Required

(a) Analyse and compare the profitability of Forever30 and Bardod. Provide calculations to support your analysis.

(b) From your calculations in part (a), explain the different business approaches the two companies have adopted.

(c) Explain how increasing the proportion of debt to assets can affect profitability ratios.

SOLUTION TO 8.2

(a)

	Forever30	Bardod
Return on assets	$275 000/$490 000 = 56.1%	$253 000/$475 000 = 53.3%
Profit margin	$275 000/$2 000 000 = 13.75%	$253 000/$1 000 000 = 25.3%
Asset turnover	$2 000 000/$490 000 = 40.8 times	$1 000 000/$475 000 = 2.1 times

(b) Both companies are similar in the return on assets that they generated. However, Forever30 seems to have a high turnover, low profit margin approach. Forever30 has a much lower profit margin than Bardod, indicating that it is making less profit per dollar of sales. Forever30, however, has a much more efficient use of assets to generate revenue, as evidenced by the asset turnover.

(c) Increasing the gearing ratio can have a positive effect on the ROE. If the ROA exceeds the cost of borrowing, then borrowing to finance assets will have a positive impact. However, if the borrowed funds are used to finance assets and the ROA is less than the cost of borrowings, then the impact will not be favourable.

8.3 Below are data extracted from the statement of profit or loss of Inspiring Art Ltd over a number of years. **LO4, 5, 6, 7**

INSPIRING ART LTD Statement of profit or loss					
	2019	2018	2017	2016	2015
Sales revenue	$115 750	$117 564	$88 263	$93 575	$85 651
Cost of sales	60 750	61 257	44 542	48 671	41 275
Gross profit	55 000	56 307	43 721	44 904	44 376
Selling expenses	(7 451)	(7 158)	(6 581)	(6 224)	(5 941)
Marketing expenses	(5 872)	(6 150)	(5 568)	(5 674)	(5 275)
Distribution expenses	(6 894)	(5 214)	(4 897)	(4 764)	(4 617)
Administration expenses	(4 751)	(4 000)	(3 596)	(3 650)	(3 700)
Profit before tax and finance costs	30 032	33 785	23 079	24 592	24 843
Finance costs	(12 500)	(11 250)	(7 650)	(8 320)	(8 635)
Finance income	8 500	7 300	5 800	6 100	4 700
Net finance income/(cost)	(4 000)	(3 950)	(1 850)	(2 220)	(3 935)
Profit before tax	**26 032**	**29 835**	**21 229**	**22 372**	**20 908**
Income tax (30%)	(7 810)	(8 951)	(6 369)	(6 712)	(6 272)
Profit after tax	**$ 18 822**	**$ 20 884**	**$14 860**	**$15 660**	**$14 636**

The comparative statement of financial position for financial year 2019 is as follows.

INSPIRING ART LTD Statement of financial position as at 31 December 2019		
	2019	2018
Current assets		
Cash and cash equivalents	$ 14 500	$ 12 451
Accounts receivable	21 750	23 675
Inventories	24 625	18 454
Other current assets	10 458	9 475
Total current assets	71 333	64 055
Non-current assets		
Property, plant and equipment	45 000	39 850
Agricultural assets	20 532	22 400
Intangible assets	25 120	21 863
Total non-current assets	90 652	84 113
Total assets	161 985	148 168
Current liabilities		
Accounts payable	28 450	22 642
Short-term borrowings	25 600	23 800
Total current liabilities	54 050	46 442
Non-current liabilities		
Long-term borrowings	42 750	46 210
Deferred tax liabilities	15 862	25 644
Total non-current liabilities	58 612	71 854
Total liabilities	112 662	118 296
Net assets	**$ 49 323**	**$ 29 872**
Equity		
Issued capital	$ 35 000	$ 20 000
Retained earnings	14 323	9 872
Total equity	**$ 49 323**	**$ 29 872**

Required

(a) Perform a trend analysis for the following statement of profit or loss items:
- revenue
- profit before tax and finance costs
- profit after tax.

(b) Calculate the ratios for the year 2019 that reflect the:
   (i) company's ability to generate income from its asset investments
   (ii) average period of time it takes for the company to sell its inventory
   (iii) dollars of current assets available to repay a dollar of current liabilities
   (iv) number of times the company's earnings before interest and tax cover its net finance expense
   (v) percentage of sales revenue dollars that result in earnings before interest and tax
   (vi) company's efficiency in generating income per dollar investments in assets
   (vii) average period of time it takes for the company to collect money from its customers.

SOLUTION TO 8.3

(a) Trend analysis

Absolute $ figures	2019	2018	2017	2016	2015
Sales revenue	115 750	117 564	88 263	93 575	85 651
Profit before tax and finance costs	30 032	33 785	23 079	24 592	24 843
Profit after tax	18 822	20 884	14 860	15 660	14 636

Trend analysis	2019	2018	2017	2016	2015
Sales revenue	135	137	103	109	100
Profit before tax and finance costs	121	136	93	99	100
Profit after tax	125	143	102	107	100

(b) Calculating ratios

Ratio	Calculation
(i) Return on assets	$= \dfrac{\text{Profit (loss)}}{\text{Average total assets}} \times 100$ $= \dfrac{\$18\,822}{(\$161\,985 + \$148\,168)/2} \times 100$ $= 12.14\%$
(ii) Days inventory	$= \dfrac{\text{Average inventory}}{\text{Cost of sales}} \times 365 \text{ days}$ $= \dfrac{(\$24\,625 + \$18\,454)/2}{\$60\,750} \times 365 \text{ days}$ $= 129 \text{ days}$
(iii) Quick ratio	$= \dfrac{\text{Current assets} - \text{Inventory}}{\text{Current liabilities}}$ $= \dfrac{\$71\,333 - \$24\,625}{\$54\,050}$ $= 0.86 \text{ times}$
(iv) Interest coverage ratio	$= \dfrac{\text{Earnings before interest and tax}}{\text{Net finance costs}}$ $= \dfrac{\$30\,032}{\$4000}$ $= 7.51 \text{ times}$

(v) Profit margin	$= \dfrac{\text{Profit (loss)}}{\text{Sales revenue}} \times 100$
	$= \dfrac{\$18\,822}{\$115\,750} \times 100$
	$= 16.26\%$
(vi) Asset turnover ratio	$= \dfrac{\text{Sales revenue}}{\text{Average total assets}}$
	$= \dfrac{\$115\,750}{(\$161\,985 + \$148\,168)/2}$
	$= 0.75$ times
(vii) Days debtors	$= \dfrac{\text{Average accounts receivable}}{\text{Sales revenue}} \times 365\,\text{days}$
	$= \dfrac{(\$21\,750 + \$23\,675)/2}{\$115\,750} \times 365\,\text{days}$
	$= 71.62$ days

COMPREHENSION QUESTIONS

8.4 Users of financial statements are interested in an entity's future profitability, asset efficiency, liquidity and capital structure. Describe the ratios that would be of interest to users and the purpose of computing these ratios. **LO4, 5, 7**

8.5 Your friend has $5000 to invest in the stockmarket and is deciding between investments in Bamboo Ltd or Panda Ltd. In the most recent reporting period, Panda Ltd made a profit after tax of $1 500 000, compared to Bamboo Ltd's after-tax profit of $750 000. On this basis, your friend believes Panda Ltd is the superior investment. Discuss your friend's investment choice. In doing so, suggest other financial data that should be considered. Identify the non-financial data that may also be of interest to inform your friend's investment decision. **LO2, 4**

8.6 When calculating the return on asset ratio, the average asset balance is used as the denominator. When calculating the debt ratio, the year-end asset balance is used as the denominator. Explain the rationale for using average asset figures for some ratios and year-end asset figures for others. **LO3**

8.7 Identify what ratios a bank lender would be particularly interested in. **LO1**

8.8 The working capital ratio for Butler Business has progressively increased from 1.2 times to 3.0 times over the past three years. Discuss whether this trend is favourable. **LO6**

8.9 Earnings before interest and tax (EBIT), rather than profit, is sometimes used as the numerator in the return on asset ratio. Discuss the rationale for using EBIT rather than profit. **LO4**

8.10 The statement of financial position for Works Ltd reveals total assets of $420 000, total liabilities of $230 000 and equity of $190 000 as at the end of the reporting period. Using these data, calculate the debt ratio, equity ratio and debt to equity ratio. Discuss why the conclusions drawn from these ratios are consistent, despite the ratio calculations generating different numbers. **LO7**

8.11 When calculating days inventory, the average inventory level is compared with the cost of sales. When calculating days debtors, the average accounts receivable balance is compared with the sales revenue. Explain why the former ratio uses cost of sales whereas the latter uses sales revenue. **LO5**

8.12 Visit the ASX website and graph the trend in JB Hi-Fi Ltd's (JBH) monthly share price over the past two years. **LO3**

8.13 Discuss three limitations of ratio analysis as a fundamental financial analysis tool. **LO10**

8.14 In its 2018 annual report JB Hi-Fi Ltd refers to the 'cost of doing business' (CODB) ratio. Paraphrase what you believe the CODB represents. **LO4**

8.15 In its 2018 annual report JB Hi-Fi Ltd provides the gross margin for each of its divisions. Discuss what factors impact on the variation in these margins across the three divisions. **LO4**

EXERCISES

★ BASIC | ★ ★ MODERATE | ★ ★ ★ CHALLENGING

8.16 ★   **LO4, 5, 6**

There are a variety of tools available to assist business owners to better understand the performance and position of their business. One such tool, provided by the ATO, allows a financial ratio comparison of an entity with that of its industry. Access the industry benchmarks used by the ATO's tool at www.ato.gov.au/Business/Small-business-benchmarks/In-detail/Benchmarks-by-industry. Assume that you own a small business with a turnover of $400 000 in the new and used car sales industry. Identify the benchmarks available for comparison purposes and discuss how you can use these benchmarks to compare the performance of your business.

8.17 ★   **LO4**

The following is a summary of key reported figures for Woolworths Ltd's business segments for 2018 and 2017. Report on the profitability of the business segments.

	Operating segment reporting (extract)			
	2018 $m		2017 $m	
	Total revenue	EBIT	Total revenue	EBIT
Australian food	37 614	1 757	36 024	1 603
New Zealand food	5 902	262	5 848	292
Endeavour drinks	8 271	516	7 913	503
Big W	3 566	(110)	3 542	(151)
Hotels	1 612	259	1 553	233
Other	222	(136)	398	(154)

Source: Adapted from Woolworths Ltd 2018, p. 73.

8.18 ★   **LO8**

The following table shows the returns and valuations of selected listed retailers as at June 2018.

	P/E (times)	Annual dividend yield (%)	EPS 2018 (cents)	EPS forecast 2019 (cents)
Woolworths Ltd	23.1	3.37	132	145
Harvey Norman Holdings Ltd	9.9	9.04	34	32
Wesfarmers Ltd	46.7	4.52	106	292
JB Hi-Fi Ltd	11.2	5.86	201	210

Source: Adapted from MarketScreener 2018.

Required

(a) Explain what is meant by 'P/E (times)'.

(b) Calculate the expected growth in EPS between 2018 and 2019 for each of the retailers.

(c) Explain the impact on a retailer's margins, inventory turnover and liquidity as a result of the retailer having a large sale offering goods at heavily discounted prices.

(d) Explain how tightly managed costs and lean inventory contribute to profit.

(e) Explain how you think the dividend yield percentage is calculated.

8.19 ★   **LO3**

The most recent annual statement of profit or loss for High Tower Enterprises is presented below. Prepare a vertical analysis of the statement.

HIGH TOWER ENTERPRISES **Statement of profit or loss**	
Income	$324 000
Expenses	
Cost of sales	141 000
Advertising expense	31 650
Insurance expense	16 800

Rent expense	24 200
Utilities expense	1 840
Depreciation	12 300
Wages and salaries	62 500
Interest expense	4 800
Total expenses	295 090
Profit	**$ 28 910**

8.20 ★   **LO3**

During 2021, Barb Ryan, the sole shareholder in Sunshine Farms Pty Ltd, decides to invest in automotive manufacturing equipment to reduce direct labour costs. She decides to fund the investment of $140 000 from retained profits. Financial data (assume average data for statement of financial position items) before and after the investment are shown below.

	Before investment	After investment
Total assets	$799 210	$929 310
Total liabilities	409 400	378 950
Shareholders' equity	389 810	550 360
Interest expense	14 000	18 000
Profit before income tax	**328 000**	**336 500**
Income tax expense (30%)	98 400	100 950
Profit	**$229 600**	**$235 550**

Required

(a) Calculate the following relationships based on the above data.

		Before	After
(i)	ROA ratio		
(ii)	ROE ratio		
(iii)	Debt to total assets ratio		
(iv)	Times interest earned ratio		

(b) Based on the single period results, will Barb be happy with the investment?

8.21 ★   **LO4**

Savannah Ltd had $84 000 of profit and incurred $16 500 in net finance costs during the recently completed period. Savannah's liabilities and owner's equity total $925 000. Assuming a 30 per cent tax rate, calculate the return on assets.

8.22 ★   **LO6**

Examine what happens to the current ratio when:
(a) an account payable is paid with cash
(b) inventory is purchased on credit
(c) money is received from a debtor.

8.23 ★   **LO4**

Examine what happens to the gross profit margin when:
(a) advertising is incurred
(b) selling prices are increased, assuming customers buy the same amount
(c) all suppliers increase their prices.

8.24 ★   **LO7**

Examine what happens to the debt ratio when:
(a) short-term debt is converted into an equivalent amount of long-term debt
(b) a major asset is sold, with part of the proceeds being used to repay debt
(c) cash is used for a share buy-back.

8.25 ★   **LO4**

Discuss what is meant by fundamental analysis and the role it plays in determining buy, hold and sell recommendations.

8.26 ★   **LO5**

If days inventory for Fab40 retail outlet was 35 days and days creditors was 12 days, calculate what the cash cycle would be if credit sales for a year amounted to $88 000 and the average trade debtors balance at the end of the year was $33 000.

8.27 ★   **LO3**

The statement of financial position for Ambre Ltd is presented below. Perform a horizontal analysis of the change (in absolute and percentage terms) between the year-end figures. Identify any significant variations that warrant further investigation and suggest why the variations have occurred.

AMBRE LTD Statement of financial position		
	2020	**2019**
Current assets		
Cash assets	$ 1178	$ 3120
Receivables	2356	2700
Inventories	1996	1362
Other current assets	2305	4354
Total current assets	7835	11536
Non-current assets		
Receivables	55	102
Inventories	150	158
Property, plant and equipment	3232	9200
Agricultural assets	20612	59910
Intangible assets	0	1563
Deferred tax assets	20	47
Other non-current assets	40	0
Total non-current assets	24109	70980
Total assets	31944	82516
Current liabilities		
Payables	1943	3872
Interest-bearing liabilities	3730	1158
Current tax liabilities	1138	1216
Provisions	1430	278
Total current liabilities	8241	6524
Non-current liabilities		
Interest-bearing liabilities	7541	26657
Deferred tax liabilities	409	757
Provisions	1	1
Total non-current liabilities	7951	27415
Total liabilities	16192	33939
Net assets	**$15752**	**$48577**
Shareholders' interest		
Contributed equity	$10144	$35655
Reserves	1104	1745
Retained earnings	4504	11177
Total equity	**$15752**	**$48577**

8.28 ★ ★   **LO5**

Coconut Plantations Pty Ltd's financial records reveal the following as at 30 June 2021.

Net sales (all credit)	$1 675 000
Cost of sales	1 025 000
Accounts receivable — beginning	93 010
Accounts receivable — ending	145 000
Inventory — beginning	175 000
Inventory — ending	170 000

(a) Assuming a 365-day year, calculate the days inventory ratio. Interpret and explain this ratio.
(b) Coconut Plantations Pty Ltd proposes to improve control of inventory and to further reduce days inventory levels by five days. If this is achieved, calculate how many times inventory would be turned over per annum. Estimate by how much the average inventory would need to be reduced.
(c) Assuming a 365-day year, calculate the days debtors ratio. Interpret and explain this ratio.
(d) Advise Jo Geter, the sole shareholder of Coconut Plantations Pty Ltd, what actions can be taken to improve collections from debtors.

Grammar Ltd reports the following information.

	$'000		$'000
Total assets	3 840	Interest revenue	220
Profit after tax	130	Interest expense	320
Current liabilities	1 140	Tax expense	90
Non-current liabilities	1 660	Current assets = 50% of total assets	

From this information, calculate and interpret the following ratios (year-end figures have to be used because the comparative year figures are not available) and prepare a report on the financial position and performance of Grammar Ltd.
(a) Liquidity ratio
(b) Return on equity
(c) Return on assets using:
    (i) profit
    (ii) EBIT
(d) Debt ratio

The statement of financial position and the statement of profit or loss for Protocol are presented below.
(a) Calculate the:
    (i) current ratio
    (ii) return on assets (use year-end figures)
    (iii) return on shareholders' funds (owner's equity; use year-end figures)
    (iv) debt to equity ratio.
(b) Prepare a presentation on the financial analysis conducted, commenting on the performance and position of Protocol.

PROTOCOL Statement of financial position as at 30 June 2019	
Assets	
Current assets	$ 40 000
Investments	10 000
Property, plant and equipment	64 000
Intangible assets	30 000
Total assets	**$144 000**
Liabilities	
Current liabilities	$ 18 000
Long-term liabilities	32 000
Total liabilities	50 000
Owner's equity	
M Wright — capital	94 000
Total liabilities and owner's equity	**$144 000**

PROTOCOL Statement of profit or loss for the year ended 30 June 2019	
Sales revenue	$ 90 000
Cost of sales	40 000
Gross profit	50 000
Operating expenses	36 000
Profit	**$ 14 000**

8.31 ★ ★   **LO4, 5, 6, 7, 9**

Selected information for two companies competing in the catering industry is presented below.

	Fine Foods	Devine
Current assets	$165 750	$251 850
Non-current assets	375 000	448 500
Current liabilities	87 900	35 250
Non-current liabilities	134 550	217 500
Equity	318 300	447 600
Profit	150 000	79 500

Required

(a) Analyse and compare the liquidity, solvency and profitability ratios of the entities.

(b) From your calculations in part (a), explain which entity is in a more favourable position.

8.32 ★ ★   **LO4, 5, 6, 7, 9**

An entity has $660 000 of assets, including current assets of $180 000. The following information has also been ascertained about the entity.

- The two owners have contributed $150 000 each.
- The entity has always distributed all the profits via a family trust.
- The entity owes $130 000 to trade creditors and other creditors.
- The remainder of the entity's financing is via a mortgage loan.
- The entity made a profit this year (before tax) of $70 000.
- The profit figure includes $30 000 of interest associated with the loan.

Required

Which of the following statements is correct?

(a) The entity's current ratio is 2:1.

(b) The entity uses more debt financing than equity financing.

(c) The entity's net assets are $530 000.

(d) The entity's debt ratio is 55 per cent.

8.33 ★ ★   **LO9**

The following table reports various financial ratios for Qantas and Virgin for 2018.

	Qantas Airways	Virgin Australia
Operating margin	9.16%	3.22%
ROE	26.14%	(48.96)%
ROA	5.44%	1.74%
Total debt/equity (D/E)	119.93%	234.53%
Current ratio	0.49	0.78
Cash per share ($)	1.09	0.17
PER	10.82	—
Net profit margin	5.74%	(12.56)%
Price/book value	2.38	1.71

Source: Adapted from Yahoo! Finance 2018.

(a) Given that the companies operate in the same industry, write a report explaining what the ratios suggest about the companies' operating, financing and investing activities.

(b) If you were contemplating an investment in either Qantas Airways or Virgin Australia, identify what other (non-financial) information would assist your investment decision and why this information is important to you.

8.34 ★ ★   **LO8, 9**

The market performance ratios for Unicycle Ltd are presented next. Calculate the entity's dividend payout ratio, interpret the ratio and explain why an investor would be interested in this ratio. Comment on Unicycle Ltd's NTAB, EPS, DPS, dividend payout and PER.

	2020	2019	2018	2017	2016
NTAB per share	$ 0.36	$ 0.52	$ 0.70	$ 0.75	$ 0.73
EPS	15.9c	17.3c	17.1c	22.1c	20.1c
DPS	9.5c	16.5c	16.5c	16.5c	15.0c
PER	22.6	13.9	14.8	14.5	17.7

8.35 ★ ★   **LO6**

It is important for businesses to have efficient processes and systems in place for collecting monies from debtors. The business and industry portal of the Queensland government (www.business.qld.gov.au/business) contains advice for offering credit and managing the risk associated with debtors. Referring to the guide, identify five actions that a business manager can take to manage debtors.

8.36 ★ ★   **LO4, 7**

You have been given the following information regarding an entity. One of your friends is interested in investing in it. Help your friend by calculating some cash-based ratios, explaining what the ratios are measuring.

Cash from operating activities	$92 000
Capital expenditure	187 500
Current liabilities	84 000
Non-current liabilities	492 500
Sales revenue	79 500
Dividends paid	22 500

8.37 ★ ★   **LO4, 6**

Fit and Fantastic Ltd produces and sells a range of fitness equipment. Its capital expenditure for the current year for new plant was $600 000 and dividends paid were $80 000. Current liabilities and non-current liabilities were $112 000 and $1 400 000 respectively. Sales for the current year were $1 050 000 and net cash flow from operating activities was $176 000. Compute and interpret the cash flow ratio, debt coverage ratio and cash flow to sales ratio.

PROBLEMS

★ BASIC | ★ ★ MODERATE | ★ ★ ★ CHALLENGING

8.38 Trend and vertical analysis ★ ★   **LO1, 3, 9**

The statement of profit or loss figures for the past five years for Victorian Manor are presented below. Using the information:

(a) prepare a trend analysis and comment on the trends

(b) prepare a vertical analysis (using revenue as the base amount) and comment on the trends

(c) identify other non-financial ratios that would be of interest to the management of Victorian Manor.

VICTORIAN MANOR Statement of profit or loss for the period 2016 to 2020					
	2016 $'000	2017 $'000	2018 $'000	2019 $'000	2020 $'000
Revenue	420 800	476 000	500 400	514 500	522 600
Interest received	2 500	2 900	3 010	2 950	2 900
Total revenue	423 300	478 900	503 410	517 450	525 500
Expenses					
Cost of food	242 000	281 800	285 200	298 900	304 500
Advertising expense	28 200	36 400	40 900	45 400	45 400
Insurance expense	15 500	17 000	17 600	17 600	22 700

	2016 $'000	2017 $'000	2018 $'000	2019 $'000	2020 $'000
Rent expense	25 000	29 500	31 800	34 100	36 400
Utilities expense	1 700	2 200	2 240	2 330	2 390
Depreciation	12 000	12 000	12 000	15 000	15 000
Wages and salaries	60 000	71 600	73 300	76 100	78 400
Interest expense	3 400	5 200	5 600	5 800	5 900
Total expenses	387 800	455 700	468 640	495 230	510 690
Profit	**35 500**	**23 200**	**34 770**	**22 220**	**14 810**

8.39 Calculating and analysing days inventory turnover, days debtors, current ratio and quick ratio ★ ★   LO5, 6, 9

Summary information from the 2021 statement of profit or loss of Coconut Plantations Pty Ltd is provided below.

Sales revenue	$1 675 000
Cost of sales	1 025 000
Gross profit	650 000
Other income	1 500
Operating expenses	315 000
Profit (before tax)	**336 500**
Income tax	100 950
Profit (after tax)	**$ 235 550**

The operating expenses include $18 000 of interest expense.

The following amounts have been extracted from the company's statement of financial positions.

	2021 $	2020 $
Cash on hand	110 977	145 367
Accounts receivable	145 000	93 010
Inventory	170 000	175 000
Prepaid expenses	25 000	4 500
Accounts payable	78 000	42 500
Accrued expenses	5 000	7 500
Income tax payable	100 950	98 400

Required

(a) Calculate and interpret the:
 (i) days inventory turnover
 (ii) days debtors
 (iii) current ratio
 (iv) quick ratio
 (v) gross profit margin
 (vi) profit (after tax) margin.

(b) If you are contemplating providing a short-term loan to Coconut Plantations Pty Ltd, discuss what these ratios reveal about the associated risk.

8.40 Limitations of ratio analysis ★ ★   LO10

Read the following quote and discuss what you think Fridson and Fernando (2002) mean by 'passively calculating standard ratios'.

> Corporations have substantial incentives to exploit the fact that accounting principles are neither fixed for all time nor so precise as to be open to only a single interpretation. Analysts, who appreciate the magnitude of the economic stakes, as well as the latitude available under the accounting rules, will see clearly that a verdict derived by passively calculating standard ratios may prove dangerously naive.

8.41 Analysing a company's market performance ★ ★ LO8

Visit the Yahoo! Finance website (http://au.finance.yahoo.com) and call up information on JB Hi-Fi Ltd (symbol: JBH.AX).

(a) Identify JB Hi-Fi Ltd's current share price (day 1), the previous day's share price (day 0) and the share price return from day 0 to day 1.

(b) You are considering purchasing shares in JB Hi-Fi Ltd. Identify the current bid and ask price for the shares.

(c) The summary information includes some market-based ratios. Explain what each of the following represents and how the ratio is calculated: price–earnings ratio; earnings per share; and market capitalisation.

(d) Review the current month's analysts' recommendations for JB Hi-Fi Ltd and comment on the market's sentiment regarding JB Hi-Fi Ltd.

8.42 Preparing financial statements from ratios ★ ★ LO4, 5, 6, 7

The following values relate to various ratios for an outdoor adventure clothing store for the most recent year. At the end of the year, total assets as per the statement of financial position were $900 000. The ratios relate to the accounts either in respect of the 12-month period or at the date of the statement of financial position for the end of the period.

Transaction	Ratio
1. Profit to total assets	10%
2. Current ratio	2.5:1
3. Acid test ratio	1:1
4. Credit sales to trade accounts receivable	7.5:1
5. Gross profit to sales revenue	25%
6. Trade accounts payable to purchases	40%
7. Credit sales to total sales revenue	75%
8. Profit margin	10%
9. Return on equity (beginning of year)	30%
10. Non-current assets to current assets	10%

Required

Assuming that there are no prepaid expenses and that trade accounts payable are the only liability, using the above information:

(a) prepare a detailed statement of profit or loss for the year, including cost of sales calculation

(b) prepare the entity's statement of financial position as at the end of the year

(c) discuss why ratios are regarded as more useful than absolute values.

8.43 Predicting statement of profit or loss and statement of financial position ★ ★ LO4, 5, 6, 7

The treasurer of Reality Ltd has recently developed a computer model to help in the prediction of profits, statement of financial position and cash flows. By entering the expected sales figure and the value of various other parameters, the model will print profit-related data and produce a statement of financial position. Given the following parameters, compose the predicted statement of profit or loss and the statement of financial position produced by the model.

Expected sales	$240 000
Gross profit as a percentage of sales	35%
Expenses as a percentage of sales	15%
Tax rate on profits	30%
Dividend payout ratio	50%
Debt to equity ratio	0.8:1
Current assets as a percentage of cost of sales	20%
Current ratio	2:1
Return on equity	15%

8.44 Interpreting ratios ★ ★   **LO4, 7, 9**

The following table provides a historical summary of key financial ratios for Homer Corporation.

Ratio	2018	2019	2020
Return on equity	10.8%	–3.1%	–1.4%
Return on assets	3.0%	–0.8%	–0.3%
Cost of sales to sales	75.6%	78.5%	74.8%
Research and development expenses to sales	6.3%	6.9%	6.6%
EBITDA to sales*	10.2%	2.3%	5.6%
Debt to total assets	72.4%	75.3%	76.9%

* EBITDA is earnings before interest, tax and depreciation.

Required

(a) With reference to the appropriate ratios, analyse the trend in Homer Corporation's profitability, providing plausible reasons for any changes.

(b) The CEO of Homer Corporation noted the following:

> Homer Corporation plans to maintain tight inventory controls heading into the crucial year-end shopping season...Homer implemented tighter inventory controls to prevent the type of punishing losses from slow demand that forced deep discounting or write-downs for unsold goods. It slashed inventory turnover during last year's October–December quarter to 38 days from 61 days a year ago.

Explain what an inventory turnover ratio is measuring and how inventory turnover impacts on Homer's profitability.

(c) Homer Corporation publishes on its website and discloses key corporate social responsibility (CSR) activities and important topics of interest to stakeholders. Describe an environmental performance indicator and a social performance indicator that may be of interest to Homer's stakeholders.

8.45 Analysing profitability, liquidity and financial stability ★ ★   **LO9**

Lincoln Indicators professes nine golden rules for successful sharemarket investing. The golden rules relate to financial health, management assessment, outlook/forecast, share price value, share price sentiment, liquidity and size, principal activities and price sensitive announcements. Details on the golden rules are available at www.lincolnindicators.com.au.

Required

(a) List the nine golden rules.

(b) Identify two listed companies in the same industry. Apply the nine golden rules investment framework and write a report judging whether these stocks satisfy the investment criteria.

8.46 Performing ratio analysis ★ ★   **LO5, 6**

The following financial statements were prepared for the management of Back2Basics Ltd. The statements contain some information that will be disclosed in note form in the general purpose financial statements (GPFS) to be issued.

BACK2BASICS LTD Statement of profit or loss for the year ended 30 June 2019	
Sales revenue	$562 500
Cost of sales	407 500
Gross profit	155 000
Expenses (including tax and finance)	90 000
Profit	**$ 65 000**

	BACK2BASICS LTD

BACK2BASICS LTD
Statement of financial position
as at 30 June 2019

Current assets		
Cash assets		$ 8 900
Receivables (all trade)	$149 625	
Less: Allowance for doubtful debts	9 450	140 175
Inventories		126 000
Total current assets		275 075
Non-current assets		
Land		31 500
Building	113 000	
Less: Accumulated depreciation	18 900	94 100
Store equipment	23 625	
Less: Accumulated depreciation	13 625	10 000
Total non-current assets		135 600
Total assets		**$410 675**
Current liabilities		
Payables (all trade)		$135 450
Income tax payable		14 490
Other		6 300
Total current liabilities		156 240
Non-current liabilities		
10% mortgage payable		31 500
Total liabilities		187 740
Equity		
Contributed capital: 6% preference shares		25 000
Ordinary shares		126 000
Retained earnings		71 935
Total equity		222 935
Liabilities and equity		**$410 675**

Additional information

1. The balances of certain accounts at the beginning of the year are as follows.

Accounts receivable (gross)	$157 500
Allowance for doubtful debts	(14 175)
Inventories	110 250

2. Total assets and total equity at the beginning of the year were $377 500 and $180 500 respectively.
3. Income tax expense for the year was $31 500. Net finance expenses were $3150.

Required

Identify and calculate the ratios that a financial analyst might calculate to give some indication of the:

(a) entity's earning ability
(b) extent to which internal sources have been used to finance asset acquisitions
(c) rapidity with which accounts receivables are collected
(d) ability of the entity to meet unexpected demands for working capital
(e) ability of the entity's earnings to cover its interest commitments
(f) length of time taken by the entity to sell its inventories.

8.47 Presenting trends and ratios ★ ★ ★   **LO3, 9, 10**

The following financial ratios and information relate to Starbucks Corporation for the period 2008 to 2017.

	Horizontal analysis %									
Statement of financial position items	2008	2009	2010	2011	2012	2013	2014	2015	2016	2017
Cash and short-term investments	5.7	11.9	22.7	27.9	24.8	28.1	17.1	13.0	15.8	18.7
Accounts receivable	5.8	4.9	4.7	5.3	5.9	4.9	5.9	5.8	5.4	6.1

(continued)

(continued)

Statement of financial position items				Horizontal analysis %						
	2008	2009	2010	2011	2012	2013	2014	2015	2016	2017
Inventory	12.2	11.9	8.5	13.1	15.1	9.6	10.1	10.5	9.6	9.5
Other current assets	7.1	7.8	7.2	5.3	5.3	4.9	5.7	2.7	2.4	2.5
Total current assets	30.8	36.5	43.2	51.6	51.1	47.5	38.8	32.0	33.2	36.8
Net PPE	52.1	45.5	37.8	32.0	32.4	27.8	32.7	32.9	31.6	34.2
Intangibles	5.9	5.9	5.2	5.9	6.6	9.9	10.5	16.9	15.6	13.8
Other long-term assets	11.2	12.1	13.8	10.6	10.0	14.8	18.0	18.1	19.6	15.2
Total assets	100.0	100.0	100.0	100.0	100.0	100.0	100.0	100.0	100.0	100.0
Accounts payable	5.7	4.8	4.4	7.3	4.8	4.3	5.0	5.5	5.1	5.4
Short-term debt	12.6								2.8	
Taxes payable		2.3	1.6	1.5	1.7	0.0	0.0	0.0	0.0	0.0
Accrued liabilities	11.1	11.5	13.1	11.3	10.2	11.0	14.1	14.1	14.0	13.5
Other short-term liabilities	9.2	9.7	8.8	8.1	10.2	31.4	9.2	9.7	9.9	10.5
Total current liabilities	38.6	28.4	27.9	28.2	26.9	46.7	28.3	29.4	31.7	29.4
Long-term debt	9.7	9.9	8.6	7.5	6.7	11.3	19.0	18.9	22.3	27.4
Other long-term liabilities	7.8	7.2	6.0	4.8	4.3	3.1	3.6	4.8	4.8	5.3
Total liabilities	56.1	45.4	42.5	40.4	37.8	61.1	51.0	53.1	58.9	62.0
Total stockholders' equity	43.9	54.6	57.5	59.6	62.2	38.9	49.0	46.9	41.1	38.0
Total liabilities and equity	100.0	100.0	100.0	100.0	100.0	100.0	100.0	100.0	100.0	100.0
Liquidity/capital structure	2008	2009	2010	2011	2012	2013	2014	2015	2016	2017
Current ratio	0.8	1.3	1.6	1.8	1.9	1.0	1.4	1.1	1.0	1.3
Quick ratio	0.3	0.6	1.0	1.2	1.1	0.8	1.0	0.7	0.7	0.9
Financial leverage*	2.3	1.8	1.7	1.7	1.6	2.6	2.0	2.1	2.4	2.6
Long-term debt/equity	0.2	0.2	0.2	0.1	0.1	0.3	0.4	0.4	0.5	0.7
Efficiency ratios	2008	2009	2010	2011	2012	2013	2014	2015	2016	2017
Days inventory	30.1	57.3	49.5	55.7	69.3	67.3	58.6	56.2	57.6	55.4
Days payables	15.6	25.0	22.5	30.3	29.5	25.4	27.3	28.5	30.3	30.6
Receivables turnover	33.6	32.6	37.3	34.0	30.5	28.4	27.6	28.4	28.7	27.3
Inventory turnover	12.1	6.4	7.4	6.6	5.3	5.4	6.2	6.5	6.3	6.6
Fixed assets turnover	3.6	3.6	4.3	4.9	5.3	5.1	4.9	5.0	4.9	4.7
Asset turnover	1.9	1.7	1.8	1.7	1.71	1.5	1.5	1.7	1.6	1.6

Source: © Morningstar, Inc. 2013. All rights reserved. Reproduced with permission; Starbucks 2014, 2015, 2016, 2017.
* Financial leverage ratio = total assets/total equity.

Required

(a) Represent the 2017 horizontal analysis of the asset section of the statement of financial position in a pie chart and comment on Starbucks' asset composition.

(b) Represent the 2017 horizontal analysis of the liability and equity sections of the statement of financial position in a pie chart and comment on Starbucks' financing of its assets.

(c) Prepare a trend line chart of Starbucks' liquidity and capital structure ratios. Discuss what this trend reveals and how it assists decision making.

(d) Prepare a trend line chart of Starbucks' efficiency ratios. Discuss what this trend reveals and how it assists decision making.

DECISION-MAKING ACTIVITIES

8.48 Qantas Airways integrates a sustainability report with its annual review. Locate the most recent sustainability report to address the following questions. The reports can be located at www.qantas.com.au. (*Hint:* Select 'Investor Centre', then 'Annual Reports' and then select the latest annual review.) From 2018, sustainability information is also available on the Sustainability Portal on the Qantas website.

(a) Discuss how Qantas defines sustainability.

(b) List the key sustainability issues identified by Qantas.

(c) Qantas selects its sustainability report content and performance measures on the basis of materiality, stakeholder interest and the Ten Principles of the United Nations Global Compact on human rights, labour, environment and anti-corruption. Define and critique five sustainability statistics reported by Qantas.

(d) Qantas presents sustainability information and statistics for the benefit of a wide range of stakeholders. Identify the stakeholder groups that would find this information relevant.

(e) Select three stakeholder groups and identify the sustainability ratios that they would be particularly interested in. Discuss what the trend in these ratios suggests about Qantas' performance in these areas.

(f) You are an accounting graduate employed by a manufacturing company. Your boss, the chief financial officer (CFO), has been requested by the board to include information in the annual report in accordance with the Global Reporting Initiative (GRI). Your boss does not know about these reporting standards and has requested you to prepare a discussion paper summarising the GRI and its benefits.

8.49 Debt collection companies Credit Corp Group and Collection House reported increases in revenue and profits for 2015, suggesting that the debt collection market is flourishing.

Speaking about Credit Corp Group's results, CEO Thomas Beregi noted that the traditional business of buying debt ledgers remained stable, but that the growth driver was the lending business, with the company's loan book growing from $63 million to $100 million and its share price closing at $13.21 — significantly higher than the $4 it traded at in 2011 (Main 2015).

Collection House's results reflect its growth strategy of growing purchased debt ledger collections, as well as growing investment in systems and analytics to improve the quality of such purchased debt ledgers. The return on this investment is evidenced by the 40 per cent higher annualised cash recovery yield for 2015 when compared to the previous two-year period (Richardson 2015).

Required

Locate the most recent annual reports of Collection House and Credit Corp Group, and other resources available, to answer the following.

(a) The debt collection industry has two main business models: debt collection with and without recourse. Explain the difference in the business models.

(b) Assume that you are an analyst. Calculate the necessary ratios for the past two years to be able to write a report on the financial performance and position of the two companies.

(c) Read the management commentary and discussion in the annual reports of the companies and identify the financial information that is referred to in the management commentary.

(d) Explain why it is important to read the Accounting Policy Notes of Collection House and Credit Corp Group to contextualise ratio analysis.

8.50 Standard & Poor's (S&P) (2018), one of the leading credit rating organisations and a publisher of financial information and research services, identifies its debt rating process as follows.

S&P undertakes quantitative and qualitative analysis in the rating assignment process, and comments that it must be remembered that a rating is, in the end, an opinion and 'the rating experience is as much an art as it is a science'. As part of the process, entities are required to provide S&P with five years of audited financial statements and the last several interim statements. The analytical process involves consideration of an entity's business risk and financial risk. In assessing the business risk, S&P is interested in an entity's industry characteristics and competitive position. The assessment of financial risk involves consideration of financial characteristics, financial policy, profitability, capital structure, cash flow protection and financial flexibility.

Standard & Poor's analyst-driven rating process

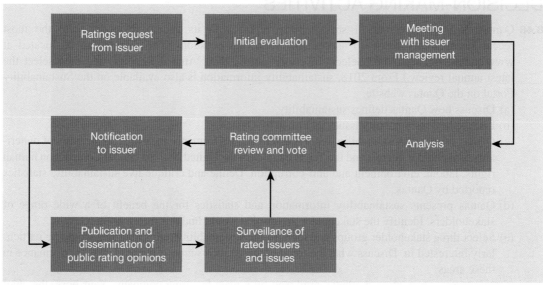

Source: Standard & Poor's 2018.

Required

(a) Explain what credit ratings are and the ratings that can be assigned to an entity.

(b) Prepare a checklist, under each of the financial risk categories, of the items or ratios that you believe S&P would investigate or calculate when assessing financial risk.

8.51 Read the following extract (Cavanagh, Saunders & Pritchard 2015) about how New South Wales winemakers have maintained their profitability.

> Maintaining premium wine prices and reacting to trends similar to the latest 'handbag' are some of the ways the wine industry can recover from struggling production profitability, according to some New South Wales winemakers.
>
> The 2015 crush was up 0.4 per cent Australia-wide, but is still slightly below the eight-year average of 1.7 million tonnes. The industry's health was detailed in the Winemakers' Federation of Australia Vintage Report for July 2015. When it came to profitability, the Hunter Valley was up 3 per cent, although the majority of the region's growers were struggling. Further inland, in the Mudgee area, zero profitability was experienced, while the Canberra area, which is also a cool climate growing region, had 1 per cent growth. Long time Canberra winemaker Ken Helm and his colleagues in the region are adamant that it is fatal to be price driven.
>
> 'Once you discount your wines, in the consumer's mind the wine is not worth what was originally asked and therefore it was overpriced,' he said. 'We have not fallen for that trap, we have maintained our prices, which we believe are fair and reflect the quality of the wine. If we continue along that line we believe the industry will continue to grow and get the respect of the consumer.'
>
> Across the range, a number of Mudgee growers are pulling out vines, as demand for their wine has slumped. This is contrary to the Canberra region where, Mr Helm points out, more land is being sought by the local growers and winemakers.
>
> Mudgee viticulturist David Lowe also looks to producing premium wines as the key, as the other areas associated with production have been exhausted. 'As an industry we have a lot of work to do,' said the former NSW Wine Industry Association President.
>
> 'I guess much of the focus over the past 10 years has been on cutting our costs, minimising our labour costs, more mechanisation. We have probably reached what we can; we can't increase the crops, our yield. That could lead to a lesser wine quality and therefore not receive the price you want for quality. The only solution I guess is to increase market demand and increase the price of our wine; the top down approach.'
>
> 'When the Australian dollar came into parity with the US dollar, it became, it made it unprofitable to export,' Mr Helm said. '[This hurt] areas which focussed on export, rather than focusing on the premium end of the market, both domestically and export.'

Required

(a) Discuss how premium winemakers have maintained their profitability in recent years.

(b) Explain why a discounting strategy may not be in a winemaker's best interest.

(c) The article refers to the Winemakers' Federation of Australia Vintage Report for July 2015. Locate this report and identify any financially based ratios reported.

(d) Summarise the Production Profitability Analysis in the report.

(e) Discuss the factors considered when predicting the future health of the Australian wine industry.

REFERENCES

Cavanagh, M, Saunders, D, & Pritchard, M (2015), 'Predicting fashion and no discounting key to profitability say New South Wales winemakers', *ABC News*, 21 July.

Fridson, M & Fernando, A 2002. *Financial statement analysis: a practitioner's guide*, 3rd edn, John Wiley & Sons, New York.

JB Hi-Fi Ltd 2018, *Preliminary final report 2018*, www.jbhifi.com.au.

JB Hi-Fi Ltd 2016, *Preliminary final report 2016*, www.jbhifi.com.au.

Main, A 2015, 'Debt collector Credit Corp Group lifts revenues and profit', *The Australian*, 5 August.

MarketScreener 2018, *Financials*, www.marketscreener.com.

Morningstar, Inc. 2015, *FinAnalysis of JB Hi-Fi Ltd*, www.morningstar.com.au.

Morningstar, Inc. 2013, *Starbucks Corporation SBUX — Key ratios*, http://financials.morningstar.com.

Richardson, T 2015, 'Are the results of Collection House Limited a strong buy sign?', 11 February, www.fool.com.au.

Standard & Poor's 2018, *Guide to credit rating essentials*, Standard & Poor's Financial Services LLC, www.understandingratings.com.

Starbucks 2017, *Annual report 2017*, https://investor.starbucks.com/financial-data/annual-reports/default.aspx.

Starbucks 2016, *Annual report 2016*, https://investor.starbucks.com/financial-data/annual-reports/default.aspx.

Starbucks 2015, *Annual report 2015*, https://investor.starbucks.com/financial-data/annual-reports/default.aspx.

Starbucks 2014, *Annual report 2014*, https://investor.starbucks.com/financial-data/annual-reports/default.aspx.

Woolworths Ltd 2018, *Annual report 2018*, www.woolworthslimited.com.au.

Yahoo! Finance 2018, *Statistics*, https://au.finance.yahoo.com.

ACKNOWLEDGEMENTS

Photo: © shironosov / Getty Images

Photo: © fizkes / Shutterstock.com

Figures 8.1, 8.2, 8.3, 8.6, 8.7: © JB Hi-Fi Ltd 2018

Problem 8.47: © Morningstar, Inc. 2013 and © Starbucks Coffee Company 2014, 2015, 2016, 2017

Decision-making activity 8.50: Figure from Standard & Poor's 'Guide to credit rating essentials', Standard & Poor's Financial Services LLC, www.understandingratings.com.

Decision-making activity 8.51: © ABC 2015

CHAPTER 9

Budgeting

LEARNING OBJECTIVES

After studying this chapter, you should be able to:

9.1 understand the importance of planning and budgeting

9.2 explain what a budget is and describe the key steps in the budgeting process

9.3 explain the different types of budgets

9.4 outline the components of a master budget and prepare a master budget

9.5 prepare a schedule of receipts from accounts receivable and a cash budget

9.6 explain the use of budgeting in planning and control

9.7 discuss the issues associated with the behavioural aspects of budgeting.

Chapter preview

This chapter explores one of the key issues associated with planning — the development of operating budgets. Planning relates to looking ahead in some kind of formal process. This process may vary from entity to entity, but the important issue is that it is formal and regular. An entity will have developed strategic plans in terms of its overall direction. These strategic plans need to be drawn up and put into operation. The focus of this chapter is how this occurs in the budgeting area, rather than a detailed study of strategic planning itself.

9.1 Strategic planning and budgeting

LEARNING OBJECTIVE 9.1 Understand the importance of planning and budgeting.

Planning has both a long-term and a short-term horizon and, most importantly, both should be linked to ensure that what happens today supports the future direction of the entity. **Strategic planning** relates to longer term planning (such as three to five years) of the entity's activities. It is usually carried out by senior management and commonly relates to broader issues such as business takeovers, expansion plans, deletion of business segments and radical product/service development. The way in which the strategic planning process is conducted depends upon a range of issues, including the industry and culture of the entity. For example, larger entities will use a rather formal process, while more creative or smaller entities may opt for a less formal process. Nevertheless, the outcomes from the process are the strategic plans of the entity and these will guide shorter term planning such as budgeting. **Budgeting** is a process that focuses on the short term (commonly one year) and results in the production of budgets that set the financial framework for that period. The planning process evaluates whether there will be sufficient resources available to achieve the strategic plan and, most importantly, whether the strategy leads to profits and thereby creates value for the entity. Budgets, therefore, operationalise the strategic plan and allow those in operational areas to understand how their work effort contributes to the entity's strategic objectives. Once the budget has been prepared, it is also used as a control tool to monitor actual results, to investigate differences between actual and budget, and to evaluate and reward performance. This budget cycle is depicted in figure 9.1.

FIGURE 9.1 Budget cycle

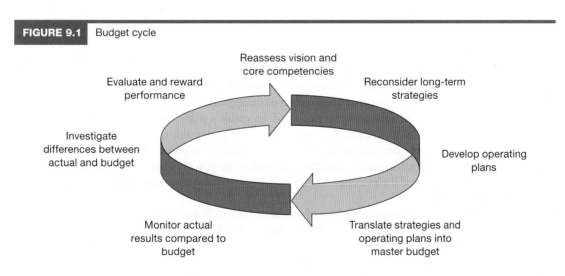

DECISION-MAKING EXAMPLE

Linking short-term and long-term decision making

SITUATION JB Hi-Fi Ltd has traditionally been known as the place to go for music, movies, TVs and computers. In 2015 it expanded its product offerings to home appliances. What factors may have led to this decision and what information would have been collected?

DECISION The decision to venture into home appliances would have been a strategic decision on the part of JB Hi-Fi Ltd management. Possible motives would have been to:
- increase profits by entering into new markets
- complement the current electronics focus
- leverage off the strong brand name and current customer base.

However, this plan had to be operationalised and strategic budgets would have been prepared to determine if financially it was the right decision for JB Hi-Fi Ltd. Information would have been collected about the potential level of sales, cost of purchasing appliances, appropriate mark-up for determining the sales price and levels of operating costs associated with rent, staffing and other factors. The development of budgets for the new venture would have enabled JB Hi-Fi Ltd management to assess whether the venture would increase wealth for the entity. While this information would have helped with the original decision, it would also serve as a key input into the annual budgets and target setting in the future.

9.2 Budgets

LEARNING OBJECTIVE 9.2 Explain what a budget is and describe the key steps in the budgeting process.

As individuals, we often look ahead and plan various aspects of our future. This planning might relate to financial matters such as an overseas trip, a new car or, as we get older, retirement. These plans will commonly involve setting short-term goals and targets in financial terms; commonly referred to as budgets. In doing so, we are engaging in the budgeting process. Similarly, entities will engage in a planning process which, among other things, requires involvement in a budgeting process.

Part of the formal planning process relates to an entity's operational plans, including short-term goals and targets. These short-term goals can be stated in financial or non-financial terms, and commonly fall under the broader heading of performance management. **Performance management** includes setting targets in other than just financial terms; for example, improving customer service, corporate governance, management techniques and human resource management. Indeed, one of the key innovations in recent years in relation to performance measurement has been the introduction of the balanced scorecard, which trumpets the use of a balanced mix of related financial and non-financial measures. These non-financial measures may be developed at two levels: first, the broader level measures, which are often referred to as critical success factors (CSFs); and second, the more specific operational measures suitable to specific segments or activities of the entity. More information on the broader topic of performance measurement can be obtained from the performance measurement chapter, which explores the balanced scorecard and non-financial measures in more depth. The following section concentrates on the expression of short-term goals and targets in financial terms. This is commonly achieved through the development of the financial budget.

A **budget** is simply the quantitative expression of an entity's plans. The nature of the entity will determine the type of budget that might be prepared but, as a minimum, it would be expected that the types of financial statements covered in the statement of financial position, the statement of profit or loss and statement of changes in equity, and the statement of cash flows chapters would be prepared in budgeted form. Budgeting and the associated planning can assist in a decision-making context in a variety of ways, including:
- putting into operation the longer term plans of an entity, such as those relating to strategy
- assessing the feasibility of strategic plans, thus creating value for the entity
- setting targets for managers
- identifying resource constraints in the budget period
- identifying periods of expected cash shortages and excess cash holdings
- assisting with short-term planning decisions, such as capacity utilisation
- providing profit forecasts and other financial data to the capital markets
- forecasting data such as sales or fees, which commonly set the level of activity for the budget period
- helping determine required inventory levels and purchasing requirements for raw materials
- planning labour and other inputs
- determining the ability of the entity to meet financing commitments.

Budgeting can assist in deciding on required inventory levels.

The budgeting process

The **budgeting process** will commonly involve a series of steps, including:
1. consideration of past performance
2. assessment of the expected trading and operating conditions
3. preparation of initial budget estimates
4. adjustment to estimates based on communication with, and feedback from, managers
5. preparation of the budgeted reports and any sub-budgets
6. monitoring of actual performance against the budget over the budget period
7. making any necessary adjustments to the budget during the budget period.

Throughout the process, communication with managers who are affected by the budgets should occur. These managers are commonly responsible for a segment of an entity, such as a division, a department or a branch. These segments may be referred to as responsibility centres and may form part of the entity structure. The level of communication in the budgeting process will vary from entity to entity, as will the level of participation sought from managers of responsibility centres in the budgeting process. For many entities, the annual budget process may take up to nine months of the year before the budget is finalised. In larger entities, there will be a budget committee that coordinates the preparation of the budget. Committee membership will include the managing director, treasurer, chief accountant and management personnel from each of the major areas of the company, such as sales, production and research.

The planning process is strengthened by considering the interrelationships between profit, cash and return on investment. Simons's (2000, p. 81) three wheels of planning highlights the impact of decisions on each. The three wheels (cash, profit and return on investment) are interlocking and turn simultaneously. For example, the entity may be able to generate more sales in the coming year. However, will there be enough cash flow to acquire the inventory to support these sales or to acquire other necessary resources? Will the increased sales lead to higher profits, which in turn will enable investment in assets that should lead to higher sales and more profits? The higher profit will lead to an increase in the return on owner's investment.

Simons highlights the need for those within the entity to work together to develop the profit plan for the coming year. The sales manager provides important information about the potential sales levels for the coming year and the operational personnel will assess whether there are the necessary resources required to achieve these sales or alternatively recommend process changes to achieve the sales goal. The financial personnel will assess both the cash flow resulting from the plans to assess the need for cash to cover day-to-day operations and the profitability of the planned activities. Overall, the interaction of the various personnel enables them to understand the impact of their decisions and to assess whether value will be created for the entity.

When not executed well, the budgeting process can produce negative, unintended consequences. For example, the budget targets may be unreasonable or too difficult to achieve. This may have a discouraging effect on the managers who prepare the budgets, those who are held accountable for budget targets and on the staff generally. The behavioural aspects of budgeting are explored later in this chapter.

9.3 Types of budgets

LEARNING OBJECTIVE 9.3 Explain the different types of budgets.

The nature of the entity will determine the type of budgets prepared. Nevertheless, budgets commonly prepared include the following.
- *Sales or fees budget*, which also serves as an important input variable for other budgets and is, therefore, often referred to as the 'cornerstone' of the budgeting process. The sales or fees budget is commonly used to set the expected level of activity for the budget period. The expected level of activity is an important consideration for many of the other budgets. This central role of the sales or fees budget is further underpinned in Simons's three wheels of planning.
- *(Operating) expenses budget*, which is commonly an aggregation from functional, sectional or departmental expense budgets, and also serves as an input variable to other budgets. For example, the expenses budget relating to the operation of the accounting department is used, along with other (e.g. marketing) departmental budgets, to build the overall operating expenses budget. It is sometimes simply called the 'cost budget'.
- *Production and inventory budgets*, which are necessary in manufacturing environments for planning production levels and managing inventory levels. There are usually sub-budgets relating to direct materials, direct labour (if any) and indirect manufacturing overhead costs.
- *Purchases budget*, for both merchandising and manufacturing entities, which will set the required level of inventory/direct materials purchases based on data from the sales budget, and possibly from the production and inventory budgets as well.
- *Manufacturing overhead budget*, which is concerned with estimating the overheads or expenses associated with production activities.
- *Budgeted statement of profit or loss*, which is essentially an aggregation of many of the other sub-budgets, including the sales budget and the operating expenses budget.
- *Cash budget*, which focuses on cash in the same way that the statement of cash flows does, and may be viewed as a statement of the expected future cash receipts and cash payments.
- *Budgeted statement of financial position*, which shows what the entity's financial position is expected to be as at the end of the period.
- *Capital budget*, which deals with expenditure relating to long-term investments. (Capital budgeting is discussed in the capital investment chapter.)
- *Program budget*, which focuses on costs associated with a specific program. This is a budget form commonly used in the government and not-for-profit sectors.

The budget structure that an entity will use depends on a range of factors. Table 9.1 provides a sample list of possible budgets for different entity settings. These budgets are commonly arranged under the umbrella of a master budget.

TABLE 9.1   Applicable budgets for sample entities

Manufacturer	Service (e.g. a hotel)	Professional services (e.g. an accounting or law entity)	Government department
Sales budget	Sales budget	Fees budget	Labour-related budget
Production budget	Labour budget	Labour budget	Expenses budget
Direct materials budget	Expenses budget	Expenses budget	Departmental/functional budget

Direct labour budget	Departmental budget	Departmental budget	Cash budget
Manufacturing overhead budget	Cash budget	Cash budget	Program budget
Non-manufacturing expenses budget	Budgeted statement of profit or loss	Budgeted statement of profit or loss	
Departmental budget	Budgeted statement of financial position	Budgeted statement of financial position	
Cash budget			
Budgeted statement of profit or loss			
Budgeted statement of financial position			

9.4 Master budget

LEARNING OBJECTIVE 9.4 Outline the components of a master budget and prepare a master budget.

A **master budget** is a set of interrelated budgets for a future period. It provides a framework for viewing the relevant budgets of an entity. While the nature of the budgets prepared will vary according to the nature of the entity and its operating environment, the master budget is commonly classified into operating budgets and financial budgets. The operating budgets usually include the sales budget and operating expenses budget, while the financial budgets commonly include the broader budgeted statement of profit or loss, the budgeted statement of financial position, the cash budget and the capital budget. The plans developed for the master budget are summarised in a set of budgeted financial statements.

To enable the budget to be used as a control tool to monitor the entity's achievement of its plans, the classification of items included in the master budget needs to mirror the entity's chart of accounts. The **chart of accounts** is the detailed listing/index that guides how transactions will be classified and recorded in the financial reporting system. It is important that the budget is developed in line with this classification structure, otherwise those within the entity will be unable to identify any budget variances by comparing actuals against budget.

Because budgets are based on forecasts about the future, complete accuracy is impossible and variances will inevitably arise. A **variance** is the difference between actual and budget results, and it can be either favourable or unfavourable. A favourable variance occurs when actual revenues are larger than budgeted or actual costs are lower than budgeted. Conversely, an unfavourable variance arises when actual revenues are lower than budgeted or actual costs are greater than budgeted. Determining the underlying reasons for a budget variance is not a straightforward exercise. For example, a favourable cost variance could be obtained by an efficient use of resources or by the use of lower quality, low-cost resources. Each entity determines the level of variance that will be tolerated before investigations are undertaken to understand the cause. Such investigations will provide the necessary feedback to inform future actions and may require a revision of the budget.

An illustration of the main components of a master budget is provided in figure 9.2. As outlined in table 9.1, the individual components that make up a master budget are specific to the entity. In the next section we illustrate the preparation of the various budgets that make up the master budget for both a service entity and a manufacturing entity.

Preparation of an operating budget for a service entity

Nicholas Cash is the owner of Advantage Tennis Coaching (ATC), a Brisbane tennis coaching clinic. The business leases a number of courts at the Brisbane Tennis Centre in Tennyson, Queensland. During its first four months of operations, the business has built up a steady flow of customers largely consisting of juniors, elite juniors and mature-aged fitness players. Before the start of the next year, Nicholas sat down with his accountant to prepare a budget for the expected operations for the next 12 months. Following is an overview of their budget preparation for the period January to December 2020.

FIGURE 9.2 Master budget illustration

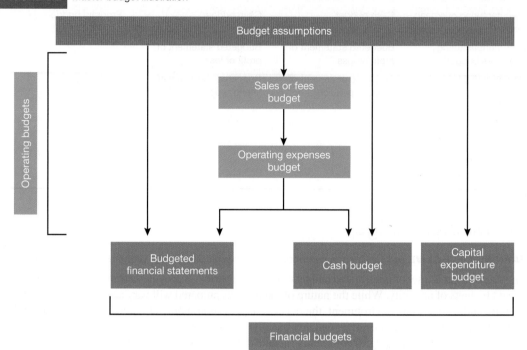

The starting point is to estimate the expected activity level for 2020. This will require market analysis to identify customer demand and then will lead to the preparation of the sales budget detailing the estimated revenue that will be generated based on forecast demand. The sales budget informs the preparation of all other sub-budgets and determines the operating level and therefore the required resources and infrastructure to support planned activities. Based on market analysis undertaken by a local agency and Nicholas's knowledge of the sector, it is expected that patronage will rise in 2020. In 2019, the number of juniors in coaching squads averaged 300 players for 26 weeks of the year. Junior coaching fees were set at $25 per week. Nicholas plans to promote his coaching services and grow this customer group by 20 per cent while holding coaching fees at the same level as in 2019. Nicholas had 20 junior elite players in 2019. He has attracted an additional five players for the 2020 year. Elite junior coaching fees in 2019 were $50 per week for 52 weeks of the year, but will be increased by 30 per cent in the next year. The mature-aged fitness customer group is very popular. In 2019 there were approximately 150 members each paying $10 per week for 48 weeks of the year. Nicholas believes he can increase adult fees by 25 per cent without loss of customers. In the new year he plans to take the junior elite squad on a circuit of local tournaments. Through sponsorships, share of prize monies and parent contributions, Nicholas expects a net return from tournaments in 2020 of $40 000.

As shown in illustrative example 9.1, the sales budget can now be prepared to determine the estimate of total revenue for 2020.

ILLUSTRATIVE EXAMPLE 9.1

Advantage Tennis Coaching sales budget

ADVANTAGE TENNIS COACHING
Sales budget
for the year ended 31 December 2020

Squad fees	Calculations	Weeks	$
Junior	(300 × 1.20) × $25	26	234 000
Junior elite	(20 + 5) × ($50 × 1.30)	52	84 500
Adult fitness	150 × ($10 × 1.25)	48	90 000
Tournaments (net)			40 000
Total revenue			**448 500**

For a service entity such as ATC another important budget will be the labour budget, as labour represents a high percentage of total operating costs in a service entity. The following employees are currently employed and the annual wage represents the enterprise bargaining agreement for 2020:
- manager and head coach × 1 @ $70 000 per annum
- senior coaches × 2 @ $40 000 per annum each
- junior coaches (casual) × 4 @ $20 per hour × 100 hours each
- receptionist (part-time, 20 hours per week) × 1 @ $30 000 per annum.

The annual wage includes all salary on-costs and benefits. To meet the planned growth in numbers of new juniors, Nicholas will employ the equivalent of 10 junior elites as junior coaches. A decision was made to employ the junior coaching staff on a casual basis due to the uncertainty relating to how successful Nicholas will be in attracting new young players. If the predicted growth is not achieved, junior coaching hours will be reduced accordingly.

Illustrative example 9.2 shows the labour budget for the year ended 31 December 2020.

ILLUSTRATIVE EXAMPLE 9.2

Advantage Tennis Coaching labour budget

ADVANTAGE TENNIS COACHING
Labour budget
for the year ended 31 December 2020

Employee category		Total salary cost
Manager and head coach	1 × $70 000	$ 70 000
Senior coaching staff	2 × $40 000	80 000
Junior coaching staff (casual)	10 × $20 × 100 hrs each	20 000
Part-time receptionist	20 hours per week	30 000
Total salary and benefits		**$200 000**

To assist with the development of the operating expenses budget, illustrative example 9.3 provides an extract of actual operating expenses from the statement of profit or loss for the three-month period to 31 December 2019.

ILLUSTRATIVE EXAMPLE 9.3

Advantage Tennis Coaching actual operating expenses extract 2019

ADVANTAGE TENNIS COACHING
Operating expenses extract from the statement of profit or loss
for the 3-month period ended 31 December 2019

Promotions and web maintenance expense	$ 2 000
Equipment depreciation expense	4 000
Utilities expenses	3 200
Court leases at Tennyson Tennis Centre	15 000
Insurance expense	3 250
Supplies expense	1 500
Interest expense	750
Total operating expenses	**$29 700**

A budget of $25 000 is to be allocated for promotion and web maintenance. The purchase of a minibus in June is planned. Depreciation on the bus and equipment is charged on a straight-line basis. The bus will cost $80 000 and have a zero residual value in eight years' time. In line with the lease agreement for tennis court hire, $6700 will be payable each month in 2020. As a result of the expected growth in numbers in the junior squad, ATC's insurer has revised the premium for 2020 to $20 000. Given that increase in numbers and in the costs of electricity and gas, it is estimated that the utilities bills will increase by 25 per cent next year. Supplies expense should be in line with 2019 actual expenditure for 3 months. The loan payable of $50 000 incurs interest at 6 per cent.

After meeting with his accountant, Nicholas developed the budgeted statement of profit or loss for 2020 as shown in illustrative example 9.4.

ILLUSTRATIVE EXAMPLE 9.4

Advantage Tennis Coaching budgeted statement of profit or loss

ADVANTAGE TENNIS COACHING
Budgeted statement of profit or loss
for year ended 31 December 2020

Sales	
Junior squad fees	$234 000
Elite junior squad fees	84 500
Adult fitness squad fees	90 000
Tournaments (net)	40 000
Total revenue	448 500
Operating expenses	
Promotion and web maintenance	25 000
Salaries	200 000
Equipment depreciation ($4000 × 4) + ($80 000 – 0)/8 × 6/12)	21 000
Utilities ($3200 × 1.25 × 4)	16 000
Lease ($6700 × 12)	80 400
Insurance	20 000
Supplies (1500 × 4)	6 000
Interest expense	3 000
Total operating expenses	371 400
Budgeted profit	**$ 77 100**

After reviewing the budget documents, Nicholas is satisfied with the budgeted profit of $77 100. From the budgeted statement of profit or loss, the two major expenses for the entity are salaries, which represent 54 per cent of the operating expenses, and the cost of leasing courts. Given that the majority of the salary cost is for permanent employees, Nicholas will have little opportunity to reduce the level of actual expenditure. Further, the opportunity to renegotiate the lease of courts will not occur until 2021. It will be important for Nicholas to focus the marketing and promotional efforts to generate the budgeted revenue, especially from the junior squads.

In the next section, we look at the preparation of the operating budgets for a manufacturing entity. Note the need to prepare additional budgets to consider the raw materials purchased and the production costs required to convert the raw materials into a finished product.

Preparation of an operating budget for a manufacturing entity

Anni Aryan is the accountant for Mountain Blue Bikes, a manufacturer of sturdy mountain bikes for intermediate-level cyclists. The company's managers are forecasting an increase in sales because of the success of its current advertising campaign. They ask Anni to create a master budget for 2019, given the forecasted sales increase.

To gather the information needed for the budget, Anni first compiles relevant data about revenues, inventories and production costs from last period's accounting records. Next, she obtains information from every department and meets with senior management to identify changes in sales volumes and prices, production processes, manufacturing costs and support department costs.

Developing the sales budget

Anni prepares the sales budget first, which is derived from the sales forecast. The sales budget represents management's best estimate of sales revenue for the budget period. A significant amount of analysis may be necessary to arrive at this estimation of sales revenue. Obviously, the sales budget will have a direct impact on profit. For example, if the sales forecast is too optimistic, the entity may purchase excessive material inventories and/or overproduce the number of units required. This may lead to additional operating costs due to the need to store more materials, not to mention the unnecessary increase in working capital requirements. Also, if there is an excess of finished goods inventory, the product may need to be sold at reduced prices. In contrast, a too-pessimistic forecast may result in insufficient materials and finished goods inventory, which could lead to a loss of sales revenue and/or a loss of customer goodwill. The marketing manager has forecast that 100 000 bikes will be sold in total at a price of $800 each and, due to the seasonal nature of the product, the sales will vary per quarter. Anni develops the sales budget detailed in illustrative example 9.5 for Mountain Blue Bikes, based on the sales pattern identified by the marketing manager.

ILLUSTRATIVE EXAMPLE 9.5

Mountain Blue Bikes sales budget

MOUNTAIN BLUE BIKES
Sales budget
for the year ended 31 December 2019

	Quarter 1	Quarter 2	Quarter 3	Quarter 4	Total
Expected sales (units)	30 000	20 000	10 000	40 000	100 000
Unit selling price	× $800	× $800	× $800	× $800	× $800
Total sales revenue	**$24 000 000**	**$16 000 000**	**$8 000 000**	**$32 000 000**	**$80 000 000**

Developing the production budget

Anni next develops the production budget. Production will be required to meet the need for both ending finished goods inventory of the mountain bikes and sales for the period. However, not all of these units will need to be manufactured, as the entity has opening finished goods inventory to offset some of these required units. According to the accounting records, the beginning finished goods inventory consists of 2500 bikes. Given the anticipated increase in sales volume, the inventory manager wants to increase the finished goods inventory to 3500 units per quarter. Anni calculates the number of bikes that will be manufactured each period, factoring in the sales forecast and both beginning and targeted ending finished goods inventory levels (illustrative example 9.6).

ILLUSTRATIVE EXAMPLE 9.6

Mountain Blue Bikes production budget

MOUNTAIN BLUE BIKES
Production budget
for the year ended 31 December 2019

	Quarter 1	Quarter 2	Quarter 3	Quarter 4	Total
Expected unit sales (refer sales budget)	30 000	20 000	10 000	40 000	
Add: Desired ending inventory	3 500	3 500	3 500	3 500	
Total required units	33 500	23 500	13 500	43 500	
Less: Beginning inventory	2 500	3 500	3 500	3 500	
Required production units	**31 000**	**20 000**	**10 000**	**40 000**	**101 000**

As a result of the analysis, it is estimated that 101 000 mountain bikes will need to be produced in 2019. This production level highlights the influence of inventory policy and sales requirements on production output. The production budget, in turn, provides the basis for determining the budgeted costs for each manufacturing cost element, as explained next.

Developing the materials budget

Once the production output has been estimated, Anni can determine the amount of materials that must be purchased for use in the manufacturing process to meet the desired finished goods inventory. The entity carries inventory of the materials used in the manufacture of the bike and the beginning materials inventory is $700 000. After discussion with the material requisitions manager, Anni is advised that the cost per unit of materials per bike to be purchased from suppliers this year is expected to be the same as last year, which was $140 per bike. Management has determined that, due to the expected sales increase, they want the ending materials inventory per quarter to be $840 000.

Given these assumptions, Anni prepares the following materials budget, which shows that a total of $14 280 000 of material will be purchased during the year (illustrative example 9.7).

ILLUSTRATIVE EXAMPLE 9.7

Mountain Blue Bikes materials budget

MOUNTAIN BLUE BIKES
Materials budget
for year ended 31 December 2019

	Quarter 1	Quarter 2	Quarter 3	Quarter 4	Total
Units to be produced (refer production budget)	31 000	20 000	10 000	40 000	101 000
Material cost per bike	× $140	× $140	× $140	× $140	
Cost of materials required for production	$4 340 000	$2 800 000	$1 400 000	$5 600 000	$14 140 000
Target ending materials inventory	840 000	840 000	840 000	840 000	
Total materials required	5 180 000	3 640 000	2 240 000	6 440 000	
Less: Beginning materials inventory	700 000	840 000	840 000	840 000	
Total cost of material purchases	**$4 480 000**	**$2 800 000**	**$1 400 000**	**$5 600 000**	**$14 280 000**

Developing the labour budget

To develop the labour budget, Anni meets with both the production manager and the human resource manager. Based on production requirements, she is advised of the labour hours required to meet the production and the type of employee skills required to undertake the tasks. Wage rates are then sourced from the payroll manager. Based on these discussions, Anni identifies that the quantity and cost of labour per mountain bike are expected to be two hours per bike at $20 per hour. Anni prepares the labour budget, which forecasts the number of total labour hours and the total labour costs required per quarter to produce the 101 000 bikes (illustrative example 9.8).

ILLUSTRATIVE EXAMPLE 9.8

Mountain Blue Bikes labour budget

MOUNTAIN BLUE BIKES
Labour budget
for the year ended 31 December 2019

	Quarter 1	Quarter 2	Quarter 3	Quarter 4	Total
Units to be produced (refer production budget)	31 000	20 000	10 000	40 000	101 000
Labour time per bike	× 2	× 2	× 2	× 2	× 2
Total required labour hours	62 000	40 000	20 000	80 000	202 000
Labour cost per hour	× $20	× $20	× $20	× $20	× $20
Total labour cost	**$1 240 000**	**$800 000**	**$400 000**	**$1 600 000**	**$4 040 000**

Developing the production overhead budget and the selling and administrative expense budget

In addition to the costs of labour and material, other production and support department costs need to be included in the budgetary process. Information collected from last year's budget and updated for current prices assists in preparing the production overhead budget and the selling and administrative expense budget, as shown in illustrative examples 9.9 and 9.10.

ILLUSTRATIVE EXAMPLE 9.9

Mountain Blue Bikes production overhead budget

MOUNTAIN BLUE BIKES
Production overhead budget
for the year ended 31 December 2019

	Quarter 1	Quarter 2	Quarter 3	Quarter 4	Total
Depreciation	$1 000 000	$1 000 000	$1 000 000	$1 000 000	$4 000 000
Supplies	1 000 000	500 000	250 000	250 000	2 000 000
Indirect labour	1 500 000	1 000 000	750 000	250 000	3 500 000
Miscellaneous	200 000	200 000	200 000	200 000	800 000
Total production overhead	**$3 700 000**	**$2 700 000**	**$2 200 000**	**$1 700 000**	**$10 300 000**

ILLUSTRATIVE EXAMPLE 9.10

Mountain Blue Bikes selling and administrative expense budget

MOUNTAIN BLUE BIKES
Selling and administrative expense budget
for the year ended 31 December 2019

	Quarter 1	Quarter 2	Quarter 3	Quarter 4	Total
Administration	$4 000 000	$4 000 000	$4 500 000	$4 000 000	$16 500 000
Marketing	4 000 000	2 000 000	3 000 000	1 000 000	10 000 000
Distribution	1 250 000	1 250 000	1 250 000	1 250 000	5 000 000
Customer service	375 000	375 000	375 000	375 000	1 500 000
Total selling and administrative expenses	**$9 625 000**	**$7 625 000**	**$9 125 000**	**$6 625 000**	**$33 000 000**

Anni will review the budget with the entity's financial controller and the budget documents will then be presented to the CEO and other department heads for consideration.

9.5 The cash budget

LEARNING OBJECTIVE 9.5 Prepare a schedule of receipts from accounts receivable and a cash budget.

Another important budget that is prepared is the cash budget. A **cash budget** is a statement of expected future cash receipts and cash payments, and enables the calculation of expected cash balances. A cash budget prepared on a month-by-month basis over the budget period is preferable, as it provides more timely information and enables closer monitoring of the cash position. The cash budget is a key component of the master budget and assists decision making by:
- documenting the timing of all estimated cash receipts and cash payments
- helping to identify periods of expected cash shortages, so corrective action can be taken
- helping to identify periods of expected cash surpluses, so short-term investments can be considered
- identifying suitable times for the purchase of non-current assets
- assisting with the planning and use of borrowed funds
- providing a framework for 'what if' analysis.

Like the statement of cash flows studied in the related chapter, the cash budget focuses on cash-related items. Cash is the lifeblood of any entity. Consequently, the use of the cash budget as a planning tool is critical in terms of providing direction, and setting financial targets and benchmarks against which performance will be evaluated. When prepared on spreadsheets, the cash budget allows alternative scenarios on the cash position of the entity to be considered. The preparation of a cash budget will identify any liquidity issues and ensure that the entity always has access to cash either through operating activities or, if needed, financing.

Illustrative example 9.11 demonstrates the preparation of a cash budget for Coconut Plantations Pty Ltd.

ILLUSTRATIVE EXAMPLE 9.11

Preparation of a cash budget

Coconut Plantations Pty Ltd is a small manufacturer of coconut-based products for sale to wholesalers and retailers in Australia. Production and sales are seasonal, with most activities occurring towards the later end of the year as customers build inventory for the summer holiday period. All sales are provided on 30-day credit terms. The cash balance at 1 January 2022 is $110 977. The following estimates have been made with respect to the first three months of operation in 2022.

Step 1. Assess expected trading and operating conditions, and gather all the necessary information.

Step 2. Prepare initial budget estimates and communicate with managers.

	January	February	March
Credit sales	$130 000	$110 000	$100 000
Purchase of raw materials	52 000	44 000	40 000
Manufacturing labour	20 000	16 500	15 000
Overhead (including $3167 per month depreciation)	8 000	6 600	6 000
Warehousing and distribution expenses	4 000	7 000	9 900
Sales and marketing expenses	5 600	4 900	3 800
Administrative expenses (incl. $417 per month depreciation)	3 750	3 500	3 000
Loan — principal		8 750	
Loan interest expense			4 500
Dividend paid			75 000

Additional information
- Past experience suggests that accounts receivable usually settle accounts according to the following pattern.
  - 50 per cent in the month following the sale
  - 40 per cent in the second month following the sale
  - 10 per cent in the third month following the sale
- Actual sales for the last three months of 2021 are as follows.
  - $210 000 in October
  - $282 000 in November
  - $303 000 in December
- Coconut Plantations pays its suppliers of raw materials in the month after purchase. Actual purchases in December are $120 000.
- As bad debts have not been an issue for Coconut Plantations, it is expected that all customers will pay their monies owing.
- The distribution-related expenses for March include an amount of $2300 that will not be paid until April.
- The marketing expenses for March include an amount of $4200 paid for advertising to be conducted in April.
- The loan interest expense will not be paid until April 2022.

For an entity that provides goods or services on credit, one of the main tasks in the preparation of a cash budget is calculating the cash receipts from the credit sales or fees generated. This is commonly shown in a **schedule of receipts from accounts receivable (debtors)**.

Step 3. Prepare a schedule of receipts from accounts receivable and other sub-budgets.

Month	Sales/fees	Receipts January	Receipts February	Receipts March
October (actual)	$210 000	$21 000 ($210 000 × 10%)	—	—
November (actual)	282 000	112 800 ($282 000 × 40%)	$28 200 ($282 000 × 10%)	—
December (actual)	303 000	151 500 ($303 000 × 50%)	121 200 ($303 000 × 40%)	$30 300 ($303 000 × 10%)
January	130 000	—	65 000 ($130 000 × 50%)	52 000 ($130 000 × 40%)
February	110 000	—	—	55 000 ($110 000 × 50%)
March	100 000	—	—	—
Total		**$285 300**	**$214 400**	**$137 300**

Totals are transferred to the cash budget. To illustrate the calculations in the schedule, if we take the actual December sales of $303 000, 50 per cent will be received in the month following the sale (January), 40 per cent in the second month (February) and the final 10 per cent in the third month (March).

Step 4. Prepare the cash budget.

Cash budget
for the three months ending 31 March 2022

	January	February	March	Total
Cash receipts				
Receipts from accounts receivable	$285 300	$214 400	$137 300	$637 000
Total cash receipts	285 300	214 400	137 300	637 000
Cash payments				
Payments to suppliers	120 000	52 000	44 000	216 000
Direct labour	20 000	16 500	15 000	51 500
Manufacturing overhead	4 833	3 433	2 833	11 099
Warehouse and distribution expenses	4 000	7 000	7 600	18 600
Sales and marketing expenses	5 600	4 900	3 800	14 300
Administrative expenses	3 333	3 083	2 583	8 999
Loan principal	0	8 750	0	8 750
Dividend paid	0	0	75 000	75 000
Total cash payments	157 766	95 666	150 816	404 248
Net cash flow	127 534	118 734	(13 516)	232 752
Bank balance at start of month	110 977	238 511	357 245	110 977
Bank balance at end of month	**$238 511**	**$357 245**	**$343 729**	**$347 729**

▨ From the receipts from accounts receivable schedule

▨ Total cash receipts less total cash payments

▨ Note that this is the bank balance at the end of March; this bank balance row is not totalled

You will notice that the 'Bank balance at start of month' row is not totalled across. In the totals column, the opening bank balance is used. Therefore, in the last column we show the total net cash flow for the period ($232 752) and then add the opening cash balance ($110 977) to estimate the final bank balance of $347 729.

Note that the focus is on cash-related items. Therefore, the distribution-related expenses to be paid in April are excluded; the marketing expense of $4200 is still included as it has been paid in the period; depreciation is not included as it does not require a cash flow; and the loan interest is excluded as it will not be paid until April. Finally, note that the bank balance at the end of one month becomes the balance at the start of the next month.

The preparation of the cash budget will enable Coconut Plantations' management to assess the liquidity of the business, given estimates of cash flow in the coming months. A review of Coconut Plantations' cash budget shows an expected positive cash position at the end of each period based on the estimates given. Coconut Plantations' management would need to assess the minimum cash balance required and then determine how best to manage any surplus cash. Given that the budget is prepared before the actual event, Coconut Plantations' management has the time to compare possible investment options. However, the availability of the 'surplus' cash is dependent on actual cash flows being in line with estimated cash flows.

9.6 Budgets: planning and control

LEARNING OBJECTIVE 9.6 Explain the use of budgeting in planning and control.

The preparation of the cash budget is an important part of the *planning process*. Once prepared, the cash budget can be used for monitoring cash performance, which is sometimes referred to as part of the *control process*. A cash budget prepared on a month-by-month basis is much more useful for this purpose than one prepared on a quarterly or yearly basis.

As each month passes, the actual cash numbers can be compared to the budget numbers. The difference between the two is called a variance. A variance report for Coconut Plantations Pty Ltd is shown in illustrative example 9.12, with 'u' representing unfavourable variances and 'f' favourable variances. This example indicates that there are problems with the entity's estimate of its operating expenses, with the majority of the actual expenses resulting in an unfavourable variance compared to budgeted amounts. The other concern for the entity is the significantly lower value of actual cash received from its customers. The current budget estimates will need to be revised in the light of these changed conditions. This will also impact upon possible investment options, as the 'surplus' cash identified in the original budget may not now eventuate.

ILLUSTRATIVE EXAMPLE 9.12

Variance report
Step 5. Compare actual performance against the budget.

Cash budget variance report
for the month ending 31 January 2022

	January budget	January actual	Variance	
Cash receipts				
Receipts from accounts receivable	$285 300	$208 200	$77 100	(u)
Total cash receipts	285 300	208 200	77 100	(u)
Cash payments				
Payments to suppliers	120 000	114 500	5 500	(f)
Direct labour	20 000	22 550	2 550	(u)
Manufacturing overhead	4 833	7 800	2 967	(u)
Warehouse and distribution expenses	4 000	4 400	400	(u)
Sales and marketing expenses	5 600	5 100	500	(f)
Administrative expenses	3 333	3 500	167	(u)
Total cash payments	157 766	157 850	84	(u)
Net cash flow	127 534	50 350	77 184	(u)
Bank balance at start of month	110 977	110 977		
Bank balance at end of month	**$238 511**	**$161 327**	**$77 184**	(u)

Actual receipts from accounts receivable are a reflection of the fees, which must be lower than expected unless there has been a change in the collections pattern

Step 6. Make any adjustments to the budget in light of any variances identified.

This might result in a reconsideration of the budget numbers for the remaining budget period. Remember that the variance report is an example of the control process, the results of which may assist with further planning.

Improving cash flow

The cash budget identifies periods of expected cash shortages. In such situations, corrective action can restore the cash position.

Cash inflow may be increased by:

- improving the collections of cash from accounts receivable — perhaps the entity needs to review its invoicing and follow-up procedures, offer incentives for prompt payment or charge interest on overdue accounts
- seeking ways to improve sales or fees — increasing advertising campaigns or changing features of the product/service to increase fees
- reducing unnecessary inventory levels — discounting obsolete inventory will generate cash
- arranging external finance — bank overdraft, accounts receivable factoring, invoice discounting
- receiving an extra capital contribution from the owners or considering a change in ownership structure
- selling excess non-current assets — a sale and leaseback arrangement may be more suitable.

Cash outflow may be reduced by:

- cutting expenses by identifying areas of waste, duplication or inefficiency
- making use of terms of credit — where purchases are made on credit, there is some benefit in using the full extent of the credit terms
- keeping inventory levels to only what is required, as excess inventory ties up cash and often adds to storage and handling costs
- deferring capital expenditures — it may be necessary to delay the acquisition of any non-current assets
- reducing the carbon footprint, which may reduce resource use and cash outflows.

To further examine budget variances, let's return to our Mountain Blue Bikes example and compare the actual operating activity against the budget expectations. The variance report is shown in illustrative example 9.13.

ILLUSTRATIVE EXAMPLE 9.13

Variance analysis for Mountain Blue Bikes

Extract from financial statements
for the year ended 31 December 2019

	Budget estimate	Actual	Variance
Sales	$80 000 000	$75 000 000	$5 000 000 (u)
Materials usage	14 140 000	14 400 000	260 000 (u)
Labour usage	4 040 000	5 000 000	960 000 (u)
Production overhead	10 300 000	11 000 000	700 000 (u)
Selling and administrative expenses	33 000 000	30 000 000	3 000 000 (f)

The analysis of the variance between actual and budget for Mountain Blue Bikes shows that the entity's actual activity did not occur as estimated in the budget. Although the entity was able to reduce expenditure in the support department costs, this was offset by lower sales and higher cost of sales. In response to these variances, Anni, the accountant, will need to discuss the budget variances with both the marketing and production personnel to try to understand the causes of the variances. After meetings with operational managers, Anni is able to ascertain that negative customer reaction to a price increase is responsible for the sales shortfall. Also, a long-term supplier went into voluntary administration and the new supplier charges more per unit for the raw material components of the bike. Support department costs were lower because new technology had not been purchased, which reduced the depreciation charge for the year. Discussion with managers about why the variances have arisen will enable corrective action to be taken (if necessary) and allow for better planning next year. Sometimes the reason for a variance is within the control of a firm and its managers, but this is not always the case.

9.7 Behavioural aspects of budgeting

LEARNING OBJECTIVE 9.7 Discuss the issues associated with the behavioural aspects of budgeting.

The behavioural aspects of budgeting and planning cover two key areas. The first relates to the style of budgeting process used by an organisation, such as the extent of participation by managers in the annual budget process. The second relates to the impact of the budget targets and plans on the behaviour, motivation and decision making of managers.

Styles of budgeting

Each organisation will have a particular style which reflects how the budgeting process is executed each year. Two common, contrasting styles are the authoritarian and participative styles of budgeting. In an **authoritarian style of budgeting**, senior management simply set the targets and the budget for unit managers. In this case, the unit managers have little say in the targets that are set and may not have any influence over the motivation of the senior management. Alternatively, in a **participative style of budgeting**, the targets and budgets are arrived at by a process of discussion and negotiation between senior management and unit managers. In this case, the unit managers have had a say in the setting of targets and the budget, and consequently are more likely to adopt 'ownership' of the targets and the budget. On the other hand, participation provides the opportunity for line managers to suggest targets and budgets which contain some 'room to move' and may result in the creation of budgetary slack. While **budgetary slack** can be explained in a number of different ways, it essentially results in targets that are a little more easily achievable than might otherwise be the case. If a number of managers engage in this practice, then the ultimate target and budget potentially becomes meaningless.[1] However, it should be noted that managers may not necessarily intend to deceive, and this may be more a function of human behaviour and nature.

Of course, one of the reasons for the existence of budget slack is that targets are used to evaluate performance through a control function; that is, when actual performance is compared to the planned performance or target. Where this performance evaluation is then linked to rewards and bonuses, the incentive for trying to influence the target setting in the first place is increased.

Finally, an interesting issue arises when we think about the options a senior manager has when the existence of budget slack is discovered. To what lengths is the manager prepared to go to remove it? Organisational practices may help contribute to the existence of budget slack. For example, where budgets are mainly set by simply adjusting last year's figures, the existence of slack might be common and may become embedded within the budget estimates. This could be overcome partly by requiring unit managers to justify their budget from scratch or from what is referred to as a 'zero base'. While this is more time consuming, it might help overcome budget slack in some circumstances.

Effect of budget targets on behaviour

This aspect of behaviour relates to the role of budget targets in motivating managers. How motivated a manager might be is influenced by a range of factors, including:

- the difficulty of the target — budget targets are best set as challenging but attainable; when a target is too difficult to achieve, the likely effect is that a manager is demotivated
- whether the manager feels 'ownership' of the target — this is influenced by the extent of input by the manager, which, as discussed above, is a function of the style of budgeting used by the organisation
- whether the manager is able to control the factors influencing the achievement of the budget target
- whether the budget estimates provide too little scope for the manager to properly execute their duties.

DECISION-MAKING EXAMPLE

Effect of targets on behaviour

SITUATION You have recently enrolled in a Bachelor of Business studying Accounting 101 and Economics 101. Upon reading the unit outlines, you learn that, in order to pass the accounting unit, you

---

[1] For those seeking some further reading on this aspect of budgeting, *Management control systems*, 4th edn, by K Merchant and W Van der Stede would be useful.

need to score 100/100 in the final exam. In contrast, the economics unit requires only a 30/100 in the final exam to pass. How will such targets influence your attendance and study approach to both units?

DECISION Obviously, your requirements for both units will lead to different reactions. For Accounting 101, you may protest that the requirement is unattainable as the benchmark set is too difficult to achieve. If unsuccessful in your attempt to change the pass criteria, you may give up, as it seems impossible to meet the benchmark. However, Economics 101's requirement may seem 'too easy' and, as a consequence, you may not attend class or put in your best effort. If you translate this to business, we can understand why benchmarks that appear too difficult may have a negative effect on employee performance. Too slack a benchmark may not encourage employees to work to their full potential and too tight a target may discourage improved performance. The challenge is to find the appropriate balance.

- Of course, the targets used to help build the budget are not set in concrete and can be revised. The use of budget targets, such as sales being linked to performance bonuses, can lead to a culture among staff where achieving the sales level is key irrespective of consequences for customers or the organisation overall.
- These negative consequences of budgeting can often be overcome through a proper process of consultation with and participation of those influenced by the budgets, as well as through a suitable allocation of responsibilities. To achieve this, the accounting department needs to work closely with the managers of various areas of the organisation. The accounting staff will act as facilitators to collect relevant information, by assisting those within the entity who are required to provide the information, and then, once collected, by preparing the relevant budget reports for dissemination throughout the organisation.

VALUE TO BUSINESS

- Budgets form an integral part of an entity's planning processes.
- The budget process will vary from entity to entity, particularly in relation to the level of participation.
- An entity's set of budgets is commonly arranged under the umbrella of a master budget.
- The cash budget focuses on cash-related items and serves as a useful tool for planning (setting targets) and control (calculating variances).

SUMMARY OF LEARNING OBJECTIVES

9.1 Understand the importance of planning and budgeting.

Planning is needed to ensure that what happens today supports the future direction of an entity. Strategic planning relates to long-term planning, while budgeting focuses on the short term (usually one year). The planning process evaluates whether the strategy leads to profits, thereby creating value.

9.2 Explain what a budget is and describe the key steps in the budgeting process.

A budget is a set of short-term goals and targets in financial terms. The key steps in the budgeting process are consideration of past performance, assessment of the expected trading and operating conditions, preparation of initial budget estimates, adjustments to estimates based on communication with and feedback from managers, preparation of the budgeted financial statements and any sub-budgets, monitoring of actual performance against the budget over the budget period and, where necessary, adjusting the budget during the budget period.

9.3 Explain the different types of budgets.

Commonly prepared budgets include the sales or fees budget, the operating expenses budget, the production and inventory budgets, the purchases budget, the budgeted statement of profit or loss, the cash budget, the budgeted statement of financial position and the capital budget.

9.4 Outline the components of a master budget and prepare a master budget.

A master budget can be viewed as a set of interrelated budgets for a future period. The master budget is commonly classified into a set of operating budgets and financial budgets.

9.5 Prepare a schedule of receipts from accounts receivable and a cash budget.

A schedule of receipts from accounts receivable is often necessary when an entity provides goods or services on credit. The schedule helps to calculate the cash expected to be received from accounts receivable in the future, based on the credit sales or fees and the normal pattern of receipts. This schedule is an important component of the cash budget, which focuses on expected future cash receipts and payments, and the expected cash levels at the end of each month, quarter or year.

9.6 Explain the use of budgeting in planning and control.

The planning aspect relates to operationalising plans and developing budget estimates and targets. The control aspect is evident in the comparison of budget with actual performance.

9.7 Discuss the issues associated with the behavioural aspects of budgeting.

The behavioural aspects of budgeting relate to the human involvement in decision making. They include the style of budgeting process used, such as authoritarian or participative; attempts by senior management to set targets that are too difficult to achieve; and attempts by unit managers to set targets that are too low.

KEY TERMS

authoritarian style of budgeting Senior management decides on targets and budgets for unit managers without their input or participation.

budget Quantitative expression of an entity's plans.

budgetary slack Budget targets that may be more easily achievable than might otherwise be the case.

budgeting Process that focuses on the short term, commonly one year, and results in the production of budgets that set the financial framework for that period.

budgeting process Process involving evaluating past performance, assessing and incorporating expectations, preparing estimates, and monitoring and adjusting budgets as required by changing circumstances.

cash budget Statement of expected future cash receipts and cash payments.

chart of accounts Detailed listing/index that guides how transactions will be classified in the financial reporting system.

master budget Set of interrelated budgets for a future period.

participative style of budgeting Targets and budgets are arrived at by discussion and negotiation between senior management and unit managers.

performance management Setting targets in other than just financial terms (e. g. customer service, corporate governance, management techniques, human resource management).

schedule of receipts from accounts receivable (debtors) Schedule calculating the cash receipts from credit sales or fees generated.

strategic planning Process relating to the longer term planning (often three to five years) of an entity's activities, including issues such as expansion plans and radical product/service development.

variance Difference between budgeted cost and actual cost.

APPLY YOUR KNOWLEDGE   *15 marks*

The accountant for Roadrunner Food Services is preparing its cash budget for November and December 2021. The accountant, Ross Leon, has collected the following information regarding expected credit sales and expected purchases of inventory on credit.

	September	October	November	December
Credit sales	$170 000	$180 000	$190 000	$210 000
Credit purchases	125 000	95 000	140 000	155 000

Ross has analysed the accounts receivable records for the past few years and has determined that customers normally pay 60 per cent in the month of sale, 30 per cent in the month following the sale and 8 per cent in the second month following the sale. The remaining 2 per cent is considered a bad debt and uncollectable.

Foods R Us, the only supplier to Roadrunner Food Services, offers a 4 per cent discount if its customers pay by the 15th day of the following month. Ross always takes advantage of this discount. Cash payment for operating expenses are expected to be $85 000 per month for November and December. The expected cash balance on 1 November is $10 000.

Required

(a) Explain to the owner of Roadrunner Food Services why a cash budget is important for the business.

3 marks

(b) Prepare a cash budget for the months of November and December 2021. *8 marks*

(c) Ross would like to purchase a new vehicle in December. The cost of the vehicle is $40 000. Based on your cash budget, what recommendations would you make regarding this purchase? *4 marks*

SELF-EVALUATION ACTIVITIES

9.1 From the following data for Gamma Services, complete a schedule of receipts from accounts receivable for the three months ending 30 June 2021.

	Actual		Estimated		
	February	March	April	May	June
Credit sales	$268 000	$252 000	$216 000	$220 000	$256 000

SOLUTION TO 9.1

Credit sales are normally settled according to the following pattern: 40 per cent in the month of sale, 30 per cent in the month following the sale and 25 per cent in the second month following the sale. Five per cent of accounts are never collected.

		April	May	June
February	$268 000	$ 66 700		
March	252 000	75 600	$ 63 000	
April	216 000	86 400	64 800	$ 54 000
May	220 000		88 000	66 000
June	256 000			102 400
Totals		$229 000	$215 800	$222 400

9.2 Nicholas Cash at Advantage Tennis Coaching has provided the following estimates for the month of January 2020.

Junior squad fees — cash	$21 000
Elite and adult squad fees — credit	7 250
Receipts from accounts receivable	5 000
Tournament sponsorship received	2500
Wages incurred (90% paid)	10 000
Court lease (paid)	3 350
Promotional expenses (50% paid)	6 500
Depreciation on equipment	650
Utility account owing	600
Payments to accounts payable for supplies	300
Loan repayment — principal	1 950
Interest charge (not paid)	125
Insurance premium paid in advance for year	10 000

The cash balance at 31 December 2019 was $4300. Prepare a cash budget for the month of January 2020.

SOLUTION TO 9.2

ADVANTAGE TENNIS COACHING
Cash budget
for January 2020

Cash receipts		
Squad fees received in cash	$21 000	
Receipts from accounts receivable	5 000	
Tournament sponsorship received	2 500	$28 500
Cash payments		
Wages	9 000	
Court lease	3 350	
Promotional expenses paid	3 250	
Payments to accounts payable	300	
Loan repayment	1 950	
Insurance premium	10 000	27 850
Excess of receipts over payments		650
Bank balance at 31 December 2019		4 300
Bank balance at end of January 2020		**$ 4 950**

COMPREHENSION QUESTIONS

9.3 Outline the importance of strategic planning. **LO1**

9.4 Discuss the benefits to an entity in preparing a budget for the coming financial year. **LO2**

9.5 Explain why it is important to link operational budgets to strategic plans. **LO2**

9.6 Outline six ways to increase cash inflow during periods of cash shortages identified in a cash budget. **LO6**

9.7 Explain why the sales budget is often referred to as the 'cornerstone' of budgeting. **LO3**

9.8 State the different types of budgets that may be prepared to construct the master budget. **LO3**

9.9 For the budgets you identified in 9.8 above, discuss the type of information provided in each budget and who in an entity would provide such information. **LO3**

9.10 Discuss the differences in the types of budgets applicable for a manufacturer compared to a service provider. **LO3**

9.11 What is a chart of accounts and what is its role in the budgeting process? **LO4**

9.12 Explain the main steps in the budgeting process. **LO4**

9.13 What does a favourable variance indicate? **LO4**

9.14 Differentiate between authoritarian and participative styles of budgeting. **LO7**

9.15 Explain the benefits of preparing a cash budget for an entity. **LO5**

9.16 Explain the similarities and differences between the cash budget and the statement of cash flows discussed in the statement of cash flows chapter. **LO5**

9.17 Explain the difference between planning and control. **LO6**

9.18 Discuss the typical role of an accountant in the budget process. **LO6**

9.19 Explain the meaning of the term 'budgetary slack'. **LO7**

EXERCISES

★ BASIC I ★ ★ MODERATE I ★ ★ ★ CHALLENGING

9.20 ★   **LO4**

Arthur Thomson Lawyers operates in the local neighbourhood and has six solicitors who work on client briefs. For the coming year, each solicitor is budgeted to work 2400 billable hours. The main areas of law work that Arthur Thomson Lawyers specialises in are conveyancing, litigation and family law. The breakdown of the billable hours per area of law is as follows.

Solicitors	Charge out rate to clients	Percentage of billable hours per area of law		
		Conveyancing	Litigation	Family law
D Arthur	$300 per hour	50%	50%	
J Thomson	$1000 per hour		100%	
C Jackson	$500 per hour	100%		
G Whu	$600 per hour		75%	25%
T Sully	$1200 per hour			100%
O Wang	$1000 per hour		100%	

Required

Prepare a sales or fees budget for the coming year based on this information.

9.21 ★   **LO5**

From the following data for Fantastic Sales, calculate the receipts from accounts receivable for September, October and November of 2021.

	Actual		Estimated		
	July	August	September	October	November
Credit sales	$105 000	$90 000	$92 000	$106 000	$87 000

Credit sales are normally settled according to the following pattern: 20 per cent in the month of the sale, 50 per cent in the month following the sale and the remainder in the second month following the sale.

9.22 ★   **LO5**

From the following data for Starlight Enterprises, calculate the receipts from accounts receivable for June, July and August of 2021.

	Actual		Estimated		
	April	May	June	July	August
Credit sales	$198 000	$206 000	$216 000	$194 000	$195 000

Credit sales are normally settled according to the following pattern: 70 per cent in the month following sale and 25 per cent in the second month following the sale. Five per cent of accounts are never settled.

9.23 ★   **LO5**

Ski Lifters is a business that provides a chairlift for tourists in the alpine region. The peak season is in winter, with the low season during the summer months. Sales are high during the winter ski season and then taper off once the season closes. Explain why preparing a cash budget might be particularly important for Ski Lifters.

9.24 ★   **LO6**

During late 2019, Ski Lifters commenced a new business in the alpine region to rent ski gear to tourists. A budget has been prepared for the coming financial year. Prepare a brief report to management on how the budget can be used as a control device to monitor actual performance.

9.25 ★   **LO7**

One of the downsides of using a participative style of budgeting is the possibility of 'budgetary slack'. Explain whether you consider the strengths of a participative style of budgeting outweigh the problems associated with budgetary slack.

9.26 ★ **LO4**

Watson Company makes specially designed coffee mugs. The entity has developed a website and is trying to switch customer behaviour to this medium. Sales for each quarter of 2020 are as follows.

Quarter ending	
31 March	$234 000
30 June	228 000
30 September	231 000
31 December	402 000

Due to the change in sales strategy, the marketing department at Watson Company expects sales to grow by 20 per cent in each quarter in 2021. The unit sales price will be the same as in 2020, at $25 per unit.

Required

Prepare a sales budget for 2021.

9.27 ★ **LO5**

Twilight Enterprises has provided the following estimates relating to the first quarter of 2021.

Cash sales	$ 88 960
Credit sales	167 624
Receipts from accounts receivable	130 840
Cash payments:	
Wages	100 040
Office furniture	27 176
Utilities expenses	11 688
Administrative expenses	29 816
Depreciation on office furniture	5 554
Receipt of loan	31 400
Credit purchases	120 456
Payments to accounts payable	98 104

The cash balance at 1 January 2021 is $24 800.

Required

Prepare a cash budget for the quarter ending 31 March 2021.

9.28 ★ **LO5**

Budget Travel plans to commence operations on 1 July 2021. The following data and estimates relate to the three months ending 30 September 2021.

	July	August	September
Initial capital	$32 000		
Fees charged (credit)	10 212	$12 321	$16 095
Fees received	5 772	7 548	11 322
Computer equipment (cash)	7 659		
Administration	1 221	1 221	1 221
Advertising and marketing	2 775	2 220	1 332
Cash withdrawals	1 332	1 332	1 332
Rent	1 776	1 776	1 776

Required

(a) Prepare a monthly cash budget for the three months ending 30 September 2021.

(b) The actual numbers for July are as follows: fees received $4200; computer equipment $8200 cash; cash withdrawals $2600 cash. All other cash budget items matched the budget. Prepare a variance report for July 2021.

9.29 ★ ★ **LO4**

Lavender Plantations Pty Limited produces and sells two types of lavender-based products: soaps and candles. Peta Mitchell, the manager, is implementing a new marketing strategy in 2022. Actual sales in 2021 are as follows.

Quarter ending	Soaps (units)	Candles (units)
31 March	6 864	3 227
30 June	8 681	5 954
30 September	9 195	7 167
31 December	10 935	9 667

Due to the change in sales strategy, Peta expects sales of both products to grow by 10 per cent in the first two quarters of 2022. In the second two quarters of 2022, the sales of soaps and candles are expected to grow by 15 per cent and 20 per cent respectively. The unit selling prices in 2021 are: soaps $40 and candles $25. The unit selling prices will remain constant in 2022.

Required

Prepare a sales budget for 2022.

9.30 ★ ★   **LO4, 6**

Garden Sculptures presents the following data relating to the expected operations for the months of January to March 2021.

	January	February	March
Credit services provided	$ 8 000	$12 000	$12 400
Receipts from accounts receivable	20 000	30 000	5 000
Cash services	1 950	2 250	3 300
Cash received from sale of old equipment		2 000	
Salaries and wages paid	8 500	8 500	8 500
Depreciation on equipment	500	500	500
Payment for supplies	2 600	3 500	2 800
Cash purchase of new equipment	20 000		
Administration costs	2 000	2 000	2 000
Credit purchase of supplies	1 900	2 150	1 890

Required

(a) Prepare a cash budget on a monthly basis for the three months ending March 2021. The cash balance at 31 December 2020 is $25 000.

(b) Explain how a variance report would help the owner of Garden Sculptures monitor the entity's cash position.

(c) The following actual cash receipts and payments occur during January: receipts from accounts receivable $15 500; new equipment $22 000; payments for supplies $3200; the other cash receipts and cash payments as per the budget. Prepare a variance report for January.

(d) What might have caused the lower than expected receipts from the accounts receivable amount?

9.31 ★ ★   **LO5, 6**

Hobby Gardens is a garden design and landscaping business. At 30 June 2021, it has a bank balance of $52 500. Provided below are estimates for receipts and payments for the three months ending 30 September 2021.

	July	August	September
Receipts			
Fees	$140 000	$160 000	$200 000
Proceeds from the sale of surplus non-current assets		100 000	
Payments			
Salaries and wages	70 000	70 000	70 000
Supplies	8 500	9 200	12 000
New equipment	144 000		
Purchase of plants	42 000	45 000	61 000

Required

(a) Prepare a monthly cash budget for the three months ending 30 September 2021.

(b) The owners are wondering what the effect would be on the cash position if they did not buy the new equipment, but instead took advantage of a new rental arrangement. The equivalent equipment would cost $12 000 per month under the rental arrangement. Redraft the cash budget to show the impact of the rental alternative. Based on the information available, should they lease or buy the equipment?

9.32 ★ ★ ★   **LO4**

Glenvale Furniture has projected sales of its product for the next six months as follows.

January	80 units
February	180 units
March	200 units
April	160 units
May	60 units
June	140 units

The product sells for $120, variable expenses are $90 per unit and fixed expenses are $1500 per month. The finished product requires 3 units of raw material and 10 hours of direct labour. The company tries to maintain an ending inventory of finished goods equal to the next two months of sales and an ending inventory of raw materials equal to half of the current month's usage.

Required

(a) Prepare a production budget for February, March and April.
(b) Prepare a forecast of the units of direct materials required for February, March and April.
(c) Prepare a direct labour hours budget for February, March and April.

9.33 ★ ★ ★   **LO4**

Golden Arbours intends to start business on the first day of January. Production plans for its first four months of operations are as follows.

January	10 000 units
February	25 000 units
March	35 000 units
April	35 000 units

Each unit requires 2 kilograms of material. The firm would like to end each month with enough raw material inventory on hand to cover 25 per cent of the following month's production needs. The material costs $7 per kilogram. Management anticipate being able to pay for 40 per cent of purchases in the month of purchase. The firm will receive a 10 per cent discount for these early payments. Management anticipate having to defer payment to the next month on 60 per cent of purchases. No discount will be taken on these late payments. The business starts with no inventories on 1 January.

Required

Determine the budgeted payments for purchases of materials for each of the first three months of operations.

9.34 ★ ★ ★   **LO4, 7**

Discuss the potential issues arising for an entity if it takes a budgetary approach in which budgetary data are imposed on business unit managers by the CEO. Contrast this with an approach whereby the budgetary data are developed in a more participatory environment.

9.35 ★ ★ ★   **LO4**

Middleton Services is preparing a master budget for the coming year. At present senior management are reviewing the inventory policies. Which budgets would be affected by policies concerning the level of inventories? Why?

9.36 ★ ★ ★   **LO4**

Brodie Ltd has undertaken its budget planning for the coming accounting period.

Budget item	Budget data
Sales	60 000 units; selling price $120
Cost of inventory	Direct materials: 2 kilograms @ $5 per kilogram Direct labour: 3 hours @ $15 per hour Indirect manufacturing costs: $4 per direct labour hour
Raw materials inventory	Beginning balance: 10 000 kilograms Ending balance: 15 000 kilograms
Raw material cost	$5 per kilogram
Selling and administration costs	$200 000

Required

Prepare a budgeted statement of profit or loss for the coming accounting period.

9.37 ★ ★ ★   **LO4**

Lavender Plantations Pty Limited produces and sells two types of lavender-based products: soaps and candles. The 2022 sales budget for the two products is as follows.

Quarter	Soaps	Candles
1	10 000	6 000
2	12 000	9 000
3	13 000	11 000
4	15 000	14 000

The beginning inventory on 1 January 2022 is expected to be 4200 units of soaps and 1200 units of candles. Management want an ending inventory each quarter equal to 60 per cent of the next quarter's sales. Sales in the first quarter of 2023 are expected to be 30 per cent higher than sales in the same quarter in 2022.

Required

Prepare separate quarterly production budgets for each product for 2022.

9.38 ★ ★ ★   **LO4**

Chalkboard was commenced by Louis Turner. Chalkboard is an innovative technology company that provides a platform for the posting of best-practice teaching videos and commentary. Its strategy is focused around being the number one *enabler* of teaching best practice using a visual medium: videos and commentary. The business provides Louis with the opportunity to combine his two passions: teaching and technology. The platform has now developed to the point where some of the videos are posted by teachers, while others are commissioned by Louis himself. He also provides some of the hardware necessary to facilitate high-quality video production. Best-practice videos now cover primary, secondary and tertiary educational settings. Revenue is generated by advertising on the platform, as well as a growing subscription service that offers premium content. While most of the cash budget items are relatively easy to predict, Louis is worried about the ones where budget and actual figures differ. He wants to invest in order to expand and wonders if he can. The cash budget for Chalkboard is as follows.

CHALKBOARD
Cash budget
for the 3 months ending 31 March 2020

	January Budget $	January Actual $	January Var. $	February Budget $	February Actual $	February Var. $	March Budget $	March Actual $	March Var. $
Anticipated receipts									
Subscriptions	22 000	24 500		20 000	21 200		18 000	15 400	
Advertising	34 000	30 500		28 000	26 500		22 000	16 000	
Total receipts	56 000	55 000		48 000	47 700		4 0000	31 400	
Anticipated payments									
Wages	21 500	21 500		21 500	21 500		21 500	21 500	
Platform costs	18 000	18 000		18 000	18 000		18 000	18 000	
Marketing	6 100	6 100		4 500	5 200		3 800	4 400	
Administration	5 400	5 400		5 400	5 400		5 400	5 400	
Total payments	51 000	51 000		49 400	50 100		48 700	49 300	
Excess (deficit) receipts over payments	5 000	4 000		(1 400)	(2 400)		(8 700)	(17 900)	
Bank balance at beginning of month	28 000	28 000		33 000	32 000		31 600	29 600	
Bank balance at end of month	**33 000**	**32 000**		**31 600**	**29 600**		**22 900**	**11 700**	

Required

(a) Calculate the variances for each of the three months.

(b) Louis is hoping to invest in some new computing technology (estimated at $12 000) during the second quarter of 2020. He is hoping not to have to borrow to do so. Do you think he has sufficient cash reserves to do this?

PROBLEMS

★ BASIC | ★ ★ MODERATE | ★ ★ ★ CHALLENGING

9.39 Issues with budgetary slack ★ ★   LO6, 7

Amy Turner is the newly appointed chief accountant at Satellite Data Components (SDC), which designs and manufactures data components for the satellite and car industries. One of Amy's early tasks is to review the budgeting and planning system. From her initial enquiries, she finds the issue of 'budgetary slack' being mentioned by a number of managers.

Required

(a) Explain what budgetary slack is and why it might be a problem.

(b) What advice would you offer to Amy regarding her course of action with respect to budgetary slack?

9.40 Effect on budgets of planned sales increase ★ ★   LO4

Michael Wallis is the marketing manager for a chain of stores specialising in electric tools for home renovators. Michael's department is preparing a sales budget for the coming year and he has issued a memo to his staff that includes a requirement for an annual increase in sales of 15 per cent for all stores. This sales increase applies to all products sold. What budget(s) would be affected by the estimated increase in sales?

9.41 Effect on entity performance from cost cutting ★ ★   LO4, 6, 7

Johnny Castles is the operational manager for Tru Blue Tours. Johnny's bonus is dependent upon the reduction of his department's operating expense budget by 10 per cent in the coming year. One initiative he has taken is to cut staff training expenditure. What implications could this decision have for Tru Blue Tours as a whole?

9.42 Use of budgeting techniques to assist strategic change ★ ★   LO5, 6

Dairy Australia Ltd's annual operating plan for 2017–2018 outlines its three-year plan following revision of its strategic direction. Access the plan (available at www.dairyaustralia.com.au) and outline how budgeting techniques have been used by Dairy Australia's accountant to assist in making the decision to rationalise operations.

9.43 Effect on cash budget of different loan repayment options ★ ★   LO5

Mona Little, the accountant for Trailers 4 Hire, is currently preparing the budget for the coming year. One of the agenda items for next week's finance meeting is consideration of whether an outstanding loan of $250 000 should be refinanced, paid out in a lump sum or extended by reducing the repayments. Discuss how the cash budget would change with each of the above options.

9.44 Understanding variance between budget estimates and actual performance ★ ★   LO6

Database Service's management expressed surprise that the budgeted profit was achieved despite actual sales being under by $75 000. Give reasons why the actual profit may have been able to match the budgeted profit.

9.45 Effect on budget of changing occupancy rates ★ ★   LO4

Holiday Manor has twenty rooms available for rent. During the month of December, its average room rate is expected to be $180 and its room occupancy 80 per cent. Due to the holiday season, the room rate is to be increased by 20 per cent and the occupancy is expected to be 95 per cent. In February, no further room rate increase is planned and occupancy is expected to be 90 per cent.

Required

(a) Calculate the budgeted room revenue for each of the three months.

(b) Discuss how the management of Holiday Manor would have determined the occupancy rates.

9.46 Budget for a restaurant ★ ★   LO4, 6

Holiday Manor has a dining room with the capacity to seat 100 guests. It is open for breakfast and lunch seven days a week. During January 2019, management forecast the seat turnover for breakfast to be 2.5 times and for lunch 2 times, with the average bill to be $20 for breakfast and $40 for lunch. Beverage revenue is usually 10 per cent of the breakfast revenue and 25 per cent of the lunch revenue.

Required

(a) Calculate the budgeted total revenue of food and beverage for January 2019.

(b) What actions could the dining room manager take to increase beverage sales?

9.47 Review of budget estimates ★ ★   LO6

As a consequence of the global financial crisis, many airlines have cut back services to various locations around Australia. Identify other entities or groups of entities that might be reviewing their budget targets during the budget period due to this reduced service by airlines.

9.48 Usefulness of a budgeting system ★ ★　　　　　　　　　　　　　　　　　**LO2, 6**

Veronica Shan owns and operates the Quality First printing company. Veronica and her staff do not engage in planning or budgeting, as they consider the business too small to warrant their attention to such matters. Recently, it has been necessary for the employees to work overtime every night in order to complete customer orders, although some customers have become frustrated and taken their business elsewhere. The backlog of orders has arisen because customers have been promised a two-day turnaround and has been compounded by the business running out of premium paper and inks.

Required

Discuss how a budgeting system would assist Quality First.

9.49 Budgeting styles ★ ★　　　　　　　　　　　　　　　　　　　　　　　　**LO6, 7**

Betty Wu is the manager of a large retail store specialising in children's clothing and accessories. As Betty is the longest serving employee, she believes that she knows what is best for the store. She does not consult with her departmental managers in relation to operational plans and prepares all budget estimates by herself. Over the past several years, unfavourable budget variances have become more significant. When questioned about the variances, departmental managers have given many excuses to explain their department's lack of performance against budget. The situation has not been helped by the high turnover of employees at all levels.

Required

(a) Comment on the style of budgeting used by Betty Wu.

(b) Suggest any improvements that could be made to the budgetary process and how such changes would benefit the store.

9.50 Target setting in budget planning ★ ★　　　　　　　　　　　　　　　　　**LO6, 7**

'Nobody ever seems to be able to hit our sales targets. Why is that?' (John Lyons, Chief Accountant of Clocktower Fashions).

John is showing his frustration at the failure of the company's store managers to meet their specific targets for sales and expenses. He says, 'We do everything for them. We don't ask them to contribute at all; our formula for target setting is well known'.

Required

Briefly outline what might be wrong with Clocktower Fashions' budget process with respect to target setting. What improvements would you suggest?

9.51 Preparation of receipts from accounts receivable schedule and cash budget ★ ★　　**LO5**

M20 Company has presented the following estimates relating to 2021 activities.

	Quarter ending			
	31 March	30 June	30 September	31 December
Sales revenue	$395 000	$445 000	$495 000	$520 000
Purchases	252 000	214 500	204 500	219 500
Cost of sales	197 500	222 500	247 500	260 000
Marketing and administration expenses	94 000	94 000	94 000	94 000
Occupancy expenses	43 500	43 500	43 500	43 500
Depreciation expense	12 200	12 200	12 200	12 200

Sales in the December quarter of 2020 are $345 000. All sales are on credit, of which 55 per cent are collected in the quarter of sale and 45 per cent in the following quarter. Purchases are on credit and entity policy is that all purchases are paid for in the same quarter. The marketing and administration expenses incurred and paid are the same. Occupancy expenses incurred and paid are usually the same, except that the electricity bill (estimated to be $700) for December 2021 will not be paid until January 2022. A major IT hardware acquisition of $13 650, to be paid for in cash, is expected in the December quarter. The bank balance at 31 December 2020 is $9225.

Required

(a) Prepare a schedule of receipts from the accounts receivable showing cash collections for each quarter of 2021.

(b) Prepare a cash budget (on a quarterly basis) for the 12 months ending 31 December 2021.

(c) Assess the cash position of the entity for 2021.

9.52 Preparation of receipts from accounts receivable schedule and cash budget ★ ★ ★　　**LO5, 6**

Realty Company prepares monthly cash budgets. Provided next is a set of relevant data extracted from existing reports and the sub-budgets for the two months of September and October 2021.

	September	October
Credit sales	$342 000	$436 000
Direct materials purchases	162 000	216 000
Direct labour	51 400	55 200
Manufacturing overhead	21 600	23 400
Marketing and administration expenses	35 000	35 000
Proceeds from sale of old equipment		8 200
Cash payment for new IT equipment	18 400	

All sales are on credit. Collections from accounts receivable normally have the following pattern: 60 per cent in the month of sale, 30 per cent in the month following the sale and 10 per cent in the second month following the sale. Fortunately, Realty Company does not have much trouble with bad debts.

Sales in June, July and August are $315 000, $286 000 and $322 000 respectively. Direct material purchases are paid for in the month following the purchase. Purchases in August are $192 000. Manufacturing overhead includes $14 500 for depreciation expense, while marketing and administration expenses include an amount of $6000 for depreciation expenses. Realty Company expects to be able to repay the principal on a $150 000 loan in October.

Required

(a) Prepare a schedule of receipts from the accounts receivable for the two months ending 31 October 2021.

(b) Prepare a cash budget for September and October 2021. The cash balance at 31 August 2021 is $12 600.

(c) As part of its longer term plans, Realty Company is hoping to commence a product reinvention program for one of its core products. The project would require an initial cash commitment of $30 000. Management is hoping to fund this from the cash flows of the business. Does this seem feasible?

9.53 Budgeting and sales increase ★ ★ ★   **LO4, 7**

At a recent finance committee meeting, the Chief Operating Officer advised the marketing department that a 10 per cent increase in sales is expected for the coming year. The increase is to apply to all product lines.

Required

(a) How will this directive impact on the preparation of next year's budget?

(b) What are the potential behavioural effects on employees from this directive?

9.54 Preparation of receipts from accounts receivable schedule and cash budget ★ ★ ★   **LO5, 6**

Glenn Stone, manager of Jarrett Car Repairers, has requested that you prepare a cash budget for the months of December and January. He has provided the following information to assist in this task.

• Projected cash balance at the end of November is $60 000.

• Actual revenue for October and November and projected revenue for December and January are as follows.

	October	November	December	January
Cash sales	$ 63 000	$ 61 000	$ 72 000	$ 60 000
Sales on credit	90 000	110 000	130 000	80 000
Total sales	**$153 000**	**$171 000**	**$202 000**	**$140 000**

• Analysis of past records shows that credit sales are collected over a three-month period, with 50 per cent being collected in the month of the sale, 40 per cent in the next month and the remainder in the following month.

• Projected expenditure during December and January is as follows.

– Selling and administrative expenses are budgeted to be $88 000 each month.

– A new car hoist will be purchased for $100 000, with a $20 000 cash payment in December and the balance to be paid in March.

– Glenn wants to maintain a minimum cash balance of $60 000.

- As more customers will want their vehicles serviced prior to Christmas, the consumables store will need more supplies. Accordingly, an order has been placed for $60 000 of inventory. This will arrive in late November and be paid in December.

Required

(a) Prepare a schedule showing receipts from customers for the credit sales.

(b) Prepare a cash budget for December and January.

(c) Prepare a report for Glenn outlining his cash position over the Christmas period. Give advice regarding any financing requirements or investment opportunities.

9.55 Budgets and performance ★ ★ ★ LO6

Willow Health provides a range of healthcare services to the local community, including home visits by nurses to elderly patients. An allied health worker, who performs a range of tasks such as housework and showering for patients, accompanies the nursing staff. When the nurses are not visiting patients, the allied health staff work at the office doing related administration work.

Each year, the centre receives a budget allocation from the state government's department of health. The objective of the home-visiting program is to enable the elderly to remain in their own homes for as long as possible. The department does not allow the centre to spend more than this allocation. The centre, in turn, allocates its budget among its various programs. The home-visiting program is approved and allocated $260 396 in 2020 and $289 476 in 2021 as follows.

	2020	2021
Nurses	$145 378	$155 019
Allied health workers	60 046	71 500
Medical supplies	18 197	21 402
Cleaning supplies	6 894	9 216
Transportation	9 068	11 144
Clinic general overhead	20 813	21 195
Total expenditures	**$260 396**	**$289 476**
Number of home visits	4 812	5 601
Average cost per home visit	54.11	51.68

The nursing staff receive a 5 per cent increase in salary one-third of the way through 2021. The allied health workers do not receive an increase in wages in either year. The prices of medical supplies increases by about 2 per cent during 2021. The prices of cleaning supplies are relatively constant across the two years.

Transportation is provided by the nurses, who are reimbursed 20 cents per kilometre. The clinic's general overhead is allocated to programs on the basis of budgeted program salaries.

Required

(a) Compare the results for 2020 and 2021. Does it appear that the financial performance has improved in 2021?

(b) If you were the general manager of the centre, what would you discuss with the head of the home-visiting program concerning the 2021 results? Explain.

(c) If you were the head of the home-visiting program, how would you respond to the concerns raised in (b) above?

9.56 Production, labour, materials and sales budgets ★ ★ ★ LO4

Bullen & Company makes and sells upmarket carrybags for laptop computers. John Crane is responsible for preparing Bullen & Company's master budget and has assembled the data below for 2021.

The direct labour rate includes wages, all employee-related benefits and the employer's share of payroll tax. Labour-saving machinery will be fully operational by March. Also, as of 1 March, the company's enterprise agreement calls for an increase in direct labour wages; this has been included in the direct labour rate.

Bullen & Company expects to have 10 000 bags in inventory at 31 December 2020 and has a policy of holding 50 per cent of the following month's projected sales in inventory.

	2021			
	January	February	March	April
Estimated unit sales	20 000	24 000	16 000	18 000
Sales price per unit	$80	$80	$75	$75
Direct labour hours per unit	4.0	4.0	3.5	3.5
Direct labour hourly rate	$15	$15	$16	$16
Direct materials cost per unit	$10	$10	$10	$10

Required

Prepare the following budgets for Bullen & Company for the first quarter of 2021. Be sure to show supporting calculations.

(a) Production budget
(b) Direct labour budget
(c) Direct materials budget
(d) Sales budget

9.57 Purchase, cost of sales, and cash collection budgets ★ ★ ★   **LO4, 5**

Quality Goods Company operates antique and second-hand goods stores throughout Victoria. Such stores are currently very popular and sales are increasing each month. It has budgeted the following sales for the indicated months.

	June	July	August
Sales on account	$1 450 000	$1 550 000	$1 650 000
Cash sales	380 000	390 000	400 000
Total sales	**$1 830 000**	**$1 940 000**	**$2 050 000**

Quality Goods Company's success in this specialty market is due in large part to the extension of credit terms and the budgeting techniques implemented by the firm's owner, Janelle Matthews. All merchandise is marked up to sell at its invoice cost plus 25 per cent. Stated differently, cost is 80 per cent of selling price. Merchandise inventories at the beginning of each month are 30 per cent of that month's forecast cost of sales. With respect to sales on account, 40 per cent of receivables are collected in the month of sale, 50 per cent are collected in the month following and 10 per cent are never collected.

Required

(a) What is the anticipated cost of sales for June?
(b) What is the beginning inventory for July expected to be?
(c) What are the July purchases expected to be?
(d) What are the forecasted July cash collections?

9.58 Preparation of sales and operating expenses budgets and budgeted statement of profit or loss statement ★ ★ ★   **LO4**

John Wilson is the owner/manager of Overnight Courier Solutions, a small transport and courier company that provides logistic services to business. John is about to start the budget process for 2021. His marketing manager has contacted customers and analysed market trends, and expects sales to online traders to increase by 30 per cent in 2021. One of the major customers has predicted that its sales will increase by 109 per cent next year. John is very confident that his business will meet the estimated sales growth for 2021. In contrast, transport to local traders is expected to increase by no more than 3 per cent in 2021. The sales activity for 2020 is as follows.

	Online traders	Local traders	Total
March quarter	$1 000 000	$ 800 000	$1 800 000
June quarter	900 000	600 000	1 500 000
September quarter	800 000	700 000	1 500 000
December quarter	1 500 000	1 100 000	2 600 000
Total	**$4 200 000**	**$3 200 000**	**$7 400 000**

Operating expenses

Given the expected increase in sales volumes for 2021, John holds meetings with the drivers and the sales personnel to identify the resources needed to support the increased activity. To assist their deliberations, the statement of profit or loss for 2020 is used as a basis for discussion.

OVERNIGHT COURIER SOLUTIONS Statement of profit or loss for the financial year ended 31 December 2020	
	$
Sales	8 200 000
Less: Operating expenses	
General administration expenses	800 000
Utilities	
— Gas	10 000
— Electricity	30 000
Wages	1 600 000
Sales commission	370 000
Loan interest	50 000
Marketing expenses	100 000
Vehicle-related expenses	2 000 000
Depreciation on vehicle fleet	800 000
Total operating expenses	5 760 000
Profit	**2 440 000**

Wages breakdown for 2020	
Annual salaries for employees are as follows:	
10 drivers @ $120 000	$1 200 000
Office manager	150 000
Administration staff × 2	100 000
Sales staff × 3	150 000
Total salaries	**$1 600 000**

Additional information

The following changes are expected in 2021.

- A new enterprise bargaining agreement is expected to be approved, which will increase salaries by 4 per cent.
- Due to uncertainty regarding the cost of fuel, an expected increase of 1 per cent is to be allowed in the budget.
- The fuel is included in the vehicle-related expenses and is 50 per cent of the expense.
- Utilities are expected to increase by 2 per cent.
- To encourage sales staff to boost sales to the expected levels, the sales commission will increase from 5 per cent to 5.5 per cent of sales.
- Marketing-related expenses are expected to increase by 25 per cent.
- General administration expenses are expected to increase by 1 per cent.
- Loan interest and depreciation for 2021 will be the same as in 2020.

Required

Prepare a sales budget, operating expenses budget and a budgeted statement of profit or loss for Overnight Courier Solutions for 2021 taking in consideration the revenue and cost changes identified by the business.

DECISION-MAKING ACTIVITIES

9.59 Go to the website for JB Hi-Fi Ltd and examine its latest annual report. Write a report to the finance manager explaining how you would prepare the sales budget.

9.60 Best Beef Burgers operates a store in Melbourne and the following is its average monthly statement of profit or loss.

	$	$
Revenue		
Food	60 000	
Beverages	20 000	80 000
Cost of sales		
Food (50% of revenue)	30 000	
Beverages (20% of revenue)	4 000	34 000
Gross profit		46 000
Operating expenses		
Wages	15 000	
Operating supplies	5 000	
Administration	3 000	
Advertising	2 500	
Repairs and maintenance of equipment	1 500	
Utilities	2 500	
Depreciation	1 000	
Interest	1 000	31 500
Profit before tax		**14 500**

The owner is currently preparing the budget for next year and is considering the following alternatives.

1. Reducing the cost of sales for food from 50 per cent to 45 per cent. This would be achieved by reducing portions and improving purchasing. There would be no other changes.
2. Cutting the food cost from 50 per cent to 45 per cent and spending an additional $1500 on advertising. The advertising should attract new customers and increase the volumes of both food and beverage revenue by 20 per cent on present levels. The new customers would also cause monthly other operating expenses to increase as follows.

Wages	$2 000
Supplies	400
Administration	200
Repairs	150
Utilities	400

Required

Prepare a budgeted average monthly statement of profit or loss for both alternatives. Advise the owner which alternative you consider best, giving reasons.

9.61 According to Telstra's 2018 Remuneration report, 40 per cent of the executive variable remuneration plan (EVP) was based on customer performance measures. Discuss the reasons why the board has linked executive remuneration to customer satisfaction ratings.

9.62 Swinton Industries operates in the IT industry, producing and selling computer and IT equipment. It is structured along functional lines (research and design, production, marketing and so on) and, for most of its history, has operated with a fairly authoritarian management style. This management style is reflected in the budget-setting process, whereby the accounting staff set budget targets in conjunction with the CEO and budgets are presented to departmental managers as non-negotiable reports. Recently there has been a change of CEO with the appointment of Wendy Ambrose. Wendy has embarked on a reorganisation aimed at a more decentralised decision-making structure. The budget-setting process is also to be conducted with a higher level of participation by departmental managers. Accounting staff have been instructed to work more closely with departmental managers on the setting of budget targets.

Required

(a) Outline the advantages of the move to a more participative-style budget process.
(b) What is the likely impact of this change on accounting staff?

9.63 A university student, Barry Ward, plans to sell atomic alarm clocks with a music function over the internet and in person during the semester to help pay his study expenses. He buys the clocks for $35 and sells them for $55. If payment by cash accompanies the personal sales (estimated to be

40 per cent of sales), he gives a 10 per cent discount. If customers include a credit card number for either internet or personal sales (30 per cent of sales), they receive a 5 per cent discount. The remaining collections are estimated as follows.

One month following	15%
Two months following	6%
Three months following	4%
Uncollectable	5%

Sales forecasts are as follows.

September	120 units
October	220 units
November	320 units
December	400 units
January	Out of the business

Barry plans to pay his supplier 50 per cent in the month of purchase and 50 per cent in the following month. A 6 per cent discount is granted on payments made in the month of purchase. However, Barry will not be able to take any discounts on September purchases because of cash flow constraints. All September purchases will be paid for in October.

Barry has 40 clocks on hand (purchased in August and to be paid for in September) and plans to maintain enough end-of-month inventory to meet 70 per cent of the next month's sales.

Required

Prepare schedules for monthly budgeted cash receipts and cash disbursements for this venture. During which months will Barry need to finance purchases?

REFERENCES

Simons, R 2000, *Performance measurement and control systems for implementing strategy*, 1st edn, Prentice Hall.

ACKNOWLEDGEMENTS

Photo: © Goodluz / Shutterstock.com
Photo: © Hero Images / Getty Images

CHAPTER 10

Cost–volume–profit analysis

LEARNING OBJECTIVES

After studying this chapter, you should be able to:

- **10.1** define fixed, variable and mixed costs
- **10.2** prepare a break-even analysis for single-product and multi-product entities
- **10.3** apply the contribution margin ratio to CVP calculations
- **10.4** explain the key assumptions underlying CVP analysis
- **10.5** discuss the uses of break-even data
- **10.6** outline the concept of operating leverage
- **10.7** assess the profitability of output when there are resource limitations
- **10.8** assess relevant information for decision making
- **10.9** analyse an outsourcing decision
- **10.10** analyse a special order decision.

Chapter preview

In this chapter, we further explore the planning activities in business entities. Following on from strategic planning and budgeting covered in the previous chapter, cost–volume–profit (CVP) analysis allows a systematic consideration of cost behaviour and the subsequent impact on profit planning. The focus is on understanding how total costs change if there is a change in activity level.

CVP analysis aids our understanding of how profits will change in response to changes in sales volumes, costs and prices, and it can help to answer queries such as the following.
- How many units need to be sold, or services performed, to break even (earn zero profit)?
- What is the impact on profit of a change in the mix between fixed and variable costs?
- How many units need to be sold, or services performed, to achieve a particular level of profit?
- What is the impact on profit of a 15 per cent increase in costs?
- Which products or services are contributing best to the entity's profit performance?

In order to answer these types of questions, management need to look forward. Consequently, CVP analysis forms a part of the planning process, as it is forward-looking. CVP analysis is critical in the start-up phase as well as at regular intervals to set and monitor profit targets. Conducting CVP analysis requires an understanding of the nature of fixed costs and variable costs. In this chapter you learn how to undertake such analysis.

Later in the chapter we examine how profitability is affected when an entity's operating capacity is limited due to insufficient resources such as labour and technology. We then identify the relevant revenues (the term 'revenues' is used in this chapter to refer to income from ordinary activities) and costs to assist with short-term decision making. In particular, we look at the financial and non-financial considerations in relation to an entity assessing either a special order or the decision to outsource a business activity to another entity.

10.1 Cost behaviour

LEARNING OBJECTIVE 10.1 Define fixed, variable and mixed costs.

Examining cost behaviour enables us to consider the way in which costs change and the main factors that influence those changes. Traditionally, costs have been classified as being fixed, variable or mixed. An understanding of these is important for basic **cost–volume–profit analysis** whereby we investigate the change in profits in response to changes in sales volumes, costs and prices.

Fixed, variable and mixed costs

The nature of fixed and variable costs relates to whether such costs are likely to alter in total with changes in activity. **Fixed costs** are commonly identified as those that remain the same in total (within a given range of activity and timeframe) irrespective of the level of activity. Typically, fixed costs include such costs as facility-sustaining costs (e.g. lease costs and depreciation charges). When levels of activity are thought of in terms of units of output, the total fixed costs remain the same but the fixed costs per unit will decrease as the number of units produced increases. This is illustrated in figure 10.1.

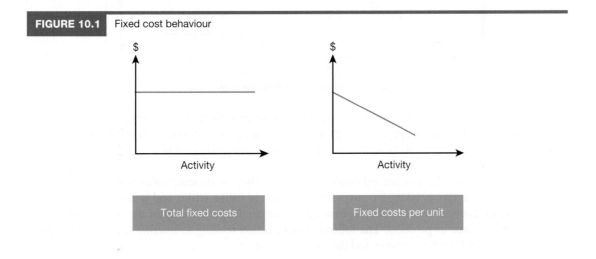

FIGURE 10.1 Fixed cost behaviour

Total fixed costs

Fixed costs per unit

Variable costs are commonly identified as those that change in total as the level of activity changes. Typically, variable costs include such costs as ingredients for a food manufacturer or fuel costs for a courier. Just as we do for fixed costs, we can consider variable costs on a total or unit basis. The difference is illustrated in figure 10.2.

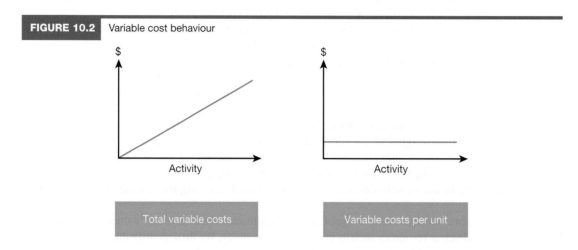

FIGURE 10.2 Variable cost behaviour

The traditional definitions of fixed and variable costs relate to the concept of the relevant range. The **relevant range** is the range of activity over which the cost behaviour is assumed to be valid. If the activity level goes outside the relevant range, then the expected behaviour of costs may change — for example, fixed costs can no longer be assumed to be fixed, as an entity may be able to renegotiate contracts or change the level of resources required to support operating activities.

Of course, the classification of costs as fixed or variable is not simple. Indeed, some costs may appear to possess both fixed and variable characteristics, in which case the costs would be classified as **mixed costs** (sometimes referred to as 'semi-fixed costs' or 'semi-variable costs'). The mixed cost relationship is illustrated in figure 10.3, which shows a mixed cost for television advertising based on a fixed amount of $10 000 to generate the advertisement and a $500 charge each time it is aired.

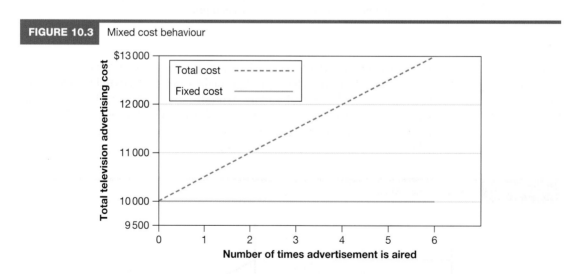

FIGURE 10.3 Mixed cost behaviour

In order to split costs into their fixed and variable components, there are a number of techniques that are available, ranging from an approach where managers can use their business knowledge to split costs to the use of more complex statistical analysis. To gain an understanding of how costs can be separated, let's consider the following example.

Coconut Plantations Pty Ltd has established an online shop to increase sales of its coconut-based products. Jo, the manager, is taking a conservative approach to online selling and is initially only offering a single product, coconut candles. She is planning to analyse the profitability of the online shop before offering a wider range of products. The following information relating to internet activity and internet charges is extracted from her accounts and the sales database.

	3 months to 31 March 2020	3 months to 30 June 2020
Number of online sales orders	5 000	5 500
Total internet charges	$150 000	$155 000

Before CVP analysis can be undertaken, we need to split the total costs into their fixed and variable components. Given our discussion of cost behaviour earlier, we know that fixed costs stay the same regardless of the level of activity while total variable costs increase in proportion to output. Therefore, the variable cost behaviour can explain why the costs of Coconut Plantations have increased by $5000 for an increased activity level of 500 online sales orders. To calculate the variable cost per order, we divide the difference in cost by the difference in activity level as follows.

Change in internet charges	$5000
Change in online orders	500 online orders
Variable cost per unit	$10 per online order

We know that total costs are equal to total fixed costs plus total variable costs. Therefore, to calculate the total fixed costs we have to deduct the total variable costs, which will be equal to the number of sales orders times $10, from the total costs. From the calculations below, we have calculated total fixed costs to be $100 000.

$$\text{For } 5000 \text{ online orders} = \$150\,000 - (5000 \text{ online sales} \times \$10) = \$100\,000$$

$$\text{For } 5500 \text{ online orders} = \$155\,000 - (5500 \text{ online sales} \times \$10) = \$100\,000$$

Coconut Plantations Pty Ltd can now use this cost behaviour knowledge to determine the total costs for any level of online orders within the relevant range. Jo now knows that costs will increase at the rate of $10 per online order due to the variable cost behaviour and that fixed costs will remain constant at $100 000. For example, if she wanted to know the total cost at 5100 online orders, we would determine the variable cost (5100 × $10) and then add the fixed cost ($100 000), which would give a total cost of $151 000.

An understanding of fixed and variable costs is necessary in order to explore break-even analysis.

10.2 Break-even analysis

LEARNING OBJECTIVE 10.2 Prepare a break-even analysis for single-product and multi-product entities.

Break-even analysis relates to calculation of the necessary level of activity required in order to break even in a given period. Break-even occurs when total revenue and total costs are equal, resulting in zero profit. There are a number of ways in which the break-even calculation can be made. (Illustrative example 10.1 explores the more popular of these.)

Break-even analysis draws on the traditional understanding of fixed and variable costs to introduce the concept of the contribution margin. The **contribution margin** is calculated by deducting the total variable costs from the total revenue. To determine the **contribution margin per unit** the variable cost per unit is deducted from the revenue per unit. We can think of the contribution margin as that amount of revenue that contributes in the first instance towards fixed costs with any excess contributing to profit. Alternatively, if the contribution margin does not cover fixed costs, then the entity is in a loss-making situation. At break-even point, the total contribution margin is equal to the fixed costs.

We now calculate break-even for single-product and multi-product entities, and highlight the differences in calculation for each.

Break-even analysis is an important tool for entities such as airlines to understand the financial impact of changing cost structures.

Break-even analysis for a single product or service

Break-even analysis for a single product is detailed in illustrative example 10.1.

Break-even analysis for a single product

Nicholas Cash, the owner of Advantage Tennis Coaching (ATC), is planning to take a squad of junior players who have reached qualifying standards to the National Tennis Australia Junior Championship. The tournament will be held on the Gold Coast in Queensland. Players will be transported to the tournament in a bus (48-seat capacity) from Brisbane and ATC will engage an additional coach to support them during the tournament. In recognition of being selected for the squad, ATC will award each player a kit bag embossed with the event and their name. Lunches will be provided.

Participation charge (parents to pay)	$150 per player
Nomination fees	$25 per player
Embossed kit bag	$35 per player
Lunches and sports drinks	$30 per player
Support coach	$1200 for the event
Bus hire from Brisbane to Gold Cost	$600 for the event

The break-even calculation (in units, or players) can be expressed as:

$$\frac{\text{Fixed costs }(\$)}{\text{Contribution margin per unit (or player) }(\$)} = x \text{ break-even (units or players)}$$

where the contribution margin (per unit, or player) is equal to the selling price (participation charge) per player less the variable costs per player.

So, for ATC the contribution margin per player is as follows.

Selling price (participation charge) per player		$150
Variable costs per unit (or player):		
Nomination fees	$25	
Embossed kit bag	35	
Lunches and drinks	30	90
Contribution margin per unit		**$ 60**

The break-even point for ATC in number of players attending the championship is:

$$
\begin{aligned}
\text{Break-even for ATC} &= \frac{\text{Fixed costs}}{\text{Contribution margin per unit}} \\
&= \frac{\$(1200 + 600)}{\$60} \\
&= \frac{\$1800}{\$60} \\
&= 30 \text{ players}
\end{aligned}
$$

CVP analysis may also be viewed in graphical form, as shown in figure 10.4.

FIGURE 10.4 Mixed cost behaviour

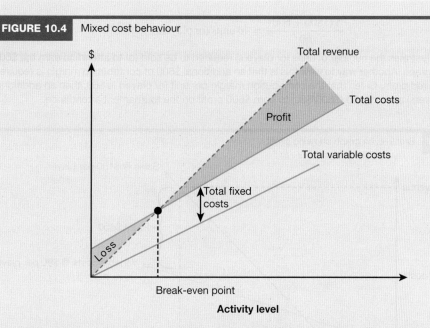

Figure 10.5 below shows the CVP graph for ATC at the break-even number of players.

FIGURE 10.5 Graphical presentation — ATC break-even point

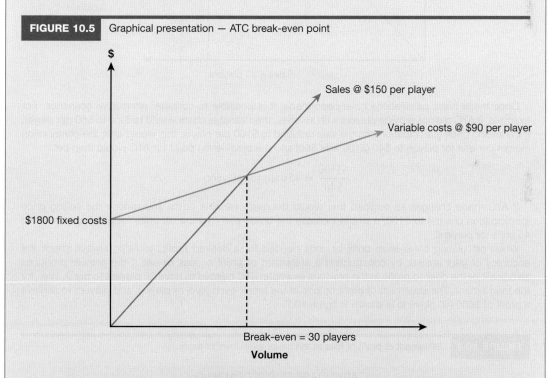

Clearly, as soon as ATC increases the number of players above 30, it begins to make a profit. It is possible to build a desired profit level into this analysis and thereby calculate the units (or players) required to be sold to achieve a particular profit. The formula for this calculation is:

$$\frac{\text{Fixed cost} + \text{Desired profit} \; (\$)}{\text{Contribution margin per unit} \; (\$)} = x \; \text{sales units to earn a desired profit}$$

For example, if ATC sets a desired profit level (prior to any income tax consideration) of $600, then the number of units (or players) required can be calculated as:

$$\frac{(\text{Fixed costs} + \text{Desired profit})}{\text{Contribution margin per unit (or players)}}$$

$$\frac{\$(1800 + 600)}{60} = 40 \text{ units (or players)}$$

Figure 10.6 illustrates the number of units (or players) required to be sold (or to attend) to earn the $600 profit in a CVP graph. Another way to view this is that an additional $600 of contribution margin is required to earn the desired profit. Given that the contribution margin per unit (or player) is $60, then an additional 10 units (or players) are required ($600/$60) to earn $600 profit on the tournament attendance.

FIGURE 10.6   Break-even graph showing profit

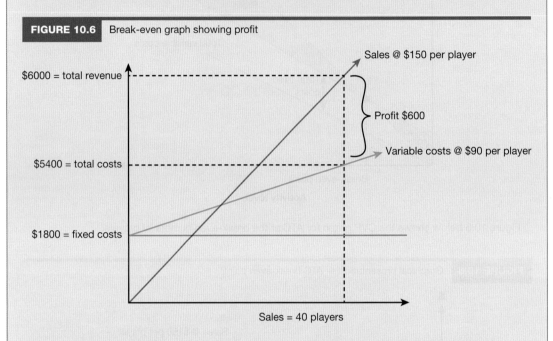

Once these basic calculations have been made, it is possible to consider alternative scenarios. For example, if ATC did not provide players with lunches, then variable costs would reduce to $60 per player. If the selling price (participation charge) was reduced to $100 per player, this would alter the contribution margin per unit (or player) to $40 ($100 less $60) and the break-even point for ATC would then be:

$$\frac{\$1800}{\$40} = 45 \text{ units (or players)}$$

If ATC made changes as outlined that would decrease variable costs and reduce the selling price (participation charge) to $100, it would increase the break-even number of units (or players) from 30 to 45 units (or players).

When calculating break-even units or units needed for a desired profit, you can always check the accuracy of your answer by constructing a statement of profit or loss to see if the answer produces zero profit or the desired profit. In the previous example, ATC needed to have 30 players to break even for the tournament. The statement of profit or loss at the break-even level of players and players to achieve a profit of $600 (40 players) is shown in figure 10.7.

FIGURE 10.7   Statement of profit or loss at the break-even level of sales

ADVANTAGE TENNIS COACHING Statement of profit or loss at the break-even level of sales (players)		
	30 players	40 players
Sales ($150)	$4 500	$6 000
Less: Variable costs ($90)	2 700	3 600
Contribution margin	1 800	2 400
Less: Fixed costs	1 800	1 800
Profit	**$ 0**	**$ 600**

CVP can be used in equation form or as a ratio. In some circumstances, the unit data may not be available or the aim may be to calculate the break-even point in total sales dollars. In such circumstances, the contribution margin ratio can be used. This is explored later in this chapter.

The break-even calculation can be viewed as an equation in the following form:

$$s(x) = vc(x) + fc \text{ for break-even and}$$
$$s(x) = vc(x) + fc + p \text{ for meeting a desired profit}$$

where:
    s = selling price per unit
    x = number of units
    vc = variable cost per unit
    fc = fixed costs
    p = desired profit

We have explored only the very basics of CVP analysis here. Each entity needs to find its own application of the concepts outlined. CVP analysis provides the opportunity for spreadsheet analysis, including 'what if' and sensitivity analysis. Indeed, some entities use quite complex modelling to identify break-even points. Moreover, some entities adapt the basics outlined here to suit their own environment. For example, transport entities speak of break-even kilometres or miles, hotels speak of break-even occupancy rates and airlines speak of break-even passenger miles or kilometres. While each of these calculations will be made at a more complex level, they still require an understanding of the fundamentals outlined here.

Another measure that can be used to assess risk associated with sales is the margin of safety. The **margin of safety** is commonly regarded as the excess of revenue (or units of sales) above the break-even point. It provides an indication of how much revenue (sales in units) can decrease before reaching the break-even point and may be calculated as:

Margin of safety in units = Actual or estimated units of activity − Units at break-even point
Margin of safety in revenues = Actual or estimated revenues − Revenues at break-even point

If the margin of safety is small, managers may put more emphasis on reducing costs and increasing sales to avoid potential loss. A larger margin of safety gives managers more confidence in making plans such as incurring additional fixed costs.

Break-even analysis for multiple products

In our previous example ATC had only one product (or tournament), so how does CVP analysis work when there is more than one product or service? CVP analysis for a multi-product entity relies on knowing or assuming the **sales mix** (i.e. how many units of each product/service are sold relative to total units sold). CVP analysis for a multi-product entity relies on the sales mix between each of the products/services remaining consistent for each scenario under consideration. The CVP calculation for a multi-product entity is shown in illustrative example 10.2.

ILLUSTRATIVE EXAMPLE 10.2

Break-even analysis for multiple products

Let's return to Coconut Plantations Pty Ltd, a small company that manufactures coconut-based products including candles, soaps and detergents. Data relating to the bricks-and-mortar sales of its three products are provided below.

	Products		
	Candles (C)	Soaps (S)	Detergents (D)
Annual volume in units (200 000 total units)	60 000	40 000	100 000
Selling price per unit	$25	$40	$20
Variable costs per unit	$15	$22	$15
Annual fixed costs are $355 000			

The problem is that Coconut Plantations Pty Ltd has not one but three contribution margins. If our basic break-even calculation is going to help, then we need to determine some kind of average contribution margin. This is where the sales mix is used to determine a **weighted average contribution margin (WACM)**. The WACM is the contribution margin after weighting the unit contribution margins by its relative sales mix. The calculation of the WACM follows.

The sales mix, along with the contribution margin per unit, is used to calculate the WACM for Coconut Plantations.

	Candles (C)	Soaps (S)	Detergents (D)	Total
Annual volume in units	60 000	40 000	100 000	
Selling price per unit	$25	$40	$20	
Variable costs per unit	$15	$22	$15	
Contribution margin	$10	$18	$5	
Sales mix[a]	0.30	0.20	0.50	
Weighted average contribution margin (WACM)[b]	3.0	3.60	2.50	9.10

$$^a\text{Calculated as } \frac{\text{Number of sales units of product}}{\text{Total number of sales units for all products}}$$

$$\text{For candles } = \frac{60\,000 \text{ units}}{200\,000 \text{ units}} = 0.30$$

$$\text{For soaps } = \frac{40\,000 \text{ units}}{200\,000 \text{ units}} = 0.20$$

$$\text{For detergents } = \frac{100\,000 \text{ units}}{200\,000 \text{ units}} = 0.50$$

[b] Sum of the contribution margin for each product multiplied by sales mix

$$\text{For candles} = \$10 \times 0.30 = \$3.00$$

$$\text{For soaps} = \$18 \times 0.20 = \$3.60$$

$$\text{For detergents} = \$5 \times 0.50 = \underline{\$2.50}$$
$$\underline{\underline{\$9.10}}$$

Unit sales required to break even can be calculated as:

$$\frac{\text{Fixed costs}}{\text{WACM per unit}}$$

$$= \frac{\$355\,000}{\$9.10}$$

$$= 39\,011 \text{ units (rounded)}$$

We can then apply the sales mix per product to the 39 011 units to determine how many of each product would need to be sold to break even.

Candles	39 011 units × 0.30	11 703
Soaps	39 011 units × 0.20	7 802
Detergents	39 011 units × 0.50	19 506
		39 011

Note that multi-product CVP analysis is of value only when the sales mix is predictable and relatively constant. Next is a statement of profit or loss for Coconut Plantations showing the contribution to fixed costs by each product at break-even using each product's sales requirements for break-even.

	Candles	Soaps	Detergents	Total
Sales volume at break-even	11 703	7 802	19 506	
Revenue (sales volume × selling price)	$292 575	$312 080	$390 120	
Less: Variable costs (sales volume × variable cost per unit)	175 545	171 644	292 590	
Contribution margin (revenue less variable costs)	117 030	140 436	97 530	$354 996
Less: Fixed costs				355 000
Profit (due to rounding)				$ 4

So far, we have not mentioned the treatment of income tax in relation to the desired profit in CVP analysis. For CVP analysis we need to use pre-tax profit. Assume Coconut Plantations plans a desired after-tax profit of $200 000. How can we determine the pre-tax amount? To calculate a pre-tax profit, we divide the after-tax profit by 1 minus the income tax rate. This conversion of after-tax profit into pre-tax profit is necessary to perform the CVP calculations. Therefore, if Coconut Plantations wants an after-tax profit of $200 000 what will be the pre-tax profit? Assuming a tax rate of 30 per cent, then:

$$\text{Pre-tax profit} = \frac{\$200\,000}{(1 - 0.30)}$$
$$= \$285\,714$$

This shows that, to earn an after-tax profit of $200 000, Coconut Plantations would need to earn a pre-tax profit of $285 714. Once the pre-tax profit target has been determined, the remainder of the CVP calculations can be conducted as described in earlier sections.

10.3 Contribution margin ratio

LEARNING OBJECTIVE 10.3 Apply the contribution margin ratio to CVP calculations.

In some circumstances, there may be insufficient data to calculate the number of units of a product required to reach the break-even point or it may not be feasible to calculate the number of units. In these circumstances, executing CVP analysis by using the contribution margin per unit is of little use. What we can use instead is the **contribution margin ratio**, the percentage by which revenue exceeds variable costs (or, alternatively, the contribution margin expressed as a percentage of revenue). It is particularly useful when seeking the total sales dollars required to break even or earn a desired profit, rather than a specific number of units.

The contribution margin ratio can be calculated as:

$$\frac{\text{Contribution margin per unit}}{\text{Selling price per unit}} \times 100 = x\%$$

or

$$\frac{\text{Total contribution margin}}{\text{Total sales}} \times 100 = x\%$$

The contribution margin ratio provides a measure of the contribution of every dollar of sales or fees to cover fixed costs and generate profit. This is demonstrated in illustrative example 10.3.

ILLUSTRATIVE EXAMPLE 10.3

Contribution margin ratio

Referring back to the data for Advantage Tennis Coaching (ATC) in illustrative example 10.1, the contribution margin ratio is calculated as:

$$\frac{(\$150 - \$90)}{\$150} = 0.40 \text{ or } 40\%$$

▶

Break-even sales can then be calculated as total fixed costs/contribution margin ratio. In ATC's case, this is:

$$\frac{\$1800}{0.40} = \$4500 \text{ in sales (total parents' contributions)}$$

We can confirm this result, as the break-even units (players) in illustrative example 10.1 were 30. At a selling price (or parent contribution) of $150, this gives total sales of $4500 (30 units or players × $150).

The contribution margin ratio can be particularly useful when individual unit price and cost data are not available or when the focus is on calculating the sales dollars required to break even. It can also be used to analyse the impact of a change in sales revenue on profit. Consider the following independent data.

	Product A	Product B	Total
Sales revenue	$20 000 000	$10 000 000	$30 000 000
Variable costs	8 000 000	5 000 000	13 000 000
Contribution margin	$12 000 000	$ 5 000 000	$17 000 000
Contribution margin ratio	0.60#	0.50+	0.567*
Fixed costs			$ 9 000 000

#$0.60 = \$12\,000\,000/\$20\,000\,000$
+$0.50 = \$5\,000\,000/\$10\,000\,000$
*$0.567 = ((\$20\,000\,000/\$30\,000\,000) \times 0.6) + ((\$10\,000\,000/\$30\,000\,000) \times 0.5)$

The break-even level of sales is equal to:

$$\frac{\$9\,000\,000}{0.567} = \$15\,873\,015$$

At this level of sales revenue, the contribution margin is equal to the fixed costs.

We can use the contribution margin ratio data to consider the impact on profit of, say, a 5 per cent increase in sales revenue. Using the example above, a 5 per cent increase in sales revenue would be $(30\,000\,000 \times 0.05) = \$1\,500\,000$. With an average contribution margin of 0.567, the additional contribution margin (and profit) would be ($1 500 000 × 0.567) or $850 500.

10.4 CVP assumptions

LEARNING OBJECTIVE 10.4 Explain the key assumptions underlying CVP analysis.

CVP analysis and break-even analysis are underpinned by a range of important assumptions. Key assumptions include the following.
- The behaviour of costs can be neatly classified as either fixed or variable.
- Cost behaviour is linear (see figures 10.1 and 10.2).
- Fixed costs remain 'fixed' over the time period and/or a given range of activity (often referred to as the relevant range).
- Unit price and cost data remain constant over the time period and relevant range.
- For multi-product entities, the sales mix between the products is constant.

If the conditions and environment for the entity fall outside these assumptions (e.g. not all costs can easily be classified as fixed or variable), then such analysis is of little benefit.

10.5 Using break-even data

LEARNING OBJECTIVE 10.5 Discuss the uses of break-even data.

Break-even data can be used to assist with a variety of decision situations, including:
- identifying the number of products or services required to be sold to meet break-even or profit targets
- allocating resources, by focusing on those products that contribute more to profits
- determining the impact on profit of changes in the mix of fixed and variable costs
- pricing products.

An interesting issue relating to break-even calculations is: what should you do if the break-even units are too high for the period in question? In other words, how does an entity reduce its risk and lower its break-even point? A range of possibilities exist.

- Are the assumptions and forecasts relating to costs reliable?
- Can costs be lowered?
- Can anything be done about price(s)?
- What would the impact be of increasing some costs (e.g. marketing) in order to achieve higher sales levels?
- Can the cost mix be altered (i.e. changing the mix between fixed and variable costs)?

10.6 Operating leverage

LEARNING OBJECTIVE 10.6 Outline the concept of operating leverage.

Operating leverage refers to the mix between fixed and variable costs in the cost structure of an entity. A knowledge of operating leverage helps in understanding the impact of changes in sales on profit. Those entities with a higher proportion of fixed costs than variable costs within their cost structure are often classified as having high operating leverage. Such entities are commonly thought to be more risky, as fluctuations in sales will produce higher fluctuations in profits for entities with high operating leverage than for entities with lower operating leverage. The reason for this is that higher fixed costs lead to a higher contribution margin; however, more sales need to be achieved to cover the fixed costs. For example, during the global financial crisis and the swine flu outbreak, airlines were struggling to break even due to their high fixed-cost structure. Passenger loads being achieved were about 71 per cent, while above 73 per cent is considered necessary for flights to be profitable. Another example was in 2012 when the Indian Pacific railway commenced its usual low-season service two months earlier than normal due to increasing competition from low-cost airlines and cruise ships. The reason given for the earlier than expected 'low season' was to remain financially viable by reducing services in a period of lower demand. Train travel has a high level of fixed costs such as hiring the locomotives, hiring the track and employment of staff, all of which occur before welcoming one paying guest.

A business with a high level of fixed costs is train travel.

Let's revisit the Advantage Tennis Coaching (ATC) example to illustrate the impact of different cost structures. ATC has variable costs that include $30 per unit (or player) for providing lunch for the players. The Tennyson Tennis Centre has a catering service that has offered to prepare lunches for a fixed fee of

$1200 per tournament regardless of the number of players. If this proposal were accepted, it would lead to a change in the cost structure, as the lunch cost would be reclassified from a variable cost to a fixed cost. The change in cost structure would also change the contribution margin as, under existing arrangements, the contribution margin per unit (or player) is $60, whereas with the proposed lunch arrangement the contribution margin would increase to $90 per unit (or player) due to the higher fixed costs. Given the different cost structures, Nicholas Cash, the owner of ATC, has a choice of which option to go with. To determine the best option, we need to work out the number of sales (or players) where ATC is indifferent to either option for providing lunch to the players. This point of indifference is the sales level (or number of players) where profits are the same for both options. To calculate this level, we divide the $1200 fixed lunch charge by the $30 variable lunch cost, which gives us the sales level (or number of players) where the lunch costs are the same. Therefore, the sales level (or number of players) at which ATC would be indifferent to the lunch options is 40 units or players. To prove this, we can prepare a statement of profit or loss for both options.

Lunch provided @ $30 per player		Contract lunch @ $1200 per tournament	
Fee (40 players × $150)	$6 000	Fee (40 players × $150)	$6 000
Less: Variable costs		Less: Variable costs	
(40 players × $90)	3 600	(40 players × $60)	2 400
Contribution margin		Contribution margin	
($60 per player)	2 400	($90 per player)	3 600
Less: Fixed costs	1 800	Less: Fixed costs	
		($1800 + $1200)	3 000
Profit	$ 600	Profit	$ 600

The statement of profit or loss shows that, at a sales level (number of players) of 40, Nicholas at ATC would be indifferent to either lunch strategy, as profits are identical. However, if the sales level changed, ATC's preference would change due to the difference in the contribution margin offered by each option. For example, if sales (number of players) fell below 40 ATC would prefer to go with the per-player lunch option, as profits would fall by only $60 per player due to the lower contribution margin. However, beyond 40 units (or players) ATC would prefer the contract lunch option, as profits would increase by $90 per unit (player) due to the higher contribution margin. The change in profit is able to be explained by the change in contribution margin.

VALUE TO BUSINESS

- CVP analysis is an important part of the planning process and serves as a useful decision-making tool.
- An understanding of fixed, variable and mixed costs is necessary to execute break-even analysis.
- Break-even analysis can be conducted for both single-product/service entities and multi-product/service entities.
- CVP analysis is underpinned by a set of important assumptions.
- The concepts of margin of safety and operating leverage provide entities with useful extensions to the basic CVP analysis and break-even calculations.

DECISION-MAKING EXAMPLE

Improving the break-even level of sales

SITUATION Prior to the opening of EastLink in Melbourne in 2008, it was forecast that 258 000 vehicles would use the tollway daily. However, in 2008 fewer than 150 000 trips were being made and at the time industrial analysts advised that at least 156 000 trips a day were needed to cover the monthly interest bill. By 2011 daily trips were on average 186 332, still well below the original forecast. Using CVP concepts, how do you think management responded to this situation?

DECISION Connect East management focused on cost efficiencies and, as a result, the cost per trip dropped from $1.72 in 2009 to $1.28 in 2010. Cost efficiencies were gained by upgrading the image-processing system, which led to a reduction in manual processing and through technical improvements to the web and contact centre channels, with the expectation that customers would elect to use self-service options. However, the actions taken were not sufficient and in 2011 the tollway was sold to foreign investors.

10.7 Contribution margin per limiting factor

LEARNING OBJECTIVE 10.7 Assess the profitability of output when there are resource limitations.

For some businesses, sales are not limited by market demand but by production/operational limitations. For example, limited production can be caused by a shortage of labour, materials, space or equipment, or any combination of these. In such cases, if the entity offers more than one product or service to customers, it needs to determine which product/service provides the most profitable use of the limited resource. In order to calculate the most profitable mix of products/services, it is necessary to calculate the **contribution margin per limiting factor**. We use an earlier example, Coconut Plantations Pty Ltd, to illustrate this situation. The following table provides financial data on the company's three products and the amount of machine time (machine hours) required to produce each.

	Products		
	Candles	Soaps	Detergents
Budgeted sales next year	60 000	40 000	100 000
Selling price per unit	$25	$40	$20
Variable costs per unit	$15	$22	$15
Contribution margin per unit	$10	$18	$5
Machine hours per unit	1 hour	4 hours	1.5 hours
Total machine hours required = 370 000 hours	60 000 hours	160 000 hours	150 000 hours

Coconut Plantations has only 270 000 machine hours available for production, which is not enough to meet all production requirements (370 000 hours). In addition, the entity is planning an advertising campaign for online customers and the marketing department wants to know which product should be promoted, as the funds available will only support one product. Therefore, it is necessary to focus on the production limitation, which in this example is machine hours, to determine how to maximise profits. The first step is to calculate the contribution margin per machine hour for each product, by dividing the contribution margin per unit by the machine hours required per unit.

	Candles	Soaps	Detergents
Contribution margin per unit	$10	$18	$5
Machine hours per unit	1 hour	4 hours	1.5 hours
Contribution margin per machine hour	$10 per hour	$4.50 per hour	$3.33 per hour

The contribution margin per machine hour highlights that, although the soap product provides the highest contribution margin per unit ($18), it only provides a contribution margin per machine hour of $4.50 compared with the candle product, which provides a contribution margin of $10 per machine hour. Therefore, when faced with a machine hour shortfall, candles will maximise the entity's profit by providing a $10 contribution margin per machine hour compared with the other products and should be the focus of the advertising campaign. To highlight how profit is maximised, let's compare the total contribution margin if only one product was produced within the 270 000 hours available.

	Candles	Soaps	Detergents
Machine hours per unit	1 hour	4 hours	1.5 hours
Total units in 270 000 hours	270 000	67 500	180 000
Contribution margin per unit	$10	$18	$5
Total contribution	$2 700 000	$1 215 000	$900 000

The total contribution is maximised by producing 270 000 units of candles, as they contribute an additional $1 485 000 profit over the soap product's contribution to profit. However, if there was no machine hour constraint, then the most profitable product would be the product that gives the highest contribution margin per unit, which for Coconut Plantations is soap, which would contribute $18 per unit to profit compared with $10 per unit of candles and $5 per unit of detergents. Therefore, in order to maximise profits, it is important that the entity identifies any constraints which may have an impact on output.

10.8 Relevant information for decision making

LEARNING OBJECTIVE 10.8 Assess relevant information for decision making.

Business decisions usually involve the selection of one alternative over another. An entity may need to choose whether to accept or reject a one-off customer order, or whether to make a product or deliver an activity in-house or purchase it externally (known as 'make or buy' or **outsourcing**). It is important that decisions are based on the right information and this requires identifying relevant costs and income. **Relevant costs** and **relevant income** are those that differ among alternative courses of action, with the focus being on identifying **incremental income** and **incremental costs**, which represent the additional income/costs resulting from an alternative course of action. It is also important to identify if there is an opportunity cost (i.e. what is given up if one alternative is chosen over another) as a result of the decision. For example, if an entity can lease out space that has become empty due to outsourcing a production activity, the loss of rental income would be considered an **opportunity cost** if the outsourcing did not take place.

However, remember that the financial analysis is only one input into the decision-making process and, together with relevant qualitative factors, forms the information package to be used by those within the entity. Relevant qualitative information may include risk-related factors such as:
- an assessment of how existing customers will react to an entity selling one-off orders at a lower price
- the quality of service delivery by the outsourced provider
- the ability for the outsourced provider to deliver when required
- the financial stability of the outsourced provider.

When both the quantitative and qualitative analyses have been considered, an informed decision can then be made to ensure the best outcome for the entity. In the next section we further explore these issues by looking at two operational decisions made by entities — outsourcing and special orders.

10.9 Outsourcing decisions

LEARNING OBJECTIVE 10.9 Analyse an outsourcing decision.

An **outsourcing decision** (also called a 'make or buy' decision when referring to a product) requires an entity to choose whether to continue producing a product component or providing a service in-house. Many entities today have chosen to outsource activities or have a component part manufactured by an external entity. For example, some universities outsource the teaching of particular industry-based software to industry experts who have up-to-date practical experience in using that software. Similarly, major car companies outsource the manufacture of many of their vehicle component parts such as seat belts, windscreens and engines. Other services commonly outsourced by entities include building maintenance, office cleaning and security. When considering an outsourcing decision, it is important to identify both **avoidable costs** (those that will no longer be incurred if the decision is made to buy) and **unavoidable costs** (those that will still be incurred under either option). Therefore, it is necessary to identify those costs that will change as a result of a business decision. Costs that do not change are unavoidable and will be incurred regardless of the decision taken.

Illustrative example 10.4 provides the financial input into the decision by a service entity of whether it should outsource a business activity to an external provider.

ILLUSTRATIVE EXAMPLE 10.4

Outsourcing a business activity

Gee Vesty Accounting Services is a suburban accounting business that provides services to local entities. Its services include the maintenance of accounting records, the preparation of financial statements and tax returns, and the provision of consulting services. Due to the increasing demand for consulting services, Gee Vesty is considering concentrating more on this service area. In order to staff the consulting activities, it is considering outsourcing the maintenance of clients' accounting records to a local bookkeeper. The following relevant information has been collected to assess this proposal.
- 1600 billable hours per year are currently being charged to clients for bookkeeping services provided.
- The charge-out rates are $200 per hour for Gee Vesty's consulting services and $50 per hour for its bookkeeping services.

- An external bookkeeper has quoted $2000 per week for 52 weeks.
- An analysis of the overhead costs identified that $500 could be avoided each week if the bookkeeping activity was outsourced.

The question could be asked as to why Gee Vesty is considering outsourcing the bookkeeping service. Given the increasing demand for consulting services, Gee Vesty is faced with the issue of how best to enable the capacity to provide these services. By outsourcing the bookkeeping activity, capacity is made available to pursue the new business opportunity without eliminating the bookkeeping service currently provided to clients. As part of the decision process, it is necessary to undertake a financial analysis to identify the revenue and costs that will be affected by the outsourcing decision.

Relevant costs and revenue

Increase in revenue	$240 000
Billable hours 1600 hours × $150 per hour ($200 − $50)	26 000
Avoidable overhead costs ($500 × 52 weeks)	266 000
Increase in cost	
Bookkeeping fee ($2000 × 52 weeks)	104 000
Net benefit to outsource	**$162 000**

The switch in billable hours from bookkeeping services to consulting services will enable the charge-out rate to increase from $50 to $200 per hour, giving rise to a $150 increase in revenue per billable hour. Analysis of the overhead expenditure identifies that the outsourcing will decrease costs by $500 each week, with a total saving of $26 000 over the year. The financial benefits gained from the outsourcing must be offset by the increase in costs resulting from the contract fee of $2000 per week. All other income and costs are irrelevant because they will not change with either option.

This analysis indicates that the outsourcing will be favourable for the entity from a financial perspective, as it is expected that profits will increase by $162 000. However, Gee Vesty will also need to consider any qualitative factors that may affect the decision. For example: How reliable is the contract bookkeeper? Does the person have the necessary experience? Can the bookkeeper complete the assigned tasks within the timeframe expected by clients? Will all billable hours currently charged to bookkeeping be taken up with consulting?

DECISION-MAKING EXAMPLE

Outsourcing

SITUATION A coastal city in northern California was faced with a decision on how best to reduce budget expenditure due to a cash shortfall as a result of a previous year budget blowout caused by a legal dispute with a developer which the city lost. Analysis of the budget records revealed that 40 per cent of its general expenditure related to the police budget. To reduce budget expenditure, the decision was made to outsource the police service. What motivated this decision?

DECISION The decision to outsource the police service enabled a cost saving of $3.5 million per year. The responsibility for police service was outsourced to a nearby city. The rationale given was that there were only about 17 violent crimes a year in the coastal city and there had been only two homicides in the past decade, both of which were solved. The outsourcing allowed the city to stretch funds while still maintaining the same level of public protection.

As mentioned earlier, a range of other, more qualitative factors may need to be considered in outsourcing decisions, particularly with respect to the management of risk-related factors. For example, a recent building collapse at a garment manufacturer in Bangladesh which killed over 1000 workers has caused many global companies to review their outsourcing decisions and put in place stricter supervision practices of their international suppliers.

Illustrative example 10.5 looks at a decision about whether Palamara Industries, a manufacturing entity, should make or buy a special flashing light needed in the manufacture of a mobile phone.

'Make or buy' decision — outsourcing a component part

Palamara Industries produces mobile phones specifically for hearing-impaired people. One of the components is a special flashing light that alerts the user to a call. The unit cost of making this light is as follows.

Variable costs per unit	
Direct material	$ 0.80
Direct labour	0.20
Indirect	0.10
Total variable costs	**$ 1.10**
Total fixed costs	
Various	$60 000

Fleet Ltd has offered to supply 100 000 units of the light for $1.40. If the offer is accepted, $10 000 of the fixed costs can be eliminated. Wong Industrial has offered to lease the factory space currently used to produce the flashing light from Palamara Industries for $560 per week.

The decision for Palamara Industries is whether to outsource production of the special flashing light component to Fleet Ltd and lease the factory space to Wong Industrial, or continue to manufacture the light in-house. Of the fixed costs, $50 000 is irrelevant to the decision as it is a cost that will be incurred regardless of the decision made by Palamara Industries. For example, the $50 000 would represent allocated costs such as factory rent, equipment depreciation and maintenance. If the $50 000 was included in the analysis, it would need to be assigned to both the make and buy options. The income from leasing the factory will be an opportunity cost if the flashing light is not outsourced, so it is relevant to this decision and reduces the cost of outsourcing the component part.

Identification of relevant costs

Cost to make	
Variable manufacturing costs ($1.10 × 100 000 units)	$110 000
Avoidable fixed costs	10 000
Total relevant costs to make	**$120 000**
Cost to outsource	
Purchase price ($1.40 × 100 000 units)	$140 000
Less: Lease income ($560 per week × 52 weeks)	(29 120)
Total relevant costs to outsource	**$110 880**

The financial analysis indicates that outsourcing will benefit Palamara by decreasing costs by $9120 ($120 000 – $110 880) and thereby increasing profits by $9120. Other factors to consider are whether Fleet Ltd can:

- deliver the lights when required
- manufacture to the same quality as that of Palamara Industries
- guarantee supply when required
- remain financially stable enough to enable ongoing supply.

Focusing on full costs, the financial analysis is as follows (you will notice that the $50 000 unavoidable cost is also now included in the outsource option).

Cost to make	
Variable manufacturing costs ($1.10 × 100 000 units)	$110 000
Fixed costs	60 000
Total costs to make	**$170 000**
Cost to outsource	
Purchase price ($1.40 × 100 000 units)	$140 000
Unavoidable fixed costs	50 000
Less: Lease income ($560 per week × 52 weeks)	(29 120)
Total costs to outsource	**$160 880**
Additional costs to make	**$ 9 120**

The decision to outsource can be motivated by many factors such as the need to reduce costs, the desire to free up capacity to pursue other ventures, or a decision to focus on core activities. Many entities today outsource the routine aspects of their accounting needs, maintenance, payroll and recruitment.

10.10 Special order decisions

LEARNING OBJECTIVE 10.10 Analyse a special order decision.

A **special order** requires an entity to consider whether it would be willing to supply goods or services at a reduced price or with special features, or a combination of both. As the label suggests, it is an order which is different from the entity's 'normal' customer orders. The answer as to whether the order should be accepted will depend on many factors, including whether the entity has unused capacity or the opportunity exists to have a long-term relationship with the customer. The time period for such decisions is short term (i.e. during the current financial period), so existing fixed costs can be considered irrelevant because any unused capacity will be within the relevant range. It is unlikely that the level of fixed-cost expenditure will be altered in the short term. Therefore, only incremental fixed costs are relevant for such a decision.

In assessing a special order, it is important to identify the entity's available capacity, also called idle capacity. **Available capacity (idle capacity)** indicates the amount of capacity an entity has available to increase output. For example, a manufacturing entity that can produce a maximum of 100 000 units (100 per cent capacity) might be producing only 90 000 units (90 per cent capacity). This indicates that the entity has available capacity of 10 000 units (10 per cent). Any order up to 10 000 units can be accepted without affecting current production or altering the existing level of fixed costs.

However, what would be the effect if a special order required 20 000 units? To accept the special order in full, the entity would need to make use of the 10 000 units available as well as directing 10 000 units from the normal production to the special order. The loss of contribution margin from the 10 000 units of normal production would be considered an opportunity cost and a relevant cost of the special order.

Furthermore, how would the entity's normal customers react if their deliveries were affected? Management would need to make a judgement about the potential effect of the decision to forgo 10 000 units of normal sales for the special order. Normal customers might react negatively to late deliveries or the knowledge that other customers were getting a better deal. The entity could increase production capacity by working overtime hours so that normal production would not be affected, but this would lead to increased costs for the special order.

Illustrative example 10.6 demonstrates the assessment of a special order for an entity with idle capacity.

ILLUSTRATIVE EXAMPLE 10.6

Special order with idle capacity

Brooks Enterprises manufactures a popular range of swimwear. Due to an anticipated increase in customer orders over the next few years, the entity has recently expanded its production capacity by 20 000 swimsuits. Its current output is 100 000 swimsuits, which sell in the market for $75 each. The current costs are as follows.

Variable costs	
Direct material	$ 800 000
Direct labour	1 200 000
Indirect	750 000
	2 750 000
Fixed costs	1 500 000
Total costs	**$4 250 000**

Based on current sales, Brooks Enterprises is generating a profit of $3 250 000. The statement of profit or loss, therefore, is as follows.

Statement of profit or loss (contribution margin format)	
Revenue	$7 500 000
Less: Variable costs	2 750 000
Contribution margin	**4 750 000**
Less: Fixed costs	1 500 000
Profit	**$3 250 000**

A local boutique, Specialised Fitters, has requested the supply of 500 swimsuits manufactured to its own design and has offered to pay $70 per swimsuit. The order would increase direct labour by 10 per cent

▶

---

and direct material by 20 per cent. In addition, $5000 would be charged for programming the machinery to cut the fabric for the new design.

Brooks Enterprises is interested in this special order, as it has available capacity of 20 000 units due to its recent expansion. Therefore, the 500 swimsuits requested by Specialised Fitters can be satisfied by the available capacity. The financial analysis considers the incremental income and incremental costs. Existing fixed costs are irrelevant, as the 500 swimsuits are within the relevant range. The unit cost for the regular swimsuits is as follows.

Variable cost per swimsuit	
Direct material ($800 000/100 000 units)	$ 8.00
Direct labour ($1 200 000/100 000 units)	12.00
Indirect ($750 000/100 000 units)	7.50
Variable cost per unit	**$27.50**

Increasing production would increase expenditure only on variable costs. The variable costs for the special order would increase to $30.30 (see calculations following). The total variable costs would increase by $15 150, with an additional $5000 required for programming the machinery. As this is a one-off order, it is assumed that the machinery would not be used for other purposes and therefore full cost recovery is required from the income generated by the special order.

Relevant costs and income of special order		
Incremental income		
500 swimsuits × $70		$35 000
Incremental costs		
Variable manufacturing costs		
Direct material (500 swimsuits × $9.60[a])	$4 800	
Direct labour (500 swimsuits × $13.20[b])	6 600	
Indirect manufacturing (500 swimsuits × $7.50)	3 750	15 150
Incremental fixed costs		
Programming of machinery		5 000
Total incremental costs		20 150
Benefit of special order (increase in profit)		**$14 850**

[a] Increase of 20% = $8 × 1.2
[b] Increase of 10% = $12 × 1.1

The financial analysis of the special order indicates that Brooks Enterprises can increase its current profits by $14 850. The statement of profit or loss incorporating the special order is as follows.

Statement of profit or loss (contribution margin format)		
	With existing sales	With special order
Revenue		
100 000 units × $75	$7 500 000	$7 500 000
500 units × $70		35 000
Total revenue	7 500 000	7 535 000
Less: Variable costs		
100 000 units × $27.50	2 750 000	2 750 000
500 units × $30.30		15 150
Total variable costs	2 750 000	2 765 150
Contribution margin	**4 750 000**	**4 769 850**
Less: Fixed costs	1 500 000	1 500 000
Additional fixed costs		5 000
	1 500 000	1 505 000
Profit	**$3 250 000**	**$3 264 850**

However, the qualitative factors also need to be considered. How would existing customers react if they discovered Specialised Fitters was purchasing the swimsuits at a lower price? Would Specialised Fitters be a potential long-term customer after this order? A final decision cannot be made until such factors are considered.

Illustrative example 10.7 demonstrates the assessment of a special order for an entity without idle capacity.

Special order with no idle capacity

Specialised Fitters has now placed another order with Brooks Enterprises, asking for the same contractual arrangements as last time. Despite the time difference, all income and costs have remained the same. However, Brooks Enterprises' anticipated new customer orders have now fully used its additional production capacity of 20 000 swimsuits. Should the order be accepted this time? The last order increased Brooks Enterprises' profits by $14 850. However, this new order has created an opportunity cost, which is the contribution margin of forgone regular sales. As the production capacity is fully utilised, the only option available to satisfy the order is to reduce current sales by 500 units. The financial analysis of the new order calculates a loss of $8900 for Brooks Enterprises if this order is accepted.

Relevant costs and income of special order	
Benefit of special order (refer to example 10.6)	$ 14 850
Opportunity cost	
Contribution margin forgone on 500 swimsuits × ($75 − $27.50)	(23 750)
Loss generated from special order	**$ (8 900)**

Therefore, Brooks Enterprises should not accept Specialised Fitters' offer. The difference between the first order (which generated a profit of $14 850) and the second order (which would result in a loss of $8900) is due to the lack of available capacity for the second order. The statement of profit or loss would change as follows.

Statement of profit or loss (contribution margin format)		
	With existing sales	With special order
Revenue		
120 000 units × $75	$9 000 000	
119 500 units × $75		$8 962 500
500 units × $70		35 000
Total revenue	9 000 000	8 997 500
Less: Variable costs		
120 000 units × $27.50	3 300 000	
119 500 units × $27.50		3 286 250
500 units × $30.30		15 150
Total variable costs	3 300 000	3 301 400
Contribution margin	**5 700 000**	**5 696 100**
Less: Fixed costs	1 500 000	1 500 000
Additional fixed costs		5 000
	1 500 000	1 505 000
Profit	**$4 200 000**	**$4 191 100**

- Relevant costs and income need to be identified for short-term decision making. Relevant costs and income are those that differ for each alternative.
- For special orders, current fixed costs are considered irrelevant because it is expected that such costs will not change within the relevant range in the short term.
- Capacity is an important determinant of opportunity costs for special order decisions.
- Avoidable costs need to be identified for outsourcing decisions.

SUMMARY OF LEARNING OBJECTIVES

10.1 Define fixed, variable and mixed costs.

Fixed costs are commonly identified as those that remain the same in total (within a given range of activity and timeframes) irrespective of the level of activity. Variable costs are commonly identified as those that change in total as the level of activity changes. Mixed costs are those that appear to possess both fixed and variable characteristics.

10.2 Prepare a break-even analysis for single-product and multi-product entities.

CVP analysis commonly requires the use of the contribution margin concept to calculate the break-even number of units. Data are needed on fixed and variable costs in order to execute the calculation. When calculating break-even for multi-product or service entities, we need to calculate the weighted average contribution margin before calculating the break-even units.

10.3 Apply the contribution margin ratio to CVP calculations.

The contribution margin ratio can be used to perform break-even calculations by focusing on the ratio of the contribution margin to sales. This can be particularly useful when seeking the total break-even sales dollars, rather than the per unit numbers.

10.4 Explain the key assumptions underlying CVP analysis.

The key assumptions underlying CVP analysis include the assumption that the behaviour of costs can be neatly classified as either fixed or variable — which may not be the case, as some costs do not behave as expected; cost behaviour is generally assumed to be linear (see figures 10.1 and 10.2); fixed costs are believed to remain 'fixed' over the time period and/or a given range of activity (often referred to as the relevant range); unit price and cost data are assumed to remain constant over the time period and relevant range; and, for multi-product entities, the sales mix between the products is assumed to be constant.

10.5 Discuss the uses of break-even data.

Break-even data can be used in a number of ways, including identifying the number of products or services required to be sold to meet break-even or profit targets; planning products and allocating resources by focusing on those products that contribute more to profitability; determining the impact on profit of changes in the mix of fixed and variable costs; and pricing products.

10.6 Outline the concept of operating leverage.

The margin of safety is commonly regarded as the excess of revenue (or units of sales) above the break-even point. It provides an indication of how much revenue (sales in units) can decrease before reaching the break-even point. Operating leverage refers to the mix between fixed and variable costs in the cost structure of an entity. A knowledge of operating leverage helps in understanding the impact of changes in revenue on profit.

10.7 Assess the profitability of output when there are resource limitations.

For some businesses, sales are not limited by market demand but by production/operational limitations including shortage of any factor such as labour, materials, space or equipment. For each output, the contribution margin per limiting factor needs to be calculated to identify the most profitable use of the limited resource.

10.8 Assess relevant information for decision making.

Relevant costs and relevant income are those that differ among alternative courses of action, with the focus being on identifying incremental income and incremental costs, which represent the additional income/costs as a result of taking an alternative course of action. It is also important to identify if there is an opportunity cost (i.e. what is given up if one alternative is chosen over another) as a result of the decision.

10.9 Analyse an outsourcing decision.

Whether it is for cost saving or other reasons, an entity may decide to outsource a product or business activity to an external provider. To assess such a decision, the entity needs to compare the in-house costs with those of the external provider. Costs that will be incurred regardless of the decision taken are unavoidable and therefore irrelevant.

10.10 Analyse a special order decision.

An entity may be requested by a new or existing customer to provide a modified product or provide an existing product at a lower cost. The motivation could be driven by a need for cash flow or a strategic move to develop relationships with new customers. In such a decision, the entity needs to compare the incremental income with the incremental cost. An opportunity cost should be considered if there is no idle capacity.

KEY TERMS

available capacity (idle capacity) Difference between maximum capacity and current operating capacity.

avoidable costs Costs avoided if an outsourcing decision is accepted.

break-even analysis Calculation of the necessary levels of activity required in order to break even in a given period.

contribution margin Calculated by deducting total variable costs from total revenue.

contribution margin per limiting factor Contribution margin per a limited resource.

contribution margin per unit Selling price per unit less variable cost per unit.

contribution margin ratio Contribution margin per unit divided by selling price per unit.

cost–volume–profit analysis Investigation of change in profits in response to changes in sales volume, costs and prices.

fixed costs Costs that remain the same in total (within a given range of activity and timeframe) irrespective of the level of activity.

incremental costs Additional costs incurred for each additional unit.

incremental income Additional income gained for each additional unit.

margin of safety Excess of revenue (or units of sales) above the break-even point.

mixed costs Costs that possess both fixed and variable characteristics.

operating leverage Mix between fixed and variable costs in the cost structure of an entity.

opportunity cost Cost of forgoing benefits that would be available if resources had been used for the next best alternative.

outsourcing Purchase of goods or services from an external party.

outsourcing decision Decision on whether to make or buy a product or service, or to outsource the production of that product or service.

relevant costs Costs that will be different under alternative courses of action.

relevant income Income that will be different under alternative courses of action.

relevant range Activity range over which fixed costs remain constant.

sales mix Number of units of each product/service sold relative to total number of units sold.

special order One-off customer order that is different from orders usually received by the entity.

unavoidable costs Costs incurred regardless of decision taken regarding outsourcing a product or service.

variable costs Costs that change in total as the level of activity changes.

weighted average contribution margin (WACM) Sum of the contribution margin of each product weighted by the relative sales mix.

APPLY YOUR KNOWLEDGE

22 marks

Juices R Us sells bottles of freshly squeezed juice to small convenience stores throughout Melbourne. Its latest statement of profit or loss for the last 12 months is as follows.

JUICES R US Statement of profit or loss		
Sales (100 000 bottles × $5)		$500 000
Less: Cost of sales (100 000 bottles × $3)*		300 000
Gross profit		200 000
Less: Other expenses		
Advertising	$10 000	
Manager's salary	50 000	
Occupancy and administration	20 000	80 000#
Profit		**$120 000**

* all variable costs
# all fixed costs

Required

(a) Calculate the contribution margin per juice bottle. **2 marks**

(b) Calculate the number of juice bottles to break even in both units and sales dollars. **2 marks**

(c) The company expects to sell 115 000 units in the coming year.

  (i) What is the margin of safety at this level of activity? **1 mark**

  (ii) How much profit will the business make for the year if its estimated level of activity is accurate? **1 mark**

(d) The company estimates that, if it reduced the selling price by $0.30 per bottle, spent an additional $20 000 on advertising for the year and improved the appearance of the juice bottle (at an extra cost of $0.15 per bottle), sales for the year would rise to 155 000 units. Using supporting calculations, advise whether the company should make these changes or retain the existing revenue and cost structure and go with the 115 000 units sales plan. **4 marks**

(e) Juices R Us could avoid the manager's salary costs by paying her $1.00 for every bottle sold. In what circumstances would Juices R Us benefit from switching to this arrangement? (Revert to original cost scenario.) **4 marks**

(f) Juices R Us is introducing a new product, exotic juice, which will sell for $5.50. The only additional variable cost is the addition of the 'special exotic' supplement at $0.50 per bottle. Other variable costs are as per the original cost scenario for the regular fresh juice bottle. Fixed costs will increase by $15 000 per year due to both administrative and production changes. Considering this information, what would be the weighted average contribution margin of 'standard juice' and 'exotic juice'? **4 marks**

(g) The sales mix is expected to be 85 per cent standard juice and 15 per cent exotic juice. What is the new break-even point for Juices R Us and the breakdown per product type? **4 marks**

SELF-EVALUATION ACTIVITIES

10.1 The table below shows selected data relevant to CVP analysis.

Selling price/unit	Variable costs/unit	Units sold	Contribution margin (total $)	Fixed costs	Profit (loss)
$ 40	?	5 000	?	$ 60 000	$ 40 000
55	$25	?	$30 000	?	0
44	22	?	?	115 000	(5 000)
?	75	2 500	72 500	28 000	?
100	?	1 000	?	60 000	(20 000)

Required

Show your understanding of basic CVP analysis by finding the missing numbers.

SOLUTION to 10.1

Selling price/unit	Variable costs/unit	Units sold	Contribution margin (total)	Fixed costs	Profit (loss)
$ 40	$20	5 000	$100 000	$ 60 000	$ 40 000
55	25	1 000	30 000	30 000	0
44	22	5 000	110 000	115 000	(5 000)
104	75	2 500	72 500	28 000	44 500
100	60	1 000	40 000	60 000	(20 000)

The answers could also have been determined by preparing a statement of profit or loss. Using the first table (row 1) above:

Sales (5000 × $40)	$200 000 (given)
Less: Variable costs	Not given
Contribution margin	Not given
Fixed costs	$60 000 (given)
Profit	$40 000 (given)

To calculate the contribution margin, we would need to add fixed costs and profit. Why would we do this? Because we know that the contribution margin is equal to the fixed costs in the first instance, with any additional contributing towards profits. Therefore, the contribution margin is $100 000 ($60 000 + $40 000). To calculate the variable costs, we know that sales less the contribution margin are equal to the variable costs. In our example, if sales are $200 000 with a contribution margin of $100 000, then variable costs are $100 000 and, given that 5000 units were sold, the variable cost per unit is $20 ($100 000/5000 units).

10.2 Waterbird Company operates a single-product entity. Data relating to the product for 2019 are as follows.

Annual volume	64 000 units
Selling price per unit	$ 50
Variable manufacturing cost per unit	18
Annual fixed manufacturing costs	640 000
Variable marketing and distribution costs per unit	12
Annual fixed non-manufacturing costs	320 000

Required
(a) Calculate total fixed costs and total variable costs per unit.
(b) Calculate the break-even units for 2019.
(c) Changes in marketing strategy are planned for 2020. This would increase variable marketing and distribution costs by $4 per unit, and reduce fixed non-manufacturing costs by $120 000 per year. Calculate the break-even units for 2020 under the new marketing strategy.

SOLUTION TO 10.2
(a) Costs per unit:

Total fixed costs	
Annual fixed manufacturing costs	$640 000
Annual fixed non-manufacturing costs	320 000
	$960 000
Total variable costs per unit	
Variable manufacturing cost	$ 18
Variable marketing and distribution	12
	$ 30

(b) Break-even units for 2019:

$$\text{Break-even units} = \frac{\$960\,000}{(\$50 - \$30)}$$
$$= 48\,000 \ \text{units}$$

(c) Break-even units for 2020:

$$\text{Break-even units} = \frac{\$840\,000}{(\$50 - \$34)}$$
$$= 52\,500 \ \text{units}$$

Therefore, the break-even units under the new plan increase by 4500 units.

COMPREHENSION QUESTIONS

10.3 Explain the difference between mixed and variable costs. Provide examples of each. **LO4**
10.4 Using examples, distinguish between fixed and variable costs. **LO1**
10.5 Discuss the circumstances in which CVP analysis might be useful. **LO5**
10.6 How can the margin of safety be used to assess risk associated with sales? **LO2**
10.7 Discuss the concept of operating leverage. **LO6**

10.8 How does the calculation of break-even differ between single-product and multi-product entities?
LO2

10.9 Explain the meaning of the term 'fixed cost' and give five examples of fixed costs.
LO1

10.10 Under what circumstances can calculating the contribution margin ratio to perform break-even analysis be useful?
LO3

10.11 How may an opportunity cost be relevant in an outsourcing decision?
LO9

10.12 What are avoidable costs and why are they important in decision making?
LO8

10.13 'Fixed costs are always irrelevant in decision making.' Discuss.
LO8

10.14 When is it necessary to calculate the contribution margin per limiting factor?
LO7

10.15 An organisation is currently operating at full capacity. Should it accept a request for a special order based on variable cost plus 40 per cent? Explain.
LO10

10.16 If an entity has a mixed cost function, a 10 per cent increase in sales volume should increase income by more than 10 per cent. Explain why.
LO5

10.17 CVP analysis and break-even analysis are underpinned by a range of important assumptions. Briefly discuss four such assumptions.
LO4

10.18 Discuss how knowledge of the break-even point and the margin of safety will assist management in the risk assessment of business operations.
LO5

10.19 Explain the importance of the relevant range in relation to cost behaviour when considering the costs of expanding business activities.
LO8

EXERCISES

★ BASIC | ★ ★ MODERATE | ★ ★ ★ CHALLENGING

10.20 ★
LO2

Find the missing figures for each of the independent cases shown below. (*Hint:* Reconstruct the statement of profit or loss for each scenario.)

Selling price/unit	Variable costs/unit	Units sold	Contribution margin (total)	Fixed costs	Profit (loss)
$ 0	(a)	20 000	$400 000	$240 000	(b)
20	$15	(c)	11 250	(d)	$ 0
10	8	(e)	(f)	3 000	(1 500)
(g)	80	2 000	24 000	16 000	(h)
15	(i)	1 500	(j)	6 500	(2 000)

10.21 ★
LO2

Find the missing figure for each of the following independent cases. (*Hint:* Reconstruct the statement of profit or loss for each scenario.)

Selling price/unit	Variable costs/unit	Units sold	Contribution margin (total)	Fixed costs	Profit (loss)
$40	$ 20	40 000	(a)	(b)	$300 000
18	(c)	10 000	$ 60 000	$ 45 000	(d)
(e)	20	50 000	250 000	(f)	0
8	6	200 000	(g)	100 000	(h)
5	(i)	250 000	(j)	230 000	20 000

10.22 ★
LO2

For each of the following independent situations, calculate the break-even point in units.
(a) Variable cost per unit of $3, annual fixed costs of $42 750 and selling price per unit of $9.
(b) Variable costs per unit of $10, annual fixed costs of $63 200 and selling price per unit of $20.
(c) Variable costs per unit of $20, annual fixed costs of $40 650 and selling price of $23.

10.23 ★
LO1, 5

Yen Rippon is about to commence operations as a beauty technician. She believes her costs can be classified as fixed or variable.
(a) Distinguish between fixed and variable costs.
(b) Outline how Yen could make use of CVP analysis to help guide her business operations.

10.24 ★
LO5

Discuss some possible options when the break-even unit target appears too difficult to achieve.

10.25 ★   **LO2**

Emy Fong has been operating a single-product firm for three years. As this product is now well established in the market, Fong is thinking about adding two new products to her range. Outline the impact of her decision on the calculation of her new break-even point.

10.26 ★   **LO10**

In the Whine Company, it costs $30 per unit ($20 variable and $10 fixed) to make a product that normally sells for $55. A foreign wholesaler offers to buy 3000 units at $35 each. The Whine Company will incur special shipping costs of $2 per unit.

Required

Assuming that the Whine Company has excess operating capacity, indicate the profit (or loss) it would realise by accepting the special order.

10.27 ★ ★   **LO7**

Lavender Plantations Pty Ltd advertises weekly specials and makes sure that the shelf space (9 metres) at the entrance to the store showcases these specials. For the current week, its three products are being advertised at special prices. Each product must be allocated shelf space.

	Candles	Soaps	Detergent
Contribution margin per product (at special price)	$10	$18	$5.50
Minimum shelf space required per product	1 metre	4 metres	2 metres

Required

How should the shelf space be allocated among the three products to maximise the profits from the weekly specials?

10.28 ★ ★   **LO10**

Gotrack Company produces compasses for cross-country skiing. The production capacity is 45 000 compasses and the company is currently operating at 85 per cent capacity. Variable manufacturing costs are $10 per unit. Fixed manufacturing costs are $425 000. The compasses are normally sold directly to Outdoor Adventures at $25 each. Gotrack has an offer from On Top Company (a foreign wholesaler) to purchase an additional 5000 compasses at $13 per unit.

Required

(a) Calculate the available production capacity.
(b) Calculate the contribution margin per unit for both the current production of compasses and the special order compasses.
(c) Should the special order be accepted? Show calculations.
(d) What is the opportunity cost if On Top required 10 000 compasses?
(e) Would you recommend the special order if On Top required 10 000 compasses?

10.29 ★ ★   **LO2, 6**

Nicholas Cash of Advantage Tennis Coaching (ATC) has received an offer from a top-ranked Australian player, Serena Novac, who wishes to spend two months in the beautiful Queensland weather and have 50 private coaching sessions with Nicholas. If the offer is accepted, Nicholas will need to hire an additional tennis court for a cost of $16 000 for two months. The following data are provided.

Coaching session fee	$650
Cost of tennis racket and gear per session for Nicholas	150
Cost for tennis balls	80

Required

(a) Calculate the number of tennis coaching sessions required for Nicholas to break even.
(b) Draw a graph to show the cost–volume–profit relationships for this special contract for ATC.
(c) If Nicholas provides 50 coaching sessions for Serena, what is the amount of profit ATC would achieve?
(d) To ensure Serena is happy with the coaching services provided, Nicholas has arranged for a number of aspiring senior players to attend sessions for match play. ATC will pay $80 per session to the match players. ATC wishes to maintain the same amount of profit with the match players as calculated in (c) above. To achieve this, Nicholas will approach the manager of Tennis Pro Shop and ask for the balls to be provided at no cost. Negotiations will then be required between the Tennyson Tennis Centre manager and Nicholas regarding the fee for the hire of the tennis

court. What is the upper limit that Nicholas should be prepared to pay for the hire of the court to maintain the amount of profit calculated in (c) above from 50 sessions?

(e) What qualitative factors should Nicholas also consider?

10.30 ★ ★   **LO2, 6**

IT Equip sells IT equipment, specialising in printers and projectors. The following statement reflects the contribution margin of each activity and overall profit levels.

	Printers	Projectors	Total
Sales	$1 548 000	$797 500	$2 345 500
Less: Variable costs	1 130 000	532 500	1 662 500
Contribution margin	**418 000**	**265 000**	**683 000**
Direct fixed costs	207 500	177 500	385 000
Common fixed costs:			
Utilities			20 000
Other administration			81 000
Profit			**$ 197 000**

Required

(a) Calculate the contribution margin ratios for each of the two areas of activity and in total.

(b) Using the total contribution margin ratio, calculate the level of sales required of each product to break even.

10.31 ★ ★   **LO2**

Information for Harbour Industries is provided below.

Average selling price per unit	$ 10.00
Average variable costs per unit:	
Cost per unit	5.00
Selling costs	1.40
Annual fixed costs:	
Selling	240 000
Administration	380 000
After-tax profit target	126 000
Tax rate	30%

Required

(a) Calculate the before-tax profit.

(b) Calculate the number of units that need to be sold in 2020 to reach the after-tax profit target.

(c) If the sales units in 2020 were 25 per cent less than required to meet the after-tax profit target, what would the after-tax profit actually be?

10.32 ★ ★ ★   **LO2**

Mermaid Enterprises operates a single-product entity. Data relating to the product for 2019 are as follows.

Annual volume	64 000 units
Selling price per unit	$ 60
Variable manufacturing cost per unit	28
Annual fixed manufacturing costs	240 000
Variable marketing and distribution costs per unit	12
Annual fixed non-manufacturing costs	720 000

Required

(a) Calculate the break-even in both dollars and units for 2019.

(b) Calculate the margin of safety in both units and sales dollars.

(c) Calculate the profit achieved in 2019 given the annual volume of 64 000 units.

(d) Changes in the marketing strategy are planned for 2020. This would increase variable marketing and distribution costs by $4 per unit, and reduce fixed non-manufacturing costs by $160 000 per year. Calculate the units that would need to be sold in 2020 to achieve the same profit as in 2019.

(e) Would you recommend the change? Explain.

10.33 ★ ★ ★
LO2

Lavender Plantations Pty Ltd management plan to introduce detergents to its product range in 2022. They have provided the following information relating to the planned activities.

	Candles	Soaps	Detergents
Sales mix (250 000 units)	75 000	50 000	125 000
Selling price	$28	$45	$20
Variable cost/unit	18	27	12
Total fixed costs = $402 800			

Required

(a) Calculate the break-even point in total units and units per product based on the 2022 data.

(b) Calculate the before tax profit (loss) that would be achieved in 2022 based on the above data.

(c) Lavender Plantations' management are concerned about increasing competition for some of its products and want to increase its sales of soaps relative to detergents. The initiative would increase annual fixed costs by $50 000 and alter the sales mix to 30 per cent for candles, 30 per cent for soaps and 40 per cent for detergents. On the available data, would you recommend the initiative?

10.34 ★ ★ ★
LO9

Terrace Company currently manufactures a sub-assembly for its main product. The costs per unit are as follows.

Direct materials	$ 4.00
Direct labour	30.00
Variable overhead	15.00
Fixed overhead (allocated)	25.00
Total	**$74.00**

Ballen Co. has contacted Terrace Company with an offer to sell it 5000 sub-assemblies for $55 each.

Required

(a) Why is it important to identify whether any of the fixed overhead is avoidable or unavoidable in order to assess the outsourcing of the sub-assembly? Explain.

(b) Should Terrace Company make or buy the sub-assemblies? Create a schedule that shows the total quantitative differences between the two alternatives. Assume all fixed overhead is unavoidable.

(c) If Terrace Company was able to eliminate $50 000 of fixed overhead, would it change your decision in (b)? Explain and show your calculations.

(d) What qualitative factors should the accountants and managers of Terrace Company consider in their 'make or buy' decision?

10.35 ★ ★ ★
LO2, 6

Blitz Nails has provided the following financial data for the last two financial periods.

	2019	2020
Nail services (units)	15 000	22 500
Sales	$1 500 000	$2 250 000
Less: Expenses	750 000	975 000
Profit	**$ 750 000**	**$1 275 000**

The manager, Jonie Matte, is beginning her planning for next year and requires the following information.

Required

(a) Calculate the break-even level of sales in both units and sales dollars.

(b) New machines are available for fast drying of nails that cost $300 000 to purchase and would lead to a reduction in variable costs of $0.50 per service. The new machines are to be depreciated $60 000 per year. What is the new break-even point in both units and sales dollars?

(c) What level of sales is required in 2021 to maintain the profit at $1 275 000 if the fast-drying machines are purchased?

10.36 ★ ★ ★   **LO10**

Flash Pty Ltd manufactures handheld egg-beaters. For the first eight months of 2020, the company reports the following operating results while operating at 80 per cent capacity.

Sales (400 000 units)	$2 000 000
Cost of sales	1 200 000
Gross profit	800 000
Operating expenses	450 000
Profit	**$ 350 000**

Cost of sales was 65 per cent variable and 35 per cent fixed. Operating expenses were 60 per cent variable and 40 per cent fixed.

In October, Flash Pty Ltd receives a special order for 20 000 egg-beaters at $6 each from Rosie Cakes located in New Zealand. Acceptance of the order would result in $5000 of shipping costs but no increase in fixed operating costs.

Required

(a) Calculate the contribution margin per egg-beater for normal sales.
(b) Calculate the contribution margin per egg-beater for the special order.
(c) What is the minimum selling price for the special order?
(d) Should Flash Pty Ltd accept the special order? Explain your answer and show calculations.

10.37 ★ ★ ★   **LO9**

Elm Ltd has been manufacturing its own shades for its camping chairs. The company is currently operating at 100 per cent capacity. Variable manufacturing overhead is charged to production at the rate of 50 per cent of direct labour cost. The direct materials and direct labour cost per unit to make the chair shades are $4 and $6, respectively. Normal production is 25 000 chair shades per year.

A supplier has offered to make the shades at a price of $6.80 per unit. If Elm Ltd accepts the supplier's offer, all variable manufacturing costs will be avoided, but $20 000 of fixed manufacturing overhead currently being charged to the chair shades will be unavoidable.

Required

(a) Should Elm Ltd accept the supplier's offer to supply the chair shades?
(b) Would your answer to (a) be different if the production capacity released by not making the chair shades could be used to produce profit of $17 500?

10.38 ★ ★ ★   **LO7**

Mansfield Ltd has recently expanded its production facility to satisfy a new customer order that will start in six months. As a consequence, it has the opportunity to make use of the spare capacity for the next six months. Financial information on the current products sold by Mansfield Ltd is as follows.

	Budget	Standard	Superior
Selling price	$40	$45	$60
Direct material	10	12	12
Direct labour ($10 per hour)	5	10	15
Variable overhead (allocated based on labour hours)	4	8	12
Fixed overhead (allocated based on machine hours)	4	8	8

Required

(a) For the next six months, the new production facility has no constraints from either a labour or machine hour perspective. Which product or mix of products should Mansfield Ltd produce using this capacity?
(b) Assess whether your answer to (a) would be different if there was a constraint in relation to the labour hours available.

10.39 ★ ★ ★   **LO2, 5**

Advantage Tennis Coaching (ATC) has been engaged to provide tennis coaching services to students at a local private girls' college. ATC has put forward a proposal to the University of Queensland's School of Human Movement (SHM) to offer some university students work experience. ATC's qualified coaches will plan the coaching program, supervise the SHM students as they implement the training program and attend the Queensland Girls' Secondary Schools Sports Association competition matches. Following are financial data relating to the proposal.

Revenue:		
Season tennis coaching fees per player (payable by college and reimbursed by parents)		$200
Season costs (variable per player):		
Sports drinks	$100	
ATC logo embossed on school kit bag	20	120
Season fixed costs — supervision by ATC coaches		6 400

Required

(a) Calculate the approximate number of school tennis players required for ATC to break even on the proposal.

(b) Calculate the contribution margin ratio.

(c) Calculate the revenue required to earn a profit of $4800.

(d) Calculate the decrease in total variable costs necessary to maintain the break-even point calculated in requirement (a) if fixed costs increase by $800. (Also calculate the per-unit decrease.)

10.40 ★ ★ ★   **LO2**

Scenario 1

The following information has been extracted from the financial statements of Vivid, a social media company. Revenue is generated through advertising on the social media platform, where the number of 'clicks' is the driver of revenue.

Item	$	Additional information
Cost of sales	200 000	60% variable
Revenue	669 900	Based on 304 500 clicks at $2.20 per click
Sales and marketing	340 000	60% variable; 40% fixed
General and administration expenses	21 000	Fixed
Occupancy and rental expenses	13 000	Fixed
Depreciation and amortisation	50 000	Fixed
Interest and finance costs	54 500	Fixed

Required

(a) Calculate the contribution margin per click.

(b) Calculate the number of clicks required to break-even.

(c) How might the management of Vivid reduce the number of clicks required to break even?

Scenario 2

Some changes have occurred: revenue pricing; fixed cost/variable cost structures; and levels of some fixed costs triggered by changes to the accommodation/office space.

Item	$	Additional information
Cost of sales	200 000	60% variable
Revenue	548 100	Based on 304 500 clicks at $1.80 per click
Sales and marketing	340 000	20% variable; 80% fixed
General and administration expenses	21 000	Fixed
Occupancy and rental expenses	13 000	Fixed
Depreciation and amortisation	20 000	Fixed
Interest and finance costs	30 000	Fixed

Required

(d) Calculate the contribution margin per click.

(e) Calculate the number of clicks required to break even.

(f) What has happened to the break-even point? Why?

PROBLEMS

★ BASIC | ★ ★ MODERATE | ★ ★ ★ CHALLENGING

10.41 Break-even analysis ★   **LO5**

'If an entity has the objective of profit maximisation, break-even analysis is not necessary.' Discuss this assertion.

10.42 Outsourcing and qualitative risks ★   **LO9**

Briefly outline some of the key qualitative risk considerations with respect to outsourcing decisions.

10.43 Special order with spare capacity ★   **LO2, 10**

Lavender Plantations Pty Ltd manufactures and sells candles, soaps and detergents, and distributes them to stores located in Australia and New Zealand. The normal selling price per carton of candles is $25; the variable cost of a carton of candles is $15. The principal of a local primary school has asked Lavender Plantations to provide 20 cartons of candles for its spring fair. The principal wants to purchase the candles at cost. Unlike regular sales, this special order of candles will not incur the average distribution costs of $3 per carton. Lavender Plantations has sufficient capacity to meet the order.

Required

(a) Calculate the contribution margin per carton of candles for those sold to the usual outlets.
(b) Calculate the variable costs per carton of candles for the special order from the local primary school.
(c) If the principal can pay no more than $12 per carton, should Lavender Plantations accept the order? Why?
(d) Would your decision change if Lavender Plantations was operating at full capacity and had to give up normal sales of candles to accept the principal's order?

10.44 Special order with spare capacity ★   **LO10**

Waffle House sells ice-cream cones in a variety of flavours. Financial data for a recent week are shown below.

Revenue (2000 cones @ $2.00)	$4 000
Cost of ingredients	1 200
Rent	700
Store attendant	1 300
Profit	**$ 800**

Waffle's manager receives a call from a university student club requesting 200 cones to be picked up in three days. The cones can be produced in advance by the store attendant during slack periods and then stored in the freezer. Each cone requires a special plastic cover that costs $0.10.

Required

(a) Discuss the quantitative information relevant to this decision.
(b) Calculate the minimum price per cone for this special order.
(c) Explain why Waffle House's manager might be willing to sell cones at the minimum selling price you calculated in (b).

10.45 Contribution margin ratio ★   **LO2, 3**

Coffee House sells specialist coffee drinks from a rented cart on the beachside on the Sunshine Coast. Provided below is a summarised version of its statement of profit or loss for July 2019.

Sales revenue		$5 500
Cost of beverages	$2 500	
Cost of napkins	550	
Rent of cart	550	
Wages	1 250	4 850
Profit		**$ 650**

The costs of beverages and napkins are classified as variable costs.

Required

(a) Calculate the contribution margin ratio.
(b) Calculate the break-even sales in dollars.

10.46 Profitability with resource limitations ⋆   **LO7**

Lavender Plantations Pty Ltd manufactures three lavender-based products, candles, soaps and detergents. On average 75 000 candles, 50 000 soaps and 125 000 detergents are sold. Next year, the company has a restricted advertising budget of $40 000, which is sufficient to effectively promote only one of its products. The marketing department estimates that average sales of candles will increase by 25 per cent if they are advertised, while average sales of soaps will increase by 20 per cent and of detergents will increase by 10 per cent if they are advertised. The following data are provided.

	Candles	Soaps	Detergents
Selling price per unit	$25	$38	$20
Variable cost per unit	$15	$22	$12
Machine hours per unit	1 hour	3 hours	1 hour
Fixed costs are estimated to be $600 000			

Required

(a) Calculate the contribution margin for each product.

(b) Calculate the contribution margin per machine hour for each product.

(c) Assuming unlimited machine hours are available, which product should be promoted in the advertising campaign?

(d) Would your answer to (c) change if there were 300 000 machine hours available for production?

(e) Prepare a statement of profit or loss after you have made your decisions in (c) and (d).

(f) Discuss when to use the contribution margins calculated in your answers to (a) and (b) above.

10.47 Relevant information for decision making ⋆ ⋆   **LO8**

Magic Dusters is considering a special order from Stay Clean Ltd for a special cleaning product for windows. One ingredient required for the product is Alpha A, which Magic Dusters has in its inventory. Magic Dusters' current products do not use Alpha A; however, it was an ingredient in one of its discontinued product lines. Alpha A was purchased at a cost of $10 per litre and could be currently sold for $5 per litre, with a replacement cost of $12 per litre.

Required

You have been requested to prepare a financial analysis of the special order from Stay Clean Ltd. Given that 1000 litres of Alpha A are required in production of this order, what is the relevant cost of Alpha A to be included in the analysis?

10.48 Relevant information for decision making ⋆ ⋆   **LO8**

Magic Dusters has also identified that another ingredient, Delta D (500 litres required), will also be used in the special order for Stay Clean Ltd (see problem 10.47). Unlike Alpha A, Delta D is currently used in normal production for Magic Dusters. The current inventory of Delta D was purchased at a cost of $20 per litre. The replacement cost is $22 if ordered in the normal schedule; however, if a rush order is required the cost will be $25. Another requirement of the supplier of Delta D is that the minimum order is 1000 litres.

Required

Analyse the cost to be included for Delta D in the following circumstances.

(a) Sufficient inventory of Delta D available to meet orders without affecting normal production.

(b) Requirement to make a rush order for Delta D to satisfy the special order.

10.49 Break-even: single product; profit calculation ⋆ ⋆   **LO2, 6**

Tartan Company is a single-product entity and provides the summary data shown below relating to its product for 2020.

Selling price per unit	$ 50
Variable manufacturing costs	24
Annual fixed manufacturing costs	250 000
Variable marketing, distribution and administration costs	8
Annual fixed non-manufacturing costs	128 000
Annual volume	24 000 units

Required

(a) Calculate the contribution margin per unit.

(b) Calculate the contribution margin ratio.

(c) Calculate the break-even in units and sales dollars for 2020.

(d) Calculate the profit earned in 2020.

(e) Tartan Company is considering changes in plant operations and the production process for 2021. The changes would result in a reduction in variable costs per unit of $6 and an increase in fixed manufacturing costs of $132 500. How many units would need to be sold to earn the same profit as in 2020? Would you recommend the changes?

(f) Prepare the statement of profit or loss for (d) and (e) above.

10.50 Profit calculation; price to achieve profit target ★ ★   **LO2**

The management of Kayla Industries have been aggressive in trying to build market share. The price was set at $5 per unit, well below the existing market price. Variable costs were $4.50 per unit and annual fixed costs in the first year were $600 000.

Required

(a) If Kayla Industries were to sell 1 million units in the first year, what profit (loss) would be achieved?

(b) If sales were to remain at 1 million in the second year, and the fixed and variable costs remained the same, what price would need to be set to achieve a profit of $25 000?

10.51 Special order with no spare capacity ★ ★   **LO10**

Soft Mats produces exercise mats for use in fitness centres. Production capacity is 40 000 mats per year. Due to a chain of fitness centres closing, Soft Mats now has spare capacity of 4000 mats per year. An international hotel chain, Mini Break, has recently contacted Soft Mats to place a one-off order for 6000 mats. Mini Break has recently remodelled a number of its hotels to incorporate fitness centres for guests.

Budgeted costs for 40 000 mats are:
- variable manufacturing costs $1 600 000
- fixed manufacturing costs $1 800 000.

Mats normally sell for $100 each, while Mini Break has offered to pay $90 per mat. Mini Break has also requested that each mat be embossed with its company logo. An embossing machine costing $40 000 would therefore need to be purchased by Soft Mats. The machine could not be used for other products.

Required

(a) From a financial perspective, should Soft Mats accept the special order? Show calculations.

(b) Would you recommend accepting the order if Soft Mats was currently operating at 95 per cent capacity? Show calculations.

(c) What other factors should be considered before the order is accepted?

10.52 Outsource computations, qualitative factors ★ ★   **LO9**

Soft Pearl Company incurs the following costs to produce 50 000 light switches for floor lamps in 2020.

Direct materials	$200 000
Direct labour	300 000
Variable manufacturing overhead	160 000
Fixed manufacturing overhead	240 000
Total manufacturing costs	**$ 900 000**

The Ignition Company has offered to supply the switches for $8 per unit. An analysis of the overhead costs has identified that, if the switches are outsourced, Soft Pearl Company would eliminate $40 000 of fixed costs and could use the released production capacity to generate additional income of $112 000 from producing a different product.

Required

(a) From a financial perspective, should the light switches be outsourced? Show calculations.

(b) What qualitative factors need to be considered in the outsourcing decision?

10.53 Outsourcing (make or buy) ★ ★ ★   **LO9**

The management of York Company have asked for your assistance in deciding whether to continue manufacturing a part or buy it from an outside supplier. The part, called Beta B, is a component of York's finished product. Analysis of the accounting records and the production data reveals the following information for the year ending June 2020.

1. The production department produced 70 000 units of Beta B.
2. Six employees were assigned to the production department and worked full-time (1920 hours each per year) producing Beta B. Each employee was paid $20 per hour.
3. The cost of materials per Beta B unit was $4.
4. Manufacturing costs directly applicable to the production of Beta B were as follows.

Indirect labour	$15 000
Utilities	3 000
Depreciation	3 600
Rates and insurance	2 000

All of the above costs would be eliminated if Beta B is purchased.
5. The lowest price for Beta B from an outside supplier is $8 per unit. Delivery cost would be $0.80 per unit and a part-time dispatch employee at $17 000 per year would be required.
6. If Beta B was purchased, the excess space would be used to store York's finished product. Currently, York rents storage space at approximately $1.60 per unit stored per year. Approximately 9000 units per year are stored in the rented space.

Required
Should York make or buy the part? Show all calculations.

10.54 Outsourcing computations, uncertainties ★ ★ ★   **LO9**

Wynham Stereos produces and sells speakers and CD players. The following information about the costs related to the systems has been collected.

Selling price per unit	$ 130	Production costs per unit		
Total fixed overhead	360 000	Direct materials		$42
		Direct labour		36
		Variable overhead		22

Wynham Stereos normally produces 25 000 of these systems per year.

The managers have recently received an offer from a New Zealand company to produce these systems for $108 each. The managers estimate that $260 000 of Wynham Stereos' fixed costs could be eliminated if it accepted the offer.

Required
(a) Perform a quantitative analysis for the decision.
(b) Identify as many uncertainties as you can for this decision.
(c) Prepare a brief report to management on your recommendations.

10.55 Break-even: single product; profit calculation; second product introduced ★ ★ ★   **LO2**

Tropical Processing is a single-product entity and provides the following summary data relating to its product for 2020.

Selling price per unit	$ 80
Variable manufacturing costs	28
Annual fixed manufacturing costs	600 000
Variable marketing, distribution and administration costs	20
Annual fixed non-manufacturing costs	360 000
Annual volume	76 000 units

Required
(a) Calculate the break-even in units and sales dollars for 2020.
(b) Calculate the profit earned in 2020.
(c) Tropical Processing is considering introducing a second product that would result in the following estimates.

	Product A	Product B	
Expected sales volume in units	70 000	30 000	
Selling price per unit	$80	$52	
Variable costs per unit	$48	$28	
Annual fixed costs			$1 243 600

(i) Calculate the number of units (in total and per product) required to break even.

(ii) Calculate the number of units (in total and per product) required — in the first year of the two products — to earn the same profit as for 2020.

10.56 Break-even; alternative cost structures ★ ★ ★ LO2, 6

The statement of profit or loss for Nambour Industries for 2019 is as follows.

NAMBOUR INDUSTRIES Statement of profit or loss for year ending 31 December 2019		
Sales revenue (200 000 units)		$2 000 000
Cost of sales		1 200 000
Gross profit		800 000
Operating costs		
Marketing and distribution	$460 000	
Administration	440 000	900 000
Profit (loss)		**$ (100 000)**

Cost behaviour seems to follow this pattern: all of the cost of sales is considered variable; 50 per cent of the total marketing and distribution costs are variable; and 40 per cent of the total administration costs are variable.

Required

(a) Calculate the number of units that need to be sold in 2019 to break even.

(b) The finance manager has developed a number of alternative plans to get the entity back into profitability. One of the plans relates to switching to a more reliable supplier of raw materials, which would increase the cost of sales per unit by $0.80. A change in marketing strategy would see variable marketing and distribution increase by $0.10, and fixed marketing and distribution decrease by $60 000. Competitive forces would allow an increase in selling price of only $0.50 per unit. On the information available, would you advise a switch to this alternative plan?

(c) Prepare a statement of profit or loss for both alternatives given in (b).

(d) Explain the concept of operating leverage as it relates to your answer in (b).

10.57 Break-even: multiple products; contribution margin ratio ★ ★ ★ LO2

McDonald Services offers three core accounting and bookkeeping services. After a cost behaviour study, the following profitability analysis has been prepared.

MCDONALD SERVICES Profitability analysis for 12 months ending 31 December 2019				
	Bookkeeping	Advisory	Account management	Total
Fees	$300 000	$160 000	$120 000	$580 000
Less: Variable costs	180 000	96 000	72 000	348 000
Contribution margin	**120 000**	**64 000**	**48 000**	**232 000**
Direct fixed costs	25 000	35 000	18 000	78 000
Common fixed costs				
Utilities				31 000
Other administration				36 000
Total fixed costs				145 000
Profit				**$ 87 000**

The management of McDonald Services estimate that the total fees mix (52% : 28% : 20%) is generally representative.

Required

(a) Calculate the contribution margin ratios for each of the three areas of activity and in total.

(b) Using the total contribution margin ratio, calculate the level of fees required to break even.

(c) Prepare a statement of profit or loss at the break-even level of fees as calculated in (b).

10.58 Break-even units; targeted profit units; changes to cost structure ★ ★ ★   **LO2, 6**

Leonardo Company has the capacity to manufacture 250 000 units annually of its only product. The following information is available.

Selling price	$130 per unit
Variable manufacturing costs	$60 per unit
Fixed manufacturing costs	$900 000 annually
Fixed marketing and administrative costs	$600 000 annually
Variable marketing and administrative costs	$20 per unit

Required

(a) Calculate the number of units that need to be sold annually to break even.

(b) How many units would need to be sold to earn a target annual profit of $600 000?

(c) In an attempt to achieve better results in the marketplace, management have been looking at changing the reward system for marketing, distribution and sales personnel. This would result in an increase in variable marketing and administrative costs by $10 per unit and would reduce fixed marketing and distribution costs by $250 000.

    (i) Calculate the number of units required to break even if management implemented the changes.

    (ii) Would you suggest management pursue the changes? Explain.

(d) 'CVP analysis is useful because it is so accurate.' Comment on this statement.

10.59 Contribution margin; break-even units ★ ★ ★   **LO2**

Katy Davis has had a passion for cycling for years. She has decided to explore turning her passion into a business. She has spent the last few months exploring the industry and collecting information to facilitate decisions about the focus of the business. For the moment, Katy Davis thinks she has raised sufficient start-up funding through family members and a somewhat generous friend.

    Katy's first option is to focus on an area of the market she believes is a bit underserviced: bikes for mid-teens, a market she labels *youth*. She has made a set of estimates as shown in Exhibit 1.

DAVIS CYCLES		
Exhibit 1 Estimates for Year 1		
Single product: youth bikes		
Item		Additional information
Bike sales volume	2400 bikes	
Average selling price	$600 per bike	
Average variable cost of bike (purchase of basic bike, additional assembly-related costs)	$350 per bike	
Sales and marketing	$92 000	60% variable; 40% fixed
General and administration expenses	$130 000	Fixed
Occupancy and rental expenses	$176 000	Fixed
Direct fixed workshop and bike costs	$90 000	Fixed

Required

(a) Calculate the contribution margin per bike.

(b) Calculate the number of bikes required to break even.

(c) Based on the evidence, will this venture be profitable? Briefly explain.

(d) Are you able to provide an estimate of current profits?

10.60 WACM; break-even units ★ ★ ★   **LO2**

Continuing the example in 10.59, the other option Katy is exploring is to offer a wider product range including two other specialist bikes: adult mountain bikes and adult road bikes. From her investigations, she realises this is a highly competitive part of the market, but thinks she needs to offer a wider range of bikes to attract the higher end buyers. Her year 1 estimates are shown in Exhibit 2.

DAVIS CYCLES			
Exhibit 2 Estimates for Year 1			
Multiple products			
	Youth	Road	Mountain
Bike sales volume	1 600	1 600	800
Average selling price	$500	$1200	$900
Average variable cost of bike (purchase of basic bike, additional assembly-related costs)	$350	$620	$590
Direct fixed workshop and bike costs	$90 000	$136 000	$164 000
Other cost items		Additional information	
Sales and marketing	$172 000	Fixed	
General and administration expenses	$190 000	Fixed	
Occupancy and rental expenses	$376 000	Fixed	

Required

(a) Calculate the weighted average contribution margin (WACM) per bike.

(b) Determine the break-even level of bikes overall and per bike type.

(c) Katy is hoping to earn a pre-tax profit of at least $400 000 in the next few years. Does this seem feasible?

(d) Katy is a little worried about her estimates around price, volume and costs. By way of illustration, she is thinking about raising the price of the youth bikes by 15 per cent with the impact of reducing sales volume by 10 per cent. At the same time, she wants to decrease the price of adult road bikes by 15 per cent with an increase in sales units of 20 per cent. What are the likely impacts on planned profits? What would you advise?

DECISION-MAKING ACTIVITIES

10.61 Barloo Company is a software producer and sales company. Currently, it pays all sales staff on a fixed base salary. Recently, management have been considering switching sales staff across to an incentive-based reward system. Barloo's chief accountant, Sasha Carter, has prepared some summarised numbers (see below) for senior management to consider.

One manager comments that he cannot see the difference, as the sales level and profit are unchanged. Sasha argues that it is the difference in cost structure that matters. She argues that the entity is better off staying with the current structure, because the increase in profit is greater when sales levels increase than it would be with the incentive rewards.

	With fixed rewards	With incentive rewards
Sales	$5 000 000	$5 000 000
Variable costs	3 000 000	4 000 000
Contribution margin	**2 000 000**	**1 000 000**
Fixed costs	1 500 000	500 000
Profit	**$ 500 000**	**$ 500 000**

Required

(a) Explain the basis of Sasha Carter's argument.

(b) Calculate the contribution margin ratio under each alternative.

(c) If sales were to increase by 10 per cent, which alternative would produce the highest increase in profit?

(d) Prepare a statement of profit or loss for each alternative.

10.62 You are the adviser to a junior achievement group in a local high school. You need to help the group make a decision about fees that must be paid to sell gardening tools at the Home and Garden Show. The group sells a set of tools for $20. The manufacturing cost (all variable) is $6 per set. The Home and Garden Show coordinator allows the following three payment options for groups exhibiting and selling at the show.

(i) A fixed booth fee of $5600.

(ii) A fee of $3800 plus 10 per cent of all revenue from tool sets sold at the show.

(iii) 15 per cent of all revenue from tool sets sold at the show.

Required

(a) Compute the break-even number of tool sets for each option.

(b) Which payment plan has the highest degree of operating leverage?

(c) Which payment plan has the lowest risk of loss for the junior achievement group? Explain.

10.63 Refresh Company produces plunge pools. Currently, the company uses internally manufactured pumps to power water jets. Refresh Company has found that 40 per cent of the pumps failed within their 12-month warranty period, causing huge warranty costs. Because of the company's inability to manufacture high-quality pumps, management are considering buying pumps from a reputable outside supplier who will also bear any related warranty costs.

Refresh Company's unit cost of manufacturing pumps is $83.75 per unit, including $17.25 of allocated fixed overhead (primarily depreciation of equipment). Also, the company has spent an average of $22 (labour and parts) repairing each pump returned. Refresh Company can purchase pumps for $92.50 per pump.

During 2020, Refresh Company plans to sell 12 800 plunge pools (each pool requires one pump).

Required

(a) Determine whether Refresh Company should make or buy the pumps, and the amount of cost savings arising from the best alternative.

(b) What qualitative factors should be considered in the outsourcing decision?

ACKNOWLEDGEMENTS

Photo: © LittlePigPower / Shutterstock.com

Photo: © Ekaterina Pokrovsky / Shutterstock.com

CHAPTER 11

Costing and pricing in an entity

LEARNING OBJECTIVES

After studying this chapter, you should be able to:

11.1 define a cost object and explain how cost information is used

11.2 classify costs into direct costs and indirect costs for individual cost objects

11.3 discuss the allocation process for indirect costs

11.4 calculate the full cost of a cost object

11.5 calculate an inventoriable product cost

11.6 discuss pricing issues for products and services.

Chapter preview

In this chapter, we look at how an entity can determine the costs incurred for specific objects such as products, services, customers, business units or geographical regions. Identifying why costs are incurred is important for cost management and decision making. Cost information is used for many purposes including price setting, profitability analysis and performance evaluation. In this chapter, we will also look at an important cost for manufacturing entities — the inventoriable product cost (the inventory value of manufactured products), which is used for financial reporting purposes. As well as costs, managers and accountants also have to manage income, and one important consideration is the price charged for goods and services. It is important that the price is both competitive and allows for profit maximisation. Later in the chapter we will look at issues relating to the pricing of goods and services.

11.1 Use of cost information

LEARNING OBJECTIVE 11.1 Define a cost object and explain how cost information is used.

A **cost** is a resource, commonly measured in monetary terms, used to achieve a particular objective. In previous chapters, we looked at the financial accounting responsibilities of an entity, where costs are classified as either expenses in the statement of profit or loss or assets in the statement of financial position. However, costs recorded in the financial statements are aggregated and do not provide sufficiently detailed information to assist in both day-to-day management and strategic management. For a moment, reflect on the financial statements discussed in previous chapters and determine whether you could answer the following questions.

- What is the profitability of individual products, services, customers or departments?
- How much does each product or service contribute to overall profit?
- How efficient are daily operations?
- Where are the opportunities for cost reduction?
- How much does it cost to service particular customer groups?
- Which product or service should be dropped?

When such questions are posed, it becomes clear that the cost information in the financial statements is too aggregated to be used for the internal management of entity activities.

It is important for an entity to understand why costs are incurred, as this allows costs to be managed and also leads to more informed decision making. This requires the costs to be assigned to the specific objects of interest to management. Consider the example of JB Hi-Fi Ltd, a large retailer of electronics, whitegoods and appliances across Australia and New Zealand. JB Hi-Fi Ltd sells products online and via 300 stores, as well as offering information technology and consulting services through its JB Hi-Fi Solutions business. To determine the profitability of each store and business segment, JB Hi-Fi Ltd would need to understand the revenue and costs of each of those stores and segments.

Whatever it is that an entity requires a separate measurement of cost for is called a **cost object**. Examples of cost objects are products, services, customers, departments, business units and geographical regions. In the case of Nokia Corporation, its 50 markets could be considered individual cost objects for the purpose of determining each market's profitability. You should note that, although an entity can view costs through these different lenses, the total costs of the entity do not change. Costs will only change if management take action to alter the level of costs incurred by the cost object.

Figure 11.1 illustrates some of the many cost objects for which an entity needs to record costs in the accounting information system.

The system used by entities to collect and report the cost of resources used by particular cost objects is known as a **costing system**. Traditionally, costing systems focused on determining the inventory value of manufactured products (the inventoriable product cost) for external financial reporting. Such systems focused on production costs only and ignored other, non-production costs such as information technology and human resources that also support the production process. So, due to an increasingly competitive business environment, coupled with an increase in the level of costs common to many cost objects, entities have been forced to take a more contemporary view when developing costing systems. To remain competitive, entities now need to understand the costs incurred at all stages of the internal value chain — from research and development, design, production and distribution to customer service. This **internal value chain** represents all the linked activities undertaken within an entity — from the inception of the product or service to the final delivery to customers.

FIGURE 11.1 Cost objects

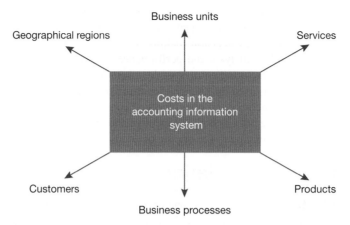

As a consequence, costing systems have been developed to support internal management, rather than simply measuring the inventoriable product cost. Such costing systems take a more contemporary approach by enabling an entity to capture costs at any stage in the value chain, and are suitable for measuring the cost of any cost object. The focus is on aligning the costs to activities in the first instance and then to cost objects. For example, consider an entity that follows the traditional approach of allocating salary costs to individual departments (e.g. allocating the salary costs of accounts payable employees to the accounts payable department). While this provides management with information about total departmental salary costs, it gives no insight into why the costs have been incurred. Such salary costs represent the employee effort in undertaking a variety of activities. For accounts payable staff, these activities would include processing invoices, assessing credit and reconciling payments against the bank account. More insight into the cost of these activities will be gained if the salary costs are assigned to the activities that make use of the costs, rather than to the department.

We will now discuss how to develop a costing system to measure the **full cost** (direct costs plus allocated indirect costs) of a cost object. Before we do this, it is necessary to understand the classification of costs as either direct or indirect in relation to the cost object of interest.

11.2 Direct costs

LEARNING OBJECTIVE 11.2 Classify costs into direct costs and indirect costs for individual cost objects.

Direct costs are those costs that can be linked directly to the cost object. Figure 11.2 shows the relationship between a direct cost and a cost object. To establish this link, an entity needs some type of tracking system to trace the cost directly to the cost object. Source documentation (whether computerised or manual) enables identification of the specific cost object that has made use of a particular resource. For example, material requisitions record the product, service, business unit or activity that requested the material items, and payroll records record employee costs against specific business units or tasks. The more costs that can be directly traced, the greater the accuracy of the costs for the cost object. However, the cost of a tracking system can be prohibitive and entities will only commit resources to tracing costs if such costs are deemed important to the entity or the cost of tracking is minimal. A **cost/benefit test** will be used by an entity to assess the costs against the benefits of a more detailed system of tracking cost information. If the cost does not exceed the benefit, then the cost will be directly traced to the cost object. If the cost is greater than the benefit, the cost will be assigned to an indirect cost category, which is discussed below.

FIGURE 11.2 Relationship of a direct cost to a single cost object

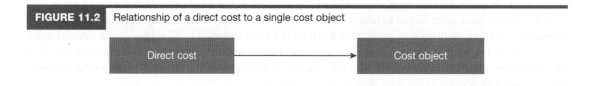

Indirect costs

Indirect costs (also referred to as **overheads**) are those costs that are used for the benefit of multiple cost objects. An indirect cost has a relationship to many cost objects. Figure 11.3 shows the relationship between an indirect cost and the many cost objects that consume the costed resource. These costs may be directly traceable to an individual cost object, but such an exercise may not always pass the cost/benefit test. For example, what would be involved in collecting information about the number of nails used in the construction of a particular house if the builder is constructing 20 houses at the same time, or the amount of glue used to laminate individual office desks? Clearly, the benefits of calculating these costs would be outweighed by the cost of doing so. The question then arises as to how these indirect costs can be allocated to the many cost objects that have made use of the resources. We will address this issue in the following section.

| **FIGURE 11.3** | Relationship of indirect cost to multiple cost objects |

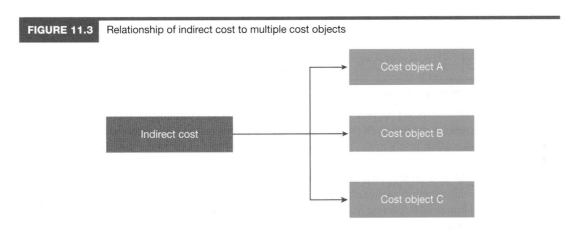

The classification of a cost as either direct or indirect will depend on the specific cost object that has been identified as the focus for the cost analysis, as well as on a cost/benefit assessment of tracing the cost. The total cost of a cost object is:

$$\text{Total cost of a cost object} = \text{Direct costs} + \text{Indirect costs}$$

Illustrative example 11.1 explores the classification of costs as direct or indirect in relation to a cost object.

ILLUSTRATIVE EXAMPLE 11.1

Classifying costs as direct or indirect

Oh Belgium! is a local rock group that performs regularly at venues around the Asia–Pacific region. Costs incurred by the group during October are listed below. Note the classification of each cost as either direct or indirect in relation to a show held at the Toff of the Town venue in Melbourne.

1. Rehearsal room hire to practise for all shows in October (indirect cost).
2. Petrol costs incurred to go to rehearsals and the shows in October (no record of kilometres travelled; indirect cost).
3. Wages of a sound engineer for each show (direct cost).
4. Advertising brochures for the shows during October (indirect cost).
5. Interest payment on loan for musical instruments (indirect cost).
6. Payments to band members for each show (direct cost).
7. Guitar strings — new set needed for each show (direct cost).

   The cost object in the Oh Belgium! example is the show held at the Toff of the Town venue in October. Only those costs that were incurred directly for this particular show are classified as direct costs — items 3, 6 and 7. All other costs (items 1, 2, 4 and 5) are classified as indirect because the expenditure is for the benefit of all shows held in October.

- Cost information assists entities in price setting, profitability analysis, performance evaluation and cost management.
- As the costs in the financial reports are aggregated, information is not provided in sufficient detail to assist in the day-to-day management of entity activities or in strategic decision making.
- To better understand why costs are incurred, the entity will allocate costs to the specific objects that caused costs to be incurred.
- To determine the full cost of a cost object, it is necessary to assign the direct costs and to allocate the indirect costs.
- With a tracking system, direct costs can be traced to specific cost objects.
- Indirect costs are incurred for the benefit of multiple cost objects and need to be allocated to individual cost objects because it is not economically feasible to trace them directly to individual cost objects.

11.3 Cost allocation

LEARNING OBJECTIVE 11.3 Discuss the allocation process for indirect costs.

As indirect costs are incurred for the benefit of multiple cost objects, determining the full cost of a particular cost object will require assigning such costs to the many cost objects that have received the benefit of the resources. **Cost allocation** refers to the process of allocating indirect costs to the cost objects that make use of the resources.

Unless required by an external party, the allocation of costs by an entity is discretionary. For example, to comply with external requirements/regulations, entities must calculate inventoriable product costs in line with International Financial Reporting Standards (IFRS). This requires the recognition of direct production costs and indirect production costs.

Some examples of the reasons why entities choose to allocate indirect costs are to:

- determine the full cost of a specific cost object in order to undertake profitability analysis, which will provide a basis for pricing decisions and assist in resource allocation decision
- allocate the cost of shared services such as accounts payable, payroll and information technology (cost assignment will remind business unit managers of the full economic impact of their decisions)
- encourage the use of central resources by business units — if managers are charged for the costs of a service (e.g. legal services and training services) whether they use it or not, they will be encouraged to use it
- encourage mutual monitoring to control costs — if a manager is to be charged for a shared service, the allocated costs will be benchmarked against external providers to ensure that the allocation is within commercial limits.

Cost drivers

In order to allocate the indirect costs to individual cost objects, an appropriate driver (or allocation base) needs to be identified to establish the link between an indirect cost and the many cost objects that make use of the resource. A **cost driver** provides a measure of activity that explains the cost object's use of the indirect cost. In contrast, an **allocation base** is simply a variable used to allocate costs from a cost pool to a cost object — there may not be a causal relationship. The accuracy of the cost allocation is increased if there is a cause-and-effect relationship between the cost driver (allocation base) and the indirect cost. That is, a change in the use of the cost driver should cause a corresponding change in the amount of cost incurred. Criteria that can be used in the selection of an appropriate cost driver include:

- cause and effect — choosing the variables that cause resources to be consumed (e.g. allocating machine costs based on the cost object's use of machine time)
- benefits received — identifying the beneficiaries of the outputs of the cost object (e.g. allocating advertising costs based on the cost object's increase in income)
- fairness or equity — selecting the costs that appear reasonable and fair
- ability to bear — allocating costs in proportion to the cost object's ability to bear them (e.g. allocating indirect costs based on a cost object's level of profit or level of income)
- behavioural — selecting a cost driver to modify behaviour (e.g. using direct labour hours to encourage a reduction in the use of labour hours).

An analysis of the above criteria shows that, if accuracy of the full cost is the objective, the cause-and-effect cost driver will be the most appropriate. All other criteria are subjective and may lead to behavioural problems. Imagine that you are the manager of the department with the highest revenue; how would you react if you were burdened with the majority of the indirect costs incurred to support all departments simply because your unit earned the most revenue? The benefits received by particular cost objects might be difficult to pinpoint; for example, how could an entity identify which particular department benefited from an entity-wide advertising campaign? The ability-to-bear criterion will burden better performing departments, while the behavioural criterion will be more focused on modifying behaviour than developing the most accurate full cost. For example, in a Victorian municipality the council charged higher rates to the owners of vacant land than to home owners; the rates were set higher to encourage construction. However, this approach to setting council rates caused much debate and dissent within the community.

A cost driver provides a useful measure of activity that helps to allocate indirect costs, such as IT, to the correct cost object.

Cost drivers can be classified as either volume drivers, resource drivers or activity drivers. **Volume drivers** use a measure of output (or volume) to assign the indirect costs; for example, labour hours, machine hours or units of output. It is assumed that indirect costs are consumed by the cost object in relation to its use of the volume driver. For example, if machine hours are selected as the cost driver, then each cost object will be assigned indirect costs in proportion to its use of machine hours. However, if indirect costs are caused by factors other than volume, then incorrect allocation may lead to cross-subsidisation between the cost objects. That is, cost objects that use more of the cost driver (but not necessarily the underlying cost) will be burdened with a higher proportion of indirect costs. This may lead to the entity making incorrect decisions. For example, if cross-subsidisation has caused incorrect measures of product profitability, an entity might attempt to boost sales on the more profitable product by allocating more of the advertising budget to promoting sales. However, this could lead to the promotion of a product that is less profitable due to the incorrect allocation of indirect costs.

Resource drivers are factors that measure resource consumption by activities. Such drivers enable costs to be assigned to activities. For example, the accounting system will have costs collected in accounts for electricity, rent, rates, salaries and so on. In the case of electricity costs may be allocated to activities based on kilowatt hours, and rent may be based on the metres of floor space where the activity takes place. **Activity drivers** are then used to assign the costs from the activities to the cost object. Activity drivers represent the attributes of the individual activities and recognise that factors other than volume cause indirect costs to be used by cost objects. For example, rather than using machine hours as the cost driver, further investigation of the processes might reveal that other factors cause the consumption of indirect costs. Such factors could be the time taken to set up the machine, the number of machine set-ups, the type of labour used, or the type of material or packaging used. Cross-subsidisation is addressed by using activity drivers, as the indirect costs are allocated to the cost objects that make use of that particular activity.

When developing a costing system based on activities, reference to an activity hierarchy can assist in identifying the most appropriate type of cost driver. The **activity hierarchy** is a framework that describes how indirect costs change with various activities. For a manufacturing entity, the hierarchy would include:

- unit level costs — costs incurred for each unit of output (e.g. the cost of electricity to operate machines)
- batch level costs — costs incurred for the benefit of a group of products simultaneously (e.g. the cost of setting up machines to manufacture batches of product)
- product level costs — costs incurred for the benefit of a specific product family (e.g. the cost of designing specific products)
- facility level costs — costs incurred for the benefit of the entire entity (e.g. the cost of operating the entity's headquarters).

The activity hierarchy shows that a volume driver would be appropriate only for a unit level cost. The specific levels in the hierarchy can be adapted to suit the characteristics of individual entities. For example, an entity might identify customer level costs to recognise costs associated with specific customers. Such costs could include specialised equipment or dedicated staff.

DECISION-MAKING EXAMPLE

Selection of appropriate allocation base

SITUATION Multimillion-dollar properties backing onto Palm Beach have experienced severe erosion due to storms and king tides. Some properties have the potential to be completely swept away. The Gold Coast City Council has a potential repair bill of more than $20 million to stop the properties being washed into the ocean. Properties will be protected by the construction of artificial reefs and the restoration of sand dunes. The Council will have to find these funds from its budget, which is partly met by the rates paid by local property owners. The question arises, how should property owners contribute towards the repair work?

DECISION Given the potential safety risk, the Council will not be able to ignore this situation. However, funds need to be found to pay for the repair work. If the Council were to raise the funds by increasing the annual rates, then the question arises as to how best to do this. Options available to the Council would include: a standard levy for all ratepayers; a levy for affected property owners only; a levy based on property values (either market value or purchase cost); or different levies for commercial, residential and vacant-land property owners.

11.4 Allocation process

LEARNING OBJECTIVE 11.4 Calculate the full cost of a cost object.

To determine the full cost for any cost object, direct costs are traced and indirect costs are allocated based on the cost object's usage of the chosen cost driver(s) (allocation base). The indirect cost allocation formula is used to calculate the rate at which indirect costs will be assigned:

$$\frac{\text{Indirect costs to be allocated}}{\text{Total cost driver usage}} = \text{Indirect cost rate per unit of cost driver}$$

The allocation process involves three phases.

1. *Structure the indirect cost allocation formula.* This requires identifying the indirect costs to be allocated and selecting the cost driver that will link the indirect cost to the cost object.
2. *Calculate the indirect cost rate.* This is done by dividing the indirect costs by the total cost driver usage.
3. *Allocate the indirect cost to the cost object.* This is calculated by multiplying the indirect cost rate by the cost object's use of the cost driver.

To develop the indirect cost allocation formula, the entity must first decide on the number of indirect cost pools in its costing system; that is, whether there is to be one or many. An indirect cost allocation formula will then be developed for each indirect cost pool. A **cost pool** is a grouping of 'similar' costs that can be classified on a departmental basis, an activity basis or on the basis of some other criterion for grouping. Breaking down the entity's costs into different cost pools indicates that different cost drivers

---

are needed to explain the cost object's resource consumption. The complexity or sophistication of the cost allocation system (i.e. the number of cost pools to be used to allocate indirect costs) will be determined by comparing the cost of collecting detailed data against the cost of error in decision making that arises from having a less accurate measure of full cost.

An entity may choose to measure the indirect costs using actual costs or budgeted costs, or even further classify them according to cost behaviour (fixed or variable). The determination of an actual **indirect cost rate** (which is the rate used to assign actual indirect costs based on a cost object's actual use of the chosen cost driver) will not be possible until the end of the financial period, when actual results are known. Also, if the actual indirect cost rate is calculated on a monthly basis, it can vary from month to month due to fluctuations in the cash-flow pattern. To overcome this delay in obtaining information and to smooth out fluctuations in cash flows, entities will often use budgeted costs to calculate a **predetermined indirect cost rate**. This is the estimated level of indirect cost divided by the estimated level of the cost driver. The use of budgeted costs will also provide a benchmark against which actual costs can be measured to assess both cost variances and performance, and to assist in budget preparation and pricing.

As the number of cost pools increases, the accuracy of the cost information is also increased, as a different cost driver will be used for allocation purposes that best explains resource consumption. However, as the number of cost pools increases, the need to collect information about individual cost drivers also increases. This will lead to an overall increase in the cost of the system due to the level of resources needed to undertake the cost assignment and data collection.

Therefore, once the cost driver has been identified for each cost pool, the total use of the cost driver for the financial period under investigation will need to be determined. Cost driver usage will be based on either the budgeted or actual usage to match the type of indirect costs to be allocated. By dividing the total indirect costs by the total use of the cost driver, a measure of the cost per unit of the cost driver will be calculated. The determination of this indirect unit cost rate allows the indirect costs to be allocated to the many cost objects that have made use of the resource. Allocation will be based on each cost object's use of the cost driver.

Determination of full cost

The identification of the indirect cost pools and related cost drivers enables the determination of the full cost for the desired cost object. Figure 11.4 illustrates the process to determine the full cost for any cost object. As mentioned earlier, the level of sophistication of the costing system — that is, the number of indirect cost pools, the classification of indirect cost pools and the cost drivers selected — will be at the discretion of each entity and determined by its information needs.

FIGURE 11.4 Overview of a simple costing system to determine the full cost of a cost object

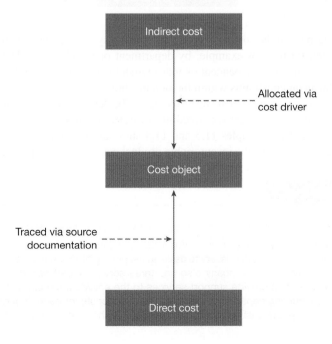

The simple costing system in figure 11.4 highlights the tracing of the direct cost via source documentation and the allocation of the indirect cost based on the cost object's use of the cost driver. Figure 11.5 further refines this simple system, with the changes being seen in the breaking up of the indirect costs into multiple cost pools (including salaries, rent and insurance).

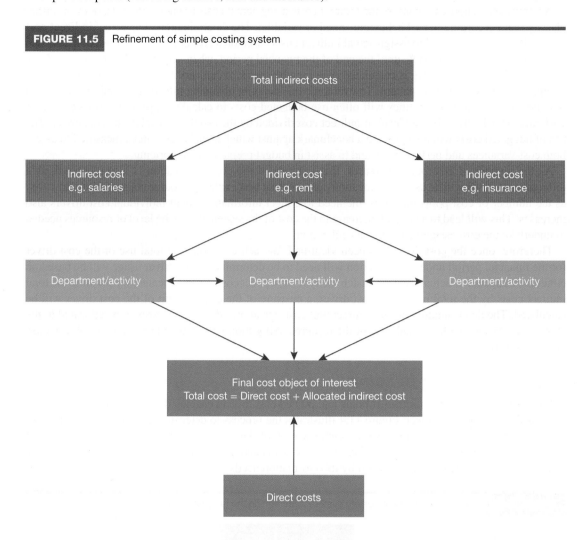

FIGURE 11.5 Refinement of simple costing system

Depending on the purpose of the costing exercise, the costing system can be structured with the indirect cost pools broken down further, for example, by department or activity. The decision on how best to structure the costing system will be dependent on management's information needs, constraints placed by external parties and financial constraints within the organisation.

Note that this process can be used to cost any cost object. The determination of a full cost using business units as the cost object of interest is demonstrated in illustrative example 11.2. This highlights the cost-assignment process. Illustrative examples 11.3 and 11.4 show the structure of a costing system used in manufacturing entities to determine the inventoriable product cost for financial reporting purposes.

ILLUSTRATIVE EXAMPLE 11.2

Determination of full cost — cost objects (business units)

Partridge Insurance Company needs to cost (fully) its operating departments: home insurance, car insurance and life insurance. This is necessary to assist in the pricing of insurance premiums for the various policies issued by the entity. The company also has three service departments — finance, personnel and computer services — that provide support services to the entity's three operating departments. An investigation by the accounting department identified the direct costs for each department (both service and operating) and appropriate cost drivers to help allocate all the costs to the cost objects (operating departments). Costs were identified for (1) each department and (2) other costs (rent, electricity and general administration) that were used for the benefit of all departments.

The *first stage* allocation involves the allocation of the other costs (rent, electricity and general administration) to all the departments. (*Note:* In this example, it is assumed that the service departments do not share resources. Further study of service departments sharing resources can be found in more advanced texts.)

An overview of the relationships between the costs and cost objects in this first stage allocation is shown in figure 11.6. You will notice that the direct costs are traced directly to each department.

FIGURE 11.6   First stage cost allocation — relationship between costs and cost objects

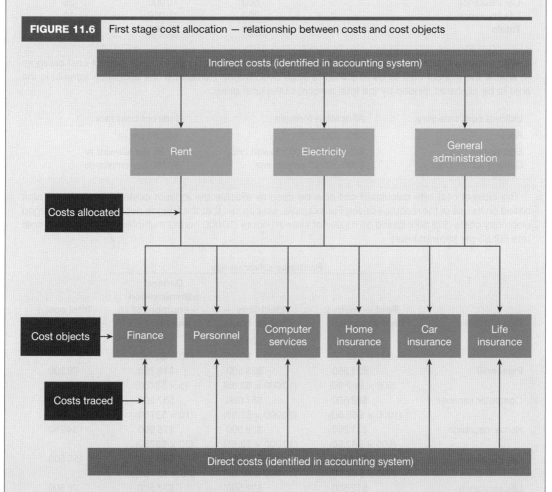

After analysis of the accounting records, the following indirect costs were identified and a suitable resource driver (allocation base) was selected.

Indirect cost category	Cost	Resource driver
Rent	$200 000	Metres floor space
Electricity	199 500	Kilowatt hours
General administration	300 000	Number of employees
Total	**$699 500**	

Therefore, to calculate the full cost of each department, the indirect costs (rent, electricity and general administration) need to be allocated to each department (both service and operating departments). To assist with the allocation, the accounting staff have undertaken a study to identify the most appropriate resource driver and have measured the total usage of the resource driver. The resource driver selected and the use of the resource driver by each department are as follows.

Department	Resource driver usage		
	Metres floor space (m²)	Kilowatt hours	Number of employees
Finance	500	10 000	10
Personnel	500	10 000	5
Computer services	1 000	20 000	10
Home insurance	500	10 000	20
Car insurance	500	10 000	25
Life insurance	200	10 000	10
Totals	**3 200**	**70 000**	**80**

With the above data, it is now possible to calculate the indirect cost rate for each indirect cost category to enable the indirect cost to be allocated to each department. Remember the allocation formula is the cost to be allocated divided by the total amount of the cost driver.

Indirect cost category	Allocation formula	Indirect cost rate
Rent	$200 000/3200 m²	$62.50 per m²
Electricity	$199 500/70 000 kilowatt hrs	$2.85 per kilowatt hr
General administration	$300 000/80 employees	$3750 per employee

The indirect cost rate calculated can now be used to allocate the indirect costs to each department based on its use of the resource driver. For example, we can see that the finance department was charged electricity costs ($28 500) based on its use of kilowatt hours (10 000 hours) multiplied by the indirect cost rate ($2.85 per kilowatt hour).

Department	Resource driver usage			Total cost allocated
	Rent — metres floor space (m²)	Electricity — kilowatt hours	General administration — number of employees	
Finance	$31 250 (500 × $62.50)	$28 500 (10 000 × $2.85)	$37 500 (10 × $3750)	$ 97 250
Personnel	$31 250 (500 × $62.50)	$28 500 (10 000 × $2.85)	$18 750 (5 × $3750)	78 500
Computer services	$62 500 (1000 × $62.50)	$57 000 (20 000 × $2.85)	$37 500 (10 × $3750)	157 000
Home insurance	$31 250 (500 × $62.50)	$28 500 (10 000 × $2.85)	$75 000 (20 × $3750)	134 750
Car insurance	$31 250 (500 × $62.50)	$28 500 (10 000 × $2.85)	$93 750 (25 × $3 750)	153 500
Life insurance	$12 500 (200 × $62.50)	$28 500 (10 000 × $2.85)	$37 500 (10 × $3 750)	78 500
Total allocated	**$ 200 000**	**$ 199 500**	**$ 300 000**	**$ 699 500**

The full cost for each department can now be calculated. As mentioned, the accounting staff were able to trace the direct costs to the departments, and from our calculations above we have allocated the indirect costs. Therefore, the total cost for each department is as follows.

Department	Indirect cost (allocated)	Direct cost (traced)	Total costs
Finance	$ 97 250	$ 52 750	$ 150 000
Personnel	78 500	41 500	120 000
Computer services	157 000	143 000	300 000
Home insurance	134 750	365 250	500 000
Car insurance	153 500	246 500	400 000
Life insurance	78 500	221 500	300 000
Total allocated	**$699 500**	**$1 070 500**	**$1 770 000**

The *second stage* of the allocation process is to allocate the service department costs to the operating departments. (*Note:* In this example, it is assumed that the service departments do not share resources. Further study of service departments sharing resources can be found in more advanced texts.) In this second stage allocation, the service department costs become the indirect cost pools and their costs need to be allocated to the cost objects, which are the operating departments. The activity cost drivers (allocation bases) chosen for allocation of the service department costs to the operating departments are: the number of invoices for the finance department; the number of employees for the personnel department; and the number of computers for the computer services department. The following information details the total cost for each service department and the total usage of the cost drivers selected to allocate service department costs.

Cost		Cost driver	
Finance	$ 150 000	Number of invoices	5 000
Personnel	120 000	Number of employees	100
Computer services	300 000	Number of computers	60
Home insurance	500 000		
Car insurance	400 000		
Life insurance	300 000		
Total costs	**$ 1 770 000**		

The cost driver usage by the three operating departments follows.

	Invoices	Employees	Computers
Home insurance	1 500	50	25
Car insurance	2 000	30	25
Life insurance	1 500	20	10
Totals	**5 000**	**100**	**60**

The above information highlights that each operating department requires the three service departments to provide services such as invoice processing, personnel services and information technology support.

The steps involved in allocating the service department costs to the three operating departments are now outlined.

Step 1. Overview of cost assignment — identifying cost objects, cost pools and cost drivers

Before commencing any calculations, it is important to understand the costing system that will be used to determine the full cost for each operating department. The first step is identifying the relevant cost objects, the number and type of cost pools, and the appropriate cost drivers by which to allocate the indirect costs. An overview of the costing system is detailed in figure 11.7. The cost objects are the three operating departments: home insurance, car insurance and life insurance. In order to determine the full cost for each of the operating departments, it is necessary to assign the indirect costs, which are the total costs of each of the three service departments (i.e. finance, personnel and computer services). Therefore, we have three indirect cost pools classified on a departmental basis measuring costs on an actual basis. Figure 11.7 highlights the second stage of the allocation process and the one-to-one relationships that exist between the direct costs and the cost objects, and the one-to-many relationships between the indirect costs and the cost objects.

The cost drivers identified to allocate the indirect costs are the number of invoices (finance department), the number of employees (personnel department) and the number of computers (computer services department). The actual usage of the cost driver is used to allocate indirect costs. The next stage in the allocation process is calculating the indirect cost rate for each cost pool.

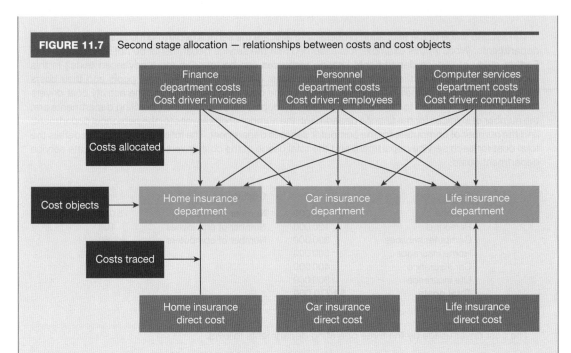

FIGURE 11.7 Second stage allocation — relationships between costs and cost objects

Step 2. Determining indirect cost rates for each cost pool

In this example, there are three cost allocation formulas — one for each of the three service department cost pools. Each allocation formula will require determination of the cost to be allocated for the accounting period and the total use of the cost drivers. The indirect cost rate can then be calculated and the indirect costs allocated according to the use of the cost driver by the individual cost objects, which in this example are the operating departments.

For the finance department the total costs are $150 000, with 5000 invoices being processed in the current accounting period. Each invoice paid by the finance department will lead to a $30 charge being assigned to the operating department to cover such costs as finance staff salaries, stationery and telephone costs. Using the same rationale for the personnel department costs and the computer services costs, charges of $1200 per employee and $5000 per computer will be used to assign costs to these operating departments.

Department (cost pool)	Allocation formula	Indirect cost rate
Finance	$150 000/5000 invoices	$30 per invoice
Personnel	$120 000/100 employees	$1200 per employee
Computer services	$300 000/60 computers	$5000 per computer

Step 3. Allocating indirect costs to the cost objects

Now that the indirect cost rate has been determined, allocation of the indirect costs can be undertaken by applying the indirect cost rate to the cost object's use of the cost driver. For Partridge Insurance Company, indirect costs are allocated according to the cost object's actual use of the cost driver. For example, the indirect cost rate for the finance department is $30 per invoice. The home insurance department raises 1500 invoices per year and so will be allocated $45 000 (1500 invoices × $30) to cover its share of the costs incurred by the finance department.

Indirect costs are assigned to individual cost objects by multiplying the indirect cost rate by the cost object's use of the cost driver.

	Home insurance	Car insurance	Life insurance
Finance	$45 000	$60 000	$45 000
	(1500 invoices × $30)	(2000 invoices × $30)	(1500 invoices × $30)
Personnel	$60 000	$36 000	$24 000
	(50 employees × $1200)	(30 employees × $1200)	(20 employees × $1200)
Computer services	$125 000	$125 000	$50 000
	(25 computers × $5000)	(25 computers × $5000)	(10 computers × $5000)
Total indirect costs	**$230 000**	**$221 000**	**$119 000**

Step 4. Determining the full cost of each cost object

The full cost for each of the cost objects can now be determined. You will notice that the total cost of $1770 000 (refer to the original information) has now been assigned to the three cost objects — the operating departments.

	Home insurance	Car insurance	Life insurance	Total costs
Indirect costs (allocated from service departments)	$230 000	$221 000	$119 000	$ 570 000
Direct costs	500 000	400 000	300 000	1 200 000
Full cost	**$730 000**	**$621 000**	**$419 000**	**$1 770 000**

This example highlights the different lenses that have been used to view the costs — the total cost for the entity, the costs of the individual departments and the full cost of each operating department.

Partridge Insurance Company can now use the data from the allocation process in many ways, for example:

- to determine the full cost of each operating unit
- to review current premiums on insurance policies
- in strategic management — making decisions about which insurance policies to offer in the future based upon the profitability analysis of each type of policy
- in cost management — if individual operating department managers believe that the charges are too high, they will pressure the service departments to lower costs.

The above process for determining the full cost of the operating departments can be used to determine the full cost of any cost object. Obviously there may be different cost pools and different cost drivers; however, the process will be the same. In the following section, we illustrate how the costing system is structured to meet the requirements of the accounting standards for determining inventory valuation for manufacturing entities.

You will notice that the data above have been presented as a spreadsheet. Spreadsheets have been used for hundreds of years and are a system of presenting data in rows and columns. Modern spreadsheets are computerised and have grown in sophistication. Spreadsheets are an essential tool of the accountant, as the ability to collect, store, manipulate and prepare reports from data is becoming easier with advanced spreadsheeting programs. The above example demonstrates how much data need to be collected for quite a simple allocation task. Extrapolate this over many time-periods, many geographical locations, many more products/departments, and you can quickly understand that data need to be collected, manipulated and reported in an efficient manner.

VALUE TO BUSINESS

- Cost information assists entities in price setting, performance evaluation and cost management.
- A cost object is anything for which a separate measurement of cost is desired.
- The full cost of a cost object is equal to direct costs plus indirect costs.
- Direct costs can be traced in an economically feasible way to a cost object.
- Indirect costs are incurred for the benefit of multiple cost objects.
- As indirect costs cannot be traced to specific cost objects in an economically feasible way, such costs need to be allocated.
- Cost drivers provide the link between the indirect cost and the cost objects.

11.5 Inventoriable product cost

LEARNING OBJECTIVE 11.5 Calculate an inventoriable product cost.

An important cost object reported in a manufacturing entity's financial reports is the inventory value of manufactured products. **Inventoriable product cost** represents the cost of converting raw material into a finished product. Accounting standards guide the preparation of financial statements and the valuation of inventory. Any costs incurred to support entity activities that are non-manufacturing in nature — such as office salaries, administration expenses and depreciation of office equipment — are treated as **period costs** (i.e. non-manufacturing costs for the current period) and expensed in the current reporting period. Therefore, the indirect costs used to calculate the inventoriable product cost are limited to indirect manufacturing (production) costs. Remember that the indirect manufacturing costs are direct costs for the manufacturing department, but indirect in relation to the individual products being manufactured.

When products are sold, the inventoriable product cost is expensed as a cost of sales. For products still remaining in inventory (i.e. unsold), the inventoriable product cost is carried into the next reporting period as a current asset (either as work-in-process inventory for incomplete goods or as finished goods inventory for completed goods) on the statement of financial position.

The type (structure) of the costing system selected to determine the inventoriable product cost is influenced by an entity's product range and processes. If an entity's products are mass produced (whereby all products go through similar processes and consume resources in the same way) or if there is only one product manufactured, the entity will use a process costing system (see figure 11.8). In the **process costing system**, direct costs are considered to be the raw materials, while the indirect costs represent the labour and other indirect manufacturing costs (the two costs are grouped into one cost pool and described as **conversion costs**). The indirect cost is allocated by averaging the indirect costs used in the process for the period. This is done by dividing the total costs by the number of units of output.

| FIGURE 11.8 | Overview of a process costing system |

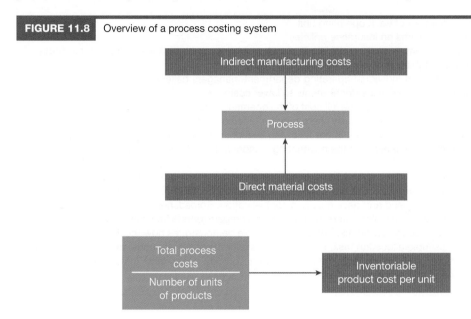

When an entity manufactures products to different customers' specifications, the costing system will need to capture the differences in resource consumption. A **job costing system** (see figure 11.9) is used when the costs need to be assigned to jobs on an individual basis. Direct costs include labour, which is used directly in the production process, and the raw materials that are converted into the finished product. Indirect manufacturing costs are all the other costs incurred in the factory.

Note that labour is classified differently under each system. In a process costing system, the same amount of labour is used for each product. Therefore, detailed records matching labour hours to particular units are not required, and labour can be treated as an indirect cost and allocated to each unit. In contrast, when products do not use the same amount of labour per product unit, separate records need to be kept that trace the labour usage to the specific jobs. This detailed recordkeeping of the job costing system allows the labour cost to be traced to individual products, and it is classified as a direct cost.

Traditionally, manufacturing costing systems pooled indirect costs on a departmental basis or into a single factory-wide cost pool. As noted earlier, the indirect cost rate can be determined using either actual costs or budgeted costs. As the inventoriable product cost is used for financial reporting purposes, it is necessary to identify any variances caused by allocating costs on a predetermined basis using budgeted costs. A **variance** is the difference between a budget cost and an actual cost. Such variances arise when an entity over- or under-estimates either the expenditure level of indirect costs assigned to the cost pool or the expected usage of the cost driver. The variances are recorded in the financial records as either overapplied or underapplied overhead. **Overapplied overhead** refers to a situation where the indirect costs applied to an inventoriable product cost are greater than the actual costs incurred. For **underapplied overhead**, the applied indirect costs are lower than the actual costs.

Illustrative examples 11.3 and 11.4 demonstrate the use of both costing systems by a manufacturing entity.

FIGURE 11.9 Overview of a job costing system

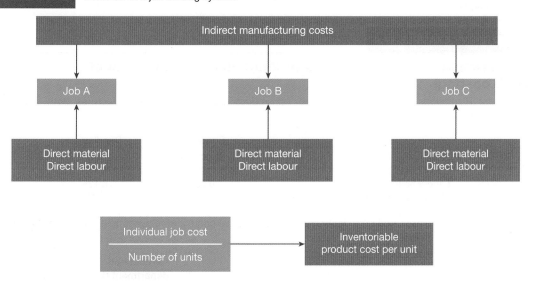

Determination of inventoriable product cost — single product (process costing)

Joanne (Jo) Geter established a private company, Coconut Plantations Pty Ltd, located on the Sunshine Coast in Queensland, to manufacture and sell a range of sustainable coconut-based products such as soaps, candles and detergents. The company commenced operations in September 2019. Assume that Jo made a cautious, risk-averse decision to manufacture only soaps initially to reduce production complexity and planned to increase the range of products gradually as feedback was obtained on production processes.

In the first four months of operation, Coconut Plantations Pty Ltd produced 15 000 soaps, of which 12 500 were sold. The following costs were recorded.

Direct material	$180 000	
Direct labour	100 000	
Manufacturing overhead	50 000	
Total manufacturing costs	**$330 000**	÷ 15 000 = $22/soap
Warehouse and distribution expenses	$ 42 000	
Sales and marketing expenses	3 000	
Administrative and finance expenses	35 000	
Total non-manufacturing costs	**$ 80 000**	

Determining the inventoriable product cost for Coconut Plantations Pty Ltd is relatively simple, as the company produced only one product, soap. A process costing system is therefore suitable, as all manufacturing costs were consumed in the same way by all units of output. The total manufacturing costs incurred in the production process for the first four months were $330 000, being direct material, direct labour and manufacturing overhead. This amount excludes the selling and administrative expenses, in line with the IFRS, as they were not 'costs' of the inventory.

The determination of the unit cost enables Coconut Plantations to value the cost of sales and inventory on hand at the end of the period as follows: $275 000 (12 500 units × $22) are expensed to cost of sales; and $55 000 (2500 units × $22) is recorded as a current asset (inventory). (Further discussion of the effects of opening and closing inventories on the determination of inventoriable product costs in a process costing system can be found in management accounting texts.)

Assume that Coconut Plantations extended its range of products in 2020 to include candles as well as soaps. The choice of costing system now depends on how resources were consumed by each product. If the indirect costs were consumed differently, an averaging approach to product costing will no longer be appropriate. In order to recognise the difference in resource consumption, Coconut Plantations would have to adopt a job costing system to determine the inventoriable product cost for each product. Illustrative example 11.4 illustrates how the costing system would change for Coconut Plantations with the introduction of the new product line, candles, which consumes resources differently to the existing product, soaps.

Determination of inventoriable product cost — multi-product (job costing)

Coconut Plantations Pty Ltd has extended its product range and now manufactures both soaps (30 000 units) and candles (20 000 units).

	Soaps	Candles
Units	30 000	20 000
Direct costs	$613 125	$276 875
Labour hours per unit	0.25	0.125
Machine hours per unit	1	1.5

Indirect costs are allocated on a departmental basis. Actual costs and relevant cost driver information for each department follow.

	Production department A	Production department B
Indirect costs	$60 000	$62 500
Cost driver	Machine hours	Labour hours
Usage of cost driver	60 000 machine hours	10 000 labour hours

To recognise the increased complexity in the process, the manufacturing section has now been separated into two departments: Department A, where the soaps and candles are moulded; and Department B, where the products are finished and wrapped. The use of departmental cost pools recognises that different cost drivers cause resource consumption in each department. Department A is machine intensive, so the use of machine hours has been identified as the appropriate cost driver; while in Department B the process is labour intensive, with labour hours being the appropriate cost driver. To illustrate the job costing system, we will now calculate the inventoriable product cost for each product.

Step 1. Understand the structure of the costing system

The first step is to understand the job costing system. Figure 11.10 outlines how costs are to be allocated to the individual products — soaps and candles. The manufacturing operation has been divided into two departments — Department A and Department B. All costs incurred by both departments are direct costs of those departments and of the manufacturing operation. Remember that the costs can be classified as direct to the manufacturing operation because there have been no costs allocated from the non-manufacturing departments.

FIGURE 11.10   Structure of the costing system

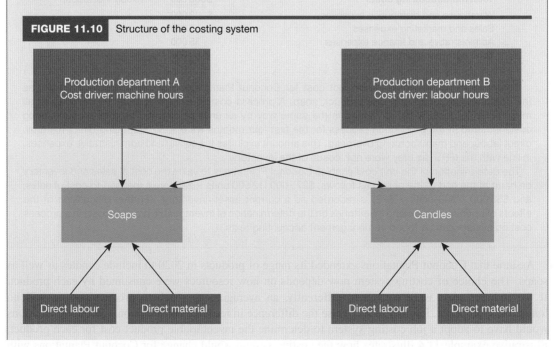

There are two direct cost pools — direct labour and direct material — which can be directly traced to the individual products. Indirect costs will be allocated based on the products' use of the cost drivers identified as causing resource consumption in Department A and Department B. The next step is to determine the indirect cost rates.

Step 2. Determine the departmental indirect cost rates

The products consume indirect costs differently, so there is more than one indirect cost pool to capture the difference in resource consumption. For products passing through Department A, the indirect costs will be allocated based on the use of machine hours. In Department B, the indirect costs will be allocated to the individual products based on the use of labour hours. The accuracy of the cost assignment will depend on the strength of the cost driver to explain resource consumption.

Department A	Department B
$60 000	$62 500
60 000 machine hours	10 000 labour hours
= $1.00 per machine hour	= $6.25 per labour hour

Step 3. Allocate the indirect costs

Multiplying the products' use of the cost driver by the indirect cost rate will complete the allocation process. For example, the soap product uses 1 hour of machine time per unit and, given the total output of 30 000 units, would have used 30 000 machine hours. Overhead will be applied at the rate of $1 per machine hour. Therefore, 30 000 machine hours at $1 per hour will result in $30 000 being applied to the soap product. These calculations, along with those for the candles, are summarised below.

	Soaps (30 000 units)	Candles (20 000 units)
Department A	$30 000	$30 000
	(($1 × 1 machine hour) × 30 000 units)	(($1 × 1.5 machine hour) × 20 000)
Department B	$46 875	$15 625
	(($6.25 × 0.25 labour hours) × 30 000 units)	(($6.25 × 0.125 labour hours) × 20 000 units)
Total indirect costs	**$76 875**	**$45 625**

Does a variance need to be identified? No, because actual indirect costs incurred and actual usage of the cost driver were used for cost determination. Variances need to be identified only if budgeted costs are used in the allocation process and they differ from actual costs. (A detailed look at the calculation of variances can be found in management accounting texts.)

Step 4. Determine the inventoriable product cost

Determination of the inventoriable cost for each product is now possible by adding the direct cost and the allocated indirect cost. The unit cost can be calculated by dividing the total inventoriable product cost by the number of units of output. The total cost of the soap product is $690 000 (direct material plus direct labour plus allocated indirect costs) divided by 30 000 units, giving a unit cost of $23.00 per unit of soap. The unit cost for candles is $16.125. These costs are summarised below.

Cost category	Soaps (30 000 units)	Candles (20 000 units)
Total indirect costs	$ 76 875	$ 45 625
Direct costs	613 125	276 875
Inventoriable product cost		
(direct costs + indirect costs)	$690 000	$322 500
Unit cost		
(inventoriable product cost / # units)	$ 23.00	$ 16.125

The degree of accuracy of the inventoriable product cost is influenced by the use of a cost driver that explains resource consumption. If we look at the soap product, we can see that in illustrative example 11.3 the unit cost was $22.00 per unit in 2019, yet in illustrative example 11.4 the unit cost has changed to $23.00. The difference relates to the introduction of a new product, changes in input prices or production efficiencies, and the change in the design of the cost system. This difference in unit cost could indicate that the costing system design is not appropriate for the entity. The current design assumes that products consume resources in the same manner in each department. Also, as a volume cost driver has been selected, the higher volume products will always be burdened with more of the indirect costs. This could suggest a need for the entity to look more closely at the selection of cost pools and cost drivers.

How will Coconut Plantations use this unit cost information?

- If the pricing policy is cost plus mark-up, the unit cost can be increased by the desired mark-up to set the selling price. However, what would be the impact if an incorrect cost driver had been used to allocate costs?
- The unit cost enables inventory valuation for financial reporting — manufacturing costs incurred for the accounting period can be divided between ending work-in-process inventory and finished goods. When goods are sold, the unit cost enables the calculation of the cost of sales.
- Coconut Plantations can determine the contribution of each product to the company's profits. This information will assist with decisions regarding product mix, production promotion and cost management strategies to improve profitability.

Illustrative example 11.4 demonstrates the determination of an inventoriable product cost using volume-based cost drivers. If products do not consume resources in relation to volume, then cross-subsidisation between products will result. To obtain a more accurate inventoriable product cost, an entity could classify the indirect manufacturing costs into activity cost pools and assign costs using activity-based cost drivers. The activity view of costs recognises that factors other than labour hours or machine hours influence resource consumption.

As mentioned, the inventoriable cost is primarily used to satisfy financial reporting requirements. The question could be asked whether this cost is appropriate for internal decision making. For more informed decision making, the determination of a full product cost would be more suitable. This would require both manufacturing and non-manufacturing costs to be assigned to the product. The process for determining the full cost of a cost object was explained earlier in this chapter; this requires the indirect cost pools to include non-manufacturing costs.

VALUE TO BUSINESS

- Manufacturing entities need to determine the inventoriable product cost for financial reporting purposes.
- An inventoriable product cost includes only manufacturing costs.
- Non-manufacturing costs are expensed in the current accounting period.
- Depending on the operating characteristics of the manufacturing entity, either a job costing or a process costing system will be used.
- Process costing is used by entities producing only one product, or multiple products that go through the same processes and consume resources in the same way.
- Job costing is used by entities manufacturing products that consume resources differently and whose costing system needs to separate costs by individual jobs.

11.6 Pricing of products and services

LEARNING OBJECTIVE 11.6 Discuss pricing issues for products and services.

As we have learned from earlier chapters, an entity's profit is determined by income less expenses (costs that have been consumed). So far in this chapter, we have examined issues in relation to cost determination. Let's now focus on how an entity sets its pricing policy for determination of the individual product/service price in order to calculate sales revenue. To maximise profits, an entity should charge customers the highest price possible, but not such a high price that the customers will buy from a competitor or decide not to purchase at all. There are two common methods of pricing — cost-based and market-based.

Cost-based pricing applies a mark-up to some calculations of the product or service cost. The cost base can be calculated in several ways. For example, some entities use a variable cost base or an average cost that includes both fixed and variable costs. Mark-ups can originate from general industry practice, be based on previous entity practices or be chosen so that the entity can earn a target rate of return on investment. Therefore, cost-based pricing will vary significantly across entities.

Market-based pricing is based on some measure of customer demand. The market price is influenced by the degree of product differentiation and competition in the market. Managers would attempt to identify what price customers are willing to pay for a product or service. An entity with many competitors will set the price at what customers would pay to any entity offering such a product or service. With less competition, where an entity is selling a more unique good or service, the entity will set the price at the maximum the market will bear.

Which pricing method is more suitable? Cost-based pricing ignores customer demand and therefore prices could be either higher or lower than what customers are willing to pay. However, one of its major benefits, at least initially, is its simplicity, as prices can be calculated from readily available data. In contrast, market-based pricing allows managers to make better decisions about sales volumes and whether to sell products or services, leading to more success in entity strategies. A disadvantage is that estimating market demand and prices is often difficult; however, this is being addressed with the use of more sophisticated information systems.

To illustrate the different pricing methods, let's return to Coconut Plantations Pty Ltd. From our costing exercise, we were able to calculate the unit cost of the soap in 2020 to be $23.00 and of the candle product to be $16.125. We could apply a cost-based pricing policy whereby we add a 50 per cent mark-up to the cost. However, given the differences in the two products, is a 50 per cent mark-up across both products appropriate? It could be that soap is a product available from competitors and, as such, the price should be in line with competitors' pricing. However, if candles were not available from competitors, Jo Geter, the manager of Coconut Plantations Pty Ltd, would want to maximise the price to be charged for this product.

Regardless of the method chosen, there are other factors that can influence the setting of product prices for individual entities or in specific circumstances.

- **Peak load pricing** — different prices are charged at different times to reduce capacity restraints. For example, cinemas charge less for movies shown early in the day or on quieter days.
- **Price skimming** — a higher price is charged for a product or service when it is first introduced. For example, when DVD players were first introduced into the market they were around $1000, whereas today we can purchase a unit for as little as $20.
- **Penetration pricing** — prices are set low when new products are introduced to increase market share. For example, Microsoft reduced the price of the Xbox to match its competition.

It should be noted that entities are not free to establish any price they wish; some pricing practices are illegal. In Australia, illegal practices include price discrimination, predatory pricing, collusive pricing and dumping. A brief discussion of these follows.

- **Price discrimination** — the practice of setting different prices for different customers.
- **Predatory pricing** — the deliberate act of setting prices low to drive competitors out of the market and then raising prices once competition is removed.
- **Collusive pricing** — two or more organisations conspiring to set prices above a competitive price.
- **Dumping** — a foreign-based entity selling products in Australia at prices below the market value in the country where the product is produced, where the price could harm an Australian industry.

Another important consideration is short-run pricing compared with long-run pricing. In the previous chapter we looked at whether or not an entity should accept a special order. In this short-run decision, we were able to ignore fixed costs, as the level of expenditure would not change in the short term, and therefore our focus was on variable costs in the decision process. We determined that the minimum price in situations where there was spare capacity was the variable cost. At this pricing level, the entity would break even on the special order. However, is this a suitable pricing practice long term? The answer is 'no' as in the long run all products should contribute towards fixed costs and profits, and so the price should incorporate a margin to cover such contributions.

SUMMARY OF LEARNING OBJECTIVES

11.1 Define a cost object and explain how cost information is used.

A cost object is anything for which a separate measurement of cost is required. Examples are customers and individual business units. Cost information is used for a variety of purposes to assist in day-to-day management and strategic management — in determining inventory values, analysing product profitability, identifying relevant costs for outsourcing decisions and so on.

11.2 Classify costs into direct costs and indirect costs for individual cost objects.

A direct cost is traceable to a particular cost object. The tracing is made possible by the implementation of a tracking system to link the cost to the cost object. An indirect cost is used for the benefit of multiple cost objects and the cost is linked to the individual cost objects by the identification of an appropriate cost driver.

11.3 Discuss the allocation process for indirect costs.

An indirect cost is used for the benefit of multiple cost objects. Therefore, an allocation of costs is necessary to enable the cost to be assigned to the many cost objects that make use of the resource. By allocating indirect costs, an entity is able to determine the full cost of the cost object.

11.4 Calculate the full cost of a cost object.

Full cost is equal to direct costs plus indirect costs. The accuracy of the full cost is strengthened by the choice of cost driver for indirect cost allocation. Cost drivers can be based on either volume or activity. Volume drivers assign indirect costs based on some measure of the volume of output; for example, units of output, direct labour hours or machine hours. In contrast, activity drivers recognise that factors other than volume will cause indirect costs to be consumed; for example, number of invoices processed, number of orders processed or time taken to set up machines.

11.5 Calculate an inventoriable product cost.

An inventoriable product cost is calculated by manufacturing entities to satisfy the requirements of having an inventory value in the financial reports, in line with International Financial Reporting Standards (IFRS). An inventoriable product cost includes only manufacturing costs. All non-manufacturing costs are expensed in the current accounting period.

11.6 Discuss pricing issues for products and services.

An entity has the option of applying either a cost-based or market-based pricing strategy for its products or services. A cost-based price will add a mark-up to a calculated cost of the product or service. A market-based price will be set at the highest possible price that a customer will pay and this will be dependent on the degree of product differentiation and competition.

KEY TERMS

activity driver Cost driver that can be either volume- or non-volume related.
activity hierarchy Framework that describes how overhead costs change with various activities.
allocation base Variable used to allocate costs from a cost pool to a cost object.
collusive pricing When two or more organisations conspire to set prices above a competitive price.
conversion cost Direct labour and overhead incurred to convert direct materials into a finished product.
cost Resource, usually measured in monetary terms, used to achieve a particular organisational objective.
cost allocation Assignment of indirect costs to the many cost objects that make use of the resources.
cost-based pricing Pricing method that applies a mark-up to some calculation of the product or service cost.
cost/benefit test Assessment of the costs and benefits of tracing costs to cost objects.
cost driver Measure of the activity, related to a cost pool, that is used to allocate costs.
cost object Object with a separately measured cost.
cost pool Collection of similar costs.
costing system System used to allocate costs to cost objects.
direct costs Costs that can be directly traced to a cost object.
dumping When a foreign-based entity sells products in Australia at prices below the market value in the country where the product is produced, and the price could harm an Australian industry.
full cost Direct costs plus allocated indirect costs.

indirect cost rate Total indirect costs (overhead costs) for the cost pool divided by the total level of the cost driver.

indirect costs (overheads) Costs that are not economically feasible to trace to the cost object.

internal value chain Linked activities undertaken within an entity — from the inception of the product or service to the final delivery to customers.

inventoriable product cost Cost of converting raw material into finished products.

job costing system System of accounting for product costs that is used by entities producing individual products or batches of products that are unique.

market-based pricing Pricing method based on some measure of customer demand.

overapplied overhead When the indirect costs applied to an inventoriable product cost are greater than the actual costs incurred.

peak load pricing When different prices are charged at different times to reduce capacity restraints.

penetration pricing Setting prices low when new products are introduced to increase market share.

period costs Costs written off in the current accounting period.

predatory pricing Setting prices low to drive competitors out of the market and then raising prices once competition is removed.

predetermined indirect cost rate Estimated level of indirect costs (overhead costs) for the cost pool divided by the estimated level of the cost driver (allocation base).

price discrimination Setting different prices for different customers.

price skimming When a higher price is charged for a product or service at the time it is first introduced.

process costing system Product costing system used by entities that produce large numbers of identical items in a continuous production process.

resource driver Cost driver that measures resource consumption by activities.

underapplied overhead When the indirect costs applied to an inventoriable product cost are less than the actual costs incurred.

variance Difference between budgeted cost and actual cost.

volume driver Cost driver that relates to the volume of output.

APPLY YOUR KNOWLEDGE
25 marks

The financial controller of Seats R Us has established indirect cost pools and cost drivers for the coming year as follows.

Indirect cost pools	Budgeted cost	Cost driver	Total level of cost driver
Machine processing	$120 000	Number of set-ups	40
Power	350 000	Machine hours	22 500
Materials handling	85 000	Materials weight	35 000 kg
Quality control	145 500	Number of units	82 000 units
Other indirect costs	184 500	Direct labour hours	14 560 hours
	$885 000		

The sales team has received an order for 1500 seats and produced them. The order requires the following.

Machine set-ups	7 set-ups
Machine hours	3250 machine hours
Materials	4250 kg
Direct labour hours	2750 hours

Required

(a) Briefly comment on the importance of a costing system to Seats R Us. **4 marks**

(b) Draw a diagram showing the current costing system framework. **2 marks**

(c) Calculate the indirect cost rate for each cost pool identified in (b). **5 marks**

(d) Assign the indirect costs to the cost object identified in (b). **5 marks**

(e) Suppose that a single indirect cost rate based on machine hours was used to allocate indirect costs. Draw a diagram showing this costing system framework and contrast it with the one in (b) above. Calculate the indirect cost rate. **3 marks**

(f) What amount of indirect costs was applied to the cost object using the indirect cost rate based on machine hours? **2 marks**

(g) Briefly comment on any differences in your answers to (d) and (f) above. **4 marks**

SELF-EVALUATION ACTIVITIES

11.1 Trans Australia Airlines has three service departments:
1. ticketing
2. baggage handling
3. engine maintenance.

The service department costs are assigned by air kilometres and are allocated to two operational departments (domestic flights and international flights) to determine the full cost of the operating departments. The following data relate to the allocations.

	Budgeted data	
	Costs	Air km
Ticketing	$4 000 000	
Baggage handling	2 000 000	
Engine maintenance	6 000 000	
Domestic flights		5 000 000
International flights		20 000 000

Required

Allocate the service department costs to the operational departments, using air kilometres as the allocation.

SOLUTION TO 11.1

Step 1. Determine indirect cost rate

As there is only one cost driver, the allocation formula will be:

$$\text{Total service department costs/Total air km}$$
$$(\$4\,000\,000 + \$2\,000\,000 + \$6\,000\,000)/(5\,000\,000 + 20\,000\,000 \text{ air km}) = \$0.48 \text{ per air km}$$

Step 2. Allocate indirect costs to the two operating departments

Domestic: 5 000 000 air km × $0.48 = $2 400 000
International: 20 000 000 air km × $0.48 = $9 600 000

11.2 SteelFab is a steel fabricator and Tough Gates has submitted an order for 1400 steel gates. Estimates have been prepared, and direct labour costs are 150 hours at $40 per hour and direct materials are $5000. SteelFab's budgeted indirect manufacturing costs for the year are $150 000. Costs are allocated using direct labour hours as the cost driver. A total of 20 000 direct labour hours has been allowed in the budget to cover expected demand.

Required

(a) Estimate the total cost of the Tough Gates order.
(b) What is the unit cost for each steel gate frame?

SOLUTION TO 11.2

(a) Estimated total cost of the Tough Gates order is as follows.

Direct labour (150 hours × $40)	$ 6 000
Direct materials	5 000
Indirect manufacturing (150 hours × $7.50*)	1 125
Total cost of order	**$12 125**

* Indirect cost rate $150 000/20 000 direct labour hours = $7.50 per direct labour hour.

(b) Unit cost for each steel gate frame is $12 125/1400 gates = $8.66 per gate.

COMPREHENSION QUESTIONS

11.3 What is a cost object? Give three examples.   **LO1**
11.4 Explain the difference between a direct cost and an indirect cost.   **LO2**
11.5 Explain the difference between a full product cost and an inventoriable product cost. **LO4, 5**
11.6 Discuss the importance of selecting an appropriate cost driver in the cost allocation process. **LO3**

11.7 Explain cost-based pricing and give an example that shows how prices would be determined using this method. **LO6**

11.8 Explain market-based pricing and give an example that shows how prices would be determined using this method. **LO6**

11.9 Cost rivers can be based on either volume or activity. Provide an example of each. **LO4**

11.10 Briefly outline four pricing practices that are illegal in Australia. **LO6**

11.11 Discuss the allocation process for indirect costs. **LO3**

11.12 Identify two factors that influence pricing decisions. **LO6**

11.13 Explain the benefits to an entity of using a costing system. **LO1**

EXERCISES

★ BASIC I ★ ★ MODERATE I ★ ★ ★ CHALLENGING

11.14 ★ **LO2**

Michelle's Tax Services has two departments, tax and audit. The tax department has two product lines, business returns and individual returns. A list of costs and three cost objects from Michelle's Tax Services are shown below.

	Cost object		
Cost	Tax department	Individual returns	Mr Cross's individual tax return
A. Subscription to personal tax-law updates publication			
B. Ink supplies for tax department photocopy machine			
C. Portion of total rent for tax department office space			
D. Wages for tax department administrative assistant			
E. Tax partner's salary			
F. Charges for long distance call to Mr Cross about personal tax return questions			
G. Tax partner lunch with Mr Cross (the tax partner has lunch with each client at least once per year)			

Required

For each cost, identify whether it is direct or indirect for each cost object.

11.15 ★ **LO3**

Hartford Company manufactures five products in a single production facility. The company uses activity cost pools to allocate indirect costs. The following activities have been identified following an analysis of the entity operations.

(a) Inventory control	(d) Machine set-up	(g) Building maintenance
(b) Raw materials	(e) Quality inspections	(h) Delivery to customers
(c) Engineering design	(f) Materials ordering	(i) Employee benefits

Required

Classify each activity cost as unit level, batch level, product level or facility level.

11.16 ★ **LO3**

Refer to exercise 11.15. For each activity, name a cost driver that might be used to assign activity costs to products.

11.17 ★ **LO3**

The Skin Care Company has one product line that is unprofitable. What circumstances might cause the entity's overall profit to be lower if the unprofitable product line was eliminated?

11.18 ★ **LO3**

Fruits on High Ltd uses three activity cost pools to assign costs to customers in order to assess customer profitability. Each activity cost pool has a unique cost driver to apply indirect costs to customers.

Activity	Cost driver	Estimated indirect costs	Estimated total usage of cost driver
Sales returns	Number of returns	$100 000	2 750 returns
Order processing	Lines on order	$275 000	275 000 lines
Rush orders	Number of rush orders	$150 000	6 000 orders

Required

Calculate the activity cost rate for each activity.

11.19 ★ ★ LO1

Megan Mitchell has recently graduated from a business school and joined the family business as an accountant. At the first management meeting with production, marketing and sales, a great deal of time is spent discussing the unit cost of products. What kinds of decisions can managers make using unit cost information?

11.20 ★ ★ LO3

Benson Manufacturing estimates the following activity for the coming year.
- Expected production 23 000 units
- Expected direct labour hours 1750 hours
- Expected manufacturing overhead $92 000.

Manufacturing overhead is allocated on the basis of direct labour hours. At the end of the financial period, the following information is collected.
- Direct labour hours 2350 hours
- Manufacturing overhead $102 000.

Required

(a) Calculate the predetermined indirect cost rate at the beginning of the year.

(b) Calculate the actual indirect cost rate for the year.

11.21 ★ ★ LO5

Refer to exercise 11.20. Benson Manufacturing's total direct labour cost was $470 000 (2350 hours × $100 per hour). There was no direct labour cost variance.

Required

(a) Calculate the total production cost.

(b) Calculate the inventoriable product cost for each unit based on:
   (i) budgeted costs
   (ii) actual costs.

11.22 ★ ★ LO3

During 2022, Lavender Plantations Pty Ltd continued to grow. The manager decided to add detergents to its existing range of soap and candles. The management accountant, Nick Gee, expressed concern regarding the accuracy of the product costing system now that the diversity of output had increased. To further understand the costs, Nick undertook an activity analysis of indirect costs. His findings were as follows.

Activity	Cost	Cost driver
Receipt of materials	$15 000	Material receipts
Machining	85 000	Machine hours
Deliveries	15 000	Number of deliveries
Machine set-up	30 000	Machine set-ups
Engineering	10 000	Engineering advice slips
Packaging	25 000	Cartons packed

The products' use of each cost driver was estimated to be as follows.

	Soaps	Candles	Detergents
Material receipts	350	50	100
Machine hours	50 000	35 000	15 000
Number of deliveries	550	150	50
Machine set-ups	750	550	200
Engineering advice slips	25	10	15
Cartons packed	1 300	450	250

Required
(a) Calculate the activity cost rate for each activity.
(b) Calculate the indirect product cost based on the activity analysis.
    Use a computerised spreadsheet package for both (a) and (b).
(c) It seems some errors occurred when estimating the cost drivers. Material receipts should have been 400 for soaps, 40 for candles and 120 for detergents, while engineering advice slips should have been 15 for soaps, 12 for candles and 18 for detergents. Re-compute (a) and (b) using your spreadsheet model.

11.23 ★ ★   **LO3**

A housekeeping support department budgets its costs at $20 000 per month plus $18 per hour. The estimated and actual hours for November provided by the housekeeping support department to three operating departments are as follows.

	Estimated hours spent cleaning	Actual hours spent cleaning
Department A	2 400	2 250
Department B	2 100	2 400
Department C	3 000	2 700
Total	**7 500**	**7 350**

Required
(a) Draw a diagram showing the structure of the costing system.
(b) Calculate the housekeeping support department's allocation rate if estimated hours is the allocation base.
(c) Calculate the housekeeping support department's allocation rate if actual hours is the allocation base.
(d) Discuss one advantage and one disadvantage of each type of allocation rate.

11.24 ★ ★   **LO3, 4**

Mercy Hospital uses a costing system to determine the cost of patients who have surgery. The hospital uses a budgeted indirect cost rate for allocating indirect costs to patient stays. In March, the operating theatre had a budgeted allocation base of 1000 operating hours. The budgeted operating theatre indirect costs were $66 000.

Patient Dwight Schuller was in the operating theatre for four hours during March. Other costs related to Schuller's four-hour surgery include the following.

Patient medicine	$ 250
Cost of nurses	3 500
Cost of supplies	800

Physician cost is not included because physicians bill patients separately from the hospital billing system.

Required
(a) Calculate the budgeted (estimated) indirect cost rate for the operating theatre.
(b) Calculate the total costs of Schuller's four-hour surgery.

11.25 ★ ★   **LO3, 5**

Richards Manufacturing estimates the following activity for the coming year.
• Expected production 20 000 units
• Expected direct labour hours 20 000 hours
• Expected manufacturing overhead $200 000.

Manufacturing overhead is allocated on the basis of direct labour hours. At the end of the financial period, the following information is collected.
• Direct labour hours 18 000 hours
• Manufacturing overhead $240 000.

Direct labour costs were $60 per hour and there was no direct labour cost variance.

Required
(a) Calculate the predetermined manufacturing overhead rate at the beginning of the year.
(b) Calculate the actual manufacturing overhead rate for the year.

(c) Calculate an inventoriable product cost based on:
  (i) budgeted costs
  (ii) actual costs.

11.26 ★ ★ ★   **LO6**

Winton Produce package and distribute three grades of animal feed. The material cost per tonne and estimated annual sales for each of the products are as follows.

Product	Material cost	Estimated sales
Super Premium	$16.00	2 000 tonnes
Premium	$12.00	3 000 tonnes
Economy	$10.00	5 000 tonnes

The indirect cost of operating the machinery used to package all three products is $40 000 per year. In the past, prices have been set by allocating the indirect costs to products on the basis of estimated sales in tonnes. The resulting total costs (material costs plus allocated fixed overhead) are then marked up by 100 per cent.

Required

(a) Calculate the price per tonne for each grade of feed using the method described for setting prices.

(b) Does the price in (a) take into account how much customers are willing to pay for the product? Explain.

11.27 ★ ★ ★   **LO3, 4**

Just Windows manufactures two product ranges: the standard range and the special range. During July, 300 standard windows and 50 special windows were manufactured and indirect production costs of $73 000 were incurred. An analysis of indirect costs revealed the following activities.

Activity	Cost driver	Total cost
Materials handling	Number of requisitions	$25 000
Machine set-ups	Number of set-ups	27 000
Quality inspections	Number of inspections	21 000
Total		**$73 000**

The cost driver volume for each product was as follows.

Cost driver	Special	Standard	Total
Number of requisitions	400	600	1 000
Number of set-ups	150	300	450
Number of inspections	200	400	600

Required

(a) Draw a diagram showing the structure of the costing system used by Just Windows.

(b) Calculate the indirect activity cost rate for each activity.

(c) Allocate the indirect manufacturing overhead costs for July to the products using the activity cost rates calculated in (b).

(d) Write a memo to the managing director of Just Windows explaining the benefits of activity-based costing.

PROBLEMS

★ BASIC ︱★ ★ MODERATE ︱★ ★ ★ CHALLENGING

11.28 Market-based pricing and customer preferences ★   **LO6**

Transrapid is a magnetically levitated train that connects Shanghai to its Pudong International Airport at a speed of 268 miles per hour. Engineers developed a system with trains departing every 15 to 20 minutes. Suppose Transrapid asked you to research customer preferences and recommend a pricing policy. It costs considerably more to have trains depart as frequently as 15 to 20 minutes apart, so a cost-based pricing schedule will result in ticket prices that are considerably higher than alternative modes of transportation.

Required

(a) In addition to customer preferences, what information would you gather before recommending a pricing policy? Explain why each item you list is relevant.

(b) Explain why it is important to understand customer preferences before building the system.

(c) Is the need to consider customer preferences different for this organisation than for another type of organisation? Why or why not?

11.29 Product pricing decisions and profitability ★   **LO5, 6**

Aluminium Industries manufactures two products: Delta and Gamma. Both products are produced on the same assembly lines and packaged with 20 units of product per package. The predicted sales are 320 000 packs of Delta and 400 000 packs of Gamma. The budgeted costs for the coming year are as follows.

	Variable cost	Fixed cost
Materials	$320 000	$640 000
Other	$480 000	$1 280 000

Each product uses 50 per cent of the variable material costs. The other costs are allocated as follows: variable costs based on machine time (Delta 160 000 hours and Gamma 80 000 hours) and fixed costs allocated evenly to both products. The management of Aluminium Industries desire an annual profit of $160 000 per product.

Required

(a) Calculate the total cost for each product.

(b) What price should be charged for each product?

11.30 Contrasting use of an activity cost driver with a volume-based cost driver ★ ★   **LO1, 3, 4**

Regional Animal Services is located in rural Queensland and treats farm animals and domestic pets. Providing veterinary care to farm animals requires travel to the individual farms in the area, while veterinary care to domestic pets is usually conducted in the surgery located in the town. One of the partners, Dr Diane Marshall, recently attended a small-business management course in Brisbane. She was particularly interested in the discussion of activity-based analysis and how this technique can better identify the costs of providing different services. Her business partner, Dr Jack Russell, likes to keep the accounting records simple and would prefer to maintain the current system of allocating indirect costs based on professional labour hours. However, the partners have reached an agreement to undertake a comparison of the current indirect cost allocation and the proposed activity cost focus. The following information is collected.

Activity cost pool	Cost driver	Estimated cost	Total expected use of cost driver	Use of cost driver* Farm animals	Use of cost driver* Domestic pets
Medication	Prescriptions	$128 000	10 000	4 600	5 400
Surgery	Operations	130 000	3 600	1 400	2 200
Travel	Kilometres	56 000	58 000	53 000	5 000
Consultations	Appointments	66 000	8 000	2 200	5 800
Administration	Professional hours	60 000	12 000	5 000	7 000
Kennel services#		80 000			
		$520 000			

* Expressed in units of measure of the driver.
# Kennel services will now be directly traced, as records will be kept of pets using this practice.

Direct costs are $300 000 for farm animals and $200 000 (prior to inclusion of kennel services) for domestic pets.

Required

(a) Identify the cost objects for the analysis.

(b) Calculate the indirect cost allocations for farm animals and domestic pets using existing methods.

(c) Determine the activity cost rates for each activity.

(d) Assign the activity cost to farm animals and domestic pets using the activity rates calculated in (c).

(e) Calculate the full (total) cost for both farm animals and domestic pets under both the traditional approach and the activity approach. (*Hint:* Include kennel services as a direct cost under the activity approach.)

(f) Compare the results in (e) — can you explain any differences?

(g) What recommendations would you make to the partners in relation to the appropriate costing system for the service?

For ease of calculation and to reduce errors, undertake parts (b) to (e) using an electronic spreadsheet program.

11.31 Profit effect of price change ★ ★   **LO6**

The accountants at French Scents decide to increase the price of a scent called Summer by 10 per cent, from $6 per bottle to $6.60. The accountants for French Scents expect the 10 per cent price increase to reduce unit sales by 20 per cent. Current sales are 200 000 bottles and total variable costs are $800 000.

Required

(a) Identify both cost-based and market-based reasons why the accountants decided to raise the price of Summer.

(b) How certain can the accountants be that volume will decline by 20 per cent if the selling price increases to $6.60? What effect does this uncertainty have on the accountants' decision to increase the selling price?

11.32 Customer profitability analysis ★ ★   **LO3, 4**

The Top Taste Cheesecake Company supplies cheesecakes to three large supermarket chains throughout Australia. Management have become concerned about the rising costs associated with the processing and dispatch of orders. An activity analysis of the indirect costs identifies the following customer-related costs.

Activity cost pool	Cost driver	Estimated indirect costs	Total expected use of cost driver*	Use of cost driver Supermarket customer 1	2	3
Orders processing	Number of orders	$100 000	450	300	100	50
Returns processing	Number of returns	$25 000	100	50	25	25
Delivery	Number of deliveries	$50 000	700	400	200	100
Rush orders	Number of rush orders	$35 000	50	10	20	20
Sales visits	Number of visits	$10 000	100	50	25	25

*Expressed in units of measure of the driver.

Sales are marked up 50 per cent on cost.

Required

(a) Draw a diagram showing the structure of the proposed costing system.

(b) Calculate the gross profit for each customer. The sales for each supermarket customer are as follows: Customer 1 — $450 000; Customer 2 — $225 000; Customer 3 — $325 000.

(c) Calculate the activity cost rate for each activity.

(d) Assign the activity costs to each of the three customers.

(e) Calculate the total (full) cost for each customer and the contribution of each to profit.

(f) Discuss the difference between the analyses in (b) and (e).

(g) Advise the management of the Top Taste Cheesecake Company as to whether any changes should be made in its relationships with customers.

11.33 Cost system design — activity analysis ★ ★ ★   **LO1, 2, 3, 4**

Suppose that Willow Daycare provides two different services — full-time childcare for preschoolers and after-school care for older children. The director would like to estimate an annual cost per child in each of the daycare programs, ignoring any facility-sustaining costs. She is considering expanding the services and wants to know whether full-time or after-school care is more profitable.

The following activities and annual costs apply to the daycare centre. Salaries and wages are $200 000. Full-time children arrive between 8 am and 9 am. Older children arrive about 3 pm. All of the children leave by 6 pm. Employees estimate that they spend about 20 per cent of their time on meal-related activities, 20 per cent supervising naps or recreation, 10 per cent on greeting and sending children home, and the rest of the time presenting educational experiences to the children. Meals and snacks cost about $40 000. Preschoolers receive two snacks and one meal per day, and the older children receive one snack per day. On average, snacks and meals do not differ in cost. Supplies cost $20 000 for the full-time childcare program and $16 000 for the after-school program. Currently, 30 children participate in full-time care and 10 children in after-school care. Because Willow Daycare maintains a waiting list for openings in its programs, the number of children in each program remains steady. The centre is open 192 days per year.

Required

(a) Identify the cost objects of interest and then choose a set of activities and cost drivers for Willow Daycare's activity-based costing system. Explain your choices.

(b) Using the activities you chose in (a), estimate the annual cost per child in each program.

(c) Do uncertainties exist about the proportion of salaries and wages that should be allocated to full-time care versus after-school care? Why or why not?

11.34 Costing in a service firm ★ ★ ★   **LO3, 4**

Zigbee & Associates is a local legal entity employing six solicitors, four paralegals and six administrative staff. The entity has a costing system that assigns costs to clients. There are two departments — legal support and commercial. The entity uses a different indirect cost rate for each department. The following information is taken from the budget for the coming year.

	Legal support department	Commercial department
Planned solicitor hours	7 000	22 400
Planned paralegal hours		12 000
Number of clients	600	2 300
Legal supplies	$34 800	$67 200
Salaries — solicitors and paralegals	$348 000	$1 640 000
Indirect costs	$232 000	$950 000

The indirect costs are allocated to the clients as follows.

- Departmental indirect costs are the numbers of solicitor and paralegal hours.
- Legal supplies are charged on a per-client basis.

The entity uses a cost-plus pricing policy with a 20 per cent mark-up.

Client Case Number FR110 has been completed and is ready for the invoice to be sent to the client. The following costs and times were recorded for the client.

- Solicitor hours — legal support 90 hours
- Solicitor hours — commercial 330 hours
- Direct cost of solicitors — $30 060.

Required

(a) Identify the type of costs included in legal supplies and department indirect costs.

(b) Calculate the indirect cost rate for each department.

(c) Calculate the indirect cost rate for legal supplies.

(d) Determine the total cost for Client Case Number FR110.

(e) Calculate the amount that the client should be invoiced for the work undertaken.

11.35 Service department cost allocation in service industries ★ ★ ★   **LO1, 3, 4, 5**

Overseas Adventures is a travel agency with 20 offices located throughout Australia. Caleb Thomas, the managing director, recently attended an accounting seminar on cost allocation. During a coffee break, he was overheard making the following comment to Veronica Wells, a local manufacturer: 'Allocating service department costs to income-producing departments is necessary only in service organisations. Your company would be wasting a lot of resources to conduct such an exercise.'

Required

As a management accountant for the manufacturing entity, how would you respond to the comment made by Caleb Thomas?

11.36 Contrast cost allocation using a volume-based cost driver and activity-based cost drivers ★ ★ ★

LO1, 2, 3, 4

Willow and Glen is a public accounting entity that offers auditing and tax services to local small entities. The partners are in dispute over who contributes the greater amount to the entity's profit. The area of contention is the allocation of indirect costs. The tax partners argue for allocating indirect costs on the basis of 40 per cent of professional labour dollars, while the audit partners argue for implementing an activity-based approach to indirect cost allocation. The partners agree to use next year's budgeted data for the purposes of analysis and comparison. Budgeted direct costs are $1 500 000 for audit services and $1 000 000 for tax services. The entity's accountant has provided the following indirect cost analysis.

Activity cost pool	Cost driver	Estimated indirect cost	Expected use of cost driver	Expected use of cost drivers per service	
				Audit	Tax
Employee training	Professional labour dollars	$209 000	$1 900 000	$1 000 000	$900 000
Administrative services	Number of reports/ forms	$76 200	2 500	600	1 900
Computing	Number of minutes	$204 000	60 000	25 000	35 000
Rental	Number of employees	$142 500	38	20	18
Travel	Travel requisitions	$128 300	Directly traced	$86 800	$41 500

The analysis has revealed that travel costs can now be considered a direct cost to the audit and tax services. Travel requisitions are to be used as the source documentation to trace these costs. The only other direct costs are professional labour costs, as shown in the table.

Required

(a) Draw a diagram contrasting the current and proposed structures of the costing system.

(b) Using the current approach to cost allocation, compute the total indirect cost assigned to each service.

(c) Using the activity approach to cost allocation, compute the activity cost rates.

(d) Assign the indirect costs to each service, using the activity cost rates calculated in (c) above.

(e) Calculate the total cost for both audit and tax services under each cost allocation method.

(f) Write a report to the partners advising which cost allocation method you would recommend.

11.37 Selection of a costing system to support financial reporting and decision making ★ ★ ★ LO3, 5

Talk2Me Communications manufactures headsets to make phones hands free. In 2020, the entity produced 30 000 units, of which 24 000 were sold. The following costs were recorded for 2020.

Direct material	$1 200 000
Direct labour	600 000
Manufacturing overhead	1 500 000
Selling expenses	150 000
Administrative expenses	240 000

Determination of the inventoriable product cost for Talk2Me Communications is relatively simple, as the entity produces only one product.

Required

(a) Identify the most appropriate costing system to value products for Talk2Me Communications' financial statements.

(b) Calculate the inventoriable product cost.

(c) Comment on the usefulness of the inventoriable product cost for decision making.

DECISION-MAKING ACTIVITIES

11.38 Blue Hills Hospital is a major hospital that serves 11 small rural communities within a 40-kilometre radius. The hospital offers all the medical and surgical services of a typical small hospital. It has a staff of 12 full-time doctors and 16 part-time visiting specialists. Blue Hills Hospital has a payroll of 120 employees consisting of technicians, nurses, therapists, managers, directors, administrators, dieticians, personal assistants, IT staff and cleaners.

Required

(a) Using your (limited, moderate or in-depth) knowledge of a hospital's operations, identify as many activities as you can.

(b) For each of the activities listed in (a), identify a cost driver that would serve as a valid measure of the resources consumed by the activity.

11.39 In recent years, slow response times and frequent repairs have plagued Jetson Engineering's computer system. The cause was a substantial increase in computer-aided design work that pushed the system beyond its intended capacity. Roberta Wilson, the production manager, decided that a new computer should be acquired to absorb some of the additional work. Surprisingly, six months after installing the new computer, she noticed that many of the engineers were continuing to use the old computer system, even though the new system had excess capacity and several features that simplified programming.

Roberta discussed the situation with the supervisors of the entity's six design teams. They explained that the finance director's office allocated the cost of each computer to their work based on the number of hours they used the computer. One responded, 'Look, the old computer didn't cost much and it's highly utilised — even the accounting department uses that machine. When the cost per hour of use is calculated, it's very low. The new machine, on the other hand, costs a lot of money and in the first couple of months we didn't use it much because it takes time to learn a new system. I was shocked when I saw how high my charges were for using the new machine. Because the cost is high and the use is low, the cost per hour charged to my work was incredible. I'll tell you something: next month we'll probably use the new computer even less. Our job performance doesn't look very good when our jobs cost a fortune to complete because of huge allocations of computer cost.

'What a mess,' Roberta sighed. 'Even though the new computer is bought and paid for and has plenty of capacity, the engineers aren't using it. Don't they realise most of the computer costs are fixed costs? Using the new computer for 200 hours a month doesn't really cost the company much more than using it for 20 hours a month.'

Required

Recommend a change in the allocation system at Jetson Engineering that will change the behaviour of the design teams.

11.40 Watson University offers an MBA program that is widely respected around the world. The tuition fee for the program always covered the costs of the program until a recent recession increased the sensitivity of students to the cost of tuition. The business school managers decide to freeze the tuition fee for the next few years. The director of the MBA program asked a cost accounting class to act as consultants for the program and make recommendations on possible ways to reduce costs or to increase the tuition fee. You are part of the student team assigned to this project.

Required

(a) Describe the steps you would take as you analysed the program, including the types of information you would like to use.

(b) Explain how you would decide on an appropriate level of tuition fee.

11.41 Your friends have decided to organise a number of functions to raise funds for a trek to a Himalayan base camp. The functions planned are: a cinema night; a disco at the local hotel; and a trivia night. As you have some knowledge of accounting, they have asked you to help them work out the financials. They are unsure about what costs should be considered in relation to the functions and what price they should charge for the tickets.

ACKNOWLEDGEMENTS

Photo: © blue jean images RF / Getty Images

Photo: © PeopleImages / Getty Images

Capital investment

Chapter preview

In this chapter, we examine how entities make decisions to invest in new assets or new projects. An Australian listed company such as JB Hi-Fi Ltd regularly makes decisions about investments in new product markets, new concept stores and new retailing outlets in shopping centres. The Qantas Group makes decisions about investments in aircraft for its passengers and air cargo operations by asking questions such as, 'Should we lease an aircraft or buy an aircraft? What size aircraft do we require for our Jetstar and Qantas passengers?' BMW Group (the German motorcycle and vehicle manufacturer) makes decisions about which models of vehicles and motorcycles to produce each year and the types of investors to target. Managers of small stores such as convenience stores face decisions such as the types of newspapers, magazines and confectionary to sell, and whether to update the store with new fixtures and fittings. The investments may be small or large, but the principles that underlie the decisions about whether to make the investments are the same, no matter the absolute size of the investment or the type of entity investing.

Three principal methods are discussed in this chapter to evaluate whether an investment in assets or projects should proceed. They are the accounting rate of return (ARR), the payback period (PP) and the net present value (NPV). The NPV method is a discounted cash-flow technique which takes into consideration the time value of money. Specifically, it recognises that $1 received in the future is worth less than $1 received now. Finally, there are important issues to be considered when calculating and applying numerical decision-support tools. Recently we have seen the emergence of Big Data and business analytics (as discussed in the first chapter), which has the potential to impact on our investment decision making. In the last section of the chapter, we discuss some of these issues.

12.1 The nature and scope of investment decisions

LEARNING OBJECTIVE 12.1 Explain the nature and scope of investment decisions.

Investment decisions are made by managers in all sorts of entities, large and small. Some of the most common features of investments are that they:

- often involve large amounts of resources in relation to entity asset bases or turnover
- involve risk and uncertainty that stem from the inability to cost projects accurately or to foresee operating revenues and costs
- often span long periods of time
- normally require a relatively large initial cash outlay and returns are received over a long period into the future
- are often difficult to reverse without the loss of substantial funds
- must be made on the basis of best available data, and the values factored into the initial decision may not prove to be correct due to the effects of unexpected external influences.

Let us look at each of these features in turn. Investments in projects and in property, plant and equipment (PPE) often involve large amounts of resources (staff time and funds) in relation to some other measure of the entity's size. JB Hi-Fi Ltd, for example, on its 2018 statement of financial position had more than $198 million of plant and equipment and the Qantas Group had $12.851 billion. The Qantas Group's PPE includes land, aircraft and engines, buildings, aircraft spare parts and leasehold improvements. For both JB Hi-Fi Ltd and the Qantas Group, the amounts of investments involved are very large and need to be made with the help of appropriate decision-support tools.

Investment decisions normally involve risk and uncertainty, with managers expected to also bear the responsibility for 'bad investments'. **Risk** in finance is defined as the measurable variation in outcomes. **Uncertainty**, on the other hand, is the unmeasurable variation in outcomes. Risk can be measured with some degree of confidence when the same decision is taken many times and the varying outcomes can be analysed, so that a measure of the variation can be made. Thereafter, the decision maker will have a better understanding of how expected outcomes may vary. BMW Group spends large amounts of funds on research and development (R&D) activities. The company employs approximately 14 047 employees in its global research and innovation network situated in 16 locations across five countries. The company expenses research costs as they are incurred. Costs of development projects are recognised as intangible assets when it is foreseeable that a product will generate future economic benefits. In 2017, R&D costs expensed were €6.1 billion, which was an increase of 18.3 per cent compared to those in 2016. BMW Group undertakes this process to help deliver the best product possible and keep up to date with innovative technologies. This strategy obviously involves risks, as there is no guarantee that saleable and successful products will be developed. Nor can BMW Group be certain about the market's desire for any new products.

Investments normally span long periods of time and require cash outlays initially, with cash inflows being received over a long future period. Consider, for example, airlines such as the Qantas Group or Virgin Australia and the large sums of cash outlaid on new aircraft. Airlines require a number of different types of aircraft (e.g. Airbus A380 and A330, and Boeing 787 Dreamliner) and they make a choice as to whether to buy or lease the aircraft. New aircraft require millions of dollars to be spent upfront or as progress payments before delivery. Returns come in from the sales of flights to passengers and freight income over several years. In 2018, the Qantas Group made $12.478 billion in capital expenditure commitments on new aircraft and building works for its passengers and also its air cargo operations. In 2017, its commitment was $11.385 billion. Qantas has certain rights within its aircraft purchase contracts which can reduce or defer the above capital expenditure.

What happens if, partway through the development of a project, the investors find circumstances have changed and they really would prefer not to be involved? Such unexpected changes might involve major changes in consumer or political values, changes in legislation governing an industry, substantial increases in infrastructure development costs or perhaps major reductions in the supply of raw materials. Normally, if projects are suspended before coming to fruition, investors stand to lose most, if not all, of their invested funds. This risk should impose great pressure on analysts and investors when they are investigating the worth of potential investment projects. There are many examples available of these types of losses. For example, making movies is a very expensive business, with a single high-budget film costing $100–200 million or more. Any expenditure incurred on a film project before the full financing is arranged will be lost if filming does not proceed. These preliminary expenses are 'sunk costs', which should not be considered in any future consideration of the same or a related project.

Many investment decisions are made before all the relevant expenditure can be properly costed because the cost information is just not available.

The process of decision making

Just as funds are normally a scarce and valuable resource in our personal lives, so too they are for business entities. Hence, entities that are successful in the long term make investment decisions very carefully and follow established decision-support procedures. At any one time, most entities will have many projects or investments available to them, and the decision as to which projects to invest in is based on assessment of the attractiveness of the returns relative to the risk.

The steps involved in making an investment decision are as follows.
1. Identify all the investment alternatives available at the time.
2. Select a decision-support tool and set the decision rule.
3. Collect the data necessary to make the decision.
4. Analyse the data.
5. Interpret the results in relation to the decision rule.
6. Make the decision.

After making the investment decision, the next step is often to arrange finance (the financing decision) and start the planning and physical implementation of the project or investment.

The investment alternatives available to any entity at any one time normally fit into one of three categories:
• new investments to increase revenue
• new technology to decrease costs
• replacement of old assets as they wear out.

One example of a new investment to increase revenue is JB Hi-Fi Ltd's investment in new stores. As at 30 June 2018, JB Hi-Fi Ltd operated 208 JB Hi-Fi/JB Hi-Fi Home stores across Australia and New Zealand, and 103 The Good Guys stores in Australia, along with online operations and JB Hi-Fi Solutions. In the 2018 financial year, eight new JB Hi-Fi and two The Good Guys stores opened and one of each closed. In 2019, the entity expects to open seven new stores. For the Qantas Group, a large proportion of its capital investment projects relate to the purchase or lease of new aircraft to replace old worn-out aircraft (e.g. replacing its Boeing 747s with Boeing 787 Dreamliners). For small entities, investment decisions can relate to moving to larger premises, acquiring a new machine or investing in a vehicle fleet.

Almost all entities make investments to decrease costs in today's environment of rapidly developing technology. In recent years we have seen the emergence of Big Data and software tools in business analytics, and these tools assist in the decision-making process. More and more companies are investing in expensive software and hardware; more efficient and more sustainable plant and machinery; cloud computing, websites and of course social media. All of these investments are made with the intent of making processes more sustainable, competitive, effective and efficient.

Finally, entities make investments to replace assets that have come to, or are nearing, the end of their effective lives. Examples are the replacement of computers, trucks, aircraft, passenger vehicles, trains, ships, factory machinery, tractors and farm machinery, and furniture and fittings. It is often the case that the new assets incorporate new technology, but this is a bonus when the primary motivation is merely to replace older worn-out assets.

The following sections of this chapter deal with the steps in the decision-making process. Thus, the next four major sections discuss the decision-support tools available, their data requirements and their decision rules. The final section examines some of the practical issues in applying these decision-support tools.

Data and information for an investment decision are given in illustrative example 12.1.

ILLUSTRATIVE EXAMPLE 12.1

The material for a decision

Coconut Plantations Pty Ltd manufactures sustainable coconut-based products. Jo Geter, the manager, has been successful in securing long-term contracts to supply a variety of retailers in Australia with quantities of soaps, candles and detergents packaged under the Habitat Eco Friendly label. To ensure an adequate supply of coconut oil, the major raw material for each product, Jo has worked out a remuneration deal for potential suppliers. Each manufacturer is offered a four-year contract to supply certified organic coconut oil. The oil is purchased at $200 per 100 litres as a standard price. Coconut oil that fails the certification process will be accepted at a 20 per cent discount.

Under these arrangements, manufacturers can expect to earn the following net cash returns. The net cash inflows shown in table 12.1 are net of raw materials, other ingredients, processing costs, manufacturing overhead and delivery. The manufacturer's own labour costs are excluded.

TABLE 12.1	Expected net cash inflows ($000)
Year	Expected net cash flows ($000)
1	30
2	60
3	50
4	40

Specialised equipment necessary to manufacture certified organic coconut oil is estimated to cost $120 000. The equipment can be sold for $60 000 on the second-hand market after four years of usage. Each supplying manufacturer will use the straight-line method of depreciation. With this information, we now have enough data to make an investment decision. Throughout the chapter, we will use these data to arrive at an investment decision for the suppliers of coconut oil using the various techniques as they are explained.

VALUE TO BUSINESS

- Investment decisions are made by managers in all sorts of entities.
- Some of the most common features of investments are that:
  - they often involve large amounts of resources in relation to entity asset bases or turnover
  - they involve risk and uncertainty
  - they often span long periods of time
  - normally, a relatively large cash outlay is required initially and returns are received over a long period into the future
  - it is often difficult to reverse investment decisions without the loss of substantial funds, so reasoned initial judgements are critical.

12.2 Accounting rate of return

LEARNING OBJECTIVE 12.2 Describe and apply the concept of the accounting rate of return (ARR).

The **accounting rate of return (ARR)** is a simple measure, which has immediate appeal to accountants and managers who are accustomed to dealing with profit figures and asset values. This measure expresses the average profit over the period of the investment as a percentage of the average investment. Thus, it uses the same methodology as the familiar return on assets (ROA) measure, which was discussed in the chapter on analysis and interpretation of financial statements. The ROA is, of course, a historical measure, while the ARR involves projected future values.

The ARR is calculated as:

$$ARR = \frac{\text{Average profit}}{\text{Average investment}}$$

Illustrative example 12.2 demonstrates the application of the ARR equation to Coconut Plantations Pty Ltd.

ILLUSTRATIVE EXAMPLE 12.2

Calculating the ARR

The cash flows (net of cash expenses) given in the Coconut Plantations information in illustrative example 12.1 are not profits for each year. The cost of using up the value of the equipment, or depreciation, must be considered. The value of equipment used up is $60 000 ($120 000 − $60 000). Depreciation of $60 000 for the four-year period, or $15 000 per year, must be deducted to arrive at profits before tax. The ARR for the Coconut Plantations contract is as follows. (The figures on the top line are in thousands, as are the figures on the bottom line, so we can ignore the thousands in our calculations.) The average investment in the equipment is the average of the values initially and at the end of four years; that is, the average of $120 000 and $60 000.

$$ARR = \frac{\text{Average profit}}{\text{Average investment}} = \frac{\dfrac{(\$30 + \$60 + \$50 + \$40 - \$60)}{4}}{\dfrac{(\$120 + \$60)}{2}} = \frac{30}{90} = 33.3\%$$

Having calculated this rate of return, manufacturers may think the contract offered by Coconut Plantations looks like a pretty good deal. What also must be considered in this case is the opportunity cost of the manufacturers' labour. **Opportunity cost** is the cost of forgoing benefits that otherwise would be available had the manufacturer not spent time manufacturing the coconut oil. If the manufacturer could earn $20 000, on average, every year for manufacturing other products in this time or working for other people, then the average profit would fall to $10 000 and the ARR to 11.1 per cent.

Decision rule for ARR

The decision rule associated with the ARR varies among entities. Most entities accept the investment with the highest ARR at the time; they set a minimum level (their required rate of return (RRR)), below which they will not consider investing. How the RRR is set varies. Some entities base the level on their own past performance, others look to industry averages and still others compare the estimated ARR with currently available yields or returns from other investments outside their industries.

Advantages and disadvantages of ARR

The advantages of the ARR measure are that it is:
- simple to calculate
- easy to understand
- consistent with the ROA measure, which entities often try to increase in an attempt to maximise owners' wealth.

The disadvantages of the ARR method are that:
- it ignores the **time value of money** and the timing of profits

---

- it ignores the importance of cash as the ultimate resource that entities cannot survive without (entities must have sufficient cash to meet their obligations on time, no matter how asset-rich they are)
- profits and costs may be measured in different ways.

Overall, the ARR is considered by most managers to be too simplistic a measure to be appropriate by itself as a decision-support tool for the application of scarce investment funds. The fact that the timing of cash flows and subsequent profits is ignored is seen as a major deficiency. The method, for example, cannot differentiate between two equally profitable projects but with unequal timing of the profits. (In reality, a project with cash surpluses early in its life is preferable to another project with cash receipts received later in its life.)

12.3 Payback period

LEARNING OBJECTIVE 12.3 Explain and use the payback period (PP) method.

Entities invest in order to make profits. Investments normally require the outlay of cash and, as noted above, cash is important to entities that want to survive. Thus, the time it takes to recoup cash expended on investment is important. If two investments were potentially equally profitable, most entities would prefer the investment where the outlaid cash was recouped earlier.

The **payback period (PP)** is the period of time necessary to recoup the initial outlay with net cash inflows. Hence, the expected net cash inflows each year are added until the sum is equal to or greater than the initial outlay. The number of years of cash surpluses necessary to be earned to equal the initial investment is the PP. This is demonstrated in illustrative example 12.3.

ILLUSTRATIVE EXAMPLE 12.3

Calculating the payback period

For the Coconut Plantations proposal, we know the initial investment in equipment is $120 000. By the end of year 1, $30 000 net cash flows have been received and, by the end of year 2, a further $60 000 in net cash flows should have been received, making $90 000 in total, with a further $30 000 cash necessary to repay the initial investment. Given that we need $30 000 of the $50 000 in year 3 to pay back the initial investment exactly, we can say the payback period is about 2.6 years (see table 12.2). (Assuming funds are received consistently at about $1000 surplus each week, it will take 30 weeks or 0.6 years to earn the required $30 000 surplus.)

TABLE 12.2   Payback decision rate

Year	Net cash flow $	Cumulative net cash flow ($)	
0	(120 000)	(120 000)	
1	30 000	(90 000)	
2	60 000	(30 000)	Payback occurs between years 2 and 3
3	50 000	20 000	
4	100 000	120 000	

Decision rule for payback period

The decision rule with PP varies among entities, but most investors have maximum periods beyond which they would not invest. Just as with ARR standards, the maximum periods might be based on past performance in that individual entity or on industry averages. The maximum periods generally vary quite markedly. For example, the PP for a major mining venture, like those undertaken by BHP Group and Bass Strait Oil Company, is much longer than the PP built into the pricing and investment decisions related to a newly developed herbicide or pharmaceutical ingredient. Similarly, the purchase of an Airbus A380 would take several years (and many flights) to pay back its initial purchase price. However, one thing is certain: the longer the PP, the greater the risk, because there is a far greater chance that some of the assumptions on which the investment decision was based will change.

Advantages and disadvantages of PP

The advantages of the PP measure are that it:
- is simple to calculate
- is easy to understand
- provides a crude measure of incorporating awareness of risk into the decision, as projects with relatively high early cash surpluses will have smaller PPs.
  The disadvantages of the PP method are that it:
- ignores the time value of money, as this method treats all cash inflows equally
- also ignores all cash inflows after payback has occurred, so that inherently more profitable investments may be rejected in favour of less profitable short-term investments given that the time horizon of analysis is restricted to the period up until the initial investment is recouped. For example, with the Coconut Plantations contract no consideration is given to cash flows beyond the PP.

Similarly to the ARR, the PP is considered to be too simplistic a measure to be used by itself as a decision-support tool. Again, it does not recognise that funds received early in the life of a project are worth more than funds received later.

VALUE TO BUSINESS

- The accounting rate of return (ARR) is based on accounting profits and the payback period (PP) is based on cash flows.
- The ARR has immediate appeal to accountants and managers, who are accustomed to dealing with profit figures and asset values. This measure expresses the average profit over the period of the investment as a percentage of the average investment.
- The PP is the period of time necessary to recoup the initial outlay with net cash inflows. If two investments are equally profitable, most entities would prefer the investment where the outlaid cash was recouped earlier.
- Both measures are simplistic and may be useful for quick analyses to sort out projects for further analysis.

12.4 Net present value

LEARNING OBJECTIVE 12.4 Discuss and calculate net present values (NPV) and apply the decision rule.

Time value of money

As discussed in the previous section, ignoring the time value of money is a major defect of both the ARR and PP tools. Discounted cash-flow techniques overcome this problem by specifically recognising that $1 received in the future is worth less than $1 received now. Suppose Andrew, a friend, borrows $1000 from you and your expectation is that he will repay you in a day or so. After you ask him for the money several times, Andrew promises to repay the funds at the end of one year. If he does so, is the $1000 received then worth the same amount to you as it is now? The answer is 'no'. This is because the $1000 will buy less in a year's time because of the change in the level of prices (inflation, which is currently about 3 per cent per year). In addition, you could invest your $1000 received today elsewhere and earn a return without taking on much risk, making the future value of the $1000 higher.

Let us say you invested at 4 per cent, so the return of $40 on your $1000 would cover the effect of inflation if it was about 3 per cent for the year, and would mean you received a net increase in funds as well. The following is a timeline showing this situation.

$1000 (present value)	$1040 (future value)
T_0 = now	T_1 = 1 year's time

The formula you used to do this calculation in your head is:

$$FV = PV(1 + i)^n$$

---

where FV = future value

PV = present value

i = interest rate/period

n = number of periods.

For example, $FV = 1040 = 1000 (1 + 0.04)^1$.

We could look at this situation from the other end — in one year's time. If Andrew pays back the $1000 then, what is the dollar value of that $1000 then given that you could have earned 4 per cent return for the year? The answer is $961.54, which is the present value (PV) of $1000 in one year's time given a discount rate of 4 per cent. The $961.54 is called a discounted cash flow. The discounted cash flow or PV is calculated by dividing the future sum by a discount factor:

$$PV = \frac{FV}{(1 + i)^n}$$

$$PV = \frac{1000}{1.04} = 961.54$$

Here, that factor is 1.04 (i.e. 1 + the relevant interest rate for the year). You can check to find if $961.54 is correct by multiplying it by 1.04 to see if you get $1000.

$961.54 (present value)	$1000 (future value)
T_0 = now	T_1 = 1 year's time

This shows that receiving $1000 in one year is the equivalent of receiving $961.54 today, assuming a rate of return of 4 per cent.

The reason for calculating the PVs of all the cash flows is so that the initial investment may be matched with the expected inflows in terms of the same units of money with the same purchasing power. A dollar that is received now has the same purchasing power as a dollar paid out now. In addition, the cash flows are adjusted for risk and the opportunity cost of capital. The cash flows used in the analysis are the net cash inflows (either positive or negative) for each period. This means that the final net cash inflow also includes any salvage value that might be gained by selling the infrastructure or materials that are left over at the completion of a project. Normally, the initial investment is taken to occur now and its value is thus a PV, unless it is a major project where development spans more than one period.

The investment decision technique involving discounting cash flows (and accounting for the time value of money) that we discuss in this chapter is the **net present value (NPV)** method. The PV of a project is the sum of the PVs of all the expected cash flows from all the individual periods. These PVs of the cash flows are calculated just as we saw above. Then, the NPV measure compares the sum of the PVs of all of the expected cash inflows from the project with the sum of the PVs of the expected cash outflows. The NPV is the PV of the net cash flows. The **discount rate** is the interest rate at which a future cash flow is converted to a PV:

$$PV = CF_1/(1 + r) + CF_2/(1 + r)^2 + CF_3/(1 + r)^3 + \ldots + CF_n/(1 + r)^n$$

$$NPV = CF_1/(1 + r) + CF_2/(1 + r)^2 + CF_3/(1 + r)^3 + \ldots + CF_n/(1 + r)^n - INV$$

where CF = the net cash flow at the end of period n

r = the selected discount rate per period

n = the number of periods

INV = the initial investment.

Decision rule for NPV

The cash flows are assumed, for simplicity, to have occurred at the end of each relevant period. This point is discussed in more detail later in this section.

The investment decision rule based on this type of financial analysis is to invest in projects (assets) if the NPV is positive (i.e. PV net CF > initial investment). This is because the positive value indicates a project that is potentially able to yield a higher return than the opportunity cost of the funds (whose value is incorporated in the discount rate). Calculating the NPV is demonstrated in illustrative example 12.4.

Calculating net present value

Let us now return to the Coconut Plantations example and assume that potential manufacturers require a 10 per cent investment return. Denominated in thousands of dollars, the NPV is calculated as follows.

$$NPV = CF_1/(1 + r) + CF_2/(1 + r)^2 + CF_3/(1 + r)^3 + \ldots + CF_n/(1 + r)^n - INV$$

$$= 30/1.1 + 60/(1.1)^2 + 50/(1.1)^3 + 100/(1.1)^4 - 120$$

$$= 27.27 + 49.58 + 37.57 + 68.30 - 120$$

$$= 62.72$$

Remember, the $100 000 in year 4 is the $40 000 from the sale of coconut oil plus the $60 000 from the sale of the second-hand machinery. The result of $62 720 is positive and indicates that, on this measure, the contract to manufacture coconut oil should be undertaken, as it will enhance the manufacturer's wealth. While a positive value for the NPV indicates that the manufacturer would be better off if it took on this project, a negative value, on the other hand, indicates that the project would not generate sufficient surplus and the manufacturer would not increase its wealth through this project.

To solve the NPV equation, with r valued at 10 per cent so that $(1 + r)$ equals 1.1, a financial calculator can be used in place of the manual steps above. Refer to appendix 12B for the calculator steps.

Discount tables

An alternative to using the formula and calculation method shown in illustrative example 12.4 is to use discount tables. A discount table showing the present value of $1 received in n periods of time is included in appendix 12A at the end of this chapter.

Look at this discount table. For period 1 and a 10 per cent discount rate, the table tells us that the discount factor is 0.909. In our example, $30 000 × 0.909 gives $27 270; and, for period 2 and a 10 per cent discount rate, the table tells us that the discount factor is 0.826. Multiplying $60 000 by 0.826 gives $49 560. The difference between that value and $49 580 is due to rounding to three decimal places.

Determining the discount rate

There are a number of factors that affect the discount rate used in investment decisions, including inflation, risk and the opportunity cost of capital.

1. Inflation

One factor in the determination of r (the discount rate) is inflation. **Inflation** is the increase in the prices of goods and services. The converse is **deflation**, which often coincides with lower levels of demand in an economy, periods of high unemployment and economic depression. It has been seldom seen in the developed economies in the last several decades. Thus, inflation at greater or lesser levels is the norm. What inflation means for investors is that their invested funds lose purchasing power while those funds are being used by the investee. Hence, an investor placing $1000 today in any investment and receiving $1000 back in three years' time will not recover the same amount of purchasing power. For example, if inflation has been on average 3 per cent per annum during those three years, then the investor will receive only $915 ($1000/1.03^3) of purchasing power in today's terms. In reality, interest rates and other returns offered in financial markets have an inflation component already incorporated. Thus, the investor does not really have to worry about this aspect of interest rates and returns. The opportunity return will take care of the inflationary impact.

2. Risk

Investment decisions involve risk. Costs may rise above what was expected, returns may fall short. A further concern is the extra element of risk associated with an individual investment. Many single investments carry more risk than groups of investments, especially if those investments have been put together carefully to manage their risk. Consider for example the Qantas Group, which has a number of business segments (i.e. Jetstar, Qantas, Qantas Freight and Qantas Frequent Flyer). All of these segments earn revenues and incur expenses, control assets and have future obligations. The Qantas Group is managing its risk by offering different products to customers (i.e. passengers) and operating in different segments of the market (e.g. passenger transport, freight and loyalty programs). However, a business focusing on one project carries more risk (e.g. a pharmaceutical company developing a new drug). From an individual investor's perspective, a single investment in one company on the share market is likely to carry more risk than, say, a deposit with a local building society, where an individual's funds would be pooled with other monies and spread among different investments. Investors who take on more risk demand higher returns as compensation for assuming that risk. Thus, more risky investments will have a risk margin added to their opportunity interest rate to arrive at a final higher discount rate which, in turn, lowers the PV.

3. Opportunity cost

Opportunity cost has been discussed in relation to a manufacturer supplying coconut oil to Coconut Plantations. Money also has an opportunity cost. If investors can place their funds in alternative investments (which they can), then directing their funds to a particular investment has an opportunity cost. The opportunity cost is the cost of forgoing the benefit from an alternative investment. If the alternative investment pays 5 per cent per annum, then the opportunity cost in making the given investment is 5 per cent.

Remember, we noted earlier that the cash flows are assumed to have been received and paid at the end of each period. This is a simplifying assumption. In reality, most projects have cash flows received and paid more or less evenly throughout the year. It is possible to incorporate this pattern of cash flows into an analysis by using specially calculated daily discount tables. However, we will not investigate this in this chapter. Just be aware that such a refinement is possible.

Advantages and disadvantages of the NPV method

The advantages of the NPV method are that it takes into account:
- all of the expected cash flows
- the timing of expected cash flows (with cash flows received sooner being more beneficial to the entity)
- cash flows only, so it is not subject to changing accounting rules and standards they way that profit figures are.

In addition, the decision rule is explicit, in that positive NPVs will increase entity value if the data are correct.

The disadvantages of the NPV method are that:
- the method relies on the use of an appropriate discount factor for the circumstances
- the actual return in terms of the percentage of the investment outlay is not revealed
- ranking of projects in terms of highest NPVs may not lead to optimum outcomes when capital is rationed.

The last two disadvantages may need further explanation. Suppose a project's cash returns have been discounted by 10 per cent and the calculated NPV is $23 450. From these data, we do not know if the project can be expected to return 11 per cent, 12 per cent, 13 per cent or 20 per cent. To understand the ranking problem, consider the following data in table 12.3.

TABLE 12.3	Outlays and NPVs for proposed projects	
Project	**Outlay ($A million)**	**NPV ($A million)**
Brisbane	100	8.2
Sydney	80	6.9
Perth	60	4.4
Melbourne	40	3.0
Adelaide	20	1.6

Is Brisbane the best project for the entity to undertake? It does have the highest NPV. However, the answer is 'no'. Supposing an entity has access to $100 million in finance, it could undertake the Brisbane project and earn $8.2 million. Alternatively, it could undertake two projects that together involve an investment not exceeding $100 million. In this case, it could undertake the Brisbane project or both the Sydney and the Adelaide projects, or both the Perth and the Melbourne projects. The NPVs of these three options are $8.2 million, $8.5 million and $7.4 million, respectively. Thus, the best decision for the entity would be to undertake both the Sydney and Adelaide projects, to earn $8.5 million. So the project with the highest NPV may not be the best project when capital is limited. Sometimes entities will invest in a range of different projects with differing NPVs as part of their long-term business strategy.

- A discounted cash-flow measure overcomes the time value of money problem, which is a major defect of both the ARR and PP tools.
- A discounted cash-flow technique specifically recognises that $1 received sometime in the future is worth less than $1 received now.
- The NPV measure compares the sum of the present values (PVs) of all of the expected cash inflows from the project with the PVs of the expected cash outflows. The NPV is the net outcome.

12.5 Practical issues in making decisions

LEARNING OBJECTIVE 12.5 Explain some of the practical issues in making investment decisions.

The tools outlined earlier in this chapter make decision making appear relatively easy. Just crunch the numbers and there is your answer! However, things are seldom as easy as they appear. In practice, the investment decision is not normally just a mechanical calculation. There are many other factors that must be taken into consideration. We have already discussed the impacts of inflation, risk and opportunity cost. In addition, many decisions and judgements must be made about:

- collecting data (including Big Data and business analytics)
- taxation effects
- finance
- human resources
- goodwill and future opportunities
- social responsibility and care of the natural environment.

Collecting data

For firms, collecting data on costs and returns is often not easy. Think back to Coconut Plantations' relatively simple coconut oil equipment investment project. In that case, finding the cost of the equipment was simple. However, some of the periodic outflows — such as equipment maintenance and insurance — are relatively easy to cost, but others are not. The quantity of electricity for running the plant to manufacture the coconut oil, for example, and its total cost are difficult to estimate. There could be unforeseen issues such as poor-quality ingredients that require additional processing to get to the desired end product — certified organic coconut oil.

And what about the returns? In order to estimate the cash inflows each year, the manufacturer needs to think about the cost of the ingredients in the process. Ingredients such as unprocessed coconut will fluctuate in price. So, as you can see from this simple example, collecting data is not as easy as it looks.

Recently, we have seen the emergence of Big Data and business analytics in the business world. As discussed in the first chapter, 'Big data is a term that describes the large volume of data — both structured and unstructured – that inundates a business on a day-to-day basis' (SAS Institute Inc. 2018). These large data sets are readily available through different databases (e.g. the Australian Bureau of Statistics, ASX, ASIC and BOM), and software packages such as Excel and Tableau can merge together and perform some very cool analytics that firms are increasingly relying on for decision making.

Taxation effects

Taxation impacts on investments. Most, if not all, developed countries have some form of income tax and many have a form of capital gains tax. Australia is no exception, with a 30 per cent flat company tax rate (27.5 per cent for SMEs) and marginal taxation rates of up to 45 per cent plus a 2 per cent Medicare levy surcharge for businesspeople and investors operating as individuals and in partnerships. Capital gains are taxed at 30 per cent for companies and, under the simplest current regime, at half marginal rates for individuals and investors operating in partnerships. Thus, the impact of taxation for a simple investment by a company is to reduce net cash annual returns by 30 per cent. Complications are introduced into cash-flow analyses with the effect of taxation benefits that stem from non-cash costs such as depreciation.

Moreover, in Australia the issue of taxation is even more complicated. Australia has the **dividend imputation scheme**, where investors in companies that pay income tax are allowed tax credits for the dividends that they receive out of company profits on which taxation has been paid. This scheme was introduced to reform the system of double taxation that had been in place. The effect of dividend imputation in relation to PV analysis of investments is that taxation is treated differently according to the legal structures of the entities involved. For example, companies fully owned by resident Australian taxpayers should not include income taxation effects in their investment appraisals, while sole traders and partners should.

Finance

Investment appraisals are undertaken on the assumption that finance will be available if the numbers are attractive enough. While this may be true some of the time — even most of the time — it is not true all of the time. Some investments, even though they look good on paper, have trouble attracting venture capital. Look, for example, at how long it took to build the Adelaide to Darwin railway. The first part of the line (Adelaide to Alice Springs) was completed about 100 years ago; the Alice Springs–Darwin part was completed only in 2004. A railway or other major infrastructure project partly completed normally represents funds lost, as it is often difficult to recover value even if the project gains enough funding to regain momentum.

Human resources

As with finance, investment appraisals are undertaken on the assumption that human resources (i.e. employees or consultants with the required skills) will be available on demand. While this may be true for most needs of the more common skills, it may not be true where highly skilled scientists, pilots, artists, computer analysts and others are needed. In addition, sometimes the undertaking of several projects at a time by an entity can overload the capacity of the current skilled workforce to produce the required output of the required quality. An example of this is an engineering entity that needs to produce specialised parts made from special alloys to very fine tolerances. The tradespeople with the fine quality skills needed may not be available at the time they are needed. Another example of human resource issues exists in universities. In the last few years, many university departments have significantly changed their course offerings and, in doing so, have had to look closely at their staff to ensure that they have the appropriate staff numbers and experience to meet the requirements to teach the new courses. In some cases, it has become evident that a university does not have enough staff with a suitable background to teach in these new areas, which has led to the cancellation of some of these new courses or the hiring of additional staff. The Qantas Group provides another example. It must continually ensure that it has the appropriate human resources to fly its large and varied fleet of planes. When the Airbus A380 was introduced, Qantas had to plan ahead to ensure that its pilots had appropriate training to fly the larger plane. In many cases, Qantas trained existing pilots of other aircraft to pilot the configuration of the A380.

Goodwill and future opportunities

Goodwill is built up over time by entities through giving customers the service and quality they demand. Service can mean fast response times, always having the necessary stock on hand, and completing supply contracts on time and at the right price. Quality in relation to goods and services normally means that the goods and services are useful and appropriate, and indeed do the job better than expected. Entities able to deliver quality service tend to build up loyalty among their customers. The loyalty may include nothing in the way of a reward for past service but be merely self-serving on the part of the customers, in that they know they will get what they want, when they want it and for the price they are prepared to pay. It may be necessary sometimes for an entity to take on projects or investments that it would rather not, in order to keep faith with its customers in the hope that such service will be recognised and there will be further mutually satisfactory business deals in the future. It is through this sort of behaviour that entities build loyal customer bases, which are assets to the entities just as much as machinery and skilled employees.

Social responsibility and care of the natural environment

Social responsibility and care of the natural environment have become important concerns for an increasing proportion of the investor community. The accounting in society chapter of this text focused on sustainability issues in accounting. Environmental issues, such as the wood-chipping of old-growth forests and the release of greenhouse gases into the environment, are important issues for both companies and their stakeholders. Investors should be aware of these issues, the possibility of changes in legislation and the need to consider this source of risk before they commit their funds.

The availability of a skilled workforce can significantly affect the investment decisions made by an entity.

Conclusion — Coconut Plantations' potential coconut oil manufacturers' investment decisions

Throughout this chapter, we have used the data given in illustrative example 12.1 to show how the various decision tools are calculated. Table 12.4 summarises the results of these calculations before we discuss the final decision.

TABLE 12.4	Decision tool results
Tool	**Result**
ARR	33.3% or 11.1% with the opportunity cost of labour included
PP	2.6 years
NPV	$62 720 with 10% discount factor

From table 12.4, all the tools seem to indicate that the coconut oil manufacturing project is a reasonably good investment. However, as noted earlier in the chapter, managers make their decisions based on their entity's past performance, their expectations, industry averages and/or current production in comparable markets. Hence, it is an individual manufacturer's decision as to whether 11.1 per cent is an acceptable return as indicated by the ARR measure. However, in an environment where many manufacturers normally make less than 5 per cent return on their assets, a double-digit return looks acceptable. Moreover, at 2.6 years the PP tool indicates a project that most managers would probably view as worth a second look. Less than three years is a short period to allow for recovery of the initial investment and would be acceptable to many decision makers.

As you have seen in this chapter, these tools take little or no account of risk, with the exception that a short PP reduces the period in which adverse factors can develop and manifest themselves. The tool that is able to incorporate risk is the discounted cash flow method — the NPV.

This NPV of more than $62 000 would be acceptable to many managers, given the initial investment of $120 000 and the fact that the investment is all in readily saleable assets with good second-hand values, no matter what their ages. The discount factor of 10 per cent incorporates an assessment of inflation, risk and alternative opportunities not taken up by undertaking this project. In conclusion, all four tools suggest that the project is worth considering and, if not undertaken immediately, then at least worth further investigation.

SUMMARY OF LEARNING OBJECTIVES

12.1 Explain the nature and scope of investment decisions.

Investment decisions are made by managers in all sorts of entities, large and small. Some of the most common features of investments are that they:
- often involve large amounts of resources in relation to entities' asset bases or turnover
- involve risk and uncertainty
- usually span long periods of time
- normally require a relatively large initial cash outlay and returns are received over a long period into the future
- are often difficult to reverse without the loss of substantial funds.

12.2 Describe and apply the concept of the accounting rate of return (ARR).

The ARR is a simple measure which expresses the average profit over the period of an investment as a percentage of the average investment. Decision makers may accept projects where the ARR exceeds a required minimum level.

12.3 Explain and use the payback period (PP) method.

Having sufficient cash is important to entities that want to survive. Thus, the time it takes to recoup cash is important. The PP is the period of time necessary to recoup the initial outlay with net cash inflows. Investors favour projects with short PPs.

12.4 Discuss and calculate net present values (NPV) and apply the decision rule.

Discounted cash-flow techniques overcome the problem of the time value of money by specifically recognising that $1 received sometime in the future is worth less than $1 received now. The NPV measure compares the sum of the present values (PVs) of all of the expected cash inflows from the project with the PVs of the expected cash outflows. The NPV is the net outcome. Positive NPVs indicate that projects are acceptable. Negative NPVs indicate that projects will not increase wealth.

12.5 Explain some of the practical issues in making investment decisions.

The tools outlined may cause decision making to appear relatively easy. In practice, there may be difficulties with the following issues:
- collecting data
- taxation effects
- finance
- human resources
- goodwill and future opportunities
- social responsibility and care of the natural environment.

KEY TERMS

accounting rate of return (ARR) Average profit over the period of the investment as a percentage of the average investment.

deflation Decrease in the prices of goods and services.

discount rate Interest rate at which a future cash flow is converted to a present value.

dividend imputation scheme Scheme that allows investors (in companies that pay income tax) credits for their share of the tax already paid by the companies.

inflation Increase in the prices of goods and services.

net present value (NPV) Sum of the present values (PVs) of the expected cash inflows from the project less the PVs of the expected cash outflows.

opportunity cost Cost of forgoing benefits that would be available if resources had been used for the next best alternative.

payback period (PP) Time necessary to recoup with net cash inflows the initial outlay.

risk Measurable variation in outcomes.

time value of money Notion that a dollar is worth more the sooner it is received, all other things being equal.

uncertainty Unmeasurable variation in outcomes.

APPLY YOUR KNOWLEDGE

38 marks

PART A

(a) Discuss the advantages and disadvantages of both the ARR and the PP. **4 marks**

(b) Examine the practical issues in making capital investment decisions. **4 marks**

(c) Distinguish between the net present value (NPV) of an investment and its future value (FV). Provide an example to explain the difference between the two amounts. **4 marks**

PART B

Chang De Silva Ltd, an Australian entity, is offered three projects for which the cash flows are as follows in thousands of dollars. The directors work on 14 per cent as their required rate of return (RRR). Assume all cash flows occur at the end of the relevant year. No scrap values are expected for any of the projects.

Project	Year 0	Year 1	Year 2	Year 3	Year 4	Year 5
X	−390	70	90	95	100	60
Y	−310	80	100	140	150	80
Z	−250	130	70	60	40	30

Required

(a) Calculate the ARR and PP for each project. **6 marks**

(b) Rank the projects and advise Chang De Silva which projects, if any, to accept. Give your reasons. **2 marks**

(c) What other information would be useful to consider as part of your investment decision? **4 marks**

PART C

Eloise Tan, a student, recently received a digital SLR camera for her 18th birthday. Over the summer months she has been busy experimenting with the lenses and taking photos of Brisbane attractions such as the Brisbane River, the Gabba, Southbank, Suncorp Stadium and the CBD. A friend has recommended that, with a little more work on her technique, perhaps Eloise could sell her photos. She has decided that the best idea and location would be the Sunday market at Southbank. She has set herself a goal of saving $30 000 over a five-year period. To improve her technique, Eloise feels she needs to do a course at a local TAFE which will cost $3000. She also will need to purchase a new ultrawide 12–35 mm lens costing $2000 and a tripod costing $1500. She thinks she can make $25 000 each year after all costs (e.g. rent of stall, materials, transport, printing and framing) are paid. After five years of selling photos, she hopes to go overseas with her savings of $30 000 and sell all her photography equipment for about $2000.

Required

(a) What is the PP for producing the photos and selling them at markets? **2 marks**

(b) If Eloise allows herself $22 000 in wages and she could earn 7 per cent elsewhere on these funds, what is the NPV for the project? **4 marks**

(c) In your opinion, should Eloise undertake this project? Why or why not? Discuss with reference to the ARR, PP and NPV. **4 marks**

(d) What are some of the risks and opportunity costs associated with this business venture? **4 marks**

SELF-EVALUATION ACTIVITIES

12.1 Nicholas Cash of Advantage Tennis Coaching (ATC) is considering the purchase of a bus to transport junior elite players to various tournaments in south-east Queensland and northern New South Wales. Purchase of the bus will require an initial cash outflow of $160 000. As a result of attending the tournaments, Nicholas believes ATC can generate net cash inflows from sponsorship deals, new player coaching fees and tournament prize money over the next four years of $48 000, $59 500, $49 000 and $72 000, respectively. In addition, the bus is estimated to have a salvage value of $60 000 at the end of year 4. Nick's required rate of return is 10 per cent.

Required

Calculate each of the following measures and comment on their significance:

(a) ARR

(b) PP

(c) NPV.

SOLUTION TO 12.1

(a) ARR = Average profit/Average investment
$$= [(\$48 + \$59.50 + \$49 + \$72 - \$160)/4]/[(\$160 + \$60)/2]$$
$$= 17.125/110$$
$$= 15.6\%$$
This looks like an acceptable return.

(b) PP = Initial investment/Net cash inflow
The initial investment is $160 000. This amount will not be recovered until the start of year 4, if cash is received evenly throughout each year. So the PP is 3.049 years. This may or may not be acceptable to the investors.

(c) (i) $NPV = CF_1/(1 + r) + CF_2/(1 + r)^2 + CF_3/(1 + r)^3 + \ldots + CF_n/(1 + r)^n - INV$

$$(\$000) = 48/(1.1) + 59.5/(1.1)^2 + 49/(1.1)^3 + 132/(1.1)^4 - 160$$
$$= 43.64 + 49.17 + 36.81 + 90.16 - 160$$
$$= 59.78$$
With an NPV at $59 780, this project looks highly acceptable.

(ii) We can also use the discount table to solve this problem:
$$NPV = -160\,000 + 490\,000 \times 0.909 + 59\,500 \times 0.826 + 49\,000 \times 0.751 + 132\,000 \times 0.683$$
$$= -160\,000 + 43\,636 + 49\,174 + 36\,810 + 90\,157$$
$$= 59\,777$$

COMPREHENSION QUESTIONS

12.2 Discuss potential investment opportunities for each of the following.   **LO1**
(a) A computer hardware manufacturer
(b) A car dealership
(c) A clothing retailer
(d) An accounting firm

12.3 Investment decisions are made by managers in all types of business entities. Describe the common features of investments that must be taken into consideration for any investment decision-making activity.   **LO1**

12.4 What is the difference between risk and return in finance?   **LO1**

12.5 What factors must be taken into consideration in determining the discount rate used in investment decisions?   **LO1, 2**

12.6 Define the ARR. What are the two components of the investment that must be known in order to perform this calculation?   **LO2**

12.7 What factors are taken into consideration in determining an appropriate ARR?   **LO2**

12.8 Discuss the factors that would lead to an investment with a shorter PP being selected.   **LO3**

12.9 Define the term 'discount rate' and explain how entities set their rates.   **LO4**

12.10 How does inflation impact on the setting of discount rates?   **LO4**

12.11 Compare the calculation of the ARR with the NPV. What advantages does the NPV have compared with the ARR?   **LO2, 5**

12.12 What impact does taxation have on investment decisions?   **LO4**

EXERCISES

★ BASIC I ★ ★ MODERATE I ★ ★ ★ CHALLENGING

12.13 ★   **LO2**

Acacia Constructions is offered two contracts on the same day for building a new retirement village and a new library complex, respectively. The contracts promise total profits of $6 million and $9 million extending over four years and five years, respectively. Each will require investment of $8 million. On the basis of the ARR, which contract is more profitable?

12.14 ★   **LO3**

Acacia Constructions (from exercise 12.13) recovers its project investment by straight-line methods so that the $5 million is recovered by the end of each project. Assuming profits are also booked in a straight-line fashion, what is the PP for each contract?

12.15 ★   **LO2, 3**

Given the analyses you have completed in exercises 12.13 and 12.14, which of the two contracts would you recommend? Why?

12.16 ★   **LO2**

Lavender Plantations Pty Ltd is contemplating acquiring a new machine to be used for a relatively short period until its new factory is built with computerised equipment installed. Two machines are being investigated as follows.

Machine	A	B
Cost ($)	95 000	140 000
Cost savings — year 1	35 000	42 500
Cost savings — year 2	38 000	50 000
Cost savings — year 3	43 000	57 500
Salvage value — end year 3	58 500	72 500

Calculate the ARR of each machine. Which machine would you recommend?

12.17 ★   **LO3**

What are the PPs for each of the machines in the Lavender Plantations exercise 12.16? What are the risks associated with these investment analyses?

12.18 ★ ★   **LO4**

What are the NPVs for the two machines in exercise 12.16 if Lavender Plantations has an RRR of 10 per cent? Demonstrate your answer using the discount table in appendix 12A at the end of this chapter.

12.19 ★ ★   **LO4, 5**

Explain what is meant by positive and negative NPV.

12.20 ★ ★   **LO4**

If a six-year project has an NPV of $400 000 with a 8 per cent discount rate, will the NPV be higher or lower with a 12 per cent discount rate?

12.21 ★ ★   **LO1, 6**

List and describe three factors that must be considered with an investment in an overseas airline.

12.22 ★ ★   **LO6**

Discuss three environmental concerns that could impact on a business manufacturing custom-made dining tables.

12.23 ★ ★   **LO6**

What is the difference between return and capital growth on an investment? Illustrate with an example of an investment in a new warehouse.

12.24 ★ ★   **LO6**

What is the difference between the profitability and liquidity of an investment?

PROBLEMS

★ BASIC | ★ ★ MODERATE | ★ ★ ★ CHALLENGING

12.25 Making an investment decision between two projects ★   **LO3, 5**

The Flametree Company has two independent projects it could invest in. The financial operations manager has completed some analysis and presented the information to the board. The board has asked you for advice. The entity uses a PP criterion of not accepting any project that takes more than 7 years to recover costs.

	Project 23	Project 24
Investment required ($'000)	400	800
Life of project (years)	10	15
PP (years)	7	11
NPV ($'000)	20	40

Required

(a) Are both projects acceptable to the entity?

(b) If the entity had a history of conservatism in its financial decision making, which project would you advise?

(c) Which project would you advise after taking only these decision-support tools into consideration? Why?

12.26 Making an investment decision on a project ★ ★   **LO2, 3, 4, 5**

An inner city amateur theatre company, Theatre Empire, is planning on performing a new take on two Shakespearean plays, *Hamlet* and *Macbeth*, at an old Brisbane theatre in the inner-city suburb of South Bank. The producers of the theatre plan on alternating the performances of the two plays for a combined total of 40 weeks, if possible. Given the size of the theatre and the expected seat-sales rate, the producers think they can gross $420 000 at the box office. The plays will cost $48 000 to mount in the first place to cover the costs of new sets, costumes and props, and the weekly running costs are expected to be $5500. Assume for the NPV that all funds are earned and paid, except the mounting costs, at the end of the 40 weeks. The sets, costumes and props are expected to realise $26 500 at the end of the run.

Required

(a) What is the ARR?

(b) What is the PP?

(c) What is the NPV if the producers can earn 12 per cent elsewhere on their funds?

(d) Would you advise the producers to go ahead or not? Why?

12.27 Deciding between two machines ★ ★   **LO2, 5**

Higgins Ltd is considering the purchase of one out of two acceptable pieces of equipment. Each design is expected to have individual advantages.

	Equipment A	Equipment B
ARR (%)	35	30

Required

(a) What additional financial information does the board need in order to make a decision?

(b) Would you rely only on this information to make a decision? If not, why not?

(c) If the calculated returns all exceed the entity's required minimum rate, which design would you recommend? Why?

12.28 Deciding on a new machine ★ ★   **LO4**

A small industrial machine costs $136 000 and is expected to earn annual net cash inflows of $58 200, $52 600, $49 500 and $42 100, before it wears out sufficiently to be unreliable and must be sold for an estimated $16 300.

Required

(a) If funds earn 11 per cent, what is its NPV?

(b) If funds earn 15 per cent, what is its NPV?

(c) Advise management on the purchase of the machine.

12.29 Deciding on a new machine ★ ★   **LO4, 5**

Emerald Ltd is considering a new machine which will reduce net cash inflow by $38 000 in the current year, but increase net cash inflow by $9000, $14 000, $18 000, $22 000, $26 000 and $26 000 in the following six years.

Required

(a) If Emerald's cost of capital is 10 per cent, what is the NPV for the machine?

(b) If Emerald's cost of capital is 20 per cent, what is the NPV for the machine?

(c) Advise management on the purchase of the machine.

12.30 Deciding on improving a process ★ ★   **LO4**

An improvement to the process in a children's shirt factory will cost $1.2 million, but will result in net cost savings of $380 000 annually for the next ten years.

Required

(a) If funds are worth 12 per cent, what is the NPV for the investment?

(b) If the shirt factory process improvements turn out to cost $1.8 million, are the process changes still worth making?

12.31 Deciding on a new venture ★ ★ ★   **LO3, 4, 5**

James Denning wants to buy a caravan rental business in the inner Melbourne suburb of Richmond. James spends $1 500 000 on the purchase of the business including caravans and further advertising and signage costs amount to $122 000. He thinks he can net $395 000 each year after all costs are paid. He will work in the business and not take a salary. After five years of this venture, he aims to sell the business and the caravans. To be conservative, he allows only $300 000 as the amount recouped.

Required

(a) What is the PP for the caravan venture?
(b) If James allows $85 000 as his own wage in his calculations and he could earn 10 per cent elsewhere on his funds, what is the NPV for the project?
(c) In your own words, what does this NPV tell us?

12.32 Deciding on a finance package ★ ★ ★   **LO5**

Tracey has just started a new IT business and is thinking of leasing a new luxury car. She has her sights on a BMW coupe. A lease company offers her a deal which comprises a $35 200 payment on delivery of the vehicle, a $21 100 payment at the end of year 1, a $24 600 payment at the end of year 2 and a $31 700 payment at the end of year 3. If Tracey wants to take over the ownership of the vehicle, she must pay another $35 200 at the end of year 3. The lease provider states that the interest rate it has charged is 16 per cent. Ignore taxation.

Required

(a) From these data, calculate the total price of the new vehicle.
(b) If the price of the new vehicle were $54 600, what is the implied interest rate for the lease?
(c) If the price of the new vehicle were $47 500, what is the implied interest rate for the lease?

12.33 Deciding between three projects ★ ★ ★   **LO2, 3, 4, 5**

The directors of Summer and Rayne, a partnership of investors, have three independent investment projects before them for consideration. Each will cost $600 000 in the first instance. The net cash inflows in thousands of dollars each year of the projects are projected to be as in the following table. There is thought to be no residual value for any of the projects. The directors work on 10 per cent as their RRR. Ignore taxation effects and assume all cash flows occur at the end of the relevant years.

Year	A	B	C
1	180	150	150
2	240	330	270
3	300	270	330
4	240	270	210

Required

(a) Calculate the three investment appraisal measures for each project.
(b) Rank the projects and advise the directors which projects, if any, to accept and give your reasons.

12.34 Deciding between three projects ★ ★ ★   **LO2, 3, 4, 5**

A company owned exclusively by residents in the New South Wales coastal community of Yamba is offered three projects for which the cash flows are as follows in thousands of dollars. The directors work on 12 per cent as their RRR. Assume all cash flows occur at the end of the relevant years. There are no salvage values factored into the expected cash flows and no salvage values are expected.

Project	Year 0	Year 1	Year 2	Year 3	Year 4	Year 5
A	−900	300	260	300	220	140
B	−800	180	180	240	260	260
C	−820	500	120	120	120	380

Required

(a) Calculate the three investment appraisal measures for each project.
(b) Rank the projects and advise the directors which projects, if any, to accept. Give your reasons.

DECISION-MAKING ACTIVITIES

12.35 Chrystina and Diana own and manage Warm and Cosy, a roadside cafe located on a main highway on the way to the snowfields in the Victorian Alps. Warm and Cosy services the tourist traffic each year and, in addition, it supplies to the local community small car parts. As the cost of purchasing stock has risen year after year and stockholding costs have also risen, Chrystina has posed the question as to whether such large stocks are worth keeping. Diana argues that they have a reputation for 'nearly always having the part needed'. She says this is a reputation worth having. Chrystina counters with the argument that they are often left with stock they specially ordered after customers 'forget' to return. Sometimes the orders are for specialised parts that are not generally in demand.

Required

(a) What are the investment issues here? Explain in terms of risk, opportunity costs and finance.

(b) How do you suggest they could solve the 'forgotten' orders problem?

(c) Is your solution likely to impact on the entity's goodwill?

12.36 Charlie Williams is a geologist working for a mining company. She spends a great deal of her time on field trips studying rocks and ground-truthing maps which have been developed from aerial and satellite surveys. Because Charlie has spent so much time in the field, she has developed her skills as an amateur field naturalist. She is well aware of the definition of 'amateur' — as a person who loves what she is doing. One day Charlie makes two exciting discoveries — on a rocky hill, she finds a colony of jewel moths long thought extinct and also strong indications of a payable gold deposit. If the gold was mined, there is a strong possibility the land disturbance would upset the feeding and breeding of the moths.

Required

(a) Should Charlie report all she has found that day? What are the issues for her?

(b) If Charlie reports both finds and further exploration suggests the mining venture would be profitable, should the entity go ahead with the mine? Assume the entity has a number of gold prospects to explore. What is your view? Explain with reference to the investment and environmental issues.

12.37 In the 12 months to June 2018, IBM recorded $18.5 billion in cloud revenue, up 23 per cent. Ginni Rometty, IBM's CEO, claimed 'more clients are engaging IBM on their journey to the cloud … This demonstrates IBM's unique leadership in providing innovative technology coupled with deep industry expertise, trust and security' (IBM 2018).

Required

(a) Discuss the risks and the potential benefits for IBM in investing in cloud computing.

(b) What are the potential issues for IBM if it decides to forgo this investment?

REFERENCES

BMW Group 2017, *Annual report 2017*, www.bmwgroup.com.

IBM 2018, 'IBM reports 2018 second quarter results', https://newsroom.ibm.com/2018-07-18-IBM-Reports-2018-Second-Quarter-Results.

JB Hi-Fi Ltd 2018, *Preliminary annual report 2018*, www.jbhifi.com.au.

Qantas Group 2018, *Annual report 2018*, www.qantas.com.au.

SAS Institute Inc. 2018, 'Big data: what it is and why it matters', www.sas.com/en_au/insights/big-data/what-is-big-data.html.

ACKNOWLEDGEMENTS

Photo: © SFIO CRACHO / Shutterstock.com

Photo: © Monkey Business Images / Shutterstock.com

Appendix 12A

(n) Periods	4%	5%	6%	8%	9%	10%	11%	12%	15%
				Discount table					
			Present value of $1 received in *n* periods of time						
1	0.961 54	0.952 38	0.943 40	0.925 93	0.917 43	0.909 09	0.900 90	0.892 86	0.869 57
2	0.924 56	0.907 03	0.890 00	0.857 34	0.841 68	0.826 45	0.811 62	0.797 19	0.756 14
3	0.889 00	0.863 84	0.839 62	0.793 83	0.772 18	0.751 22	0.731 19	0.711 78	0.657 52
4	0.854 80	0.822 70	0.792 09	0.735 03	0.708 43	0.683 01	0.658 73	0.635 52	0.571 75
5	0.821 93	0.783 53	0.747 26	0.680 58	0.649 93	0.620 92	0.593 45	0.567 43	0.497 18
6	0.790 31	0.746 22	0.704 96	0.630 17	0.596 27	0.564 47	0.534 64	0.506 63	0.432 33
7	0.759 92	0.710 68	0.665 06	0.583 49	0.547 03	0.512 16	0.481 66	0.452 35	0.375 94
8	0.730 69	0.676 84	0.627 41	0.540 27	0.501 87	0.466 51	0.433 93	0.403 88	0.326 90
9	0.702 59	0.644 61	0.591 90	0.500 25	0.460 43	0.424 10	0.390 92	0.360 61	0.284 26
10	0.675 56	0.612 91	0.558 39	0.463 19	0.422 41	0.385 54	0.352 18	0.321 97	0.247 19
11	0.649 58	0.584 68	0.526 79	0.428 88	0.387 53	0.350 49	0.317 28	0.287 48	0.214 94
12	0.624 60	0.556 84	0.496 97	0.397 11	0.355 54	0.318 63	0.285 84	0.256 68	0.186 91
13	0.600 57	0.530 32	0.468 84	0.367 70	0.326 18	0.289 66	0.257 51	0.229 17	0.162 53
14	0.577 48	0.505 07	0.442 30	0.340 46	0.299 25	0.263 33	0.231 99	0.204 62	0.141 23
15	0.555 26	0.481 02	0.417 27	0.315 24	0.274 54	0.239 39	0.209 00	0.182 70	0.122 89
16	0.533 91	0.458 11	0.393 65	0.291 89	0.251 87	0.217 63	0.188 29	0.163 12	0.106 87
17	0.512 37	0.436 30	0.371 26	0.270 27	0.231 07	0.197 85	0.169 63	0.145 64	0.092 93
18	0.493 63	0.415 52	0.350 34	0.250 25	0.211 99	0.179 86	0.152 82	0.120 04	0.080 81
19	0.474 64	0.395 73	0.330 51	0.231 71	0.194 49	0.163 51	0.127 68	0.116 11	0.070 27
20	0.456 39	0.376 89	0.311 80	0.214 55	0.178 43	0.148 64	0.124 03	0.103 67	0.061 10

Appendix 12B

Calculating net present value

To solve the problem in illustrative example 12.4, clear your calculator and enter the following information.

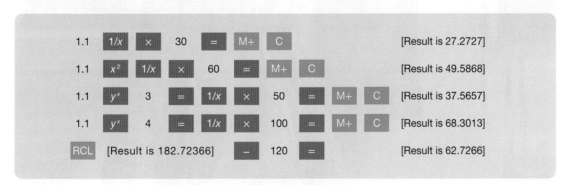

Note that, on some calculators, the y^x button is shown as $^\wedge$ and the $1/x$ button is shown as x^{-1}. M+ is the memory-in button, C is the clear button and RCL is the memory recall button.

CHAPTER 13

Financing the business

LEARNING OBJECTIVES

After studying this chapter, you should be able to:

13.1 discuss the management of net working capital

13.2 outline the issues underlying the management of cash

13.3 discuss the management of accounts receivable

13.4 identify the issues with respect to the management of inventories

13.5 compare the sources of short-term finance

13.6 compare the sources of long-term debt finance

13.7 explain equity finance instruments and their roles

13.8 discuss hybrid financial instruments

13.9 describe the use of international finance

13.10 describe new funding opportunities for business such as crowdfunding, ICOs, angel investors and microcredit.

Chapter preview

A major concern for every business entity is the way the entity is financed. It is important for managers to select appropriate funding as all entities need funding, no matter how small or large their turnover or asset base. The chapter begins with a discussion of working capital and introduces the underlying principle that guides the sourcing of funds for various entity uses. This principle forms the foundation for all later discussion. The chapter then moves on to examine the roles and management of cash, accounts receivable and inventories, building upon knowledge that was presented in the chapter on the statement of financial position. The sources of short-term finance are discussed, followed by the sources of long-term finance from both financial institutions and financial markets. Next, hybrid financial instruments are explored. The chapter then discusses other traditional methods of finance including equity instruments and international finance. The chapter concludes by outlining new funding areas for business including crowdfunding, initial coin offerings (ICOs), angel investors and microcredit.

13.1 Managing net working capital

LEARNING OBJECTIVE 13.1 Discuss the management of net working capital.

Working capital is defined as the funds invested in current assets. You should recall that **current assets** are the assets an entity expects to be able to convert into cash in the normal course of business within the next 12 months. Thus, current assets include cash, accounts receivable (debtors) and inventory (stock). Another relevant concept is **net working capital**, which is current assets minus current liabilities. **Current liabilities** are debts that will be paid within the next 12 months (or accruals that will be shortly reversed). Current liabilities normally include trade creditors or accounts payable, accrued expenses, taxation liabilities, short-term debt such as commercial bills, and provisions for current liabilities such as dividends declared but not yet paid.

In managing the level of net working capital, the entity is concerned with three aspects:
- maintaining liquidity
- the need to earn the required rate of return on assets
- the cost and risk of short-term funding.

Liquidity is a measure of the ease of conversion of an asset into cash. Thus, cash is 100 per cent or totally liquid. Bank current account balances normally have high liquidity, in that the depositor can write a cheque and have that document (which is really an instruction to the bank) accepted as cash. On the other hand, a term deposit at a bank has lower liquidity, as the depositor must either wait until the term expires or 'break' the term by asking for the funds back and incurring a high financial penalty for doing so.

Entities need liquidity to pay their bills on time. As you can readily appreciate, entities really run on trust and short-term credit, and entities want to be paid by their accounts receivable or they themselves may be in danger of failure. Therefore, being able to maintain that trust within the immediate business environment by paying bills on time is vitally important.

In order to maximise their wealth, investors have a rate of return that they require from investments. The rate of return was discussed in the previous chapter. This requirement applies not only to long-term capital investments, but also to working capital. Thus, working capital must play its part. If working capital is allowed to increase to an inappropriately high level, it can reduce the average rate of return on equity.

Another aspect that entities must manage is the cost and risk of current liabilities. An entity can increase its holdings of cash, accounts receivable and inventory at any time, so long as it is able to contract for adequate funds to finance the expansion. The finance has a cost, normally comprising both fees and interest, and the financial manager must be convinced that the benefits to the entity exceed the cost.

Deciding the appropriate level of net working capital

How does a manager decide the appropriate level of net working capital; that is, the level where the entity maintains the ability to meet its financial obligations on time? To achieve this, many entities use the **hedging principle**. This is based on the idea of matching the maturity of a source of funding with its use. The financial manager has control over the maturity of loan contracts, which are entered into for funding, and so can match loan maturities to expected cash inflows. Thus, a retail store preparing for the Christmas trading period may have to pay supply invoices by 7 December. To pay the bills, the manager could arrange for 30-day funding, repayable on 6 January, on the basis that the store will have recouped all of the outlays, plus earned a profit margin, by that date. The funding will cost, say, 5 per cent per annum, or 0.41 per cent for the 30 days. The interest charge is an additional cost of doing business, but it ensures the entity is able to pay its bills on time and maintain a good reputation.

In order to make the hedging principle more useful, it is useful to think in terms of permanent, temporary and spontaneous sources of funding. **Permanent funding** comprises funding with maturities greater than one year and includes long-term debt, leases and ordinary shares. **Temporary funding** essentially comprises the short-term formal sources of finance, such as commercial bills and bank loans. **Spontaneous sources of funding** are those that arise in a substantially unplanned and unstructured way in the ordinary course of business. Examples are trade creditors and the various forms of accrued expenses. Accrued expenses include wages, interest and taxes. Accrued wages are a significant source of spontaneous finance because employees are effectively lending funds free of charge to their employers every pay cycle until payday. Similarly, the withholding of pay-as-you-go (PAYG) tax instalments from employees' pay, as Australian taxation law requires, until the subsequent payment of the total of these instalments to the Australian Taxation Office (ATO) monthly or quarterly gives entities a significant source of free funding.

The principles for using these permanent, temporary and spontaneous classifications to advantage are:
• permanent assets should be financed with permanent and spontaneous sources of funding
• temporary assets should be financed with temporary sources of funding.

Why is it a good idea to finance permanent assets with spontaneous sources of funding? The answer stems from the fact that there remains a core level of funding that is virtually fixed, even though the balances of the various types of spontaneous funding are continually changing. Thus, if the totals of spontaneous funding from all sources over several periods are $140 000, $180 000, $160 000, $140 000 and $180 000, the core level of $140 000, which comprises the minimum level that is always available, may be treated virtually as permanent funding.

However, the hedging principle does not give any guidance as to the level of net working capital that provides the optimal return. Such an assessment involves several cost–benefit analyses. The cost of holding additional cash is the opportunity cost of forgoing higher returns available elsewhere, and the benefit is the reduced expectation of illiquidity. For example, consider a business with a large sum of cash sitting in its company bank account. While it may be prudent to have that sum of money available for any unexpected expenditures, it could also be invested elsewhere; for example, expanding the business into a new geographical area, purchasing new machinery to double output or investing in a joint venture. The cost of carrying higher accounts receivable and inventory is, again, an opportunity cost if internally financed, or a true cash cost of the additional external funding necessary, while the benefits stem from increasing sales, both currently and in the future. Hence, finding the appropriate levels of accounts receivable and inventory, especially, is more a matter of trial and error. In the final analysis, entities must maintain an adequate level of working capital, depending on individual circumstances, to ensure that business is not disrupted and continuity is maintained in a smooth and efficient manner.

The absolute value of working capital is an important measure (e.g. at the end of the June 2018 reporting period, the retail chain JB Hi-Fi Ltd held $1.2 billion and the Qantas Group held $3.7 billion), but that measure alone does not show whether the amount of working capital held is appropriate for the business. We obviously need to know what demands might be placed on these assets — in other words, how do current liabilities compare and what are the arrangements in place to repay that debt?

Net working capital gives us a clear or remaining value after current financial obligations (liabilities) are deducted. As at June 2018 for the companies noted above, JB Hi-Fi Ltd's management regarded $293.3 million as appropriate net working capital and the Qantas Group showed a net working capital of −$3.9 billion (being a proportion of current assets to current liabilities of 132 per cent and 49 per cent respectively). Qantas Group had negative net working capital; however, close examination of the components of current liabilities for the Qantas Group reveals a large amount of revenue received in advance. In fact, if we deduct the amount of revenue received in advance from total current liabilities, the recalculated net working capital becomes $0.1 million (102 per cent). These examples reflect the decisions that have been made by each entity's management regarding the levels of cash, accounts receivable and inventory held. They show that a wide range of values is considered appropriate for each entity's particular cash flow patterns and environment.

VALUE TO BUSINESS

• Net working capital is current assets minus current liabilities.
• In managing the level of net working capital, an entity is concerned with three aspects:
  – maintaining liquidity

- the need to earn the required rate of return on assets
- the cost and risk of short-term funding.
- Liquidity is a measure of the ease of conversion of an asset into cash.
- Entities need liquidity to pay their bills on time and maintain business confidence.
- If working capital is allowed to increase to an inappropriately high level, it can reduce the average rate of return on equity.
- The short-term loans component of current liabilities has a cost, normally comprising both fees and interest, and the financial manager must be convinced that the benefits to the entity exceed the cost.
- To decide an appropriate level of net working capital, many entities use the hedging principle. This principle is based on the idea of matching the maturity of a source of funding with its use.
- Entities categorise funding as permanent, temporary and spontaneous, and use a matching principle to decide appropriate levels.
- The principles for using the permanent, temporary and spontaneous classifications to advantage are:
  - permanent assets should be financed with permanent and spontaneous sources of funding
  - temporary assets should be financed with temporary sources of funding.

13.2 Managing cash

LEARNING OBJECTIVE 13.2 Outline the issues underlying the management of cash.

Entities manage cash with regards to the following issues:
- the need to have sufficient cash
- the timing of cash flows
- the cost of cash
- the cost of not having enough cash.

The need to have sufficient cash

An entity must always have sufficient cash on hand to meet its financial obligations. This means having enough cash to pay wages and taxes, and bills as they come due, and sufficient cash or near-cash (deposits, commercial bills or pre-approved credit) to meet expected bills in the immediate future. The contrasting position is described as being insolvent. An **insolvent entity** is unable to pay its bills or meet its financial obligations on time.

Managers face a trade-off between risk and return when contemplating how much cash to hold. Cost may be minimised by holding as little cash as possible, but risk is increased. A manager overseeing the cash position of an entity can cut cash holdings so that they just cover contemplated expenses, but what would happen if an unexpected bill was received? Liquid funds would have to be arranged quickly and such speedy accommodations normally cost more than planned increases in liquidity. On the other hand, a manager might hold excess cash 'just in case'. What is the cost of this? The cost is the return forgone by holding cash and not investing in the short-term money market. The return on cash-in-hand is zero; the return on money market funds may be 4–5 per cent per annum.

The timing of cash flows

Cash flows come into an entity from a number of sources, including:
- cash sales
- credit sales, when the accounts receivable eventually pay their accounts
- sales of used or unwanted assets
- capital injections
- short-term loans
- long-term loan funding.
  Cash flows out of the entity to service needs include:
- purchase of inventories
- purchase of labour, materials and other services
- purchase of assets (fixed or intangible)
- payment of taxes.

The timing of most of these flows is normally variable, the only exceptions probably being the payment by the entity of wages and taxes. Entities can plan the timing of the purchase and sale of assets, and the requirements for capital injections, to suit their needs. Similarly, in contracting for loans or placing funds in the short-term money market, an entity can negotiate the timing that best suits its own needs.

How does the entity know what timing is most appropriate? The major tool is the cash budget discussed in the budgeting chapter. The cash budget is a detailed plan of expected cash receipts and cash payments that may be drawn up on a daily, weekly, monthly or annual basis. The cash budget highlights any probable cash surpluses or deficits, and allows the manager to plan for investing surpluses or providing for deficits in plenty of time so that the most advantageous arrangements may be made.

The cost of cash

The cost of holding cash may be thought of in terms of the:
- opportunity cost of holding currency or cash deposits, rather than short-term securities
- cost of ensuring the physical security of currency.

Where a manager keeps additional funds in currency on hand or as cash-at-bank in a demand (cheque) account, the return will be zero or close to it. The cost of keeping funds in those forms is the return forgone from not investing in the short-term market. Similarly, funds kept in seven-day deposits or one-month securities normally involve the sacrifice of returns possible from a longer period. Moreover, there is normally a high cost to keeping currency physically secure.

Electronic alternatives to settling transactions in currency or by writing cheques, such as EFTPOS, direct entry, payWave/PayPass and the use of debit and credit cards, have greatly reduced the amounts of currency handled by entities. Some entities no longer even accept cash payments. This has reduced some costs, but has increased costs elsewhere; for example, bank interchange and merchant fees.

The cost of not having enough cash

The cost of not having enough cash at the required time may be a loss of the business. For example, Amcor Ltd suspended its development phase because it needed a new injection of cash. A deficit in cash has the potential to become a permanent condition — insolvency. The penalty for insolvency is normally the winding up of the entity. This was evident in 2011 with the liquidation of Borders Group, which had operated 511 stores globally. In the decade prior it had expanded into many new markets, yet not all of the stores were profitable. The large number of unprofitable stores impacted on the overall performance and the ability of Borders to pay its debts. This, combined with people spending less on luxury purchases like books and music, and the emergence and attraction of online companies, led to the demise of Borders Group.

Temporary cash shortages may be overcome by arranging emergency loans. However, as a general rule, the more desperate the need, the higher the cost of emergency funds.

VALUE TO BUSINESS

- Entities manage cash with regards to these issues:
  - the need to have sufficient cash to meet commitments
  - the timing of cash flows
  - the cost of cash
  - the cost of not having enough cash.
- An entity must always have sufficient cash on hand to meet its financial obligations if it does not wish the business community to regard it as insolvent.
- Entities can plan the timing of many types of cash flows, the main exceptions being the payment of wages and taxes.
- The cost of holding cash comprises the opportunity cost of holding currency or cash deposits rather than short-term securities, and the cost of ensuring the physical security of currency. On the other hand, the cost of not having enough cash at the required time may be a loss of business.

13.3 Managing accounts receivable

LEARNING OBJECTIVE 13.3 Discuss the management of accounts receivable.

Accounts receivable are a normal and often a significant asset class for many entities. In 2018, JB Hi-Fi Ltd had 16.9 per cent of its current assets represented by accounts receivable and the Qantas Group had 24.5 per cent. Even retail stores that you might think would not have receivables do extend credit to their favoured customers.

Benefits and costs of granting credit

Why do entities sell goods or provide services to their customers on the promise that they will be paid, when they are well aware of the chance that some customers will not pay? Recently we have also seen the introduction of 'buy now, pay later' schemes for everyday items such as haircuts, alcohol, food and health services to further entice customers to make purchases. Consider a department store which chose to have a cash-only policy. The store would be losing a great number of potential customers just because it did not offer flexible means of payment. As with most financial decisions, there are both benefits and costs, and managers face a trade-off between the costs and benefits of providing credit. With careful management, benefits can be maximised and costs minimised.

The benefits of granting credit include:
- increasing sales, because of:
  - attracting new customers from other cash-only suppliers
  - encouraging customers to bring planned purchases forward
  - attracting impulsive purchases
  - attracting customers who would not otherwise have purchased
- reducing the cost of making sales, such as in the case where counter staff merely fill out delivery dockets and specialist pricing staff calculate the actual charges.

The costs of granting credit include the:
- opportunity cost of the funds being tied up, as there is no direct return to the funds
- cost of the (hopefully small) proportion of slow payers and bad debts; even with the best of credit rating and collection systems, there will normally be a small percentage of accounts receivable who are slow to pay or do not pay at all
- cost of administering the system, including office staff, stationery, postage, telephone and, possibly, specialist collection services.

Determinants of the level of accounts receivable

The value of accounts receivable carried by any entity depends on a number of policies and processes that the entity determines and manages. Figure 13.1 gives a diagrammatical overview of these determinants. This section discusses each of the determinants in turn.

FIGURE 13.1 Determinants of the level of accounts receivable

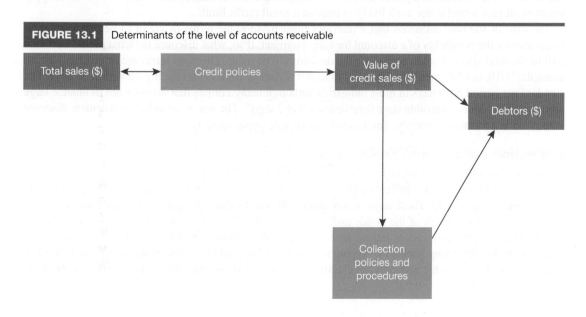

Total sales

The value of total sales has an impact on the value of credit sales, so long as the entity exercises a policy of offering sales on credit. Thus, it follows that the greater the total sales, the greater the credit sales and so the greater the value of accounts receivable.

Moreover, as we saw in the previous section, credit policies also have an impact on total sales.

Credit policies

Credit policies determine the value of credit sales. Credit policies may be broken up conveniently into four aspects, all of which must be managed. These aspects are all decision variables, in that managers are free to make whatever decisions or policies they think best to achieve the entity's objectives. The four aspects are:

- deciding to offer credit or not
- selecting suitable creditworthy customers
- setting credit limits
- deciding payment terms.

Competition in markets normally forces suppliers to offer similar services and trading terms. The stronger the competitive pressures, the more likely it is that no entity can stand out from the pack by offering significantly less advantageous selling terms. If an entity's competitors offer credit, it too will be forced to offer credit sales. Additionally, in terms of pure economics, it is highly likely that the marginal sales revenue from credit-induced sales at normal profitable prices, initially at least, will exceed the marginal cost of these sales. In other words, an entity not offering credit sales at all is very likely reducing its potential profitability.

Entities seeking to determine the creditworthiness of potential customers face different tasks, depending on the size and status of the applicant customer. Very large entities may be rated by the global ratings agencies such as Moody's Investors Service and Standard & Poor's (S&P), and these ratings are publicly available. Other agents, such as Equifax (Australia's leading data intelligence and insights company) and Dun & Bradstreet, collect data on the operations, financial standing and credit history of many entities, and sell this information to entities which require it.

Many entities ask potential credit customers to fill in a credit-scoring questionnaire. Such a questionnaire asks for information on the age and stability of the customer entity, details of any past credit difficulties, bank account details and so on. More sophisticated entities may use more complex credit-scoring models. These models rely on quantifying the answers to questions that ask about issues considered to be determinants of creditworthiness, and combining the quantitative data into a model. The data are compared with past experience in that particular industry. Often, if a company is applying for credit terms, a director's personal guarantee will be requested.

Entities granting credit normally set an upper credit limit, either explicitly or implicitly. The credit limit is set with regards to the level of knowledge of the customer and the expected size of the sales during any period. Thus, a new customer, about whom little is known, may have a relatively small credit limit imposed. On the other hand, a potato grower contemplating a new contract with Woolworths Ltd to supply potatoes all year round is not at all likely to impose a small credit limit.

The final of the four decisions that a manager must make is the terms of credit to be offered. Credit terms involve the possibility of a discount for early payment; if so, what discount for what period and what will be the total allowed credit period are the decisions to be made. Discount terms are often stated as, for example, '1/10, net 30', meaning 1 per cent discount if paid in 10 days and net if paid within 30 days. The standard net period is 30 days in most industries, although many entities that do not want to finance large amounts of accounts receivable state their term as 'net 7 days'. The aim of granting a settlement discount is to provide a monetary incentive for accounts receivable to pay quickly.

Collection policies and procedures

What can a supplier do to ensure it collects the highest possible proportion of its accounts receivable? The answer is to have written policies and procedures in place, monitor the ageing of accounts and apply the procedures rigorously. These days, when almost all entities have computerised accounting packages (following the introduction of the goods and services tax (GST), which forced many smaller entities to install electronic systems), accessing an accounts receivable ageing schedule is easy, as such schedules are standard in accounting packages. Ageing schedules identify which accounts are unpaid and overdue. Additionally, these overdue accounts are classified by the period overdue; for example, 30 days, 60 days, 90 days and so on.

Entities may judge the effectiveness of their collection policies and procedures by making use of ratio analysis, as discussed in the analysis and interpretation of financial statements chapter. The most useful ratio is the days debtors turnover, which is the ratio that indicates how long on average it takes for the cash to be collected from accounts receivable. When calculating this ratio, ideally the credit sales figure rather than total sales should be used, as accounts receivable arise only from credit sales. The ratio gives the number of days of the sales value that remain outstanding. This number may then be compared with those of previous periods for the same entity and industry benchmarks.

A decreasing average collection period (ACP) may indicate more effective collection processes — which is good, but may also indicate that too much time and effort are being put into collections or that credit policy has become so restrictive that the entity is missing out on sales. Conversely, an increasing ACP may indicate less effectiveness in collections, too little expenditure or too lenient a credit policy.

Another measure of the success of collection policies is the percentage of bad debts — this percentage is calculated as bad debts divided by sales for the same period. As above, an entity may compare this value with the values computed for previous periods or against industry benchmarks. The same comments relate to either decreasing or increasing values as noted above for decreasing or increasing ACPs.

Level of credit sales

Now that we have examined sales revenue, credit policies and collection policies and procedures, we can review all of the determinants of the level of accounts receivable. Credit policies to some extent affect total sales; and total sales, when considered in conjunction with credit policies, determine the value of credit sales. Credit sales increase the value of accounts receivable at any point of time, but efficient collection policies decrease the value of accounts receivable.

VALUE TO BUSINESS

- The benefits to entities of granting credit include:
  - increasing sales, because of:
    - attracting new customers from other cash-only suppliers
    - encouraging customers to bring planned purchases forward
    - attracting impulsive purchasers
    - attracting customers who would not otherwise have purchased at all
  - reducing the cost of making sales, such as by having counter staff merely fill out delivery dockets and specialist pricing staff calculate the actual charges.
- But granting credit has costs, which include the:
  - opportunity cost of the funds tied up, as there is no direct return to the funds
  - cost of the (hopefully small) proportion of slow payers and bad debts, as even with the best of credit rating and collection systems there will normally be a small percentage of accounts receivable who are slow to pay or do not pay at all
  - cost of administering the system, including office staff, stationery, postage, telephone and, possibly, specialist collection services.
- The level of accounts receivable is determined by total sales, credit policies and collection policies.

13.4 Managing inventories

LEARNING OBJECTIVE 13.4 Identify the issues with respect to the management of inventories.

Inventories or stock are normally a component of current assets for entities involved in the manufacturing or sale of goods. Manufacturers hold raw material inventory so that production can be carried out without undue hold-ups should there be any disruption in the normal course of supply. A manufacturing company such as BMW Group has 17.8 per cent of current assets in the form of inventories. Retail entities hold inventory to ensure that sales can be effected immediately. JB Hi-Fi Ltd keeps over 73.6 per cent of its current assets in the form of inventories. Entities selling services, on the other hand, normally have insignificant values of inventories, as their inventories are limited to such items as office supplies and vehicle maintenance supplies. Qantas Group, for example, has about 9.5 per cent of its current assets in the form of inventories.

Types of inventories

The types of inventories include:

- raw materials
- work-in-progress
- finished goods.

The purpose of holding these inventory types is essentially the same. Raw materials are held by all types of manufacturers to ensure that production can be carried out without delay should there be interruption in normal supply. Work-in-progress (WIP) consists of goods (or services) where some of the required work operations have been completed and others have not. Normally, the more complex the transformation process, the more likely an entity will have WIP inventories. Finished goods are held as a buffer between production and sales. Inventories are allowed to increase when sales fall, to avoid cutting staff and production. Conversely, inventories fall when unexpected increases in sales are not immediately reflected in increased production, which may mean the payment of overtime costs.

Benefits and costs of holding inventories

Managing inventories is an art, although there are techniques that managers can use to transform much of the role into a science. Suppose you manage a convenience store on the Melbourne–Albury truck route and you sell a wide variety of products, including fuel, oil, vehicle spare parts, fast food, ice-cream, sweets, drinks and newspapers. How much of each type of these goods should you hold? What are the benefits and what are the costs of holding the inventory?

The benefits of holding inventory are:

- sales are made and profits gained
- cross-sales are made and profits increased (truck drivers stop for fuel, but also buy meals, drinks, ice-cream and newspapers)
- goodwill is built up ('that place always has what you want') and no-inventory costs are avoided ('that place never has what you want, let's go elsewhere').

However, there are costs that must be balanced against the benefits. The costs of holding inventory include:

- ordering costs
- holding costs.

Ordering costs include the time and cash costs involved in placing orders, freight costs and quantity discounts forgone if only small orders are made. In general, the larger the order, the smaller and less significant will be the sum of these costs. However, making only large orders may not be possible because of the nature of the goods. Large orders also increase holding costs.

Holding costs include:

- storage and display costs
- insurance costs
- deterioration and obsolescence
- wholesale price changes
- theft
- financing costs.

Storage costs can be high for some types of goods. The different sugars held by the listed company Sugar Australia, for example, must all be held in specially built silos, which must be weatherproof, vermin-proof and, possibly, climate-controlled. Inventory should be insured unless the manager believes the entity can afford to lose the lot or that the risk is so small that losing the lot is hardly possible. When wholesale prices change, the value of inventory changes. A drop in wholesale prices represents a cost, if selling prices must be immediately dropped due to competitive pressure. Theft or shoplifting occurs in practically all retail situations and, indeed, in almost all entities. Anecdotally, employees are responsible for a significant proportion of inventory thefts.

Finally, there are the financing costs. Funds tied up in inventory could be invested elsewhere. If the best alternative investment yields 5 per cent per annum, then the financing cost of holding inventory is 5 per cent per annum, or $50 per $1000 of inventory. In practice, the best alternative investment is probably an investment elsewhere in the entity, but it may be an investment externally on the short-term money market.

In making decisions about the levels of inventory to be held, the manager must trade off all these costs against the benefits. Normally, holding inventory is an incremental thing. As entities become established, turnover improves, cash flow improves and inventory tends to build up as managers see the need to hold more of a particular product or another.

Inventory management techniques

Two techniques are commonly used to manage inventory levels:
* maintaining a minimum level of inventory
* managing the average turnover period.

Many managers maintain either an explicit or implicit minimum level of inventory. The level is explicit when documented in inventory-management records and implicit when the requisite level is an idea or 'feeling' on the part of the manager.

The second technique involves managing the average inventory turnover period (ITP):

$$\text{Inventory turnover} = \frac{\text{Average inventory}}{\text{Cost of sales}} \times 365 = x\,\text{days}$$

The value calculated with this equation is in units of days. Hence, from their experience managers can decide on a number of days for inventory to be held as optimum for the business. For example, the data in figure 13.2 relate to JB Hi-Fi Ltd for the period 2015 to 2018.

| FIGURE 13.2 | JB Hi-Fi Ltd's inventory and cost data ($ million) |

Item	2015	2016	2017	2018
Inventory	478	546	860	891
Average inventory	468	512	703	875
Cost of sales	2 853	3 089	4 398	5 384
Number of times (per year)	6.10	6.03	6.26	6.15
Inventory turnover (days)	59	60	58	59

Source: Data from JB Hi-Fi Ltd's annual reports (2015–2018).

DECISION-MAKING EXAMPLE

Controlling inventory turnover levels

SITUATION Using the data from the figure above, discuss JB Hi-Fi Ltd's inventory management. If JB Hi-Fi Ltd wanted to reduce the turnover to an average of 55 days, what strategies could it employ?

DECISION It is clear from the figure above that the management of JB Hi-Fi Ltd have instituted a policy to keep strict control of inventory levels. The average period it takes to sell the whole of the inventory purchased by the entity varied from 58 days to 60 days during the period 2015 to 2018. Reducing the turnover in days is conducive to increasing profits, as funds are not tied up in inventory for a long period. For JB Hi-Fi Ltd, we must remember that the business specialises in a range of products from cheaper items such as CDs to more expensive items such as computers. A reduction in days could result from an increase in cost of sales or a decrease in average inventory. Both would result in a decrease in the number of days (increase in turnover). Basically, for JB Hi-Fi Ltd to reduce its turnover in days (increase its turnover in number of times), it needs to either sell more or carry less inventory. Selling more inventory can be achieved by discounting inventory or offering incentives to customers such as '3 for 2' deals. Reducing inventory levels can be achieved by not carrying as much floor inventory, particularly carrying less of the expensive inventory such as home cinemas. This would also reduce other costs for JB Hi-Fi Ltd such as storage, inventory loss and insurance.

The need to reduce the funds tied up in inventory over long periods of time is especially relevant to the concept of the just-in-time (JIT) philosophy, which was originally developed by the Toyota Motor Company of Japan in the 1960s. Reduction of inventories provides the benefit of savings in holding costs. However, reduction of inventories also exposes inefficiencies in management, as the unplanned changes in inventories no longer mask such problems.

- Inventories are held to ensure that production and sales may be carried out without delay and as a buffer between production and sales.
- The benefits of holding inventories are:
  - sales are made and profits gained
  - cross-sales are made and profits increased
  - goodwill is built up and no-inventory costs are avoided.
- The costs of holding inventory include ordering and holding costs.
- Two techniques are commonly used to manage inventory levels:
  - maintaining a minimum level of inventory
  - managing the inventory turnover period.

13.5 Sources of short-term finance

LEARNING OBJECTIVE 13.5 Compare the sources of short-term finance.

Remember, in our discussion of the management of working capital, that we looked at the hedging principle and noted that temporary assets should be funded with temporary or short-term funds. The most common sources of short-term finance for entities are:

- accrued wages and taxes
- trade credit
- bank overdrafts
- commercial bills and promissory notes
- factoring or debtor/invoice/trade finance
- inventory loans or floor-plan finance.

Accrued wages and taxes

Accrued wages and PAYG withholding instalments are examples of spontaneous sources of finance. An entity such as a private hospital pays a high proportion of its cash expenses as wages and salaries. Consider such an entity with a $2 million fortnightly wage bill. On average, this entity effectively owes its employees $1 million all the time. This $1 million of funding is provided free of charge.

Trade credit

Trade credit is possibly the most important source of short-term finance for entities. This is because such credit arises during the normal course of business and is normally extended without formal agreement. Moreover, trade credit is normally unsecured and requires nothing additional to normal accounting practices for its successful management. Trade credit these days is most likely to be offered on a net 30-days or even net 7-days basis. This means that the full amount of the invoice must be paid within 30 days or 7 days. Often, where a customer makes many purchases within the monthly accounting period, a statement of account is sent out to the customer at the end of the month and then the customer has 30 days to pay the whole amount.

The management of trade credit should be built into an entity's accounting systems and processes. For example, the entity might have an internal rule that one week's invoices are batched on Fridays (or any other selected day) and paid on the third Friday following the batch day. This means that no invoice will remain unpaid for longer than 30 days. Such a system allows a measure of control. An alternative system that exhibits control but is extremely costly in terms of both labour costs and the opportunity cost of cash — and so is not favoured by large entities — is to pay all invoices upon receipt.

Because managers need to monitor this function of their business, they need a single measure that gives them information about how their business (and office processes) are performing. Such a measure is the creditors turnover. Illustrative example 13.1 demonstrates how this measure is calculated for Turner Ltd.

$$\text{Creditors turnover} = \frac{\text{Average trade creditors} \times 365}{\text{Credit purchases}} = x\,\text{days}$$

Calculating the creditors turnover

During the last five years, Turner Ltd had the following trade creditors at balance date and made the following credit purchases (in $ million).

Item	2014	2015	2016	2017	2018
Trade creditors	400	416	436	468	556
Credit purchases	3 660	3 940	4 220	4 710	5 658

What is the trend in average settlement period?

First, we must find the average trade creditors value for each available year. These are the last four years, as we do not have the information to compute average creditors for 2014. The average for 2015 is 408 [(400 + 416)/2] and, for the following three years, 426, 452 and 512 respectively. We can now substitute into the equation and compute the average settlement periods for the four years, as follows.

Item	2014	2015	2016	2017	2018
Average trade creditors	n/a	408	426	452	512
Credit purchases	n/a	3 940	4 220	4 710	5 658
Creditors turnover (days)	n/a	37.8	36.8	35.0	33.3

From these data, it is apparent that Turner Ltd keeps strict control of trade creditors (an average of 35 days) and has put effort into bringing the average settlement period down. Entities that do not have adequate control over their creditors face interest on overdue accounts and the possibility of losing the trade creditor as a major supplier of their product or service to the entity.

Bank overdrafts

An **overdraft** is normally a loan facility attached to a current account. The loan is drawn down only as required, when cheques or transfers made on the account exceed positive balances. The intention of overdraft finance is that the balance in the account will fluctuate between being positive and negative from day to day, as cash flows into and out of the entity.

Commercial bills and promissory notes

Commercial bills and promissory notes are discount securities. That is, the borrower receives funds less than the face value, with the face value repaid at maturity. The difference between the funds received by the borrower and the funds eventually repaid to the lender represents interest and fees. The price of bills (PV) is calculated using the compound interest formula, manipulated so that the PV is the unknown factor, as in the equation below.

$$PV = \frac{FV}{(1 + i)}$$

where PV = the price of the bill or funds lent

FV = the face value of the bill

i = the interest rate for the period of the bill

Thus, a $100 000 180-day bill funded to yield 6 per cent per annum would be priced at $97 126.04. To arrive at this value, the nominal annual interest rate of 6 per cent is first reduced to the rate for a 180-day period, that is, $\frac{180}{365} \times 0.06 = 0.029\,59$. Then:

$$PV = \frac{100\,000}{1.029\,59}$$

$$= \$97\,126.04$$

There are normally three parties to the issue of a bank-accepted commercial bill (BAB). An entity (the borrower, party 1) wanting to access the bill market normally approaches the bank and makes a request. The bank draws up a bill and then finds an investor (the 'discounter', party 2) to fund the loan. The bank then 'accepts' the bill, which means it guarantees that the bill will be honoured at maturity. The bank assumes the credit risk on the bill in return for a fee and becomes the 'acceptor' (party 3).

Promissory notes (PNs) are similar to BABs, but they are not endorsed by an acceptor. The borrower is the only party that is responsible for the repayment of the debt. As there is no other party involved in guaranteeing repayment, the raising of finance by means of PNs tends to be restricted to larger entities with good reputations and excellent credit ratings.

Factoring or debtor/invoice/trade finance

Financial institutions have been inventive in finding ways to use the security of debtors to back business loans. The variety includes:
- guaranteeing a general line of receivables or specific invoices
- factoring.

With guaranteeing a general or specific line of receivables, the borrower offers its debtors either in total or in part as security for a loan. This method is simple and inexpensive to implement. However, as the lender has no control over the quality of the debts and there may be some potentially bad debts included, normally the loan on a general line does not exceed a rate of 70–75 per cent of the total invoices. With the guarantee of receivables, customers know nothing of the financial arrangements that are being made on the basis that they will pay their bills on time. The borrowing entity collects its debts in the normal way and repays the financier according to the conditions underlying each cash advance.

The second method of using accounts receivable as security is quite different. **Factoring** gives the lender (the 'factor') the right to collect the cash owing on invoices. Essentially, the factor discounts the invoices and hands over the cash. It then collects the amounts owed by the borrowing entity's customers. In some cases, the factor buys the invoices outright as well as the right to collect the funds owing. In other cases, the factor gives a loan, collects the outstanding amounts, subtracts its fees and the loan amount, and then returns the balance to the borrower. Factoring fees may be quite high. A fee of 5 per cent, for example, when converted to a nominal annual basis, becomes 64 per cent if the 5 per cent is for the use of the funds for 30 days.

Factoring has been growing strongly in the last 20 years or so, both in Australia and worldwide. In 2011, the value of factoring in Australia was more than $93 billion. Australia's use of factoring reduced in 2013 to $65 billion. It has since increased on a yearly basis, exceeding $77 billion in 2016. The worldwide value of factoring in 2017 reached over US$3 trillion (AUD4.2 trillion) (Factors Chain International 2018). Factoring and discounting are normally highly suitable for entities that have rapid sales growth, that are unable to fund large orders or seasonal peaks and that regularly exceed their current overdraft limits and are fully borrowed against fixed assets. Factoring and discounting are not suitable for entities with disproportionate levels of trade disputes or retailers with myriad small sales.

Inventory loans or floor-plan finance

The final asset able to be used to secure short-term finance is inventory. The quality of inventory as a security depends on its nature. Essentially, quality, age, perishability and marketability all impact on the usefulness of inventory as security for a loan. Think of some examples where you would not like to lend funds with that sort of inventory as the security.

The most important example of inventory finance is floor-plan finance, which is very commonly found in the motor vehicle (cars, trucks and motorbikes) retail sector. Examples in Australia include GE Capital, NAB Asset Finance and Macquarie Leasing.

The lending arrangements with floor-plan finance involve three parties: the lender, the manufacturer and the borrower (the retail dealer). After the initial contracts outlining each party's responsibilities are in place, the dealer places an order with the manufacturer, who then contacts the lender to see if the dealer's credit for that amount is good. If so, the order is filled, the dealer gets the inventory and the lender receives the invoice to pay. Until the inventory is sold, the dealer pays interest on a monthly basis to the lender and has an obligation to repay the principal as soon as the inventory is sold.

Floor-plan finance is commonly found in the motor vehicle retail sector.

- The most common sources of short-term finance for entities are:
  - accrued wages and taxes
  - trade credit
  - bank overdrafts
  - commercial bills and promissory notes
  - factoring or debtor/invoice/trade finance
  - inventory loans or floor-plan finance.
- Accrued wages and taxes, as well as trade credit, are the most important source of short-term finance for entities. This is because the funding arises during the normal course of business, is free of charge and is extended without formal agreement.
- A bank overdraft is normally a loan facility attached to a current account. The loan is drawn down only as required, when cheques or transfers made on the account exceed positive balances.
- Bank-accepted commercial bills (BAB) are a common form of short-term finance where banks guarantee for lenders the repayment of their funds. Banks arrange the transactions and charge fees for their services.
- Promissory notes (PNs) are similar to BABs, but they are not endorsed by an acceptor. As there is no other party involved in guaranteeing repayment, the raising of finance by means of PNs tends to be restricted to larger entities with good reputations and excellent credit ratings.
- Debtors may be used as security to back business loans by:
  - guaranteeing a general line of receivables or specific invoices
  - factoring.
- Factoring gives the lender (the 'factor') the right to collect the cash owing on invoices. The factor discounts the invoices and hands over the cash. It then collects the amounts owing by the borrowing entity's customers.
- Inventory is also used as security for business loans. The most important example of inventory finance is floor-plan finance, which is commonly found in the motor vehicle (cars, trucks and motorbikes) retail sector.

13.6 Sources of long-term debt finance

LEARNING OBJECTIVE 13.6 Compare the sources of long-term debt finance.

Again, remember the hedging principle suggests that permanent assets should be funded with long-term funds. Long-term debt finance is supplied to borrowers either through financial institutions acting as intermediaries or directly by the debt markets.

Intermediated finance

Australian entities tend to look to financial institutions, in the first instance, as suppliers of intermediated finance. While larger entities with standing in the community (or internationally) are able to access financial markets and financial institutions for funds, smaller entities typically approach one or several financial institutions for long-term funding.

For long-term funding purposes, most financial institutions offer:
- fixed-rate business loans
- variable-rate business loans
- instalment loans
- interest-only loans
- fully drawn advances
- lease finance.

Fixed-rate and variable-rate business loans

Fixed-rate business loans are available from most of the major financial institutions. Many institutions prefer loans in the range from $100 000 to $2 million. Terms are usually given for up to 25 years. After the expiry of the initial period, the rate may be fixed for a further period or converted to a variable rate. These loans may be unsecured, secured with entity assets or secured with residential property. The availability of acceptable security naturally affects the interest rate charged. Repayment conditions are negotiated to suit the business conditions of customers. Variable-rate business loans are also available from most of the major financial institutions and amounts available vary up to about $2 million. Terms are available up to 25 years. Interest rates vary in line with changes in the markets and depending on security and loan terms and conditions. The lender will also assess the risk of the entity to determine the excess interest rate the entity is charged over and above a base rate. Many financial institutions offer flexible drawdown of the contracted loan amounts and flexible repayment schedules. JB Hi-Fi Ltd reported $469.34 million of unsecured bank loans for the reporting period ended June 2018.

Instalment loans

Instalment loans differ from business loans in that fixed repayment schedules are negotiated at the outset. Minimum loan amounts vary between financial institutions and may be as low as $10 000 with some suppliers and $50 000 with others. The loan periods also vary between suppliers, but are often in the range of 1–15 years.

Interest-only loans

Interest-only loans are taken out to finance special situations. During the term of the loan only interest is paid, while the repayment of the principal amount is made in full at the expiry of the term. These types of loans are suitable for situations where, say, an asset is bought (and used) for a specific period, with the expectation that it will be sold at the end of the period. The sale of the asset then provides funds to repay the loan. Thus, the payment of interest in the intervening period may be considered a holding cost for owning the asset.

Fully drawn advances

Fully drawn advances (FDAs) are a major form of entity financing. Amounts available from some institutions may vary from as low as $5000 up to any amount at all. Terms are normally for up to 10 years. Rates are normally variable. Often, financial institutions will set a system where interest is charged to a separate account, while the FDA account merely keeps track of the balance of the principal. Normally, a regular repayment schedule is set up, so that the balance in the FDA account decreases continually over the term of the loan. FDA loans are usually secured.

Leases

Leasing is a significant form of finance for entities. The major financial institutions provide a full range of leasing options and products to complement their other loans and to assist entities with financing specific assets such as motor vehicles, construction and manufacturing plant, and IT and office equipment. What is meant by the term 'lease'? A **lease** is a contract by which an owner of an asset ('the **lessor**') allows another person or entity ('the **lessee**') the use of the asset for a specific period in return for rent or lease payments.

Two examples of leases are novated leases and hire-purchase agreements. A **novated lease** involves a three-party agreement between an employee, an employer and a financial institution. Novated leases are normally used to provide motor vehicles to employees as part of salary packages. The cost of providing the vehicle is part of the employee's salary, but is paid directly to the financial institution. The employee is able to select the vehicle of their choice and to reduce their annual taxable income. The financial institution is able to claim from the ATO the GST component of the new price of the vehicle, and this credit effectively reduces the lease payments. Novated leases are normally fully portable between employers, at least from the point of view of the financial institutions.

In this case, the underlying asset is owned by the financier and used by the customer in return for a rental payment. The rental or lease payments are tax deductions for the customer. There are no tax deductions for interest or depreciation, and there is no guarantee of ownership of the asset at the end of the period by the customer. The fact that there is no such guarantee, however, does not mean that the customer cannot purchase the asset. Often, they do, by paying a final lump sum, 'balloon' or residual payment.

In contrast, under a **hire-purchase agreement** a financial institution buys the asset required by the customer, then hires it to the customer for use during the agreed period. At the end of the period, the deal is settled by the payment of any outstanding balances and ownership of the asset passes to the customer. The payments made by the lessee are treated as ownership costs, and deductions are allowable for interest and depreciation. Consistent with this view, ownership at the expiry of the terms of the agreements resides not with the financial institution but with the lessee.

All of the forms of leasing discussed here may be classified as finance leases. **Finance leases** are non-cancellable contractual obligations to make payments in return for the use of an asset for the majority of its useful life, and are essentially just one of many forms of financing the use of assets. The lessee party to a finance lease enjoys most of the benefits of ownership and is normally responsible for maintenance and upkeep. Conversely, some leases may be classed as **operating leases**, which are contractual agreements that are cancellable upon giving notice and tend to be of much shorter term than the useful life of the asset. These include the sorts of agreements that you might enter into for the hire of a car for a two-week holiday, the hire of a floor-sander or, indeed, the rental of a house.

Debt finance from the Australian market

Entities wanting to raise debt finance from the Australian market have corporate bonds, notes and debentures to choose from as methods of finance. To a great extent, these securities are similar methods of financing; the differences mainly lie in their historical roles. Essentially, borrowing entities issue bonds, notes or debentures as proof that debts exist. After that, if the securities are traded, the security itself (the physical piece of paper) or the proof of registration with issues, which is electronically recorded, merely acts as proof of current ownership. Naturally, the owner of a bond at maturity is the entity that receives the repayment of face value from the issuer.

Corporate bonds

Corporate bonds grew in popularity in Australia during the 1990s. These are bonds that are issued by entities to raise funds in order to expand the business. Corporate bonds are unsecured, so good credit ratings by the ratings agencies — Moody's Investors Service and S&P — are extremely important to potential issuers of bonds. This market has grown strongly in the last few years. The Australian Securities Exchange (ASX) website www.asx.com.au has full details of corporate bonds, product specifications, prospectus summaries and prices.

Debentures and unsecured notes

Debentures are issued by entities to raise debt funds. Debentures may be offered to large institutional investors by way of a private issue or issued to the public after the full details of the issue and the entity are given in a prospectus. Information of interest with regards to the issue includes the total amount of the issue, the maturity dates (normally 1–10 years), redemption details, the interest rate offered (normally fixed), interest payment dates and the security that is being offered to investors should the entity become insolvent.

Unsecured notes are also issued by financial institutions. These have similar characteristics to debentures, except that they are unsecured. Because they are unsecured, they carry a higher coupon to compensate investors for the higher risk. These unsecured notes normally take the form of a certificate issued by the borrower, made out to the lender for the amount invested. Where issues are not traded, investors must wait until maturity of each issue to be repaid their funds.

VALUE TO BUSINESS

- Long-term debt finance is supplied to borrowers through financial institutions as intermediated finance or directly by debt markets.
- For long-term funding purposes, most financial institutions offer:
  - fixed-rate business loans
  - variable-rate business loans
  - instalment loans
  - interest-only loans
  - fully drawn advances
  - lease finance.
- Entities wanting to raise debt finance from the Australian market may choose as the financing medium:
  - corporate bonds
  - debentures and unsecured notes.

13.7 Equity finance

LEARNING OBJECTIVE 13.7 Explain equity finance instruments and their roles.

Owners may at times wish to expand their entities or liquidate some or all of their ownership rights. They achieve this by selling ownership rights to other investors. The media by which ownership rights are packaged, sold (and bought) and transferred are ordinary shares and preference shares. Ordinary shares are by far the more common of the two. All companies issue ordinary shares; some, but not all, companies issue preference shares.

Ordinary shares

As explained in the accounting in society chapter, **ordinary shares** are the main type of share by which companies divide and sell ownership rights to investors. Ordinary shares have an initial issue price but, after that time, their price is set by the secondary market.

In the case of private companies, ownership is normally still divided up into shares, but often there may be as few as five or ten shares only in each company. The value of each such share is usually very difficult to ascertain. Additionally, as these are often family-owned companies, there may be a family tradition or unwritten principle that the shares are not sold outside the family.

Ordinary shares have no fixed maturity date, unlike most forms of debt. The shares continue to exist so long as the entity exists. However, individual shares may undergo transformations such as share consolidations or share splits. The payments attaching to shares are dividends, the amounts of which are not guaranteed. Directors decide upon and declare dividends, normally twice a year, after the profitability of the company for the relevant period has been calculated. However, if there are no or insufficient profits after interest and taxes have been paid, dividends may not be paid, and ordinary shareholders do not have any cumulative rights. Dividends may also not be paid if there is insufficient cash in the entity.

Ordinary shares rank last in the event of the winding-up of a company. The claims of people holding debt (the senior-ranked debt being paid first) are settled first, followed by the claims of preference shareholders. In most insolvencies, ordinary shareholders receive no repayment of their invested funds at all, because the pool of cash accumulated through the liquidation of assets is insufficient to pay out in full all those who rank above them. This chance increases the risk associated with ordinary shares. The collapse of Borders Group is a good example of a situation where the remaining assets of the group were put into a liquidating trust for payment of taxes and professional fees. The ordinary shareholders were left with nothing.

One of the major attractions of ordinary shares is their limited liability. If shareholders were held responsible and liable for all the actions of the employees of the companies in which they had invested funds, most reasonably risk-averse people would not invest in shares, but would merely invest in debt securities. The securities exchanges as we know them today would not exist! Thus, limited liability for shareholders enables companies to raise equity capital where otherwise they would be unable to do so. Shareholders are liable only to the extent of their subscribed capital in the case of initial shareholders, and to the extent of the price paid for shares in the case of later shareholders.

Preference shares

Preference shares are a hybrid form of capital, just as the convertible notes discussed above are a mix of debt and equity. Preference shares tend to lean more towards equity than debt. Issuers are able to attach different sets of rights to their issues of preference shares, so debt and equity characteristics vary between securities. Preference shares are legally regarded as equity, even if their economic substance for accounting purposes deems them to be debt, and preference dividends are regarded as a distribution of profits, not a tax-deductible expense.

Preference shares rank ahead of ordinary shares for repayment in the event of the winding-up of a company. Additionally, the payment of preference share dividends ranks ahead of the payment of ordinary dividends. Moreover, preference shares usually have a fixed dividend (e.g. 10 per cent of the issue price) rather than a dividend which fluctuates according to the profitability of the company. Preference shares are usually not issued as partly paid. In this, they mimic debt. A company issuing preference shares does so to collect the full amount of funds that they represent at the time of issue.

Companies issue preference shares to gain the following advantages.
- Ownership rights are not diluted by the issue of preference shares, while the preference shares do not normally have voting rights attached to them.
- Non-participation, being the norm, gives companies certainty in the cost of this form of funding.
- Cumulative or non-cumulative non-payment of preference dividends cannot pose the solvency risk of debt.
- The fixed cost of preference share capital allows companies to enhance earnings per ordinary share.

Rights and options

A **rights issue** is the issue of new shares to existing shareholders. The 'rights' terminology refers to the entitlement of existing shareholders to subscribe. Normally, there is a benefit attached to the right, in that the new issue of shares is made available at a price that is below the current market price.

Most rights issues are **renounceable rights issues**. That is, shareholders are free to sell their rights to subscribe on the market. (Some are **non-renounceable rights issues**, which means investors are not able to sell the rights even though they may decline to subscribe more funds.) The value of each right to subscribe to one share naturally depends on the discount implied with the rights subscription price.

Another method that companies use to raise further capital is that of options. An **option** to purchase shares is the right to subscribe to shares at a price and time that are predetermined. Companies issue options for four main purposes:
- to set in place a programmed raising of funds in the future
- to reward and motivate employees so that their financial health is aligned with that of the company
- as an additional benefit attached to an equity issue to make the current issue more attractive, but also to put in place the opportunity to raise more capital
- as an additional benefit attached to a debt contract to secure the funds or to benefit from a lower interest rate.

VALUE TO BUSINESS

- Owners of companies may at times wish to expand their business or liquidate some or all of their ownership rights by selling ownership rights or shares to other investors.
- Ownership rights are traded and transferred by means of ordinary shares and preference shares.
- All companies issue ordinary shares; some, but not all, companies issue preference shares.
- Another method which companies use to raise further capital is by means of rights and options, which confer the right to subscribe to shares in the future at a price and time which are predetermined.

13.8 Hybrid finance

LEARNING OBJECTIVE 13.8 Discuss hybrid financial instruments.

Hybrid debt securities are securities that have characteristics of both debt and equity. The main hybrid securities are convertible notes and convertible preference shares. **Convertible notes** convert to the issuer's ordinary shares, while **convertible preference shares** also convert at maturity to the issuer's ordinary shares. The major difference between the two is that convertible notes pay interest, while convertible preference shares pay dividends, which are usually fully franked. With both types of securities, however, the issuer receives cash only on issue. Eventual conversion to ordinary shares is a cashless transaction. The classification of hybrid instruments in the statement of financial position is problematic.

Convertible notes

Convertible notes, while all converting ultimately to the issuer's ordinary shares, nevertheless are issued with varying conditions. However, as entities issuing convertible notes are generally interested in claiming tax deductions for the interest payable on them, these notes are normally issued with conditions that are acceptable to the ATO under the relevant legislation. Chief among these conditions are that:
- the interest rate is fixed
- note-holders, not issuers, decide when to convert notes to ordinary shares
- conversion must take place between two and ten years from the date of issue, so long as the note maturity is not less than two years.

The notes are normally unsecured and often subordinated, but some notes may not be issued with these conditions. Subordinated notes are issued when an entity has several issues of similar notes and wishes to indicate precedence in redemption should the entity fail.

Convertible preference shares

Convertible preference shares (CPS) are preference shares that the owner can exchange for a certain number of ordinary shares. CPS generally do not convert to ordinary shares in a fixed ratio, such as one for one or one for two, as is the case with convertible notes. Normally, the conversion ratio is calculated by taking into account the volume-weighted average sale price on the ordinary shares on the market in the past 5 to 20 days before the conversion date. Additionally, a discount rate of 2.5–10 per cent is applied to the average market price to enhance the conversion ratio, to increase the benefits to the investor.

> **VALUE TO BUSINESS**
>
> - Hybrid debt instruments are instruments that have characteristics of both debt and equity.
> - The principal hybrid instruments are convertible notes and convertible preference shares.
> - Both convertible notes and convertible preference shares convert at maturity to the issuer's ordinary shares.
> - The main difference between the two is that convertible notes pay interest, while convertible preference shares pay dividends, which are usually fully franked.
> - The issuer receives cash only on issue and the eventual conversion to ordinary shares is a cashless transaction.

13.9 International sources of funding

LEARNING OBJECTIVE 13.9 Describe the use of international finance.

Australia and New Zealand as nations have traditionally relied heavily on overseas capital as a source of funds to assist in their development. Their need for international capital stems directly from their inability, for various reasons, to save enough themselves and therefore to provide sufficient homegrown capital. Foreign investment occurs when overseas investors make direct equity investments and lend directly, or make portfolio investments in equities or debt. **Direct investment** is defined by the Reserve Bank of Australia (RBA) as capital invested in an entity by an investor that has significant influence over the key policies of the entity. An example of a direct equity investment is the establishment of Virgin Blue in Australia. In contrast, **portfolio investment** is assumed to mean that the investor has no control over the key policies of the entity. Australian and New Zealand companies can attract international funding by offering securities for sale in overseas markets and attracting foreign investors to purchase securities in Australian and New Zealand markets. For example, both Woolworths Ltd and Telstra Corporation have raised debt in foreign capital markets and denominated in foreign currencies.

VALUE TO BUSINESS

- Australia and New Zealand as nations have traditionally relied heavily on overseas capital as a source of funds to assist in their development.
- Foreign investment occurs when overseas investors make direct equity investments and lend directly, or make portfolio investments in equities or debt.
- Direct investment is defined by the RBA as capital invested in an entity by an investor that has significant influence over the key policies of the entity.
- Portfolio investment means that the investor has no control over the key policies of the entity.

13.10 New funding opportunities for business

LEARNING OBJECTIVE 13.10 Describe new funding opportunities for business such as crowdfunding, ICOs, angel investors and microcredit.

In the past decade, some new and exciting finance opportunities have become available for businesses. These sources of finance are gaining popularity among different types of business structures and sizes. Funding opportunities today are much less formal than the traditional types of finance such as debt versus equity, floor-plan finance and factoring. They can be short or long term and can suit various business structures. These new funding opportunities include crowdfunding, ICOs, angel investors and microcredit.

Crowdfunding

Crowdfunding is a source of finance for a business project where a large group of people come together through the internet and pledge small amounts of money for the initial phase of the project. The first crowdfunding platform was launched in 2012, but the first instance of crowdfunding was back in the late 1990s when a rock band funded a tour through advertising to its loyal fans. Popular crowdfunding platforms include Kickstarter, Indiegogo and Circleup. In 2017 alone, $34 billion was raised in crowdfunding.

Initial coin offerings

Initial coin offerings (ICOs) are a type of funding using cryptocurrencies. In 2013, the first ICO (also known as token sales) was sold and since then ICOs have grown in popularity and raised many billions of dollars. ICOs can be an important source of funding for new companies that sell their underlying crypto tokens in exchange for bitcoin and ether. This process is very similar to an IPO (initial public offering) except that in an IPO's case it is shares that are purchased in a company, not crypto tokens. Successful ICO projects include Ethereum selling $18 million in tokens in 2014, Aragon selling $25 million in tokens and Status.im selling $270 million in tokens.

Angel investors

Angel investors are another source of finance for start-up businesses that has also vastly increased in popularity in recent years. An **angel investor** is a private investor who provides the capital for a business. Many of them use crowdfunding as a means to invest or form groups with other angels to share insights and consolidate their investment capital. In recent years, angel investors have invested over $23 billion in funds to over 67 000 businesses (Cremades 2018).

Microcredit (microloans)

Microcredit is a form of finance to small-business owners or individuals. The recipients of microcredit are unable to secure loans through traditional financial institutions. In recent years, these loans have been issued to small-business owners with little or no capital in developing countries such as Uganda, Indonesia, Nicaragua and Serbia. Success stories include a Ugandan couple who have developed a home solar-lighting system through microcredit and a farmer in Nicaragua who has grown an orchard of 60 000 fruit trees with the help of microcredit.

SUMMARY OF LEARNING OBJECTIVES

13.1 Discuss the management of net working capital.

Working capital is the funds invested in current assets. Net working capital is current assets minus current liabilities. In managing the level of net working capital, entities are concerned with maintaining liquidity, the need to earn the required rate of return on assets, and the cost and risk of short-term funding. Entities use the hedging principle to match the source of funding with the use of that funding.

13.2 Outline the issues underlying the management of cash.

Issues that entities must manage with regards to cash include the need to have sufficient cash, the timing of cash flows, the cost of cash and the cost of not having enough cash. Entities must have sufficient cash on hand to meet their bills on time. The timing of cash flows may be manipulated to some extent, in order to have sufficient cash at all times and to optimise the returns to cash. The cost of holding cash is the opportunity cost of holding liquid deposits, but the cost of not holding sufficient cash may be the cost of arranging emergency loans or could be the ultimate penalty: insolvency and business cessation.

13.3 Discuss the management of accounts receivable.

Accounts receivable provide benefits for entities, but they also involve costs. The value of accounts receivable carried by any entity depends on a number of policies and processes that the entity determines and manages. These policies and processes include credit policies and collection policies and procedures. Credit policies include the decision to offer credit, selecting suitable customers, setting credit limits and deciding payment terms. Collection procedures include the monitoring of ageing accounts and putting in place steps to exert pressure on customers to pay.

13.4 Identify the issues with respect to the management of inventories.

Managing inventories is an art, although there are techniques managers may use to transform much of the role into a science. Inventories are held to facilitate production and sales. The cost of holding inventories includes both ordering and holding costs. Inventories may be managed by entities holding minimum levels at all times, while other entities use just-in-time (JIT) techniques to reduce costs.

13.5 Compare the sources of short-term finance.

The most common sources of short-term finance for entities are accrued wages and taxes, trade credit, bank overdrafts, commercial bills and promissory notes, factoring or debtor/invoice/trade finance, and inventory loans or floor-plan finance.

13.6 Compare the sources of long-term debt finance.

Long-term debt finance is supplied to borrowers through financial institutions as intermediaries or directly by debt markets. Most entities tend to look to financial institutions as suppliers of intermediated finance in the first instance. For long-term funding purposes, most financial institutions offer fixed- and variable-rate business loans, instalment loans, interest-only loans, fully-drawn advances and lease finance. Entities wanting to raise debt finance from the Australian market have corporate bonds, notes and debentures to choose from as the financing media.

13.7 Explain equity finance instruments and their roles.

Ordinary shares are the standard security by which companies divide and sell ownership rights to investors who wish to buy part-ownership of the entities. Ordinary shares have an initial issue price but, after that time, their price is set in the secondary market by the interaction of supply and demand. Most larger public companies are listed on the securities exchange, but private entities are not, no matter what their size. One of the major attractions of ordinary shares is their limited liability. Preference shares are a hybrid form of capital, just as convertible notes are a mix of debt and equity. Preference shares tend to lean more towards equity than debt. Additionally, companies raise funds through the issue of rights and options.

13.8 Discuss hybrid financial instruments.

Hybrid debt securities are securities that have characteristics of both debt and equity. The main hybrid securities are convertible notes and convertible preference shares. Both convertible notes and convertible preference shares convert to the issuer's ordinary shares. The major difference between the two is that convertible notes pay interest, while convertible preference shares pay dividends, which are usually fully franked. With both types of securities, however, the issuer receives cash only on issue. Eventual conversion to ordinary shares is a cashless transaction.

13.9 Describe the use of international finance.

Countries like Australia and New Zealand have traditionally relied heavily on overseas capital as a source of funds to assist in their development. Their need for international capital stems directly from their inability to save enough and therefore to provide sufficient homegrown capital. Foreign investment in industry occurs when overseas investors make direct equity investments and lend directly, or make portfolio investments in equities or debt.

13.10 Describe new funding opportunities for business such as crowdfunding, ICOs, angel investors and microcredit.

In recent years, there has been much growth in new and innovative sources of finance such as crowdfunding, ICOs, angel investors and microcredit. These provide opportunities for new start-ups and also individuals (in particular those from developing countries) who are contemplating setting up small businesses but cannot access traditional sources of finance.

KEY TERMS

angel investor A private investor who provides the capital for a business.

convertible notes Notes that convert to the issuer's ordinary shares.

convertible preference shares Shares that convert at maturity to the issuer's ordinary shares.

corporate bonds Unsecured loans that are contracted directly with investors in the debt markets and normally available only to entities with acceptable credit ratings.

crowdfunding A source of finance for a business project where a large group of people come together through the internet and pledge small amounts of money for the initial phase of the project.

current assets Cash and other assets that are expected to be converted to cash or used in an entity within one year or one operating cycle, whichever is longer.

current liabilities Obligations that can reasonably be expected to be paid within one year or one operating cycle.

debentures Loan instruments that are normally secured by a fixed or floating charge over assets.

direct investment Capital invested in an entity by an investor with significant influence over the key policies of the entity.

factoring Funding method that gives the lender the right to collect the cash owing on invoices.

finance leases Non-cancellable contractual obligations to make payments in return for the use of an asset for the majority of its useful life.

fully drawn advances (FDAs) Loans initially drawn down to the full amount and repaid over the term of the loan by a fixed repayment schedule.

hedging principle Matching the maturity of a source of funding with its use.

hire-purchase agreement Involves a financial institution buying the asset required by the customer, then hiring it to the customer for use during the agreed period in return for hire/rental payments.

hybrid debt securities Securities that have characteristics of both debt and equity.

initial coin offerings (ICOs) A type of funding using cryptocurrencies rather than shares.

insolvent entity Entity that is unable to pay its bills or meet its financial obligations on time.

instalment loans Loans with fixed repayment schedules that are negotiated at the outset.

lease Contract by which an owner of an asset allows another person or entity the use of the asset.

lessee Person or entity that leases an asset.

lessor Owner of a leased asset.

liquidity Ability of an entity to meet its short-term financial commitments.

microcredit A form of finance to small-business owners or individuals who are unable to secure loans through traditional financial institutions.

net working capital Current assets less current liabilities.

non-renounceable rights issues Rights issues where investors are not able to sell the rights even though they may decline the right to subscribe more funds.

novated lease Involves a three-party agreement between an employee, an employer and a financial institution to provide a motor vehicle to the employee as part of a salary package.

operating leases Contractual agreements that are cancellable upon given notice and tend to be of much shorter term than the useful life of the asset.

option Right to subscribe to shares at a price and time that are predetermined.

ordinary shares Most commonly traded type of shares in Australia. Holders of ordinary shares are part-owners of a company and may receive payments in cash (called dividends). This class of shares has no preferential rights to dividends or capital on winding up.

overdraft Loan facility attached to a current account.

permanent funding Funding with maturity greater than one year.

portfolio investment Investment where the investor has no control over the key policies of the entity.

preference shares Shares with characteristics of both debt and equity. They rank before ordinary shares in the event of liquidation of a company and usually receive a fixed rate of return.

renounceable rights issues Rights issues where shareholders are free to sell their rights to subscribe on the market.

rights issue Issue of new shares to existing shareholders.

spontaneous sources of funding Sources of funding that arise in a substantially unplanned and unstructured way in the ordinary course of business.

temporary funding Short-term formal sources of finance.

working capital Difference between current assets and current liabilities.

APPLY YOUR KNOWLEDGE
37 marks

PART A

(a) Explain the advantages and disadvantages of using factoring or discounting. *4 marks*

(b) Discuss what type of businesses would benefit from floor-plan finance. *4 marks*

(c) Graham Ltd is a profitable manufacturing company in the clothing industry and currently has a net working capital of 150 per cent. Cockcroft Ltd commenced operations this year in the biotechnology industry and is currently trialling a new pharmaceutical drug to cure cancer. Cockcroft Ltd's net working capital is 15 per cent. Provide reasons why these two entities could have vastly different net working capital and how both could still be in existence in five years' time. *4 marks*

PART B

(a) The following table illustrates key figures from Robertson Ltd's statement of profit or loss and statement of financial position for the five-year period ending 30 June 2020.

Item	2016	2017	2018	2019	2020
Trade creditors	680	850	1 020	1 190	1 360
Credit purchases	3 400	3 740	4 080	4 250	2 312

Calculate the creditors turnover (in days) for Robertson Ltd for the years 2017 to 2020. Describe the trend over the four-year period. Comment on the trend above if Robertson Ltd's average credit limit with its suppliers is 30 days. *9 marks*

(b) Robertson Ltd requires external finance to fund a new business venture which will be developed over the next five years. The company is considering the options of an instalment loan and an interest-only loan. Discuss the advantages and disadvantages of both of these forms of finance. *6 marks*

(c) Robertson Ltd is also considering a 180-day commercial bill at 7 per cent yield including fees. The face value of the commercial bill is $400 000. How much will Robertson Ltd receive? *5 marks*

(d) Robertson Ltd's average collection period for its accounts receivable is 45 days. Its credit terms are 30 days. What strategies can Robertson Ltd implement to reduce its collection period to a period closer to its credit terms? *5 marks*

SELF-EVALUATION ACTIVITIES

13.1 David Ltd has introduced a new credit policy of '5/10, net 30' in an effort to reduce the value of its accounts receivable and the number of days the debts remain outstanding.

Required

(a) How much is payable by Cheens Ltd for a $120 000 invoice paid on the eighth day after issue for goods purchased?

(b) The cash forgone by David Ltd is a cost that purchased a benefit of how many days earlier payment if Cheens Ltd had always paid on the 30th day?

SOLUTION TO 13.1

(a) $\$120\,000 - (0.05 \times \$120\,000) = \$114\,000$

(b) Benefit $= 30 - 8 = 22$ days

13.2 Shelley Ltd provides you with the following inventory and cost data for the three years ending December 2020.

Item	2018	2019	2020
Average inventory	90	120	150
Cost of sales	440	500	550
Inventory turnover (days)			

Required

(a) Calculate the inventory turnover for 2018 to 2020.

(b) Describe the trend of inventory turnover during this three-year period.

SOLUTION TO 13.2

(a)

Item	2018	2019	2020
Average inventory	90	120	150
Cost of sales	440	500	550
Inventory turnover (days)	4.88	4.16	3.66

(b) The inventory turnover for Shelley Ltd decreased from 4.88 times to 3.66 times per year. When converted to a daily rate, this is approximately 74 days in 2018 and 99 days in 2020. So, in 2020 the inventory is turning over only just more than three times per year and the turnover has significantly slowed during the three-year period. Depending on the type of business and its industry, this is probably not a satisfactory trend. Shelley Ltd will need to investigate the reasons for this decrease. There could have been a major change in inventory mix during this period, which could explain the decrease in ratio (e.g. is Shelley Ltd selling more expensive items that are slower to convert to sales?).

13.3 During the past five years, Delta Ltd had the following average trade creditors at balance date and made the following purchases (in millions).

Item	2017	2018	2019	2020	2021
Average trade creditors	800	1 000	1 200	1 400	1 600
Credit purchases	4 000	4 400	4 800	5 000	5 200

Required

(a) Calculate the creditors turnover in times per year.

(b) Calculate the creditors turnover in days.

(c) Comment on the trend in creditors turnover.

SOLUTION TO 13.3

(a) and (b)

Item	2017	2018	2019	2020	2021
Average trade creditors	800	1 000	1 200	1 400	1 600
Credit purchases	4 000	4 400	4 800	5 000	5 200
Creditors turnover (times)	5.0	4.4	4.0	3.6	3.3
Creditors turnover (days)	73.0	83.0	91.3	102.2	112.3

(c) It is obvious from the calculations illustrated above that the average settlement time is decreasing in number of times per year but increasing in number of days. In 2017 the average time to settle creditors was 73 days and in 2021 the average time increased to 112 days. This is clearly not a satisfactory situation for Delta Ltd. The company needs to examine whether the credit terms have increased over this time (i.e. whether the trade creditors are being more generous to Delta Ltd, or the increase in days is more a case of poor cash management practices and insufficient cash).

COMPREHENSION QUESTIONS

13.4 Differentiate between working capital and net working capital. Provide examples of both current asset and current liability accounts that would be taken into consideration to determine net working capital for a bakery. **LO1**

13.5 Which of the following entities do you think would have the greatest proportion of working capital held as cash? Why? **LO1**
(a) Local butcher
(b) Hardware store
(c) Stallholder at a weekend market selling handicrafts

13.6 Which of the following entities do you think would have the greatest proportion of working capital held as accounts receivable? Why? **LO1**
(a) Local butcher
(b) Hardware store
(c) Stallholder at a weekend market selling handicrafts

13.7 Which of the following entities do you think would have the greatest proportion of working capital held as inventory? Why? **LO1**
(a) Local butcher
(b) Hardware store
(c) Stallholder at a weekend market selling handicrafts

13.8 As production manager for a hoodie manufacturing company, how would you react regarding your inventory levels in the following circumstances? **LO4**
(a) Continual breakdowns in the machine used to weave the fabric for the hoodies.
(b) Unreliable outsourced final colouring of the hoodies.
(c) Reduction in interest rates.
(d) Unreliable supplier of fabric for the hoodies.

13.9 As inventory manager in a retail-chain warehouse, how would you react regarding your inventory levels in the following circumstances? **LO4**
(a) Sudden volatility in sales.
(b) Continual short deliveries by suppliers.
(c) Managerial suggestions to reduce the number of product lines.
(d) Increase in interest rates.

13.10 If you had just started a business and were in the early development phase, which forms of short-term credit would you try to maximise? Why? **LO5**

13.11 What is a novated lease? How is it markedly different from other leases? **LO6**

13.12 Summarise the advantages and disadvantages of owning ordinary shares in a company compared with financing the company through a loan. **LO6, 7**

13.13 Distinguish between rights and options. **LO7**

EXERCISES

★ BASIC | ★ ★ MODERATE | ★ ★ ★ CHALLENGING

13.14 ★ **LO5**

Mike and Andy is a clothing store for teenagers. It is chronically short of cash, so arranges a 120-day bank-accepted commercial bill (BAB). According to the theory of management of assets, what use should it put this money to?

13.15 ★ **LO2, 5**

How can a profitable, fast-growing entity such as Mike and Andy be chronically short of cash?

13.16 ★ **LO2**

Mike and Andy has on average $150 000 of employees' pay, tax withheld and superannuation contributions in its hands at all times. What use should it make of these funds?

13.17 ★ ★ **LO2, 3, 5**

Pineapple Plantations Pty Ltd manufactures sustainable, Pineapple-based products for sale to wholesalers and retailers around Australia and New Zealand. Dave Geitz, the manager, has a goal of increasing the market share of the company. Strategies to achieve this goal are increasing marketing and promotional activities, and offering attractive credit terms to new customers. The implementation of both strategies has been successful. Pineapple Plantations is enjoying an upsurge in sales and its accounts receivable balances have increased dramatically. The company now needs to increase its regular orders for raw materials. Dave is concerned that the company will not have sufficient cash available to pay the resultant supplier invoices when they fall due. What is your advice to Pineapple Plantations regarding the financing of the supplier invoices?

13.18 ★ ★   **LO2**

'Entities must juggle the costs of holding cash with the costs of not having enough.' Explain the issues involved.

13.19 ★ ★   **LO3**

Explain, with numerical examples, four aspects of an entity's credit policies and how decisions regarding each impact on the value of accounts receivable at any time.

13.20 ★ ★   **LO3**

After thinking about how this could be done, explain the processes an entity might use to collect its debts.

13.21 ★ ★   **LO4**

Give examples of inventories of retail products that would incur high costs for each of the following.
(a) Storage and display
(b) Insurance
(c) Deterioration or obsolescence
(d) Theft

13.22 ★ ★   **LO5**

Before reforms were put in place during the 1980s, many entities allowed their overdraft accounts to remain continually overdrawn. Banks reformed the situation by advising these clients to contract for longer term funding. Provide an example of a company's circumstances that would necessitate entering into an overdraft arrangement with a bank.

13.23 ★ ★ ★   **LO6**

Explain the advantages to all parties of a novated lease.

13.24 ★ ★

Explain the trend in crowdfunding over the past five years. What types of businesses are commonly financed by crowdfunding?   **LO10**

13.25 ★ ★

Explain what is meant by an ICO. Differentiate between IPOs and ICOs.   **LO10**

13.26 ★ ★

A friend is thinking about starting a company manufacturing small robots for household chores. Explain to your friend the different types of finance that would be available to him.   **LO10**

PROBLEMS

★ BASIC | ★ ★ MODERATE | ★ ★ ★ CHALLENGING

13.27 Managing accounts receivable ★ ★   **LO3**

Coconut Plantations Pty Ltd manufactures sustainable, coconut-based products for sale to wholesalers and retailers around Australia and New Zealand. Jo Geter, the manager, has a goal of increasing the market share of the company. Strategies to achieve this goal are increasing marketing and promotional activities, and offering attractive credit terms to new customers. The implementation of both strategies has been successful. Coconut Plantations is enjoying an upsurge in sales and its accounts receivable balances have increased dramatically to average $140 000 on most trading days of the year. If Jo could reduce the accounts receivable balance, she believes the company could increase its inventory, sales and profitability. But Jo is concerned about exerting too much pressure on its accounts receivable for fear of losing customers.

Required

(a) How could Coconut Plantations encourage its credit customers to pay earlier?
(b) If Coconut Plantations' accounts receivable management strategies result in average accounts receivable reducing to $90 000, how would this lead to increases in sales and profitability?

13.28 Managing payroll ★ ★ **LO5**

CuteIT makes smartphone covers. The employee payroll averages $600 000 per week. CuteIT would like to extend the pay cycle to fortnightly. The manufacturing workers union argues that the company is saving payroll-handling costs of $10 000 and receives other benefits. If short-term funding earns 10 per cent per annum, quantify the other benefits.

13.29 Managing cash ★ ★ **LO2**

Volley Ltd has $1 million spare cash from commissions earned during the busy pre-Christmas season. Staff are paid a retainer, as well as part of the commissions earned through sales. Volley Ltd is aware from past experience that sales fall off during winter and there will be a cash deficit then. Volley Ltd finds it can invest the funds for six months by taking a two-month term deposit at 5.0 per cent per annum and rolling it over twice, a three-month deposit at 5.2 per cent per annum rolled over once or a straight six-month term deposit at 5.5 per cent per annum. Advise Volley Ltd on the best course of action.

13.30 Managing accounts receivable ★ ★ **LO1, 3**

Baxter Ltd reported $200 million in credit sales in 2017–18 and 2018–19. Average accounts receivable dropped from $25 million to $20 million over the two periods.

Required

(a) Assuming 220 trading days each year, how has debtors turnover changed?

(b) Explain why this might have occurred.

13.31 Managing trade creditors ★ ★ **LO1, 5**

Lavender Plantations Pty Ltd manufactures Lavender-based products and commenced operations in 2019. Production and sales have grown consistently. Here are data for the last four years (in $ thousand).

Item	2019	2020	2021	2022
Trade creditors	6.6	85.0	156	170
Credit purchases	370	1 300	1 320	1 500

Required

(a) Compute the creditors turnover for Lavender Plantations Pty Ltd's trade creditors for the last three years.

(b) How would you explain the differences or similarities in creditors turnover values each year?

13.32 Managing trade creditors ★ **LO1, 5**

Toowong Ltd has been growing relatively slowly in a mature industry. Its trade creditor and credit sales data for the last five years (in $ million) are shown below.

Item	2017	2018	2019	2020	2021
Trade creditors	190	205	251	297	345
Credit purchases	2 103	2 290	2 413	2 505	2 670

Required

(a) Compute the creditors turnover for Toowong Ltd's trade creditors for the last four years.

(b) What does this ratio trend tell you about the company?

13.33 Arranging short-term finance ★ ★ **LO5**

Advantage Tennis Coaching (ATC) in Brisbane offers coaching for junior, elite and mature tennis players. Nicholas Cash, the sole proprietor, has identified that the business cycle will be seasonal, with most activities in the spring and summer months. As a result, he is predicting that net working capital will be negative from the beginning of April to the end of September. Nicholas arranges with his bank for funds to finance net working capital during this period. He requires 180-day money and about $60 000. His bank offers commercial bills at 5 per cent yield, including fees.

Required

(a) How much does ATC receive?

(b) How much must the business repay?

13.34 Managing equity finance ★ ★ **LO7**

Rosedale Ltd is a listed company with 30 million shares issued. It wants to raise more capital by means of a rights issue. The current market price is $6 and the subscription price is $5. The

---

rights will be issued on the basis of 1:5. How much will Rosedale raise if all rights are taken up, disregarding any transaction costs?

13.35 Analysis of profitability, liquidity and financial structure ★ ★ LO1, 2, 7

JB Hi-Fi Ltd's 2018 statement of financial position provides the following data.

	2018 $m	2017 $m
Non-current assets	1 281.2	1 292.3
Current assets	1 210.5	1 167.5
Total assets	**2 491.7**	**2 459.8**
Equity	947.6	853.5
Non-current liabilities	626.9	720.9
Current liabilities	917.2	885.4
Total equity and liabilities	**2 491.7**	**2 459.8**

Source: JB Hi-Fi Ltd 2018, p. 56.

In 2018, JB Hi Fi Ltd earned record revenue (increased by 35.3 per cent) and the EPS (earnings per share) increased by 31.5 per cent. JB Hi-Fi Ltd's profit after tax was $233.2 million in 2018 and $172.4 million in 2017.

Required

(a) Comment on JB Hi-Fi Ltd's profitability and liquidity situation.

(b) Analyse and comment on JB Hi-Fi Ltd's financing structure in the 2017–18 period.

13.36 Arranging short-term finance ★ ★ ★ LO5

Katelyn Ltd arranges a 91-day commercial bill: 91 days because the 90th day was a Sunday. The face value is $200 000 and Katelyn receives $197 010. What is the yield?

DECISION-MAKING ACTIVITIES

13.37 Base Company buys in sand, gravel, cement powder and steel reinforcement. These raw materials cost about $15 million most years. Base Company has recently enjoyed a surge in sales after it liberalised its credit policies. The result of the change in credit policies is that the value of accounts receivable has risen and management have decided to hold higher levels of raw material inventories. As a result, Base Company is experiencing something of a cash squeeze. The financial manager thinks a $250 000 commercial bill will give the entity time to sort out the increased accounts receivable problems. This finance will cost 8 per cent per annum. The sales manager comes up with another idea, of slowing down creditor payments to an average 45 days to match the increase in accounts receivable. Alternatively, Base Company has been in contact with a factoring company that has offered to take over a proportion of the accounts receivable at a rate of 80 per cent of the original accounts receivable balance (i.e. a 20 per cent discount). What plan of action do you suggest for Base Company? What are the advantages and disadvantages of each of the three strategies that have been put forward?

13.38 Plush Cruiser Ltd builds luxury houseboats. The entity needs funds for expansion. It could take out a fixed-rate or variable-rate business loan over, say, 25 years. An alternative is issuing new shares to investors in the form of a rights issue. Explain the issues relating to these two different forms of finance. In your answer, refer to current interest rates relating to fixed- and variable-rate loans, and also what the potential costs are of offering shares via a rights issue. What other factors relating to Plush Cruiser Ltd need to be taken into account in order to arrive at the best decision for the company?

13.39 Pozible is a crowdfunding site for creative, community and passion projects. Go to the website at www.pozible.com.

Required

(a) What are the benefits of joining a crowdfunding community like Pozible?

(b) How much money has been raised in pledges?

(c) Choose an area such as creativity, social good or side projects, and search online for the top five projects in that area. Summarise the projects' objectives, funds raised and future strategies.

REFERENCES

BMW Group 2017, *Annual report 2017*, www.bmwgroup.com.

Cremades, A 2018, 'How angel investors and angel groups work', *Forbes*, www.forbes.com/sites/alejandrocremades/2018/09/25/how-angel-investors-and-angel-groups-work.

Factors Chain International (FCI) 2018, 'Statistics', https://fci.nl/en/solutions/statistics2018.

JB Hi-Fi Ltd 2018, *Preliminary final report 2018*, www.jbhifi.com.au.

JB Hi-Fi Ltd 2017, *Annual report 2017*, www.jbhifi.com.au.

JB Hi-Fi Ltd 2016, *Annual report 2016*, www.jbhifi.com.au.

JB Hi-Fi Ltd 2015, *Annual report 2015*, www.jbhifi.com.au.

Qantas Airways Ltd 2018, *Annual report 2018*, www.qantas.com.au.

ACKNOWLEDGEMENTS

Photo: © StockRocket / Getty Images

Photo: © Nestor Rizhniak / Shutterstock.com

Problem 13.35: © JB Hi-Fi Ltd 2018

Performance measurement

LEARNING OBJECTIVES

After studying this chapter, you should be able to:

14.1 explain the importance of measuring organisational performance and outline common frameworks and reports used to assess and report organisational performance

14.2 outline common organisational structures, responsibility centres and reasons for divisional performance evaluation, and generate divisional performance reports

14.3 apply investment centre performance evaluation measures such as return on investment (ROI), residual income (RI) and economic value added

14.4 examine the use of environmental and social performance measurement

14.5 discuss the issues surrounding individual performance measurement

14.6 assess the use of non-financial performance measures.

Chapter preview

This chapter discusses performance measurement. Many aspects of an entity can be measured, including the performance of the entity as a whole, specific divisions or even individual employees. Linking the performance measurement system to organisational objectives ensures that the focus is on the goals of the entity. Contemporary performance measurement systems include a balance between financial and non-financial measures, and between short-term and long-term measures. There is also a growing expectation that environmental and social performance should be measured and reported. Such measures should be simple to apply and understand, and should link the operations with strategy and encourage beneficial behaviour.

Performance measurement tools covered in this chapter include the balanced scorecard, environmental and social measures, and financial measures such as return on investment, residual income and economic value added. Non-financial performance measures and issues relating to individual performance measurement are also discussed.

14.1 Organisational performance measurement

LEARNING OBJECTIVE 14.1 Explain the importance of measuring organisational performance and outline common frameworks and reports used to assess and report organisational performance.

Organisational performance measurement forms part of the overall management process. This includes developing goals to support the achievement of an entity's mission, transforming those goals into strategies and then measuring performance. Decisions need to be made regarding the types of business an entity should be involved in, how the entity can compete within the chosen markets, how the entity should be structured internally and what processes can be used to harness resources efficiently and effectively. The performance evaluation of the efficiency and effectiveness of the entity's strategies, structures and processes is integral to the achievement of its mission.

For example, JB Hi-Fi Ltd's mission statement focuses on its principal activity: 'The retailing of home consumer products, with particular emphasis on consumer electronics, electrical goods, car sound systems and music, games and movies.' The company needs to formulate strategies, structure the entity and design processes to ensure the efficient and effective use of resources in achieving its mission.

A **mission statement** or vision is simply a short statement that sets out the overall philosophy and objectives of the entity. It is normally quite abstract, but concrete goals and measures can be formulated from it. The design of an entity's strategies is formulated from the mission or vision statement, which in turn lays the foundation for the direction and control of the entity's resources. Performance measurement helps evaluate the entity's success and provides feedback for future action. This cyclic process of goal setting and evaluation helps motivate people and entities towards goal achievement, and in adjusting and refining future goals and practices.

Performance measurement systems could include measures to evaluate the performance of the entity as a whole, organisational divisions or segments, individual managers and employees, customers, products/services, environmental and social performance, suppliers or processes. In fact, any aspect that can help meet the attainment of the entity's goals can be evaluated.

The whole entity's performance is monitored in various ways. Earlier chapters reviewed the preparation and presentation of general purpose financial statements (GPFS). The production of the financial statements gives a good evaluation of the financial success of an entity. Financial statements are prepared based on standards for the purpose of providing general users with financial performance information. Publicly listed entities produce an annual report which contains GPFS as well as other key data that external users can evaluate. Increasingly, entities are also reporting their environmental and social performance in corporate social responsibility (CSR) reports. Sustainability reporting, including the **integrated report** and environmental reporting frameworks, was discussed in the first chapter.

Performance evaluation of an entity is not restricted to that reported for external purposes. Internal performance evaluation is also undertaken and can use information from a variety of sources — internal or external to the entity, accounting or non-accounting, financial (quantitative) or non-financial (qualitative).

Balanced scorecard

Various performance frameworks have been developed to help entities focus on the factors that drive successful attainment of goals and corresponding performance measures. One such framework is the

---

balanced scorecard, developed by Robert Kaplan and David Norton. The balanced scorecard framework is presented in figure 14.1, with an example applied to the hypothetical company Electronic Circuits Inc. (ECI) shown in figure 14.2. The **balanced scorecard** provides a set of performance measures that reflect an entity's goals and strategies. The framework includes measures from four perspectives.

1. *Financial.* How do we create value for our shareholders?
2. *Customer.* What do new and existing customers value from us?
3. *Internal operations.* What processes must we excel at to achieve our financial and customer objectives?
4. *Innovation and improvement activities.* How can we continue to improve and create value?

FIGURE 14.1 The balanced scorecard framework

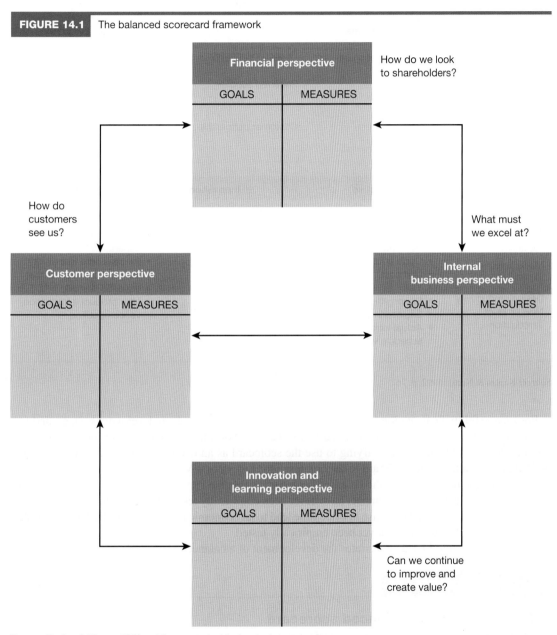

Source: Kaplan & Norton 1992, p. 72.

The balanced scorecard framework implies that traditional financial performance measures are inadequate to capture the entire performance of the entity alone. There is a need to include both short-term and long-term measures, as well as financial and non-financial measures. This is made clear by Kaplan and Norton (1992, p. 72), who compare the balanced scorecard to:

> the dials and indicators in an airplane cockpit. For the complex task of navigating and flying an airplane, pilots need detailed information about many aspects of the flight. They need information on fuel, air speed,

altitude, bearing, destination, and other indicators that summarize the current and predicted environment. Reliance on one instrument can be fatal.

FIGURE 14.2	ECI's balanced business scorecard

Financial perspective		**Customer perspective**	
Goals	Measures	Goals	Measures
Survive Succeed	• Cash flow • Quarterly sales growth and operating income by division • Increased market share and ROE	New products	• Per cent of sales from new products • Per cent of sales from proprietary products
Prosper		Responsive supply	• On-time delivery (defined by customer)
		Preferred supplier	• Share of key accounts' purchases • Ranking by key accounts
		Customer partnership	• Number of cooperative engineering efforts

Internal business perspective		**Innovation and learning perspective**	
Goals	Measures	Goals	Measures
Technology capability	• Manufacturing geometry vs. competition	Technology leadership	• Time to develop next generation
Manufacturing excellence	• Cycle time • Unit cost • Yield	Manufacturing learning Product focus	• Process time to maturity • Per cent of products that equal 80% sales
Design productivity New product introduction	• Silicon efficiency • Engineering efficiency • Actual introduction schedule vs. plan	Time to market	• New product introduction vs. competition

Source: Kaplan & Norton 1992, p. 76.

For successful implementation of a balanced scorecard, an entity needs to develop its strategy first and ensure that top management are committed to its success. Not allowing adequate resources, including training, for its implementation or trying to use the scorecard as an extra level of top-down control will undermine the value of the scorecard to the organisation (Lewy & du Mee 1998).

One of the main criticisms of the balanced scorecard is that the causal relationships between some of the measures and their economic impact have never been empirically tested. For example, will an increase in customer satisfaction or a decrease in cycle time lead to an economic benefit? Logically the relationship may seem plausible, but it has not yet been empirically tested.

Illustrative example 14.1 demonstrates the development of a balanced scorecard.

ILLUSTRATIVE EXAMPLE 14.1

Development of a balanced scorecard

The Fun Hats Company specialises in manufacturing hats. Its main market is the production of hats for companies. That is, corporate clients order hats with their company logo on them in whatever shape and colour they choose. They use the hats for promotional purposes. This has been quite a lucrative market for the company. Its other (older) markets include department stores and specialty stores that want to buy hats. The company has grown quite rapidly, and proper planning and processes have fallen by the wayside in the frenetic pace of everyday operations.

The directors of the company have decided to spend some time thinking about their strategy and performance. They believe the balanced scorecard framework will help them achieve their goals by linking their vision, goals and processes to performance measures. The directors have determined that their vision is: 'To be known as the name synonymous with hats of quality, fun and distinctive appeal'. They now need to develop goals, and the relevant measures and drivers, to support that vision (see table 14.1).

TABLE 14.1   Fun Hats Company — balanced scorecard measures and drivers

Goals	Measures	Drivers
1. Financial perspective		
Improve shareholder value	Economic value added	• Divisional profit
	Market profitability	• Contribution margin per product and contribution per customer group
	Cash flow	• Debtors turnaround
Increase market share	Market share	• New markets obtained • New customers obtained
2. Customer		
Increase customer satisfaction	Customer satisfaction measure	• Number of customer complaints • Customer satisfaction survey
New products	Percentage of sales from new products	• Number of new products
New customers	Percentage of sales from new customers	• Number of new customers
3. Internal operations		
Decrease customer response time	Customer response time	• Number of steps from customer order to delivery • Delivery time
Improve quality	Spoilage and rework (in dollars)	• Defective units produced • Time spent on rework
	Quality training and documentation	• Update manuals • Number of employees undertaking quality training
Reduce stock levels	Raw materials inventory (in dollars)	• Number of suppliers • Number of supplier agreements
	Finished goods inventory (in dollars)	• Warehouse utilisation
4. Innovation and improvement		
Empower workforce	Employee satisfaction survey	• Employee benefits, facilities and challenges
	Employee suggestions	• Number of employee suggestions
	Employee performance	• Number of employees receiving bonuses
Enhance training and development	Develop skills and knowledge	• Number of employees attending training

The measures and drivers are used to monitor the progress towards the goals, and they should be communicated throughout the entity. A measure is sometimes referred to as a key performance outcome (KPO) and helps convey how successfully managers have achieved the stated goal. A driver is more operational in nature and helps ascertain what will influence the measure. For example, the number of new customers obtained will help drive the market share measure. Measures and drivers are two types of **key performance indicator (KPI)**, which is a performance measure that is critical to the success of an entity. Walsh (1996) argues that it is important not only to measure an outcome, but also to link the outcome with operational processes (drivers) to gain an understanding of the actual business processes. He states (p. 11):

> KPOs (outcomes) are those measures which indicate progress towards corporate objectives; they are what the business is expected to deliver. KPDs (drivers) are those measures which have a direct influence on the outcomes; they are the drivers of outcomes.

This suggests that the driver should be the focus of efforts: improve the driver and the outcome will also improve. For example, an increase in the number of new products to market will increase the percentage of new sales from new products.

There have been criticisms that the balanced scorecard framework does not encourage environmental and social performance measurement. However, given that its objective is to link strategy with performance measurement, the balanced scorecard can be expanded to include the environmental and social goals important to the entity. Two approaches could be adopted. The first incorporates the sustainability success factors and KPIs within each of the four original dimensions. Figure 14.3 shows this approach.

FIGURE 14.3	Balanced scorecard measures for sustainability

Financial perspective	**Customer perspective**
• Percentage of sales revenues from 'green' products • Recycling revenues • Energy costs • Fines and penalties for pollution	• Number of product recalls • End of customer use recycling volume • Number of warranty claims
Internal business perspective	**Innovation and learning perspective**
• Percentage of suppliers certified • Volume of hazardous waste • Packaging volume • Number of community complaints • Cost of minority business purchases	• Diversity of workforce and management • Number of volunteer hours • Cost of employee benefits • Percentage of employees trained regarding sustainability

Source: Adapted from Epstein & Wisner 2006.

The second approach increases the number of perspectives. For example, Möller and Schaltegger (2005) suggest adding a 'non-market perspective'. This non-market perspective links the goals, measures and drivers relating to the environmental and social strategy to the vision of the entity. The choice of approach and the goals, measures and drivers to include would depend on the specific opportunities and challenges of the entity. The main advantage of adding a fifth dimension is that it reinforces the importance of the environmental and social dimensions to the entity's core values and mission.

VALUE TO BUSINESS

- Measuring performance helps to evaluate the achievement of an entity's objectives, and also serves to consolidate the efforts of employees and harness them to the entity's goals.
- The balanced scorecard provides a measure of performance based on financial data, customer satisfaction, internal operations, and innovation and improvement levels.
- Environmental and social goals can also be incorporated into an entity's balanced scorecard.
- The balanced scorecard is designed to encourage the use of a wide range of measures to gauge performance. It is linked to the identification of performance drivers that are used to monitor progress towards the entity's goals.

14.2 Divisional performance measurement

LEARNING OBJECTIVE 14.2 Outline common organisational structures, responsibility centres and reasons for divisional performance evaluation, and generate divisional performance reports.

The **organisational structure** is the structure taken by an entity to help direct and control its resources for the attainment of its mission. It also helps to delineate the level of responsibility and authority of a division. The structure an entity forms depends on the nature of its business, the products or services it delivers, and its processes, customers and geographical spread. Common structural forms include functional, geographical or enterprise structures, or combinations of these. Figure 14.4 contains some examples.

JB Hi-Fi Ltd segments its business according to brand and geographical location. Quite simply, it has a New Zealand segment, an Australian segment and its The Good Guys segment. Below this level, the company can evaluate performance per store. The performance measurement system of an entity normally aligns with its structure. That is, each division, group or segment identifies its contribution to the overall goal of the entity and is evaluated on the basis of this contribution.

A manager is normally charged with coordinating the resources of a **business unit**. ('Segment', 'division' and 'business unit' are terms used interchangeably.) The manager of the business unit is therefore responsible for its performance. The division of an organisation, and the subsequent appointment of managers responsible for the performance of the divisions, help to:

- localise decision making, thus improving the timeliness of and access to information
- improve the commitment and motivation of managers to the entity
- free central management time for strategic long-term planning
- assign responsibility and authority to divisional managers.

Once structured into segments or divisions, an entity needs to monitor and evaluate the performance of the segments and the managers and employees within them. Care must be taken when designing performance measurement systems to ensure that individual managers are held accountable only for factors within their control. Individual managers in charge of business units must be set clear boundaries of responsibilities. This means that the results or performance outcomes upon which a manager is to be held accountable can be influenced primarily by that specific manager.

Generally, business units can be classified into four different types of responsibility centres.

1. **Cost centre** — a division of an entity that is solely responsible for providing a product or service at minimal cost. Types of cost centres include manufacturing or service departments such as a manufacturing plant, a maintenance department and a personnel department. The performance of such managers is normally evaluated on cost factors. For example, a typical performance measure for a cost centre manager would include variance analysis (i.e. budgeted costs less actual costs).

2. **Revenue centre** — a division of an entity that is solely responsible for generating a target level of revenue. Revenue centre managers may be able to influence the price, market and volume of products. The manager of a marketing or sales division would be evaluated on the level of revenue achieved (budgeted revenue less actual revenue) and to some extent on customer awareness and satisfaction.

3. **Profit centre** — a division of an entity that is solely responsible for both cost inputs and revenue and therefore the profit of a division. Depending on the scope of their responsibility, profit centre managers would be in charge of production costs/methods, suppliers, prices of products/services and markets. For example, a profit centre manager might be in charge of a geographical location or product line. These managers are evaluated on overall profit achieved through controlling costs and raising revenue (e.g. by comparing budgeted profits to actual profits) and by managing cash flows (measured by cash inflows less cash outflows).

4. **Investment centre** — a division of an entity that is solely responsible for costs, revenues (and therefore profit) and investment in assets. An investment centre manager could be in charge of a geographically located division or a whole enterprise within a large corporation. This is the most sophisticated form of responsibility centre and a manager's performance is assessed on the division's overall contribution to the entity's goal. Normally, this is based on comparing profit to the assets invested, but additional measures would be appropriate under a balanced scorecard framework. For example, variance analysis as well as cash flow considerations could be used.

When evaluating the performance of divisions, both controllable and non-controllable revenues and costs should be identified. Controllable costs are those costs a manager can influence. For example, a cost centre manager can exert influence over the purchase, quantity and storage of raw materials, but will have no influence over the overhead charged to the centre by the head office. Controllable and non-controllable costs should be separated in performance reporting.

FIGURE 14.4 Organisational structures

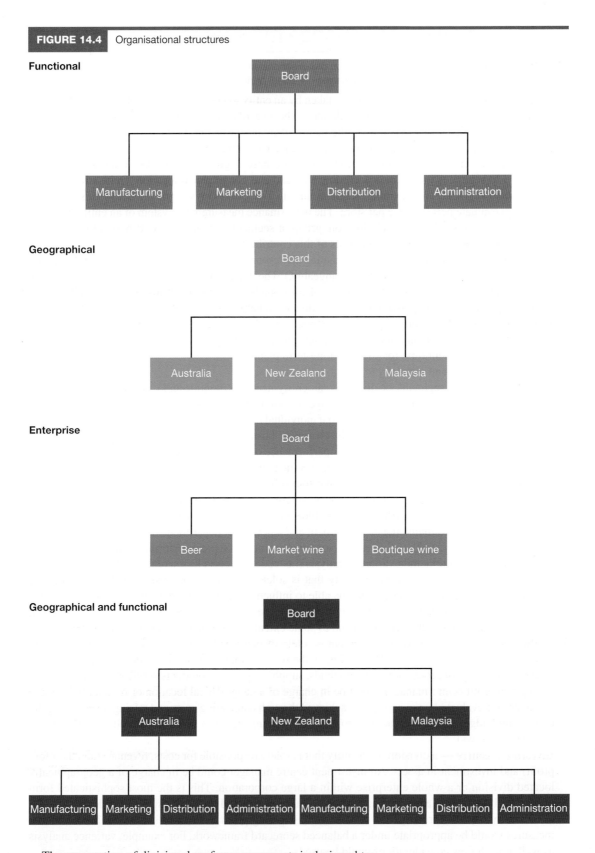

The preparation of divisional performance reports is designed to:
1. help evaluate a division's performance
2. provide a guide for the pricing of products and services
3. evaluate the level of investment in each division.

These three objectives are discussed in the following sections.

Divisional performance evaluation

The first objective of preparing divisional performance reports is to evaluate a division's performance. Generally, a contribution margin format is used when reporting on divisional performance. This is shown in illustrative example 14.2.

Divisional performance evaluation

The format of a divisional report in table 14.2 shows each division's revenue, costs and contribution to the whole organisation. The main requirement in presenting the report is to distinguish between controllable and non-controllable costs. Direct revenues and direct costs are easily traceable to each division. They are items that come under the direct influence of the divisional manager. Each divisional manager's performance evaluation should be based on the divisional margin, as they have control only over the revenues and costs above the divisional margin line. Costs below the divisional margin line are costs that are not incurred directly by the division. Such costs are not controlled by the division but are instead allocated to the division. They include common costs and corporate headquarters costs. Recall from the chapter on costing and pricing in an entity, the discussion on tracing direct costs and allocating indirect costs.

TABLE 14.2   Fun Hats Company — divisional performance report

FUN HATS COMPANY Divisional performance report				
	Corporate	Department stores	Specialty stores	Total
Sales	$990 000	$400 000	$520 000	$1 910 000
Variable costs	470 000	420 000	370 000	1 260 000
Contribution margin	**520 000**	**(20 000)**	**150 000**	**650 000**
Fixed cost	120 000	50 000	80 000	250 000
Divisional margin	**400 000**	**(70 000)**	**70 000**	**400 000**
Common costs				200 000
Profit				$ 200 000

The report shows that the corporate division is contributing $400 000 and the specialty stores division $70 000 in profit, while the department stores division is making a loss of $70 000.

Pricing guide

The second objective of preparing divisional performance reports is to provide a guide for the pricing of products and services. The report in table 14.2 shows common costs of $200 000. A share of this cost is normally allocated to each division, even though the divisional managers do not have any control over such costs. This is done mainly for pricing determination. When setting the prices of their products, divisional managers must remember that the prices have to cover the entity's total costs and operations. These include the entity's common costs. The other benefit of allocating the common costs is to increase awareness of the total entity costs and operations. Figure 14.5 lists the reasons why companies allocate common costs.

FIGURE 14.5   Pros and cons of the allocation of corporate and other common costs to divisions

Pros

1. To remind profit centre managers that indirect costs exist and that profit centre earnings must be adequate to cover some share of those costs.
2. To encourage the use of central services that would otherwise be underutilised.
3. To stimulate profit centre managers to put pressure on central managers to control service costs.
4. To acknowledge that divisions would incur such costs if they were independent units or if services were not provided centrally.

The difficulty in allocating common costs is determining the basis for allocation. The direct costs of each division can easily be traced to each division, but how can the common costs be allocated fairly to each division? Should they be allocated based on factory floor space, revenues or investment? Common costs must be allocated arbitrarily, because there is no true cause/effect basis upon which to allocate them. This was discussed in the chapter on costing and pricing in an entity. Illustrative example 14.3 provides an example where common costs are allocated according to floor space.

ILLUSTRATIVE EXAMPLE 14.3

Divisional performance with common costs allocated

Using the information from illustrative example 14.2, assume that the majority of common costs arise from the building in which the factory is housed (i.e. rates, insurance and so on). Therefore, it has been decided to allocate common costs according to floor space. Based on this allocation, the corporate division will be allocated 900/2000 × $200 000 = $90 000 in common costs. The department stores division and the specialty stores division will be allocated $30 000 and $80 000 respectively. After the allocation, the profit (loss) for each division is as follows: corporate division $310 000; department stores division ($100 000); and specialty stores division ($10 000). This is depicted in table 14.3.

TABLE 14.3   Fun Hats Company — divisional performance report with common costs allocated

FUN HATS COMPANY Divisional performance report (common costs allocated)				
	Corporate	Department stores	Specialty stores	Total
Sales	$ 990 000	$ 400 000	$520 000	$1 910 000
Variable costs	470 000	420 000	370 000	1 260 000
Contribution margin	**520 000**	**(20 000)**	**150 000**	**650 000**
Fixed cost	120 000	50 000	80 000	250 000
Divisional margin	**400 000**	**(70 000)**	**70 000**	**400 000**
Allocated common costs	90 000	30 000	80 000	200 000
Profit	**$ 310 000**	**$(100 000)**	**$ (10 000)**	**$ 200 000**
Floor space	900 m^2	300 m^2	800 m^2	2 000 m^2
Investment level	**$2 200 000**	**$ 75 000**	**$225 000**	**$2 500 000**

The divisional margin of the department stores division shows a loss of $70 000, indicating that this division's revenues are not covering its direct costs, let alone making any contribution to the entity's common costs. The fact that sales are not covering variable costs indicates that the products haven't been priced correctly. Sadly, at times the focus on sales revenue as a performance measure takes the spotlight away from what the product or service or division is actually contributing to the entity. Products or services that are not priced appropriately or are heavily discounted may lead to greater revenue but lower profits. That is, the more you sell, the more you lose. It is easy to sell items cheaply. However, a performance measurement system should reward good performance.

If prices cannot be increased and costs cannot be reduced, then closing the department needs to be considered. If the department closed, the variable costs would disappear in the short term, but some of the fixed divisional costs might remain. However, these costs would disappear in the long term and the closure of the department stores division would improve the overall performance of the organisation by $70 000. The $30 000 in common costs would then need to be allocated to the other divisions.

The specialty stores division, although showing a positive divisional margin, is now showing a loss once the common costs are allocated. This may signal a need to rethink pricing, the common cost allocation method or whether the division is operating efficiently (can it reduce costs?).

Evaluation of investment level

The third objective of preparing divisional performance reports is to evaluate the performance of the division in relation to the level of investment. This evaluation may result in an increase or decrease of investment funds into a division. This could include expanding a division, closing a division or redistributing investment funds. An evaluation of both the short-term and long-term consequences of divisional closure is needed. In our example, two divisions are making a loss (see table 14.3). At first glance, it may seem that closing each of these divisions should increase the overall performance of the organisation by the loss amounts. However, it is necessary to examine what costs would disappear if the divisions were closed. If the specialty stores division closed, the $80 000 in common costs would need to be allocated to the remaining departments. The divisional margin for the specialty stores division shows it is contributing $70 000 towards the common costs and this would be forgone if the division were closed. So it is worthwhile investigating whether the performance could be improved to ensure that the specialty store division can contribute to the bottom line after allowing for common costs. Further, consideration needs to be given to the level of investment. The entity has $225 000 invested in the specialty store division. Would the entity be better off investing the funds elsewhere? The next section addresses this more fully.

VALUE TO BUSINESS

- The organisational structure of an entity is designed to direct and control resources, and to clearly delineate the level of responsibility and authority of a division. These divisions could be functional, geographical or enterprise-based groups.
- Responsibility centres are business units coordinated by a manager. They may take the form of a cost centre, a revenue centre, a profit centre or an investment centre.
- Divisional performance evaluation is designed to evaluate a division's performance, achievement of goals, and contribution to the performance of the organisation as a whole.
- It also provides a guide for the pricing of products and services and a measure of the level of investment in each division.

14.3 Investment centre performance evaluation

LEARNING OBJECTIVE 14.3 Apply investment centre performance evaluation measures such as return on investment (ROI), residual income (RI) and economic value added.

As indicated previously, the evaluation of investment centre performance is based on the economic return relative to the invested resources. Three common investment centre measures are:
- return on investment (ROI)
- residual income (RI)
- economic value added (EVA).

Illustrative example 14.4 demonstrates the application of these three measures. You will notice that some of the ratios presented were discussed in the chapter on analysis and interpretation of financial statements. In addition, this section introduces some new ratios used by management for internal decision making.

ILLUSTRATIVE EXAMPLE 14.4

Investment centre performance evaluation
The divisional performance report and relevant asset and liability amounts for the Fun Hats Company are shown in table 14.4.

▶

TABLE 14.4   Fun Hats Company — divisional performance report and asset values

FUN HATS COMPANY Divisional performance report and asset values				
	Corporate	Department stores	Specialty stores	Total
Sales	$ 990 000	$ 400 000	$520 000	$1 910 000
Variable costs	470 000	420 000	370 000	1 260 000
Contribution margin	**520 000**	**(20 000)**	**150 000**	**650 000**
Fixed cost	120 000	50 000	80 000	250 000
Divisional margin	**400 000**	**(70 000)**	**70 000**	**400 000**
Common costs	90 000	30 000	80 000	200 000
Profit	$ 310 000	$(100 000)	$ (10 000)	$ 200 000
Current assets	$1 000 000	$ 75 000	$ 50 000	$1 125 000
Non-current assets	1 400 000	75 000	200 000	1 675 000
Total assets	2 400 000	150 000	250 000	2 800 000
Accumulated depreciation	200 000	75 000	25 000	300 000
Assets book values	2 200 000	75 000	225 000	2 500 000
Current liabilities	$ 110 000	$ 36 750	$ 12 600	$ 159 350
Floor space	900 m^2	300 m^2	800 m^2	2 000 m^2

Return on investment for a division

The formula for **return on investment (ROI)** is:

$$\text{Return on investment (ROI)} = \frac{\text{Profit}}{\text{Divisional investment}}$$

In our Fun Hats Company example, the ROI for each of the three divisions would be as follows.

		Corporate		Department stores		Specialty stores
ROI =	$\dfrac{\text{Divisional margin}}{\text{Divisional investment}}$ =	$\dfrac{\$400\,000}{\$2\,200\,000}$	=	$\dfrac{(\$70\,000)}{\$75\,000}$	=	$\dfrac{\$70\,000}{\$225\,000}$
	=	18.2%	=	(93.3%)	=	31.1%

The above indicates that the specialty stores division is performing better than the corporate or department stores divisions relative to the level of investment. An entity's desired ROI level will depend on the type of industry the entity operates within, the current economic conditions and the current lifecycle phase of each division.

Further analysis of the ROI can be conducted using the **Du Pont ROI**, which is the return on sales multiplied by the investment turnover for divisions. This formula was used at the Du Pont Corporation in the early 1900s to conduct divisional evaluations. It is also referred to as the Du Pont Method and the Du Pont Formula.

$$\text{Du Pont ROI} = \text{Return on sales} \times \text{Investment turnover}$$

$$\frac{\text{Profit}}{\text{Investment}} = \frac{\text{Profit}}{\text{Sales}} \times \frac{\text{Sales}}{\text{Investment}}$$

Applying this formula to each of our divisions would give the following.

ROI		=	Return on sales	×	Investment turnover
Corporate	$\dfrac{\$400\,000}{\$2\,200\,000}$	=	$\dfrac{\$400\,000}{\$990\,000}$	×	$\dfrac{\$990\,000}{\$2\,200\,000}$
	18.2%	=	40.4%	×	0.45 times
Department stores	$\dfrac{(\$70\,000)}{\$75\,000}$	=	$\dfrac{(\$70\,000)}{\$400\,000}$	×	$\dfrac{\$400\,000}{\$75\,000}$
	−93.3%	=	−17.5%	×	5.3 times
Specialty stores	$\dfrac{\$75\,000}{\$225\,000}$	=	$\dfrac{\$70\,000}{\$520\,000}$	×	$\dfrac{\$520\,000}{\$225\,000}$
	31.1%	=	13.46%	×	2.31 times

The above calculations show that the corporate division has an investment turnover of 0.45 times. **Investment turnover**, sometimes called **asset turnover**, is a ratio that measures the amount of sales generated relative to the level of investment. This means that every dollar invested in the corporate division has generated $0.45 in revenue. The **profit margin**, sometimes referred to as the return on sales, is a ratio that measures profit relative to sales for a division. The profit margin of 40.4 per cent indicates that every sales dollar acquired by the corporate division has turned into $0.404 in divisional profit. Overall, the corporate division has a higher profit margin but a lower asset turnover than the other divisions.

Compare the ratios presented above (ROI, profit margin and asset turnover) to the formulas for return on assets (ROA), profit margin and asset turnover presented in the chapter on analysis and interpretation of financial statements. Note the similarities and the differences. In the chapter on analysis and interpretation of financial statements, profit is defined as 'after-tax profit'. The formulas presented in this chapter are quite general and show that the concept can be specifically adjusted to suit financial statement analysis (as was the case in the analysis and interpretation of financial statements chapter) or to divisions or segments.

The asset turnover of the department store division is 5.3 times. This indicates that it generated $5.30 in sales for every dollar invested, which is good relative to the other divisions. However, its return on sales is poor, indicating that it cannot turn these sales into profit. It needs to increase selling prices and/or control variable costs more tightly. In the longer term, fixed costs should be scrutinised.

It is useful to conduct the above analysis of divisions and other entities in similar industries to ascertain good performance and to point to possible improvements. For instance, comparing the profit margins of the corporate and specialty stores divisions (40.4 per cent compared to 13.46 per cent) indicates that the prices in the specialty stores division might be too low or its operating costs too high. Further, comparing the asset turnovers of the corporate and specialty stores divisions (0.45 times compared to 2.31 times) suggests that the assets in the corporate division are not generating enough sales. Therefore, assets (e.g. cash, inventory, receivables, equipment, property) may need to be reduced.

Using ROI as a performance indicator has the following advantages.
- ROI is easy to use and understand.
- It links profit with the investment base, thereby increasing awareness of asset management and discouraging overinvestment.
- The relationship between assets held in the statement of financial position and the profit in the statement of profit or loss can be easily determined.

Using ROI as a performance indicator has the following disadvantages.
- ROI is a percentage measure, not a measure of absolute values. For instance, the ROI calculations above indicated that the specialty stores division was a better performer than the corporate division, yet the corporate division contributed $400 000 while the specialty stores division contributed $70 000. Therefore, ROI should not be used as the sole measure of performance.
- ROI does not consider divisions that are different in size or type. Comparisons for performance evaluation are useful only if made between divisions of similar size and type.
- Divisional managers can manipulate ROI by decreasing the investment base relative to the segment profit. For example, managers might delay investing in new equipment that would increase the investment base (the denominator) or purchase cheaper, substandard equipment. The use of ageing or suboptimal equipment might increase ROI in the short term but could be detrimental to performance in the long term.
- ROI use could result in suboptimal decision making. Managers might reject an investment opportunity because it could decrease overall ROI. For example, assume the specialty stores division has an opportunity to expand into another geographical market with an investment requirement of $50 000 and an expected segment return of $12 500. The expected ROI of this expansion would be 25 per cent and the existing ROI for the corporate division of 31.1 per cent would be reduced to 30 per cent by this new investment. The reduction in the ROI might make the manager reluctant to take on the investment even though it would have a positive impact on the company overall.

The disadvantages discussed above result from ROI being a short-term performance measure. There is a need to include long-term performance measures in combination with the ROI when assessing performance.

Residual income

The formula for **residual income (RI)** is:

Residual income (RI) = Profit before tax − (Required rate of return × Investment)

Unlike the ROI, the RI method is expressed in absolute dollars. An examination of the RI formula shows that a charge for capital (i.e. the required rate of return) is subtracted from the divisional contribution. This alleviates the problem of managers making suboptimal decisions based on a decrease in ROI. The use of a suitable charge based on the organisation's expected returns will result in managers accepting investment opportunities that give an ROI that is higher than the charge for capital. The calculation of residual income is demonstrated in illustrative example 14.5.

ILLUSTRATIVE EXAMPLE 14.5

Residual income

In our Fun Hats Company example, the RI for each of the three divisions (assuming a required rate of return of 15 per cent) would be as follows.

Division		RI		
Corporate	$400 000	−	(0.15 × $2 200 000)	=	$70 000
Department stores	−$70 000	−	(0.15 × $75 000)	=	−$81 250
Specialty stores	$70 000	−	(0.15 × $225 000)	=	$36 250

The above calculations indicate that, after a suitable charge for capital, the corporate division is contributing $70 000 and the specialty stores division is contributing $36 250. The department stores division is not contributing enough to cover the charge for capital, which is 15 per cent. Remember that the ROI for the corporate division is 18.2 per cent, 31.1 per cent for the specialty stores division and −93.3 per cent for the department stores division. Consideration needs to be given to the suitability of the 15 per cent expected return in the current economic climate. That is, how does this return compare with other investment alternatives? It may be that the attainment of a 15 per cent return in the current economic climate is reasonable given the level of risk associated with the investment.

Revisiting the investment opportunity presented earlier for the specialty stores division, the use of RI would result in the specialty stores division accepting the investment opportunity of expanding to another geographical area. Recall that the expansion would require an additional $50 000 investment and was predicted to contribute $12 500 to the entity. The RI would be:

Residual income (RI) = Profit before tax − (Required rate of return × Investment)
= ($70 000 + $12 500) − [15% × ($225 000 + $50 000)]
= $41 250

This is an increase of $5000 on the current RI of $36 250, so the manager of the specialty stores division would accept the investment opportunity.

Using RI as a performance indicator has the following advantages.
- It minimises the suboptimal decision making that could result from the use of ROI. A manager would take on a new investment opportunity if the dollar return was greater than the charge for the extra capital invested.
- The charge for capital can vary across divisions based on the risk of the venture being pursued in each division.

Using RI as a performance indicator has the following disadvantages.
- It can still encourage short-term decision making.
- The required rate of return or a suitable charge for capital may not be easy to determine.

Economic value added

Economic value added (EVA)[1] was developed by the company Stern Stewart & Co and is a registered trademark. Like RI, this measure is based on the economic increase in an organisation's value after a suitable charge for capital is subtracted. The formula for the EVA is as follows.

$$EVA = \text{Profit after tax (PAT)} - (\text{Cost of capital} \times \text{Capital})$$

Compare this formula to the RI formula presented earlier.

$$\text{Residual income (RI)} = \text{Profit before tax} - (\text{Required rate of return} \times \text{Investment})$$

The use of profit after tax (PAT) takes into account all returns to the division prior to any financing charges. (Note, therefore, to add back interest expense in the PAT calculation.) Regardless of how the investment is financed, all returns and expenses are accounted for in the PAT. How the investment is financed is considered in the second part of the equation through the 'Cost of capital × Capital' component.

It is argued that the EVA measure is a true measure of economic profit, since it subtracts from earnings a suitable charge for capital. By doing this, all costs to the entity are considered. The logic of its use rests on the importance of ensuring that managers act in the best interests of the owners of the entity. If the purpose of an entity is to maximise the wealth of its owners, then using the EVA as a performance measure will ensure that managers make decisions that increase the owners' economic wealth.

The EVA is calculated from the financial accounting figures, with adjustments made to reflect the conservative basis of accounting measurement. Stern Stewart has developed more than 100 adjustments that can be made to both profit and capital, depending on the nature of the entity. It is argued that in reality only a handful of adjustments will be made, as some would not have a significant effect on the resulting EVA. This flexibility in the use of adjustments could also be seen to allow for manipulation of the measure.

Some of the adjustments include the following.

- *Adding back the research and development (R&D) costs.* It is argued that these costs should be capitalised and written off in the financial years in which they bring benefits, not when they are incurred. The amount spent on R&D should be seen as an investment, rather than an expense.
- *Adding back the marketing costs.* For the same reason stated above, the costs spent on marketing should be capitalised and written off over the years in which the benefit accrues.

Illustrative example 14.6 demonstrates the calculation of the EVA.

ILLUSTRATIVE EXAMPLE 14.6

The calculation of the EVA for the Fun Hats Company is demonstrated in table 14.5.

TABLE 14.5   **Fun Hats Company — calculation of the EVA**

	Corporate	Department stores	Specialty stores
Assets	$2 200 000	$75 000	$225 000
Less: Current liabilities	110 000	36 750	12 600
= Long-term assets	$2 090 000	$38 250	$212 400
× Weighted average cost of capital	15.4%	15.4%	15.4%
=	$321 860	$5 890	$32 710
PAT	= $400 000 × (1 − 0.30) = $280 000	= −$70 000 × (1 − 0.30) = −$49 000	= $70 000 × (1 − 0.30) = $49 000
EVA	= $280 000 − $321 860 = −$41 860	= −$49 000 − $5 890 = −$54 890	= $49 000 − $32 710 = $16 290

The PAT used is the segment profit adjusted for tax. In our example, the tax rate is 30 per cent. Capital refers to long-term assets and is calculated as total assets less current liabilities. Some adjustments may be made to this based on the judgement of those involved. As mentioned earlier, over 100 possible adjustments have been put forward by Stern Stewart.

▶

---

1 EVA is a registered trademark of Stern Stewart & Co. More information can be found at www.sternstewart.com.

> The use of the weighted average cost of capital (WACC) is used regularly in finance-related decisions. The WACC is calculated on the entity's cost of equity and debt. In our example, the WACC was assumed to be 15.4 per cent. The actual WACC calculation is beyond the scope of this chapter.

The advantages of using the EVA as a performance indicator are similar to those for residual income. They include the following.
- It minimises suboptimal decision making. That is, subtracting the charge for capital focuses managers' attention on the economic value added to the entity. It is argued that this helps managers make decisions similar to those they would make if they were the owners.
- The charge can vary to take into account various risk levels.
- Adjustments can be made to the components within the equation to suit the specific circumstances of each division.

The disadvantages of using the EVA as a performance indicator include the following.
- The modifications to the formula are complex.
- The modifications could be seen as being manipulated.
- It is still a short-term economic performance indicator based on financial accounting data.

ROI, RI and EVA compared

The three measures for each of our divisions are compared in table 14.6.

TABLE 14.6   Fun Hats Company — ROI, RI and EVA compared

	ROI	RI	EVA
Corporate	18.2%	$70 000	−$41 860
Department stores	−93.3%	−$81 250	−$54 890
Specialty stores	31.1%	$36 250	$16 290

Under the ROI and EVA calculations, the specialty stores division is the higher performer; under the RI calculation, however, the corporate division is the higher performer. The ROI calculation indicates that the specialty stores division has the highest yield relative to the investment base. This indicates a good use of assets. The RI and EVA are calculated in absolute terms and they attempt to overcome the goal congruence problem encountered with ROI. Goal congruence problems arise when the goals of the entity are not in line with the goals of the individual manager. Recall that with ROI a manager may reject an investment proposal — even though the proposal would give an ROI favourable to the owners of the entity — because the proposal would reduce the overall ROI obtained by the manager. RI and EVA are both based on the principle of deducting a charge for capital, but RI is based on pre-tax profits and the EVA is based on after-tax profits. This illustrates that, although the corporate division seems to be performing well, it has not increased the economic value of the investment when tax is considered. An inspection of the corporate division's assets in table 14.4 reveals a high proportion of current assets. This could lead to a review of its inventory policy, debtors' policy and cash-on-hand requirements.

The investment base

To calculate the ROI and RI, the **investment base** was needed. This is the value of the investment that is used in ratio analysis. There is some choice as to what investment base can be used. It could be the:
- gross book value (original cost)
- net book value (written-down value)
- market value (current cost).

The investment base used can alter the ROI and RI outcomes. Using written-down values will produce more favourable ROI and RI calculations over time as the value of the investment in assets is depreciated. That is, if profit remains constant, the decrease in the investment base will increase the ROI and RI over time. Such an increase may delay investment in new assets, and the subsequent retention of old assets may adversely affect the efficiency and effectiveness of operations over the long term. However, the use of the original cost may not represent a true reflection of the actual investment in the entity. It may encourage the premature disposal of assets to ensure that the latest equipment is being used to earn the profit; that is, equipment might be replaced before it should be.

Using the market value rather than the book value means that the investment base is being valued on current costs rather than historical costs. (Note that both written-down value and original cost are historical costs.) The advantage of this method is that the derived profit is based on current prices and costs, so the investment base should also be based on current costs. Further, the use of market value is based on the opportunity cost principle. That is, the return we are receiving is based on today's costs compared to the return that we could be receiving if the investment base was invested elsewhere.

To illustrate the differences in the investment base, table 14.7 contains the written-down value, original cost and market value for the specialty stores division of the Fun Hats Company. The ROI and RI have been calculated on these values. Recall that the specialty stores division made a divisional margin of $70 000 and the company's desired rate of return when calculating the RI is 15 per cent. The results show that using the different investment base can alter the performance results quite drastically, so care must be taken when choosing the investment base.

TABLE 14.7 Effect of differences in investment bases

	Value	ROI	RI
Written-down value or net book value	$225 000	31.1%	$36 250
Original cost or gross book value	$250 000	28%	$32 500
Market value	$300 000	23.3%	$25 000

As discussed earlier, the EVA uses long-term assets (total assets less current liabilities) as its investment base and adjustments are made depending on the type of entity.

VALUE TO BUSINESS

- The evaluation of investment centre performance is based on the economic return relative to the invested resources.
- Return on investment (ROI) = Profit/Investment.
- Du Pont ROI = Return on sales × Investment turnover.
- Residual income (RI) = Profit before tax − (Required rate of return × Investment).
- EVA = Net operating profit after tax − (Cost of capital × Capital).

14.4 Environmental and social performance

LEARNING OBJECTIVE 14.4 Examine the use of environmental and social performance measurement.

The above section highlighted some of the key financial performance measures. This section gives an overview of some of the typical environmental and social performance measures. As discussed in the first chapter, sustainability reporting is growing in importance. A number of frameworks were presented to help external reporting of environmental and social performance. It is also important to measure environmental and social performance for internal reporting. In 2001, the United Nations Division for Sustainable Development (UNDSD) published *Environmental management accounting procedures and principles* to help management accountants deal with the extensive information available on environmental data. In order to assess environmental and social dimensions, there was a need to develop, track and monitor KPIs. The UNDSD relied on ISO 14031 *Environmental management — Environmental performance evaluation — Guidelines* for definitions of these environmental indicators. The ISO 14031, updated in 2013, specifies two categories of environmental performance.

1. *Environmental condition indicator (ECI), which provides information about the local, regional, national or global condition of the environment that could be affected by the entity.* Water and air quality are

typical concerns that are monitored via environmental condition indicators. Some companies may monitor this, but normally this is monitored by government agencies. For instance, a government may monitor the noise levels around airports, the water quality of major river systems to check for overfertilisation, emissions surrounding power stations or soil quality around major farming land.

2. *Environmental performance indicators (EPIs) consisting of:*

   (a) *operational performance indicator (OPI), which provides information about the environmental performance of an organisation's operations.* Material, energy and water consumption and waste and emission amounts are typical indicators.

   (b) *management performance indicator (MPI), which provides information about the management's efforts to influence an organisation's environmental performance.* Examples are staff training, certification, environmental audits and cases of non-compliance.

Just like financial data, these indicators can be expressed in absolute figures, percentages, as ratios or as an index to some base year. They are also more meaningful when monitored over time, compared to benchmarks and other sites and standards. In setting up an environmental performance information system, there is a need to consider the purpose of such a system, the types of environmental and social concerns most relevant to the entity, the access to information systems and expertise that will help measure, collect and store the information, and the stakeholders to whom the information needs to be communicated in order to improve environmental performance. In a similar manner to those applied to financial information, the UNDSD has put forward some basic principles to be applied. They are:

- relevance
- understandability
- target orientation
- consistency
- comparability
- balanced view
- continuity.

The suitability of indicators would differ from organisation to organisation and be driven by the organisation's strategic goals. This would then be linked to financial performance measures such as ROI, RI or economic value (which were covered earlier in the chapter).

Eco-efficiency

Related to environmental outcomes is the concept of **eco-efficiency**. The Organisation for Economic Co-operation and Development (OECD) (1998, p. 7) states that eco-efficiency 'expresses the efficiency with which ecological resources are used to meet human needs'. Schaltegger and Burritt (2000, p. 358) further elaborate, stating that eco-efficiency is the 'ratio between value added and environmental impact added, or between an economic performance indicator and an ecological performance indicator'. The purpose is to integrate the ecological impact with economic information. Simply recording environmental information, without integration into the traditional accounting system, may not bring about the change required or the understanding on the entity's bottom line. For instance, recording a reduction in the energy used may be worthwhile, but putting a cash value on that reduction shows both the environmental and financial impacts of the goal of energy reduction.

The basic formula is:

$$\text{Eco-efficiency} = \frac{\text{Value added}}{\text{Environmental impact added}}$$

The numerator in the indicator is related to the economic dimension, while the denominator is related to the ecological dimension. The result will show the environmental impact added per chosen unit of economic performance. The environmental performance (measured as the environmental impact added) can be assessed from the socio-political perspective or the natural science perspective. It can be applied to many types of environmental and social information. The 'eco' refers to both ecology and economics, and is sometimes referred to as E^2 efficiency. It could be quite general, such as the residual income per workforce diversity improvement, the EVA per unit of contribution to global warming or the taxes paid per ozone depletion unit. It could also be quite specific, such as the cost per litre of oil consumed, the revenue per tonne of forest consumed or the shareholder value per unit of CO_2 emitted. The main principle of its use is the link between an environmental or social issue and a relevant economic metric. Like all performance indicators, it becomes more real and understandable when benchmarked over time and across industry sectors, and when compared to best practice.

Sustainability report card

The balanced scorecard developed by Kaplan and Norton (1992) was presented earlier in the chapter. As noted, there were two approaches to including sustainability in the original scorecard: (1) incorporating sustainability measures in each of the original dimensions; or (2) adding a new sustainability dimension. A further adaptation is the sustainability report card, which reports solely on sustainability. This is illustrated in figure 14.6.

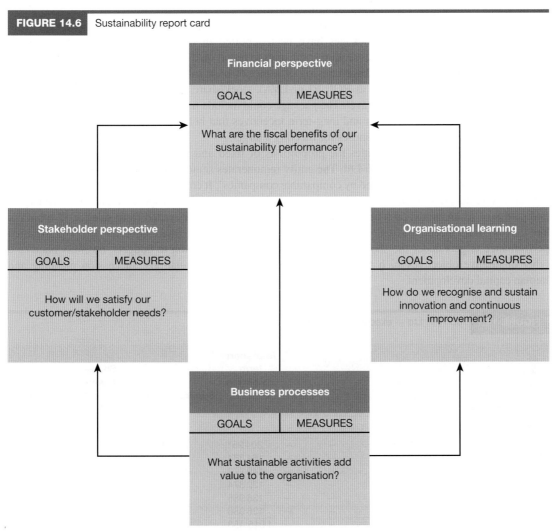

FIGURE 14.6 Sustainability report card

Source: KPMG 2002.

14.5 Individual performance measurement

LEARNING OBJECTIVE 14.5 Discuss the issues surrounding individual performance measurement.

There is a well-known saying: 'Companies don't succeed; people do.' Companies are artificial entities and do not perform any physical function (the company itself brings owners, workers and resources together under a legal structure). The people working within a company perform multiple tasks, individually and in teams, to accomplish the organisation's goals. Performance measurement at the individual level should highlight to the employees what tasks are important. For example, a sales assistant may be required to assist customers and make sales. Including both tasks in a performance measurement system helps managers communicate this to the employee. The performance system may include a customer satisfaction measure and a dollar sales measure. If only the sales dollars were measured, then the sales assistant might focus on making as many sales as possible with little regard to customer service and needs — and the customer might never return. Such short-term gains would not be good for the entity in the longer term.

Another consideration of the performance measurement system is the reward system, specifically, the choice between individual and team-based rewards. Some entities encourage teamwork by including rewards based on team, department or company-wide performance. Such an approach has the advantage of encouraging employees to work together and hopefully achieve synergies that individuals could not achieve working alone. Criticisms of such an approach include the difficulty of managing individuals who shirk their responsibilities, knowing the team overall will pick up the slack; and managing individuals within teams who have no incentive to excel individually.

Of special interest under individual performance measurement is executive performance compensation. Some very large compensation packages have been reported in recent years. Changes to company regulations and accounting standards require companies to report on director and executive compensation. Generally, an executive salary package consists of a mix of base salary, incentives based on achieving certain measurement targets (such as ROI, RI or EVA), stock/share options and other benefits such as superannuation, company car and travel. The package could include financial and non-financial measures, and also encourage both short-term and long-term incentives that help achieve the entity's goals. Short-term incentives typically include bonuses for meeting a target.

For example, figure 14.7 illustrates the proportions of fixed and performance-based components of executive compensation at JB Hi-Fi Ltd. The entity remunerates senior executives by evaluating 'performance and data on remuneration paid by comparable companies'. It comprises (a) fixed remuneration; and (b) variable remuneration consisting of: (i) short-term incentives (based on specified performance targets and paid 80% as an annual cash bonus and 20% in shares which are restricted from sale for 12 months); and (ii) long-term incentives (options under the JB Hi-Fi Ltd Executive Share Option Plan). The specified performance targets under the short-term incentives include comparison to budgets, business plans and other qualitative objectives such as corporate governance, investor relations, succession planning and human capital development.

FIGURE 14.7   JB Hi-Fi Ltd — executive compensation

2018	Salary and fees $	Bonus[2] $	Other[1] $	Total short-term employee benefits $	Superannuation $	Share-based payments[2] $	Total $
Non-executive directors							
G. Richards	304 951	—	—	304 951	20 049	—	325 000
B. Laughton	164 384	—	—	164 384	15 616	—	180 000
W. Tang	149 772	—	—	149 772	14 228	—	164 000
R. Uechtritz	122 374	—	—	122 374	11 626	—	134 000
S. Goddard	136 986	—	—	136 986	13 014	—	150 000
M. Powell	136 986	—	—	136 986	13 014	—	150 000
	1 015 453	—	—	1 015 453	87 547	—	1 103 000
Group executives							
R. Murray	1 245 871	999 622	28 187	2 273 680	24 712	1 063 151	3 361 543
C. Trainor	892 770	580 114	33 000	1 505 884	23 750	497 240	2 026 874
T. Smart	931 219	602 904	29 308	1 563 431	20 049	657 865	2 241 345
N. Wells	552 981	349 992	20 000	922 973	24 712	287 171	1 234 856
T. Carter	503 942	320 826	20 000	844 768	24 712	266 947	1 136 427
J. Saretta	503 942	323 662	19 808	847 412	25 000	170 343	1 042 755
	4 630 725	3 177 120	150 303	7 958 148	142 935	2 942 717	11 043 800
	5 646 178	**3 177 120**	**150 303**	**8 973 601**	**230 482**	**2 942 717**	**12 146 800**

[1] Car allowances.
[2] Performance based.
Source: JB Hi-Fi Ltd 2018, p. 36.

JB Hi-Fi Ltd, Australia's largest home entertainment retailer, evaluates its executive compensation on comparative positions in similar companies and industries.

VALUE TO BUSINESS

- The performance of divisional units of a business can be further evaluated on an individual level.
- Individual performance measures are designed to capture performance on multiple tasks, individual and team-based rewards, and short- and long-term rewards.

14.6 Non-financial performance evaluation

LEARNING OBJECTIVE 14.6 Assess the use of non-financial performance measures.

The use of financial performance measures alone is insufficient to gauge organisational success. A common analogy used to highlight the importance of multiple measures of performance is that of a football player. Focusing solely on the scoreboard will not provide the full picture. Information such as tackles, injury rates, penalties, fielding positions, scoring success and so on all helps to inform and provide feedback for future action. Likewise, an entity needs to understand operating, market and employee indicators, as well as overall financial performance measures.

The integrated report and the balanced scorecard frameworks discussed earlier in this chapter support the need to balance financial and non-financial measures of performance. There is a need to identify an organisation's value proposition and then develop a scorecard or dashboard process to collect and monitor KPIs that gauge value creation and the trade-offs made. It is context specific and a creative process for any organisation. **Non-financial performance measures** are part of the suite of measures, but are generally more operational in nature. They have the following benefits.

- They are more user-friendly and relevant to non-management employees.
- They are more likely to lead to longer term performance gains, as they tend to be linked more readily to the organisation's goals.
- They tend to diminish the likelihood of myopic management decision making, as they usually promote more long-term thinking.
- They can identify problems in a more timely fashion and locate the entity's problems and benefits.

- They can be easily structured to suit an organisation's goals.
- They can be benchmarked easily.

  Non-financial performance measures have the following disadvantages.
- They are subjective in nature.
- Including too many measures can impede understanding and be costly to collect, so there is a need to limit the number of measures.
- Inappropriate measures can be chosen.
- There is no proven cause-and-effect link between non-financial measures and economic success.
- Various measures give conflicting results.

The choice of non-financial performance measures should be linked to the organisation's goals; the measures should be well defined, easily understood and based on reliable data. Once relevant measures are chosen, appropriate benchmarks must be established. Benchmarks could include past performance, a target, or competitor or industry measures. The number of measures used should be limited, as too many measures may become meaningless and end up overwhelming instead of enlightening the user.

DECISION-MAKING EXAMPLE

Non-financial performance indicators

SITUATION You are the manager of a pizza chain. Over the last year, you have noticed a change in customer groups from families to teenagers. The families would come in to purchase a family meal and were highly likely to get takeaway, but when they did eat in, they would be in the store only for the duration of the meal. The teenagers, however, spend a lot of time in the pizzerias, but do not spend a lot of money. This seems to be having an adverse effect on the number of families that come to the stores and therefore the chain's overall profitability. You decide to implement a strategy to encourage the families back and to minimise the number of teenagers hanging around. Decide upon the types of factors that could be used in your strategy and suggest some non-financial performance indicators to measure their effect.

DECISION The objective would be to collect information about your pizza chain that differentiates the two customer groups, then concentrate on the factors most favoured by the families. The measurements of these factors become your KPIs. Research into the food and drink choices of teenagers and families could help determine what changes to the menu items might be necessary. Tallies of food items bought by the different groups could be collected. The time spent in each store by each group could also be tallied. A ratio of time in store to dollar spend could be used for each group. Customer surveys could be carried out to determine what types of food and service delivery each group expects. Advertising spend focused on each type of customer group could be investigated and collected.

Figure 14.8 gives examples of non-financial performance measures.

FIGURE 14.8	Non-financial performance measures

Operating performance measures

Quality — customer satisfaction

- Number of defective products shipped
- Customer response time
- Warranty claims
- Number of customer complaints
- On-time deliveries
- Number of return visits/orders
- Customer return visits
- Customer survey

Quality — supplier

- Percentage of defects per delivery
- Frequency of defective supplies
- Number of late deliveries

Quality — internal measures

- Number of defects per product/product run
- Measure of scrap and rework in the production process
- First-pass yields and process yields in the production process
- Number of suggestions from employees
- Process downtime

Inventory

- Number of inventoried items
- Inventory turnover
- Warehouse space reduction
- Warehouse space utilisation

Material and scrap

- Target versus actual material use
- Actual quantity of product scrapped

Equipment and maintenance

- Machine use and capacity
- Equipment productivity
- Machine availability
- Maintenance hours
- Time between failure

Delivery and throughput

- Production and delivery lead time
- On-time delivery
- Overdue deliveries
- Process times
- Set-up times
- Throughput time
- Number of component parts

Employee performance measures

- Employee morale: percentage of absenteeism, staff turnover
- Health and safety: injury rate, workers compensation claims
- Employee skill: age and experience statistics, percentage of trained staff, staff educational qualifications
- Employee productivity: labour efficiency, output measures

Market performance measures

- Market share growth (percentage and volume)
- Market leadership
- Market vulnerability

Traditionally, non-financial performance measures were reported internally only. However, given the growing emphasis on the need to disclose environmental and social performance indicators publicly, there has been an increase in the reporting of non-financial measures. Many organisations publicly report various non-financial measures in their sustainability and CSR reports. This provides an avenue for linking non-financial performance with financial performance. A good example of this linkage can be found in the IAG *Annual review 2018* (available at www.iag.com.au/results-and-reports/FY2018/index.html), which presents both financial and non-financial measures aligned with IAG's strategies and values.

SUMMARY OF LEARNING OBJECTIVES

14.1 Explain the importance of measuring organisational performance and outline common frameworks and reports used to assess and report organisational performance.

Measuring the performance of an entity helps to ascertain the achievement of the entity's objectives. The performance of the entity can be reported using general purpose financial statements (GPFS), social and environmental reports, and integrated reports. An entity can also use a framework such as the balanced scorecard to help link its strategy to key performance metrics.

14.2 Outline common organisational structures, responsibility centres and reasons for divisional performance evaluation, and generate divisional performance reports.

Common organisational structures include functional, geographical and enterprise-based groups. Responsibility centres include cost centres, revenue centres, profit centres and investment centres. The preparation of divisional performance reports is designed to help evaluate the division's performance, to provide a guide for the pricing of products and services, and to evaluate the level of investment in each division.

14.3 Apply investment centre performance evaluation measures such as return on investment (ROI), residual income (RI) and economic value added.

Common measures to evaluate investment centre performance include return on investment (ROI), Du Pont ROI, residual income (RI) and economic value added (EVA).
- ROI = Profit/Investment
- Du Pont ROI = Return on sales × Investment turnover
- Residual income (RI) = Profit before tax – (Required rate of return × Investment)
- EVA = Net operating profit after tax – (Cost of capital × Capital)

    For the purposes of ROI and RI calculation, 'investment' can be defined as original cost, written-down value or current cost.

14.4 Examine the use of environmental and social performance measurement.

The measurement of environmental and social performance is needed to promote business sustainability.

14.5 Discuss the issues surrounding individual performance measurement.

There is a need to incorporate individual performance measures that capture the performance on multiple tasks, individual and team-based rewards, and short- and long-term rewards.

14.6 Assess the use of non-financial performance measures.

Non-financial performance measures are measures that do not have a finance focus and are normally operational. Incorporating non-financial measures in the evaluation system can give more information about performance.

KEY TERMS

balanced scorecard Performance measure that weighs performance from four perspectives: financial, customer, internal business processes, and innovation and learning.

business unit Division or segment of an entity.

cost centre Division of an entity that is solely responsible for providing a service or product at minimal cost.

Du Pont ROI Measure of performance based on economic return relative to invested resources, calculated as ROI = Return on sales × Investment turnover.

eco-efficiency A focus on the efficient use of resources to minimise their impact on the environment.

economic value added (EVA) Short-term financial performance measure of the economic value created over a specified time period.

integrated report A report that presents the value creation of an entity's strategy, governance, performance and prospects.

investment base Value of the investment that is used in ratio analysis.

investment centre Division of an entity that is responsible for costs, revenues and investment in assets.

investment turnover (asset turnover) Ratio measuring the amount of sales generated relative to the level of investment.

key performance indicator (KPI) Performance measure that is critical for the success of an entity.

mission statement Short statement that sets out the overall philosophy and objectives of an entity.

non-financial performance measures Performance measures that are not financial in nature but are generally more operational.

organisational structure Structure taken by an entity to help direct and control its resources for the attainment of its mission.

profit centre Division of an entity that is solely responsible for both cost inputs and revenue, and therefore the profit of a division.

profit margin Profitability ratio calculated as profit divided by sales revenue.

residual income (RI) Short-term financial performance measure of the income or profit over the required return on investment.

return on investment (ROI) Performance measure calculated as profit divided by investment.

revenue centre Division of an entity that is solely responsible for generating revenue.

APPLY YOUR KNOWLEDGE

23 marks

JB Hi-Fi Ltd's focus is on creating shareholder value. In its 2018 preliminary final report, the company states that the cornerstone of its success is its ability to consistently offer everyday low prices through economies of scale, high stock turnover and low cost of doing business.

Required

(a) Suggest what indicators JB Hi-Fi Ltd would use to evaluate its performance.   *4 marks*

(b) Given its concentration on delivering consistently low prices to consumers, suggest what factors would be dominant in the company's balanced scorecard.   *4 marks*

(c) Compute the Du Pont ROI, RI and EVA for JB Hi-Fi Ltd for 2018. Relevant data (in millions) are as follows.   *10 marks*

Sales	$6 854.3
Before tax profit	$334.5
After tax profit	$233.2
Finance expenses	$16.6
Total assets	$2 491.7
Current liabilities	$917.2
Required rate of return	10%[1]
WACC	9.3%[2]

[1] Assumed for the purposes of this question.
[2] Calculated based on 30 per cent tax rate, 7 per cent cost of debt, 10 per cent assumed cost of equity, market capitalisation as at June 2018 and non-current borrowings.
Source: Data from JB Hi-Fi Ltd 2018.

(d) JB Hi-Fi Ltd reported in its 2018 *Preliminary final report* (p. 31) an increase in shareholder value as follows. Compare the EVA computed in part (c) with the shareholder value computed by JB Hi-Fi Ltd. Comment on the difference.   *3 marks*

		2018	2017
1.	Consolidated sales ($m)	6 854.3	5 628.0
2.	Consolidated profit attributable to members of the parent entity ($m)	233.2	192.2
3.	Basic earnings per share (cents)	203.1	172.1
4.	Shareholder value created:		
	Company share price at the end of the reporting period ($)	22.52	23.37
	Market capitalisation ($m)	2 587.2	2 674.0
	Enterprise value[i]	2 984.5	3 160.0
	Movement in enterprise value during the financial year ($m)	(175.5)	717.5
	Dividends paid to shareholders during the financial year ($m)	151.6	119.1
	Shareholder value created[ii]		
	– per annum ($m)	(23.9)	836.6
	– cumulative	**3 904.2**	**3 928.1**

[i] Enterprise value is measured as the sum of market capitalisation and net debt.
[ii] Shareholder value created is measured as the increase in the enterprise value, plus cash dividends paid during the financial year.
Source: JB Hi-Fi Ltd 2018, p. 31.

(e) Figure 14.7 in this chapter lists the company's executive compensation for 2018. Does the type of executive compensation align with the company's focus on creating shareholder value? Explain your answer. **2 marks**

SELF-EVALUATION ACTIVITIES

14.1 The Grant family has been in the printing business for three generations. The family prides itself on knowing the industry and being at the forefront of technological advances. This technological edge has helped maintain its name as the business leader in printing services. However, it has not always been profitable and over the years the company's focus on technology has sometimes overridden the need to be cost effective and efficient. The business also places high importance on customer satisfaction, as repeat business and word of mouth advertising help maintain sales levels. It is also mindful of its environmental and community obligations.

To remain competitive, the Grant family has sought your help in designing a performance framework to capture the key factors that drive its success. You are required to draw up a balanced scorecard that will help the family focus.

SOLUTION TO 14.1

Goals	Measures	Drivers
1. Financial perspective		
Improve overall financial value	Profitability	• Divisional profit
	Cash flow	• Debtors turnaround • Inventory (in dollars)
Cost efficiency	Labour costs	• Employee hours
	Raw material cost	• Value of raw material • Number of different inventory items
2. Customers		
Increase customer satisfaction	Customer satisfaction measure	• Repeat customers • Number of customer referrals • Customer satisfaction survey • On-time deliveries
Market share	Market share	• New customers obtained
3. Internal operations		
Customer response time	Customer response time	• Number of steps from customer order to delivery • Delivery time
Improve quality	Spoilage and rework (dollar values)	• Defective units produced • Time on rework
	Quality training and documentation	• Update manuals • Number of employees undertaking quality training
Reduce stock levels	Raw materials inventory (dollar values)	• Number of suppliers • Number of supplier agreements
	Finished goods inventory (dollar values)	• Warehouse utilisation

4. Innovation and improvement

Empower workforce	Employee satisfaction survey	• Employee benefits, facilities and challenges
	Employee suggestions	• Number of employee suggestions
	Employee performance	• Number of employees receiving bonuses
Technological edge	Skill and knowledge training sessions	• Machinery comparison with competitors
	Machinery investment	• Machinery comparison with competitors

5. Non-market perspective

Environment	Reduce CO_2 emissions and energy use	• % of plant on green power • Dollars invested in solar power
Community	Reduce water consumption	• Capacity of rain water tanks
	Sponsorship of community and sporting clubs	• $ of services given to non-profit community and sporting associations

14.2 McDonald is a development company that builds infrastructure such as roads, bridges and rail networks, as well as large commercial, retail and mining buildings. Information pertaining to the two divisions is presented. The common costs are allocated on the number of employees and the corporate costs are allocated on sales revenue.

	Roads and infrastructure	Buildings
Sales	$4 250 000	$2 500 000
Number of employees	10 000	9 250
Variable costs	$1 750 000	$1 250 000
Fixed costs	$1 500 000	$ 875 000

Common costs amounted to $577 500 for the year and the corporate costs were $405 000. You are required to draw up a divisional performance report.

SOLUTION TO 14.2

	Roads and infrastructure	Buildings	Total
	$'000	$'000	$'000
Sales	4 250	2 500	6 750
Variable costs	1 750	1 250	3 000
Contribution margin	**2 500**	**1 250**	**3 750**
Fixed cost	1 500	875	2 375
Divisional margin	1 000	375	1 375
Common costs[a]	300	278	578
Corporate costs[b]	255	150	405
Profit	**445**	**(53)**	**392**

[a] $577 500/(10 000 + 9250 employees) = $30 per employee.
[b] $405 000/(4 250 000 + 2 500 000) = 0.06 per sales dollar or 6 per cent.

14.3 The information below relates to Highland Incorporated.

	Division A $	Division B $
Total assets	2 000 000	10 000 000
Current liabilities	500 000	3 000 000
Divisional profit margin	400 000	1 500 000
Sales	1 900 000	13 000 000

Required

(a) Calculate the Du Pont ROI for each division.

(b) If the charge for capital is 17 per cent, what is the RI for each division?

(c) If the WACC for both divisions is 13 per cent, calculate the EVA. The tax rate is 30 per cent.

SOLUTION TO 14.3

(a)

ROI	=	Profit margin	×	Investment turnover
Profit/Investment	**=**	**Profit/Sales**	**×**	**Sales/Investment**
Division A				
$400 000/$2 000 000	=	$400 000/$1 900 000	×	$1 900 000/$2 000 000
20%	=	21%	×	0.95 times
Division B				
$1 500 000/$10 000 000	=	$1 500 000/$13 000 000	×	$13 000 000/$10 000 000
15%	=	11.5%	×	1.3 times

(b)

Profit	−	Required rate of return × Investment	=	RI
Division A				
$400 000	−	0.17 × $2 000 000	=	$60 000
Division B				
$1 500 000	−	0.17 × $10 000 000	=	−$200 000

(c)

PAT	−	WACC × (Total assets − Current liabilities)	=	EVA
Division A				
$400 000 × (1 − 0.3)	−	0.13 × ($2 000 000 − $500 000)	=	$85 000
Division B				
$1 500 000 × (1 − 0.3)	−	0.13 × ($10 000 000 − $3 000 000)	=	−$140 000

COMPREHENSION QUESTIONS

14.4 Why measure organisational performance? **LO1**

14.5 What is the balanced scorecard framework? **LO1**

14.6 What is the main criticism of the balanced scorecard framework? **LO1**

14.7 Discuss the four types of responsibility centres. **LO2**

14.8 What are the terms used interchangeably for a business unit? What is the responsibility of the manager of the business unit? **LO2**

14.9 What are the three purposes of preparing divisional performance reports? **LO2**

14.10 List some typical goals and performance measures for a balanced scorecard. **LO3**

14.11 List the formulas for the three basic financial performance indicators used to measure divisional performance. **LO3**

14.12 Describe economic value added (EVA). **LO3**

14.13 List the advantages and disadvantages of ROI, RI and EVA. **LO3**

14.14 Identify the three categories of environmental indicators as outlined by ISO 14031. **LO4**

14.15 List the principles espoused by the United Nations Division for Sustainable Development when designing an environmental performance system. **LO4**

14.16 Explain the concept of eco-efficiency. **LO4**

14.17 Outline a typical executive performance compensation package. **LO5**

14.18 Outline the reason for implementing a team-based reward structure and the disadvantages in doing so. **LO5**

14.19 Outline the advantages and disadvantages in using non-financial performance indicators. **LO6**

14.20 Discuss the basic principles in choosing non-financial performance indicators. **LO6**

EXERCISES

★ BASIC I ★ ★ MODERATE I ★ ★ ★ CHALLENGING

14.21 ★   **LO2**

A division of a global multinational company reports sales of $1 075 000, variable costs of $500 000, traceable fixed costs of $387 500, allocated regional common costs of $75 000 and allocated corporate costs of $37 500. Prepare a divisional performance report.

14.22 ★   **LO2**

Feather Pillows Ltd has three divisions: Hard, Medium and Soft. Corporate expenses of $72 000 are allocated to divisions based on sales. Data for the current quarter are as follows.

	Sales	Direct variable costs	Direct fixed costs
Hard	$ 72 000	$43 200	$12 000
Medium	120 000	60 000	16 800
Soft	96 000	48 000	24 000

Required

Prepare a division performance report using a format similar to table 14.3.

14.23 ★   **LO3**

You have been presented with a proposal to invest $200 000 into a company (using $100 000 of borrowed funds). In the first year of operations, the net operating profit after tax is expected to be approximately $46 000 in total. No shift in debt or equity is expected over the three years. The WACC is calculated at 13 per cent.

Calculate the EVA.

14.24 ★   **LO3**

The following data relate to the Chinese Division of Hangzhou Incorporated.

Sales	$360 000
Direct variable costs	$120 000
Direct fixed costs	$80 000
Average invested capital	$400 000
Required rate of return	20%

Required

Determine the:

(a) return on investment

(b) residual income.

14.25 ★ ★   **LO4**

For each of the following stakeholder groups, give an example of an eco-efficiency indicator.

(a) Shareholders

(b) Government

(c) Top management

(d) Site management

(e) Project management

(f) Divisional management

(g) Product management

14.26 ★ ★   **LO3**

A division reports divisional margin/profit of $180 000, residual income of $36 000 and investment for the period of $1 440 000. What is the minimum return being required by management?

14.27 ★ ★   **LO3**

A division has profit of $20 250, sales of $247 500 and an investment base of $112 500. If the required charge for capital is 20 per cent, determine the:

(a) profit margin
(b) asset turnover
(c) return on investment
(d) relationship between the three measures in (a) to (c)
(e) residual income.

14.28 ★ ★   **LO3**

A segment of Canine Holdings reports sales of $280 000 and a profit of $60 000. The data below also relate to this segment of Canine Holdings.

Total assets	$650 000
Accumulated depreciation	$150 000
Net assets book value	$500 000
Current market value	$1 250 000

Required

Determine the return on investment if the investment base is valued at:

(a) original cost
(b) written-down value
(c) market value.

14.29 ★ ★   **LO1**

For each of the five perspectives of the balanced scorecard, list two possible objectives, a measure and a driver. Arrange your answer as follows.

	Objective	Measure	Driver
Financial perspective			
Customer			
Internal operations			
Innovation and improvement			
Non-market perspective			

14.30 ★ ★   **LO6**

One common objective is quality. Listed below are businesses that regard quality as a strategic objective. For each business, list two performance measures that could help capture the strategic objective of quality.

(a) A bus company
(b) A day care centre
(c) A legal firm
(d) A financial planner
(e) A company that manufactures office equipment
(f) A shop that sells footwear

14.31 ★ ★   **LO1**

A family business has built a chain of coffee shops. The basic underlying principles of the chain, which has helped it to grow, are cost effectiveness, quality of service and product innovation. Determine two performance measures for each of these success factors.

14.32 ★ ★   **LO3**

The data below have missing values. Determine the missing values indicated by the letters (a) to (i).

	Division 6	Division 7	Division 8
Return on investment	(a)	28%	19%
Profit margin	15%	18%	(g)
Asset turnover	5	(d)	3
Sales	(b)	$69 000	(h)
Investment	$370 000	(e)	$41 000
Profit	(c)	(f)	(i)

14.33 ★ ★ LO5

Select a company in your region and search its website for its mission statement. Investigate the information on the website to discover what factors drive the company's success and any related information about its overall performance.

Further review its annual report and investigate how senior management and the board of directors are paid. Comment on whether the remuneration process would be effective in enhancing the company's long-term performance.

14.34 ★ ★ LO4

Refer to the company you selected in exercise 14.33 and investigate the environmental and social information it provides. This may be in its annual report, in its CSR report or on its website. What are the company's environmental and social concerns? How is it addressing these concerns? List some performance measures the company uses to assess its performance against its corporate and social goals.

14.35 ★ ★ LO1

Critique the two approaches to incorporating environmental and social performance in the balanced scorecard.

14.36 ★ ★ LO3

Information for the three divisions of the Hampton Corporation follows.

	Horses	Camels	Dogs
Profit before interest and taxes	$650 000	$89 000	$141 000
Assets	$3 020 000	$211 000	$1 100 000
Current liabilities	$640 000	$57 000	$121 100
Weighted average cost of capital	15.8%	13.5%	9.2%

Required

Assuming that the tax rate is 30 per cent, calculate the EVA for each division.

PROBLEMS

★ BASIC | ★ ★ MODERATE | ★ ★ ★ CHALLENGING

14.37 Balanced scorecard ★ LO1

The four perspectives of the balanced scorecard are internal operations, innovation and improvement, financial and customer. A list of goals and measures is presented below. Match each goal with one of the four perspectives, then match each measure with the most appropriate goal.

Goals	Measures
• Develop employee skills	• ROI
• Increase shareholder value	• Product cost per unit
• Increase market share	• Profit per salesperson
• Introduce new products	• Statistics on gender, race and age of workforce
• Improve manufacturing quality	• Training hours per employee
• Improve technological edge	• Percentage of on-time deliveries
• Ensure on-time delivery by suppliers	• Customer profitability
• Improve sales per customer/customer group	• Number of patents
• Decrease rework time	• Energy costs
• Improve community engagement	• Employee turnover rate
• Diversify workforce	• Earnings per share
• Reduction of energy use	• Number of rework hours
	• Profit margin
	• Percentage of defective products
	• Number of new customers
	• Technological comparison with competitors
	• Number of volunteer hours

14.38 EVA ★ **LO3**

The statement of financial position and the statement of profit or loss for Lavender Plantations Pty Ltd are presented below.

LAVENDER PLANTATIONS PTY LTD
Statement of financial position
as at 31 December 2021

Current assets	
Cash on hand	$110 977
Accounts receivable	145 000
Inventory	170 000
Prepayments	25 000
	450 977
Non-current assets (net)	
Plant and equipment	450 000
Office equipment	28 333
	478 333
Total assets	929 310
Current liabilities	
Accounts payable	78 000
Accrued expenses	5 000
Income tax payable	100 950
Dividend payable	75 000
	258 950
Non-current liabilities	
Loan	120 000
Total liabilities	378 950
Net assets	**$550 360**
Owners' equity	
Share capital	$200 000
Retained profits	350 360
Total equity	**$550 360**

LAVENDER PLANTATIONS PTY LTD
Statement of profit or loss
for year ended 31 December 2021

Sales		$1 675 000
Cost of sales		1 025 000
Gross profit		650 000
Other income		1 500
Warehouse and distribution	77 000	
Sales and marketing	105 000	
Administrative expenses	115 000	297 000
Profit before interest and tax		354 500
Interest		18 000
Profit before tax		**336 500**
Tax @ 30%		100 950
Profit after tax		**$ 235 550**

The WACC is 15 per cent.

Required

Calculate the EVA.

14.39 Individual performance measurement ★ **LO5**

You work for a fruit and vegetable manufacturer that has three divisions: juice, canned and fresh. Rewarding performance has been on the agenda for the last few management meetings and it has been proposed that the company would benefit from creating an employee reward system with a profit-sharing component. The proposal is for the company to pool 3 per cent of its profits each month, to be paid out to employees at the end of the year based on their existing salaries. It is thought this approach would encourage commitment to the organisation and help employees strive for better results.

There will be a vote for the current proposal at the next management meeting.

Required

(a) Discuss the advantages and the disadvantages of the proposal.

(b) Outline an alternative reward system.

14.40 Non-financial performance measurement ★ LO6

You have been assigned a consulting job with a medium-sized agricultural company that specialises in supplying seedlings to nurseries. The entity is divided into divisions based on geographical location. Currently the management of each division are evaluated on its ROI.

Your investigations at the entity reveal its mission is to be 'the number-one provider of quality plant stock in the southern hemisphere'. You also note that the entity has identified customer satisfaction, product quality and product innovation as hallmarks of success. However, recently the company's profits have been declining.

You notice a positive attitude at the plant propagation laboratories during your field visits, but at the distribution centres there appears to be some discontent, resulting in a lot of lost stock and customer complaints.

Required

(a) Explain how a performance measurement system can affect an entity's success.

(b) For each of the identified factors — customer satisfaction, product quality and product innovation — outline some non-financial performance indicators that could help focus work effort at the agricultural company.

(c) You explain to management that a focus on operational issues relating to customer satisfaction, product quality and product innovation should help improve profit in the longer term. What other success factor should be included in the entity's mission and performance measurement system?

14.41 Divisional performance report ★ LO2

Pineapple Plantations Pty Ltd is located on the Sunshine Coast in Queensland and manufactures sustainable, pineapple-based products for three different markets. The business has grown from a backyard hobby for the owner, Dave Geitz, to quite a large manufacturing concern. The company is structured into three distinct divisions aligned with each market, as shown.

	Soaps	Candles	Detergents
Sales	$950 000	$570 000	$380 000
Contribution margin ratio	60%	50%	55%
Fixed costs	$180 000	$160 000	$120 000
Divisional investment	$700 000	$250 000	$150 000

Common costs for the year totalled $300 000 and were allocated based on sales.

Required

Prepare a divisional performance report based on the information supplied.

14.42 Du Pont ROI, RI and EVA ★ ★ LO3

Global Enterprises is a division of an international conglomerate. The following information relates to its performance.

Target profit margin	12%
Target asset turnover	1.34 times
Charge for capital	14%
Weighted average cost of capital	12.40%
Income tax rate	30%
Investment	$22 600 000
Total assets	$28 050 000
Current liabilities	$820 000
Sales	$23 200 000
Variable costs	$8 960 000
Fixed costs	$10 460 000
Allocated common and corporate costs	$1 636 000

CHAPTER 14 Performance measurement **523**

Required

(a) Calculate the divisional margin for the year.

(b) Calculate the Du Pont ROI and evaluate the performance of Global Enterprises in relation to the expected performance.

(c) Calculate the RI.

(d) Calculate the EVA.

(e) Why are the RI and the EVA different?

(f) Discuss the appropriateness of the use of ROI, RI and EVA as performance measures.

14.43 Common cost allocation ★ ★   **LO2**

Susan is a divisional manager with the Generator Company. Her performance report shows a positive divisional margin, but a loss for the year. Susan has complained to the CEO about the common costs that were charged to her division and she has questioned the method of doing so. If her division were not charged or were allocated common costs in a different way, she would have a favourable profit figure and so would be awarded her bonus. Should Susan's bonus be awarded based on the profit figure? Why or why not?

14.44 Environmental and social performance indicators ★ ★ ★   **LO2**

Suggest indicators that could be used to assess an improvement in efficiency in each of the following areas.

(a) Reducing the amount of energy used in production of goods and services.

(b) Reducing the material intensity of the production of goods and services.

(c) Maximising the sustainable use of renewable resources.

(d) Reducing the dispersion of any toxic material.

(e) Reducing the amount of water used in the production of goods and services.

(f) Increasing the literacy rate of employees.

(g) Improving the health and wellbeing of employees.

(h) Contributing to crime prevention in the local area.

14.45 ROI and RI ★ ★ ★   **LO6**

Refer to the information supplied in problem 14.41. The management of Pineapple Plantations Pty Ltd have come across a further investment opportunity. They do not want to develop a separate division, so one of the existing divisions would need to take responsibility for the new investment opportunity. Management estimate that the new opportunity would require an investment of $90 000 to deliver sales this year of $120 000, with variable costs estimated at $86 500 and fixed costs at $20 000.

Required

(a) At present, divisional performance is evaluated based on ROI. If this is the case, which division would want to take over the new investment opportunity?

(b) If the company changed its performance evaluation criteria to encompass RI based on a charge for capital of 14 per cent, which division would now want to take over the new investment opportunity?

14.46 Performance measurement manipulation ★ ★ ★   **LO3**

For each of the scenarios below, indicate the effect (increase, decrease or no effect) it would have on ROI, RI, profit margin and asset turnover.

(a) Equipment is sold for $20 000. It is currently valued on the books at $25 000 and was originally acquired for $50 000. Sales will not be affected.

(b) The charge for capital is increased from 12 per cent to 15 per cent.

(c) A piece of equipment is purchased that will replace some manual operations. Therefore, the labour required will be reduced and costs will be lowered. It is expected that operating costs will be reduced by 5 per cent overall.

(d) Some obsolete inventory is written down.

(e) A production manager produces 6000 more units of product than was planned. The increase in production does not increase sales.

(f) An end-of-year marketing boost increases sales by 10 per cent. This increases profit.

14.47 Environmental information management systems ★ ★ ★   **LO4**

'Information management is an essential component of an environmental and social performance measurement system.' Discuss whether you agree with this statement.

14.48 EVA and balanced scorecard ★ ★ ★ **LO1, 3**

Enviro Solutions Pty Ltd operates three divisions that supply products and services relating to water. The two older divisions produce and supply water hardware such as pumps, pipes and tanks. The new division is a service division. It supplies consultancy services to government and large corporations on the preservation and best use of water resources.

Enviro Solutions Pty Ltd uses the EVA to measure divisional performance. Its results over the last year are as follows.

	Consultancy services	Tanks	Pumps and pipes
Sales	$2 145 000	$38 550 000	$8 520 000
Divisional margin	1 800 000	7 800 000	1 470 000
EVA	555 000	1 845 000	840 000

In a management performance meeting, concern was expressed about the use of the EVA as the sole measure for consultancy services performance. It was agreed that this was a growth area, but that sales growth had slowed dramatically over the last year. Investigation revealed that some competitor companies had managed to sustain their initial growth through the current year in contrast to the slowing sales of Enviro Solutions Pty Ltd. It was concluded that the performance of the consultancy services division was poor in the current growth market.

Required

(a) Consider whether the use of the EVA as the sole performance measure is suitable in the current circumstances.

(b) Consider whether the introduction of a balanced scorecard could facilitate a focus on the growth strategy.

14.49 Divisional performance measurement — short-term behaviour ★ ★ ★ **LO3**

Fit Solutions is a provider of personal exercise equipment. One division of Fit Solutions produces a product called Fab Abs, a specialised piece of equipment that exercises the abdominal region. Most of the components for the Fab Abs are sourced from various entities, warehoused and retrieved during production runs. Some components are made by the division.

The divisional report shows that the division made sales of 24 000 units at a price of $80 each. The variable costs were $50 per unit, with fixed costs of $380 000.

The entity calculates managers' bonuses on the profit. The manager of the Fab Abs division wants to receive as big a bonus as possible. To ensure that the divisional margin is reported at its highest possible level, the manager has been producing more units of the Fab Abs than required according to sales forecasts. Producing more units has the effect of increasing the ending inventory, which in the statement of profit or loss reduces the cost of sales amount. This in turn increases the divisional margin. The extra production of Fab Abs then has to be stored, thus increasing the need for warehouse space.

Required

(a) Comment on the strategy of the manager to produce more units of product than needed in order to adjust the closing inventory and raise the divisional profit. Is this practice in the best interests of the entity's long-term survival?

(b) Discuss the use of divisional margin as a performance measure.

DECISION-MAKING ACTIVITIES

14.50 Read the following article by Brown (2008).

> Beginning with the June 28, 2007 issue, *Rolling Stone* magazine became the first mass-marketed magazine to print on carbon-neutral paper. The special June issue of the magazine included a series of features devoted to the climate change issue, including a broad-based interview with former Vice President Al Gore, and an in-depth report on global warming solutions by environmental advocate Robert F. Kennedy Jr.

Studies have demonstrated that paper manufacturing accounts for the majority of a publication's total carbon footprint. *Rolling Stone* prints on Catalyst Cooled paper, an Electracote™ lightweight coated paper, manufactured in Port Alberni, British Columbia. Catalyst Cooled paper adds no net carbon dioxide to the environment.

How is this accomplished? Well before the climate change issue had captured the public's attention, Catalyst Paper undertook a thorough review of its operations, with an eye to identifying emissions reductions opportunities. As a result, the company was able to reduce its greenhouse gas emissions by approximately 70 per cent compared to the 1990 Kyoto Protocol baseline year, equivalent to taking 250 000 cars off the road every year. These direct greenhouse gas reductions were accomplished through a range of measures, including energy efficiency and replacing a significant portion of fossil energy use with biofuels.

To address the residual greenhouse gas emissions footprint for the paper produced for *Rolling Stone* magazine, Catalyst engaged ERA Ecosystem Restoration Associates Inc. (ERA), a recognised pioneer in community-based climate mitigation programming. ERA, whose community-based programming is directed toward restoring forest ecosystems, offset the remaining direct greenhouse gas emissions associated with paper production through a carefully chosen forest ecosystem restoration project in the District of Maple Ridge, British Columbia. ERA is also exploring and developing opportunities for ecosystem restoration and avoids deforestation projects in South America and Africa.

In addition to the positive impacts this programming has on atmospheric carbon, ecosystem restorations offer a range of environmental co-benefits, including: improved storm-water management, fish and wildlife habitat enhancement, native biodiversity restoration, and endangered species refuges.

Socio-economic co-benefits include local employment, a boost to local economies supporting the restorations, and education.

What has been the response?
While some organizations resist the concept of offsetting, informed individuals and established commentators realize that offsetting, while not the entire solution, represents an essential element of sustainability and climate mitigation. Furthermore, as in the case of Catalyst Paper, offsetting generally follows voluntary efforts by companies and organizations to reduce their environmental footprints. In practice, offsetting companies are usually already at the top of the list of environmental performers.

The leadership and ingenuity of forward-thinking companies like Catalyst Paper, ERA, and other leaders in the space, are providing focus and substance to advancing sustainability in business and communities. *Rolling Stone* magazine, while the first, will certainly not be the last major publication, or business, to face head-on the challenges of climate change and sustainability. In becoming an 'early reducer', *Rolling Stone* magazine has been able to tangibly reduce its environmental footprint, while sustaining its position as the 'go to' publication for the latest in music reviews, in-depth interviews, respected political commentary, and award-winning investigative journalism.

Required

(a) How did *Rolling Stone* magazine achieve a carbon-neutral paper? Why did *Rolling Stone* choose to reduce its emissions by concentrating on paper? Can you think of other printing processes that are harmful to the environment?

(b) Catalyst Paper helped *Rolling Stone* achieve its claim. Hypothesise what the culture and vision of this company would be with regards to sustainability. Review Catalyst Paper's website www.catalystpaper.com and make a conclusion about whether your hypothesis is correct.

(c) A number of companies offer a carbon-offsetting option when purchasing their services (e.g. some airlines). Formulate your opinion on the concept of carbon offsetting by reforestation. What do you think are the pros and cons of such an approach?

14.51 CEO remuneration packages have courted much controversy. These packages are normally divided into a base salary and incentive payments. The incentive payments are usually aligned with the financial performance of the company, and are made up of bonuses and share options. However, critics believe that many managers are only concerned with maximising their own wealth and so are working to increase the short-term financial performance, rather than the long-term growth and sustainability of the company.

Critics say that incentive payments deplete the value of the company and sacrifice cash, that the link between payments and performance is tenuous, and that it is easy to compensate good performance but boards falter when it comes to dealing with poor performance. However, defenders say that a few big incentive payments to some poor performers are overshadowing the deserved payments to hard-working, high-performing managers.

Required

(a) Appraise the need for an individual to earn millions of dollars each year.

(b) A number of high-profile companies came under attack for excessive CEO payment. Major banks fell into that category. The CEO of ANZ, for instance, received $4.26 million in 2017. His fixed remuneration was $2.1 million and his variable remuneration was $2.16 million, which included a cash incentive of $1 million. In addition, the board allowed non-monetary benefits to cover his 'car parking and taxation services'. Profit attributable to shareholders was up 12 per cent to $6406 million for 2017 and the total dividends paid during the year dropped by 7.8 per cent even though both the interim and final dividends paid were constant at 80 cents (ANZ 2017). Discuss whether you feel the CEO of ANZ earned his pay during 2017. Comment on whether or not a company should pay its employees' personal expenses such as car parking, life insurance and tax services.

(c) Boards and shareholders (at the AGM) decide on CEO pay. Speculate on why they agree to pay such large sums.

(d) When companies don't do well, hypothesise why their CEOs don't lose their jobs.

(e) Most CEOs are paid a combination of a base salary plus share bonuses and options. What is the reason that boards like to have their CEOs own shares in the company?

REFERENCES

ANZ 2017, *2017 annual report,* http://shareholder.anz.com/sites/default/files/2017_anz_annual_report.pdf.

Brown, L 2008, 'Case study: going green without the moss', *Awareness into action,* www.awarenessintoaction.com.

Dean, G, Joyce, M & Blayney, P 1991, *Strategic management accounting survey,* University of Sydney, Sydney.

Epstein, MJ & Wisner, PS 2006, 'Actions and measures to improve sustainability', in MJ Epstein & KO Hanson (eds), *The accountable corporation,* vol. 3, Praeger, Westport, CT, pp. 207–34.

Fremgen, J & Liao, S 1981, *The allocation of corporate indirect costs,* National Association of Accountants, New York.

International Organization for Standardization (ISO) 2013, *ISO 14031:2013 Environmental management — environmental performance evaluation — guidelines,* www.iso.org.

JB Hi-Fi Ltd 2018, *Preliminary final report 2018,* www.jbhifi.com.au.

Kaplan, RS & Norton, DP 1992, 'The balanced scorecard: measures that drive performance', *Harvard Business Review,* Jan–Feb, pp. 71–9.

KPMG 2002, *Beyond the numbers: how leading organisations are linking values with value to gaincompetitive advantage,* KPMG, Amsterdam.

Lewy, C & du Mee, L 1998, 'The ten commandments of balanced scorecard implementation', *Management Control and Accounting,* April, pp. 34–6.

Möller, A & Schaltegger, S 2005, 'The sustainability balanced scorecard as a framework for eco-efficiency analysis', *Journal of Industrial Ecology,* vol. 9, no. 4, pp. 73–83.

Organisation for Economic Cooperation and Development (OECD) 1998, 'Eco-efficiency, ENV/EPOC/MIN(98)7', Environment Ministerial Steering Group, OECD, Paris, France.

Ramadan, S 1989, 'The rationale for cost allocation: a study of UK divisionalised companies', *Accounting and Business Research,* Winter.

Schaltegger, S & Burritt, R 2000, *Contemporary environmental accounting: issues concepts and practice,* Greenleaf, Sheffield, UK.

United Nations Division for Sustainable Development 2001, *Environmental management accounting procedures and principles,* United Nations, New York.

Walsh, P 1996, 'KPIs revisited: parts 1 & 2', National Management Accounting Conference, CPA Australia, May, pp. 1–16.

ACKNOWLEDGEMENTS

Photo: © Pressmaster / Shutterstock.com

Photo: © TK Kurikawa / Shutterstock.com

Figures 14.1, 14.2: © *Harvard Business Review*

Figure 14.5: Dean, Joyce & Blayney 1989; Fremgen & Liao 1981; Ramadan 1989. © Wiley

Figure 14.6: © KPMG 2002

Figure 14.7 and Apply your knowledge question: © JB Hi-Fi Ltd 2018

Decision-making activity 14.50: Brown 2008. © Catalyst Paper

APPENDIX

Appendix

JB Hi-Fi Ltd 2018 — Consolidated financial statements and notes (abridged)

STATEMENT OF PROFIT OR LOSS
for the financial year ended 30 June 2018

		Consolidated	
	Notes	2018 $m	2017 $m
Revenue		6,854.3	5,628.0
Cost of sales		(5,384.1)	(4,397.5)
Gross profit		1,470.2	1,230.5
Other income		1.1	2.0
Sales and marketing expenses		(695.1)	(580.1)
Occupancy expenses		(305.7)	(248.6)
Administration expenses		(42.2)	(36.2)
Acquisition transaction and implementation expenses		–	(22.4)
Other expenses		(77.2)	(75.3)
Finance costs	5	(16.6)	(10.7)
Profit before tax		334.5	259.2
Income tax expense	6	(101.3)	(86.8)
Profit for the year attributable to Owners of the Company		233.2	172.4
		Cents	*Cents*
Earnings per share			
Basic (cents per share)	3	203.09	154.30
Diluted (cents per share)	3	201.11	152.94

The above statement of profit or loss should be read in conjunction with the accompanying notes.

STATEMENT OF PROFIT OR LOSS AND OTHER COMPREHENSIVE INCOME
for the financial year ended 30 June 2018

	Consolidated	
	2018 $m	2017 $m
Profit for the year	233.2	172.4
Other comprehensive income		
Items that may be reclassified subsequently to profit or loss		
Changes in the fair value of cash flow hedges (net of tax)	1.9	(1.1)
Exchange differences on translation of foreign operations	(1.3)	(0.1)
Other comprehensive income/(loss) for the year (net of tax)	0.6	(1.2)
Total comprehensive income for the year attributable to Owners of the Company	233.8	171.2

The above statement of profit or loss and other comprehensive income should be read in conjunction with the accompanying notes.

61

	Notes	Consolidated 2018 $m	2017 $m
ASSETS			
Current assets			
Cash and cash equivalents		72.0	72.8
Trade and other receivables	8	204.7	193.6
Inventories	7	891.1	859.7
Other current assets	9	42.7	41.4
Total current assets		1,210.5	1,167.5
Non-current assets			
Plant and equipment	10	198.0	208.2
Intangible assets	11	1,037.3	1,037.3
Other non-current assets	9	45.9	46.8
Total non-current assets		1,281.2	1,292.3
Total assets		2,491.7	2,459.8
LIABILITIES			
Current liabilities			
Trade and other payables	12	665.3	644.7
Deferred revenue	13	150.5	141.8
Provisions	14	83.5	76.3
Other current liabilities	15	8.3	9.0
Current tax liabilities		9.6	13.6
Total current liabilities		917.2	885.4
Non-current liabilities			
Borrowings	17	469.4	558.8
Deferred revenue	13	103.7	99.6
Deferred tax liabilities	6	5.7	16.1
Provisions	14	12.5	11.8
Other non-current liabilities	15	35.6	34.6
Total non-current liabilities		626.9	720.9
Total liabilities		1,544.1	1,606.3
Net assets		947.6	853.5
EQUITY			
Contributed equity	18	441.7	438.7
Reserves	19	42.7	33.2
Retained earnings		463.2	381.6
Total equity		947.6	853.5

The above balance sheet should be read in conjunction with the accompanying notes.

STATEMENT OF CHANGES IN EQUITY
for the financial year ended 30 June 2018

Consolidated	Notes	Contributed equity $m	Equity settled benefits reserve $m	Foreign currency translation reserve $m	Hedging reserves $m	Common control reserve $m	Retained earnings $m	Total equity $m
Balance at 1 July 2016		49.3	27.3	5.0	0.9	(6.1)	328.3	404.7
Profit for the year		–	–	–	–	–	172.4	172.4
Cash flow hedges (net of tax)		–	–	–	(1.1)	–	–	(1.1)
Exchange difference on translation of foreign operations		–	–	(0.1)	–	–	–	(0.1)
Total comprehensive income for the year		–	–	(0.1)	(1.1)	–	172.4	171.2
Issue of shares under share option plans	18	1.7	–	–	–	–	–	1.7
Share issue costs (net of tax)	18	(6.5)	–	–	–	–	–	(6.5)
Dividends provided for or paid	4	–	–	–	–	–	(119.1)	(119.1)
Issue of shares under entitlement offer	18	394.2	–	–	–	–	–	394.2
Share-based payments - expense		–	5.3	–	–	–	–	5.3
Share-based payments - income tax		–	2.0	–	–	–	–	2.0
Balance at 30 June 2017		438.7	34.6	4.9	(0.2)	(6.1)	381.6	853.5
Balance at 1 July 2017		438.7	34.6	4.9	(0.2)	(6.1)	381.6	853.5
Profit for the year		–	–	–	–	–	233.2	233.2
Cash flow hedges (net of tax)		–	–	–	1.9	–	–	1.9
Exchange difference on translation of foreign operations		–	–	(1.3)	–	–	–	(1.3)
Total comprehensive income for the year		–	–	(1.3)	1.9	–	233.2	233.8
Issue of shares under share option plans	18	3.0	–	–	–	–	–	3.0
Dividends provided for or paid	4	–	–	–	–	–	(151.6)	(151.6)
Share-based payments - expense		–	7.8	–	–	–	–	7.8
Share-based payments - income tax		–	1.1	–	–	–	–	1.1
Balance at 30 June 2018		441.7	43.5	3.6	1.7	(6.1)	463.2	947.6

The above statement of changes in equity should be read in conjunction with the accompanying notes.

63

	Notes	Consolidated 2018 $m	2017 $m
Cash flows from operating activities			
Receipts from customers		7,551.9	6,205.5
Payments to suppliers and employees		(7,130.5)	(5,908.8)
Interest received		0.5	1.7
Interest and other finance costs paid		(15.0)	(9.3)
Income taxes paid		(114.8)	(98.5)
Net cash inflow from operating activities	16	292.1	190.6
Cash flows from investing activities			
Payment for business combination, net of cash acquired	25	–	(836.6)
Payments for plant and equipment	10	(54.4)	(49.1)
Proceeds from sale of plant and equipment		0.4	0.2
Net cash (outflow) from investing activities		(54.0)	(885.5)
Cash flows from financing activities			
Proceeds from issues of shares	18	3.0	395.9
(Repayment)/proceeds of borrowings		(89.7)	450.0
Payments for debt issue costs		(0.8)	(1.7)
Share issue costs		–	(9.2)
Dividends paid to owners of the Company	4	(151.6)	(119.1)
Net cash (outflow) inflow from financing activities		(239.1)	715.9
Net (decrease) increase in cash and cash equivalents		(1.0)	21.0
Cash and cash equivalents at the beginning of the financial year		72.8	51.9
Effects of exchange rate changes on cash and cash equivalents		0.2	(0.1)
Cash and cash equivalents at end of year		72.0	72.8

The above statement of cash flows should be read in conjunction with the accompanying notes.

64

NOTES TO THE FINANCIAL STATEMENTS

for the financial year ended 30 June 2018

***

Contents of the notes to the consolidated financial statements

1 ABOUT THIS REPORT

These are the consolidated financial statements of JB Hi-Fi Limited (Company or parent entity) and its controlled entities. JB Hi-Fi Limited and its controlled entities together are referred to in this financial report as the Group. For the purposes of preparing the consolidated financial statements the Company is a for-profit entity.

(a) Basis of preparation

These general purpose financial statements have been prepared in accordance with Australian Accounting Standards and interpretations issued by the Australian Accounting Standards Board and the *Corporations Act 2001*.

(i) Compliance with IFRS

The consolidated financial statements of JB Hi-Fi Limited also comply with International Financial Reporting Standards (IFRS) as issued by the International Accounting Standards Board (IASB).

(ii) Historical cost convention

These financial statements have been prepared under the historical cost convention, except for financial assets and liabilities (including derivative instruments), and certain classes of plant and equipment which are measured at fair value.

(iii) Corporation information

JB Hi-Fi Limited is a company limited by shares, incorporated and domiciled in Australia. Its registered office and principal place of business is Level 4, Office Tower 2, Chadstone Place, Chadstone Shopping Centre, 1341 Dandenong Road, Chadstone, Victoria.

The financial statements were authorised for issue by the directors on 13 August 2018.

(b) Rounding off of amounts

The Company is of a kind referred to in ASIC Corporations (Rounding in Financial/Directors' Reports) Instrument 2016/191, dated 24 March 2016, and in accordance with that Corporations Instrument, amounts in the financial report are rounded off to the nearest hundred thousand dollars, unless otherwise stated.

(c) Sections

The notes in these financial statements have been organised into the following sections to help users find and understand the information they need to know:

(i) **Group Performance:** focuses on the results and performance of the Group;

(ii) **Operating Assets and Liabilities:** provides information on the assets and liabilities used to generate the Group's performance;

(iii) **Capital Structure and Risk Management:** outlines how the Group manages its capital and various financial risks;

(iv) **Group Structure:** explains aspects of the group structure and how any changes have affected the financial position and performance of the Group; and

(v) **Other Disclosures:** provides information on items which require disclosure to comply with Australian Accounting Standards and other regulatory pronouncements.

(d) Critical accounting estimates and assumptions

Estimates and judgements used in the preparation of these financial statements are continually evaluated and are based on historical experience and other factors, including expectations of future events that may have a financial impact on the Group and that are believed to be reasonable under the circumstances.

The estimates and assumptions that have a significant risk of causing a material adjustment to the carrying amounts of assets and liabilities within the next financial year are included in the following notes:

Judgement Area	Note
Impairment of goodwill and other intangible assets	11
Business combination	25

GROUP PERFORMANCE

2   SEGMENT INFORMATION

(a)   Description of segments

Management has determined the operating segments based on the reports reviewed by the Group Chief Executive Officer that are used to make strategic and operating decisions.

The Group Chief Executive Officer considers the business primarily from a brand and geographic perspective. On this basis, management has identified three reportable segments, JB Hi-Fi Australia (JB Aust), JB Hi-Fi New Zealand (JB NZ) and The Good Guys (TGG). The Group Chief Executive Officer monitors the performance of these three segments separately. The Group does not operate any other brand or in any other geographic segment.

(b)   Segment information provided to the Group Chief Executive Officer

The segment information provided to the Group Chief Executive Officer for the reportable segments for the year ended 30 June 2018 is as follows:

2018	JB Aust $m	JB NZ $m	TGG $m	Total $m
Revenue from external customers	4,539.7	213.3	2,101.3	6,854.3
EBITDA	333.6	0.8	77.3	411.7
Total segment assets	1,152.5	51.6	1,346.4	2,550.5
Additions to plant and equipment	30.9	1.2	22.3	54.4
Depreciation and impairment	41.3	3.4	16.4	61.1
Total segment liabilities	1,033.2	17.1	552.6	1,602.9

2017	JB Aust $m	JB NZ $m	TGG $m	Total $m
Revenue from external customers	4,148.6	221.0	1,258.4	5,628.0
EBITDA	302.0	0.6	57.7	360.3
Total segment assets	1,141.8	52.2	1,289.3	2,483.3
Additions to plant and equipment	37.6	1.8	9.7	49.1
Depreciation and impairment	39.5	19.0	11.2	69.7
Total segment liabilities	1,075.9	14.4	539.5	1,629.8

Note that the amounts disclosed for TGG from the prior period are from the date of acquisition on 28 November 2016 until 30 June 2017. Refer to note 25 for further details.

(i)   EBITDA

The Group Chief Executive Officer assesses the performance of the operating segments based on a measure of EBITDA. This measurement basis excludes the effects of interest revenue, finance costs, income tax, depreciation, amortisation, impairment, and non-operating intercompany charges.

A reconciliation of EBITDA to profit before income tax is provided as follows:

	Consolidated 2018 $m	Consolidated 2017 $m
EBITDA pre-transaction and implementation costs	411.7	360.3
Transaction and implementation costs	–	(22.4)
EBITDA	411.7	337.9
Interest revenue	0.5	1.7
Finance costs	(16.6)	(10.7)
Depreciation and impairment	(61.1)	(69.7)
Profit before income tax from continuing operations	334.5	259.2

67

2 SEGMENT INFORMATION (continued)

(b) Segment information provided to the Group Chief Executive Officer (continued)

(ii) Segment assets and liabilities

The amounts provided to the Group Chief Executive Officer with respect to total assets and liabilities are measured in a manner consistent with that of the financial statements. These assets and liabilities are allocated based on the operations of the segment or the physical location of the asset.

Reportable segments' assets and liabilities are reconciled to total assets and liabilities as follows:

	Consolidated	
	2018 $m	2017 $m
Segment assets	2,550.5	2,483.3
Intersegment eliminations	(58.8)	(23.5)
Total assets as per the balance sheet	2,491.7	2,459.8
Segment liabilities	1,602.9	1,629.8
Intersegment eliminations	(58.8)	(23.5)
Total liabilities as per the balance sheet	1,544.1	1,606.3

(c) Product information

The Group operates in one product and services segment, being the sale of consumer electronics products and services, including televisions, audio equipment, computers, cameras, telecommunications products and services, software, musical instruments, whitegoods, cooking products, heating and cooling products, small appliances, kitchen accessories and information technology and consulting services.

	Consolidated	
	2018 Cents	2017 Cents
3 EARNINGS PER SHARE		
Basic (cents per share)	203.09	154.30
Diluted (cents per share)	201.11	152.94

	Consolidated	
	2018 $m	2017 $m
(a) Reconciliation of earnings used in calculating earnings per share		
Basic earnings per share		
Profit for the year attributable to owners of the Company	233.2	172.4
Diluted earnings per share		
Profit for the year attributable to owners of the Company	233.2	172.4

3 EARNINGS PER SHARE (continued)

	Consolidated	
	2018 *Number* *m*	*2017* *Number* *m*
(b) Weighted average number of shares used as the denominator		
Weighted average number of ordinary shares used as the denominator in calculating basic earnings per share	114.8	111.7
Adjustments for calculation of diluted earnings per share:		
Options	1.1	1.0
Weighted average number of ordinary and potential ordinary shares used as the denominator in calculating diluted earnings per share	115.9	112.7

(c) Information concerning the classification of securities

Options

Options granted under the Company's share option plans are considered to be potential ordinary shares and have been included in the determination of diluted earnings per share to the extent to which they are dilutive (1,131,023 options are considered dilutive (2017: 993,326), 130,453 are considered anti-dilutive (2017: 237,311)). The options have not been included in the determination of basic earnings per share. Details relating to the options are set out in note 29.

	2018		2017	
	Cents per share	*$m*	*Cents per share*	*$m*
4 DIVIDENDS				
Recognised amounts				
Final Dividend - previous financial year	46.00	52.8	37.00	36.7
Interim Dividend - current financial year	86.00	98.8	72.00	82.4
	132.00	151.6	109.00	119.1
Unrecognised amounts				
Final Dividend - current financial year	46.00	52.8	46.00	52.8

In respect of the financial year ended 30 June 2018, the directors have recommended the payment of a final dividend of 46.0 cents per share. The record date is 24 August 2018.

All dividends declared and subsequently paid by the Company are franked to 100% at the 30% corporate income tax rate.

	Consolidated	
	2018 *$m*	*2017* *$m*
(a) Franking account balance		
Franking credits available for subsequent reporting periods based on a tax rate of 30.0% (2017: 30.0%)	270.6	221.5

The above amounts represent the balance of the franking account as at the end of the financial year, adjusted for franking credits that will arise from the payment of the amount of the provision for income tax.

The impact on the franking account of the dividend recommended by the directors since year end, but not recognised as a liability at year end, will be a reduction in the franking account of $22.6 million (2017: $22.6 million).

69

		Consolidated	
		2018 $m	2017 $m
5	**EXPENSES**		
	Profit before income tax includes the following specific expenses:		
	Finance costs		
	Interest on loans	15.0	9.6
	Fair value loss on interest swaps designated as cash flow hedges - transfer from equity	0.5	0.4
	Other interest expense	1.1	0.7
		16.6	10.7
	Rental expense relating to operating leases		
	Minimum lease payments	193.1	152.4
	Employee benefits expenses		
	Share-based payments - expense	7.8	5.3
	Defined contribution superannuation expense	53.9	43.6
	Other employee benefits	634.0	520.7
		695.7	569.6
6	**TAXATION**		
(a)	**Income tax expense**		
	Current tax	90.9	78.3
	Deferred tax	10.4	8.5
		101.3	86.8
(b)	**Numerical reconciliation of income tax expense to prima facie tax payable**		
	Profit from continuing operations before income tax expense	334.5	259.2
	Tax at the Australian tax rate of 30.0% (2017: 30.0%)	100.4	77.8
	Effect of expenses that are not deductible in determining taxable profit	2.3	9.8
	Effect of different tax rates of subsidiaries operating in other jurisdictions	0.1	0.4
	Effect of other deductibles in determining taxable profit	(1.4)	(1.3)
	Other	(0.1)	0.1
	Tax expense	101.3	86.8
(c)	**Amounts recognised directly in equity**		
	The following current and deferred amounts were charged directly to equity during the period:		
	Current tax		
	Tax effect of employee share options in reserves	(1.1)	(2.0)
	Deferred tax		
	Tax effect of hedge gains/(loss) in reserves	0.8	(0.5)
	Tax effect of share issue costs charged to issued capital	–	(2.7)
		(0.3)	(5.2)

70

6   TAXATION (continued)

	Consolidated	
	2018 $m	2017 $m
(d) Deferred tax		
The balance comprises temporary differences attributable to:		
Deferred tax assets		
Provisions	35.6	35.2
Inventories	8.1	7.8
Deferred revenue	45.0	45.4
Other	10.7	1.1
	99.4	89.5
Deferred tax liabilities		
Brand names	(85.2)	(85.2)
Prepayments	(19.9)	(20.4)
	(105.1)	(105.6)
Net deferred tax liabilities	(5.7)	(16.1)

Movements - Consolidated	Provisions $m	Inventories $m	Deferred revenue $m	Brand names $m	Prepayments $m	Other $m	Total $m
At 1 July 2016	22.4	3.0	–	(12.9)	–	(4.7)	7.8
Business combination	11.5	3.4	45.3	(72.3)	(20.9)	(1.7)	(34.7)
Charged to income	1.3	1.4	0.1	–	0.5	5.2	8.5
Charged to equity	–	–	–	–	–	2.3	2.3
At 30 June 2017	35.2	7.8	45.4	(85.2)	(20.4)	1.1	(16.1)
At 1 July 2017	35.2	7.8	45.4	(85.2)	(20.4)	1.1	(16.1)
Charged to income	0.4	0.3	(0.4)	–	0.5	9.6	10.4
At 30 June 2018	35.6	8.1	45.0	(85.2)	(19.9)	10.7	(5.7)

(e)   Recognition and measurement

Current tax

Current tax represents the amount expected to be paid to taxation authorities on taxable income for the period, using tax rates enacted or substantively enacted at the reporting date and any adjustment to tax payable in respect of previous years. Current tax for current and prior periods is recognised as a liability (or asset) to the extent that it is unpaid (or refundable).

Deferred tax

Deferred tax is accounted for using the balance sheet liability method, providing for temporary differences between the carrying amounts of assets and liabilities under financial reporting and taxation purposes. Deferred tax is measured at the rates that are expected to apply in the period in which the liability is settled or asset realised, based on tax rates enacted or substantively enacted at the reporting date.

Deferred tax assets and liabilities are not recognised if the temporary difference arises from the initial recognition (other than in a business combination) of assets and liabilities in a transaction that affects neither the taxable profit nor the accounting profit or in relation to the initial recognition of goodwill.

A deferred tax asset is recognised only to the extent that it is probable that future taxable profits will be available against which the deductible temporary differences or unused tax losses and tax offsets can be utilised. Deferred tax assets are reduced to the extent that it is no longer probable that the related tax benefit will be realised.

71

6   TAXATION (continued)

(e)   Recognition and measurement (continued)

Deferred tax (continued)

Deferred tax assets and liabilities are offset when they relate to income taxes levied by the same taxation authority and the Group intends to settle its current tax assets and liabilities on a net basis.

Income tax is recognised in the statement of profit or loss except to the extent that it relates to items recognised directly in equity, in which case, the tax is also recognised directly in equity.

(f)   Tax consolidation legislation

The Company and its wholly owned Australian resident entities are part of a tax consolidated group and are therefore taxed as a single entity. The head entity within the tax consolidated group is JB Hi-Fi Limited. The members of the tax consolidated group are identified at note 22.

Tax expense/income, deferred tax liabilities and deferred tax assets arising from temporary differences of the members of the tax consolidated group are recognised in the separate financial statements of the members of the tax consolidated group using the 'separate taxpayer within group' approach by reference to the carrying amounts in the separate financial statements of each entity and the tax values applying under tax consolidation. Current tax liabilities and assets and deferred tax assets arising from unused tax losses and relevant tax credits of the members of the tax consolidated group are recognised by the Company (as head entity in the tax consolidated group).

Where the tax contribution amount recognised by each member of the tax consolidated group for a particular period is different to the aggregate of the current tax liability or asset and any deferred tax asset arising from unused tax losses and tax credits in respect of that period, the difference is recognised as a contribution from (or distribution to) equity participants.

(g)   Nature of tax funding and tax sharing agreements

Entities within the tax consolidated group have entered into a tax funding arrangement and a tax sharing agreement with the head entity. Under the terms of the tax funding arrangement, JB Hi-Fi Limited and each of the entities in the tax consolidated group have agreed to pay a tax equivalent payment to or from the head entity, based on the current tax liability or current tax asset of the entity. Such amounts are reflected in amounts receivable from or payable to other entities in the tax consolidated group.

The tax sharing agreement entered into between members of the tax consolidated group provides for the determination of the allocation of income tax liabilities between the entities should the head entity default on its tax payment obligations or if an entity should leave the tax consolidated group. The effect of the tax sharing agreement is that each member's liability for tax payable by the tax consolidated group is limited to the amount payable to the head entity under the tax funding agreement.

JB Hi-Fi calculates deferred taxes in relation to investments within the tax consolidated group using the 'change in tax status' view. This view results in no deferred tax being recognised until such time as an entity leaves the tax consolidated group.

72

OPERATING ASSETS AND LIABILITIES

	Consolidated	
	2018 $m	2017 $m
7 INVENTORIES		
Finished goods	891.1	859.7

(a)   Recognition and measurement

Inventories are stated at the lower of cost and net realisable value. Costs are assigned to individual items of inventory on the basis of weighted average costs. Costs of inventories are determined after deducting rebates and discounts. Net realisable value represents the estimated selling price less all estimated costs necessary to make the sale.

Determining the net realisable value of inventories relies on key assumptions that require the use of management judgement. These key assumptions are the variables affecting the expected selling price and are reviewed annually. Any reassessment of the selling price in a particular year will affect the cost of goods sold.

	Consolidated	
	2018 $m	2017 $m
8 TRADE AND OTHER RECEIVABLES		
Trade receivables	56.6	54.2
Allowance for doubtful debts	(1.1)	(0.7)
	55.5	53.5
Non-trade receivables	149.2	140.1
	204.7	193.6

(a)   Terms and conditions

Trade receivables

The average credit period on account sales of goods is 30 days. No interest is charged on trade receivables. An allowance has been made for estimated irrecoverable amounts arising from a review of individual debtors. Credit insurance is carried for most commercial debtor accounts. Trade receivables are recognised at amortised cost less provision for impairment.

Non-trade receivables

Non-trade receivables principally represent rebates receivable from suppliers for purchases of inventories. No amount is considered irrecoverable from suppliers and therefore no allowance has been made.

	Consolidated	
	2018 $m	2017 $m
(b) Ageing of trade receivables		
Not past due	50.8	48.2
Past due but not impaired:		
0 - 30 days	3.7	4.0
31 - 60 days	1.0	1.3
61 - 90 days	–	–
91+ days	–	–
	55.5	53.5

73

8   TRADE AND OTHER RECEIVABLES (continued)

	Consolidated	
	2018 $m	2017 $m
(c) Movements in allowance for doubtful debts		
Balance at the beginning of the year	0.7	0.5
Provision for impairment recognised during the year	0.5	0.3
Receivables written off during the year as uncollectable	(0.1)	(0.1)
	1.1	0.7
(d) Ageing of impaired trade receivables		
0 - 31 days	–	–
31 - 60 days	0.6	0.1
61 - 90 days	0.4	0.5
91+ days	0.1	0.1
	1.1	0.7

(e)   Collectability of trade receivables

Collectability of trade receivables is reviewed on an ongoing basis. An allowance account (provision for impairment of trade receivables) is used when there is objective evidence that the Group will not be able to collect all amounts due according to the original terms of the receivables. The amount of the impairment allowance is the difference between the asset's carrying amount and the amount expected to be collected.

The amount of the impairment loss is recognised in profit or loss within other expenses. When a trade receivable for which an impairment allowance had been recognised becomes uncollectible in a subsequent period, it is written off against the allowance account. Subsequent recoveries of amounts previously written off are credited against other expenses in profit or loss.

The Group has not impaired all debts that are past due at the reporting date as the Group considers the majority of these amounts to be recoverable. The Group does not hold any collateral over trade receivables with the exception of retention of title for certain customers.

	Consolidated	
	2018 $m	2017 $m
9 OTHER ASSETS		
Current		
Prepayments	31.8	29.8
Other	10.9	11.6
	42.7	41.4
Non-current		
Prepayments	45.9	46.8
	45.9	46.8

Prepayments includes payments made in relation to The Goods Guys Gold Service Extras program and general prepaid expenses.

74

	Plant and equipment $m	Leasehold improvements $m	Total $m
10 PLANT AND EQUIPMENT			
At 1 July 2016			
Cost	259.0	160.4	419.4
Accumulated depreciation and impairment	(138.5)	(97.3)	(235.8)
Net book amount	120.5	63.1	183.6
Year ended 30 June 2017			
Opening net book amount	120.5	63.1	183.6
Acquisitions through business combination	35.0	0.2	35.2
Additions	33.5	15.6	49.1
Disposals	(4.5)	(0.2)	(4.7)
Depreciation charge	(35.6)	(18.3)	(53.9)
Impairment charge	(0.7)	(0.4)	(1.1)
Closing net book amount	148.2	60.0	208.2
At 30 June 2017			
Cost	310.6	173.9	484.5
Accumulated depreciation and impairment	(162.4)	(113.9)	(276.3)
Net book amount	148.2	60.0	208.2
Year ended 30 June 2018			
Opening net book amount	148.2	60.0	208.2
Exchange differences	(0.4)	(0.2)	(0.6)
Additions	35.9	18.5	54.4
Disposals	(2.2)	(0.7)	(2.9)
Depreciation charge	(40.8)	(19.6)	(60.4)
Impairment charge	(0.6)	(0.1)	(0.7)
Closing net book amount	140.1	57.9	198.0
At 30 June 2018			
Cost	336.4	188.1	524.5
Accumulated depreciation and impairment	(196.3)	(130.2)	(326.5)
Net book amount	140.1	57.9	198.0

(a) Recognition and measurement

Plant and equipment and leasehold improvements are stated at cost less accumulated depreciation and impairment (if any). Cost includes expenditure that is directly attributable to the acquisition of the item.

Depreciation is provided on plant and equipment and leasehold improvements. Depreciation is calculated on a straight line basis so as to write off the net cost of each asset over its expected useful life to its estimated residual value. The estimated useful lives, residual values and depreciation method are reviewed at the end of each annual reporting period, with the effect of any changes recognised on a prospective basis.

The following estimated useful lives are used in the calculation of depreciation:

- Leasehold improvements   1 to 15 years
- Plant and equipment   1.5 to 15 years

Plant and equipment and leasehold improvements are tested for impairment whenever events or changes in circumstances indicate that the carrying amount may not be recoverable.

An impairment loss is recognised for the amount by which the asset's carrying amount exceeds its recoverable amount. The recoverable amount is the higher of an asset's fair value less costs to sell and value in use. For the purposes of assessing impairment, assets are grouped at the lowest levels for which there are separately identifiable cash inflows which are largely independent of the cash inflows from other assets or groups of assets (cash-generating units).

An item of plant and equipment is derecognised upon disposal or when no future economic benefits are expected to arise from the continued use of the asset. Any gain or loss arising on the disposal or retirement of an item of plant and equipment is determined as the difference between the sales proceeds and the carrying amount of the asset, and is recognised in other expenses in the profit or loss.

75

	Goodwill $m	Brand names $m	Location premiums $m	Rights to profit share $m	Total $m
11 INTANGIBLE ASSETS					
Year ended 30 June 2017					
Opening net book amount	49.5	43.1	2.4	3.5	98.5
Additions - business combination (note 25)	712.2	241.3	–	–	953.5
Impairment charge	(14.7)	–	–	–	(14.7)
Closing net book amount	747.0	284.4	2.4	3.5	1,037.3
Year ended 30 June 2018					
Opening net book amount	747.0	284.4	2.4	3.5	1,037.3
Impairment charge	–	–	–	–	–
Closing net book amount	747.0	284.4	2.4	3.5	1,037.3

(a) Recognition and measurement

Goodwill represents the excess of the cost of an acquisition over the fair value of the Company's share of the net identifiable assets acquired at the date of acquisition.

Brand names, location premiums and rights to profit share are assessed as having indefinite useful lives. This assessment reflects management's intention to continue to utilise these intangible assets into the foreseeable future. Each period, the useful life of these assets are reviewed to determine whether events and circumstances continue to support an indefinite useful life assessment for the assets.

Intangible assets that have an indefinite useful life are carried at cost less accumulated impairment losses.

(b) Impairment testing

Intangible assets that have an indefinite useful life are not subject to amortisation and are tested annually for impairment, or more frequently if events or changes in circumstances indicate that they might be impaired.

An impairment loss is recognised for the amount by which the asset's carrying amount exceeds its recoverable amount. The recoverable amount is the higher of an asset's fair value less costs to sell and value in use. For the purposes of assessing impairment, assets are grouped at the lowest levels for which there are separately identifiable cash inflows which are largely independent of the cash inflows from other assets or groups of assets (cash-generating units). Non-financial assets other than goodwill that suffered an impairment are reviewed for possible reversal of the impairment at the end of each reporting period.

For the purposes of impairment testing, goodwill is allocated to each of the Group's cash-generating units ('CGUs'), or groups of CGUs, expected to benefit from the synergies of the business combination.

If the recoverable amount of the CGU (or groups of CGUs) is less than the carrying amount of the CGU (or groups of CGUs), the impairment loss is allocated first to reduce the carrying amount of any goodwill allocated to the CGU (or groups of CGUs) and then to the other assets in the CGU (or groups of CGUs) pro rata on the basis of the carrying amount of each asset in the CGU (or groups of CGUs). An impairment loss recognised for goodwill is recognised immediately in profit or loss.

On disposal of an operation within a CGU, the attributable amount of goodwill is included in the determination of the profit or loss on disposal of the operation.

The carrying amount of goodwill and brand names is allocated to the following cash-generating units (CGUs) or groups of CGUs for impairment testing purposes:

	Consolidated	
	2018 $m	2017 $m
Goodwill		
The Good Guys	575.6	575.6
JB Hi-Fi Australia	163.3	163.3
Impact Records (store acquisition)	1.7	1.7
JB Solutions division (Commercial)	6.4	6.4
JB Hi-Fi New Zealand	–	–
	747.0	747.0

76

11 INTANGIBLE ASSETS (continued)

(b) Impairment testing (continued)

	Consolidated	
	2018 $m	2017 $m
Brand names		
The Good Guys	241.3	241.3
JB Hi-Fi Australia	43.1	43.1
	284.4	284.4

The recoverable amount of each CGU (or group of CGUs) has been determined based on value in use calculations which use cash flow projections from financial budgets approved by the Board. The cash flows beyond the budget period have been extrapolated using a steady 2.5% long term growth rate (2017: 2%) which is consistent with the projected long term average growth rate for the consumer products market. The discount rate used in the calculations is 10.0% for JB Hi-Fi Australia, Impact Records and JB Solutions division (2017: 10.0%), 10.5% for JB Hi-Fi New Zealand (2017: 10.5%) and 10.5% for The Good Guys (2017: 10.5%).

The key assumptions used in the value in use calculations include sales growth, gross margin, cost of doing business (CODB) and the discount rate. The assumptions are based on past experience and the Company's forecast operating and financial performance for each CGU (or group of CGUs). The discount rate is derived from the Group's weighted average cost of capital, adjusted for varying risk profiles.

	Consolidated	
	2018 $m	2017 $m
12 TRADE AND OTHER PAYABLES		
Trade payables	582.0	580.7
Goods and services tax (GST) payable	37.3	24.1
Other creditors and accruals	46.0	39.9
	665.3	644.7

Trade payables and other creditors and accruals represent liabilities for goods and services provided to the Group prior to the end of financial year which are unpaid. Trade and other payables are stated at amortised cost. The amounts are unsecured and are usually settled within 45 days of recognition.

	Consolidated	
	2018 $m	2017 $m
13 DEFERRED REVENUE		
Current		
Deferred revenue	150.5	141.8
	150.5	141.8
Non-current		
Deferred revenue	103.7	99.6
	103.7	99.6

Deferred revenue relates to unfulfilled services to be performed under The Good Guys Gold Service Extras program, unredeemed gift cards and customer deposits. Refer to note 31(a) for revenue recognition accounting policy.

77

	Consolidated	
	2018 $m	2017 $m
14 PROVISIONS		
Current		
Employee benefits	78.2	71.4
Lease provision	5.3	4.9
	83.5	76.3
Non-current		
Employee benefits	7.3	7.3
Lease provision	5.2	4.5
	12.5	11.8

(a) Recognition and measurement

Provisions are recognised when the Group has a present obligation (legal or constructive) as a result of a past event, it is probable that the Group will be required to settle the obligation, and a reliable estimate can be made of the amount of the obligation.

The amount recognised as a provision is the best estimate of the consideration required to settle the present obligation at reporting date, taking into account the risks and uncertainties surrounding the obligation. Where a provision is measured using the cash flows estimated to settle the present obligation, its carrying amount is the present value of those cash flows.

(i) Employee benefits

Liabilities for wages and salaries, including non-monetary benefits, are recognised in respect of employees' services up to the end of the reporting period and are measured at the amounts expected to be paid when the liabilities are settled. The liability for annual leave and unpaid bonuses are recognised in the provision for employee benefits. All other short-term employee benefit obligations are presented as payables.

Contributions to defined contribution superannuation plans are expensed when employees have rendered services entitling them to the contributions.

The liability for long service leave is recognised in the provision for employee benefits and measured as the present value of expected future payments to be made in respect of services provided by employees, up to the end of the reporting period. Expected future payments are discounted using the Australian corporate bond discount rate curve as published by Milliman with terms to maturity and currency that match, as closely as possible, the estimated future cash outflows.

Management judgement is applied in determining the following key assumptions used in the calculation of long service leave at balance date:

- future increases in wages and salaries;
- future on cost rates; and
- experience of employee departures and period of service.

(ii) Lease provision

The lease provision includes the Group's best estimate of the amount required to return the Group's leased premises to their original condition, taking into account due consideration of the Group's past history of vacating stores and the Group's best estimate of onerous lease obligations.

78

	Consolidated	
	2018 *$m*	*2017* *$m*
15 OTHER LIABILITIES		
Current		
Lease accrual	2.8	2.9
Lease incentive	5.2	4.8
Other financial liabilities	0.3	1.3
	8.3	9.0
Non-current		
Lease accrual	15.0	14.8
Lease incentive	20.6	19.8
	35.6	34.6

(a) Lease accrual

Leases in which a significant portion of the risks and rewards of ownership are not transferred to the Group as lessee are classified as operating leases. Payments made under operating leases (net of any incentives received from the lessor) are charged to the statement of profit or loss on a straight line basis over the period of the lease. The lease accrual represents the difference between the expense incurred and the payments made.

(b) Lease incentives

In the event that lease incentives (for example rent free periods and upfront capital contributions) are received to enter into operating leases, such incentives are recognised as a liability. The aggregate benefits of incentives are recognised as a reduction of rental expense on a straight line basis over the period of the lease.

79

CAPITAL STRUCTURE AND RISK MANAGEMENT

16   NOTES TO THE CASH FLOW STATEMENT

For the purposes of the cash flow statement, cash and cash equivalents includes cash on hand and in banks, net of outstanding bank overdrafts.

(a)   Reconciliation of net cash inflow from operating activities to profit

	Consolidated	
	2018 $m	2017 $m
Profit for the year	233.2	172.4
Depreciation and amortisation	60.4	53.9
Impairment of plant and equipment	0.7	1.1
Impairment of goodwill	–	14.7
Non-cash employee benefits expense - share-based payments	7.8	5.3
Net loss on disposal of non-current assets	2.5	4.5
Fair value adjustment to derivatives	1.9	(1.1)
Change in operating assets and liabilities net of effects from acquisition of businesses:		
(Increase) decrease in inventories	(33.0)	(56.3)
(Increase) decrease in current receivables	(10.7)	3.0
(Increase) decrease in other current assets	(0.4)	(3.0)
(Decrease) increase in deferred tax liabilities	(10.4)	(8.5)
(Decrease) increase in current payables	22.4	(14.7)
(Decrease) increase in current provisions	7.3	4.2
(Decrease) increase in other current liabilities	(0.7)	1.4
(Decrease) increase in deferred revenue	12.8	15.0
(Decrease) increase in non-current provisions	0.7	(0.2)
(Decrease) increase in other non-current liabilities	0.7	2.2
(Decrease) increase in current tax liabilities	(3.1)	(3.3)
Net cash inflow from operating activities	292.1	190.6

17   BORROWINGS

Unsecured non-current

Bank loans	469.4	558.8

Reconciliation of liabilities arising from financing activities

Opening borrowings	558.8	
Repayment of borrowings	(89.7)	
Debt issue costs paid	(0.8)	
Amortisation of debt issue costs	1.1	
	469.4	

In June 2018, the Group restructured its multi-tranche term debt facilities, resulting in a reduction in its multi-tranche term debt facilities by $100.0 million to $550.0 million. In conjunction with the restructure of the term debt facilities, the Group also entered into a new $30.0 million trade finance facility which is renewable annually. Refer to note 20(b) for further details on the Group's financing facilities.

In line with the Group's financial risk management policy, the Group has utilised an interest rate swap and interest rate cap over approximately 50% of the Group's borrowings to mitigate the risk of changing interest rates on the variable rate debt held.

17   BORROWINGS (continued)

(a)   Recognition and measurement)

Borrowings are initially recognised at fair value, net of transaction costs incurred. Borrowings are subsequently measured at amortised cost.

Borrowings are classified as current liabilities unless the Group has an unconditional right to defer settlement of the liability for at least 12 months after the reporting date, and intends to do so.

The Group monitors compliance with its financial covenants on a monthly basis and reports compliance on a semi-annual basis to the banks. The Group has complied with all such requirements during the current and previous year.

	Parent entity		Parent entity	
	2018 Shares	2017 Shares	2018 $m	2017 $m
18 CONTRIBUTED EQUITY				
(a) Share capital				
Ordinary shares - fully paid	114,883,372	114,421,403	441.7	438.7

Ordinary shares issued are classified as equity and are fully paid, have no par value and carry one vote per share and the right to dividends. Incremental costs directly attributable to the issue of new shares are shown in equity as a deduction, net of tax, from the proceeds.

If the entity reacquires its own equity instruments, for example, as the result of a share buy-back, those instruments are deducted from equity and the associated shares are cancelled. No gain or loss is recognised in the profit or loss and the consideration paid, including any directly attributable incremental costs (net of income taxes), is recognised directly in equity.

(b)   Movements in ordinary share capital

Date	Details	Number of shares	$m
1 July 2016	Opening balance	98,947,309	49.3
	Issue of shares under the entitlement offer	15,046,182	394.2
	Share issue costs (net of tax)	–	(6.5)
	Issue of shares under share option and deferred STI plans	427,912	1.7
30 June 2017	Closing balance	114,421,403	438.7
1 July 2017	Opening balance	114,421,403	438.7
	Issue of shares under share option and deferred STI plans	461,969	3.0
30 June 2018	Closing balance	114,883,372	441.7

(c)   Share options

In accordance with the provisions of the Company's share option plans, as at 30 June 2018, executives and non-executive management have options over 1,333,919 ordinary shares (which were all unvested), in aggregate, with various expiry dates.

As at 30 June 2017, executives and non-executive management had options over 1,359,199 ordinary shares (which were all unvested), in aggregate, with various expiry dates.

Share options granted under the Company's share option plans carry no rights to dividends and no voting rights.

81

18   CONTRIBUTED EQUITY (continued)

(d)   Capital management

The Board reviews the capital structure on an ongoing basis. The Group's objective is to maintain an optimal capital structure which seeks to reduce the cost of capital and to ensure the Group has access to adequate capital to sustain the future development of the business.

In order to maintain or adjust the capital structure, the Group may adjust the level of dividends paid to shareholders, return capital to shareholders, buy back shares, issue new shares or sell assets to reduce debt.

As part of its capital management program, the Group monitors the return on invested capital and the gearing ratio. The Group defines return on invested capital as earnings before interest and tax (EBIT) divided by the sum of total equity plus net debt and the gearing ratio as term debt excluding capitalised borrowing costs, plus bank overdrafts, divided by earnings before interest, taxation, depreciation, amortisation and impairment (EBITDA).

The Board has adopted a policy of monitoring the dividend payout ratio and targeting a payout ratio of 65% of net profit after tax as it seeks to strike a balance between shareholder returns and ensuring adequate capital is retained for the growth of the business so as to maximise long term shareholder returns.

There were no changes in the Group's approach to capital management during the year.

The Group's return on invested capital and gearing ratios as at 30 June 2018 and 30 June 2017 were as follows:

	Consolidated	
	2018 $m	2017 $m
Return on invested capital		
Profit before tax	334.5	259.2
Net finance costs	16.1	9.0
EBIT	350.6	268.2
Borrowings	469.4	558.8
Cash and cash equivalents	(72.0)	(72.8)
Net debt	397.4	486.0
Total equity	947.6	853.5
Invested capital	1,345.0	1,339.5
Return on invested capital	26.1%	20%
Gearing		
Term debt	470.3	560.0
EBIT	350.6	268.2
Depreciation and impairment	61.1	69.7
EBITDA	411.7	337.9
Gearing	1.14	1.66
19 RESERVES		
Equity-settled benefits	43.5	34.6
Common control reserve	(6.1)	(6.1)
Hedging reserves	1.7	(0.2)
Foreign currency translation reserve	3.6	4.9
	42.7	33.2

82

19 RESERVES (continued)

(a) Nature and purpose of reserves

(i) Equity-settled benefits

The equity-settled benefits reserve arises on the grant of share options to executives and non-executive management under the Company's share option plans. Further information about share based payments is in note 29 to the financial statements.

(ii) Common control reserve

The common control reserve represents the excess of the purchase consideration over the balance of a non-controlling interest at the date a change in ownership of a subsidiary occurs.

(iii) Hedging reserves

Hedging reserves include gains and losses recognised on the effective portion of cash flow hedges with respect to the Group's interest rate swaps, caps and forward foreign exchange contracts as described in note 31(b), in addition to gains and losses recognised on the effective portion of foreign currency loans in previous periods designated as net investment hedges.

The cumulative deferred gain or loss on the interest rate swaps, caps and forward foreign exchange contracts is recognised in the profit or loss when the hedged transaction impacts the profit or loss. The gains and losses deferred due to the net investment hedge are recognised in the profit or loss when the foreign operation is disposed.

(iv) Foreign currency translation

Exchange differences relating to the translation of the Group's foreign controlled entities from their functional currencies into Australian dollars are brought to account directly to the foreign currency translation reserve, as described in note 31(c).

20 FINANCIAL RISK MANAGEMENT

The Group's activities expose it to a variety of financial risks, including market risk (foreign currency and interest rate risk), liquidity risk and credit risk.

The Group seeks to minimise the effects of these risks, by using various financial instruments, including derivative financial instruments. The Group does not enter into or trade financial instruments, including derivative financial instruments, for speculative purposes. The use of financial derivatives is governed by the Group's policies approved by the Board of directors, which provide written principles on the use of financial derivatives.

The Group is exposed to some foreign currency risk as The Good Guys purchase some private label product denominated in foreign currencies. In order to minimise this risk, the Group holds forward foreign exchange contracts.

The Group holds the following financial assets and liabilities at reporting date:

	Consolidated	
	2018 *$m*	*2017* *$m*
Financial assets		
Cash and cash equivalents	72.0	72.8
Trade and other receivables	204.7	193.6
Forward foreign exchange contracts	1.0	–
	277.7	266.4
Financial liabilities		
Trade and other payables	665.3	644.7
Bank loans	469.4	558.8
Interest rate swaps and caps (net settled)	0.3	0.6
Forward foreign exchange contracts	–	0.7
	1,135.0	1,204.8

83

20   FINANCIAL RISK MANAGEMENT (continued)

(a)   Market risk

(i)   Foreign exchange risk management

The majority of the Group's operations are denominated in the functional currency of the country of operation therefore minimising the impact of further foreign currency risk. That is, transactions and balances related to the Australian operations are denominated in Australian dollars and transactions and balances related to the New Zealand operations are denominated in New Zealand dollars.

The Group undertakes some transactions denominated in foreign currencies; consequently, exposures to exchange rate fluctuations arise. Exchange rate exposures are managed within approved policy parameters utilising forward foreign exchange contracts.

Forward foreign exchange contracts

It is the policy of the Group to enter into forward foreign exchange contracts to cover specific foreign currency payments (normally USD or EUR) for future purchases.

The following table details the forward foreign exchange contracts outstanding at the end of the reporting period:

	30 June 2018			30 June 2017		
Consolidated	Weighted average exchange rate	Foreign currency m	Notional value A$m	Weighted average exchange rate	Foreign currency m	Notional value A$m
Forward exchange contracts						
- buy USD (cash flow hedges)	0.78	14.1	18.1	0.75	25.6	34.2
- buy Euro (cash flow hedges)	0.64	2.4	3.8	0.67	4.3	6.4

Summarised sensitivity analysis

The carrying value of forward foreign exchange contracts is an asset of $1.0m (2017: liability of $0.7m). Using a sensitivity of 10% movement in exchange rates results in an immaterial impact on the carrying value.

(ii)   Cash flow and fair value interest rate risk

The Group is exposed to interest rate risk as it borrows funds at floating interest rates. The risk is managed by the Group by maintaining an appropriate mix between fixed and floating rate borrowings through the use of interest rate swap and cap contracts. Hedging activities are evaluated regularly to align with interest rate views and defined risk appetite, ensuring optimal hedging strategies are applied, by either positioning the balance sheet or protecting interest expense through different interest rate cycles.

Interest rate swap and interest rate cap contracts

Under interest rate swap and cap contracts, the Group agrees to exchange the difference between fixed and floating rate interest amounts calculated on agreed notional principal amounts. Such contracts enable the Group to mitigate the risk of changing interest rates on the cash flow exposures on the issued variable rate debt held. The fair value of interest rate swaps and caps at the reporting date is determined by discounting the future cash flows using the forward interest rate curves at reporting date and the credit risk inherent in the contract.

The following tables detail the notional principal amounts and interest rate swap and cap contracts outstanding as at reporting date and weighted average interest rates based on the outstanding balances and applicable interest rates throughout the financial year:

	30 June 2018		30 June 2017	
Consolidated	Weighted average interest rate %	Balance $m	Weighted average interest rate %	Balance $m
Bank loans	3.01%	470.3	2.95%	560.0
Interest rate swaps and caps (notional principal amount)	3.15%	228.4	3.10%	250.0
Net exposure to cash flow interest rate risk		698.7		810.0

84

20 FINANCIAL RISK MANAGEMENT (continued)

(a) Market risk (continued)

(ii) Cash flow and fair value interest rate risk (continued)

The interest rate swaps and caps settle on a monthly basis and the Group settles the difference on a net basis. The interest rate swap and cap contracts are designated as cash flow hedges in order to reduce the Group's cash flow exposure resulting from variable interest rates on borrowings. The interest rate swaps, caps and the interest payments on the loan occur simultaneously and the amount deferred in equity is recognised in profit or loss over the period that the floating interest payments impact profit or loss.

Summarised sensitivity analysis

The carrying value of interest rate swap and caps was $0.3m (2017: $0.6m) and borrowings was $469.4m (2017: $558.8m). Using a sensitivity of 50 basis points results in an immaterial impact on the carrying values.

(b) Liquidity risk

Ultimate responsibility for liquidity risk management rests with the Board of directors, who assess the Group's short, medium and long term funding and liquidity management requirements. The Group manages liquidity risk by maintaining adequate reserves, banking facilities and reserve borrowing facilities and by continuously monitoring forecast and actual cash flows.

Financing arrangements

The Group had access to the following undrawn borrowing facilities at the end of the reporting period:

	Consolidated	
	2018 $m	2017 $m
Unsecured bank overdraft facility:		
amount used	16.7	5.1
amount unused	72.5	84.4
	89.2	89.5
Unsecured trade finance facility:		
amount used	–	–
amount unused	30.0	–
	30.0	–
Unsecured indemnity guarantees:		
amount used	4.9	7.4
amount unused	4.0	1.5
	8.9	8.9
Unsecured bank loan facilities (term debt):		
amount used[i]	470.3	560.0
amount unused	79.7	90.0
	550.0	650.0
Headroom in total borrowing facilities (excluding security indemnity guarantees)	182.2	174.4

(i) Face value of term debt (excluding capitalised borrowing costs).

85

20   FINANCIAL RISK MANAGEMENT (continued)

(b)   Liquidity risk (continued)

Maturities of financial liabilities

The following tables detail the Group's remaining contractual maturity for its financial liabilities. The tables have been drawn up based on the undiscounted cash flows of financial liabilities based on the earliest date on which the Group can be required to pay. The table includes both principal and estimated interest cash flows.

Cash flows for financial liabilities without fixed amount or timing are based on the conditions existing at the reporting date.

2018	Less than 6 months $m	6 - 12 months $m	Between 1 and 2 years $m	Between 2 and 5 years $m	Over 5 years $m	Total $m	Weighted average effective interest rate %
Financial liabilities							
Trade and other payables	665.3	–	–	–	–	665.3	–
Bank loans	7.1	7.1	205.4	281.6	–	501.2	3.01%
Interest rate swaps and caps (net settled)	0.1	0.2	–	–	–	0.3	3.15%
	672.5	7.3	205.4	281.6	–	1,166.8	

2017	Less than 6 months $m	6 - 12 months $m	Between 1 and 2 years $m	Between 2 and 5 years $m	Over 5 years $m	Total $m	Weighted average effective interest rate %
Financial liabilities							
Trade and other payables	644.7	–	–	–	–	644.7	–
Bank loans	8.3	8.3	206.2	369.5	–	592.3	2.95%
Interest rate swaps and caps (net settled)	0.3	0.2	(0.1)	–	–	0.4	3.10%
Forward foreign exchange contracts	0.5	0.2	–	–	–	0.7	
	653.8	8.7	206.1	369.5	–	1,238.1	

(c)   Credit risk management

Credit risk refers to the risk that a counterparty will default on its contractual obligations resulting in financial loss to the Group. The Group has endeavoured to minimise its credit risk by dealing with creditworthy counterparties. The Group's exposure and the credit ratings of its counterparties are continuously monitored and the aggregate value of transactions concluded is spread amongst approved counterparties.

The Group does not have any significant credit risk exposure to any single counterparty or any group of counterparties having similar characteristics.

The carrying amount of financial assets recorded in the financial statements, net of any allowance for impairment, represents the Group's maximum exposure to credit risk.

86

20   FINANCIAL RISK MANAGEMENT (continued)

(d)   Fair value of financial instruments

The only financial assets or financial liabilities carried at fair value are interest rate swaps, interest rate caps and foreign currency forward contracts.

All these instruments are considered to be Level 2 financial instruments because, unlike Level 1 financial instruments, their measurement is derived from inputs other than quoted prices that are observable for the assets or liabilities, either directly (as prices) or indirectly (derived from prices).

The interest rate swaps and caps fair value was obtained from third party valuations derived from discounted cash flow forecasts of interest rates from observable yield curves at the end of the reporting period and contract interest rates.

The foreign currency forward contracts fair value was obtained from third party valuations derived from discounted cash flow forecasts of forward exchange rates at the end of the reporting period and contract exchange rates.

There were no transfers between levels 1, 2 and 3 for recurring fair value measurements during the financial year.

The carrying amount of other financial assets and financial liabilities recorded in the financial statements approximate their fair values.

21   COMMITMENTS

(a)   Non-cancellable operating leases

The Group has entered into operating lease agreements in relation to its stores and some minor operating leases in relation to plant and equipment. Store leases have terms of between five to fifteen years, with, in some cases, an option to extend. Operating lease contracts generally contain market review clauses in the event that the Group exercises its option to renew. The Group does not have an option to purchase the leased asset at the expiry of the lease period.

	Consolidated	
	2018 $m	2017 $m
Commitments for minimum lease payments in relation to non-cancellable operating leases are payable as follows:		
Within one year	157.5	146.0
Later than one year but not later than five years	405.3	395.4
Later than five years	121.6	142.2
	684.4	683.6

87

GROUP STRUCTURE

22 SUBSIDIARIES

The consolidated financial statements incorporate the assets, liabilities and results of the following principal subsidiaries in accordance with the accounting policy described below:

		Ownership interest	
Name of entity	Country of incorporation	2018 %	2017 %
Parent entity			
JB Hi-Fi Limited ^	Australia		
Subsidiaries			
JB Hi-Fi Group Pty Ltd ^	Australia	100	100
Clive Anthonys Pty Ltd	Australia	100	100
JB Hi-Fi (A) Pty Ltd ^	Australia	100	100
Rocket Replacements Pty Ltd	Australia	100	100
JB Hi-Fi Education Solutions Pty Ltd ^	Australia	100	100
JB Hi-Fi Group (NZ) Limited	New Zealand	100	100
JB Hi-Fi NZ Limited	New Zealand	100	100
JB Hi-Fi (B) Pty Ltd ^	Australia	100	100
The Muir Electrical Company Pty Ltd ^	Australia	100	100
The Muir Electrical Service Co Pty Ltd ^	Australia	100	100
The Good Guys Discount Warehouses (Australia) Pty Ltd ^	Australia	100	100
Muir Group Employee Share Plan Pty Ltd ^	Australia	100	100
The Muir Finance Company Pty Ltd ^	Australia	100	100
M.E.W. (Australia) Pty Ltd ^	Australia	100	100
The Muir Electrical Company Pty Ltd as Trustee of the Muir Investment Unit Trust ^	Australia	100	100
The Good Guys Discount Warehouses (Australia) Pty Ltd as Trustee of the various store Trusts	Australia	100	100
Home Services Network Pty Ltd ^	Australia	100	–

Notes:

(i)   JB Hi-Fi Limited is the head entity within the tax consolidated group.

(ii)   All Australian entities are members of the tax consolidated group.

(iii)   Entities identified with '^' are party to a deed of cross guarantee.

(iv)   Home Services Network Pty Ltd was incorporated on 18 October 2017 and became a party to the deed of cross guarantee on 12 June 2018.

(v)   The Company has a trust to administer the Company's share options plans. This trust is consolidated, as the substance of the relationship is that the trust is controlled by the Company.

(a) Principles of consolidation

(i)   Subsidiaries

Subsidiaries are all entities which are controlled by the Company. Control is achieved when the Company:

- has power over the investee;

- is exposed, or has rights, to variable returns from its involvement with the investee; and

- has the ability to use its power to affect its returns.

The Company reassesses whether or not it controls an investee if facts and circumstances indicate that there are changes to one or more of the three elements of control listed above. Subsidiaries are fully consolidated from the date on which control is transferred to the Group. They are de-consolidated from the date that control ceases. Intercompany transactions, balances and unrealised gains on transactions between Group companies are eliminated. Unrealised losses are also eliminated. Non-controlling interests in the results and equity of subsidiaries are shown separately in the consolidated financial statements. Investments in subsidiaries are accounted for at cost, less any impairment, in the separate financial statements of JB Hi-Fi Limited.

22   SUBSIDIARIES (continued)

(a)   Principles of consolidation (continued)

(ii)   Changes in ownership interests

The Company treats transactions with non-controlling interests that do not result in a loss of control as transactions with equity owners of the Company. A change in ownership interest results in an adjustment between the carrying amounts of the controlling and non-controlling interests to reflect their relative interests in the subsidiary. Any difference between the amount of the adjustment to non-controlling interests and any consideration paid or received is recognised in a separate reserve within equity attributable to owners of JB Hi-Fi Limited (the common control reserve).

23   DEED OF CROSS GUARANTEE

The subsidiaries identified with a '^' in note 22 are parties to a deed of cross guarantee under which each Company guarantees to each creditor payment in full of any debt in accordance with the deed of cross guarantee. By entering into the deed, the subsidiaries who are party to the deed have been relieved from the requirement to prepare and lodge an audited financial report under ASIC Corporations (Wholly-owned Companies) Instrument 2016/785.

The consolidated statement of profit or loss, statement of profit or loss and other comprehensive income and balance sheet of the entities party to the deed of cross guarantee are provided as follows:

	2018 $m	2017 $m
(a) Consolidated statement of profit or loss, statement of profit or loss and other comprehensive income		
Statement of profit or loss		
Revenue	4,895.6	4,383.2
Cost of sales	(3,845.0)	(3,322.6)
Gross profit	1,050.6	1,060.6
Other income	114.2	6.4
Sales and marketing expenses	(503.2)	(546.5)
Occupancy expenses	(205.0)	(183.5)
Administration expenses	(34.0)	(29.9)
Acquisition transaction and implementation expenses	–	(18.7)
Finance costs	(16.4)	(10.5)
Other expenses	(68.9)	(49.8)
Profit before income tax	337.3	228.1
Income tax expense	(102.1)	(76.3)
Profit for the year	235.2	151.8
Statement of profit or loss and other comprehensive income		
Profit for the year	235.2	151.8
Other comprehensive income		
Items that may be reclassified to profit or loss		
Changes in the fair value of cash flow hedges (net of tax)	1.9	(1.1)
Other comprehensive income for the year (net of tax)	1.9	(1.1)
Total comprehensive income for the year	237.1	150.7

89

23   DEED OF CROSS GUARANTEE (continued)

	2018 $m	2017 $m
(b) Balance sheet		
Current assets		
Cash and cash equivalents	69.3	77.0
Trade and other receivables	295.9	196.5
Inventories	606.6	579.1
Other current assets	13.2	15.2
Total current assets	985.0	867.8
Non-current assets		
Plant and equipment	161.1	178.0
Deferred tax assets	63.5	21.4
Intangible assets	83.8	83.8
Other non-current assets	1,084.7	1,095.2
Total non-current assets	1,393.1	1,378.4
Total assets	2,378.1	2,246.2
Current liabilities		
Trade and other payables	644.9	627.3
Deferred revenue	60.3	55.4
Current tax liabilities	9.6	9.7
Provisions	89.8	75.9
Other current liabilities	7.2	12.7
Total current liabilities	811.8	781.0
Non-current liabilities		
Borrowings	462.1	558.8
Deferred revenue	6.2	–
Provisions	12.4	8.8
Other non-current liabilities	32.5	25.2
Total non-current liabilities	513.2	592.8
Total liabilities	1,325.0	1,373.8
Net assets	1,053.1	872.4
Equity		
Contributed equity	453.0	450.0
Reserves	44.6	33.8
Retained earnings	555.5	388.6
Total equity	1,053.1	872.4

90

	Parent Entity	
	2018 $m	2017 $m
24 PARENT ENTITY		
Assets		
Current assets	–	0.8
Non-current assets	517.7	496.1
Total assets	517.7	496.9
Liabilities		
Current liabilities	14.1	15.4
Total liabilities	14.1	15.4
Shareholders' equity		
Contributed equity	441.7	438.7
Reserves	43.5	34.6
Retained earnings	18.4	8.2
	503.6	481.5
Profit for the year	161.8	124.5
Total comprehensive income	161.8	124.5

91

25 BUSINESS COMBINATION

(a) Summary of acquisition

There were no acquisitions in the year ending 30 June 2018.

During the year ending 30 June 2018, the provisional accounting for the acquisition of The Good Guys was finalised.

Details of the purchase consideration, and finalised fair values of the net assets acquired and goodwill at the date of acquisition are as follows:

		$m
(i)	The assets and liabilities assumed at the date of the acquisition:	
	Current assets	
	Cash and cash equivalents	23.5
	Trade and other receivables	79.7
	Inventories	257.0
	Other current assets	34.3
	Non-current assets	
	Plant and equipment	35.2
	Brand name	241.3
	Other non-current assets	44.8
	Current liabilities	
	Trade and other payables	(302.2)
	Deferred revenue	(86.6)
	Provisions	(26.1)
	Current tax liabilities	(8.3)
	Other current liabilities	(1.8)
	Non-current liabilities	
	Deferred revenue	(94.7)
	Provisions	(5.6)
	Deferred tax liability	(34.7)
	Other non-current liabilities	(7.9)
	Net identifiable assets acquired	147.9
(ii)	The goodwill arising on the acquisition was as follows:	
	Purchase consideration	860.1
	Less: value of net identifiable assets acquired	(147.9)
	Goodwill arising on acquisition	712.2

92

26 COMPARATIVE BALANCES

In this annual report, comparative balances have been restated to reflect the finalisation of the accounting for the acquisition of The Good Guys. The following table illustrates the quantum of the fair value adjustments recognised during the year and their impact on the prior year comparatives presented in this annual report.

Consolidated	30 June 2017 $m	30 June 2017 (Restated) $m
Balance sheet (extract)		
Cash and cash equivalents	72.8	72.8
Trade and other receivables	196.6	193.6
Inventories	859.9	859.7
Other current assets	41.4	41.4
Plant and equipment	208.2	208.2
Intangible assets	1,026.6	1,037.3
Other non-current assets	46.8	46.8
Total assets	2,452.3	2,459.8
Trade and other payables	647.8	644.7
Deferred revenue	141.8	141.8
Provisions	75.4	76.3
Other current liabilities	9.0	9.0
Current tax liabilities	11.8	13.6
Non-current borrowings	558.8	558.8
Non-current deferred revenue	99.6	99.6
Non-current deferred tax liabilities	8.2	16.1
Non-current provisions	11.8	11.8
Other non-current liabilities	34.6	34.6
Total liabilities	1,598.8	1,606.3
Net assets	853.5	853.5
Contributed equity	438.7	438.7
Reserves	33.2	33.2
Retained earnings	381.6	381.6
Total equity	853.5	853.5

27 RELATED PARTY TRANSACTIONS

(a) Parent entity and equity interests in related parties

The parent entity of the Group is JB Hi-Fi Limited, a listed public company, incorporated in Australia.

(b) Equity interests in related parties

Details of the percentage of ordinary shares held in subsidiaries are disclosed in note 22.

(c) Key management personnel

Disclosures relating to key management personnel are set out in the Directors' report.

(d) Terms and conditions of transactions with related parties other than key management personnel or entities related to them

Sales to, and purchases from, related parties for goods and services are made in arm's length transactions at normal prices and on normal commercial terms.

93

OTHER DISCLOSURES

	Consolidated	
	2018 $'000	2017 $'000
28 KEY MANAGEMENT PERSONNEL DISCLOSURES		
The aggregate compensation of the key management personnel of the Group is set out below:		
Short-term employee benefits	8,974	8,865
Post-employment benefits	230	278
Share-based payments expense	2,943	1,978
	12,147	11,121

Detailed remuneration disclosures are provided in the remuneration report on pages 31 to 53.

29 SHARE-BASED PAYMENTS

(a) Group share option plans

The Group has ownership-based remuneration schemes for executives and non-executive management (excluding non-executive directors). In accordance with the provisions of these schemes, executives and non-executive managers within the Group are granted options to purchase parcels of ordinary shares at various issue prices or to acquire shares at a zero exercise price.

Details of the features of outstanding share options are provided in the remuneration report on page 50.

The following reconciles the outstanding share options granted under the Group's share option plans at the beginning and end of the financial year:

	Balance at start of the year Number	Granted during the year Number	Exercised/ lapsed during the year Number	Balance at end of the year Number	Vested and exercisable at end of the year Number
2018					
Outstanding Share Options with an exercise price	404,054	–	(221,855)	182,199	–
Outstanding Zero Exercise Price Options	955,145	464,840	(268,265)	1,151,720	–
	1,359,199	464,840	(490,120)	1,333,919	–
Weighted average exercise price of those with an exercise price	$15.53	–	$13.75	$17.69	–

	Balance at start of the year Number	Granted during the year Number	Exercised/ lapsed during the year Number	Balance at end of the year Number	Vested and exercisable at end of the year Number
2017					
Outstanding Share Options with an exercise price	732,889	–	(328,835)	404,054	–
Outstanding Zero Exercise Price Options	893,486	446,499	(384,840)	955,145	–
	1,626,375	446,499	(713,675)	1,359,199	–
Weighted average exercise price of those with an exercise price	$14.65	–	$12.75	$15.53	–

The weighted average remaining contractual life of share options outstanding at the end of the period was 1,222 days (2017: 1,218 days).

94

29 SHARE-BASED PAYMENTS (continued)

(a) Group share option plans (continued)

Fair value of options granted

Equity settled share based payments with employees are measured at the fair value of the equity instrument at grant date. The weighted average fair value of options granted during the year ended 30 June 2018 was $21.48 (2017: $24.71). The fair value at grant date is determined using a Black-Scholes option pricing model that takes into account the exercise price, the term of the option, the expected exercise date based on prior years' experience, the share price at grant date, the expected price volatility of the underlying share, the expected dividend yield and the risk-free interest rate.

The expected life used in the model has been adjusted, based on management's best estimate, for the effects of non-transferability, exercise restrictions and behavioural considerations.

The expected price volatility for options granted during the year ended 30 June 2018 is based on the daily closing share price for the number of years preceding the issue of the series, that matches the years to vesting as all of these options are expected to be exercised as soon as they vest.

Detailed share option disclosures for all options series granted and exercised during the year are provided in the remuneration report on pages 31 to 53.

Share based payments expense

The fair value determined at the grant date of the equity-settled share based payments is expensed on a straight line basis over the vesting period, based on the Group's estimate of shares that will eventually vest, with a corresponding increase in equity.

At each reporting date the Group estimates the number of equity instruments expected to vest. The number of equity instruments that are expected to vest is based on management's assessment of the likelihood of the vesting conditions attached to the equity instruments being satisfied. The key vesting conditions that are assessed are earnings per share targets and required service periods. The impact of any revision in the number of equity instruments that are expected to vest is recognised as an adjustment to the share based payments expense with the corresponding adjustment to the equity-settled benefits reserve in the reporting period that the revision is made.

	Consolidated	
	2018 $'000	2017 $'000
30 REMUNERATION OF AUDITORS		
Audit and other services		
Audit and review of group financial statements	607	589
Audit and review of subsidiary financial statements	44	31
Audit of accounting for the acquisition of The Good Guys	10	68
Other services	–	35
Total remuneration for audit and other services	661	723

The auditor of the Group is Deloitte Touche Tohmatsu.

95

31 SUMMARY OF OTHER SIGNIFICANT ACCOUNTING POLICIES

The remaining principal accounting policies adopted in the preparation of these financial statements that have not already been disclosed are set out below. These policies have been consistently applied to all the years presented, unless otherwise stated.

(a) Revenue recognition

Revenue is measured at the fair value of the consideration received or receivable. Amounts disclosed as revenue are net of returns, trade allowances, rebates and amounts collected on behalf of third parties.

The Group recognises revenue when the amount of revenue can be reliably measured, it is probable that future economic benefits will flow to the entity and specific criteria have been met for each of the Group's activities as described below. The Group bases its estimates on historical results, taking into consideration the type of customer, the type of transaction and the specifics of each arrangement.

Revenue is recognised for the major business activities as follows:

(i) Sale of goods

Revenue from the sale of goods is recognised when the Group has transferred to the buyer the significant risks and rewards of ownership of the goods. Risks and rewards are considered passed to the buyer at the point of sale if the goods are taken by the customer at that time, or on delivery of the goods to the customer.

(ii) Commissions

When the Group acts in the capacity of an agent rather than as the principal in a transaction, the revenue recognised is the net amount of commission made by the Group.

(iii) Rendering of services

Revenue from a contract to provide services is recognised by reference to the portion of services provided in accordance with the contract. Revenue from time and material contracts is recognised at the contractual rates as labour hours are delivered and direct expenses are incurred.

(b) Derivatives and hedging activities

Derivatives are initially recognised at fair value on the date a derivative contract is entered into and are subsequently remeasured to their fair value at the end of each reporting period. The accounting for subsequent changes in fair value depends on whether the derivative is designated as a hedging instrument, and if so, the nature of the item being hedged. The Group designates certain derivatives as either:

*   hedges of a particular risk associated with the cash flows of recognised assets and liabilities and highly probable forecast transactions (cash flow hedges); or
*   hedges of a net investment in a foreign operation (net investment hedges).

The Group documents at the inception of the hedging transaction the relationship between hedging instruments and hedged items, as well as its risk management objective and strategy for undertaking various hedge transactions. The Group also documents its assessment, both at hedge inception and on an ongoing basis, of whether the derivatives that are used in hedging transactions have been and will continue to be highly effective in offsetting changes in fair values or cash flows of hedged items.

The fair values of various derivative financial instruments used for hedging purposes are disclosed in note 20. Movements in the hedging reserve in shareholder's equity are shown in the statement of changes in equity.

(i) Cash flow hedge

The effective portion of changes in the fair value of derivatives that are designated and qualify as cash flow hedges is recognised in other comprehensive income and accumulated in reserves in equity. The gain or loss relating to the ineffective portion is recognised immediately in profit or loss within other income or other expenses.

Amounts accumulated in equity are reclassified to profit or loss in the periods when the hedged item affects profit or loss. The gain or loss relating to the effective portion of interest rate swaps hedging variable rate borrowings is recognised in profit or loss within 'finance costs'.

96

31 SUMMARY OF OTHER SIGNIFICANT ACCOUNTING POLICIES (continued)

(b) Derivatives and hedging activities (continued)

(i) Cash flow hedge (continued)

When a hedging instrument expires or is sold or terminated, or when a hedge no longer meets the criteria for hedge accounting, any cumulative gain or loss existing in equity at that time remains in equity and is recognised when the forecast transaction is ultimately recognised in profit or loss. When a forecast transaction is no longer expected to occur, the cumulative gain or loss that was reported in equity is immediately reclassified to profit or loss.

(ii) Net investment hedges

Hedges of net investments in foreign operations are accounted for similarly to cash flow hedges.

Any gain or loss on the hedging instrument relating to the effective portion of the hedge is recognised in other comprehensive income and accumulated in reserves in equity. The gain or loss relating to the ineffective portion is recognised immediately in profit or loss within other income or other expenses.

Gains and losses accumulated in equity are reclassified to profit or loss when the foreign operation is partially disposed of or sold.

(c) Foreign currency translation

(i) Functional and presentation currency

Items included in the financial statements of each of the Company's entities are measured using the currency of the primary economic environment in which the entity operates ('the functional currency'). The financial statements are presented in Australian dollars, which is JB Hi-Fi Limited's functional and presentation currency.

(ii) Transactions and balances

Foreign currency transactions are translated into the functional currency using the exchange rates prevailing at the dates of the transactions. Foreign exchange gains and losses resulting from the settlement of such transactions and from the translation at year end exchange rates of monetary assets and liabilities denominated in foreign currencies are recognised in profit or loss, except when they are deferred in equity as qualifying cash flow hedges and qualifying net investment hedges, or are attributable to part of the net investment in a foreign operation.

(iii) Group companies

The results and financial position of foreign operations (none of which has the currency of a hyperinflationary economy) that have a functional currency different from the presentation currency are translated into the presentation currency as follows:

- assets and liabilities presented are translated at the closing rate at the date of that balance sheet;

- income and expenses are translated at average exchange rates (unless this is not a reasonable approximation of the cumulative effect of the rates prevailing on the transaction dates, in which case income and expenses are translated at the dates of the transactions); and

- all resulting exchange differences are recognised in other comprehensive income.

On consolidation, exchange differences arising from the translation of any net investment in foreign entities, and of borrowings and other financial instruments designated as hedges of such investments, are recognised in other comprehensive income. When a foreign operation is sold or any borrowings forming part of the net investment are repaid, the associated exchange differences are reclassified to profit or loss, as part of the gain or loss on sale.

Goodwill and fair value adjustments arising on the acquisition of a foreign operation are treated as assets and liabilities of the foreign operation and translated at the closing rate.

97

31   SUMMARY OF OTHER SIGNIFICANT ACCOUNTING POLICIES (continued)

(d)   Goods and Services Tax (GST)

Revenues, expenses and assets are recognised net of the amount of associated GST, unless the GST incurred is not recoverable from the taxation authority. In this case it is recognised as part of the cost of acquisition of the asset or as part of the expense.

Receivables and payables are stated inclusive of the amount of GST receivable or payable. The net amount of GST recoverable from, or payable to, the taxation authority is included with other receivables or payables in the balance sheet.

Cash flows are presented on a gross basis. The GST components of cash flows arising from investing or financing activities which are recoverable from, or payable to, the taxation authority, are presented as operating cash flows.

(e)   New accounting standards and interpretations

In the current year, the Group has adopted all of the following new and revised Standards and Interpretations issued by the Australian Accounting Standards Board (the AASB) that are relevant to its operations and effective for the current annual reporting period:

(i)   AASB 2016-1 *Amendments to Australian Accounting Standards - Recognition of Deferred Tax Assets for Unrealised Losses*

(ii)   AASB 2016-2 *Amendments to Australian Accounting Standards - Disclosure Initiative: Amendments to AASB 107*

(iii)   AASB 2017-2 *Amendments to Australian Accounting Standards - Further Annual Improvements 2014-2016*

(iv)   AASB 1048 *Interpretation of Standards*

The Group has applied the amendments to AASB 107 for the first time in the current year. The amendments require an entity to provide disclosures that enable users of financial statements to evaluate changes in liabilities arising from financing activities, including both cash and non-cash changes. The Group's liabilities arising from financing activities consist of borrowings. A reconciliation between the opening and closing balances of these items is provided in note 17. Consistent with the transition provision of the amendments, the Group has not disclosed comparative information for the prior period.

Other than the additional disclosure noted above, the adoption of these new and revised Standards and Interpretations did not have any material financial impact on the amounts recognised and the disclosures presented in the financial statements of the Group.

At the date of authorisation of the financial report, the following relevant Standards and Interpretations were issued but not yet effective:

The effects of the following Standard are still being determined:

(i)   AASB 16 *Leases* (effective 1 January 2019)

AASB 16 is effective for periods beginning on or after 1 January 2019 and therefore will be effective in the Group's financial statements for the year ending 30 June 2020. AASB 16 introduces a comprehensive model for the identification of lease arrangements and accounting treatments for both lessors and lessees. AASB 16 will supersede the current lease guidance including AASB 117 *Leases* and the related interpretations when it becomes effective.

AASB 16 distinguishes leases and service contracts on the basis of whether an identified asset is controlled by a customer. Distinctions of operating leases (off balance sheet) and finance leases (on balance sheet) are removed for lessee accounting, and is replaced by a model where a right-of-use asset and a corresponding liability have to be recognised for all leases by lessees (i.e. all on balance sheet) except for short-term leases and leases of low value assets.

The right-of-use asset is initially measured at cost and subsequently measured at cost (subject to certain exceptions) less accumulated depreciation and impairment losses, adjusted for any remeasurement of the lease liability. The lease liability is initially measured at the present value of the lease payments that are not paid at that date. Subsequently, the lease liability is adjusted for interest and lease payments, as well as the impact of lease modifications, amongst others.

The new requirement to recognise a right-of-use asset and a related lease liability is expected to have a significant impact on the amounts recognised in the Group's consolidated financial statements.

The classification of cash flows will also be affected as operating lease payments under AASB 117 are presented as operating cash flows; whereas under the AASB 16 model, the lease payments will be split into a principal and an interest portion which will be presented as financing and operating cash flows respectively. Furthermore, extensive disclosures are required by AASB 16.

98

31   SUMMARY OF OTHER SIGNIFICANT ACCOUNTING POLICIES (continued)

(e)   New accounting standards and interpretations (continued)

During the financial year, the Group has made progress in preparing for the implementation of the new leases standard in a number of areas including:

- identification of leases and contracts that could be determined to include a lease;

- collation of lease data required for the calculation of the impact assessment;

- identification of areas of complexity or judgement relevant to the Group;

- identification of necessary changes to systems and processes required to enable reporting and accounting in accordance with the new standard; and

- development of initial estimates for discount rates.

As at 30 June 2018, the Group has non-cancellable operating lease commitments of $684.4m (30 June 2017: $683.6m). AASB 117 does not require the recognition of any right-of-use asset or liability for future payments for these leases; instead, certain information is disclosed as operating lease commitments in note 21. A preliminary assessment indicates that these arrangements will meet the definition of a lease under AASB 16, and hence the Group will recognise a right-of-use asset and a corresponding liability in respect of all these leases unless they qualify for low value or short-term leases upon the application of AASB 16.

A reliable estimate of the financial impact on the Group's consolidated results is dependent on a number of unresolved areas, including:

- choice of transition method;

- refinement of approach to discount rates;

- estimates of lease-term for leases with options; and

- conclusion of data collection.

In addition, the financial impact is dependent on the facts and circumstances at the time of transition. For these reasons, it is not yet practicable to determine a reliable estimate of the financial impact on the Group.

The effects of the followings Standards and Interpretations are not expected to be material:

(i)   AASB 15 *Revenue from Contracts with Customers*, and the relevant amending standards (effective 1 January 2018)

AASB 15 is effective for periods beginning on or after 1 January 2018 and therefore will be effective in the Group financial statements for the year ending 30 June 2019. The standard establishes a principles-based approach for revenue recognition and is based on the concept of recognising revenue for performance obligations only when they are satisfied and the control of goods or services is transferred. In doing so, the standard applies a five-step approach to the timing of revenue recognition and applies to all contracts with customers, except those in the scope of other standards. It replaces the separate models for goods, services and construction contracts under the current accounting standards.

The majority of Group sales are for goods sold in store, online and to commercial customers, where there is a single performance obligation and revenue is recognised at the point of sale or, where later, delivery to the end customer. There is no material impact from the adoption of AASB 15 on these sales. The revenue recognition approach historically applied by the Group for other services related sales that contain multiple performance obligations are consistent with the principles of AASB 15 meaning there will be no material impact from the adoption of AASB 15.

(ii)   AASB 9 *Financial Instruments*, and the relevant amending standards (effective 1 January 2018)

AASB 9 replaces AASB 139 *Financial Instruments: Recognition and Measurement*. The standard is effective for periods beginning on or after 1 January 2018 and therefore will be effective in the Group financial statements for the year ending 30 June 2019. AASB 9 introduces new requirements for the classification and measurement of financial assets and financial liabilities, a new model for recognising impairment provisions based on expected credit losses and new hedge accounting requirements.

We have aligned hedge accounting documentation with the new standard, and do not anticipate any impact on our current hedging relationships. In relation to credit losses, the primary change relates to provisioning for potential future credit losses on our financial assets. We do not expect this to have a significant impact on the Group's financial statements.

31   SUMMARY OF OTHER SIGNIFICANT ACCOUNTING POLICIES (continued)

(e)   New accounting standards and interpretations (continued)

The effects of the followings Standards and Interpretations are not expected to be material: (continued)

(iii)   AASB 2016-5 *Amendments to Australian Accounting Standards - Classification and Measurement of Share-based Payment Transactions* (effective 1 January 2018)

(iv)   AASB 2018-1 *Amendments to Australian Accounting Standards - Annual Improvements 2015 - 2017 Cycle* (effective 1 January 2019)

(v)   AASB 2018-2 *Amendments to Australian Accounting Standards - Plan Amendment, Curtailment or Settlement* (effective 1 January 2019)

(vi)   Interpretation 23 *Uncertainty over Income Tax Treatments* (effective 1 January 2019)

32   EVENTS OCCURRING AFTER THE REPORTING PERIOD

There have been no matters or circumstances occurring subsequent to the end of the financial year end, that have significantly affected, or may significantly affect, the operations of the Group, the results of those operations or the state of affairs of the Group or economic entity in future financial years.

100

INDEX

Note: Figures and tables are indicated by italic *f* and *t*, respectively, following the page reference.